BILATERAL INVESTMENT TREATIES

BILATERAL INVESTMENT TREATIES

HISTORY, POLICY, AND INTERPRETATION

KENNETH J. VANDEVELDE

OXFORD
UNIVERSITY PRESS

OXFORD
UNIVERSITY PRESS

Oxford University Press, Inc., publishes works that further Oxford University's objective of excellence in research, scholarship, and education.

Oxford New York
Auckland Cape Town Dar es Salaam Hong Kong Karachi Kuala Lumpur Madrid
Melbourne Mexico City Nairobi New Delhi Shanghai Taipei Toronto

With offices in
Argentina Austria Brazil Chile Czech Republic France Greece Guatemala Hungary
Italy Japan Poland Portugal Singapore South Korea Switzerland Thailand
Turkey Ukraine Vietnam

Published by Oxford University Press, Inc.
198 Madison Avenue, New York, New York 10016

Library of Congress Cataloging-in-Publication Data

Vandevelde, Kenneth J.
Bilateral investment treaties : history, policy, and interpretation / Kenneth J. Vandevelde.
p. cm.
Includes bibliographical references and index.
ISBN 978-0-19-537136-9 (hardback : alk. paper)
1. Investments, Foreign—Law and legislation. 2. Treaties. I. Title.
K3830.V37 2010
332.67'32—dc22 2009047000

---

1 2 3 4 5 6 7 8 9

Printed in the United States of America on acid-free paper

Note to Readers
This publication is designed to provide accurate and authoritative information in regard to the subject matter covered. It is based upon sources believed to be accurate and reliable and is intended to be current as of the time it was written. It is sold with the understanding that the publisher is not engaged in rendering legal, accounting, or other professional services. If legal advice or other expert assistance is required, the services of a competent professional person should be sought. Also, to confirm that the information has not been affected or changed by recent developments, traditional legal research techniques should be used, including checking primary sources where appropriate.

(Based on the Declaration of Principles jointly adopted by a Committee of the American Bar Association and a Committee of Publishers and Associations.)

Summary of Contents

Contents

Chapter 9

Access

Chapter 10

Due Process

Chapter 1

Introduction

Fifty years ago, Germany and Pakistan concluded the first bilateral investment treaty (BIT), styled as a treaty "for the Promotion and Protection of Investments." By 2009, more than 2600 such treaties had been concluded, with at least 179 countries a party to at least one BIT.[1] This book assesses the half century of international lawmaking represented by the BITs.

In the years immediately following the conclusion of the first German BIT, several other European countries inaugurated their own BIT programs, concluding treaties with developing countries most commonly in Africa, sometimes in Asia, and occasionally in Latin America. Typically, the European country prepared a model negotiating text that it presented to potential treaty partners as a basis for negotiation. Thus, the BITs concluded by any one developed country tended to be similar, although the models evolved over time. Further, these models were influenced by various draft conventions for the protection of foreign investment and by each other, with the result that the entire network of BITs was characterized by remarkable uniformity in principle, although some variety in language. The models have evolved, but the evolution of different models has occurred in parallel directions. In time, developing countries began to conclude BITs among themselves and these often were based on existing BITs already concluded with developed countries, although BITs between developing countries sometimes omitted provisions that were common in BITs drafted by developed countries. Each of these circumstances preserved the uniformity of the BIT network. As a result of this uniformity, the network of twenty-six-hundred BITs is characterized by an essential coherence. The treaties are structured by a set of core principles.

BITs are drafted to address a specific circumstance: that of an investor of one state (the home state) locating assets in the territory of another state (the host state). History demonstrated the vulnerability of the foreign investor in that circumstance and thus

1 UNCTAD identified 2608 BITs as of the end of 2007. *See* United Nations Conference on Trade and Development, "Recent Developments in International Investment Agreements (2007–June 2008)," *IIA Monitor* No. 2 (2008), available at http://www.unctad.org.

BITs are remedial documents, drafted to ameliorate the condition of these investors and their investments. The remedy provided by BITs is that they ensure that the treatment of foreign investment is subject to the rule of law.

The success of a BIT program depends upon the willingness of host states to accept the legal obligations imposed by the treaties. The inducement offered to host states is that BITs promote economic development by establishing a more liberal international investment regime. More specifically, BITs purport to create conditions under which foreign investors are more likely to enter the host state market.

1.1 THE CORE PRINCIPLES OF THE BITS

The decision of a foreign investor to enter a foreign market might be analogized to the decision of an athlete to compete in a game held in unfamiliar territory. Such an athlete would want certain assurances.

First, before preparing to compete, the athlete would want an assurance that he or she would be deemed eligible to participate. This is the principle of *access*.

Second, the athlete would want an assurance that the competition would be governed by rules, that is, the result of the game would not be determined by arbitrary factors, but by reference to principles. This is the principle of *reasonableness.*

Third, the athlete would want an assurance that the rules would not be changed after the game began. This is the principle of *security.*

Fourth, the athlete would want an assurance that the rules would not favor one participant over another or, to use a colloquial expression, that the playing field would be level. This is the principle of *nondiscrimination.*

Fifth, the athlete would want an assurance that he or she would be informed of the rules that would govern the competition before the game began. This is the principle of *transparency.*

Finally, the athlete would want an assurance that the game would be supervised by an impartial referee. This is the principle of *due process.*

These six principles—access, reasonableness, security, nondiscrimination, transparency, and due process—are the core principles of BITs. The treaties vary in the degree to which they further these principles. For example, they provide much greater assurances of security than of transparency. Further, as will be seen in the following chapters, a particular BIT provision may rest on more than one core principle. For example, some BITs guarantee a right of nondiscrimination with respect to the establishment of investment, a provision that is based on the principles of both access and nondiscrimination. Ultimately, however, these six core principles provide the conceptual foundation on which virtually all BITs rest.

I have argued elsewhere[2] that five of these principles—all those but access—have in common that they are elements of the concept of the rule of law. In requiring that investment be treated in accordance with these principles, BITs essentially require that

2 *See* Kenneth J. Vandevelde, "*A Unified Theory of Fair and Equitable Treatment*," (forthcoming)

investment be treated in a way that is consistent with the rule of law. Promoting the rule of law with respect to foreign investment may be regarded as the primary function of a BIT. BITs are instruments by which host states embrace liberal legalism. Because they create obligations that cannot be altered merely be modifying domestic legislation, BITs function to some extent like foundational or constitutional documents that create a long term legal framework within which the host country must apply its international investment law and policy.

In their preambles, BITs profess that they seek to promote economic prosperity through facilitating foreign investment flows.[3] The belief that facilitating foreign investment flows will promote economic prosperity rests on liberal economic theory. As will be seen,[4] a liberal investment regime also rests on several of the core BIT principles, specifically, access, nondiscrimination, security, due process, and transparency. Promoting a liberal investment regime thus may be regarded as a second major function of a BIT.[5]

Capital exporting states created the BITs to protect their investment abroad and, to a lesser degree, to facilitate the establishment of additional such investments. The protection and facilitation of investment abroad, according to liberal economic theory, will promote economic prosperity. Capital importing states have agreed to conclude BITs in order to attract foreign investment that will promote economic development. Both states see in an embrace of liberal legalism and liberal economics a means to achieve these purposes.

BITs rarely impose obligations of any significance on the capital exporting state. For the capital exporting state, the cost of concluding a BIT is little more than the transaction costs involved in its negotiation.

BITs impose significant obligations on capital importing states, however. These states thus have greater reason to consider the probable effectiveness of a BIT in attracting foreign investment that will promote economic development. A capital importing state rationally could conclude a BIT without accepting in principle the validity of either liberal legalism or liberal economics. Rather, a capital importing state could regard the conclusion of a BIT as a pragmatic act necessary to attract or retain particular investments whose presence the state believes to be beneficial.[6]

---

3 *See* Section 3.1.

4 *See* Section 3.1

5 This very feature of BITs has been a source of criticism. *See* Amr A. Shalakany, "Arbitration and the Third World: A Plea for Reassessing Bias Under the Specter of Neoliberalism," 41 *Harvard International Law Journal* 419 (2000); Jose E. Alvarez, "Critical Theory and the North American Free Trade Agreement's Chapter Eleven," 28 *Inter-American Law Review* 303 (1996–1997); Ibironke T. Odumosu, "The Law and Politics of Engaging Resistance in Investment Dispute Settlement," April 2007, available at http://www.ssrn.com.

6 In particular, a state may believe that providing investors with the benefits of a BIT is necessary because other states with which it competes for investment already have done so and thus declining to conclude BITs would place it at a competitive disadvantage. Some evidence exists that this is the motive for concluding BITs in at least some cases. *See* Zachary Elkins, Andrew T. Guzman, and Beth Simmons, "Competing for Capital: The Diffusion of Bilateral Investment Treaties, 1960–2000," available at http://www.ssrn.com; A game theoretic model supporting this theory has also been developed. *See* Christoph Engel, "Governments in Dilemma: A Game

Alternatively, a capital importing state may conclude BITs as part of a genuine commitment to liberalism, that is, a belief that a liberal investment regime under the rule of law is in the national interest, apart from any specific investment that is induced by the treaty. To such a state, BITs reflect principles that have intrinsic value.

A state could incorporate the substance of BIT obligations in its domestic legislation and thereby offer precisely the same protections without concluding a BIT. Such legislation, however, is subject to amendment and thus investors cannot rely upon the continued existence of any protections that the legislation provides. The contribution of the BIT, then, is that it publicly obligates the host state to a particular kind of conduct. That is, it brings greater security and transparency to the investment climate than could be achieved by domestic legislation alone. BITs, in other words, have both a stabilizing and a signaling effect. In this way, BITs reduce risk to investors.[7] Further, where a government believes that BIT principles have intrinsic value, it may wish to conclude a network of BITs in order to commit the state to these principles over the long term and to build public support for them. In this case too, the BIT has a stabilizing effect, although here the stabilization is not only for the purpose of reassuring foreign investors, but of preserving a particular set of host state policies. The signal sent is not only to foreign investors, but to domestic constituencies as well.

As this suggests, a capital importing state's decision to conclude a BIT may be pragmatic or principled. Where the decision is pragmatic, the state regards BIT obligations as concessions made in exchange for obtaining additional foreign investment. Where the decision is principled, the state regards BIT obligations as merely codifying policies that the state should adopt in any event. The role of the BIT in either case is to stabilize these obligations, either to reassure investors or to prevent an easy reversal of the underlying policies, and to publicize the stabilization. Of course, the reassurance provided by stabilizing the commitments and the signal sent by publicizing them both are more credible, and thus more effective, if the decision to conclude a BIT appears to be principled rather than pragmatic.

1.2 THE CONTENT OF THE BITS

A provision of an investment agreement may relate to investment in any of four ways.[8] Such a provision may *protect* investment, such as where it guarantees compensation for expropriation; it may *liberalize* investment, such as where it grants foreign investors a right to establish investment; it may *promote* investment, such as where it

Theoretic Model for the Conclusion of Bilateral Investment Treaties, available at http://www.ssrn.com.

7 *See* Kenneth J. Vandevelde, "Investment Liberalization and Economic Development: The Role of Bilateral Investment Treaties," 36 *Columbia Journal of Transnational Law* 501 (1998).

8 This typology is based on a study I performed for UNCTAD in 1997–98, on which UNCTAD based its monograph *Scope and Definition*, published in 1999 as one of the first monographs in UNCTAD's Series on Issues in International Investment Agreements.

provides investment insurance; or it may *regulate* investment, such as where it prohibits corrupt payments by investors.

Nearly all of the provisions of a typical BIT protect investment, while a few BITs include provisions that liberalize investments. BITs rarely contain significant obligations to promote investment. Rather, promotion occurs, if at all, through the guarantee of protection. Promotion is merely a consequence of protection. BITs virtually never regulate investment. For these reasons, this book will refer to BITs as investment protection agreements, acknowledging that a BIT provision occasionally may liberalize or promote investment, but that most provisions are structured to protect investment. As will be seen, liberalization provisions in BITs have increased over time, although their role continues to be minor. Most criticisms of BITs have rested on either the claim that the protection provisions are too rigorous or the claim that necessary regulatory provisions are lacking.

The content of most BITs follows a typical pattern. Similar provisions appear in more or less the same order in nearly every BIT.

The first article usually defines certain critical terms. BITs protect investment owned or controlled by investors of one party that is located in the territory of the other party. The most important terms defined therefore are "investment" and "investor."

Next, a typical BIT includes very modest promotion and liberalization provisions. The typical promotion provision requires each party to promote or encourage investment of investors of the other party, without imposing any more specific obligation, while the typical liberalization provision requires each party to admit investment of investors of the other party in accordance with its own laws, an obligation to admit investment only if its own laws already so require.

The bulk of the BIT consists of investment protection provisions. Such provisions provide protection that is either absolute or relative. Relative treatment provisions define the treatment that must be provided by reference to the treatment provided to some comparator. In a broad sense, such provisions generally require that similar investments be treated similarly. Absolute treatment provisions define the treatment that must be provided without reference to the treatment provided to any other investment or investor. Treatment required by the absolute standards in some cases may be more favorable than that required by the relative standards and in other cases it may be less favorable.

Absolute and relative treatment provisions can be further categorized as either general or specific. General standards apply to the treatment of covered investment in virtually any situation, such as where a BIT prohibits any act of discrimination with respect to an investment. Specific standards apply to a narrower range of circumstances, such as where a BIT prohibits discrimination with respect to compensation for losses sustained through armed conflict. This distinction is not entirely rigid, in that a general treatment standard may be subject to some exceptions that diminish the generality of its application while a specific treatment standard may be potentially applicable to an enormous variety of circumstances. The distinction thus is useful perhaps for purposes of exposition and organization, but has no substantive consequence.

The first protection provisions encountered in the BIT typically are general absolute treatment provisions. These establish an absolute level of protection that must be accorded by the host state in every circumstance. The most common such provision guarantees fair and equitable treatment to covered investment. Other common provisions require that investment be accorded full protection and security, prohibit unreasonable or discriminatory measures that impair investment,[9] and require that the host state observe any obligations that it has assumed with respect to investment.

The next protection provisions that appear are general relative treatment provisions. The most common such provision requires that covered investment receive treatment no less favorable than the treatment accorded to investment of investors of any third country, a standard known as most favored nation (MFN) treatment. Another very common such provision requires that covered investment receive treatment no less favorable than the treatment accorded to investment of investors of the host country, a standard known as national treatment. Frequently, these two provisions are followed by a clause setting forth exceptions to this general obligation, typically for matters relating to taxation or obligations assumed under an agreement establishing an economic integration organization.

These general provisions usually are followed by a series of absolute or relative treatment provisions addressing more specific situations. One such provision imposes conditions on the expropriation of covered investment, most notably that full compensation be paid. A second such provision requires nondiscriminatory treatment with respect to compensation for losses attributable to war or civil disturbance. In some BITs, this provision also requires full compensation for certain losses caused by requisitioning or destruction during war or civil disturbance. A third such provision guarantees a right of free transfer of payments related to an investment. These are the most common provisions. A few BITs include a prohibition on performance requirements, or confer on investments the right to hire the managerial or professional personnel of their choice or to gain entry into the host state of investors or employees of the investment. Occasionally, provisions intended to promote transparency or access to courts are included.

These substantive provisions typically are followed by two dispute resolution provisions. The first includes the host state's consent to the arbitration of investment disputes with the investor, a provision generally known as the investor-state disputes provision. The second includes each party's consent to the arbitration of disputes between the two BIT parties concerning the interpretation or application of the BIT, a provision generally known as the state-state disputes provision.

After the disputes provisions, many BITs include a provision that confirms that the BIT does not diminish the level of protection guaranteed under any other instrument, whether domestic law, contract, or a treaty. Often, BITs include a provision confirming that the treaty applies to existing investments, but not to disputes that arose prior to the treaty's entry into force. Some BITs include a provision setting forth certain general exceptions, such as an exception for measures to protect a state's essential security interests. The final provision of a BIT prescribes how it shall enter into force and how it may be terminated. In some cases, this provision states that, in the event of

9 This provision combines an absolute and a relative treatment standard.

termination, covered investment will continue to be protected for some extended period of time, such as ten years or more.[10]

Many typical provisions do not appear in all BITs, while some BITs contain provision that may be unique to BITs of a particular country. These differences to date have been of relatively little consequence.[11] Where a provision is omitted, substantially the same protection is often provided by a different provision.[12] Further, the MFN treatment provision entitles investment protected by one BIT of a country to claim the protection accorded by any other BIT of that country, thereby negating the effect of an omission of a particular provision from a particular BIT. While the language of provisions of a particular type varies, in most cases, these variations have not been treated by tribunals as significant.[13] At least in practice, then, it is quite possible to speak of a typical BIT, a treaty that includes the provisions usually found in a BIT.

The provisions of the BITs generally are cumulative. That is, a host state's compliance with one provision does not excuse its obligation to comply with another provision. For example, if a BIT requires national and MFN treatment, the host state may not elect which standard to apply. Rather, its treatment of covered investment must comply with both standards. As already noted, the model BITs of many countries have evolved, although generally in parallel directions. First, the earliest BITs contained fewer provisions than later BITs. Although nearly every provision that is now considered typical appeared in at least a few BITs in the 1960s, some provisions did not become common until much later. The investor-state disputes provision did not appear at all until the late 1960s. The effect of increasing the number of provisions generally has been to strengthen the BITs. Second, some provisions have become more complex and detailed over time. For example, the investor-state disputes provision initially contained little more than consent to arbitration before the International Centre for Settlement of Investment Disputes (ICSID), while more recent forms of that provision often include consent to arbitration before multiple fora and address a range of other procedural concerns. Some recent BITs also have specified substantive protections in much greater detail than earlier BITs, often for the purpose of clarifying their scope or content. Third, BITs more often include liberalization commitments than in the past. For example, some BITs guarantee national treatment with respect to the right to establish investment and prohibit the imposition of certain performance requirements as a condition of the establishment of investment. The provision on

10 *See, e.g.*, Austria-Armenia BIT, Art. 27(3) (ten years); Indonesia-Algeria BIT, Art. XIII (ten years); Italy-Nicaragua BIT, Art. XIV(2) (five years); Netherlands-Ethiopia BIT, Art. 14(3) (fifteen years).

11 Most of the provisions that are unique to the BITs of a particular country have not been the subject of investor-state arbitrations, suggesting that these provisions have not been of great practical significance to date.

12 For example, as will be seen in Sections 5.2.1, 5.2.3, and 7.5, even if the prohibition on unreasonable or discriminatory measures is omitted, the fair and equitable treatment standard provides similar protection.

13 The major exception has been the most favored nation (MFN) treatment provision, where differences in the language sometimes have been significant in determining whether the provision applies to dispute resolution provisions. *See* Section 7.2.3.

free transfers, which has both a protection and a liberalization role, is much less often subordinated to local law in later BITs than in earlier BITs. Fourth, some recent BITs have included more provisions intended to promote transparency in the treatment of investment and in investor-state arbitration. Thus, the BITs taken as a whole have become more protective, more liberalizing, more transparenting and more complex over time.

Because BITs impose few, if any, obligations on the capital exporting country, they are sometimes characterized as unbalanced treaties. In a formal sense, this characterization is inaccurate because both parties are equally obligated by a BIT. The characterization is accurate in a substantive sense, to the extent that investment flows principally in only one direction between the two parties. In the early years of the BIT programs, the great majority of BITs were between a developed and a developing country and investment nearly always flowed in only one direction between the two parties, if it flowed at all. The sense of imbalance was heightened by the disparity in bargaining power between the developed country and the developing country, evidenced by the fact that many BITs differed little from the model text proposed by the developed country. Since the 1990s, however, BITs between developing countries have become common, as developing countries seek to increase the stabilizing and signaling effect of their BIT programs or to protect their own outward investment. As this suggests, some developing countries have become significant exporters of capital. Thus, one no longer can assume that a BIT is between two countries in which one has investments in the other, but the latter has none in the former. Many developing countries have drafted their own model BIT and these models often differ in only small ways from the models prepared by developed countries. As these events have occurred, the sense of imbalance between parties in the BITs has diminished.

The discussion of BITs as unbalanced between the parties, of course, rests to some degree on the premise that BITs are concluded for pragmatic reasons. This conception regards BITs as containing obligations that perhaps were grudgingly conceded by the capital importing state in the hope of obtaining additional investment, a conception that usually was accurate in the early years of BIT programs. Since the end of the 1980s, however, at least some capital importing countries have become more likely to conclude BITs on principled grounds, as they have come to embrace the core principles reflected in BITs.[14] Where BITs are concluded on principled grounds, the treaty

14 The distinction between pragmatism and principle should not be overstated. A country's commitment to liberal principles typically rests on the assumption that liberal principles serve its interests. That is, a principle commitment is often ultimately a pragmatic one. As will be seen in Chapter 2, even those countries with the strongest commitment to liberalism at times question or weaken their commitment when liberalism seems not to serve their interests. The distinction is not meaningless, however. A principled embrace of liberalism results in the application of liberal principles in a generally consistent way, without questioning in each instance whether that application serves one's interests, while a pragmatic embrace of liberalism results in the application of liberal principles in specific instances because they are believed to serve one's interest in those instances. Further, the principled liberal may maintain a commitment to liberalism even when self-interest repeatedly seems to dictate otherwise, believing that liberal principles will be vindicated in the long run, while a pragmatic liberal will abandon

commitments may be regarded less as concessions than as codifications of policies that the parties have decided should be adopted entirely apart from their effect on particular investments. In this case, a BIT would not be regarded as an unbalanced granting of concessions, but as a mutual commitment to certain principles. Indeed, developed countries typically provide strong protections for investment under their domestic law and thus compliance with BIT substantive obligations may require little, if any, change in their domestic laws and policies. For them, the sense of having made a concession is particularly weak. Even where a country's commitment to its BIT program rests purely on pragmatic considerations, its reasons for concluding a BIT in recent years may have expanded to include the protection of its own outward investments. Thus, the sense of having granted concessions to inward investment is offset by the sense of having gained protection for outward investment. For these reasons as well, the sense of imbalance between parties in the BITs has diminished.

Because the BITs impose obligations on the host state that inure to the benefit of foreign investors, these treaties sometimes are characterized as unbalanced as between the host state and the investor. The argument is that BITs, in addition to prescribing rights for investors and investments, also should impose obligations on investors and investments, such as an obligation to comply with host state law. That is, BITs should regulate as well as protect investment. Foreign investors and investments in the territory of a host state, however, already are within the jurisdiction of the host state, obliged to comply with host state law, and are subject to penalties under host state law if they fail to do so. Indeed, BITs were regarded as necessary precisely because foreign investments and investors are subject to the control of host state governments. BITs exist to curb the discretion of host state governments with respect to foreign investment.

Host countries may be concerned not only that BITs impose too few obligations on investors, but that they impose too many on the host states. Thus, the critical question for any capital importing country preparing to conclude a BIT is whether the BIT preserves sufficient regulatory discretion for the host state.

Host states may retain regulatory discretion under a BIT in any of three ways. First, they may narrow the scope of the BIT's application. For example, by narrowly defining the term "investment," a party may exclude many or even most assets from the protection of the BIT, retaining complete discretion to regulate those assets. As discussed in Section 4.2.1, this alternative has several potential disadvantages. It may deter investment that would have contributed to the host state's economic development and it calls into question the host state's commitment to investment protection as a matter of principle and thus its commitment to promoting the rule of law. It is a crude approach in that it includes or excludes investment by very broad categories, such as all portfolio investment, categories that are likely to be highly over-inclusive in at least some respects. It also lacks flexibility in that the parties make a permanent decision at

---

liberal principles in a particular case if they seem disadvantageous in that case. Thus, my use of this distinction in the text is intended to reflect the difference between countries that make a commitment to BIT principles on a consistent long-term basis and those that adopt them only episodically.

the time the BIT is concluded to exclude certain investments from protection. As will be seen, very few BITs adopt this approach.

Second, host states may limit the access provisions of the BIT, reserving the right to screen investment or to place conditions on its entry. This is the approach adopted by most BITs. Rather than excluding entire categories of investment from BIT protection, the host state reserves the power to decide whether to admit any particular investment and, if so, which conditions the investment will be required to meet. This allows the host state to realize some of the benefits of a broad definition of investment, such as granting general protection as a matter of principle and permitting the treaty to apply to new forms of investment as they come into existence, while limiting the actual scope of the treaty's application. That is, host states limit the scope of the access principle, but make deeper commitments to the security, reasonableness, nondiscrimination, transparency, and due process principles. These are the principles identified with the rule of law. The prevalence of this approach thus reflects the BIT's primary function as promoting the rule of law with respect to foreign investment.

The third approach is to grant a broad right of access to foreign investment, but to adopt more carefully calibrated substantive provisions. For example, if the volatility of portfolio investment is a concern, rather than excluding portfolio investment from the definition of investment or imposing limitations on the admission of portfolio investment, the currency transfers provision could be drafted with exceptions for exigent economic circumstances. Similarly, if the host state is concerned about the ability of local enterprises to compete with foreign investment in certain sectors of the economy, the host state could reserve the right to derogate from the obligation of national treatment in those sectors, at least for some specified period of time.

This approach gives a broader scope to the access principle, but then limits the other core BIT principles in various ways. In effect, it trades protection for liberalization. That is, it encourages host states to admit more foreign investment, while retaining a greater right to regulate the investment once established. To the extent that countries pursue this third approach rather than the second, they give relatively more weight to the function of the BITs in promoting a liberal investment regime and relatively less weight to the function of the BITs in promoting the rule of law. This third approach is not common in the BITs, reflecting the fact that promoting a liberal investment regime remains a secondary goal to promoting the rule of law.

Under the typical BIT, host states in fact retain considerable discretion to regulate foreign investment. First, they may exclude foreign investment entirely or admit it subject to many conditions. Further, once investment is admitted, the typical BIT allows most host-state conduct that is reasonably related to legitimate host-state regulatory objectives, that is nondiscriminatory, and that is consistent with any prior commitments to the investor. Host-state conduct that destroys the value of an investment requires payment of compensation and host states generally must allow the investor free transfer of payments related to an investment. Some affirmative obligations of transparency and due process are also imposed, although these obligations do not restrict the substance of the obligations imposed on foreign investment by host-state regulations. Within these general limitations, the host state retains broad power to regulate.

The awards of tribunals in investor-state arbitrations have confirmed the breadth of host-state regulatory discretion under a BIT. Host states have prevailed in a majority of the claims brought by investors. Where claims brought to date have been successful, with few exceptions they have been based on host-state conduct that was discriminatory, politically motivated, or retaliatory, rather than based on legitimate host-state regulatory objectives; that constituted the seizure of, destruction of, or failure reasonably to protect the claimant's property; that violated an obligation of the host state, in the form of either a contract or an assurance upon which the claimant reasonably relied, or that involved a failure of the host state to make clear its laws or policies applicable to the claimant. A host state that acts on the basis of legitimate regulatory policies, that does not discriminate, that keeps its commitments, that does not seize or destroy investment, that exercises reasonable care to protect investment, that is transparent with respect to its laws and policies, and that provides due process in its courts has had little to fear from investor-state arbitral tribunals. The conduct that tribunals have required in their awards is little more than adherence to the basic principles of the rule of law, principles that states should follow in any event.

1.3 THE PLAN OF THIS BOOK

This book seeks to describe the content of the BITs while placing them in the historical and policy context the brought them into existence. The content of the BITs, of course, is defined not only by the text of the treaties, but also by the arbitral awards interpreting the text. In short, understanding the BITs necessitates an understanding of the history, policy and interpretation of these agreements.

Following this introductory chapter, Chapter 2 describes the emergence in treaty practice over the past two centuries of the six core BIT principles, taking account of how international economic and political events have shaped treaty practice with respect to those principles.

Chapter 3 explains the BITs as instruments of liberal economics and liberal legalism, with primary emphasis on the former. Economic policy is emphasized in that chapter because BITs are justified in their preambles by their economic effects. Chapter 3 thus explores the economic theory underlying the BITs and summarizes some of the relevant empirical evidence. Much less attention is allocated to BITs as instruments of liberal legalism because that topic, in effect, is the subject of the rest of the book. Chapter 3, however, does summarize some of the empirical evidence concerning the impact of the rule of law on economic development as well as the evidence more specifically on the impact of BITs. The chapter makes the case that the BITs are more effective instruments of liberal legalism than of liberal economics, although they have a policy foundation in liberal economics and are liberalizing to some degree. It argues that promoting the rule of law with respect to foreign investment is the primary function of the BITs, while promoting a liberal investment policy is a secondary function.

Chapter 4 describes the scope of protection afforded by the BITs. It describes provisions that define terms such as "investment" and "investor" as well as provisions that limit the scope of BIT protections in other ways.

The remaining six chapters address each of the six core BIT principles in turn. The convention in this field is to organize treaty analyses by treaty provision. The approach taken here is to organize the analysis by principle. Each of the six chapters introduces a core BIT principle and then discusses the most important treaty provisions that reflect that principle. In that way, I hope to demonstrate the essential coherence of the BITs, characterizing them as a reflection of core principles underlying liberal legalism and liberal economics, rather than as merely a collection of provisions that in some way protect, promote, liberalize, or regulate investment. Such an approach, it is hoped, will contribute toward the development of a general theory of the BITs. A better theoretical understanding of the BITs promotes the sound application of BIT principles to the operation of the treaties themselves and ensures that their application furthers the rule of law and liberal economics.

Several BIT provisions rest on multiple core principles. To avoid repetition, such provisions are often discussed primarily in connection with one principle, often the first principle to which the provision seems relevant. They may be more briefly discussed in connection with other principles.

The discussion of each of the provisions addressed in Chapters 4 through 10 typically begins with a description of the structure of the provision and some of the underlying policies that shaped the provision, with particular emphasis on the six core BIT principles. With more than twenty-six-hundred BITs having been concluded, every variation in language cannot possibly be described, but the reader will find the most common forms of the provision and some of the noteworthy variations. My regret that all the variations cannot be mentioned is palliated by the recognition that most variations in language have not significantly affected the interpretation of the provision.

Next, the origin and evolution of the provision is described. The goal is to identify the process by which the provision achieved its contemporary form(s) and became a typical element of the BITs. In many cases, these events had occurred no later than the end of the 1980s. Thus, the historical discussion focuses primarily on those countries that inaugurated BIT programs between 1959 and the end of the 1980s and whose BIT programs have influenced the development of BITs worldwide over the past half century. This necessarily skews the discussion toward the BIT practice of several western European states and the United States, although Kuwait figures prominently in the historical discussion because it launched a BIT program in the 1960s. The inevitably Eurocentric nature of a historical discussion that concludes at the end of the 1980s is lamentable. Yet, to write a complete history of each clause, describing the variations in language introduced by each country, if any, would require vastly more space than is available here. Thus, the historical discussion ends once the process by which the principal contemporary forms of the provision emerged has been described.

Finally, the awards of investor-state arbitral tribunals interpreting and applying each provision are summarized. As has been noted already, in most cases, differences in the language of the provision have not been very significant in the interpretation of the provisions. The awards often are reasoned almost as if each provision existed in an ideal form, which found its expression in various ways in different treaties. This approach has much to commend it. First, many of the most influential BIT models drew on common sources and were drafted by countries sharing for the most part a common investment policy. Given that the language of the provisions often is somewhat vague and general in any event, little reason exists to believe in most cases that minor changes in language were meant to alter significantly the meaning of the provision. Such changes often reflected little more than stylistic preferences or perhaps attempts to state more clearly that which was presumed to be the meaning of the provision. Second, the BIT principles of security, nondiscrimination, and transparency are best served where similarly worded provisions are given a single meaning, allowing investors and host states relying on language that differs in minor ways from language previously interpreted by tribunals some assurance that small differences in language are unlikely to have substantive effect. The fact that these provisions have been treated as reflecting a few ideal types rather than an infinitely varied body of law also vindicates to some degree the organization of this book in which provisions are grouped by the core BIT principle that they reflect. It validates the central thesis that BIT provisions can be understood as requiring that foreign investment be treated, at least to some degree, in accordance with these six principles.

As the name of this book indicates, the discussion is limited to bilateral investment treaties. The limitation may seem to some extent arbitrary, because obligations similar or virtually identical to those contained in BITs are sometimes incorporated in free trade agreements or other kinds of economic integration agreements.[15] Yet, because BITs address only investment-related issues while economic integration agreements address a much wider range of issues, the policy considerations underlying a BIT negotiation may be quite different from those underlying the negotiation of an economic integration agreement. Thus, a book such as this one that grounds the analysis on investment policy quite sensibly can limit its scope to treaties that are united by common policy considerations and that may be distinguished from other treaties raising broader or additional policy concerns. Occasional references are made to some of these other agreements, particularly the North American Free Trade Agreement (NAFTA), where they have influenced BIT practice. Further, where a clause common to BITs also appears in a different type of agreement, such as the NAFTA, the Energy Charter Treaty, or the Association of Southeast Asian Nations (ASEAN) Agreement on Promotion and Protection of Investments, tribunals generally interpret the clause without regard to whether it appears in a BIT or another type of agreement. For this reason, the discussion of arbitral practice freely draws on awards in cases not involving BITs, including a few cases not involving any international investment treaty or agreement at all. At the same time, because the book purports to address arbitral practice under the BITs, little attention has been given to awards applying other treaties or customary international law, where those awards have not significantly BIT practice. For example, an extensive jurisprudence has been produced by the Iran-United States Claims Tribunal, applying the provisions of the friendship, commerce, and navigation treaty between the United States and Iran. While a few of these awards have been cited repeatedly in BIT arbitrations, especially in the early arbitrations when few BIT awards

15 I have written about these provisions in a 2005 study, which formed the basis of UNCTAD's monograph *Investment Provisions in Economic Integration Agreements*, published in 2006.

existed, the great majority have never been cited in any BIT arbitration. Thus, this body of jurisprudence, as significant as it is in its own right, is not discussed here.[16]

1.4 CITATIONS TO BITS, AWARDS, AND LITERATURE

References to particular BITs appear on nearly every page of this volume. To conserve space and to promote the readability of the text, this book does not cite each BIT by its formal title. Rather, BITs uniformly are cited simply by using the names of the two parties separated by a hyphen and followed by the abbreviation "BIT." For example, the first BIT ever concluded, that between Germany and Pakistan, is cited as the "Germany-Pakistan BIT." The text of the great majority of the BITs, including those cited in this book, may be found on the Web site of the United Nations Conference on Trade and Development (UNCTAD), http://www.unctad.org. The researcher should click on the link for "Investment and Enterprise," then for "Foreign Direct Investment," followed by "International Investment Agreements" and then "IIA Databases." The text of some BITs is also available in a looseleaf series, *Investment Promotion and Protection Treaties*, compiled by the International Centre for Settlement of Investment Disputes (ICSID) and published by Oceana.

The following pages also include innumerable references to awards and decisions issued by investor-state arbitral tribunals. Once again, to conserve space and to promote readability, these awards and decisions are cited not by the full name of the case, but by an abbreviated name, typically a word or two identifying the claimant, or the first named claimant if more than one is involved in the dispute, and the name of the respondent state. The name of the parties is followed by a parenthetical reference to the BIT or BITs at issue in the case. The full text of these awards may be found on either of two Web sites. One is maintained by Oxford University Press and may be found at http://www.investmentclaims.com. The other is maintained by Professor Andrew Newcombe at the University of Victoria and may be found at http://ita.law.uvic.ca. UNCTAD also maintains a database on investor-state arbitrations, which contains an abstract of certain information about each case, such as the issues decided in the case. This database may be found in the same manner as the UNCTAD database described in the paragraph above. The majority of the awards have been issued by the International Centre for the Settlement of Investment Disputes (ICSID) tribunals. The text of many of the ICSID awards may be found on the ICSID website at http://www.worldbank.org/icsid.

Finally, extensive use has been made of the economic literature, especially in Chapter 3. A great deal of this literature is widely distributed, at least initially, online through the Social Science Research Network and thus in many cases the citation

---

16 For a recent assessment of this jurisprudence, see Christopher S. Gibson and Christopher R. Drahozal, *The Iran-U.S. Claims Tribunal at 25* (2007). For an earlier assessment by a member of the tribunal, see Charles N. Brower and Jason D. Brueschke, *The Iran-United States Claims Tribunal* (1998).

merely notes that the paper is available at http://www.ssrn.com, where it can be found easily by searching by title.

1.5 APOLOGIES, ALIBIS, AND ACKNOWLEDGEMENTS

I began writing this book in 1994. Two years before I had published a book on the U.S. BIT program, *United States Investment Treaties: Policy and Practice*, drawing upon my experience in the 1980s as a U.S. BIT negotiator and as an advocate on behalf of private claimants before the Iran-United States Claims Tribunal. I believed that a similar book should be written on BIT programs generally. By midyear, I had a partial draft completed when the dean of my law school resigned and I was asked to serve as the dean of the law school on a temporary basis pending the selection of a permanent dean. A year later, in June 1995, I was offered an appointment as the permanent dean, which I accepted, intending to remain only a couple of more years to complete the projects that I had begun as acting dean. As it happened, that same month, I was invited to speak at a European Commission sponsored conference linked to the negotiation of the OECD Multilateral Agreement on Investment (MAI). After my presentation, Karl Sauvant of UNCTAD introduced himself and asked me if I would write a book on the BIT programs for UNCTAD, although he was contemplating something much shorter than my planned project. Realizing that my administrative duties as dean were preventing me from making progress on my book, I accepted Karl's offer to write a much shorter version of the book for UNCTAD. I submitted a manuscript to UNCTAD in the fall of 1995. Soon, however, the attention of the investment community turned to the MAI negotiations, it appeared to some that BITs were becoming obsolete, and my manuscript was shelved. As the world knows, the MAI negotiations failed and in 1998 UNCTAD published my manuscript under the title *Negotiating Bilateral Investment Treaties in the Mid-1990s*, although with substantial revisions and additions by others.

That book began an enormously rewarding relationship with UNCTAD. As it happened, in 1996, my law school separated from its parent institution and I became the president as well as the dean of the school, which only increased the time demands of the position. Although I could never find the time to write a book of this length, I was able to prepare a number of shorter studies that have been published over the years by UNCTAD, including *Scope and Definition*, published in 1999 as one of the first books in UNCTAD's Series on Issues in International Investment Agreements, *Investment Provisions in Economic Integration Agreements*, published in 2006 with additional contributions by Victoria Aranda and Hamet El Kady, and, most recently, *International Investment Rule-Making: Stocktaking, Challenges and the Way Forward*, published in 2008. All of these works published by UNCTAD are, of course, the product of UNCTAD's rigorous peer review process and all were significantly revised in that process. They are mentioned here not to claim authorial credit (because they are UNCTAD publications), but because the reader may notice that many of the ideas in this book first appeared in my work for UNCTAD.

Meanwhile, I found it much more difficult to extricate myself from law school administration than I had imagined it would be when I accepted a temporary appointment in 1994. Finally, in 2005, after eleven years, I won my freedom. I began work immediately on two projects: a second book on the U.S. BIT program, *U.S. International Investment Agreements*, which was published in early 2009 by Oxford University Press, and this book. The book on the U.S. BITs was intended to commemorate the 30th anniversary of the inauguration of the U.S. BIT program, which was in 2007, but two years was not sufficient time to write and publish the book. Nevertheless, it covers the U.S. BIT program from 1977 to 2007. This book commemorates the fiftieth anniversary of the first BIT, signed in 1959, and with a little good fortune it will appear very close to the anniversary date of that BIT.

Although this book bears my name, I am conscious of the dozens of wonderful friends and colleagues who have so generously shared their knowledge of international investment law with me over the years. Their ideas pervade these pages. I began my work in this field as an attorney in the U.S. Department of State and so my first debt is to those in that office with whom I had the honor to work on investment affairs either then or since. I want to acknowledge especially Jose Alvarez, Andrea Bjorklund, Jo Brooks, Mark Clodfelter, John Crook, Scott Gudgeon, Jim Hackney, Jack Lange, Barton Legum, Meg Pickering, Pat Norton, Dan Price, Ken Propp, Lucy Reed, Art Rovine, Laura Rundlet, Jon Schwartz, Jamie Selby, David Small, David Stewart, and Larry Tu, and, at the Iran-United States Claims Tribunal, Howard Holtzman, Charlie Brower, and David Caron.

As already noted, I have been fortunate in having the opportunity to work on a number of investment-related projects with UNCTAD, the preeminent international organization in this field. I have profited greatly from numerous discussions and projects with the very talented and dedicated individuals there, including in particular Victoria Aranda, Hamed El-Kady, Khalil Hamdani, Anna Joubin-Bret, Joachim Karl, Marie-Estelle Rey, Karl P. Sauvant, Joerg Weber, and James Zhan.

I have had associations with a variety of others in this field whose work has illuminated my own. These associations have been more extensive in some cases than others, but I have learned from all of them. I am grateful to Barry Appleton, Bill Dymont, Roberto Echandi, Argyris Fatouros, Mark Koulen, Howard Mann, Peter Muchlinski, Luke Eric Peterson, Maryse Robert, Jeswald Salacuse, Pierre Sauve, Christoph Schreuer, Margrete Stevens, Gaetan Verhoosel, Thomas Walde, Todd Weiler, and Katia Yannaca-Small. I want to say a special word about Professor M. Sornarajah, with whom I was privileged to share a dais on several occasions and with whom I have walked the streets of capital cities on at least four continents. He and I bring different perspectives to the field, but he is an early pioneer and his book *The International Law on Foreign Investment* is indispensable to anyone wishing to understand the development of international investment law from a developing country perspective.

The literature in this field is growing rapidly and, in the past two years, several books have appeared on the subject of international investment law that have been of great assistance to all of us working in this field. For a discussion of the entire field of international investment law, read the excellent book *Principles of International Investment Law* by Rudolf Dolzer and Christoph Schreuer, published in 2008. A basic introduction to the field for the nonspecialist is *International Investment, Political Risk and Dispute Resolution*, by Noah Rubins and N. Stephan Kinsella, published in 2005. Expert discussions of the arbitral jurisprudence may be found in both *Investor-State Arbitration* by Christopher F. Dugan, Don Wallace, Jr., Noah D. Rubins, and Borzu Sabahi, published in 2008, and *International Investment Arbitration: Substantive Principles*, by Campbell McLachlan, Laurence Shore, and Matthew Weiniger, published in 2007. Literally two days before my manuscript was due at the publisher, I received in the mail a book focusing specifically on investment treaties, *Law and Practice of Investment Treaties: Standards of Treatment* by Andrew Newcombe and Lluis Paradell, published in 2009. Time did not permit me to read it before delivering my manuscript, although I glanced at portions (and even cited a passage), but it is clearly an excellent contribution to the literature. Meg N. Kinnear, Andrea K. Bjorklund, and John F. G. Hannaford have written a terrific book dealing solely with the NAFTA, which is not a BIT, but the NAFTA investor-state arbitral awards have been very influential in the practice of investor-state arbitral tribunals formed under the BITs. Their book, *Investment Disputes under NAFTA*, was originally published in 2006; it is a looseleaf and was updated most recently in 2009.

This book, as the name implies, differs from those described above in that it focuses exclusively on BITs and the arbitral awards interpreting them, it organizes the discussion around core principles rather than specific treaty provisions, and it considers at length the ways in which the BITs emerged from their historical and policy contexts. In its exclusive focus on the BITs, it builds on my study for UNCTAD already mentioned above and the very early book by Rudolf Dolzer and Margrete Stevens, *Bilateral Investment Treaties*, published in 1995, which is a wonderful introduction to the texts of the BITs, although it was written before the deluge of investor-state arbitral awards. I should add that my 1990s study for UNCTAD was updated by UNCTAD in 2007 with the publication of *Bilateral Investment Treaties 1995–2006: Trends in Investment Rulemaking*, an excellent study for anyone interested in the most recent trends in the treaty texts. To supplement that book, which deals only with the treaty texts, UNCTAD published in 2008 a very thoughtful study of the arbitral awards, entitled *Investor-State Dispute Settlement and Impact on Investment Rulemaking*. While I have tried to discuss the context in which the BITs have appeared, those who are interested in a much richer understanding of the environment in which BITs function must read Peter Muchlinski's *Multinational Enterprises and the Law*, the second edition of which appeared in 2007 or, for a perspective from the previous decade, *The Multilateral Investment System and Multinational Enterprises* by Thomas L. Brewer and Stephen Young, published in 1998, with an updated paperback edition published in 2000. Several very good edited volumes also have appeared in the past couple of years and I have cited many of the contributions to these volumes in the pages that follow.

This book also builds on several of my writings published under my own name and portions of this manuscript have appeared elsewhere. I wish to thank the *American Journal of International Law*, the *Harvard International Law Journal*, the *Michigan*

Journal of International Law, and the *U.C. Davis Journal of International Law and Policy* for permission to reuse material that they previously published.[17]

As indicated at the beginning of this section, I have been at work continuously on this book over a period of four years. In many cases, research was conducted years before the information was incorporated into the manuscript. I have no doubt that errors have crept into that process and that readers will find them. I regret any inconvenience they cause, I take full and sole responsibility for them, and I invite you to bring them to my attention. I may be reached at kennethv@tjsl.edu.

17 *See* "The Political Economy of a Bilateral Investment Treaty," 92 *American Journal of International Law* 621 (1998); "The Economics of Bilateral Investment Treaties," *41 Harvard International Law Journal 469 (2000); "A Brief History of International Investment Agreements," 12 UC Davis Journal of International Law and Policy* 157 (2005); and "Sustainable Liberalism and the International Investment Regime," 19 *Michigan Journal of International Law* 373 (1998).

Chapter 2

History

2.1 THE COLONIAL ERA: 1820–1944

The birth of the modern system of international law based on the sovereign nation state generally is traced to the Peace of Westphalia in 1648, ending the Thirty Years War. By that time, treaty protection of foreign property already was an element of international practice. For example, Article 24 of the Treaty of Munster, one of the treaties that established the Peace of Westphalia, required restitution of all goods seized or confiscated during the war.[1] This article was based on an even earlier provision, Article 13 of the Twelve Years Truce, concluded in 1609.[2] Other provisions of the treaty imposed numerous qualifications on the restitution obligation of Article 24, including in particular the exclusion of movable property.[3]

These provisions reflected the fact that alien property commonly was seized during time of war. The seizure of property was justified as a way of weakening the enemy, as security for debts, or as punishment. When the war ended, in most cases without any agreed attribution of guilt, the justifications for the seizures lapsed, leading both parties to agree to the restitution of confiscated property.[4] Thus, by the early 1600s, the principle of restitution of at least some property after a war was established.[5] Indeed, restitution clauses can be found as early as the Peace of Bretigny, concluded in May of 1360, during the Hundred Years War.

By the time of Westphalia, property at risk of seizure could include foreign investment, which already existed in several forms. One important form of foreign investment in the seventeenth century consisted of plantations established by the European powers

1 *See* Randall Lesaffer and Erik-Jan Broers, "Private Property in the Dutch-Spanish Peace Treaty of Munster (30 January 1648)," Tilburg University Legal Studies Working Paper No. 002/2007, July 2007, available at http://www.ssrn.com.

2 *Id.*

3 *Id.*

4 *Id.*

5 *Id.*

in their colonies in the New World beginning in the sixteenth century.[6] Another form was the trading companies established by the British, Dutch, and Danish, also as early as the sixteenth century, such as the Muscovy Company and the Dutch East India Tea Company. These companies, organized as joint stock companies, were given monopoly trading privileges by their governments and exercised some powers that were political rather than commercial in nature. Companies also were established for purposes not only of trade, but of colonial settlement. The first permanent English settlements in what would become the United States were established by the Virginia Company starting in 1607.

By the seventeenth century, London had a functioning international stock market in which stocks and bonds were traded by investors from both the British Isles and the European continent.[7] The London stock market was not the first, however. Securities were traded in Italian cities in the fourteenth century and in a few other cities, notably Antwerp and Amsterdam, by the fifteenth century.[8]

2.1.1 The Emergence of a Global Economy: 1820–1914

Despite the existence of some forms of foreign investment, the international economy of 1648 was only slightly integrated. Prior to 1820, international capital flows were "only a trickle."[9] The amount of world trade also was modest. In 1820, only about 1 percent of the world's goods moved in international trade.[10] Thus, it is only after the 1820s that the colonial era also becomes in a significant way an era of international investment.

The 1820s began a process of globalization that would profoundly transform the international economy in half a century. The transformation was triggered by at least three major events. The first was the end of the Napoleonic Wars in 1815, which began a century of relative peace within Europe that would not end until the outbreak of World War I in 1914, at which time the globalization process would come to an abrupt end.

A second triggering event was the industrial revolution, which generated large surpluses of goods for export and created an enormous demand for imported raw materials, such as cotton for British textile mills. The industrial revolution also reduced transportation costs, making it feasible to integrate distant markets, thus facilitating international trade. Railroad construction began in Britain and the United States in the 1830s, and rapidly spread to other countries. Steamships also began to appear in the 1830s.[11] Reduced transportation costs facilitated as well the international migration

---

6 *See* Philip D. Curtin, *The Rise and Fall of the Plantation Complex: Essays in Atlantic History* (1998).

7 B. Mark Smith, *A History of the Global Stock Market From Ancient Rome to Silicon Valley* 22 (2003).

8 *Id.*, at 12–13.

9 Jeffrey G. Williamson, "Winners and Losers Over Two Centuries of Globalization," NBER Working Paper 9161, September 2002, available at http://www.ssrn.com.

10 Alan M. Taylor, "Globalization, Trade and Development: Some Lessons from History," NBER Working Paper No. 9326, November 2002, available at http://www.ssrn.com.

11 Geoffrey Jones, *Multinationals and Global Capitalism* 25 (2005).

of people, which essentially was unrestricted legally. Between 1820 and 1914, sixty million Europeans immigrated to New World.[12]

A third triggering event was the displacement of mercantilism by liberal economic theory. Mercantilism, the dominant economic theory of the sixteenth through the eighteenth centuries, held that the purpose of economic policy was to promote national wealth, which was measured by the amount of gold in the national treasury. Exports were to be promoted, because they brought gold into the country, while imports were to be avoided, because they resulted in a loss of gold. Mercantilists favored substantial regulation of the economy and the use of state-chartered monopolies, such as the trading companies already mentioned. Adam Smith's *Wealth of Nations*, published in 1776, argued that the wealth of a nation was measured by its productivity and convinced many that liberal economic policies, including free competitive markets and free international trade, would better promote national wealth, an argument that was strengthened by the writings of other classical economists, most notably David Ricardo, in the first decades of the nineteenth century. Great Britain would formally adopt a policy of free trade with the repeal of its grain tariffs known as the "corn laws" in 1846.

By the 1820s, the European powers already were in the practice of concluding bilateral treaties of friendship, commerce, and navigation (FCN)[13] The United States had been concluding such treaties since the 1770s.[14] These treaties were intended principally to establish trade relations between the parties, although a few provisions addressed foreign property incidentally.

The BIT principles of access, nondiscrimination, security, and due process could be found in FCN treaty practice by this time. Indeed, FCN treaty practice throughout the nineteenth century and into the twentieth century largely only reaffirmed principles in place in the 1820s. Transparency does not appear to have been an explicit goal of the FCN treaties, nor were these treaties yet explicitly concerned with the principle of reasonableness.

The principle of access was reflected in treaty provisions guaranteeing to nationals of one party the right to reside and trade in the territory of the other party,[15] although in some treaties the right did not apply to those places from which foreigners generally were excluded[16] and sometimes the right was accompanied by the stipulation that the

12 Kevin H. O'Rourke, "Globalization and Inequality: Historical Trends," NBER Working Paper 8339, June 2001, available at http://www.ssrn.com.

13 Although these treaties often were titled as treaties of friendship, commerce, and navigation, other terms were used. For example, the words "peace" or "amity" sometimes were used in lieu of "friendship." Thus, the term "FCN treaty" is a generic one.

14 *See* Kenneth J. Vandevelde, *U.S. International Investment Agreements* 19 (2009). The first U.S. model FCN was approved by Congress in September 1776, a little more than two months after the United States declared independence from Great Britain. *Id.*

15 *See, e.g.*, Treaty of Commerce, Great Britain-Morocco, June 14, 1801, 56 Consolidated Treaty Series 95.

16 *See, e.g.*, Treaty of Commerce and Navigation, Great Britain-Portugal, Feb. 19, 1810, Art. II, 61 Consolidated Treaty Series 41; Treaty of Amity, Commerce and Navigation between Great Britain and Mexico, December 26, 1826, Art. II, 77 Consolidated Treaty Series 39; Treaty of Amity and Commerce between Great Britain and Brazil, August 17, 1827, Art. IX, 77 Consolidated Treaty Series 375. For a mid-century example, *see* Treaty of Friendship,

foreign national was subject to local law.[17] As this suggests, the right of access was for persons entering the territory with their property, primarily for purposes of trade. Trade in the 1820s was heavily regulated and obtaining access for trade and shipping was the principal concern of the FCNs. Capital inflows were not restricted and thus no need existed to obtain a right of access for investment, even if the amounts had been large enough to merit attention.

The principle of nondiscrimination also was commonly applied in the FCNs of this era. For example, many FCNs guaranteed MFN treatment with respect to taxes and fees,[18] while some treaties guaranteed MFN treatment with respect to trade generally.[19] As the century progressed, some treaties guaranteed to foreign nationals MFN treatment generally.[20] Less common, but still found in these early treaties, was the right to national treatment, such as the right to national treatment with respect to trade.[21] Treaties sometimes guaranteed national treatment with respect to the protection of property[22] or with respect to the treatment in the courts.[23] Thus, the nondiscrimination

---

Commerce and Navigation between the Hanseatic Cities and Venezuela, March 31, 1860, Art. II, 122 Consolidated Treaty Series 53.

17 *See, e.g.*, Treaty of Amity between the United States and Prussia, July 11, 1799, Art. II, 55 Consolidated Treaty Series 15; Treaty of Commerce and Exchange between Great Britain and the Netherlands, March 17, 1824, Art. 1, 74 Consolidated Treaty Series 87. For a mid-century example, *see* Treaty of Navigation and Commerce between Hanover and the United States, June 10, 1846, Art. 10, 100 Consolidated Treaty Series 1; Treaty of Friendship, Commerce and Navigation between the Hanseatic Cities and Venezuela, March 31, 1860, Art. II, 122 Consolidated Treaty Series 53; Treaty of Friendship, Commerce and Navigation between Paraguay and the Zollverein, August 1, 1860, Art. II, 122 Consolidated Treaty Series 283.

18 *See, e.g.*, Treaty of Amity between the United States and Prussia, July 11, 1799, Art. II; Treaty of Commerce and Navigation, Great Britain-Portugal, Feb. 19, 1810, Art. III, 61 Consolidated Treaty Series 41.

19 *See, e.g.*, Treaty of Commerce and Navigation, Great Britain-Portugal, Feb. 19, 1810, Art. VI, 61 Consolidated Treaty Series 41; *See, e.g.*, Treaty of Amity, Commerce and Navigation between Sweden and Norway and the United States, Sept. 4, 1816, Art. 1, 66 Consolidated Treaty Series 307; Treaty of Amity, Commerce and Navigation between Great Britain and Rio de la Plata, February 2, 1825, Art. II, 75 Consolidated Treaty Series 75.

20 *See, e.g.*, Treaty of Amity, Commerce and Navigation between Denmark and Liberia, May 21, 1860, Art. IV, 122 Consolidated Treaty Series 127.

21 *See, e.g.*, Commercial Convention between Denmark and Great Britain, June 16, 1824, Art. 2, 74 Consolidated Treaty Series 173; Convention of Friendship, Commerce and Navigation between the United States and Denmark, April 26, 1826, Art. 2, 76 Consolidated Treaty Series 191.

22 *See, e.g.*, Treaty of Friendship, Alliance, Commerce and Navigation between Chili and the United Provinces of Rio de la Plata, November 20, 1826, Art. VIII, 76 Consolidated Treaty Series 481; Treaty of Amity, Commerce and Navigation between Great Britain and Mexico, December 26, 1826, Art. VIII, 77 Consolidated Treaty Series 77. For mid-century examples, *see* Treaty of Amity, Commerce and Navigation between Liberia and Denmark, May 21, 1860, Art. IV, 122 Consolidated Treaty Series 127; Treaty of Friendship, Commerce and Navigation between Paraguay and the Zollverein, August 1, 1860, Art. XV, 122 Consolidated Treaty Series 283.

23 *See, e.g.*, Treaty of Amity, Commerce and Navigation between Great Britain and Mexico, December 26, 1826, Art. VIII, 77 Consolidated Treaty Series 77; Treaty of Amity and Commerce between Great Britain and Brazil, August 17, 1827, Art. VI, 77 Consolidated Treaty Series 375. For mid-century examples, *see* Treaty of Navigation and Commerce between

principle sometimes was combined in a particular treaty provision with principles of access, security, or due process.

The principle of security would have applied to investment, to the extent that any investment existed, but was generally directed at protecting the private property of foreign nationals, which would have included land, buildings, vessels, household effects, and merchandise for trade. FCNs guaranteed protection to property or sometimes "commerce," using a variety of formulations, such as "the most complete security and protection,"[24] "the most complete protection and security,"[25] "full and perfect protection,"[26] or "complete and perfect protection."[27]

Although the portion of an FCN related to property protection was small, the principle of investment security was well established. For example, Article 6 of the 1795 FCN between the United States and Spain required each party to "endeavor by all means in their power to protect and defend all Vessels and other effects belonging to the Citizens or Subjects of the other [and to] use all their efforts to recover and cause to be returned to the rightful owners the Vessels and effects which may have been taken from them . . . whether they are at war or not with the Power whose Subjects have taken possession of the said effects."[28] John Quincy Adams, who served as both President and Secretary of State, explained with respect to Article 6, "There is no principle of the law of nations more firmly established than that which entitles the property of strangers within the jurisdiction of another country in friendship with their own to the protection of its sovereign by all efforts in its power. This common rule of intercourse between all civilized nations has, between the United States and Spain, the further and solemn sanction of an express stipulation by treaty."[29]

The protection of property against seizure during time of war remained a concern as it had been for centuries. Treaties sometimes guaranteed compensation for any property confiscated during hostilities.[30] Alternatively, they might require that property be

---

Hanover and the United States, June 10, 1846, Art. 10, 100 Consolidated Treaty Series 1; Treaty of Friendship, Commerce and Navigation between the Hanseatic Cities and Venezuela, March 31, 1860, Art. II, 122 Consolidated Treaty Series 53.

24 *See, e.g.*, Treaty of Amity, Commerce and Navigation between Sweden and Norway and the United States, Sept. 4, 1816, Art. 1, 66 Consolidated Treaty Series 307.

25 *See, e.g.*, Treaty of Amity, Commerce and Navigation between Great Britain and Rio de la Plata, February 2, 1825, Art. II, 75 Consolidated Treaty Series 75; Treaty of Amity, Commerce and Navigation between Colombia and Great Britain, April 18, 1825, Art. II, 75 Consolidated Treaty Series 195.

26 *See, e.g.*, Treaty of Amity, Commerce and Navigation between Great Britain and Mexico, December 26, 1826, Art. VIII, 77 Consolidated Treaty Series 77.

27 *See, e.g.*, Treaty of Friendship, Commerce and Navigation between Paraguay and the Zollverein, August 1, 1860, Art. X, 122 Consolidated Treaty Series 283.

28 *See, e.g.*, Treaty of Friendship, Limits and Navigation between Spain and the United States, signed Oct. 27, 1795, 55 Consolidated Treaty Series 9.

29 Quoted in Charles Lipson, *Standing Guard: Protecting Foreign Capital in the Nineteenth and Twentieth Centuries* 9 (1985).

30 *See, e.g.*, Treaty of Amity between the United States and Prussia, July 11, 1799, Art. XXIII. For a mid-nineteenth-century example, *see* Treaty of Friendship, Commerce and Navigation

restored to the owner.[31] In some cases, they simply prohibited the confiscation or sequestration of at least certain types of foreign owned property[32] or they might allow confiscation of certain property only on a national treatment basis.[33] The FCNs sometimes guaranteed safe conduct out of the territory for foreign nationals and their property during hostilities, if they preferred to leave.[34] Some FCNs applied the expropriation provision to seizures of property even if not linked to hostilities and required compensation for any such seizures.[35]

The principle of due process was established by this time as well. The primary form of dispute resolution was in local courts. Thus, early FCNs sought to ensure that foreign nationals had the right to appear in local courts. One formulation, for example, guaranteed to foreign nationals "free and open access to the Courts of Justice" including the right to employ the counsel of their choice and national treatment in the courts.[36] Access to the courts at least on a national treatment basis and the right to employ the counsel of one's choice continued to appear in later FCNs.[37]

FCNs also could provide for international arbitration between the two parties. The 1794 FCN between the United States and Great Britain contained an arbitration clause

---

between the Hanseatic Cities and Venezuela, March 31, 1860, Art. III, 122 Consolidated Treaty Series 53.

31 *See, e.g.*, Treaty of Peace and Commerce and Secret Treaty of Alliance between Great Britain and Turkey, Jan. 5. 1809, Art. III. 60 Consolidated Treaty Series 323; Treaty of Amity, Commerce and Navigation between Great Britain and Mexico, December 26, 1826, Art. VIII, 77 Consolidated Treaty Series 77.

32 *See, e.g.*, Treaty of Amity, Commerce and Navigation between Great Britain and Mexico, December 26, 1826, Art. VIII, 77 Consolidated Treaty Series 77. For a mid-century example, *see* Treaty of Friendship, Commerce and Navigation between Paraguay and the Zollverein, August 1, 1860, Art. XIV, 122 Consolidated Treaty Series 283.

33 *See, e.g.*, Treaty of Amity, Commerce and Navigation between Great Britain and Mexico, December 26, 1826, Art. VIII, 77 Consolidated Treaty Series 77. For a mid-century example, *see* Treaty of Friendship, Commerce and Navigation between Paraguay and the Zollverein, August 1, 1860, Art. XIV, 122 Consolidated Treaty Series 283.

34 *See, e.g.*, Treaty of Amity between the United States and Prussia, July 11, 1799, Art. XXIII. For a mid-nineteenth-century example, *see* Treaty of Friendship, Commerce and Navigation between Paraguay and the Zollverein, August 1, 1860, Art. XIV, 122 Consolidated Treaty Series 283.

35 *See, e.g.*, Treaty of Peace, Amity, Navigation and Commerce between Colombia and the United States, October 3, 1824, Art. 5, 74 Consolidated Treaty Series 455 (requires "sufficient indemnification" for seizures of vessels, cargoes, merchandise and effects for a military expedition or "any public or private purpose whatever"); Treaty of Peace, Amity, Commerce and Navigation between the Central American Federation and the United States, December 5, 1825, Art. 7, 75 Consolidated Treaty Series 433; Treaty of Peace, Friendship, Navigation and Commerce between the United States and Venezuela, January 30, 1836, Art. 8, 86 Consolidated Treaty Series 1.

36 *See, e.g.*, Treaty of Amity, Commerce and Navigation between Great Britain and Mexico, December 26, 1826, Art. VIII, 77 Consolidated Treaty Series 77.

37 *See, e.g.*, Treaty of Navigation and Commerce between Hanover and the United States, June 10,1846, Art. 10, 100 Consolidated Treaty Series 1; Treaty of Friendship, Commerce and Navigation between Paraguay and the Zollverein, August 1, 1860, Art. X, 122 Consolidated Treaty Series 283.

that covered disputes involving, among other things, the confiscation of property.[38] Between 1799 and 1804, that clause resulted in more than five hundred arbitral awards.[39] The year after the United States signed its FCN with Great Britain, it signed one with Spain that also included a provision for arbitration of claims, in this case claims by U.S. citizens for losses caused by Spain in its war with France.[40] State-state arbitration continued to be used as an occasional means of settling property disputes throughout the nineteenth century. The United States-Mexican Mixed Claims Commission of 1868, for example, arbitrated more than two thousand claims between 1871 and 1876.[41] One commentator has estimated that between 1829 and 1910 the United States entered into approximately forty arbitrations with Latin American countries alone.[42] Another commentator estimated that between 1840 and 1940, more than sixty arbitral commissions were established to resolve disputes arising from injuries to foreign nationals.[43]

The general practice during the nineteenth century was to establish arbitral tribunals only to resolve existing claims. Thus, nineteenth-century FCNs, which provided prospective protection, typically did not include any kind of arbitration clause or method of resolving treaty-related disputes through the use of binding, third-party procedures.

These FCNs nevertheless did contemplate that disputes over alleged breaches of the treaty would arise. The method of dispute resolution that they seemed to anticipate, however, was not arbitration but war. To the extent that the FCNs addressed the possibility of disputes, their approach was to require the parties to seek a negotiated solution before resorting to war. Thus, a provision that appeared in several nineteenth-century FCNs stated that

> [i]f, unfortunately, any of the articles contained in this treaty should be violated or infringed in any way whatever, it is expressly stipulated that neither of the two contracting parties shall ordain or authorize any acts of reprisal, nor shall declare war against the other,. . . until the said party considering itself offended shall have laid before the other a statement of such injuries or damages,. . . demanding justice and satisfaction, and the same shall have been denied, in violation of the laws and of national right.[44]

As the comment from John Quincy Adams indicates, some provisions of the FCNs were regarded as merely codifying rules of customary international law. Yet, the FCNs of the nineteenth century did not reflect all the customary principles applicable to the

---

38 *See, e.g.*, Treaty of Amity, Commerce and Navigation, November 19, 1794, 8 Stat. 116, T.S. No. 105.

39 Mark Janis, *An Introduction to International Law* 92 (1988).

40 Treaty of Friendship, Limits and Navigation between Spain and the United States, signed Oct. 27, 1795, Art. XXI 55 Consolidated Treaty Series 9. Art. XXI.

41 Janis, *supra* note 39, at 93.

42 Summers, "Arbitration and Latin America," 3 *California Western International Law Journal* 1, 7 (1972).

43 Ian Brownlie, *Principles of Public International Law* 500 (6th ed. 2003).

44 General Treaty of Amity, Commerce and Consular Privileges, United States-El Salvador, Dec. 6, 1870, Art. 37th, 18 Stat. 725, T.S. No. 310.

protection of foreign property. For example, the reasonableness principle was already present in customary law, as reflected in a rule that arbitrary or discriminatory interference with contracts was a ground for international responsibility,[45] a rule that was not found explicitly in the FCNs.

The process of globalization that began in the 1820s entailed a substantial increase in international investment flows. Much of this was stimulated by the need for capital to build infrastructure in the New World. As already noted, railroad construction began in the 1830s and British investors financed much of the infrastructure development in the Americas. American railroads in the nineteenth century not uncommonly were 40 to 50 percent foreign-owned.[46] The percentage of gross fixed capital formation composed of inward foreign investment between 1870 and 1913 was 37 percent in Canada, 70 percent in Argentina and 75 percent in Mexico.[47] By 1913, one-third of British capital was held overseas.[48] Much of the investment was in the developing world. While in 1830 two-thirds of British investment was in Europe, by 1900, only 5 percent was.[49]

Most foreign investment in the nineteenth century was portfolio investment, principally in the form of bonds, because global communications were not yet adequate to make substantial direct investments possible. Two changes in particular combined to promote the expansion of foreign direct investment.

The first was technological. Samuel Morse obtained his patent for telegraphy in 1839 and almost immediately the telegraph began to link countries. London and Paris were linked in 1852 and a trans-Atlantic cable was in operation by 1866.[50]

The second was legal. Western European countries and the United States in mid-century adopted general incorporation laws, allowing individuals to pool their capital in a limited liability corporation formed for essentially any legitimate business purpose.[51] Previously, incorporation of a limited liability company required a special charter from the legislature. The alternative form of business enterprise, the partnership, left each investor personally liable for all debts of the enterprise in the event of a business failure and thus discouraged risky ventures. The sole proprietorship, another alternative, did not allow the pooling of capital and left the proprietor personally liable for the debts of the proprietorship. The corporate form, by contrast, allowed investors

---

45 *See* Harvard Research in International Law, "Responsibility of States for Damage Done in Their Territory to the Persons or Property of Foreigners," 23 *American Journal of International Law Special Supplement* 133, 169–173 (1929) (describing nineteenth-century state practice).

46 Smith, *supra* note 7, at 90.

47 Kevin H. O'Rourke, "Globalization and Inequality: Historical Trends," NBER Working Paper 8339, June 2001, available at http://www.ssrn.com.

48 *Id.* The figure was already as high as 17 percent in 1870.

49 Smith, *supra* note 7, at 87.

50 Jones, *supra* note 11, at 25.

51 Britain adopted a general incorporation law in 1856, France in 1867, Spain in 1869, Germany in 1870, Belgium in 1873, and Italy in 1883. Smith, *supra* note 7, at 73–74. The adoption of such laws in the United States cannot be linked to a single year because such laws were adopted at the state level.

to pool capital while limiting their risk to the amount of capital they contributed, thus encouraging the establishment of larger ventures abroad.

Some transnational enterprises did exist prior to the mid-nineteenth century, such as the specially chartered trading companies already mentioned. Further, British insurance companies began to establish affiliates in other countries in the late eighteenth century.[52] By the 1830s, however, multinational enterprises began to emerge in other sectors of the economy, such as banking and manufacturing[53] and then the extraction of natural resources.[54] By 1914, one third of all foreign investment was direct investment.[55] Foreign direct investment accounted for 9 percent of world gross domestic product, a figure that would not be exceeded until the early 1990s.[56] In 1914, about 55 percent of the stock of foreign direct investment was in the primary sector, with 20 percent in railroads and 15 percent in manufacturing.[57] Foreign direct investment typically was greenfield investment. Often the investor possessed new technology that it was seeking to exploit in a new market and few potential targets for acquisition existed.[58]

In 1914, about a fourth of foreign investment was in the United States, Canada and Western Europe, another approximately 10 percent was in Eastern Europe and the rest was in the developing world.[59] About 95 percent of the investment came from Western Europe, the United States and Japan.[60] Thus, international investment flowed predominantly from developed to developing countries. The developing countries, however, were not the poorer countries of Asia or Africa, but the more prosperous countries of the Western Hemisphere.

As this suggests, capital sought out countries abundant in natural resources and human capital, rather than cheap labor.[61] Thus, international investment flows tended to increase inequality among countries, as it moved from one relatively prosperous country to another, a process that left the least prosperous countries behind. At the same time, at least among the more prosperous countries, international migration tended to equalize income distributions.[62]

International investment flows prior to 1914 were not subject to legal restrictions. Indeed, countries sought foreign investment to finance the building of railroads and utilities and to develop natural resources. After the 1870s, some countries grew relatively more protectionist with respect to trade than they had been in the immediately preceding decades and for the first time some restrictions on international migration began to appear. Any new barriers to trade or migration, however, were not accompanied by new legal barriers to investment.

---

52 Jones, *supra* note 11, at 114.

53 *Id.* at 20.

54 *Id.* at 45.

55 O'Rourke; *supra* note 47; Jones, *supra* note 11, at 21.

56 O'Rourke, *supra* note 47.

57 *Id.*

58 Jones, *supra* note 11, at 148–149.

59 Jones, *supra* note 11, at 23.

60 *Id.*, at 22.

61 Williamson, *supra* note 9, at 27.

62 *Id.* at 25–26.

Further, the developed countries, led by Great Britain, promoted an international economic system that actually facilitated the free flow of capital. British investors could earn returns on their investments abroad much higher than at home, typically 50 to 75 percent higher.[63] In the railroad sector, the return on foreign investment was twice what it was on investment in Britain.[64] Thus, Britain had a strong interest in promoting capital mobility.

This system of capital mobility, as it crystallized in the 1870s, was based on the gold standard. Under the gold standard, countries established the value of their currency in relation to gold and promised to exchange their currency for gold on demand. Thus, by definition, currencies on the gold standard were freely convertible.

The gold standard, however, imposed potentially severe constraints on economic policy. Such a system required countries to maintain reserves of gold and it limited the extent to which a country could expand its money supply. Further, if a country's imports significantly exceeded exports, gold would flow out of the country, endangering its ability to continue to redeem the currency. A country thus would be forced to adopt policies to reverse the flow, the effect of which might be to induce a recession or a deflation of the currency. In effect, a country was expected to allow wages and prices to fluctuate in order to maintain the value of the currency. For example, a country suffering from an excess of imports would allow wages and prices to fall until its exports became cheap enough to attract foreign buyers and imports became too expensive for consumers to purchase, at which point exports would rise, imports would fall, and the outflow of gold would be reversed. In a sense, adherence to the gold standard required a country, in order to maintain its commitment to free convertibility, to place its international commitments above its control over domestic economic policy. Falling wages, of course, imposed hardships on labor while falling prices could bankrupt farmers. Thus, during these periods of deflation, tremendous popular pressure to abandon the gold standard could arise. Opposition to the gold standard, however, arose from the rigidity of the money supply, which tended in the late nineteenth century to produce almost continuous deflation in the absence of new discoveries of gold, rather than from the mobility of international capital. Few objected to foreign ownership of assets in principle.

Capital flows also were encouraged by the international legal environment. The developed countries had embraced the principle that seizures of foreign property were unlawful unless accompanied by full compensation and they were willing to enforce this principle by force, if necessary. Developing countries did not necessarily agree in principle. Most notably, Carlos Calvo, an Argentine jurist, advocated in the latter half of the nineteenth century what became known as the Calvo Doctrine, under which foreign investors were not entitled to treatment any more favorable than that accorded by the host country to its own investors and that disputes concerning injuries to foreign

---

63 Jeffrey A. Frieden, *Global Capitalism* 50 (2006).

64 *Id.*

investors were within the exclusive jurisdiction of national courts.[65] Nevertheless, prior to 1914, no large scale expropriations of foreign property occurred.[66]

Yet, foreign investment was by no means free of political risk. As has been noted, most foreign investment prior to 1914 was portfolio investment, principally in the form of bonds.[67] Bond defaults were a persistent problem in Latin America during the nineteenth century. At the end of the 1820s, for example, an estimated 20 to 25 percent of all foreign bonds held by investors in Britain, France, and Germany were in default.[68] Similarly, in 1880, half of the bonds purchased by British investors from Latin American debtors were in default.[69] The usual remedy was to refuse to provide further credit. A debtor in default would be delisted from the stock exchange until it reached a settlement with its creditors.

Creditors might well hope for support from their governments in collecting debts, but they could not be assured that such support would be forthcoming. In refusing one request for assistance in 1848, Viscount Palmerston explained that, "The British Government has considered that the losses of imprudent men who have placed mistaken confidence in the good faith of foreign Governments would prove a salutary warning to others."[70] The premise was that it was better to suffer an occasional default than to destabilize a government that largely protected trade and investment.[71] Further, a refusal to support investors in their collection efforts would tend to discourage reckless investments, avoiding what modern economists would call a moral hazard.[72]

Home states nevertheless sometimes did utilize military force to protect foreign investments. Foreign investment in developing countries prior to World War I tended to be located along the coast, where it was easily protected by naval forces.[73] Even portfolio investment often was secured by the proceeds from customs houses located in port cities.[74] Military force thus could be highly effective. Between 1820 and 1914, Great Britain used military force at least forty times in Latin America to protect its subjects and their property.[75]

The use of military action to protect foreign investment produced a crisis in 1902, when Germany, Italy, and the United Kingdom blockaded Venezuela's ports and threatened further military action if the Venezuelan government failed to pay debts owed to the respective citizens of the three nations. The Argentine foreign minister, Luis Drago, responded by proposing the Drago Doctrine, under which armed intervention to collect

---

65 *See* Donald R. Shea, *The Calvo Clause: A Problem of Inter-American and International Law and Diplomacy* 17–20 (1955).

66 Jones, *supra* note 11, at 25.

67 O'Rourke, *supra* note 47.

68 Barry Eichengreen, *Capital Flows and Crises* 28 (2003).

69 Lipson, *supra* note 29, at 46.

70 Quoted in *id.* at 44.

71 *Id.* at 45.

72 *Id.* at 48–49.

73 *Id.* at 147.

74 *Id.*

75 *Id.* at 54.

public debts was a violation of international law.[76] The Drago Doctrine was widely accepted in Latin America and Drago urged the United States to support it as well.

In 1904, however, U.S. President Theodore Roosevelt issued a statement that became known as the Roosevelt Corollary to the Monroe Doctrine, in which European intervention in the Americas to coerce payment of debts was prohibited. The United States, however, reserved the right to use military action in the Western Hemisphere to force payment of debts.[77] Indeed, the United States intervened in Latin America on repeated occasions during the first third of the twentieth century to protect foreign property, until the Good Neighbor Policy of the Franklin Roosevelt Administration ended the practice in 1933.[78]

The United States contended that to adopt the Drago Doctrine would only discourage European investors, to the detriment of Latin American countries. Those countries, however, were unwilling to abandon the Drago Doctrine and the issue was placed on the agenda of the 1907 Hague Peace Conference. The conference ultimately adopted a modified version of the Drago Doctrine, known as the Porter Doctrine, after General Horace Porter, the head of the U.S. delegation, which proposed the doctrine. The Porter Doctrine stated that military intervention to coerce payment of debts was prohibited unless the debtor country refused to submit the dispute to arbitration or, having arbitrated the claim, failed to comply with the award. The modified language, calling for international arbitration, was inconsistent with the Calvo Doctrine and thus unacceptable to most Latin American countries. The Hague Conference, of course, assumed the existence of an international legal obligation to pay the debts, but sought to encourage legal rather than military means of debt collection.

Apart from military remedies, an investor's state might exercise diplomatic protection on behalf of its investor, a process also known as espousal. The legal theory underlying espousal is that an injury to a national is also an injury to that national's state. Thus, where a host state injured the property of an investor, the investor's own state could claim that it had been wronged. That is, it could espouse the claim of the investor. Under customary law, home states have complete discretion to decide whether to espouse a claim. Thus, as in the case of military intervention, espousal was available only if the investor's home state was willing to assist the investor.[79]

FCN treaty practice on the eve of World War I was not dramatically different than it had been a century before. Yet, some important changes were evident after the turn of the century. First, the right of nondiscrimination with respect to trade and commerce in some treaties was expanded to include a right of nondiscrimination with respect to engaging in industry.[80] Thus, treaties were beginning to recognize a right of establishment that went

---

76 *See, e.g.*, Edward M. Borchard, "Limitations on Coercive Protection," 21 *American Journal of International Law* 303 (1927); Luis M. Drago, "State Loans in Their Relation to International Policy," 1 *American Journal of International Law* 692 (1907).

77 *See* Armin Rappaport, *A History of American Diplomacy* 223–229 (1975); Lipson, *supra* note 29, at 63.

78 *Id.* at 228–229, 324.

79 For a more detailed discussion of espousal, *see* Section 10.1.

80 *See, e.g.*, Treaty of Commerce between Bulgaria and Russia, March 8, 1905, Art. I, 198 Consolidated Treaty Series 143.

beyond trade offices to include such activities as manufacturing and mineral extraction. The right of access, however, generally was not yet absolute, but only a right of nondiscrimination. Second, FCNs sometimes conferred rights on companies, particularly the right of access to courts.[81] Third, after the conclusion of the 1899 Hague Peace Conference and the establishment of the Permanent Court of Arbitration, countries began to conclude general arbitration treaties[82] and sometimes to include arbitration clauses in their FCNs.[83] Such clauses appeared occasionally in nineteenth-century FCNs,[84] but, as already noted, were not typical. Fourth, FCNs sometimes included provisions requiring nondiscriminatory treatment with respect to the protection of at least certain forms of intellectual property.[85] Fifth, some protection for the transfer of funds occasionally could be found. For example, an 1881 FCN between the United States and Serbia guaranteed the right to "export proceeds of the sale of property" without paying higher duties than nationals of the host state or any third state.[86]

Thus, the principle of access was expanding to include investment not incident to trade, the principle of nondiscrimination was being applied in new contexts, and neutral dispute resolution, or the principle of due process, was becoming a standard feature of FCN agreements. Security provisions, by contrast, were not much changed from those of a century before. Reasonableness and transparency provisions still were virtually nonexistent. The scope of treaty application, however, was expanding to confer rights on corporations as well as individuals.

2.1.2 The Global Economy Collapses: 1914–1944

In 1914, the international investment regime, the victim of three of the most important events of the twentieth century, collapsed. Although efforts to create a new global economy would begin in 1944, some eighty years would pass before capital markets would achieve the same level of integration that they enjoyed in 1914.

---

81 *See, e.g.*, Treaty of Commerce between Bulgaria and Russia, March 8, 1905, Art. IV, 198 Consolidated Treaty Series 143.

82 *See, e.g.*, Arbitration Convention, Belgium-Spain, January 23, 1905, 198 Consolidated Treaty Series 1; Arbitration Convention, Spain-Norway and Sweden, January 23, 1905, 198 Consolidated Treaty Series 3; Arbitration Convention, Great Britain-Netherlands, February 15, 1905, 198 Consolidated Treaty Series 121; Arbitration Convention, Denmark-Russia, March 1, 1905, 198 Consolidated Treaty Series 129; Arbitration Convention, United States-Peru, December 5, 1908, Art. I, 36 Stat. 2169, T.S. No. 528; Arbitration Convention, United States-Norway, April 4, 1908, Art. I, 35 Stat. 1994, T.S. No. 499; Arbitration Convention, United States-Netherlands, May 2, 1908, Art. I, 36 Stat. 2148, T.S. No. 519.

83 *See, e.g.*, Treaty of Commerce and Navigation between Great Britain and Cuba, May 4, 1905, Art. XIX, 198 Consolidated Treaty Series 265.

84 *See, e.g.*, Treaty of Amity, Commerce and Navigation, United States-Congo, January 24, 1891, Art. XIII, 27 Stat. 926, T.S. No. 60.

85 *See, e.g.*, Treaty of Friendship and Commerce between Great Britain and Serbia, January 26, 1880, Art. V, 156 Consolidated Treaty Series 231; Treaty of Commerce and Navigation between Great Britain and Cuba, May 4, 1905, Art. XVI, 198 Consolidated Treaty Series 265.

86 Treaty of Commerce, United States-Serbia, October 14, 1881, Art. II, 22 Stat. 963, T.S. No. 319.

The first of the great events that destroyed the international investment regime was World War I. One important casualty of the war was the gold standard, upon which rested the entire system of capital mobility. As the European powers spent enormous amounts to finance the war, they were unable to keep their commitment to free convertibility and gradually one by one they abandoned the gold standard and adopted exchange controls.

It was not only the principle of access that suffered during the war. As in prior wars, countries seized enemy property, but these now included much greater quantities of investment than in the past. Thus, the principles of nondiscrimination and security suffered as well.

The war shattered the spirit of international cooperation and the commitment to the free flow of capital that had allowed the creation of a global economy in the nineteenth century. The Treaty of Versailles, ending the war, was intended to punish Germany and thereby kept alive wartime animosities. The treaty imposed on Germany an obligation to pay reparations to the European allied powers, which it increasingly was unable to do. The allies owed debts to the United States, which they too were having difficulty servicing. In 1914, the United States was the world's largest debtor, but by 1919 it was the world's largest creditor. The allies suggested that they would relieve Germany of some of its obligations if the United States in turn would forgive their loans, but the United States forgave only a portion of the debt.

In this atmosphere, countries abandoned the liberalism of the pre-war era and increasingly pursued nationalist economic policies that promoted their domestic economic interests, regardless of the effect on other states. While nineteenth-century economic nationalists and their mercantilist predecessors had seen international trade and investment as ways of increasing wealth and thus power, economic nationalists of the 1920s stressed national self-sufficiency as the means to national power. Some countries adopted import substitution industrialization policies in which they sought to develop domestic industries that would produce goods previously imported. The receptivity to foreign investment that was virtually universal before 1914 vanished and, in the 1920s, restrictions on foreign investment became increasingly common. Restrictions on inward investment would prevent foreign competition with new domestic industries. Countries also adopted exchange controls, in some cases to keep domestic capital from seeking higher rates of return abroad so that it could be used for economic development in the home country.[87] Countries also adopted multiple exchange rates, allowing the use of a more favorable rate for those engaged in activity consistent with the government's economic policies.[88] For example, a company might be allowed to purchase foreign currency cheaply if needed for raw materials not available at home, while a company seeking to import goods that could be supplied at home would have to pay more for the foreign currency necessary for the purchases. In short, governments found that exchange rates could be used as an alternative to protectionist tariffs. Tariffs, however, rose as well.

---

87 Frieden, *supra* note 63, at 207.

88 *Id.* at 207–208.

The second great event that destroyed the global economy of the pre-war era was the Great Depression, which only deepened the economic distress and encouraged further autarky. The Smoot-Hawley Tariff of 1930 raised American tariffs to unprecedented levels, drastically reducing imports. By 1932, just two years after the Smoot-Hawley Tariff was enacted, world trade was at only one-third of 1929 levels.[89] Unable to export to the United States, European countries could not obtain dollars needed to repay their war debts. The tariff also invited retaliation and, as global trade slumped, the world fell more deeply into depression.

The difficult conditions in which foreign investment had operated in the 1920s were only exacerbated by the Great Depression. To reduce competitive pressures, many manufacturing companies formed cartels that controlled prices and production levels.[90] In the 1930s, governments adopted severe regulations of the banking sector in particular, limiting foreign ownership of banks or expropriating foreign owned banks in developing countries.[91] Exchange controls, which were widespread during the Great Depression, prevented investors from transferring profits and dividends into a convertible currency and thus discouraged foreign investment flows.

Yet foreign investment, especially in the manufacturing sector, did manage to spread during this time, although investors needed to navigate a labyrinth of regulations. The rise of protectionist tariffs encouraged companies to establish overseas affiliates in countries protected by high tariffs, in order to sell to those markets without having to pay the tariffs. Where they could not repatriate their earnings because of exchange controls, investors would reinvest the funds in the local economy. Most of this manufacturing investment, however, was in developed countries. The collapse of the global economy to a great extent had removed developing countries from the flow of international investment.

After the war, many of the developed countries had sought to restore the gold standard. The gold standard, however, severely impeded the efforts of countries to address the depression. Adherence to the standard precluded using monetary policy to stimulate the economy and orthodox economic theory of the day condemned deficit spending.[92] Further, adherence to the gold standard, with its free convertibility, transmitted financial shocks throughout the economy. Rumors that interest rates might fall in one country would lead investors to move their funds to a different country, thus converting the rumor to a self-fulfilling prophecy.[93] As capital fled, banks failed. Capital flight also required the investor to convert its funds into the currency of the country where it planned to invest the money and this act would drain gold from the treasury of the country where the investment formerly had been. To prevent depletion

---

89 *Id.* at 185. Protectionism and then war would continue to diminish world trade so that by 1950 exports as a percentage of world GDP stood at 5 percent, about the same figure as in 1870. World Bank, *Globalization, Growth, and Poverty* 27 (2002).

90 Jones, *supra* note 11, at 90.

91 *Id.* at 135–136.

92 Frieden, *supra* note 63, at 182.

93 *Id.* at 182.

of its gold supply, the country would have to raise interest rates to encourage investors to reinvest.[94] Higher interest rates would only further inhibit recovery.

As a result, the Great Depression ended the gold standard permanently. By the 1930s, governments no longer were willing to allow deflation and unemployment as the price of maintaining the gold standard.[95] The United Kingdom abandoned the gold standard in 1931, while the United States suspended gold convertibility in 1933, formally abandoning the gold standard in 1937. Generally, those countries that tried to remain on the gold standard the longest suffered the most. For example, between 1932 and 1935, industrial production in countries not on the gold standard grew by 6 percent a year, while it declined by 1 percent a year in countries still on the gold standard.[96] As countries abandoned the gold standard, some adopted exchange controls while others allowed their currency to devalue. Both devices represented efforts to achieve macroeconomic stability, although by different routes. The experience of the late 1920s and early 1930s discredited the gold standard, creating the conditions for a shift to a new, more interventionist policy on capital movements after World War II.[97]

The Great War and the Great Depression had profoundly challenged the international community's commitment to the principles of access and nondiscrimination (and to security during the war). The third great event of the twentieth century that contributed to the destruction of the pre-war international investment regime was the Russian Revolution of 1917, leading to the establishment of a communist government in the world's largest country. The revolution, like the other events, would curtail access, but also would have a long term effect on the principle of security.

By 1918, the new Soviet government had repudiated its foreign debt and begun a process that gradually would result in the nationalization of all property within its territory, which included large amounts of foreign investment, perhaps two-thirds of all French and Belgian foreign investment.[98] In 1921, the Soviet government acknowledged that it was obligated to pay compensation to foreign investors, but only on the condition that allied governments pay compensation for losses sustained as a result of foreign military interventions during the civil war that followed the revolution. Because the Soviet government estimated the amount of the losses attributable to foreign military intervention to be about four times the value of the claims of foreign investors,[99] the Soviet position essentially amounted to a demand for reparations that could be reduced by the amount of investor claims. The device of demanding an offset against the amount of compensation owed set a precedent that would be followed in subsequent decades when expropriating countries argued that the amount of compensation should be offset by various amounts, such as new, retroactive taxes.[100]

---

94 *Id.* at 183.

95 Maurice Obstfeld and Alan M. Taylor, *Global Capital Markets: Integration, Crisis, and Growth* 145 (2004).

96 Frieden, *supra* note 63, at 191.

97 Obstfeld and Taylor, *supra* note 95, at 145.

98 Jones, *supra* note 7, at 27.

99 Lipson, *supra* note 29, at 67.

100 *Id.*

The Soviet expropriations also were noteworthy for their scale. Past expropriations generally involved the seizure of individual investments, while the Soviet Union essentially abolished the very concept of private property and took title to all means of production in the economy. This eventually would lead to the argument that the obligation to pay compensation did not apply, or at least did not apply in the same way, to the expropriation of an entire sector of the economy, such as all banks. In this view, where the expropriation was nondiscriminatory, no compensation was owed.

The war and the Soviet expropriations had generated a large number of claims for loss of property. Other claims arose as a result of a series of agrarian land expropriations commenced by Mexico in 1915. Although claims for expropriations by communist governments would be resolved, if at all, through negotiated settlements between states, other claims were submitted to arbitral tribunals or to the Permanent Court of International Justice. These tribunals and the court generated a number of important awards and judgments during the 1920s. Perhaps the most important of these was the *Case Concerning the Factory at Chorzow*,[101] which established that an unlawful expropriation requires restitution or compensation sufficient to eliminate the effects of the wrongful act. Seventy years later, when claims were submitted to investor-state arbitration under the BITs, claimants and respondents alike would rely upon the jurisprudence generated during the early decades of the twentieth century and particularly in the 1920s.

In 1930, building on the work of several conferences held during the 1920s, the League of Nations held the First Conference for the Codification of International Law at The Hague. Three topics were selected for codification: nationality, territorial waters, and the responsibility of states for damage done in their territory to the person or property of foreigners. In preparation for the conference, acting on behalf of a project known as the Harvard Research on International Law, Edwin Borchard produced a Draft Convention on the Responsibility of States for Damage done in their Territory to the Person or Property of Foreigners,[102] which became known as the 1929 Harvard Draft. The conference was the least successful with respect to the work on state responsibility. Delegates found that while an extensive jurisprudence on the subject existed, this jurisprudence "[was] not known or [was] not understood in the same way in all countries, and . . . its authority [was] not universally acknowledged in the same degree."[103] Thus, "a sharp divergence of views on the fundamental aspects of the subject was evident from the start, and but slight progress was ever made toward reconciling the divergence."[104] Although a majority of the 42 delegations were prepared to formulate certain standards required by international law, seventeen of the delegations, principally those from Latin America and Eastern Europe, believed that foreigners should not enjoy better treatment in a country than its own nationals. Ultimately, majority support was obtained for only two articles, one on denial of justice

101 (Germany v. Poland), P.C.I.J., Ser. A, No. 17 (1928).

102 23 *American Journal of International Law Special Supplement* 133 (1929).

103 Manley O. Hudson, "The First Conference for the Codification of International Law," 24 *American Journal of International Law* 447, 459 (1930).

104 *Id.*

and one on due diligence. The rules of the conference, however, required a two-thirds majority for the adoption of an article and thus nothing was adopted.

Latin American states continued to maintain that foreign investors were entitled to nothing better than national treatment. At the Seventh International Conference of American States held in Montevideo in 1933, the states adopted the Convention on the Rights and Duties of States.[105] Article 9 of the convention provided that "Nationals and foreigners are under the same protection of the law and the national authorities, and the foreigners may not claim rights other or more extensive than those of the nationals."

In 1938, Mexico expropriated foreign oil interests in its territory. This merely was the latest in the long series of expropriations dating back to 1915, although the earlier expropriations had involved agrarian lands. U.S. Secretary of State Cordell Hull sent a diplomatic note demanding "prompt, adequate and effective" compensation, but the Mexican government, consistent with the Calvo Doctrine, declined to recognize any obligation to pay foreign investors when its own nationals were not compensated.[106] Further, Mexico contended that international law did not require compensation when the expropriations were of a general nature. The United States, however, took little action to compel compensation. The Roosevelt administration was more concerned with the looming war in Europe and feared that U.S. sanctions would wreck Mexico's economy, destabilize the government, disrupt mutually beneficial trade between the two countries, and invite retaliation against other U.S. investments.

In the two decades after the end of World War I, the innovations in FCNs that had been adopted in the decades prior to World War I became common in treaty practice. In other words, the inter-war period was less a period of innovation than of consolidation. The right to engage in industry as well as trade on an MFN basis appeared in many FCNs.[107] Inter-war FCNs occasionally granted national treatment with respect to the right to engage in commerce and industry.[108] The interwar FCNs did see an expansion in the rights accorded to companies from mere recognition and access to courts to include MFN treatment.[109] Treaties sometimes specified that the right to MFN treatment

---

105 165 L.N.T.S. 19 (1933).

106 *See* Section 6.5.2.

107 *See, e.g.*, Commercial Agreement between Germany and Spain, July 25, 1924, Art. 6, 41 L.N.T.S. 363 (1925–26); Treaty of Commerce and Navigation between Japan and the Kingdom of the Serbs, Croats and Slovenes, November 16, 1923, Art. II, 42 L.N.T.S. 99 (1925–26); Treaty of Commerce and Navigation between Greece and Finland, December 18, 1926, Art. I, 70 L.N.T.S. 89; Treaty between the Economic Union of Belgium-Luxembourg and the Kingdom of Serbs, Croats and Slovenes, December 16, 1926, Arts. 1 and 3, 70 L.N.T.S. 371 (1928); Convention of Commerce and Navigation, February 25, 1927, Art. 1, 71 L.N.T.S. 25; Convention of Commerce and Navigation between Denmark and Spain, January 2, 1928, Art. 3, 71 L.N.T.S. 271; Treaty of Commerce between the Kingdom of Hungary and the German Reich, July 18, 1931, Art. 1,150 L.N.T.S. 111 (1934).

108 *See, e.g.*, Treaty of Commerce and Navigation between Guatemala and Italy, September 15, 1926, Art. 2, 70 L.N.T.S. 175 (1928); Treaty of Commerce and Navigation between Brazil and Uruguay, August 25, 1933, Art. I, 176 L.N.T.S. 372 (1937).

109 *See, e.g.*, Treaty of Commerce and Navigation between Greece and Finland, December 18, 1926, Art. II, 70 L.N.T.S. 89; Treaty of Commerce and Navigation between Guatemala and Italy, September 15, 1926, Art. 7, 70 L.N.T.S. 175 (1928); Treaty between the Economic

was limited to "similar" or "like" companies.[110] Provisions relating to currency transfers, rare before World War I, started to appear with some frequency during the interwar period. The typical provision guaranteed that the proceeds from the sale of property could be freely exported without being subject to higher duties than nationals of the host state would pay.[111] Provisions for the arbitration of disputes between the parties concerning the interpretation or application of the treaty continued to appear,[112] although they were by no means universal. Some FCNs specified that the disputes would be submitted to the Permanent Court of International Justice.[113] Another innovation during the interwar period was the appearance of exceptions for frontier traffic and customs unions.[114] Apart from FCN practice, countries continued as they had in the nineteenth century to constitute mixed claims commissions to arbitrate existing claims for injuries to foreign nationals, often as a result of violence or war. After World War I, these commissions, particularly those formed to resolve claims for war damages against Germany, sometimes permitted the claimants to submit their claims to the tribunal directly.[115] Some earlier tribunals had permitted individuals to appear

---

Union of Belgium-Luxembourg and the Kingdom of Serbs, Croats and Slovenes, December 16, 1926, Art. 6, 70 L.N.T.S. 371 (1928); Convention of Commerce and Navigation between Greece and Latvia, February 25, 1927, Art. 2, 71 L.N.T.S. 25; Convention of Commerce and Navigation between Denmark and Spain, January 2, 1928, Art. 9, 71 L.N.T.S. 271; Treaty of Commerce and Navigation between Estonia and Finland, April 11, 1931, Art. IV, 124 L.N.T.S. 217; Treaty of Commerce between the Kingdom of Hungary and the German Reich, July 18, 1931, Art. 5,150 L.N.T.S. 111 (1934).

110 *See, e.g.*, Treaty of Commerce and Navigation between Greece and Finland, December 18, 1926, Art. II, 70 L.N.T.S. 89 (similar); Treaty between the Economic Union of Belgium-Luxembourg and the Kingdom of Serbs, Croats and Slovenes, December 16, 1926, Art. 6, 70 L.N.T.S. 371 (1928)(similar); Convention of Commerce and Navigation between Greece and Latvia, February 25, 1927, Art. 2, 71 L.N.T.S. 25 (like); Treaty of Commerce and Navigation between Estonia and Finland, April 11, 1931, Art. IV, 124 L.N.T.S. 217 (similar).

111 *See, e.g.*, Treaty of Commerce and Navigation between Guatemala and Italy, September 15, 1926, Art. 3, 70 L.N.T.S. 175 (1928); Treaty between the Economic Union of Belgium-Luxembourg and the Kingdom of Serbs, Croats and Slovenes, December 16, 1926, Art. 4, 70 L.N.T.S. 371 (1928).

112 *See, e.g.*, Treaty between the Economic Union of Belgium-Luxembourg and the Kingdom of Serbs, Croats and Slovenes, December 16, 1926, Art. 29, 70 L.N.T.S. 371 (1928); Convention of Commerce and Navigation between Greece and Latvia, February 25, 1927, Art.19, 71 L.N.T.S. 25; Treaty of Commerce and Navigation between Estonia and Finland, April 11, 1931, Art. XVIII, 124 L.N.T.S. 217; Treaty of Commerce between the Kingdom of Hungary and the German Reich, July 18, 1931, Art. 28,150 L.N.T.S. 111 (1934).

113 *See, e.g.*, Convention of Commerce and Navigation between Denmark and Spain, January 2, 1928, Art. 11, 71 L.N.T.S. 271.

114 *See, e.g.*, Treaty of Commerce and Navigation between Japan and the Kingdom of the Serbs, Croats and Slovenes, November 16, 1923, Art. XVII, 42 L.N.T.S. 99 (1925–26); Convention of Commerce and Navigation between Greece and Latvia, February 25, 1927, Art. 18, 71 L.N.T.S. 25.

115 Baron Legum, "The Innovation of Investor-State Arbitration under NAFTA," 43 *Harvard International Law Journal* 531, 535 (2002).

through counsel to argue their claims, although the injured party's home state at least formally was the claimant.[116]

In summary, several features consistently characterized the international investment regime in the Colonial Era in the nineteenth and early twentieth centuries. First, trade and property protection provisions appeared in the same agreement. In the Colonial Era, states generally did not negotiate separate treaties for the protection of property or investment. Second, the emphasis of the treaties was on establishing commercial relations. Property protection provisions were present in the treaties, but were clearly secondary in importance, and often incidental, to the creation of commercial relations.[117] Third, the principles of security, nondiscrimination, access, and due process were established elements of treaty practice throughout this era. Fourth, the kinds of provisions in use evolved only slightly from the early nineteenth century to the early twentieth century. Fifth, the scope of treaty protection was limited, particularly where the treaties provided no means for enforcement. Thus, the nonlegal mechanisms of military force and diplomacy remained important means for protecting foreign investment.

The seeming continuity in treaty practice, however, masked underlying changes in the operation of the international economy. The period after 1914 had witnessed serious challenges to the principles of access, nondiscrimination and security in daily practice. After 1914, governments everywhere adopted restrictions on cross-border movements of capital and, for the first time, large scale expropriations of foreign investment had occurred not as a war measure, but as an instrument of economic policy.

2.2 THE COLD WAR ERA: 1944–1989

The outbreak of World War II initially only aggravated the incursions on the principles of access, nondiscrimination, and security wrought by World War I, the Great Depression, and the Russian Revolution. With respect to security, World War II, like prior wars, was witness to widespread expropriations of the property of enemy aliens. Germany and Japan lost all their foreign investment as a result of their defeat in the war.

The war led to greater restrictions on currency transfers. By March 1940, of the principal currencies of the world, only the U.S. dollar and the Swiss franc still were convertible.[118] During the war, capital mobility was at a nadir, with most countries operating on the basis of bilateral payment arrangements.[119] By 1947, nearly four hundred such bilateral agreements were in force.[120] The principle of nondiscrimination was in shambles.

---

116 *Id.*

117 *See* Samuel Bemis, A Diplomatic History of the United States 25–29, 65–84, 101–110, and 200–202 (1965) (describing the early history of the FCN agreements, including their purpose).

118 Obstfeld and Taylor, *supra* note 95, at 146.

119 *Id.* at 145.

120 *Id.* at 151.

The end of the war, however, produced three events with long-term consequences for the international investment regime. The first of these events was the decision of the eventually victorious allies, even before the war ended, to construct a new post-war international economic order that would avoid the extreme nationalism of the years after 1914 and return to the liberal principles of the decades before 1914. The new order would be shaped by the most powerful economy at the end of the war, the United States.

U.S. post-war policy was driven in part by the fact that U.S. industry had become highly competitive and export oriented. Exports were twice as important to the U.S. economy at the end of the war as before, while competition from imports was weaker.[121] U.S. policy also was driven, however, by an ideological commitment to economic liberalism, particularly free trade.[122] U.S. policy makers believed that recent history had demonstrated that an integrated world economy would promote prosperity, while the protectionist policies of the inter-war years had exacerbated the Great Depression.[123] They also believed that free trade would promote peace, while the nationalist policies of the interwar years had led only to war. U.S. Secretary of State Cordell Hull noted that "it is a fact that war did not break out between the United States and any country with which we had been able to negotiate a trade agreement. It is also a fact that, with very few exceptions, the countries with which we signed trade agreements joined together in resisting the Axis. The political line-up followed the economic line-up."[124]

As early as 1941, John Maynard Keynes of Great Britain and Harry Dexter White of the United States began to exchange proposals for a system that would replace the gold standard. The new system would be designed to ensure both exchange rate stability, which the gold standard had assured, and macroeconomic stability, which the gold standard had not. To achieve both, countries would need to restrict capital movements to some degree. Both plans assumed government intervention rather than a self-regulating capital market.

In July 1944, the United Nations Monetary and Financial Conference met at the Mount Washington Hotel in Bretton Woods, New Hampshire, and adopted a plan based predominantly on Dexter's proposal. This new order was to promote free trade, but not an entirely free movement of capital. Thus, states were expected to impose some restrictions on inward investment and controls on capital transfers. In effect, the gold standard was inverted. Under the gold standard, capital flowed freely between countries, but governments lost control over their monetary policy. Under the Bretton Woods system, governments would maintain control over their monetary policy and capital movements would be restricted. Like the gold standard, however, the Bretton Woods system assumed fixed exchange rates. More specifically, the Bretton Woods system contemplated that currencies would have fixed values in relation to the dollar and the dollar would be convertible to gold at $35 per ounce. Currencies other than the

---

121 Frieden, *supra* note 63, at 262.

122 Rondo Cameron, *A Concise Economic History of the World* 370–371 (3d ed. 1997).

123 Bernard Hoekman and Michael Kostecki, *The Political Economy of the World Trading System* 2–3 (1995).

124 Quoted in Frieden, *supra* note 63, at 254–255.

dollar had a gold par value, but this was derived from their relation to the dollar. Although the value of currencies was expected to remain stable, the system permitted currencies to be revalued periodically, if necessary. The International Monetary Fund was created to provide loans to governments needing financing to maintain the value of their currency against short-term pressures. If it appeared that a currency was overvalued substantially, then with IMF approval member countries could adjust the value of their currency.

Article VIII of the IMF Articles of Agreement allowed exchange controls on current transactions only with the approval of the IMF. Current transactions, of course, are linked to trade. Countries had learned in the 1920s how to use currency controls as a means of protectionism and the goal of the IMF was gradually to eliminate that possibility by ensuring the free convertibility of payments in relation to international trade, thereby removing a potential trade barrier.

Article VI(3) of the IMF Articles of Agreement, however, explicitly authorized exchange controls with respect to capital transactions. The architects of the system believed that capital mobility had been a major aggravating factor in the Great Depression. The Bretton Woods system was intended to offer the exchange rate stability associated with the gold standard, while avoiding the rigidity that had prevented countries from pursuing their macroeconomic objectives. The greater control over macroeconomic policy would come at the price of reduced capital mobility.

As it happened, even current account convertibility was difficult for countries to achieve in the period immediately after the war. At the end of the war, only the U.S. dollar was freely convertible for current transactions. For this reason, Article XIV allowed states to defer their acceptance of the Article VIII obligation of free transfer of payments related to current transactions during a transitional period. The principal European currencies became fully convertible for current transactions in 1958, but achieving convertibility for capital transactions was a much slower process. Only in the 1970s did most Western European countries begin to remove controls on capital transactions. The United Kingdom ended them in 1979, Japan in 1980, Australia and New Zealand in 1983, the Netherlands in 1985, France, Sweden, and Denmark in 1989, Norway, Belgium and Luxembourg in 1990, Finland and Austria in 1991, Portugal and Ireland in 1993, and Iceland in 1994.[125] Even today about twenty IMF members are still subject to Article XIV rather than Article VIII.

Private investors had become reluctant to invest in public works projects, such as railroads and ports, because of the length of time required before they could receive a return on their investment.[126] The solution for this problem was another institution approved at Bretton Woods, the International Bank for Reconstruction and Development, which evolved into the World Bank. The bank would finance public works projects that were necessary to attract private capital, but that themselves would be difficult to finance through private investment.

---

125 Sweta C. Saxena, "A Survey of Issues Related to Capital Account Liberalization," available at http://www.ssrn.com.

126 Frieden, *supra* note 63, at 258.

The Bretton Woods conference also recognized the need for an international organization to promote international trade, but the conference was attended principally by finance ministers rather than trade officials and thus work on such an organization was deferred. The negotiation of a charter for an International Trade Organization (ITO) began in London in 1946 and was completed in Havana in March 1948 with the adoption of the Havana Charter. Meanwhile, in order to began a process of immediate tariff reductions, parallel negotiation of a General Agreement on Tariffs and Trade (GATT)[127] had been launched in Geneva. The GATT negotiation was successfully concluded in October 1947. The GATT was expected to be a temporary agreement that eventually would be displaced by the work of the ITO. The U.S. Congress, however, refused to ratify the Havana Charter, in part because the American business community believed that the investment protection provisions had been weakened too much at the insistence of developing countries.[128] Thus, the GATT by default became the principal instrument for the liberalization of trade. The GATT contained no provisions on investment, but it shifted the primary legal framework for international trade relations from bilateral to multilateral agreements and set in motion successive rounds of negotiations aimed at worldwide trade liberalization.[129] Thus, entry into force of the GATT created a major multilateral organization with competence over trade, but not investment. Investment would need to be treated outside the GATT framework, which to a large extent meant separately from trade.

The second event after the end of World War II that shaped the international investment regime was the spread of communism into Eastern Europe and China. All foreign investment in those countries was nationalized and further access by foreign investors was curtailed. These new communist countries generally argued that no compensation for expropriated foreign property was owed, emphasizing that a restructuring of the national economy along communist or socialist lines was a different phenomenon than the seizure of isolated parcels of property within a liberal economic system. Ultimately, about a third of the world's population would live under communist regimes and these regimes would launch a powerful critique of liberal investment policy over the next forty years. That is, these countries not only would oppose the application of BIT principles in their own territories, but would argue forcefully to other countries, particularly developing countries, that economic relations with the developed countries of Western Europe and North America were inherently exploitative and that the best path to economic development lay in extensive state regulation of the economy rather than through the free market.[130] The communist countries eventually resolved compensation claims by foreign investors by negotiating lump sum settlements with the investors'

127 General Agreement on Tariffs and Trade, Oct. 20, 1947, 61 Stat. 3689, 55 U.N.T.S. 188.

128 Hoekman & Kostecki, *supra* note 123, at 12–13; Jones *supra* note 11, at 221–222.

129 The most recent to conclude was the Uruguay Round, which ended in December 1993. *See* John Croome, *Reshaping the World Trading System* (1995). The World Trade Organization is now engaged in the Doha Round of multilateral trade negotiations.

130 *See generally* E. Wayne Nafziger, *The Economics of Developing Countries* 106–108 (3d ed. 1997); John Rapley, *Understanding Development: Theory and Practice in the Third World* 18–20 (1996).

home countries under which all claims were extinguished in exchange for a single payment that each home state could distribute among its investors as it deemed appropriate. Although the lump sum settlement agreements sometimes were cited by developing countries as state practice supporting a rule that expropriation required less than full compensation, developed countries responded that these settlements were pragmatic efforts to resolve an international dispute and not a recognition that the amount paid was the amount owed in principle.[131]

The third event that shaped the international investment regime in the period after World War II was the end of colonialism, which led to the creation of scores of newly independent but economically undeveloped countries.[132] These newly independent states were fiercely protective of their independence[133] and some of them came to regard foreign investment as a form of neocolonialism because it involved foreign control over the means of production.[134] Concerns also were expressed that foreign investors would interfere in the domestic political affairs of the host state.[135]

Many of the newly independent countries turned to the import substitution industrialization policies that Latin America had adopted in the 1930s, under which they would seek to produce needed goods and services locally rather than importing them from developed countries. Latin America originally adopted these policies during a period when the entire world was turning toward economic nationalism and thus few alternatives existed. By the end of World War II, however, the elites in these countries had become accustomed to protection. Strong ideological justifications for these policies were available, ranging from appeals to national power and pride on the right to denunciations of neocolonialism on the left. Although foreign direct investment created the greatest concern because it involves a foreign presence in the host state's territory, even trade with developed countries was viewed with suspicion, the fear being that trade between developed and developing countries would result in the exploitation of the latter.[136] Thus, Latin American countries erected high tariffs, funded subsidies for industry, and in some cases adopted multiple exchange rates to discourage the importation of any product that had a domestic substitute. Latin American governments also took control of much of the infrastructure and natural resources sector, which allowed them to provide domestic industry with subsidized inputs. These policies were embraced in the new nations of Asia and Africa, where governments took control of key sectors of the economy, raised tariffs, and adopted highly interventionist strategies. Often, import substitution industrialization was identified with socialism, sometimes with an

---

131 The classic treatment of this topic is Richard B. Lillich and Burns H. Weston, *International Claims: Their Settlement By Lump Sum Agreements* (1975). For a later study of the phenomenon of lump sum settlements, *see* Burns H. Weston, Richard B. Lillich and David J. Bederman, *International Claims: Their Settlement By Lump Sum Agreements 1975–1995* (1999).

132 The number of countries more than tripled as a result of decolonialization after the war. David S. Landes, *The Wealth and Poverty of Nations* 431 (1999).

133 M. Sornarajah, *The International Law on Foreign Investment* 12 (1994).

134 Dean Hanink, *The International Economy: A Geographic Perspective* 234 (1994).

135 Michael P. Todaro, *Economic Development* 534 (5th ed. 1994); Robert Gilpin, *The Political Economy of International Relations* 247–248 (1987).

136 Barry W. Poulson, *Economic Development: Private and Public Choice* 39 (1994).

ethnic identity. Governments spoke of Arab socialism or of African socialism. Where economic relations with other countries were desired, developing countries would seek to form them with other developing countries.[137] The hostility to foreign investment was particularly visible in the Middle East, where Iran nationalized the oil industry in 1951, Egypt nationalized the Suez Canal in 1956, and Syria and Iraq nationalized foreign assets in the early 1960s.[138]

In short, each of the three major events shaping the post-war investment regime produced a different faction in the international debate over investment policy. The efforts by the United States and its European allies produced a faction of "first world" countries that were the most developed economically and that generally favored a liberal investment regime, although nationalist and Marxist voices in these countries would influence their policies and limit adherence to liberal principles. The spread of communism produced a faction of "second world" countries that pursued industrialization through central planning and that rejected the free market policies of the first world as inequitable and a façade behind which the first world would perpetuate its dominance of the global economy. The end of colonialism produced a numerically large faction of "third world" countries that were economically underdeveloped and often politically fragile and that were seeking to develop economically in a way that was consistent with their newly found independence.

Suspicions about foreign investment initially were not limited to the communist and developing countries. In the years following the war, restrictions on inward foreign investment and exchange controls that had emerged in the interwar years were retained by many developed countries. The United States did not add significant new restrictions on inward investment after the war, but those that were adopted before the war remained.[139]

Despite these restrictions, some international investment flows did resume after the war, with nearly all international investment originating in a few developed countries of the first world. Initially, most of this investment consisted of U.S. companies establishing affiliates in Canada and Western Europe, increasingly through acquisitions, although most foreign direct investment was still greenfield investment.[140] British and Dutch manufacturing firms also ventured abroad.[141] Indeed, between the end of World War II and the 1980s, the United States, the United Kingdom, and the Netherlands were the source of between two-thirds and three-fourths of all foreign direct investment.[142]

In the 1950s, the relative importance of foreign investment in the primary sector began to decline.[143] One reason was host state policies of asserting national control over natural resources. In a number of cases, host countries expropriated foreign

---

137 Starting in the 1960s, developing countries made numerous attempts to create preferential trading arrangements among themselves, most of which were unsuccessful. Dominick Salvatore, *International Economics* 314–315, 323–325 (5th ed. 1995).

138 Jones, *supra* note 11, at 211.

139 *Id.* at 206.

140 *Id.* at 150.

141 *Id.* at 93.

142 *Id.* at 231.

143 *Id.* at 67.

investment in the natural resource sector, such as tin in the 1950s, copper in the 1960s and 1970s, and oil in the 1950s through the 1970s.[144] By the 1980s, half of the mineral production in developing countries was state-owned.[145]

Most international capital was invested in developed countries. In 1950, the foreign capital stock of developing countries was only 4 percent of income, which was less than half the level of 1870.[146] Before the war, the United States had three times as much investment in Latin America as in Europe, but by the 1960s it had three times as much invested in Europe and Japan as in Latin America.[147] With foreign investment shifting from the natural resources sector to the manufacturing and services chapter, investors were drawn to countries with developed human capital and infrastructure, large markets, and secure investment climates. Cultural and geographic proximity also influenced locational decisions.

By 1971, the Bretton Woods system no longer was sustainable.[148] American deficit spending in the 1960s to finance the war in Vietnam and the new social programs of the Lyndon Johnson administration was causing inflation. While the prices of American goods were rising, the value of the dollar on the international market was held constant by the Bretton Woods system. That is, a given quantity of foreign currency bought the same number of dollars as always, but the dollars could purchase less than before. Thus, consumers in other countries no longer could afford to buy the increasingly expensive American goods, and U.S. exports fell. At the same time, inflation in the United States pushed up wages and thus Americans with their larger nominal incomes in dollars could buy larger amounts of foreign currency, which encouraged them to purchase imports, travel, or invest abroad. As exports fell and imports rose, the United States began to experience sustained trade deficits. Anticipating that the United States would eventually be forced to devalue the dollar in order to reduce or eliminate the trade deficits, foreign holders of dollars no longer wished to keep a currency that was about to be devalued. The United States was met with a torrent of demands for gold in exchange for dollars, which threatened to drain the nation's gold reserves. In fact, in the first seven months of 1971, the United States lost about one-third of its gold reserves.[149] The United States could attempt to end these demands by raising interest rates and cutting government spending, which would halt the inflation, reduce the trade deficit and encourage those outside the United States to hold dollars in order to earn the higher return, but these policies also would push the country into a recession. U.S. President Richard Nixon had attributed his loss of the 1960 presidential election to John F. Kennedy to the fact that the United States was in a recession during the election, and he was determined to avoid a recession during his 1972 reelection campaign. Unwilling to sacrifice domestic prosperity or his reelection to prolong the life of the

---

144 *Id.*

145 *Id.*

146 World Bank, *Globalization, Growth, and Poverty* 25, 27 (2002).

147 Frieden, *supra* note 63, at 293.

148 The following paragraph draws on Frieden, *supra* note 63, at 339–346.

149 David K. Eiteman, Arthur I. Stonehill, and Michael H. Moffett, *Multinational Business Finance* 33 (8th Edition 1998).

Bretton Woods system, on August 15, 1971, President Nixon took the dollar off the gold standard, effectively destroying the Bretton Woods system. Efforts were made to salvage the system, but by 1973 a return to Bretton Woods clearly was not possible.

The collapse of the Bretton Woods system meant that countries no longer had a uniform method of setting their exchange rates. Some countries allowed the exchange rate to "float," that is, to be set by the market. These countries would adopt the macroeconomic policies they wished, but they no longer would guarantee the stability of their currency in international markets. Countries, of course, are not indifferent to the value of their currency. A country's wealth is denominated in its own currency and a decline in the value of the currency essentially diminishes the value of its assets. Further, when a currency loses value, debt owed in a foreign currency becomes more expensive to service. Investments abroad become more expensive to make and foreign-made goods become more expensive to purchase. At the same time, a gain in the value of a country's currency raises the prices of its goods in world markets and limits its ability to export goods, while lowering the price of goods denominated in other currencies, thus making imports cheaper to purchase. Thus, domestic producers face greater difficulty selling their goods abroad and face greater competition from imports. For these reasons, a country that chooses to allow its currency to float might nevertheless periodically intervene in the market, buying or selling currency in order to raise or lower the exchange rate and thereby keep it in a certain range. Alternatively, the country might adjust interest rates in order to make its currency more or less desirable in world markets.

Other countries, seeking to stabilize the value of their currency, would "peg" their currency, meaning that the currency would have a stated value in relation to another currency, often the U.S. dollar. Maintaining the peg required that the central bank buy or sell currency to keep the market price close to the pegged rate. As this suggests, some small deviation from the stated rate is permitted. If countries allowed capital to flow freely across borders, then pegging one country's currency to another country's would mean that the monetary policy of the latter country would control the economy of the first country.

In short, in a world of capital mobility, countries effectively have two choices: they can maintain control over their monetary policy and sacrifice currency stability by adopting a floating exchange rate or, alternatively, they can stabilize their currency with a pegged exchange rate and lose control over their monetary policy. The only way to escape this dilemma is to restrict capital movements. By closing its capital account, a country may set its own monetary policy while maintaining a stable currency, but it will lose the benefits of foreign investment. Many countries have sought to balance all of these considerations through a compromise, known as a managed float. A managed float in theory permits the market to set the exchange rate, but only within a specified range. The less a country intervenes, the more the managed float functions like a floating rate. The more a country intervenes, the more the managed float functions like a pegged rate. In fact, a floating rate, a managed floating rate, and a pegged rate essentially all represent points along a continuum rather than rigidly distinct categories. They differ in the degree to which the government will intervene to control the value of the currency.

As capital mobility has increased, the trilemma whereby a country cannot simultaneously have capital mobility, a fixed exchange rate, and control over its economic policy, has become of enormous consequence to countries. A country that has chosen to peg its currency may be forced to endure a severe recession in order to maintain the peg. Yet, if it allows the exchange rate to float, any indication in the market that the rate is about to fall could trigger a massive sell-off of the currency, converting the rumor into a self-fulfilling prophecy. As the value of the currency in international markets falls, the burden of its external debt increases. That is, capital mobility may force a choice between a recession or increased debt.

While the collapse of the Bretton Woods system was changing state practice with respect to capital mobility, *i.e.*, with respect to the principle of access, the policies of the Soviet bloc and many developing countries were threatening the security of investment, as well as the principle of nondiscrimination. Thus, the security of foreign investment diminished in the post-war world. Outside of the communist world, expropriation remained an exceptional phenomenon before the 1960s.[150] In the first years of the 1960s, fewer than ten expropriations a year occurred in the developing world. The number accelerated in the late 1960s, however, with between twenty and thirty occurring in some years. By the early 1970s, more than fifty expropriations a year were occurring in developing countries. The wave peaked in 1975, when more than eighty expropriations occurred. Many of these expropriations reflected indigenization policies by former colonies, particularly in Africa.[151] Half the expropriations during the 1970s occurred in Africa.[152] Zambia, Uganda, and Sudan each expropriated more than thirty foreign enterprises.[153] Throughout the 1960s and 1970s, host states unilaterally repudiated concession agreements with foreign investors, acts that were treated as expropriations of the contracts.[154] Many of these concession agreements had been entered into by colonial governments and granted rights over natural resources to foreign investors for long periods of time. For example, the Sheikh of Kuwait, at a time when Kuwait was a British protectorate, entered into a concession agreement with an American oil company for a period of sixty years during which the royalty to be paid was two shillings and six pence for each barrel of oil, an amount that could not be changed except by mutual agreement.[155] Ghana entered into a concession agreement granting rights to prospect for gold for one hundred years.[156] The cancellations of concession agreements, particularly those involving oil exploration and production, resulted in another wave of important international arbitrations, mostly in the 1970s, although a few occurred in the 1950s and 1960s.[157]

---

150 The data in this paragraph are taken from Jones, *supra* note 11, at 214.

151 Lipson, *supra* note 29, at 110.

152 *Id.* at 110.

153 *Id.*

154 B.A. Wortley, *Expropriation in Public International Law* 57 (1977).

155 Sornarajah, *supra* note 133, at 31.

156 *Id.*

157 *See, e.g., Petroleum Development Ltd. v. The Sheikh of Abu Dhabi*, 18 International Law Reports 144 (1951); *Sapphire International Petroleums Ltd. v. National Iranian Oil Company*, 35 International Law Reports 136 (1963); *BP Exploration Company Ltd. v. Libya*, 53 International

By the late 1970s, the number of expropriations in developing countries had fallen to fewer than twenty per year, although the number spiked in 1979 because of the Islamic revolution in Iran. One reason for the decline in the number of expropriations in the latter part of the 1970s was that the expropriation of the natural resource sector, where foreign ownership was especially sensitive politically, was essentially complete by the end of the 1970s.[158] Further, the results of early expropriations were disappointing and by the end of the 1970s developing countries were beginning to consider alternatives to expropriation.

Meanwhile, in the early 1970s, the developing and communist countries mounted an effort in the United Nations General Assembly, where they held a vast numerical majority, to establish recognition of their right to expropriate foreign investment without payment of full value for the expropriated assets. On May 1, 1974, the General Assembly adopted the Declaration of the New International Economic Order (NIEO),[159] which declared that states have "[f]ull permanent sovereignty" over their natural resources and other economic activities.[160] State sovereignty includes "the right of nationalization or transfer of ownership to its nationals."[161] The Declaration did not specify any obligation to pay compensation. On December 12, by a vote of 120–6 with 10 abstentions,[162] the General Assembly adopted the Charter of Economic Rights and Duties of States.[163] Article 2.2(c), which was adopted by a separate vote of 104–16, with 6 abstentions,[164] declared that each state has the right "[t]o nationalize, expropriate or transfer ownership of foreign property, in which case appropriate compensation should be paid by the State adopting such measures, taking into account its relevant laws and regulations and all circumstances that the State considers pertinent."[165] The Charter thus stated that compensation should be paid, not that it must be paid, and that

---

Law Reports 297 (1979); *Texaco Overseas Petroleum Company (TOPCO) and Californian Asiatic Oil Company v. Libya*, 53 International Law Reports 389 (1979); *Libyan American Oil Company (LIAMCO) v. Libya*, 20 International Legal Materials 1 (1981); *Kuwait v. American Independent Oil Company (AMINOIL)*, 21 International Legal Materials 976 (1982).

158 Jones, *supra* note 11, at 214.

159 Declaration on the Establishment of a New Economic Order, G.A. Res. 3201(S-VI), U.N. GAOR, 6th Special Sess., 229th mtg., Agenda Item 7, U.N. Doc. A/RES/3201(S-VI) (1974), reprinted in 13 *International Legal Materials* 715 (1974).

160 *Id.* at para. 4(3).

161 *Id.*

162 The six states that voted in opposition were Belgium, Denmark, the Federal Republic of Germany, Luxembourg, the United Kingdom, and the United States. The ten states that abstained were Austria, Canada, France, Ireland, Israel, Italy, Japan, the Netherlands, Norway, and Spain.

163 Charter of Economic Rights and Duties of States, G.A. Res. 3281 (XXIX), U.N. GAOR, 29th Sess., 2315th mtg., Agenda item 48, U.N. Doc. A/RES/3281(XXIX) (1975), *reprinted in* 14 *International Legal Materials* 251 (1975).

164 The sixteen states that voted in opposition were Austria, Belgium, Canada, Denmark, Federal Republic of Germany, France, Ireland, Italy, Luxembourg, Japan, the Netherlands, Norway, Spain, Sweden, the United Kingdom, and the United States. The six states that abstained were Australia, Barbados, Finland, Israel, New Zealand, and Portugal.

165 *Id.*, art. 2, para. 2 (c).

the amount of compensation would be based on national law, which might not provide for any compensation, rather than on international law.[166]

That same year, developing countries launched a movement within the United Nations to draft a Code of Conduct for Transnational Corporations, an international instrument that would establish norms to govern the conduct of transnational corporations. Developed countries insisted that the code also should include protections for foreign investment. After years of disagreement over the content of the code, the United Nations suspended negotiations in 1992. The Organization for Economic Cooperation and Development (OECD) responded to the proposed U.N. code of conduct by adopting in 1976 a Declaration on International Investment and Multinational Enterprises, to which was annexed a set of Guidelines for Multinational Enterprises. Neither the proposed U.N. code of conduct or the OECD declaration, however, has had a significant impact on the operation of multinational enterprises[167] or the development of BITs. That is, these efforts did not lead to the inclusion of investment regulation provisions in BITs.

Developed countries responded to the threat of uncompensated expropriation by proposing international agreements for the protection of foreign investment.[168] The United Nations Charter, adopted at the end of the war, had prohibited the use of military force[169] except in self-defense,[170] which rendered the use of force to collect debts or

---

166 *See generally*, Charles N. Brower & John B. Tepe, Jr., "The Charter of Economic Rights and Duties of States: A Reflection or a Rejection of International Law?" 9 *International Lawyer* 295 (1975); Burns H. Weston, "The Charter of Economic Rights and Duties of States and the Deprivation of Foreign Owned Wealth," 75 *American Journal of International Law* 437 (1981).

167 Raymond Vernon, *In the Hurricane's Eye* 184–185 (1998).

168 The BIT programs as they emerged in the early years are described in: Rudolf Dolzer and Margrete Stevens, *Bilateral Investment Treaties* (1995); Kenneth J. Vandevelde, *U.S. International Investment Agreements* (2009); Kenneth J. Vandevelde, "U.S. Bilateral Investment Treaties: The Second Wave," 14 *Mich. J. Int'l L.* 621 (1993); Mohamed I. Khalil, "Treatment of Foreign Investment in Bilateral Investment Treaties," 8 *ICSID Rev.* 339 (1992); Robert K. Paterson, "Canadian Investment Promotion and Protection Treaties," 29 *Canadian Y.B. Int'l L.* 373 (1991); Jeswald Salacuse, "BIT by BIT: The Growth of Bilateral Investment Treaties and Their Impact on Foreign Investment in Developing Countries," 24 *Int'l Law* 655 (1990); Kenneth J. Vandevelde, "The Bilateral Investment Treaty Program of the United States," 21 *Corn. Int'l L. J.* 201 (1988); Adeoye Akinsanya, "International Protection of Foreign Direct Investment in the Third World," 36 *Int'l & Comp. L. Q.* 58 (1987); Eileen Denza & Shelagh Brooks, "Investment Protection Treaties: United Kingdom Experience," 36 *Int'l & Comp. L. Q.* 908 (1987); Palitah T.B. Kohona, "Investment Protection Agreements: An Australian Perspective," 21 *J. World Trade L.* 79 (1987); T. Modibo Ocran, "Bilateral Investment Protection Treaties: A Comparative Study," 8 *N.Y.L.Sch. J.* Int'l *& Comp. L. Q.* 401 (1987); M. Sornarajah, "State Responsibility and Bilateral Investment Treaties," 20 *J. World Trade L. 79* (1986); Pamela B. Gann, "The U.S. Bilateral Investment Treaty Program," 21 *Stan. J. Int'l L.* 373 (1985).

169 United Nations Charter, Art. 2(4) (providing in part that "[a]ll members shall refrain in their international relations from the threat or use of force against the territorial integrity or political independence of any state. . . .")

170 United Nations Charter, Art. 51 (declaring that "[n]othing in the present charter shall impair the inherent right of individual or collective self-defense if an armed attack occurs against a

protect investment illegal under international law.[171] Given the serious deficiencies of customary international law as a means of protecting international investment,[172] treaties offered potentially the most effective means for preventing uncompensated expropriations.

The negotiation of FCN treaties had resumed as soon as the war ended. The post-war FCNs generally addressed the same issues in much the same way as the inter-war FCNs. Notable exceptions were the treaties of the Soviet Union and the United States, which were among the first countries to inaugurate FCN programs.

The Soviet FCNs included only very limited investment protection provisions. They provided for MFN treatment with respect to trade, industrial or other economic activity, but this obligation was subject to local law.[173] They also granted to those engaged in these activities a general right of MFN treatment.[174] Thus, the Soviet Union's FCNs largely included little more than a limited right of nondiscrimination with respect to access and treatment generally. They did not provide for investment security or dispute resolution. Some Soviet FCNs merely guaranteed that companies organized under the law of one party would be recognized in the territory of the other party and have the right to appear in the courts of that other party.[175]

The U.S. FCNs, by contrast, included the most elaborate provisions on investment ever seen in an FCN, although they applied their protections to "property" rather than "investment." Notably, the post-war U.S. FCNs extended the same investment-related protections to companies that they extended to individuals.[176] Earlier agreements had

---

Member of the United Nations until the Security Council has taken the measures necessary to maintain international peace and security.")

171 Even before the adoption of the U.N. Charter, the use of force to collect debts had become increasingly controversial. For example, Article I of the Hague Convention of 1907 had outlawed the use of force to collect contract debts owed to private citizens of one state by the government of another state unless the debtor state refused to submit the dispute to arbitration. Hague Convention of 1907, Oct. 18, 1907, 36 Stat., T.S. No. 536. The American delegation to the conference that drafted the convention had supported this provision. *See* VI Green Hackworth, *Digest of International Law* 152 (1943).

172 International investment law as late as the period immediately following the Second World War has been characterized as "an ephemeral structure consisting largely of scattered treaty provisions, a few questionable customs, and contested general principles of law." Jeswald W. Salacuse and Nicholas P. Sullivan, "Do BITs Really Work? An Evaluation of Bilateral Investment Treaties and Their Grand Bargain," 46 *Harvard International Law Journal* 67, 68 (2005).

173 *See, e.g.*, Treaty of Commerce and Navigation between the USSR and Czechoslovakia, December 11, 1947, Art. 13; 247 U.N.T.S. 35; Treaty of Commerce and Navigation between the USSR and Bulgaria, April 1, 1948, Art. 16., 247 U.N.T.S. 96.

174 *See, e.g.*, Treaty of Commerce and Navigation between the USSR and Czechoslovakia, December 11, 1947, Art. 13; 247 U.N.T.S. 35; Treaty of Commerce and Navigation between the USSR and Bulgaria, April 1, 1948, Art. 16, 247 U.N.T.S. 96.

175 *See, e.g.*, Treaty of Commerce between the USSR and Switzerland, March 17, 1948, Art. 10, 247 U.N.T.S. 73; Treaty of Commerce and Navigation between the USSR and Italy, December 11, 1948, 247 U.N.T.S. 181.

176 *See* Herman Walker, Jr., "Provisions on Companies in United States Commercial Treaties," 50 *American Journal of International Law* 373 (1956).

protected principally individuals. Protection for companies had emerged in FCN practice only at the beginning of the twentieth century and typically had involved little more than rights to recognition, MFN treatment and access to courts. The conclusion of the post-war U.S. FCNs with important investment provisions reflected the fact that investment protection for the first time had become a primary goal of the FCN agreements.[177]

The post-war U.S. FCNs also were innovative in that they required each party to provide "equitable treatment"[178] or, in some treaties, "fair and equitable treatment" to the persons, property, enterprises, and other interests of nationals and companies of the other party.[179] References to fair and equitable treatment long had been present in treaty practice. For example, an 1801 FCN between Russia and Sweden guaranteed to foreign nationals "bienveillance, justice et equity."[180] The U.S.-Netherlands interwar FCN required that a state-created monopoly accord "fair and equitable treatment" to the commerce of the other party.[181] The post-war U.S. FCNs, however, established the standard as a regular component of treaty practice. The post-war U.S. FCNs also incorporated a new standard that prohibited a party from adopting unreasonable or discriminatory measures that would impair legally acquired rights or interests of nationals or companies of the other party.[182] As the latter standard in particular makes clear, the post-war U.S. FCNs were introducing the principle of reasonableness into investment treaty practice.

At the same time, the post-war U.S. FCNs also brought together the principal investment security provisions that had emerged in prior FCN practice. First, the post-war U.S. FCNs guaranteed to foreign owned property "the most constant protection and security,"[183] a long-established standard in FCN practice.

Second, the post-war U.S. FCNs included the most elaborate provision on expropriation yet seen in FCN practice. It permitted expropriation only if the expropriation was accompanied by prompt, adequate, and effective compensation, although the typical language read "prompt payment of just compensation . . . in an effectively

---

177 Kenneth J. Vandevelde, *U.S. International Investment Agreements* 22 (2009).

178 Treaty of Friendship, Establishment and Navigation, United States-Luxembourg, February 23, 1962, ("Luxembourg-United States FCN") Art. I, 14 U.S.T. 251, T.I.A.S. No. 5306; Treaty of Friendship, Commerce, and Navigation, United States-Ireland, January 21, 1950, ("Ireland-United States FCN") Art. V, 1 U.S.T. 785, T.I.A.S. No. 2155.

179 *See, e.g.*, Treaty of Friendship, Commerce, and Navigation, United States-Netherlands, March 27, 1956, ("Netherlands-United States FCN") Art. I(1), 8 U.S.T. 2043, T.I.A.S. No. 3942 (fair and equitable treatment).

180 Treaty of Amity, Commerce and Navigation, Russia-Sweden, Art. VI, 56 Consolidated Treaty Series 1.

181 Treaty of Commerce between the United States of America and the Netherlands, December 20, 1935, Art. VIII, 178 L.N.T.S. 239.

182 *See, e.g.*, Luxembourg-United States FCN, *supra* note 178, Art. IV(2); Ireland-United States FCN, *supra* note 178, Art. V.

183 *See, e.g.*, Netherlands-United States FCN, *supra* note 179, Art. VI(1); Ireland-United States FCN, *supra* note 178, Art. VIII(2).

realizable form." They also required that the expropriation be for a public purpose, nondiscriminatory and in accordance with due process of law.[184]

Third, the post-war U.S. FCNs adopted elaborate restrictions on exchange controls. They required each party to accord national and MFN treatment to nationals and companies of the other party with respect to currency transfers.[185] In addition, the parties were prohibited from imposing exchange controls that unnecessarily harmed or arbitrarily discriminated against the investment of nationals and companies of the other party.[186] Further, they regulated the circumstances under which even nondiscriminatory restrictions on currency exchange could be imposed. The provision in these treaties is described in greater detail in Section 6.7.2.

The post-war U.S. FCNs also embraced the principle of nondiscrimination. They required the host country to provide nationals and companies of the other party with national and MFN treatment with respect to the right to engage in various commercial, industrial, and financial activities.[187] They also prohibited discrimination against covered investment in the procurement of goods by the parties and enterprises that they own or control,[188] which occasionally had been a concern in some prior FCNs.

The post-war U.S. FCNs, through their guarantee of MFN and national treatment with respect to engaging in commercial, industrial, and financial activities, recognized the principle of access. Although a right of national treatment occasionally had appeared in the counterpart provision of earlier FCNs, these earlier agreements usually had guaranteed only MFN treatment. Thus, the post-war U.S. FCNs established a right of access more broadly than had prior agreements.

The post-war U.S. FCNs contained an important qualification to the right of nondiscrimination and hence to the right of access as well. The qualification permitted the treaty parties to carve out certain sectors of the economy in which nationals and companies of the other party would not have the right to national treatment.[189] The purpose of the qualification was to permit each party to reserve certain sectors of the economy to its own nationals. These treaties usually provided that sectoral limitations were to be imposed on an MFN basis.[190] Moreover, new limitations generally were not to apply to enterprises already existing when the limitations became effective.[191]

---

184 *See, e.g.*, Netherlands-United States FCN, *supra* note 179, Art. VI(4); Luxembourg-United States FCN, *supra* note 178, Art. IV(3);

185 *See, e.g.*, Netherlands-United States FCN, *supra* note 179, Art. XII(1).

186 *See, e.g.*, Netherlands-United States FCN, *supra* note 179, Art. XII(4).

187 *See, e.g.*, Netherlands-United States FCN, *supra* note 179, Arts. VII(1) and (4); Ireland-United States FCN, *supra* note 178, Arts. VI(1)(a) and VI(3).

188 *See, e.g.*, Treaty of Friendship and Commerce, United States-Pakistan, Nov. 12, 1959, ("Pakistan-United States FCN") Art. XVIII(2), 12 U.S.T. 110, T.I.A.S. No. 4683, 404 U.N.T.S. 259.

189 *See, e.g.*, Netherlands-United States FCN, *supra* note 179, Art. VII(2); Luxembourg-United States FCN, *supra* note 178, Art. VI(2).

190 *See, e.g.*, Netherlands-United States FCN, *supra* note 179, Art. VII(4). But MFN treatment was not always guaranteed. *See, e.g.*, Luxembourg-United States FCN, *supra* note 178, Art. VI.

191 *See, e.g.*, Luxembourg-United States FCN, *supra* note 178, Art. VI(2); Netherlands-United States FCN, *supra* note 179, Art. VII(2).

As has been seen, early FCNs had contained an access provision under which the nationals of each party were entitled to enter and reside in the territory of the other party. In the era when those FCNs were concluded, countries generally did not restrict immigration. In the 1920s, however, many countries, including the United States, adopted immigration restrictions. For example, immigration to the United States between 1914 and 1950 was six million persons, which was only 40 percent of that between 1870 and 1914.[192] Thus, U.S. FCNs no longer could grant to nationals of the other party a right to enter and reside in U.S. territory. U.S. immigration law, however, did provide for the granting of visas for persons entering the territory for the purpose of developing or directing an investment. Thus, the U.S. postwar FCNs authorized entry for those purposes,[193] subject to the right of either party to apply measures necessary to maintain public order or protect the public health, morals and safety. This reservation of right, in effect, meant that the treaty right remained subject to U.S. immigration laws.

Another related provision guaranteed the right to employ "accountants and other technical experts, executive personnel, attorneys, agents, and other specialists of their choice"[194] This language was a successor to a provision that had appeared in many prior FCNs.

The post-war U.S. FCNs also embraced the principle of due process. As in the case of some prior FCNs, they required each party to provide nationals and companies of the other party with MFN and national treatment with respect to access to courts of justice and administrative tribunals and agencies in pursuit and defense of their rights.[195] They also provided for state-state dispute resolution. Specifically, they included a provision that any dispute between the parties involving the interpretation or application of the treaty not resolved by diplomacy was to be submitted to the International Court of Justice, unless the parties agreed to settlement by some other peaceful means.[196]

Although the FCNs of other countries tended not to address property protection as comprehensively as the U.S. BITs, the kinds of provisions seen in prior FCNs continued to appear in many of the FCNs of the 1950s. First, the principle of nondiscrimination continued to be standard in FCN practice. A provision guaranteeing MFN treatment with respect to the right to engage in industrial and other kinds of activities was common.[197]

---

192 World Bank, *Globalization, Growth, and Poverty* 27 (2002).

193 *See, e.g.*, Netherlands-United States FCN, *supra* note 179, Art. II(1); Pakistan-United States FCN, *supra* note 188, Art. II(1). *See generally* Wilson, "Treaty Investor Clauses in Commercial Treaties of the United States," 44 *American Journal of International Law* 366 (1950).

194 *See, e.g.*, Treaty of Friendship, Commerce, and Navigation, United States-Japan, April 2, 1953, ("Japan-United States FCN") Art. VIII(1), 4 U.S.T. 2063, T.I.A.S. No. 2863, 206 U.N.T.S. 143.

195 *See, e.g.*, Pakistan-United States FCN, *supra* note 188, Art. V(1); Japan-United States FCN, *supra* note 194, Art. IV(1); Netherlands-United States FCN, *supra* note 179, Art. V(1).

196 *See, e.g.*, Japan-United States FCN, *supra* note 194, Art. XXIV(2); Netherlands-United States FCN, *supra* note 179, Art. XXV(2).

197 *See, e.g.*, Treaty of Commerce between the Republic of India and the Royal Kingdom of Afghanistan, April 4, 1950, Art. 1, 167 U.N.T.S. 105; Treaty of Amity between China and Spain, February 19, 1953, Art. V, 181 U.N.T.S. 81.

The principle of security was present as well. Provisions on expropriation were more common than in the past and typically required just compensation[198] or prompt, adequate, and effective compensation.[199] Whereas earlier FCNs had addressed expropriation in a variety of ways, with provisions that ranged from prohibitions on certain expropriations to requirements of restitution to requirements of compensation, the post-war FCNs reflected a consensus that expropriation was permissible, although certain conditions, such as the payment of compensation, were imposed. In part, this change seemed to reflect the fact that expropriations no longer were seen as acts likely to occur principally as reprisals during war time, which either should be prohibited entirely or perhaps reversed when peace came, but rather as acts likely to occur during time of peace as part of a country's economic policy.

Under these FCNs, companies incorporated under the laws of one party were to be recognized in the territory of the other, were to be permitted access to courts, and were to receive MFN treatment.[200] FCNs not concluded by the United States sometimes adopted the U.S. innovation of applying investment-related provisions to companies to the same extent that they were applied to individuals,[201] but often they did not.[202]

Efforts to develop investment protection treaties also were undertaken at the multilateral level almost immediately after the war. In 1948, the International Law Commission published the Draft Statute of the Arbitral Tribunal for Foreign Investment and the Draft Statute of the Foreign Investment Court.[203] These provided for investor-state arbitration of certain investment disputes. Although neither statute ever was adopted, they demonstrated the recognition not only of the importance of the due process principle, but of the need for a means by which investment disputes could be resolved without the involvement of the host state.

The following year, the International Chamber of Commerce proposed the International Code of Fair Treatment for Foreign Investment. The chamber had been seeking to develop a draft convention on the protection of foreigners since the 1920s.[204] The code guaranteed nondiscriminatory treatment of investment, granted a right of free transfer of certain payments related to an investment, required fair compensation for expropriated investment and provided for ICC arbitration of disputes concerning the code. The code, however, was never adopted.

---

198 Treaty of Commerce between the Republic of India and the Royal Kingdom of Afghanistan, April 4, 1950, Art. 3, 167 U.N.T.S. 105.

199 *See, e.g.*, Treaty of Commerce between Japan and Czechoslovakia, December 15, 1959, Art. IV, 383 U.N.T.S. 277.

200 *See, e.g.*, Treaty of Commerce between the Republic of India and the Royal Kingdom of Afghanistan, April 4, 1950, Art. 8, 167 U.N.T.S. 105.

201 *See, e.g.*, Agreement on Commerce between Japan and the Federation of Malaya, May 10, 1960, Arts. II, III and IV, 383 U.N.T.S. 293.

202 *See, e.g.*, Treaty of Friendship between Thailand and Indonesia, March 3, 1954, Art. IV, 213 U.N.T.S. 297; Treaty of Amity between the Republic of China and the Republic of El Salvador, Dec. 9, 1954, Art. VI, 214 U.N.T.S. 217.

203 Reprinted in United Nations Conference on Trade and Development, 3 International Investment Instruments: A Compendium 259 (1996).

204 *See* Andrew Newcombe and Lluis Paradell, *Law and Practice of Investment Treaties: Standards of Treatment* 16–17 (2009).

In the mid-1950s, Hermann J. Abs, a German banker who served on the boards of no fewer than 24 German corporations, including Deutsche Bank, Daimler-Benz, and Lufthansa, and Lord Hartley Shawcross, a British lawyer and politician, began a process of formulating a set of principles for the protection of foreign investment. Germany had lost most of its foreign investment after World War II as part of negotiated settlements for war damages. Abs, who represented Germany in those negotiations, was especially aware of the political risks to which foreign investment was exposed.[205] Lord Shawcross, in an interesting set of ironies, had been born in Germany and, as Britain's Attorney General after the war, had served as a prosecutor at the Nuremberg war trials. In 1959, the collaboration of the German and the Briton culminated in the Draft Convention on Investments Abroad, which contained many of the provisions that would be found in early BIT practice, including requirements of fair and equitable treatment, most constant protection and security, and the observance of obligations in relation to investments, a prohibition on unreasonable or discriminatory measures and uncompensated expropriations, and provisions for both state-state and investor-state dispute resolution. The convention was proposed for adoption by the Organization for European Economic Cooperation (OEEC), which had been formed in 1948 to develop a plan for European economic recovery and to supervise the distribution of U.S. aid to Europe under the Marshall Plan. The draft convention was never adopted, however.

In 1961, Professors Louis Sohn and Richard Baxter of the Harvard Law School published the Draft Convention on the International Responsibility of States for Injuries to Aliens.[206] Their draft was based on the 1929 report drafted by Edwin Borchard in preparation for the 1930 League of Nations codification conference and was known as the 1961 Harvard Draft. Although the Harvard Draft became a highly influential summary of customary international law, it did not greatly influence treaty practice.

Meanwhile, realizing that no multilateral instrument on investment was likely to be adopted in the near term, Germany chose to seek investment protection through bilateral agreements. On November 25, 1959, Germany concluded its first BIT, with Pakistan.[207] Three weeks later, on December 16, Germany concluded its second BIT, with the Dominican Republic, which became the first BIT to enter into force, on June 3, 1960.

The German BITs included provisions that addressed many of the same issues that had been addressed in the post-war U.S. FCNs.[208] Like these FCNs, the BITs included requirements of fair and equitable treatment, full protection and security, and national and MFN treatment, prohibited unreasonable or discriminatory measures, uncompensated expropriation and some restrictions on free transfers, and provided for state-state

205 Rudolf Dolzer and Christoph Schreuer, *Principles of International Investment Law* 18 (2009). Salacuse and Sullivan, *supra* note 172, at 73.

206 55 *American Journal of International Law* 545 (1961).

207 United Nations Conference on Trade and Development (UNCTAD), *Bilateral Investment Treaties in the Mid-1990s* 8, 177 (1998).

208 The contents of these early BITs are discussed in Chapters 4 through 10 in sections headed "Origins," which discuss the emergence and evolution of particular BIT provisions.

dispute resolution, although before an *ad hoc* arbitral tribunal rather than the International Court of Justice as in the post-war U.S. FCNs. Thus, the early BITs embraced the principles of security, nondiscrimination, reasonableness, and due process. The BITs differed from the FCNs, however, in that they addressed investment-related issues exclusively. Further, whereas the FCNs typically protected property, the BITs generally protected investment. The BITs also included weaker access provisions than the U.S. post-war FCNs.

Other Western European countries quickly followed Germany's lead. France concluded its first BIT in 1960,[209] Switzerland[210] in 1961, the Netherlands[211] in 1963, Italy[212] and the Belgium-Luxembourg Economic Union[213] in 1964, Sweden[214] and Denmark[215] in 1965, and Norway[216] in 1966.

The emergence of BITs, however, did not represent a complete and immediate departure from the earlier FCN practice. Many of the bilateral treaties concluded in the early 1960s that are now treated as BITs were commercial or economic treaties that addressed topics in addition to investment. In their broader scope, these treaties resembled to some extent the U.S. FCNs of the 1950s, although they typically were far less elaborate than the post-war U.S. FCNs.

For example, Switzerland commenced its BIT program in 1961 by concluding a BIT with Tunisia. The following year, however, Switzerland began to conclude treaties of commerce, investment protection, and technical cooperation.[217] As the title implies, these treaties addressed issues relating to trade and economic and technical cooperation, as well as investment. Switzerland continued to use this form of treaty with some countries until the 1970s.[218] Switzerland also continued to conclude BITs and these departed in some respects from the investment provisions of the Swiss commerce, investment and technical cooperation treaties.

Similarly, the Netherlands concluded a convention for the encouragement and protection of investment in 1963, but the bilateral treaties it concluded over the next decade were styled as economic cooperation agreements or economic and technical cooperation agreements. Only in the mid-1970s did the Netherlands BITs become consistently styled as treaties for the encouragement and protection of investment and omit the provisions unrelated to investment. For example, its 1971 "BIT" with Malaysia addressed maritime shipping, taxation, intellectual property, and commercial exhibitions, as well as investment.

---

209 UNCTAD, *supra* note 207, at 175. The agreement was with Chad. The French BITs of the 1960s, however, never entered into force and thus, for all practical purposes, the French BIT program did not commence until the early 1970s.

210 *Id.* at 205. The agreement was with Tunisia.

211 *Id.* at 192. The agreement was with Tunisia.

212 *Id.* at 184. The agreement was with Guinea.

213 *Id.* at 163. The agreement was with Tunisia.

214 *Id.* at 204. The agreement was with the Ivory Coast.

215 *Id.* at 172. The agreement was with Madagascar.

216 *Id.* at 193. The agreement was with Madagascar.

217 *See, e.g.*, Switzerland-Niger BIT; Switzerland-Guinea BIT; Switzerland-Ivory Coast BIT.

218 *See, e.g.*, Switzerland-Mauritania BIT.

The first three Danish BITs, concluded in 1965 and 1966, were each titled as a "commercial accord" and included trade and navigation provisions as well as investment provisions. With the conclusion of its BIT with Indonesia in 1968, however, Denmark began to use a title that referred to the protection and encouragement of investment and to omit the trade provisions.

The first three Swedish BITs, concluded with Ivory Coast in 1965, Madagascar in 1966, and Senegal in 1967, similarly were each titled as a commercial accord and included provisions on trade and navigation. The Swedish BIT program went into a hiatus in 1967, after which Sweden concluded no more BITs until 1978. When Sweden concluded its fourth BIT, with Egypt in 1978, the trade and navigation provisions were omitted.

The United States had launched its post-war FCN program in 1946. It continued to negotiate FCNs for the next twenty years, a period within which 21 agreements were concluded.[219] In 1966, the United States concluded its final FCNs, with Togo and Thailand. The 1960s thus saw BITs displace the FCNs.

The Organisation for European Economic Co-operation (OEEC) had been superseded in 1961 by the OECD, which included a broader membership than had the OEEC. Although the OEEC never adopted the Abs-Shawcross convention, the OECD continued to deliberate over multilateral rules for investment protection. In 1962, the OECD produced the Draft Convention on the Protection of Foreign Property, which was revised and adopted in 1967, but never opened for signature. Thus, the BITs continued to be the principal legal instrument for the protection of foreign investment.

Although the access principle was not prominent in the earliest BITs, it remained a part of investment treaty practice. In 1961 the OECD adopted the Code of Liberalization of Capital Movements and the Code of Liberalization of Current Invisible Operations.[220] The codes applied only to transactions among the OECD members. They required the parties to eliminate progressively restrictions on capital movements and on current invisible transactions, described as invisible because they relate to trade in services or financial transactions rather than trade in goods.

In the 1970s, the dramatic increase in the number of expropriations and the adoption of the NIEO and CERDs resolutions triggered several new BIT programs. The United Kingdom[221] concluded its first BIT in 1975, Austria[222] its first in 1976 and Japan[223] its

219 For a discussion of the modern FCNs, *see* Henry C. Hawkins, *Commercial Treaties and Agreements: Principles and Practice* (1951); Robert Reubert Wilson, *The International Law Standards in Treaties of the United States* (1953); Robert Reubert Wilson, *United States Commercial Treaties and International Law* (1960); Herman Walker, Jr., "Modern Treaties of Friendship, Commerce and Navigation," 42 *Minnesota Law Review* 805 (1958); Herman Walker, Jr., "Treaties for the Encouragement and Protection of Foreign Investment: Present United States Practice," 5 *American Journal of Comparative Law* 229 (1956); Robert R. Wilson, "A Decade of New Commercial Treaties," 50 *American Journal of International Law* 927 (1956); Robert R. Wilson, "Postwar Commercial Treaties of the United States," 43 *American Journal of International Law* 262 (1949); Robert R. Wilson, "Property-Protection Provisions in United States Commercial Treaties," 45 *American Journal of International Law* 83 (1951).

220 The codes may be found at http://www.oecd.org.

221 UNCTAD, *supra* note 207, at 211. The agreement was with Egypt.

222 *Id.* at 161. The agreement was with Romania.

223 *Id.* at 185. The agreement was with Egypt.

first in 1977. The United States inaugurated its BIT program in 1977, the first year of the Carter Administration, although it did not successfully complete a BIT negotiation until 1982.[224]

The BITs of the 1960s and 1970s were relatively uniform in content and were characterized by several distinctive features.[225] First, the BITs, as their name implies, dealt exclusively with investment. The developed countries recognized that trade was now principally within the province of the GATT, leaving investment to be treated alone in a bilateral treaty. Other factors, however, also militated in favor of treaties restricted solely to investment. For example, the inclusion of noninvestment issues, it was feared, would make the treatments too complex and difficult to conclude because of disagreements over unrelated issues,[226] a fear seemingly validated by the demise of the FCN programs. At the same time, the desire of developing countries to obtain concessions in noninvestment areas might induce them to conclude BITs containing investment obligations that they could not honor, with the result that conclusion of the treaty might offer investors false security.[227] At least in the United States, it was hoped that the BITs would reflect a genuine commitment to investment protection on which investors could rely.[228]

Second, BITs were negotiated principally between a developed and a developing country.[229] The FCNs often, although not always, had been between two developed countries. The BITs were intended to protect the investment of the developed country in the territory of the developing country.[230] Typically, a BIT model negotiating text was drafted by the developed country and offered to the developing country for signature, with the final treaty text reflecting only relatively minor changes from the original draft.[231] This persistent pattern added an ideological dimension to the treaties. Although both parties formally assumed the same obligations, the BITs were perceived as nonreciprocal because in practice the obligations all fell on the developing country party.[232]

Third, the motivation for the developing country to conclude a BIT in most cases was to attract investment from the developed country.[233] The theory was that offering a secure legal framework for foreign investment would induce foreign investors to invest.

---

224 Kenneth J. Vandevelde, "The Bilateral Investment Treaty Program of the United States," 21 *Cornell International Law Journal* 201, 209–211 (1988).

225 *See generally* UNCTAD, *supra* note 207, at 71; Dolzer & Stevens, *supra* note 168.

226 Vandevelde, *supra* note 224, at 210.

227 Vandevelde, *supra* note 177, at 26, 31–32.

228 Vandevelde, *supra* note 224, at 211–212.

229 UNCTAD, *supra* note 207, at 8–19.

230 *Id.* at 1.

231 For a discussion of the U.S. experience in this regard, *see* Vandevelde, *supra* note 224, at 211–213. For a general discussion of BIT negotiations, *see* Kenneth J. Vandevelde, "Treaty Interpretation from a Negotiator's Perspective," 21 *Vanderbilt Journal of Transnational Law* 281 (1988).

232 Sornarajah, *supra* note 133, at 227.

233 UNCTAD, *supra* note 207, at 5.

Fourth, the motivation for the developed country to conclude a BIT was to obtain protection for its foreign investment.[234] Whereas the FCN agreements had been concerned principally with establishing economic relations, the BITs were a defensive reaction to past expropriations of existing investments without payment of full compensation.[235]

Fifth, the protections provided by the BITs were similar to those that had been provided in the post-war U.S. FCNs. Typically, they contained a promise of "fair and equitable treatment" for covered investment, a commitment to pay prompt, adequate, and effective compensation for expropriation of covered investment, and restrictions on exchange controls. The full protection and security standard found in many FCNs and the prohibition on unreasonable or discriminatory measures found in post-war U.S. FCNs also was included in many BITs. Although the U.S. FCNs had guaranteed nationals of each party national and MFN treatment with respect to the right to engage in various economic enterprises, most of the BITs did not guarantee to investors of one party the right to establish investment in the territory of the other party,[236] although they sometimes guaranteed the right to MFN or national treatment for investment once established. The U.S. BITs that appeared in the 1980s were an exception, promising national and MFN treatment with respect to the right to establish investment. Like the FCNs, the early BITs contained a provision for settlement of disputes between the parties, although the BITs typically provided for submission of the disputes to an *ad hoc* arbitral tribunal rather than, as in many FCNs, the International Court of Justice. The U.S. BITs in the 1980s incorporated transparency provisions into a BIT for the first time, thus introducing the transparency principle into investment treaty practice, although transparency provisions relating to trade had appeared in the GATT and in the U.S. post-war FCNs.

One major innovation in the BITs was the inclusion, starting in the late 1960s, of a provision in which the host state consented to arbitration of disputes with investors concerning covered investments. This provision was prompted by the conclusion of a 1965 convention establishing the International Centre for Settlement of Investment Disputes (ICSID),[237] an entity affiliated with the World Bank. ICSID was created as a venue for the arbitration of disputes between investors and host state governments. For the first time, investors had an effective remedy for unlawful actions by host states that injured their investments that did not depend upon local courts in the host state or action by their home state. In providing the investor with a legal remedy that was not

234 *Id.* at 2–6.

235 Vandevelde, *supra* note 224, at 24–27.

236 In the United States BITs, the guarantees of national and most favored nation treatment applied to the right to establish investment. Thus, covered investors were entitled to establish investment in the host state as long as nationals of the host state or of any third state were permitted to do so. Such a provision, however, is not typical of most BITs. *See* UNCTAD, *supra* note 207, at 46.

237 Convention on the Settlement of Investment Disputes Between States and Nationals of Other States, March 18, 1965, 17 U.S.T. 1270, T.I.A.S. No. 6090.

conditioned upon espousal, these BIT provisions depoliticized investment disputes. That is, they placed investment protection in the realm of law rather than politics.[238]

Presumably because of the perceived nonreciprocal nature of the treaties and the skepticism of many developing countries toward foreign investment, the network of BITs remained somewhat limited. From 1959 to 1969, only 75 BITs worldwide were concluded, fewer than 7 per year.[239] From 1970 to 1979, the rate grew slightly to just over 9 per year and 92 BITs were concluded.[240] The rate more than doubled in the 1980s to more than 21 BITs concluded each year, for a total of 219 during that decade.[241] Still, from 1959 until 1989, only 386 agreements were concluded, an average of about 1 per month worldwide.[242]

2.3 THE GLOBAL ERA: 1990–PRESENT

The new global economy that the United States and its allies had sought to create at the end of World War II finally emerged at the end of the 1980s, although without the Bretton Woods system that had collapsed some 15 years before. At the end of the 1980s, most countries of the world joined a new international consensus in support of a liberal international investment policy.[243] Ironically, the demise of economic nationalism with respect to international investment flows at the beginning of the 1990s may have resulted from the ascendancy of economic nationalism in the 1970s and its subsequent discrediting in the same way that economic nationalism in international trade was discredited after World War II by the disastrous effects of economic nationalism during the interwar years.

In 1973, the year before the General Assembly reaffirmed the right of permanent sovereignty over natural resources in the NIEO Declaration, the members of the Organization of Petroleum Exporting Countries (OPEC) exercised their sovereignty over their natural resources by quadrupling the price of oil on the world market. One consequence was that many developing countries suddenly were forced to borrow money to purchase oil and other imports.

Another consequence was that the OPEC countries rapidly acquired from the sale of oil very large quantities of dollars that they deposited in banks around the world. The banks were only too willing to lend these dollars to developing countries, with the result that in the early 1970s many developing countries began to accumulate substantial external debts. For example, the external debt of all developing countries grew

---

238 *See* Ibrahim F. I. Shihata, "Towards a Greater Depoliticization of Investment Disputes," 1 *ICSID Review—Foreign Investment Law Journal* 1 (1986).

239 UNCTAD, *supra* note 207, at 9.

240 *Id.*

241 *Id.*

242 A list of BITs concluded from the inception of the program through 1989 may be found in *id.*, at 159–217.

243 For a more extended discussion of some of the events that led to this consensus, *see* Kenneth J. Vandevelde, "Sustainable Liberalism and the International Investment Regime," 19 *Michigan Journal of International Law* 373 (1998).

from $68.4 billion in 1970 to $635.8 billion in 1980, an almost tenfold increase in just ten years. Thus, in the 1970s, bank lending became a much more important component of international investment flows. In the period prior to World War I, most international lending took the form of bonds. Between 1973 and 1982, bank loans constituted more than half of all capital flows to emerging markets.[244]

Meanwhile, the Islamic Revolution in Iran in 1979 triggered a second oil shock that doubled energy prices, setting off the most severe worldwide recession in five decades. The recession in turn reduced demand for developing country exports, thereby curtailing the ability of these countries to earn foreign currency to service the debt incurred during the 1970s.

The debt burden on developing countries was aggravated by the economic policies of the Reagan administration in the United States, which combined deficit spending with a restrictive monetary policy. As a result of the surge in the U.S. budget deficit, during the three years between 1982 to 1985, the United States changed from the world's largest creditor to the world's largest debtor.[245] The United States financed its budget deficits by selling bonds, which meant that the United States was competing with developing countries for debt financing. Unable to compete with the United States, developing countries could not borrow additional funds from private investors to refinance their debts.[246]

The restrictive monetary policy and competition for capital pushed up interest rates and thereby heightened the burden of the accumulated debt on developing countries. U.S. budget deficits also impaired the economic recovery in Europe, which defeated the efforts of developing countries to bolster their exports and earn foreign currency to pay off their external debt. Capital shortages in developing countries were exacerbated by massive capital flight,[247] as the deteriorating economic situation in developing countries prompted wealthy nationals to invest their money abroad.[248]

These events converged in the early 1980s to trigger the third-world debt crisis. The crisis began in August 1982, when Mexico announced that it could not make its payments on its $80 billion debt.[249] Banks that had lent extensively to developing countries suddenly were threatened with collapse.[250] In 1982, when the debt crisis erupted, the amount owed by the major debtors to U.S. banks amounted to 255 percent

---

244 Eichengreen, *supra* note 68, at 40.

245 *See* Steven Husted & Michael Melvin, *International Economics* 314 (3rd ed. 1995); Lester C. Thurow & Laura D'Andrea Tyson, "The Economic Black Hole," 67 *Foreign Policy* 3 (1987).

246 Jeffrey E. Garten, "Gunboat Economics," 63 *Foreign Affairs* 538, 546 (1984).

247 For example, it is estimated that capital flight accounted for all but $12 billion of Mexico's $96 billion foreign debt in 1985. Todaro, *supra* note 135, at 463–464.

248 Currencies in developing countries became overvalued (partially as a result of falling exports). This in turn gave rise to fears that the currency would be devalued in the future, leading to efforts to invest funds in more stable currencies abroad. Husted & Melvin, *supra* note 245, at 407.

249 *See* Samuel Britain, "A Very Painful World Adjustment," 61 *Foreign Affairs* 541, 548 (1982).

250 *Id.*

of bank capital.[251] The comparable figure for U.K. banks was 119 percent and for German banks 50 percent.[252]

Ultimately, the collapse was averted by a combination of refinancing with funds borrowed from the World Bank and the International Monetary Fund and debt forgiveness under the Brady Plan in 1989 and the early 1990s. The Brady Plan, named for U.S. Secretary of the Treasury Nicholas F. Brady, called for reducing developing countries' debt to commercial banks by 20 percent, combined with increased lending by the World Bank and the IMF.[253] The debt crisis of the 1980s, however, reduced the availability of private lending,[254] which, by 1980, had accounted for half of all capital flows to developing countries.[255]

Under other circumstances, developing countries might have replaced commercial loans with loans from multilateral development agencies, such as the World Bank, the Inter-American Development Bank, the African Development Bank and the Asian Development Bank. The early 1980s, however, saw reductions in developmental assistance, largely at the behest of the Reagan administration.[256] In 1984, for example, the United States insisted on a 40 percent reduction in lending by the International Development Agency, the World Bank entity that lends to the poorest nations.[257] Between 1980 and 1987, U.S. contributions to multilateral development banks dropped from $2.3 billion annually to $1.1 billion.[258]

Further, the loans that were available through the World Bank and other public lenders were conditioned on the adoption by the loan recipients of strict macroeconomic structural adjustment policies that required painful currency devaluations and reductions in budget deficits.[259] Developing countries that in the past might have equated foreign direct investment with external control of their economy or even neocolonialism found that international lending institutions could exercise far more control over their economies than foreign direct investors.

These reductions in lending combined with capital flight sharply diminished the capital available to developing countries to finance economic development. In fact, the net inflow of private capital into developing countries in the 1980s was only about

---

251 Eichengreen, *supra* note 68, at 42.

252 *Id.*

253 Subrata Ghatak, *Introduction to Development Economics* 443–449 (3d ed. 1995); Salvatore, *supra* note 137, at 355.

254 *See* Rapley, *supra* note 130, at 37–38; Jahangier Amuzegar, "Dealing with Debt," 68 *Foreign Policy* 140, 141–142 (1987); Samuel Britain, "A Very Painful World Adjustment," 61 *Foreign Affairs* 541, 541–548 (1982); Pedro-Pablo Kucynski, "Latin American Debt," 61 *Foreign Affairs* 344, 350–351 (1982).

255 Barry W. Poulson, *Economic Development: Private and Public Choice* 450–451 (1994).

256 Garten, *supra* note 246, at 552–554.

257 *Id.* at 553.

258 See John W. Sewell & Christine E. Contee, "Foreign Aid and Gramm-Rudman," 65 *Foreign Affairs* 1015, 1022 (1987). Total U.S. foreign assistance actually increased during this period, but only because of the sharp increase in military assistance, which more than offset the decrease in economic development assistance. *Id.*

259 Nafziger, *supra* note 130, at 562–574; Jahangir Amuzegar, "The IMF Under Fire," 64 *Foreign Policy* 98 (1986).

60 percent of what it had been in the late 1970s.[260] Unable to borrow sufficient funds and with their domestic savings fleeing abroad, developing countries found foreign private direct investment one of the few remaining sources of capital available.

Just as developing countries found themselves forced to turn to private foreign investment as a source of capital, the possibility of achieving development through economic integration seemed to be confirmed by another set of events: the performance of several East Asian economies, specifically Japan, the four "Asian Tigers" (Hong Kong, Republic of Korea, Singapore, and Taiwan), and the three "Dragon Economies" of Southeast Asia (Indonesia, Malaysia, and Thailand). During the period from 1965 to 1990, these eight Asian economies grew at a rate that was three times the rate in Latin America and twenty-five times the rate in sub-Saharan Africa.[261] These eight economies were characterized by a number of common features, prominently among them high rates of private investment and an emphasis on production for export.[262] The so-called East Asian Miracle amply demonstrated the constructive role that foreign investment and global integration could play in a developing economy and seemed to prove the benefits of export led growth relative to import substitution industrialization.[263]

Import substitution industrialization policies simply had not worked as well as had been hoped.[264] Every country must import at least a few things that are not available locally, whether raw materials, machinery, or intermediate products. As countries industrialized, their need for inputs grew. The industrialization, however, had been promoted through internal tax breaks and subsidies and most countries pursuing import substitution industrialization policies operated chronic budget deficits. They financed the deficits by inflating the currency, which made their exports more expensive. As exports fell, countries would experience trade deficits. Trade deficits could be remedied by raising interest rates and devaluing the currency, but these measures would trigger a recession. They also would make exports more attractive in foreign markets, which would trigger new growth. As the economy improved, more imports would be needed and the cycle would start again. Countries following these policies saw continuous waves of budget deficits, inflation and recession.

The final step in the emergence of the contemporary consensus was the collapse of the Soviet bloc at the end of the 1980s.[265] The Soviet-style planned economy had been

---

260 *See* Eduardo Fernandez-Arias & Peter J. Montiel, "The Surge in Capital Inflows to Developing Countries: An Analytical Overview," 10 *World Bank Economic Review* 51 (1996).

261 *See* World Bank, *The East Asian Miracle: Economic Growth and Public Policy* 2 (1993).

262 *Id.* at 40–42.

263 *Id.* at 22–23, 37–38, 40–43; Alex E. Fernandez Jilberto & Andre Mommen, "Setting the Neoliberal Development Agenda," in *Liberalization in the Developing World* 1, 3–4, (Alex E. Fernandez Jilberto & Andre Mommen, eds. 1996).

264 This paragraph draws on Frieden, *supra* note 63, at 351–356.

265 On the disintegration of the Soviet bloc, *see* Michael Mandelbaum, "Coup de Grace: The End of the Soviet Union," *Foreign Affairs*, Winter 1991–92, at 164; Michael Mandelbaum, "The Bush Foreign Policy," *Foreign Affairs*, Winter 1990–91, at 5; Coit D. Blacker, "The Collapse of Soviet Power in Europe," *Foreign Affairs*, Winter 1990–91, at 88.

the principal ideological alternative to free market capitalism during the Cold War Era.[266] The decision by virtually the entire communist world to abandon planned economies in favor of free markets delegitimized central planning, leaving liberal economics as seemingly the only effective model for economic growth.[267]

The combined effect of these events was the emergence of a consensus in the developing world about the desirability of attracting foreign investment through free market policies.[268] Developing countries also realized that attracting foreign investment would require them to compete for it. A 1985 study found intense competition among developing countries to attract foreign investment, with some countries offering as many as thirty different incentives to attract a particular investment.[269] Even where developing countries remained skeptical of the free market, the structural adjustment policies required of them by international financial institutions left many of them with no alternative but to liberalize their economies.[270]

Developing countries abandoned the hostility to foreign investment that had characterized the Cold War Era and openly sought to attract foreign investment by creating a favorable environment for such investment.[271] The policies that they had employed during the Cold War Era of hostility to foreign investment, import substitution industrialization, and closed markets to foreign goods, services, and capital appeared to have been a mistake.[272] Discussions of a New International Economic Order and the right to expropriate without payment of compensation disappeared.[273] Latin American countries abandoned the Calvo Doctrine and concluded BITs imposing international minimum standards for the protection of foreign investment and providing for international arbitration of investment disputes.[274] Developing countries rushed to attract foreign investment by demonstrating their support for market capitalism in general and a secure investment climate in particular.

Changes in attitude toward foreign investment were accompanied in the 1990s by a revolution in information technology, which permitted instantaneous transmission of virtually unlimited amounts of information to anywhere in the world and thus greatly facilitated the establishment and management of both direct and portfolio investment.

---

266 Nafziger, *supra* note 130, at 540–549; Rapley, *supra* note 130, at 70.

267 Rapley, *supra* note 130, at 70; Mark Kramer, "Eastern Europe Goes to Market," 86 *Foreign Policy* 134 (1992).

268 See Richard Caves, *Multinational Enterprise and Economic Analysis* 249 (2d. ed. 1996); Hanink, *supra* note 134, at 234; Jilberto & Mommen, *supra* note 263, at 19–20.

269 Caves, *supra* note 268, at 220.

270 Jilberto & Mommen, *supra* note 263, at 5–8, 24.

271 *See* Kenneth J. Vandevelde, "Investment Liberalization and Economic Development: The Role of Bilateral Investment Treaties," 36 *Columbia Journal of Transnational Law* 501, 502–503 (1998).

272 Jeswald W. Salacuse, "From Developing Countries to Emerging Markets: A Changing Role for Law in the Third World," 33 *International Lawyer* 875, 882–886 (1999).

273 *See* Thomas Waelde, "Requiem for the 'New International Economic Order'" in *Festschrif Fuer Ignaz Seidl-Hohenveldern* 771 (Gerhard Hafner et al., eds. 1998).

274 For example, Bolivia and Uruguay concluded BITs in 1987, Argentina and Venezuela in 1990, and Chile and Peru in 1991. UNCTAD, *supra* note 207, at 160, 164, 167, 195, 214, 215.

The volume of investment flows soared, from approximately $200 billion in 1990 to more than $1800 billion in 2007.[275] The revolution in information technology also gave investors the ability to construct highly sophisticated mathematical formulae for assessing risk and return, leading to the development of more complex investment instruments, particularly derivatives, and allowing the securitization of a wide range of debts. Thus, the 1990s saw not only an explosion in the quantity of international investment flows, but a change in their nature as well, as risks incurred in one part of the world were quickly spread around the globe. Financial markets became deeply integrated, a process that was facilitated by the deregulation of the financial services sector in a number of developed countries starting in the 1980s.

Concluding BITs that guaranteed protection for foreign investment offered a mechanism for signaling a desire to attract these new flows of foreign investment and for providing a more secure environment for such investment.[276] Further, some developing countries recognized that their efforts to attract foreign investment represented a reversal of policy and that foreign investors might well be skeptical about the permanence of this reversal. The long-term commitments represented by the BITs thus were also a means of enhancing the credibility of their new policies. BITs were useful as instruments of both liberal economics and liberal legalism.

Starting in the late 1980s, the number of BITs concluded accelerated dramatically. While fewer than four hundred BITs had been concluded in the thirty years from 1959 to 1989,[277] during the next fifteen years some two thousand BITs would be concluded.[278] More than twenty-six-hundred such treaties now exist, with more than twenty-two-hundred having been concluded since 1990.[279]

The Cold War Era had witnessed a separation of trade and investment in international agreements. The FCNs, with their mixture of trade and investment provisions, disappeared from state practice and were replaced by BITs that addressed investment-related concerns exclusively. Although the Global Era saw an explosion in the number of BITs, it also featured the reintegration of trade and investment concerns in some treaties. In 1992, Canada, Mexico, and the United States concluded the North American Free Trade Agreement (NAFTA), which contained an investment chapter modeled after the BITs. This established a precedent that would be widely followed in the ensuing years. As the trend toward liberalization continued and states sought deeper integration than they believed that they were able to achieve within the GATT or WTO framework or with agreements limited to investment,[280] bilateral and regional trade agreements with investment-related provisions greatly proliferated in number.

---

275 UNCTAD, *World Investment Report* 2008 3 (2008).

276 UNCTAD, *supra* note 207, at 6.

277 *Id.* at 9.

278 UNCTAD, *Recent Developments in international investment agreements (2007–June 2008), IIA Monitor* No. 2 (2008). UNCTAD had counted 259 agreements by the end of 2007.

279 *Id.*

280 *See* Richard E. Feinberg, "The Political Economy of United States' Free Trade Agreements," 26 *World Economy* 1019 (2003); Jong-Wha Lee, Innwon Park and Kwanho Shin, Proliferating Regional Trade Arrangements: Why and Whither?" October 15, 2004, available at http://www.ssrn.com; John Whalley, "Recent Regional Agreements: Why So Many, Why So Much Variance

By June 2008, approximately two-hundred-sixty economic integration agreements with investment chapters had been concluded.[281] Complementing these trade agreements is the Energy Charter Treaty,[282] which addresses investment, trade, and other issues in the energy sector. Concluded in 1994, the Energy Charter Treaty entered into force in 1998, with 46 countries having ratified it as of mid-2009.

The mixing of trade and investment provisions in the same agreement reflected changes in the nature of economic activity. Trade and investment no longer were seen as substitutes but as complements. The traditional view was to regard the establishment of a foreign subsidiary as a means for delivering goods or services to a foreign market, particularly when high tariffs or high transportation costs made export to that market unattractive.[283] In that view, foreign investment was an alternative to trade. In the Global Era, however, investment increasingly was seen not as a means of replacing trade, but of promoting it. Foreign subsidiaries, once established, were often links in a large chain of production, importing raw materials and parts from other subsidiaries and exporting a product to still other subsidiaries for distribution or perhaps for further refinement.[284] In effect, vertically integrated investment increasingly supplanted horizontally integrated investment. Deeper economic integration thus required lowering barriers both to trade and to investment. As a result, states negotiated bilateral and regional trade agreements that included investment related provisions. This, in turn, meant the return of the "package deal." The inclusion of investment in a larger group of concessions allowed the parties to offer concessions on investment in exchange for concessions in other areas.[285]

This process of deeper economic integration began to occur among states with dissimilar economic circumstances. In the Cold War Era, economic integration agreements typically were concluded among states at similar levels of economic development, with the most notable example being the European Community,[286] which later evolved into the European Union.[287] In 1990, two highly developed states, the United States and Canada, launched the negotiation of the North American Free Trade Agreement (NAFTA)

---

in Form, Why Coming So Fast, and Where Are They Headed?" CESifo Working Paper No. 1790, June 2006, available at http://www.ssrn.com.

281 United Nations Conference on Trade and Development, *Recent Developments in International Investment Agreements (2007–June 2008), IIA Monitor* No. 2 (2008).

282 34 International Legal Materials 360 (1995).

283 United Nations Conference on Trade and Development, *World Investment Report 1996: Investment, Trade and International Policy Arrangements* 79 (1996).

284 *Id.* at 103.

285 For discussions of the use of the package deal in the negotiation of the NAFTA, *see* Frederick W. Mayer, *Interpreting NAFTA: the Science and Art of Political Analysis* (1998).

286 The European Community was formed in the 1950s consisting of six West European states: Belgium, France, the Federal Republic of Germany, Italy, Luxembourg, and the Netherlands. Denmark, Ireland, and the United Kingdom joined in 1973, Greece in 1981, and Spain and Portugal in 1986. Thus, in the Post-Colonial Era, the European Community consisted solely of developed, West European countries.

287 The European Community became the European Union following the entry into force of the Treaty of European Union in 1993.

with Mexico, a developing country.[288] The European Union undertook to expand its membership to include the transitional economies that formerly were part of the Soviet bloc.[289] Free trade agreements with investment-related provisions between developed and developing states also appeared. By mid 2005, they accounted for 39 percent of all preferential trade agreements with investment provisions.[290]

Part of the explanation for this trend was that the old distinction between capital exporting developed countries and capital importing developing countries was blurring. A number of developing countries had achieved considerable economic success and were becoming significant exporters of capital.[291] For example, in 2007, Singapore's stock of foreign direct investment abroad was larger than that of several developed countries, including Austria, Finland, Greece, Ireland, Luxembourg, and Portugal.[292] Brazil's stock was larger than that of all of those countries except Ireland.[293] Mexico, South Korea, and Turkey have joined the OECD, with other countries moving in that direction. At the same time, developed countries were becoming major capital importers. For example, the total stock of foreign direct investment in the United States grew from $83 billion in 1980 to $2.8 trillion in 2007.[294] OECD countries in the 1950s accounted for 75 percent of world GDP, but by 2008 accounted for only 55 percent.[295]

The growing power of developing countries was reflected in the sudden emergence of sovereign wealth funds. For example, by 2008, approximately forty countries operated sovereign wealth funds, two-thirds of which were less than ten years old,[296] although the oldest, the Kuwait Investment Authority, dated from 1953. About 75 percent were based in the Middle East or Asia and only 15 percent were based in OECD countries.[297] The funds were created for a variety of purposes, including to stabilize commodity prices and to fund pensions. About two-thirds of their assets were

288 *See generally* Maxwell A. Cameron & Brian W. Tomlin, *The Making of NAFTA: How the Deal Was Done* (2000); Mayer, *supra* note 285.

289 In 2004, the European Union added eight members that were former Soviet bloc nations. These were the Czech Republic, Estonia, Hungary, Latvia, Lithuania, Poland, the Slovak Republic, and Slovenia. Former Soviet bloc states currently seeking membership are Bulgaria, Romania, Croatia, and the Former Yugoslav Republic of Macedonia. Two other states joined the European Union in 2004: Cyprus and Malta. Turkey is also currently seeking membership.

290 United Nations Conference on Trade and Development, *Research Note: Recent Developments in International Investment Agreements* 11 (2005).

291 *See* Karl P. Sauvant, "New Sources of FDI: The BRICs," 6 *Journal of World Investment and Trade* 639 (2005); Andrew F. Cooper, Agata Antkiewicz and Timothy M. Shaw, "Economic Size Trumps All Else? Lessons from BRICSAM," The Centre for International Governance Innovation, Working Paper No. 12, December 2006, available at http://www.ssrn.com.

292 UNCTAD, *World Investment Report 2008* 257–260.

293 *Id.*,

294 *Id.* at 257.

295 Javier Santiso, "Sovereign Development Funds: Key financial actors of the shifting wealth of nations," OECD Emerging Markets Network Working Paper, October 2008, available at http://www.ssrn.com.

296 Anna Gelpern, "A Sovereign Wealth Turn," Sept. 22, 2008, available at http://www.ssrn.com.

297 Santiso, *supra* note 295.

thought to rest on oil revenues,[298] but they were also funded from central bank reserves or other revenue sources including privatization receipts. These funds attracted attention because of the amount of money they included and because they operated in markets where governments in the past had not operated on a large scale. The size of sovereign wealth funds in 2008 was estimated to exceed $3 trillion.[299] The largest such fund was believed to have about $875 billion invested.[300]

Further, whereas economic integration agreements in the past generally had been regional, the new free trade agreements with investment chapters often were between states in different regions.[301] Indeed, as of mid-2005, 44 percent of all preferential trade agreements with investment-related provisions were between countries in different regions.[302]

Thus, in the Global Era, the distinctions that had characterized the Cold War Era collapsed. For example, investment policy lost the ideological division that had characterized the Cold War Era. While in the Cold War Era many had seen BITs as unequal treaties to which developed countries reluctantly and perhaps unwisely adhered in order to attract foreign investment,[303] in the Global Era states almost universally adopted the view that foreign investment could promote economic prosperity and set about jointly creating legal frameworks that would promote and protect international investment flows.

Similarly, while, in the Cold War Era, BITs were between a capital exporting developed country and a capital importing developing country, in the Global Era, the number of BITs between developing countries grew remarkably as developing countries became capital exporters, often to other developing countries.[304] By the end of 2007, slightly more than one-fourth of all BITs were concluded between developing countries.[305]

Investment provisions no longer are confined to BITs, as they were in the latter part of the Cold War Era. In the Global Era, investment provisions appear in agreements that potentially address a range of topics, including trade in goods, trade in services, and competition policy. The reintegration of trade and investment in treaty practice is also reflected in efforts by the GATT's successor organization, the World Trade Organization (WTO), which came into existence on January 1, 1995, to adopt investment-related treaties at the multilateral level. The Havana Charter, drafted at the

---

298 Mathias Audit, "Is the Erecting of Barriers Against Foreign Sovereign Wealth Funds Compatible with International Investment Law?" Society of International Economic Law Working Paper No. 29/08, July 2008, available at http://www.ssrn.com.

299 Santiso, *supra* note 295.

300 Audit, *supra* note 298.

301 For example, the United States has concluded free trade agreements outside the Western Hemisphere with Israel, Jordan, Singapore, Australia, and Morocco.

302 UNCTAD, *supra* note 290, at 10.

303 *See, e.g.*, Andrew T. Guzman, "Why LDCs Sign Treaties That Hurt Them: Explaining the Popularity of Bilateral Investment Treaties," 38 *Virginia Journal of International Law* 639 (1998).

304 By the end of the 1990s, one-third of all foreign direct investment in developing countries came from other developing countries. UNCTAD, *World Investment Report 2004: The Shift Toward Services* 20.

305 UNCTAD, *supra* note 278, at 3.

beginning of the Cold War Era, had contemplated that the proposed International Trade Organization would have some competence over investment related issues, but the ITO had never come into existence. The completion of the Uruguay Round of GATT negotiations in 1994, however, resulted in the creation of the World Trade Organization the following year to administer the GATT and related agreements, including three agreements directly related to investment. The first of these agreements is the General Agreement on Trade in Services (GATS),[306] which is intended to remove barriers to cross-border trade in services. Services are sometimes provided internationally through the establishment of an office or subsidiary by a service provider of one country in the territory of another country, in effect, by the establishment of foreign investment in the country where the services are to be consumed. The GATS explicitly applies to the delivery of services through such a "commercial presence."[307] Thus, a GATS commitment to allow trade in a certain service sector through a commercial presence amounts to a commitment to allow the establishment of foreign investment. Further, GATS commitments concerning the treatment that the service provider will receive constitute commitments to protect foreign investment.[308] Thus, the WTO potentially has jurisdiction over all foreign investment in the service sector of the economy. The potential significance of this agreement is reflected in the fact that, as of 2007, the stock of foreign direct investment in the services sector was $7.7 trillion, compared with the $3.5 trillion stock of foreign direct investment in the manufacturing sector.[309]

The second investment-related WTO agreement is the Agreement on Trade Related Investment Measures[310] (TRIMs). The TRIMs agreement prohibits the imposition on foreign investment of certain trade distorting performance requirements, specifically, those that are inconsistent with the GATT's national treatment obligation and its prohibition on quantitative restrictions.

The third investment-related WTO agreement is the Agreement on Trade Related Intellectual Property Rights[311] (TRIPs). The TRIPs agreement obligates the parties to provide certain protection for intellectual property, a form of investment.

---

306 General Agreement on Trade in Services, Apr. 15, 1994, Agreement Establishing the World Trade Organization, Annex 1B, Legal Instruments—Results of the Uruguay Round, vol. 31, *reprinted in* 33 International Legal Materials 44 (1994).

307 Article I.2 of the GATS provides that

> For purposes of this Agreement, trade in services is defined as the supply of a service . . . (d) by a service supplier of one Member, through commercial presence in the territory of another Member.

308 For example, Article II requires most favored nation treatment of trade in services, Article III imposes certain obligations of transparency with respect to trade in services, Article VI imposes restrictions on domestic regulation of trade in services, and Article XI limits states' ability to restrict payments for current transactions relating to trade in services.

309 United Nations Conference on Trade and Development, *World Investment Report 2008* 207 (2008).

310 Agreement on Trade Related Investment Measures, Apr. 15, 1994, Agreement Establishing the World Trade Organization, Annex 1B, Legal Instruments—Results of the Uruguay Round, vol. 31.

311 Agreement on Trade-Related Aspects of Intellectual Property Rights, Apr. 15, 1994, Agreement Establishing the World Trade Organization, Annex 1C, Legal Instruments—Results of the Uruguay Round, vol. 31 (1994).

As this suggests, the very purpose of investment agreements is changing. While, in the Cold War Era, BITs were intended to protect investment of developed countries in the territory of developing countries primarily against expropriation, in the Global Era investment agreements increasingly are intended to liberalize investment flows. They have become instruments of globalization, removing barriers to trade and investment, much in the same way that the FCNs of the eighteenth and nineteenth centuries sought to establish commercial relations between countries.

The Global Era also has been characterized by periodic reactions against the process of globalization. Consistent with the observation above that the distinctions that characterized the Cold War Era are dissolving, many of these reactions have come from the developed countries that most strongly promoted the creation of a liberal international investment regime during the Cold War Era.

One such reaction occurred in the mid-1990s when the OECD states attempted to negotiate a multilateral agreement on investment (MAI). The intention was that such an agreement would be concluded among the OECD states initially, but then be opened to signature by other states at a later date.[312] It was thought that perhaps the growing consensus with respect to international investment policy finally would make a multilateral agreement possible. Such an agreement repeatedly had eluded successful conclusion, dating back to the failure of the Havana Charter, but including as well the failure of the 1959 Abs-Shawcross convention and the 1967 OECD draft convention to be opened for signature. The MAI negotiations also failed, however.[313] The countries among which the consensus on investment policy is perhaps the strongest, ironically, were unable to agree on a multilateral version of a BIT. The failure of that effort, however, may have been in part the result of that very consensus. That is, because these states already provide a favorable environment for investment as a matter of national policy, most of the participants had little to gain in the way of protection from the agreement and thus, once negotiations were underway, the focus shifted to that which they would be conceding, particularly in the way of access.[314] As the MAI came to be seen as involving mainly concessions rather than gains, the impetus to continue diminished. Meanwhile, various nongovernmental organizations opposed to economic globalization, many based in developed countries, initiated a campaign against the MAI, raising the political price of achieving an agreement.[315] At the same time, the business community, which also perceived that little would be gained by the agreement, failed to provide countervailing support for the MAI.[316] Many developing countries also were critical of the OECD MAI negotiations because they were excluded from participation. In 1998, the parties simply abandoned the negotiations. The failure

312 On the initiation of the OECD negotiations, see Organisation for Economic Cooperation and Development, *Towards Multilateral Investment Rules* (1996).

313 On the failure of the MAI negotiations, *see* Edward M. Graham, *Fighting the Wrong Enemy: Antiglobal Activists and Multinational Enterprises* (2000); UNCTAD, *Lessons from the MAI* (1999).

314 UNCTAD, *supra* note 313, at 23–25.

315 *Id.*

316 *Id.*

of these negotiations demonstrated the extent to which the access principle remained one of the most difficult even for developed countries to incorporate into legally binding international instruments.

Meanwhile, in 1996, the WTO decided at its ministerial conference in Singapore to establish a working group on trade and investment. When the Doha round of multilateral trade negotiations began in 2001, investment was placed on the agenda. By this time, the MAI negotiations had failed and the more inclusive WTO appeared to be the more likely forum for the development of a multilateral instrument on investment. Progress in the Doha Round was slow, however, and in 2004, as part of an effort to focus the negotiations on fewer goals, investment was removed from the agenda.

Reactions to the process of globalization also resulted from the occurrence of several financial crises in the 1990s. These included crises in Latin America in 1994–95, in Asia in 1997–98, and in Russia and Brazil in 1998. The crises occurred in countries that had opened their economies to foreign investment, including countries that had pursued sound macroeconomic policies and had enjoyed strong economic growth. For example, the Asian crisis began in Thailand, the budget of which was in surplus during the years preceding the crisis. Because of Thailand's rapid growth, foreign banks had been willing to lend large amounts to Thai banks, which in turn wrote loans to domestic investors who made highly speculative investments, especially in real estate and in finance.[317] Thailand had pegged its currency, the baht, to a basket of currencies in which the U.S. dollar was dominant. The appreciation of the U.S. dollar in 1997 caused the Thai currency to appreciate, which weakened Thai exports and diminished the inflow of foreign currency necessary to service the external debt. As Thai foreign currency reserves fell, lenders anticipated a devaluation of the baht and fled, which forced the very devaluation lenders had feared. The panic spread throughout the region to Malaysia, Indonesia, South Korea, and the Philippines. These five economies, which in 1996 had net private capital inflows of $93 billion, experienced a net outflow in 1997 of $12.1 billion.[318] This reversal was the equivalent of 10 percent of their combined Gross Domestic Product.[319] The devaluation resulting from the currency crisis caused the value of assets to fall and private borrowers became overextended, leading to a banking crisis. Borrowers went bankrupt and the affected economies plunged into recessions. The IMF provided emergency financing, but conditioned upon increased interest rates and reduced government expenditures, measures that deepened the recession.[320] The crisis then spread to Russia and Brazil because both countries also had overvalued currencies and large amounts of debt, prompting investors to flee those countries as well.[321] The ramifications of the crisis continued into the next decade.

---

317 See Gerald M. Meier, *Biography of a Subject: An Evolution of Development Economics* 154 (2005).

318 Sweta C. Saxena, "A Survey of Issues Related to Capital Account Liberalization," available at http://www.ssrn.com.

319 *Id.*

320 For a detailed and fascinating account of the role of the IMF in the crisis of 1997 and 1998, see Paul Blustein, *The Chastening* (2003).

321 Charles P. Kindleberger and Robert Aliber, *Manias, Panics and Crashes: A History of Financial Crises* 141 (5th ed. 2005).

The Asian crisis had triggered a slowing of capital flows to emerging markets. The 1999 devaluation of the currency in Brazil, a major Argentine export market, combined with the appreciation of the U.S. dollar, to which Argentina had pegged its currency, in tandem with the reduced capital inflows, contributed to a severe economic crisis in Argentina in 2001–2002. Measures taken by Argentina to address the crisis led to the filing of dozens of claims against Argentina, which as a result has been the respondent in at least 48 investor-state arbitrations, more than any other country. The Asian crisis demonstrated that, in a global economy, even countries that had pursued sound macroeconomic policies in the past were not insulated from a financial crisis and that a crisis in one country quickly could spread to others, on even distant continents.

These crises had tended to occur in countries that had open capital accounts and fixed exchange rates. Many observers were convinced that these countries had opened their capital accounts prematurely[322] and one of the most common recommendation for avoiding such crises in the future was to impose capital controls.[323] The crises thus called into question the access principle.

Not everyone agreed, however. Some reached the opposite conclusion: that the crises were the result of too little deregulation and much of the distress was attributable to misguided government policies.[324] For example, in maintaining their fixed exchange rates, rather than allowing them to float in response to market forces, countries had caused their currencies to appreciate too much. Thailand ultimately spent $24 billion attempting to maintain the value of its overvalued currency, before abandoning the effort and allowing the baht to float in the market.[325] As a result, apart from imposing capital controls, the most common recommendation for avoiding future crises was to abandon fixed exchange rates.[326]

Both sides drew support from the contrast between the crisis economies and India, which had maintained stronger capital controls. Growth following the crisis was faster in Thailand and South Korea than in India, although India had avoided effect of the crisis entirely.[327] The comparison for some suggested that openness is best in the long run, but for others suggested the value of controls. Even the World Bank, however, has recognized that countries must have regulatory policies in place before removing controls on financial investment.[328] Some observers go farther and call for a new international financial architecture.[329] In any event, the debate over opening the capital account continued and the access principle remained controversial.

---

322 Eichengreen, *supra* note 68, at 3.

323 Saxena, *supra* note 318.

324 Eichengreen, *supra* note 68, at 3.

325 Charles P. Kindleberger and Robert Aliber, *Manias, Panics and Crashes: A History of Financial Crises* 141 (5th ed. 2005).

326 Saxena, *supra* note 318.

327 Kristin J. Forbes, "Capital Controls: Mud in the Wheels of Market Efficiency," 25 *Cato Journal* 153 (2005).

328 Meier, *supra* note 317, at 159.

329 *See, e.g.*, Blustein, *supra* note 320, at 375–392; Meier, *supra* note 317, at 155–160; Barry Eichengreen, *Toward a New International Financial Architecture: A Practical Post Asia Agenda* (1999).

The hazards of globalization again became apparent when a global financial crisis, generally described as the worst since the Great Depression, erupted in July 2007. This crisis was triggered by the loss of confidence in the value of securitized home mortgages in the United States. Housing prices had risen to the point that the market no longer could sustain them and, as the value of housing fell, many homeowners discovered that the debt they owed was greater than the value of their homes, prompting them to default on their debt. Institutions that had invested heavily in mortgages faced collapse and the effects rippled throughout the tightly integrated global financial market. As this book goes to press, the crisis had not yet affected the network of BITs, although the value of foreign direct investment flows were estimated by UNCTAD to have fallen by more than 20 percent in 2008 alone.[330] The crisis again demonstrated that no country was immune from an economic crisis and that a crisis in any part of the world could spread elsewhere.

The emergence of sovereign wealth funds in the late 1990s also has stimulated concerns about the access principle. The worry, in particular, is that the funds may make investment decisions based not on economic, but political, considerations. Several developed countries, including Canada, Australia, and the United States, adopted legislation to permit screening of sovereign wealth funds in order to exclude them from sensitive sectors of the economy, such as critical infrastructure or energy, or to ensure that such funds will operate according to commercial considerations. At the international level, the IMF undertook to develop a code of conduct to ensure the transparency of SWFs.[331] In October 2008, an international working group of sovereign wealth funds presented to the IMF a set of 24 principles, known as the "Santiago Principles," intended to promote transparency.

Adverse reactions to the globalization process have not been limited to the access principle. On July 8, 1987, the first claim arising under a BIT, *AAPL v. Sri Lanka*, a claim arising under the United Kingdom-Sri Lanka BIT, was submitted to investor-state arbitration, resulting in an award against Sri Lanka on June 27, 1990. For the first decade after the *AAPL* claim was submitted, few other claims followed. The entry into force of the NAFTA in 1994, however, imposed obligations similar to those that appeared in a BIT among countries that had enormous quantities of investment in each other's territory and a strong tradition of judicial dispute settlement. Just short of the third anniversary of the entry into force of the NAFTA, Metalclad Corporation notified Mexico of its intent to submit a claim under the NAFTA to investor-state arbitration. By the next year, both Mexico and Canada were named as respondents in NAFTA claims and the United States was named in 1998. Very quickly, the United States, which had been among the most ambitious proponents of FCNs and BITs in the Cold War Era, found itself a respondent in several claims based on a variety of routine acts of government, including a ban on a hazardous substance, a couple of state court

330 United Nations Conference on Trade and Development, "Global FDI in Decline Due to Financial Crisis, and A Further Drop Expected," UNCTAD Investment Brief Number 1 (2009).

331 *See generally* Justin O'Brien, "Barriers to Entry: Foreign Direct Investment and the Regulation of Sovereight Wealth Funds," 42 *International Lawyer* 1231 (2008).

judgments in commercial disputes, and a domestic content requirement in a federal procurement law. In 1999, in reaction to these claims, the United States halted BIT negotiations and began to reevaluate its model BIT, a process that was not completed until 2004. Meanwhile, in 2002, the United States Congress enacted a series of negotiating objectives for the investment chapters of free trade agreements, objectives that also would be taken into account in future BIT negotiations. Notable among these objectives was that investment agreements grant foreign investors in the United States no greater substantive rights than U.S. investors receive under U.S. law. One might be tempted to conclude that the United States had embraced the Calvo Doctrine, although that would not be an entirely accurate characterization. The United States did not challenge the existence of an international minimum standard, but rather took the position that that standard provided no greater protection than the highly protective corpus of U.S. law. In any event, two years later, when the United States published its 2004 BIT model negotiating text, language had been included clarifying the meaning of certain provisions, including the fair and equitable treatment standard and the expropriation provision. New clauses also were included elaborating greatly upon the procedures to be followed in investor-state arbitrations and, in particular, authorizing the BIT parties by joint agreement to control the decisions of investor-state arbitral tribunals on certain issues.[332] Thus, the reaction in the United States rested on concerns about the strength of the reasonableness, security and due process principles in the BITs. Interestingly, the Congressionally enacted negotiating objectives actually advocated greater use of the transparency principle, although as applied to the investor-state arbitral process rather than host state treatment of covered investment. Some of the U.S. revisions to its model BIT have been adopted in the BITs of other countries, most notably Canada, but as of 2009 most of the U.S. innovations could be found in only a very small number of BITs.

Although a handful of BIT claims had been submitted to arbitration prior to 1997, the NAFTA claims triggered a flood of investor-state arbitrations. By the end of 2008, just more than a decade after the first NAFTA claims were submitted to arbitration, the number of known treaty-based claims had risen to 318, with 78 countries having been named as respondents.[333] By that same date, 109 of the cases had been concluded, with the investor prevailing about half the time.[334] More than 45 of the claims submitted to arbitration arose under the NAFTA and more than 20 arose under the Energy Charter Treaty.[335] The country most often named as a respondent, however, was Argentina, as a result of measures it took during its 2001–2002 economic crisis.

These claims generated a body of arbitral practice that illuminated the meaning of many of the BIT provisions, although in some cases the interpretations were controversial. For example, on July 31, 2001, the three NAFTA parties acting through the NAFTA Free Trade Commission issued an interpretation of Article 1105 of the

---

332 *See* Section 10.2.1.8.

333 United Nations Conference on Trade and Development, *Latest Developments in Investor-State Dispute Settlement* 2 (2009).

334 *Id.*

335 *Id.* at 4.

NAFTA that was intended to correct what all three parties regarded as incorrect interpretations of the NAFTA by claimants and tribunals.[336] In 2007, Bolivia announced that it was withdrawing from ICSID and other Latin American countries threatened to do so. That same year, Ecuador notified ICSID that it would not consent to investment disputes involving natural resources. In 2008, Ecuador announced its intention to withdraw from more than a dozen of its BITs. Brazil, having signed 14 BITs during the 1990s, after seeing the surge of investor-state arbitrations, declined to ratify its BITs and thus none of the Brazilian BITs entered into force. Yet, as already noted above, Brazil has become a major capital exporter and, by 2008, the Brazilian government was under increasing pressure from Brazilian investors to ratify the BITs and thereby obtain for them protection for their investments abroad. In any event, despite occasional adverse reactions to the process of investor-state arbitration or to particular awards, in 2009 the vast majority of countries remained committed to the BIT principle of due process. More than one hundred forty countries are parties to the ICSID convention and awards of compensation issued against host states appear to be paid routinely.[337]

The Global Era, finally, is characterized by the number of countries that are now part of the BIT network. Some 179 countries are now party to at least one BIT.[338] The BIT network has truly become global and the six core BIT principles have gained some degree of acceptance in every part of the world.

---

336 *See* Section 5.4.

337 Although systematic data on the frequency with which awards are paid are scarce. *See* Susan D. Franck, "Empirically Evaluating Claims About Investment Treaty Arbitration," 86 *North Carolina Law Review* 1 (2007).

338 United Nations Conference on Trade and Development, "Recent developments in international investment agreements (2007–June 2008)," *IIA Monitor* No. 2 (2008), available at http://www.unctad.org.

Chapter 3

Policy

A state's foreign investment policy generally is an element of its larger economic policy, particularly its understanding of the proper role between the state and economic activity. At the time that the modern nation state emerged in the sixteenth and seventeenth centuries as the principal form of political organization in Europe, the prevailing theory of international political economy was mercantilism, which advocated extensive state regulation of economic activity to ensure that such activity promoted the interests of the state. Theorists such as Nicolo Machiavelli and Thomas Hobbes laid the theoretical groundwork for the absolutist state, in which all considerations were subordinate to *raison d'état.* Mercantilists regulated international economic activity to ensure that it enriched the state. Imports, which were thought to impoverish the state because they caused a loss of gold, were discouraged by the enactment of protective tariffs. Exports, which were thought to enrich the state because they caused an influx of gold, were encouraged, in some cases by subsidies. Economic activities beneficial to the state often were promoted through state grants of monopoly privileges.

3.1 ECONOMIC LIBERALISM

Economic liberalism emerged in the eighteenth century as a critique of mercantilism. As a growing merchant class challenged the power of the European monarchs, liberal political theorists, notably John Locke, rejected the Hobbesian concept of an absolutist state and argued that the state existed to promote individual liberty. Liberal economic theorists, particularly Adam Smith and David Ricardo, sought to demonstrate that free, competitive markets would result in the greatest prosperity for all. Smith, for example, believed that a nation increased its wealth by increasing its productivity, rather than merely accumulating gold. He argued that the interventionist policies of the mercantilists promoted inefficiency and thereby diminished productivity. Liberal economics thus has been concerned more with increasing the production of new wealth than with determining the distribution of existing wealth. Mercantilism, by contrast, largely had been concerned with increasing a state's share of the available wealth.

Liberal economics as developed by Smith and Ricardo advocated a policy of free trade, under which states do not interfere with the movement of goods and services across borders. The mechanism by which free trade increases productivity is that it permits each state to specialize in the production of goods and services in which it has a comparative advantage and then trade its products for other products that it wants but cannot produce as efficiently. Through economies of specialization and scale, a state maximizes its productivity.

Liberalism also has advocated the free movement of capital across borders. Economic liberals, however, do not in all cases favor increased foreign investment. Rather, the liberal doctrine in essence is that the state should permit the market to determine the direction of international investment flows.

Although liberal economic theory demolished mercantilism, liberal economics did not remain unchallenged. Mercantilism was succeeded in the nineteenth century by economic nationalism, which also held that economic policy should promote the national interest, while abandoning the mercantilist emphasis on the accumulation of gold. Economic nationalists, like their mercantilist antecedents, are willing to regulate economic activity to the extent necessary to further the national interest, particularly by increasing the nation's share of the available wealth. The national interest, of course, is determined by those who, at any given moment, hold power within the state. Thus, the national interest may become identified with the interests of particular groups and the goal of increasing the share of available wealth may become identified more specifically with increasing the wealth of those particular groups rather than the nation as a whole. Economic nationalists of the nineteenth century, like the mercantilists before them, advocated a protectionist trade policy to diminish imports and promote exports, in order to increase the market share of local manufacturing and agriculture. Economic nationalists in the nineteenth century did not oppose inward foreign investment because such investment could contribute to the development of transportation and utilities, which were necessary for industrialization. They did sometimes oppose outward foreign investment, fearing the loss of capital that was needed in the domestic economy.

Liberal economic theory also was challenged by Marxist economics, which emerged in the nineteenth century as a critique of liberalism and which was embraced in a particular form by Russia after its 1917 revolution and later by other members of the communist bloc. The Marxist contention was that increasing efficiency would lead to a surplus of capital, causing the return to investors to diminish over time. To maintain profitability, investors would be forced to invest abroad in developing countries, where the relative scarcity of capital would permit them to earn a higher return on their investment. The result would be the industrialization of the developing world, which was a necessary step in the transition from feudalism to capitalism and then ultimately to socialism. Early Marxist theory thus saw foreign investment as beneficial to developing countries. The benefits to developed countries, however, would be uneven, leading to international conflict over the control of markets in developing countries. In any event, at least in the nineteenth century, all of the prevailing theories of international political economy regarded inward international investment flows as generally beneficial to the host states.

World War I triggered a triumph of a new form of economic nationalism in which the national interest was identified with economic self-sufficiency and even isolationism. Nearly every country adopted protectionist trade policies and, for the first time, countries began to restrict foreign investment.[1] The Marxists who gained power in the Soviet Union seized foreign property without payment of compensation and terminated inward investment flows.

After the World War II, the developed countries led by the United States sought to create a new international economic order founded on liberal principles. Economic liberalism, however, continued to face challenges from nationalists and Marxists.

Post-war national policy in the third-world countries of Africa, Asia, and Latin America emphasized political independence and economic development. Many of these countries pursued economic nationalist policies in the form of import substitution industrialization, under which developing countries promoted enterprises that would manufacture goods to displace imports from developed countries. In this way, it was argued, the developing countries would achieve economic self-sufficiency, which was a corollary to their political independence. Further, the argument continued, producing goods domestically for the domestic market would promote domestic employment and, in effect, keep a country's wealth within its territory, thereby promoting economic development.

Marxists began to emphasize the potentially detrimental effects of foreign investment on developing countries. Twentieth-century "neo-Marxists" developed the dependency theory of foreign investment, which regards foreign investment as a form of neocolonialism that subjects the local economy to foreign control and promotes underdevelopment. Dependency theorists called for reducing the economic ties between developed and developing countries, policies that could entail both the exclusion of new foreign investment and the expropriation of existing foreign investment.

Particularly within developing countries, economic nationalists, with their emphasis on nation building and economic self-sufficiency, have found common cause with Marxist economists, who advocate a more equal distribution of wealth within the international community. These theorists share an inward-looking philosophy, one that favors using local producers to supply goods and local markets to consume them and that is generally suspicious of foreign investment. They support intervention in the economy when necessary to ensure that foreign investment, if not excluded entirely, conforms to their political goals of promoting national independence and the economic development of less-developed countries. They also have tended to place greater emphasis on increasing a country's share of the available wealth, rather than increasing the total production of wealth.

From their inception, the BITs almost inevitably were identified with a particular economic theory. The first BITs were drafted and proposed by developed countries seeking to protect their overseas investment against the interventionist policies of developing countries. Developed countries proposed the negotiation of BITs providing for prompt, adequate and effective compensation for expropriation as an antidote to

---

1 *See* Section 2.1.2.

economic nationalist assertions that expropriated investors were entitled to no more than national treatment and Marxist claims that no compensation at all was owed. The developed countries promoting BIT negotiations were market economies that in general espoused liberal economic theory, even if they departed from it in practice on some occasions.

Further, BITs present themselves as quintessentially liberal documents. The typical BIT cites two goals in its preamble: the creation of favorable conditions for investment by nationals and companies of one party in the territory of the other, and increased prosperity in both states.[2] The avowed purpose of a BIT thus may be distilled to five words: increased prosperity through foreign investment. The preamble affirms the basic liberal doctrine that free movement of capital will yield greater productivity.

Liberal economics advocates the use of competitive markets, rather than government regulations, to allocate investment flows. A properly functioning market economy, however, requires a particular relationship between the market and the states. With respect to investment policy, that relationship can be described in general terms by three principles.

As a first principle, the state must intervene in society to establish and protect private rights of property and contract.[3] In other words, the state must create the legal framework that makes it possible for parties to bargain effectively. More specifically, the state must ensure that the parties have secure rights that they can agree to exchange and the state must enforce those exchanges to which the parties agree. Private property and contract rights must be protected against infringement by both public and private actors. This is the principle of *investment security*.

As a second principle, the state must defer to the market's allocation of resources. That is, having created the legal framework for the market, the state must allow the market to guide the allocation of resources within the society. This is the principle of *investment neutrality*.

As a third principle, the state may intervene in the market when necessary to correct market failures. Put another way, the state should defer to the market as long as the market is functioning properly. Where the market is not functioning properly, the state may intervene to remedy the failure. This is the principle of *market facilitation*.

Economic theory recognizes a number of possible market failures. One example is that of a public good. A public good generally is defined as an activity that benefits all persons and the enjoyment of which by one person is in no way diminished by that

---

2 The United Kingdom-Armenia BIT, for example, states in its preamble that the two parties

> Desiring to create favorable conditions for greater investment by nationals and companies of one State in the territory of the other State;
>
> Recognizing that the encouragement and reciprocal protection under international agreement of such investments will be conducive to the stimulation of individual business initiative and will increase prosperity in both States;
>
> Have agreed as follows:

3 *See* generally Paul H. Rubin, "Growing a Legal System in the Post-Communist Economies," 27 *Cornell International Law Journal* 1 (1994); Tamar Frankel, "The Legal Infrastructure of Markets: The Role of Contract and Property Law," 73 *Boston University Law Review* 389 (1993).

of another. Examples include an effective legal system and physical infrastructure, such as highways. Because everyone enjoys a public good, specific individuals may try to take advantage of public goods produced by others rather than expending their own resources to contribute to the production of the good, the problem of the so-called "free rider." For this reason, an unregulated market may not produce the socially optimal quantity of a public good and the state must therefore provide these goods.

Similarly, the state may intervene to counteract inefficiencies caused by positive or negative externalities. A positive externality is a benefit enjoyed by a person other than the one who produced it. Markets will undersupply a good or service that produces positive externalities because the producer does not reap the full benefits of the good or service and thus does not have sufficient incentive to produce the socially optimal amount. An example is employee training, which benefits all future employers, although the cost is fully borne by the current employer. A negative externality is a detriment suffered by a person other than the one who produces it. Markets will oversupply goods or services that produce negative externalities because the producer does not have to pay for all the adverse consequences of the good or service and thus has no disincentive to produce more than the socially optimal amount. An example is pollution, the costs of which are borne by many persons other than the producer. In a liberal system, governments may intervene to provide, encourage, or subsidize positive externalities, such as education, and to prohibit or regulate negative externalities, such as pollution.

Yet another example of a market failure is anticompetitive behavior, such as monopolies or cartels. Where a single producer exists, by definition competition has been eliminated from the market. In the case of a cartel, multiple producers exist, but they agree not to compete against each other. Governments often intervene to halt or prevent anticompetitive behavior, such as by prohibiting the merger of two companies whose combination would have too great of an adverse impact on competition within the market where they operate.

Still another example of a market failure is an information asymmetry, that is, a situation in which one party has significantly more information than another, such that bargaining between the parties is not adequately informed. Markets can allocate resources efficiently only if the parties understand the value of the exchanges that they are making. Governments adopt an array of policies to correct information asymmetries, such as securities regulations to require companies the stock of which is publicly traded to disclose information about their financial circumstances and consumer protection regulations to require companies to disclose information about the nature of the products they sell or even to warrant the products against hidden defects.

The ability of a BIT to accomplish its professed purpose of promoting economic prosperity through economic development depends upon two causal linkages. First, a BIT must increase international investment. Second, international investment must promote economic prosperity.

As it happens, these causal linkages are the subject of different components of liberal investment policy. More specifically, a liberal investment policy may be disaggregated into a microeconomic and a macroeconomic policy. Microeconomic policy addresses the operation of capital markets and, in particular, how they allocate investment flows.

Thus, the first causal linkage on which BITs rest is a question of microeconomic policy. Macroeconomic policy addresses the effects of different transactions, including investment flows, on the economy as a whole. Thus, the second causal linkage on which BITs rest is a question of macroeconomic policy. The next two sections describe the microeconomic and macroeconomic theory, respectively, underlying the liberal investment policy of the BITs.

3.1.1 Microeconomic Theory

The simplest explanation of how the market allocates capital is simply that the market permits an investor to find the most efficient use of its capital, i.e., the highest return, which may be in another country. Although this explanation would seem to imply that investment always moves in one direction, from the low return to the high return country, with additional elaboration it also explains capital movements in both directions between two countries. Two-way investment may be explained by the fact that investors also seek to minimize risks through diversification and by the fact that investors may have different assessments of the expected return in a particular country and the associated risk. Further, as will be seen below, it also may be explained by other factors as well, such as efforts to rationalize the entire production process of a multinational enterprise or to achieve economies of scale by expanding production into foreign markets.

Investment usually is categorized as either direct or portfolio investment. The distinction between the two is that direct investment entails control of the enterprise in which the investment is made, while portfolio investment does not. Thus, an investor who owns a few shares of stock in a corporation generally has portfolio investment, while an investor who owns enough stock to exercise control over the corporation has direct investment. Investment sometimes is characterized as direct investment if the investor owns as little as 10 percent of the stock in a company. Portfolio investment includes not only equity interests that are too small to be controlling, but also nonequity interests in a company, such as loans and bonds.

Foreign direct investment, as distinguished from foreign portfolio investment, presents special questions in that the direct investor seeks not just a high return on its investment, but control over the investment. Economists have developed theories to explain when an investor will seek investment abroad in the form of direct, as opposed to portfolio, investment. The prevailing theory is one originally articulated by John Dunning and generally know as the "eclectic theory" or the "OLI theory." This theory posits that the decision to establish or acquire foreign direct investment is the result of ownership, location and internalization factors. For a foreign direct investment to make economic sense, all three factors must be present. First, the investor owns some asset, such as technology or management expertise, that gives it a competitive advantage. Second, the asset can best be employed through investment in a foreign location. For example, the high cost of shipping may mean that producing a good in the country where it will be marketed is more profitable than producing it in the home country for export to that same market. Of course, the locational advantage in theory could be exploited without establishing an enterprise abroad. For example, the owner of the asset could license the technology to a producer in the destination country so that the foreign producer manufacturers the product for local sale and pays the asset owner a licensing fee. In this way, the owner of the asset avoids the cost of learning to operate in an unfamiliar location and reduces the risk of discriminatory treatment by the host state based on the owner's foreign nationality. Given these alternative ways of exploiting asset and locational advantages, foreign direct investment will occur only if the third element, internalization, is present. Specifically, exploitation of the asset abroad, but within the firm, is advantageous relative to exploitation outside the firm. For example, if the asset is a technology, the owner may fear that licensing the technology will result in its theft and the creation of a local rival. In that case, producing the good through foreign direct investment offers internalization advantages in the form of control over the technology, with the result that foreign direct investment may be preferable to licensing.

Foreign direct investment is often classified as either efficiency-seeking or market-seeking. As will be explained below, these two forms of investment represent different ways in which the investor uses control of the enterprise to exploit asset, locational, and internationalization factors so as to increase return. In particular, a higher return may be achieved through reductions in costs. In fact, in a perfectly competitive market, the only way to increase profits is to lower costs. Production costs may be reduced through control of the investment in either of at least two ways, one tied to efficiency-seeking investments and the other tied to market-seeking investments.

First, the direct investor may lower costs by establishing investments in locations that offer cheaper inputs, such as abundant natural resources or low-wage labor, that can be incorporated into the production process, thus improving the efficiency of the enterprise. These efficiency-seeking investments are generally associated with vertically integrated enterprises.[4] Because they are part of a production chain stretching across frontiers, they tend to be export-oriented. In such cases, investments are established not because of the return that each will generate, but because of their role in rationalizing, and thereby increasing the return generated by, the entire production process,[5] a role that depends upon investor control of each part of the process. This explains in part the phenomenon of two-way investment, as enterprises place assets in the location that will generate the highest return for the entire enterprise.

An enterprise could obtain cheaper inputs though mechanisms other than acquiring control over a foreign direct investment. For example, the enterprise could import the needed inputs to its home state for use at an existing facility. Vertical integration, however, through control of foreign direct investment, that is through internalization, assures a more reliable source of supply than importing from an unaffiliated company.

---

4 Some theorists recognize a third kind of investment: resource-seeking. An example would be an investment to mine copper. A resource is merely a type of input and investments that are located near the resource are efficiency-seeking investments, in the same way that investments that are located near another input, such as inexpensive labor, are also efficiency seeking.

5 Thus, there is an empirical correlation between low wages and the existence of subsidiaries established for exporting. United Nations Conference on Trade and Development, *The Determinants of Foreign Investment: A Survey of the Evidence* 29, 42, (1992).

Vertical integration thus reduces costs in a way that is also consistent with diminishing risk. Because intrafirm trade involves lower transaction costs than interfirm trade,[6] vertical integration may be more efficient than importing from an unaffiliated company, resulting in further reductions in production costs. Intrafirm trade also permits the minimization of tax liability through the use of transfer pricing.[7] As this suggests, control over an investment can be crucial to increasing the investor's return while minimizing risk.

A second way that an investor may seek to lower costs through control over foreign direct investment is by increasing production, thus achieving economies of scale. Increased production is feasible if the investor can obtain access to larger markets, such as by establishing production facilities abroad near the markets they will serve. These "market-seeking" investments offer a partial explanation for two-way investment, particularly between two developed countries. Market-seeking investments often are associated with horizontally integrated enterprises, in which the investor replicates production facilities around the globe in new markets.

An enterprise could obtain access to foreign markets through mechanisms other than acquiring control over a foreign direct investment. For example, an enterprise could obtain access to the market by exporting to it or by licensing its products to a local producer. In many cases, however, neither exporting nor licensing can provide the same advantages as the establishment of foreign direct investments.

Foreign direct investment may be preferable to exporting, for example, where transportation costs are high or where the market is protected by trade barriers. An enterprise alsc may choose horizontal integration over trade with unaffiliated companies because of the reduced transaction costs of an internal market, that is, a market internal to the firm. Further, certain types of services, by their nature, must be performed (i.e., produced) at the point of consumption and cannot be exported. For example, a law firm representing a client before a tribunal located in the host state must perform the service in the host state.

Foreign direct investment may be preferable to licensing, for example, where the investor is concerned about the security of proprietary technology in the hands of a licensee, where the technology is particularly complex, or where quality control is of special importance, such as in the case of a good to be sold under a well-established trademark. Or, the investor may be concerned that a licensee over time will become a

---

6 Intrafirm trade in effect allows companies to create internal markets that avoid imperfections, such as information asymmetries, found in the external market.

7 A transfer price is the price charged by one corporate affiliate to another for the purchase of a good or service. Because the entities are affiliated, the price may differ from the market price. Multinational enterprises sometimes manipulate transfer prices in order to shift profits from affiliates in high tax jurisdictions to affiliates in low tax jurisdictions. *See* Andres B. Bernard, J. Bradford Jensen, and Peter K. Schott, "Transfer Pricing by U.S.-Based Multinational Firms," August 2006, available at http://www.ssrn.com. The authors of the study found that multinational firms based in the United States report large differences in prices for arms'-length and related-party exports. The authors found that "[t]hese differences exist even for the same product produced by the same firm shipped to the same country in the same month by the same mode of transport."

future competitor and thus horizontal integration offers the investor the opportunity to protect its market share. As these examples suggest, horizontal integration, like vertical integration, permits the investor to reduce costs in a way that is consistent with minimizing risk. Other considerations, of course, may prompt a producer to choose licensing over foreign direct investment. For example, the producer may lack sufficient information about the foreign market to permit entry or may have insufficient capital to establish an investment. Alternatively, the market may be too small to allow entry by the investor at a minimally efficient scale. In these situations, licensing provides the best means for the producer to gain access to the market. The empirical literature suggests that producers generally prefer establishing subsidiaries to licensing, but will turn to licensing if the establishment of direct investment is not feasible.[8] Once again, control over the enterprise may be critical to increasing return while reducing risk.

Control thus is a critical element of the rationale for establishing foreign direct investment. Indeed, the establishment of foreign direct investment may not involve the movement of capital at all, only a shift in control. A foreign direct investment may be established or acquired with capital borrowed in the host state. The effect is that the investor has not brought additional investment into the host state, but merely obtained control over assets already in the state.

Portfolio investment, by definition, offers a way to increase return without exercising control over the company in which the investment is made. Foreign portfolio investment also offers mechanisms for risk reduction, particularly through geographic diversification. The investor, for example, may invest either in companies located in different regions or in a single company with subsidiaries in multiple regions, an approach that may involve lower transaction costs than investment in multiple companies. Geographic diversification also reduces location specific risks, including in particular exchange risk, which is a primary source of risk in the international economy.[9]

3.1.2 Macroeconomic Theory

Liberal economics also offers an explanation of how foreign investment, once drawn to a particular economy by the market, promotes economic development. Economists attribute productivity, at any given level of technological development, to a combination of three factors of production: capital, comprising plants and equipment; land, including natural resources; and labor, essentially human physical and mental effort.

---

8 Richard E. Caves, *Multinational Enterprise and Economic Analysis* 169 (2d ed. 1996).

9 Exchange risk is simply the risk of loss as a result of changes in exchange rates. For example, assume that an investor wishes to invest one million dollars in a country that uses currency X, which has an exchange rate of two to the dollar. Thus, the investor exchanges one million dollars for two million X and invests it in the country. Now assume that the exchange rate changes so that currency X is traded at the rate of four to the dollar. When the investor wishes to withdraw the two million X from the country, it will be able to obtain only five hundred thousand dollars for the two million X. Thus, half of the original investment will have been lost through adverse changes in the exchange rate.

Increased productivity is achieved by increasing any one of the factors of production or by changing the level of technological development.

Productivity cannot continually increase, however, without an eventual increase in capital, again assuming a fixed level of technological development. An eventual increase in capital is essential for continued development because of the law of diminishing returns. The law of diminishing returns states that if units of a factor of production are added to fixed amounts of other factors of production, eventually each unit added will yield diminishing marginal returns. Thus, for example, if a society continues to add more labor to a fixed amount of land and capital, eventually the amount of additional output yielded by each additional unit of labor will fall. At some point, additional labor will yield no further output and, in fact, may even cause output to decline. In short, a state may increase productivity by increasing the labor supply, but only to a point. Further gains in productivity may be achieved only by increasing one of the other factors of production or by changing the level of technological development. In fact, increases in capital assets in nonwestern countries have been estimated to account for 50–90 percent of all economic growth.[10]

Foreign investment can increase productivity through its contribution to each of the factors of production. First and most obviously, a state can augment its capital supply by attracting private investment from abroad. To the extent that it contributes to the tax base, private investment may create public as well as private capital. The capital supply also can be increased through domestic saving, but developing countries may not be able to generate sufficient saving to supply the needed capital.

Foreign investment generally is denominated in a foreign currency, which means that the foreign investor may bring foreign exchange to the economy. The availability of foreign exchange enables a state to purchase scarce natural resources from other states where those resources are more abundant and thereby increase the "land" available to it.

Foreign direct investment also can enhance the productivity of labor, the third factor of production. As noted above, where the level of capital is fixed, additional units of labor produce diminishing marginal returns. In an earlier era of high labor mobility, labor could seek out capital. In the contemporary world, where migration is carefully limited, the productivity of labor can be increased by bringing capital to labor, that is, by establishing foreign investment.[11] By increasing the capital to labor ratio, foreign investment should increase the return to labor as labor becomes more scarce relative to capital. Foreign direct investment can especially improve the productivity of labor by providing training to indigenous workers in technical or managerial skills.[12] Further, some of this expertise will be transferred to other firms as these workers change jobs

---

10 E. Wayne Nafziger, *The Economics of Developing Countries* 86–124 (3d. ed. 1997); Barry Poulson, *Economic Development: Private and Public Choice* 25–49 (1994).

11 Gerald M. Meier, *Biography of a Subject: An Evolution of Development Economics* 109 (2005).

12 In general, transnational corporations engage in relatively high worker training. United Nations Transnational Corporations and Management Division (UNTCMD), *Formulation and Implementation of Foreign Investment Policies* 19 (1992).

over time.[13] In addition, the evidence is that employment with multinational enterprises is less volatile, that is, more secure, than employment with national firms.[14] The evidence is also "overwhelming" that multinational enterprises pay higher wages than national firms.[15]

Foreign direct investment may improve the level of technological development of an economy.[16] It has been argued that most of the increase in the productivity of industrialized nations is the result of technological progress, rather than capital accumulation, and thus the technological contribution eventually may be more important than the infusion of capital.[17] The impact of new technology, like that of worker training, can be multiplied by spillover effects on other firms,[18] although some studies have questioned the extent of such spillovers.[19] Spillovers are unlikely to occur, for example, where a country lacks sufficient absorptive capacity.[20] Thus, technological spillovers are more likely to occur in middle and upper income countries.[21]

Foreign investment may increase productivity by increasing the competitiveness of local industry. The empirical evidence is that local firms become more competitive following the arrival of foreign subsidiaries.[22] Foreign direct investment may stimulate local innovation by creating new markets, by positive demonstration effects and by forcing local firms to innovate to remain competitive.

---

13 Such transfers are minimized because there are not strong inducements to leave. UNCTAD, *World Investment Report 1994* 204 (1994). The empirical evidence suggests that multinational firms do in fact typically pay above the prevailing wage, provide training for local employees and increase the number of host state nationals employed in engineering and managerial positions. Caves, *supra* note 8, at 228; UNCTAD, *supra, at* 197, 221–222; Subrata Ghatak, *Introduction to Development Economics* 49–78 3d ed. 1995). This is for a variety of reasons, including both the desire to attract the best local employees and the desire to avoid criticism for exploiting local workers. UNCTAD, *supra*, at 198; UNTCMD, *supra* note 12, at 27. Indeed, transnational corporations have been known to improve worker conditions in foreign subsidiaries, such as barring child labor. UNCTAD, *supra*, at 201; UNTCMD, *supra* note 12, at 18–19.

14 Giorgio Barba Navaretti and Anthony J. Venables, *Multinational Firms in the World Economy* 45 (2004).

15 *Id.* at 44.

16 Greenfield investments are more likely to provide employee training and import new technology. UNCTAD, *supra* note 13, at 219.

17 Dominick Salvatore, *International Economics* 188 (5th ed. 1995); Michael P. Todaro, *Economic Development* 107 (5th ed. 1994); Yujuro Hayami, *Development Economics* 38–39, 111–112 (1997).

18 Caves, *supra* note 8, at 184–185; Edward Graham, *Global Corporations and National Governments* 123–130 (1996). The empirical evidence suggests that spillovers may occur through vertical rather than horizontal linkages, that is, through the transfer of knowledge to suppliers or customers. *See* M. Ayhan Kose, Eswar Prasad, Kenneth Rogoff, and Shang-Jin Wei, "Financial Globalization: A Reappraisal," IMF Working Paper WP/06/189, August 2006.

19 *See, e.g.*, Rossitza B. Wooster and David S. Diebel, "Productivity Spillovers from Foreign Direct Investment in Developing Countries: A Meta-Regression Analysis", April 2006, available at http://www.ssrn.com.

20 Navaretti and Venables, *supra* note 14, at 46.

21 *Id.*

22 Caves, *supra* note 8, at 184–185; Ghatak, *supra* note 13, at 168.

Foreign direct investment also may increase the productivity of an economy by facilitating international trade. First, a state's ability to produce goods for trade depends on its endowment of capital, labor, land, and technology.[23] As already noted, foreign investment can augment the supply of the factors of production and thereby facilitate a state's production of goods for export. Further, foreign subsidiaries can trade with their parent companies at lower transaction costs than with unaffiliated companies, thus facilitating international trade. Moreover, to the extent that barriers to trade exist, they can be circumvented by capital movements. A state that cannot export to another state may establish a subsidiary in the latter to manufacture its products for local consumption.

The advantages of trade, in turn, are three-fold. Trade allows states to specialize in goods in which they have a comparative advantage, thus generating output at the least cost; it allows states to achieve economies of scale by increasing the size of the market; and it generates efficiency through competitive pressure. International trade by multinational firms can add a further element of efficiency because, as noted above, multinational firms often make intrafirm exchanges of goods, services and knowledge with lower transaction costs than would be associated with a similar exchange between two unaffiliated firms. As transnational corporations have grown in size and numerosity, intrafirm trade has become an increasingly greater part of international trade. One-third of all world trade in goods is now estimated to be intrafirm.[24] An estimated 80 percent of trade in services is intrafirm.[25]

Liberal economic theory suggests that the home state also gains from the export of capital, again because of the law of diminishing returns. A state that has an abundance of capital will find that, at any given level of technological development, each additional unit of capital brings a smaller return because of limits on the growth of the other factors of production. By investing in countries with a lower endowment of capital relative to other factors of production, the investor may be able to obtain a higher rate of return on the investment. Geographic diversification of investment reduces the investor's risk as well.

Outward foreign direct investment can increase exports from the home country as a result of trade between the parent and its foreign subsidiaries.[26] In general, international integration increases the efficiency of a company, thus making it more competitive on

---

23 The traditional view was that productivity at any given level of technology depends on the endowments of land, labor, and capital. Because technology was assumed to be a constant, it was not treated as a factor of production. Modern economics, however, treats technology as a variable determining productivity, whether classified as a factor endowment or not.

24 Todaro, *supra* note 17, at 529; UNCTAD, *supra* note 13, at 143.

25 *Id.* at 141.

26 Organisation for Economic Cooperation and Development, *Open Markets Matter: The Benefits of Trade and Investment Liberalization* 21 (1992); Graham, *supra* note 18, at 40. For the home state, the effects of outward investment appears to neutral to moderately positive, as the loss of jobs is compensated for by increased competitiveness and growth of exports to affiliates. UNCTAD, *supra* note 13, at 169. Subsidiaries also may be established overseas as a defensive measure when there has been import penetration in the home country. UNCTAD *supra* note 5, at 31.

the world market. The benefits to the home state in these respects parallel those to the host state.

As the foregoing suggests, economic liberals espouse an outward looking policy that regards integration into the global economy as conducive to economic development. They favor the removal of barriers to transfrontier investment flows that inhibit market-driven global integration and diminish the production of wealth.

3.2 THE CRITIQUE OF ECONOMIC LIBERALISM

Economic liberalism has been critiqued by economic nationalists, who emerged as successors to the mercantilists, and by Marxists, who emerged in opposition to liberalism. The collapse of the Soviet Union at the end of the 1980s largely delegitimized its economic system as a model for other countries to follow. Although some elements of the Marxist critique continue to influence policy makers, no important part of the international community now operates predominantly from a Marxist perspective. Thus, this section will address principally the nationalist critique of liberalism, although elements of Marxist thought have influenced this critique. As has been noted, the left and the right often have found common cause in their critique of liberalism.

In general, the critique contains two elements. The first is that economic liberalism may not bring the promised increase in productivity, whether because of market failures or other reasons. Second, even assuming that economic liberalism increases productivity worldwide, it may have unacceptable distributional consequences for particular states. That is, some states may see their share of the available wealth decline, at least relatively. As has been noted, economic nationalism, like Marxism, is concerned principally with the distributional consequences of economic activity.

Turning to the first element, critics argue that, for a number of reasons, inward investment may not necessarily increase production. As an initial matter, foreign investment may not increase the capital stock because it may result simply from foreign acquisition of existing investment. Indeed, foreign investment may even reduce domestic saving and investment, as where it drives out local competition, potentially resulting in a net depletion of capital. It also may not bring foreign currency to the local economy if it is financed locally,[27] a strategy that may be employed to reduce the risk of loss associated with currency devaluation or expropriation.

Even where foreign investment does initially contribute to foreign currency reserves, it can serve to deplete such reserves even in the short run[28] by importing more than

---

27 That is, the foreign investor borrows local currency to establish or acquire the investment, repaying the loan with local currency generated by the investment. Dean Hanink, *The International Economy: A Geographical Perspective* 215 (1994); Bo Sodersten and Geoffrey Reed, *International Economics* 469 (3d ed. 1994). Foreign subsidiaries, as they mature, tend to rely increasingly on internal funding, rather than capital from the foreign parent, to finance expansion. Caves, *supra* note 13, at 159.

28 Poulson, *supra* note 10, at 459. Salvatore, *supra* note 17, at 178. The payback period for a company is generally between five and ten years. *Id.* at 378.

it exports,[29] by generating large profits that are repatriated by the foreign investor,[30] or by incurring abroad other costs such as royalties, management fees, or interest on loans.[31]

Foreign direct investment also may have a deleterious effect on labor, such as where a multinational enterprise acquires a local firm and then transfers high-skill technical or managerial positions to its headquarters in the home state[32] or replaces local managers with expatriates.[33] Indeed, as explained below, efforts to increase the productivity of an enterprise through technological advancement may decrease employment, even if it also improves the efficiency of the enterprise. Further, where an investment requires highly skilled employees, if the host state is unable to supply an adequate labor supply, the investment may have no alternative but to use expatriates.[34]

The potential technological benefits of foreign direct investment may be limited by a number of factors. First, for a variety of reasons, including economies of scale and of proximity and fears of leakage, multinational firms generally perform most research and development in the home state.[35] An investment made to access the local market may introduce technology that is obsolete or unsuited to produce goods of the quality

---

29 In general, transnational enterprises import more than their domestic counterparts, often from foreign affiliates. Caves, *supra* note 13, at 232; UNTCMD, *supra* note 12, at 21–22. There are numerous reasons for the propensity of transnational enterprises to import, including the fact that local products may be of insufficient quality or more expensive because they are produced on a small scale or in a protected market or because products from foreign affiliates can be acquired at lower transaction costs. *Id.* The investment may import intermediate products from its foreign affiliates at inflated prices, thus aggravating the foreign exchange problem. Todaro, *supra* note 17, at 532.

30 Hanink, *supra* note 27, at 233; Todaro, *supra* note 17, at 532; UNTCMD, *supra* note 12, at 22. Even if all returns on the investment were reinvested, liquidation of the investment may result in a withdrawal of foreign currency several times larger than the amount of foreign currency originally invested.

31 Todaro, *supra* note 17, at 532. Over a longer term, the worsening of the state's balance of trade will be met by a devaluation of its currency, which will make imports more expensive, encourage exports and correct the balance of trade. The state, however, will be left with a weaker currency, in effect impoverishing its economy and the devaluation can lead to capital flight. *Id.* at 459, 463.

32 Foreign direct investment may siphon off research and development firms, savings, and talent. Salvatore, *supra* note 17, at 384.

33 More than half of senior management positions in foreign affiliates in developing countries are filled by expatriates. UNCTAD, *supra* note 13, at 238. Indeed, establishment of foreign direct investment usually compels the use of expatriate technical and managerial personnel. Franklin R. Root, *International Trade and Investment* 590 (1994). Nevertheless, transnational corporations do increase the total number of local nationals employed in managerial and technical positions, UNTCMD, *supra* note 12, at 19, and they usually attempt to open positions to local personnel as quickly as possible. Root, *supra*, at 590.

34 Navaretti and Venables, *supra* note 14, at 280. They note, for example, that investments in oil producing countries often required skills unavailable in the local work force. Oil typically is extracted using expatriate personnel and exported raw, with refining occurring elsewhere.

35 In fact, only about 10 percent of all research and development is performed abroad, Caves, *supra* note 13, at 165, although this percentage appears to be increasing. UNCTAD, *supra* note 13, at 237.

needed for export. Alternatively, the importation of foreign technology may prevent the development of linkages with potential domestic suppliers and thereby reduce technological progress. Multinational firms may not attempt to adapt technology to local conditions. The technology may be capital intensive and thus have the effect of reducing employment by displacing local enterprises that were more labor intensive or of increasing costs of production where expensive machinery cannot be used efficiently, while at the same time using precious domestic financial resources and foreign currency.

The second element of the critique is that, even where the promised productivity materializes, increased productivity and economic development are not the same thing. Economic development theory has emphasized that economic development requires both increased productivity and a distribution of wealth that is equitable to some degree. Economic liberalism promises only the former.

The distributional consequences of foreign investment can be both internal and external. Foreign direct investment redistributes wealth and power internally because some members of the society will benefit more than others.[36] For example, better educated urban populations[37] or politically dominant ethnic groups[38] or regions[39] may reap disproportionate benefits, with the result that the investment merely widens existing gaps between the wealthy and the poor.[40] Alternatively, the establishment of new investment may introduce new sources of wealth, power, and opportunity that destabilize the position of traditional elites.[41]

Foreign direct investment redistributes wealth and power externally because it transfers to persons who are outside the national political system control over local assets that may be important to the host state's military defense, cultural identity, or other vital interests. The host state may fear a variety of consequences, ranging from

---

36 Foreign direct investment, for example, may be opposed by potential local competitors who may be unable to compete with much larger transnational enterprises. Ghatak, *supra* note 13, at 169.

37 Todaro, *supra* note 17, at 534. One study found that liberalization of foreign investment regimes favored the export sector of the local economy and larger local firms, while disfavoring labor unions and farmers. Alex E. Fernandez Jilberto & Barbara Hogenboom, "Mexico's Integration in NAFTA: Neoliberal restructuring and changing political alliances," in *Liberalization in the Developing World: Institutional and Economic Changes in Latin America, Africa and Asia* 150–151 (Alex E. Fernandez Jilberto & Andre Mommen, eds. 1996).

38 *See* Amy L. Chua, "The Privatization—Nationalization Cycle: The Link Between Markets and Ethnicity in Developing Countries," 95 *Columbia Law Review* 223 (1995). Improvements in income may also be gender-biased. Todaro, *supra* note 17, at 153.

39 Liberalization in Mexico has disfavored the poorer southern states. Jilberto & Hogenboom, *supra* note 37, at 155.

40 Todaro, *supra* note 17, at 533; Poulson, *supra* note 10, at 459. The fact that foreign investments generally pay relatively high wages has been cited as an indication that foreign investment exacerbates inequality, particularly between urban and rural sectors of the economy. Ghatak, *supra* note 13, at 169.

41 UNTCMD, *supra* note 12, at 25–26. Thus, for example, economic liberalization has been successfully opposed by traditional elites in Cameroon. *See* Piet Konings, "The Post Colonial State and Economic and Political Reforms in Cameroon," in Jilberto & Mommen, *supra* note 37, at 244–263.

political intervention to cultural imperialism. Marxist economists have even characterized foreign investment as a neocolonialization of the host state.

The discussion thus far has centered principally on concerns about the impact of foreign direct investment. Foreign portfolio investment raises a different set of concerns, revolving primarily around its potentially volatile nature. Specifically, the concern is that portfolio investment tends to be procyclical. For example, if the value of the currency begins to fall, portfolio investors will transfer their investment out of the economy quickly, thereby aggravating the drop in exchange rates. Indeed, portfolio investment may be withdrawn based on nothing more than the rumor of an impending change in the exchange rate or the interest rate. At the same time, sudden influxes of portfolio investments may discourage the establishment of more desirable foreign direct investment[42] or may result in an overvalued currency and thereby reduce exports.

The critique of liberalism challenges the benefits to the home state of outward investment flows as well. Outward investment flows may create a shortage of capital needed for domestic investment, raising the cost of financing and slowing economic growth. The loss of capital also may result in a lower return to labor, as labor becomes more abundant relative to capital, and a net decrease in employment as the marginal return to labor falls below its cost.[43] The shift of capital abroad may mean that the return generated by the capital will now be taxed abroad, with a potential loss in tax revenue for the home state.[44] Investment abroad may result in shrinkage of the home state's technological base, leading to a loss in the competitive position of the home state or perhaps even compromising its national security. And, while foreign direct investment does appear initially to promote exports, over time the overseas capacity may displace exports. Outward investment also may be objectionable on political grounds, such as where it flows to and benefits hostile states.

3.3 DEVELOPMENT ECONOMICS

Economic liberalism began essentially as a theory of economic development. Adam Smith's *On the Wealth of Nations*, the foundational document for economic liberalism, was written to address the question of how to promote economic growth.[45] The issue for Smith and indeed for all economists until the end of World War II was how the relatively more developed countries, particularly those of Europe, could achieve greater prosperity.

---

42 Ana Maria Fernandes, "Neoliberalism and Economic Uncertainty in Brazil," in Jilberto & Mommen, *supra* note 37, at 112.

43 Salvatore, *supra* note 17, at 378. This is really just a corollary to the law of diminishing returns. As any one factor of production diminishes, the return to other factors also diminishes. In economic theory, this is known as the Rybcynski theorem. *Id.* at 187.

44 *Id.* at 379, 383. There is an extensive network of double taxation treaties intended to ensure that foreign investors are not taxed twice on the same income. *See* Organisation for Economic Cooperation and Development, *Model Tax Convention on Income and on Capital* (1998).

45 Nilanjan Ghosh, "The Road from Economic Growth to Sustainable Development: How was it traversed?" available at http://www.ssrn.com.

With the end of colonialism after World War II, economists began to address the question of how to end the poverty that was characteristic of most nations of the world. Early development economists assumed that industrialization was the path to economic development and thus the issue was how to promote industrialization. Capital formation was recognized as critical to industrialization and governments in developed countries stepped forward to provide foreign aid either directly or through international financial institutions that would promote capital formation. Economists theorized that economic development proceeded through a series of stages, one of which was the "take-off" stage, in which an economy achieved the critical mass of capital necessary to catapult it out of poverty. They sought to achieve a "big push," a massive infusion of capital that would trigger the take-off stage and lead to industrialization. As discussed in Section 2.2, many developing countries embraced policies, rooted in economic nationalism or Marxism, that emphasized economic self-sufficiency and a highly interventionist state. Development economists of the immediate post-war era agreed that state planning must play a major role in development to ensure that available resources were used effectively.

Classic liberal economics seemed to some post-war development economists to be largely irrelevant to the condition of most developing countries. Liberalism had emerged in countries that already enjoyed a certain level of prosperity. It spoke of deference to the markets and the use of prices to signal how resources should be allocated, but large parts of many developing countries had pre-market economies. Lord John Maynard Keynes, perhaps the most influential liberal economist of the mid twentieth century, had focused his attention on the problem of a developed economy stuck in an equilibrium position characterized by high unemployment. The problem of developing countries, however, was not that they were trying to reverse a recession or depression, but that they had not yet achieved a modern economy.[46]

By the end of the 1970s, however, the failures of early development economics had become evident. Growth throughout the developing world was disappointing and inequality between countries, after diminishing for a period in the 1950s and in the 1970s, would widen again in the 1980s. The interventionist policies adopted by developing countries in the years after World War II came under heavy criticism. A new generation of economists attributed many of the failures of economic development to misguided government planning. By the end of the 1980s, development policy was dominated by a convergence of views that became known as the "Washington Consensus,"[47] so named because it reflected the consensus of the U.S. Treasury Department and Washington-based international financial institutions, notably the International Monetary Fund and the World Bank. After several decades in which development economists tried different versions of central planning, the Washington Consensus represented a return to liberalism, albeit a fundamentalist version of liberalism.[48] The market fundamentalists of the Washington Consensus emphasized fiscal discipline; trade and financial

46 Meier, *supra* note 11.

47 The term was coined by John Williamson in 1990.

48 Kimberly Ann Elliott, Debayani Kar, and J. David Richardson, "Assessing Globalization's Critics: Talkers Are No Good Doers???" undated manuscript available at http://www.ssrn.com.

liberalization; privatization; and deregulation. Reduced to its essence, the Washington Consensus was an almost libertarian approach to development under which state enterprises should be privatized and private enterprises should be deregulated, including the elimination of barriers to international trade and investment. Governments should avoid budget deficits and overvalued currencies. While economic liberalism dating back to Adam Smith had recognized the existence of market failures, within liberalism different views have existed as to the extent to which the government should intervene in the market to correct these failures. Market fundamentalists regard government intervention as almost always creating more problems than it solves and thus oppose most such interventions. That is, the principle of market facilitation was given a greatly diminished importance under the Washington Consensus. Economic difficulties were regarded as the result of too much rather than too little government involvement in the market.[49]

Events, however, were not kind to the Washington Consensus. States that adhered most faithfully to its tenets in many cases did not experience as much growth as many states that were less fundamentalist in their approach. For example, Latin American countries were perhaps the strictest adherents and they enjoyed less growth than East Asian countries that relied more heavily on state enterprises and state directed development.[50] Further, as discussed in Section 2.3, some of the countries that had opened their economies the most suffered from severe financial crises in the 1990s.

As a result, while liberalism still dominates development policy, the Washington Consensus has been displaced by a less fundamentalist version of liberalism that recognizes the necessity of government regulation to ensure the proper functioning of the market, a version of liberalism that resurrects the principle of market facilitation. That is, markets require sound institutions under the rule of law. For example, the prevailing development economics still calls for opening the capital account, but the opening requires proper sequencing to ensure that prudential regulations are in place first. Indeed, the crisis in the U.S. financial sector in 2008–2009 requiring massive government intervention in areas such as banking and insurance seemed to confirm that regulations may be inadequate even in highly developed economies. This new development economics, contrary to development economics in the 1950s and 1960s, recognizes the centrality of competitive markets to promoting economic development, but also recognizes that markets operate in an institutional context. Thus, good governance and, in particular, the establishment of the rule of law have become central elements of development economics.[51]

As will be seen in the next section, the empirical evidence seems to validate this less fundamentalist version of liberalism, one that acknowledges the role for an activist state in constituting and regulating the market and that has revived the principle of

---

49 Todaro *supra* note 17, at 85–86; Rhys Jenkins, "Theoretical Perspectives and the Transnational Corporation," in *International Political Economy* 442–443 (C. Roe Goddard, John Passe-Smith, and John Conklin, eds. 1996).

50 Dani Rodrik, "Growth Strategies," September 2003, available at http://www.ssrn.com.

51 Meier, *supra* note 11, at 131–132. Meier explains that "[d]evelopment is no longer seen primarily as a process of capital accumulation but rather as a process of organizational change." *Id.* at 127.

market facilitation. Nearly all states pursuing successful development strategies have embraced legal protection of property rights, market-based incentives subject to varying degrees of regulation, and policies to promote macroeconomic stability.[52] Economic development thus rests on both economic and legal liberalism. That is, BIT principles have become critical to economic development.

3.4 THE EMPIRICAL EVIDENCE

Development economists have subjected many of the disputes between liberals and their critics and between the more and less fundamentalist versions of liberalism to empirical investigation. This section summarizes some of the empirical evidence particularly on the macroeconomic effects of foreign investment. Discussion of the microeconomic question, the effect of BITs on foreign investment flows, is deferred to Section 3.6.

3.4.1 Foreign Investment and Growth

The first major critique of liberal investment policy is that foreign investment does not promote economic growth. Economists, in fact, have investigated extensively the role of foreign investment from both private and public sources in creating growth. The evidence appears to be that private foreign investment does promote growth, under the right circumstances.

3.4.1.1 Private Investment Some economists have approached the issue of whether foreign investment promotes growth at a high level of generality, asking whether the process of globalization promotes economic growth. The evidence is that it does.[53] The countries that are the most integrated into the global economy are the wealthiest and those least integrated have grown the least.[54] Globalization, however, is a complex process. For purposes of investment policy, the relevant question is whether investment flows promote growth.

Empirical research confirms that foreign direct investment also promotes economic growth, although it has a stronger impact in countries with higher levels of education, those that have liberalized trade, and those that have more developed financial institutions.[55]

---

52 Dani Rodrik, "Growth Strategies," September 2003, available at http://www.ssrn.com.

53 Axel Dreher, "Does Globalization Affect Growth?" October 2002, available at http://www.ssrn.com.

54 *Id.*

55 M. Ayhan Kose, Eswar Prasad, Kenneth Rogoff, and Shang-Jin Wei, "Financial Globalization: A Reappraisal," IMF Working Paper WP/06/189, August 2006, available at http://www.ssrn.com. Xuan-Vinh Vo and Jonathan A. Batten, "The Importance of Social Factors when assessing the impact of foreign direct investment on economic growth," IIIS Discussion Paper No. 179, 2007, available at http://www.ssrn.com. Studies often consider large numbers of countries to increase sample size, but this can result in the pooling of countries for which FDI works

This is consistent with more general research indicating that growth is associated with developed public infrastructure,[56] school enrollment, trade openness, and financial deepening.[57] Macroeconomic policies matter as well.[58] The implication is that efforts to attract investment must be accompanied by other reform efforts. Most studies have found that portfolio equity flows also have a significant positive impact on economic growth.[59]

Yet, empirical research also repeatedly seems to confirm the weakness of most generalizations and the contingent nature of solutions.[60] The combination of policies that seems to work in one case may not work in another. Different combinations of policies may work equally well in different countries. Foreign direct investment can promote growth, but it does not do so in every case.[61]

For example, host countries are more likely to attract technology intensive foreign direct investment if they have developed legal systems that protect property rights[62] and they are more likely to benefit from technology transfers if they have more developed human capital.[63] Efficiency-seeking foreign direct investment is most likely to

---

differently, disguising the effects that it has on certain groups of countries and not others. *See* Bruce A. Bonigen and Miao Wang, "Inappropriate Pooling of Wealthy and Poor Countries in Empirical FDI Studies," NBER Working Paper 10378, March 2004, available at http://www.ssrn.com.

56 On the importance of infrastructure, see Yuko Kinoshita and Chia-Hui La, "On the Role of Absorptive Capacity: FDI Matters to Growth," William Davidson Institute Working Paper No. 845, Nov. 2006, available at http://www.ssrn.com.

57 Elena Ianchovichina and Pooja Kacker, "Growth Trends in the Developing World: Country Forecasts and Determinants," World Bank Policy Research Working Paper 3775, November 2005, available at http://www.ssrn.com; *See also* Peter Nunnenkamp and Julius Spatz, "Foreign Direct Investment and Economic Growth in Developing Countries: How Relevant Are Host-Country and Industry Characteristics?" Kiel Working Paper No. 1176, July 2003, at 3, available at http://www.ssrn.com (noting the importance of education, sound institutions, and trade openness).

58 Evan Osborne, "Unlucky or Bad? Economic Policy and Economic Growth," The Institute of Social and Economic Research, Osaka University, Discussion Paper No. 583, May 2003, available at http://www.ssrn.com.

59 The literature is surveyed in M. Ayhan Kose, Eswar Prasad, Kenneth Rogoff, and Shang-Jin Wei, "Financial Globalization: A Reappraisal," IMF Working Paper WP/06/189, August 2006, available at http://www.ssrn.com.

60 Dani Rodrik, "Growth Strategies," September 2003, available at http://www.ssrn.com.

61 Although studies do not always find a positive correlation between foreign direct investment and economic growth, when countries are grouped according to various characteristics, the correlation is commonly positive for countries meeting certain criteria. *See* Nicholas Apergis, Katerina Lyroudi, and Athanasios Vamvakidis, "The Relationship between Foreign Direct Investment and Economic Growth: Evidence from Transition Countries," undated paper available at http://www.ssrn.com; Eddy Lee and Marco Vivarelli, "The Social Impact of Globalization in the Developing Countries," IZA DP No. 1925, January 2006, available at http://www.ssrn.com.

62 Martin Gonzales-Eiras and Jose Mauricio Prado, Jr., "Determinants of Capital Intensive and R&D Intensive Foreign Direct Investment," May 15, 2007, available at http://www.ssrn.com.

63 Peter Nunnenkamp and Julius Spatz, "Foreign Direct Investment and Economic Growth in Developing Countries: How Relevant Are Host-Country and Industry Characteristics?"

succeed where a country is open to trade.[64] Market-seeking foreign direct investment may deplete foreign exchange reserves as profits are repatriated and may crowd out local investment, although it also can raise the competitiveness of local industry.[65]

The quality of the investment also has been a subject of inquiry. Not a great deal of empirical research has been conducted to identify which types of foreign direct investment are of the highest quality, that is, the most conducive to long-term growth. In general, however, greenfield investment is more directly correlated with economic growth than foreign investment established through mergers and acquisitions, which seems to promote growth only when the host country has adequate levels of human capital.[66] As this indicates, the contribution that different types of investment can make to growth is likely to vary depending upon the circumstances of the host country.[67]

Some research has examined a special case of investment: state enterprises undergoing privatization. One study identified 2459 privatization deals in 121 countries worth approximately $1.11 trillion between 1977 and 1999.[68] Although one important impetus for privatization is to reduce public debt, privatizations are also undertaken for other reasons, such as to thwart redistributionist policies of the left by allowing middle class investment in the privatized enterprises.[69] Privatized investments, of course, are not necessarily acquired by foreign investors and thus this research is only of indirect relevance to the issue of the effect of inward foreign investment.

In any event, the study found that the success of privatization rests on a variety of factors, including the credibility of the government, the strength of legal institutions, and the liquidity of the stock market.[70] Privatization in competitive sectors generally improves the performance of the enterprise, but the evidence is more mixed in infrastructure privatization, where success depends upon proper regulatory frameworks.[71] Infrastructure privatizations have been more likely to improve efficiency in Latin America and East Asia and in the telecommunications and electricity sectors.[72] Privatizations of infrastructure have been less likely to improve efficiency in low-income countries with weak institutional frameworks and in the water sector, where

---

Kiel Working Paper No. 1176, July 2003, at 3, available at http://www.ssrn.com; Chengang Wang, Xiaming Liu and Yingqi Wei, "Impact of Openness on Growth in Different Country Groups," 2004, available at http://www.ssrn.com.

64 Nunnenkamp and Spatz, *supra* note 63.

65 *Id.* at 7.

66 Miao Wang and M. C. Sunny Wong, "What Drives Economic Growth? The Case of Cross-Border M&A and Greenfield FDI Activities," available at http://www.ssrn.com.

67 *See* Laura Alfaro and Andrew Charlton, "Growth and the Quality of Foreign Direct Investment: Is All FDI Equal?" May 2007, available at http://www.ssrn.com.

68 Domenico Siniscalco, Bernardo Bortolotti, and Marcella Fantini, "Privatisation Around the World: New Evidence from Panel Data," CESifo Working Paper No. 600, FEEM Working Paper No. 77.2001, October 2001 at 2. In only 30 percent of the cases, however, was a majority of the stock sold.

69 *Id.* at 2, 5.

70 *Id.* at 40.

71 Sunita Kilkeri and Aishetu Fatima Kolo, "Privatization: Trends and Recent Developments," World Bank Policy Research Working Paper 3765, November 2005, available at http://www.ssrn.com.

72 *Id.*

rates are especially sensitive.[73] Instances where privatizations were reversed, however, have been few in number.[74]

Some studies have examined the relationship among economic liberalism, democracy, and economic development. Democracy does seem to promote economic development, but it does so more effectively if the country has liberalized its economy first.[75] Economic liberalism lays a foundation for greater economic growth once a country democratizes.

3.4.1.2 Public Investment As discussed in Section 2.3, developing countries increasingly turned to foreign investment in the 1980s, as developmental assistance aid diminished in availability. Even where developmental assistance is available, however, persistent doubts exist that foreign aid contributes to growth.[76] One recent study by analysts at the IMF, for example, found "little evidence of a robust positive impact of aid on growth."[77] Further, it found "virtually no evidence that aid works better in better policy or institutional or geographical environments, or that certain kinds of aid work better than others."[78] Because the results were reasonably uniform across different subcategories of aid, the study inferred that different kinds of aid are highly fungible, suggesting that governments "seem to view all forms of aid as going to a common pot and act accordingly."[79]

One explanation offered for the apparent failure of foreign aid is that aid is merely substituted for other public investment, thereby offsetting any positive effect from the aid.[80] One study argued that the reason aid does not contribute to growth is that the influx of funds results in an overvalued exchange rate, which impedes the growth of manufacturing exports.[81] Others have suggested that those in power appropriate the resources for themselves, which leads them to weaken democratic institutions while also undermining any effect of the aid on growth.[82] although one analyst argued on the

---

73 *Id.*

74 *Id.*

75 Torsten Persson and Guido Tabellini, "Democracy and Development: The Devil in the Details," CESifo Working Paper No. 1672, Feb. 2006, available at http://www.ssrn.com; Francesco Giavazzi and Guido Tabellini, "Economic and Political Liberalizations," IGIER Working Paper No. 264, July 2004, available at http://www.ssrn.com.

76 The "voluminous literature" on whether aid contributes to growth is cited in Raghuram G. Rajan and Arvind Subramanian, "Aid and Growth: What Does the Cross-Country Evidence Really Show?" IMF Working Paper WP/05/'17, June 2005, available at http://www.ssrn.com.

77 *Id.* at 5.

78 *Id.*

79 *Id.* at 19.

80 Santanu Chatterjee, Paoloa Giuliano, and Ilker Kaya, "Where Has All the Money Gone? Foreign Aid and the Quest for Growth," IZA Discussion Paper No. 2858, June 2007, available at http://www.ssrn.com.

81 Raghuran G. Rajan and Arvind Subramanian, "What Undermines Aid's Impact on Growth?" Oct. 2005, available at http://www.ssrn.com.

82 Siemon Djankow, Jose G. Montalvo, and Marta Reynal-Querol, "The Curse of Aid," March 2006, available at http://www.ssrn.com; Sarantis Kalyvitis and Irene Vlachaki, "More Aid,

basis of empirical evidence that foreign aid actually decreases corruption.[83] A look at the effect of aid on economic institutions also found no effect.[84]

The effect of aid on growth may even be negative. That is, foreign aid may be counterproductive.[85] Aid, for example, may disguise the effect of bad policy choices, allowing or even encouraging governments to continue to pursue policies that are harmful in the long term[86] and reducing accountability.[87] The volatile and unpredictable nature of aid also has been blamed for the failure of aid to promote growth.[88]

The issue is not settled, however. Analysts continue to consider whether, if all aid does not promote growth, certain types of aid at least are growth enhancing. One study, for example, argues that developmental aid, as opposed to geopolitical aid, does promote growth over the long run and that this effect has been overlooked by studies that aggregate the two types of aid.[89]

Not all countries have been successful in attracting significant amounts of foreign investment. For the present, developmental assistance may be their only important source of international capital. Severe doubts about the effectiveness of foreign aid, however, only serve to emphasize the importance of creating a climate that will facilitate private investment.

3.4.2 Foreign Investment and Inequality

The second major critique of a liberal investment policy is that foreign investment has adverse distributional consequences. More specifically, it has been argued, foreign investment promotes inequality because it benefits only a portion of those in the host country. A more particular concern is that foreign investment does little for the poor. Some have argued that foreign investment flows can increase inequality between countries as well.

An analysis of the effects of foreign investment on inequality requires a determination of how inequality is to be measured. Studies distinguish between two measures of inequality: inequality between countries and inequality within countries. One type of

---

Less Democracy? An Empirical Examination of the Relationship between Foreign Aid and the Democratization of Recipients," July 2007, available at http://www.ssrn.com.

83 Jose Tavares, "Does Foreign Aid Corrupt?" Sept. 2001, available at http://www.ssrn.com.

84 Decio Coviello and Foumeen Islam, "Does Aid Help Improve Economic Institutions?" World Bank Policy Research Working Paper 3990, August 2006, available at http://www.ssrn.com.

85 Andros Kournellos, Chih Ming Tan, Xiabo Zhang, "Is the Relationship Between Aid and Economic Growth Nonlinear?" September 22, 2006, available at http://www.ssrn.com.

86 Charles Kenny, "What is Effective Aid? How Would Donors Allocate It?" World Bank Research Working Paper 4005, September 2006, at page 6, available at http://www.ssrn.com.; Miroslav Prokopijevic, "Why Foreign Aid Fails," undated paper available at http://www.ssrn.com.

87 Kalyvitis and Vlachaki, *supra* note 82.

88 Ales Bulir and A. Javier Hamann, "How Volatile and Unpredictable Are Aid Flows, and What Are the Policy Implications," IMF Working Paper WP/01/167, October 2001, available at www.ssrn.com.

89 Sanjay G. Reddy and Camelia Menoiu, "Development Aid and Economic Growth: A Positive Long-Run Relationship", July 11, 2006, available at http://www.ssrn.com.

inequality may increase while the other decreases. For example, economic integration in theory could reduce inequality between countries, so that the income earned by the poorest countries rises relative to that earned by the richest countries, while inequality within some countries could increase, such that, for example, the income received by the wealthiest citizens in that country increased relative to that received by the poorest citizens. A situation in which this might occur can easily be imagined. Consider the case of an economic integration agreement between a wealthy country and a poor country. Following liberalization, employment for low-wage unskilled workers in the poor country rises, as that country gains access to the market of the wealthy country. Unskilled workers in the wealthy country lose jobs to their lower paid competitors in the poor country. At the same time, professionals and highly skilled workers in banking, insurance, software design, and technology intensive industries gain income as they obtain access to the market of the poor country, while their competitors in the poor country are displaced by developed country firms with which they cannot compete. The result would be reduced inequality in the poor country and increased inequality in the wealthy country. Depending upon the relative size of the changes in income flows between the two countries, the income difference between the two countries could increase or diminish.

The consensus seems to be that most income inequality is attributable to inequality between countries rather than inequality within countries.[90] In measuring inequality between countries, one must decide whether to count countries or people, that is, whether to count each country equally or weight countries by population. This question obviously is critical because of enormous differences in population between countries. It is particularly critical now because China and India, the two most populous nations, have experienced dramatic economic changes in recent years not experienced by many other developing countries. Thus, for example, an increase in income earned by China could more than compensate for losses in income experienced by all of sub-Saharan Africa. If all countries are counted equally, one would conclude that income within this sample of developing countries had fallen. If countries are weighted by population, one would conclude that income within this sample had risen. Because ultimately the concern about income inequality is a concern about the welfare of people, most studies weight countries by population.

Inequality may be measured in relative or in absolute terms. Measures of relative inequality consider the proportion of income earned by the wealthiest and the poorest. Measures of absolute inequality consider the difference in income earned by the wealthiest and the poorest. For example, imagine a country in which the wealthiest

---

90 Steven Brakman and Charles van Marrewijk, "It's a Big World After All," CESifo Working Paper No. 1964, April 2007, available at http://www.ssrn.com (suggesting that 70 percent of inequality is due to between country inequality and 30 percent is due to within country inequality); Giovanni Andrea Cornia, "The Impact of Liberalisation and Globalisation on Income Inequality in Developing and Transitional Economies," CESifo Working Paper No. 843, January 2003, available at http://www.ssrn.com (60–90 percent of inequality is attributable to between-country income inequality); Kevin H. O'Rourke, "Globalization and Inequality: Historical Trends," NBER Working Paper 8339, June 2001, available at http://www.ssrn.com.

earn an average of $5000 annually, while the poorest earn an average of $500 annually. In relative terms, the difference between the wealthiest and the poorest is indicated by the ratio of 10 to 1. In absolute terms, the difference is indicated by the amount of $4500. Now imagine that the average income of every person in the country doubles. The wealthiest would earn $10,000 annually while the poorest would earn $1000 annually. In relative terms, inequality has not changed. The ratio of income earned by rich and poor remains 10 to 1. In absolute terms, however, the difference has doubled, from $4500 to $9000. In this example, everyone in the country benefited from a doubling of income. Yet, because of the increase in absolute inequality, the poor justifiably could feel that they were falling behind.

Since 1820, when the processes that would lead to the globalization of the late nineteenth century began, relative inequality between countries (weighted by population) has risen substantially. It rose continuously from 1820 to 1950, then fell during the 1950s, rose in the 1960s, was stable in the 1970s, but began to decline around 1979, just after China began its economic reforms in December 1978. Global inequality declined in the 1980s and 1990s,[91] but much of the trend toward reduced inequality is attributable to growth in China and India.[92] Although some have seen rising inequality between countries since the 1820s as evidence that liberalism aggravates inequality, as these data indicate, inequality rose even during the 1920s and 1930s, when countries aggressively pursued autarkic policies and liberalism was in eclipse. Indeed, it was precisely during the interwar era of autarky when income gaps widened at the highest rates.[93]

The declining inequality between countries in recent decades reflects both slowing growth rates in developed countries and increasing growth rates in some developing countries. Growth rates for industrialized countries have fallen since the 1960s, while growth rates for developing countries, after declining in the 1970s and 1980s, rebounded in the 1990s.[94] By the 1990s, developing countries were enjoying growth rates higher than those of industrialized countries. Not all developing countries were participating in the accelerated growth, however. Sub-Saharan Africa actually experienced negative per capita income growth in both the 1980s and the 1990s, while the transitional economies also experienced negative growth in the 1990s.[95] Further, much of the positive performance of the developing countries is again attributable to China and India. Overall, the growth rate of countries in recent decades has varied tremendously with effective growth strategies being context-specific.[96] That is, as already noted in Section 3.4.1.1, the strategy that promotes growth in one country may not be effective in another.

---

91 Brakman and Marrewijk, *supra* note 90.

92 *Id.* at 19; Albert Berry and John Serieux, "All About the Giants: Probing the Influences on Growth and Income Inequality at the End of the 20th Century," CESIFO Working Paper No. 840, January 2003, at 12–14, available at http://www.ssrn.com; The view that inequality declined in the 1980s and 1990s is not unanimous. *See* Cornia, *supra* note 90.

93 Meier, *supra* note 11, at 145.

94 Berry and Serieux, *supra* note 92; David Dollar, "Globalization, Poverty, and Inequality Since 1980," World Bank Research Working Paper 3333, June 2004, available at http://www.ssrn.com.

95 Berry and Serieux, *supra* note 92, at 8.

96 Dani Rodrik, "Growth Strategies," September 2003, available at http://www.ssrn.com.

Studies also have examined the effect of globalization on inequality within countries. In 1955, Simon Kuznets argued that economic growth leads initially to increased inequality within a country as the economy shifts from agricultural to industrial production, after which inequality decreases as the industrial labor force comes to predominate.[97] Empirical research, however, generally has not confirmed the Kuznets Curve[98] or at least has found that it is a better descriptor of the experience in Europe than in Asia or Latin America.[99]

The overall trend from the 1820s until the present has been one of declining inequality within countries.[100] In the 1980s and 1990s, however, inequality within countries worldwide has changed little. It has improved in some countries and worsened in others and these various trends have largely offset each other.[101]

Some have argued that rising inequality within a country, when it occurs, is attributable to the fact that globalization has not proceeded far enough. For example, the North American Free Trade Agreement led to increased income inequality within Mexico, but much of this was because of a boom along the U.S. border that was not replicated throughout the country.[102] China experienced a large increase in inequality in the mid 1980s, largely attributable to gaps between urban and rural areas and between coastal and interior regions.[103] Thus, it may be argued, the solution for inequality within these countries is not to disengage from the globalization process that boosted income in some regions, but to find a way to integrate the rest of the country into that process.

In general, relative income inequality within a country is not correlated with economic growth.[104] That is, a growing economy may decrease relative inequality in a country or increase it. The process of globalization in general seems to have exacerbated wage inequality in developed countries because of a decline in the wages of less skilled workers,[105] but it has had only a negligible effect on wage inequality within developing countries.[106]

---

97 Simon Kuznets, "Economic Growth and Income Inequality," 65 *American Economic Review* 1 (1955).

98 *See, e.g.*, Garth Frazer, "Inequality and Development Across and Within Countries," undated paper available at http://www.ssrn.com.

99 Daron Acemoglu and James A. Robinson, "The Political Economy of the Kuznets Curve," September 2000, available at http://www.ssrn.com.

100 Kevin H. O'Rourke, "Globalization and Inequality: Historical Trends," NBER Working Paper 8339, June 2001. The data regarding measures of inequality within countries are less clear than data on inequality between countries. Brakman and Marrewijk, *supra* note 90, available at http://www.ssrn.com.

101 Dollar, *supra* note 94, at 21–24; Berry and Serieux, *supra* note 92, at 17–22.

102 *Id.* at 14.

103 *Id.*

104 Martin Ravallion, "Competing Concepts of Inequality in the Globalization Debate," World Bank Policy Research Working Paper 3243, March 2004, at 5, available at http://www.ssrn.com; Ravallion, "Pro-Poor Growth: A Primer," World Bank Policy Research Paper 3242, March 2004, available at http://www.ssrn.com.

105 Dollar, *supra* note 94, at 24.

106 Axel Dreher and Noel Gaston, "Has Globalization Increased Inequality?" June 2006, available at http://www.ssrn.com.

When the inquiry shifts from the effects of globalization to the effects of foreign direct investment, empirical research suggests that inward foreign direct investment does increase inequality within developing countries,[107] but that the effect fades over time.[108] An increase in inequality seems particularly likely where low levels of education prevent the poor from participating in technology intensive industries.

Foreign direct investment in general does result in higher wages, which improves the welfare of the population as a whole.[109] Further, increases in foreign direct investment and especially growth in the export sector seem to be associated with reductions in poverty.[110] Yet, the wealthy may benefit disproportionately and the increase in absolute inequality often raises concerns.[111] In developed countries, by contrast, inward foreign direct investment is correlated with a decrease in wage inequality.[112]

While, as already noted, economic growth is not correlated with changes in *relative* inequality within countries, the evidence suggests that economic growth does tend to increase *absolute* inequality.[113] Increases in absolute inequality, of course, will contribute to the sense of a widening gap between rich and poor. Absolute inequality can be reduced through economic contraction, but this also will increase the number of people living in poverty.[114] Alternatively, public policies, such as educational subsidies, could be of use in reducing inequality.[115] In particular, the development of the financial sector has been shown to be positively correlated with economic growth and reductions in income inequality.[116] A more developed financial sector also appears to have a disproportionately large positive effect on the growth of industries characterized by small firms[117] because it removes growth constraints from small firms.

Critics of globalization often focus their attention less on whether it increases inequality, and more on whether it aids the poor. Typically, the poor are defined by reference to some absolute standard, intended to identify those whose position in the

---

107 Parantap Basu and Alessandra Guaruglia, "Foreign Direct Investment, Inequality and Growth," undated 2005 paper, available at http://www.ssrn.com.

108 Paolo Figini and Holger Gorg, "Does Foreign Direct Investment Affect Wage Inequality? An Empirical Investigation," IZA DP No. 2336, September 2006, available at http://www.ssrn.com.

109 *Id.* at 16.

110 Ann Harrison, "Globalization and Poverty," October 2005, at 9, available at http://www.ssrn.com.

111 Figini and Gorg, *supra* note 108, at 16.

112 *Id.* at 15.

113 Martin Ravallion, "Competing Concepts of Inequality in the Globalization Debate," World Bank Policy Research Working Paper 3243, March 2004, available at http://www.ssrn.com.

114 *Id.* at 25.

115 Parantap Basu and Alessandra Guaruglia, "Foreign Direct Investment, Inequality and Growth," undated 2005 paper, available at http://www.ssrn.com.

116 Thorsten Beck, Asli Demirguc-Kunt, and Ross Levine, "Finance, Inequality and Poverty: Cross-Country Evidence," World Bank Policy Research Working Paper 3338, June 2004, available at http://www.ssrn.com.

117 Thorsten Beck, Asli Demirguc-Kunt, Luc Laeven, and Ross Levine, "Finance, Firm Size, and Growth," November 30, 2004, available at http://www.ssrn.com.

income hierarchy is so low as to be considered unacceptable, at least morally.[118] The poor are those whose economic circumstances must be improved.

Measures of poverty raise complex methodological issues.[119] For example, defining poverty to mean having an income below a certain level does not measure shifts in income among persons below that level. Thus, the total number of the poor might be unchanged and yet the circumstances of the poor might well have changed. At the international level, extreme poverty has been defined as earning less than $1 a day.

In the Global Era, the number of those living in extreme poverty has fallen. For example, the percentage of the world population living on less than $1 a day in developing countries has fallen from 40.3 percent in 1981 to 21.3 percent in 2001.[120] Put another way, the number of those living in extreme poverty fell by 375 million from 1981 to 2001, even as world population rose by 1.6 billion,[121] although the decline in the number of poor worldwide is attributable to a large extent to reductions in China.[122] Sub-Saharan Africa actually experienced an increase in the number of those living below $1 a day during that period, although the percentage of the population below that level fell.[123]

The issue for many is how to ensure that growth benefits the poor. Where inequality is high, the poor tend to benefit the least from growth.[124] If the poor are to benefit, their capacity to participate in growth must be improved. The proper policies in this regard will vary from country to country, but the evidence suggests that rural infrastructure development, the provision of health and education services, and better access to credit are likely to be effective in many cases.[125]

Leaving aside the intrinsic value of a broader distribution of wealth, a reduction in inequality may promote growth for the economy as a whole. Most studies of the issue have concluded that inequality inhibits growth.[126] Further, the negative effect of inequality on growth is higher in developing countries, although the effect seems to

---

118 Poverty has been defined as meaning that "one cannot afford certain pre-determined consumption needs." Martin Ravallion, "Pro-Poor Growth: A Primer," World Bank Policy Research Working Paper 3242, March 2004, available at http://www.ssrn.com. Those pre-determined consumption needs, however, are based on the level of development within the society as a whole.

119 *Id.*

120 Dollar, *supra* note 94, at 17. *See also* Ravallion, *supra* note 113, at 6.

121 *Id.* at 18.

122 Shahua Chen and Martin Ravallion, "Absolute Poverty Measures for the Developing World, 1981–2004," World Bank Policy Research Working Paper 4211, April 2007, available at http://www.ssrn.com.

123 *Id.*

124 *See* Martin Ravallion, "Pro-Poor Growth: A Primer," World Bank Policy Research Working Paper 3242, March 2004, available at http://www.ssrn.com.

125 *Id. See also* Martin Ravallion, "Inequality *is* Bad for the Poor," World Bank Policy Research Working Paper 3677, August 2005, available at http://www.ssrn.com; Ann Harrison, "Globalization and Poverty," October 2005, available at http://www.ssrn.com.

126 The literature is summarized briefly in Laura de Dominicis, Henri L.F. deGroot, and Raymond J.G.M. Florax, "Growth and Inequality: A Meta-Analysis," undated paper available at http://www.ssrn.com.

vary over time.[127] Again, the effects are likely to be different for different countries. Yet, a number of growth inhibiting consequences of inequality have been documented. Inequality increases corruption, which deters investment.[128] It also can promote instability and fear of redistribution, which similarly deters investment.[129] It results as well in an ineffective use of human capital.[130]

3.4.3 Environmental and Labor Concerns

Many environmentalists have expressed the concern that developing countries, in their efforts to attract foreign investment, will weaken or at least fail to strengthen environmental protection standards. The assumption is that such standards impose costs on business operations and that foreign investors, in their desire to lower costs, will seek to locate their investments where costs attributable to environmental regulations are lowest. Indeed, it is feared, developing countries may even engage in competitive reductions in environmental standards, a phenomenon that has been called a "race to the bottom." The result would be lower environmental standards throughout the world.[131] The concern is a plausible one. Foreign investors do invest abroad to reduce costs and environmental standards do increase costs. A race toward environmental degradation clearly would justify a careful reexamination of foreign investment policy.

Yet, reasons exist for doubting whether such a race is being run to any significant extent. First, the costs imposed by environmental regulations are only one element of a foreign investor's location decision, which may be much more influenced by a wide range of other considerations, such as the political and economic stability in the proposed site of the investment, the availability of trained labor, the extent of physical infrastructure, the size of the local market, and the proximity to other export markets.

---

127 *Id. See also* Francisco H.G. Ferreira and Michael Walton, "Inequality of Opportunity and Economic Development," World Bank Policy Research Working Paper 3816, January 2006, available at http://www.ssrn.com. .

128 Richard H. McAdams, "Economic Costs of Inequality," in *The Role of Race in Law, Markets, and Social Structures* (E.C. Jordan & C. J. Ogletree, eds. 2007); Bert Denolf, "The Impact of Corruption on Foreign Direct Investment," 9 *Journal of World Investment and Trade* 249 (2008) (finding the effect on foreign investment to be "mildly negative"). On the problem of corruption with respect to foreign investment, *see* Hilmar Raeschke-Kessler and Dorothee Gottwald, "Corruption," in, *The Oxford Handbook of International Investment Law* (Peter Muchlinski, Frederico Ortino, and Christoph Schreuer, eds. 2008).

129 McAdams, *supra* note 128.

130 *Id.*

131 In theory, developed countries might participate in the race as well, hoping to keep investment from leaving by lowering their own environmental standards. This assumes an incoherent policy in which a developed country negotiates BITs to promote investment flows and then lowers environmental standards to discourage those very flows. In any event, a developed country seeking to prevent outward investment could do so in ways other than lowering politically popular environmental protection standards, such as through adverse tax treatment of income earned through investments abroad.

Ultimately, the level of environmental protection in a large number of cases may not be a significant consideration in the investment decision.[132] Second, economists have found that economic development tends initially to cause deterioration in the environment, but then to promote environmental quality, a phenomenon known as the environmental Kuznets Curve.[133] Different explanations have been offered, including that economic development tends to proceed through stages in which countries move toward cleaner industries over time and that environmental quality is a luxury good that countries will seek once they have sufficient resources.[134] The latter explanation, it has been argued, assumes effective government regulation and the rule of law.[135] Indeed, one study found that foreign direct investment raises the level of environmental regulation when government corruptibility is low, but may lead to the creation of pollution havens when corruptibility is high.[136] Third, multinational enterprises, precisely because they are under suspicion and scrutiny, may feel obliged to be more sensitive to environmental concerns than would domestic investment. Thus, in this view, economic development through foreign investment in the long run likely will encourage environmental protection.

In short, theory does not provide an unambiguous prediction. One can construct plausible accounts that predict a race to the bottom and plausible accounts that any such race is unlikely to occur. In any event, numerous empirical studies to date have been unable to document the existence of an environmental race to the bottom.[137] If such a race is occurring, the evidence of it is weak.

---

132 Jeffery Frankel, "The Environment and Economic Globalization," in *Globalization: What's New?* 129 (Michael Weinstein, ed. 2005). The argument is not that it is never a consideration, but that it may often be less important than other considerations.

133 Salvatore Bimonte, "Model of Growth and Environmental Quality: A New Evidence of the Environmental Kuznets Curve," April 2001, available at http://www.ssrn.com; Jeffrey Frankel, "Kyoto and Geneva: Linkage of the Climate Change Regime and Trade Regime," Kennedy School of Government Working Paper Series, Oct. 2004, available at http://www.ssrn.com; Marzio Galeotti, "Economic Development and Environmental Protection," Sept. 2003, available at http://www.ssrn.com; Jeffery Frankel, "The Environment and Economic Globalization," in *Globalization: What's New?* 129 (Michael Weinstein, ed. 2005). The Kuznets Curve originally was developed to describe the phenomenon whereby economic growth initially increases inequality and then decreases it. *See* Section 3.4.2.

134 Marzio Galeotti, "Economic Development and Environmental Protection," Sept. 2003, available at http://www.ssrn.com; Frankel, *supra* note 133, at 129.

135 Frankel, *supra* note 133, at 129.

136 Matthew A. Cole, Robert J. R. Elliott, and Per G. Fredriksson, "Endogenous Pollution Havens: Does FDI Influence Environmental Regulation?" University of Nottingham Research Paper 2004/20, available at http://www.ssrn.com.

137 *See, e.g.*, World Bank, *Globalization, Growth, and Poverty* 16 (2002); Zhihao Yu, "A Theory of Strategic Vertical FDI and the Missing Pollution-Haven Effect," Oct. 2001, available at http://www.ssrn.com; Matthias Busse, "Trade, Environmental Regulations and the World Trade Organization: New Empirical Evidence," World Bank Policy Research Working Paper 3361, July 2004, available at http://www.ssrn.com; Judith M. Dean, Mary E. Lovely, and Hua Wang, "Are Foreign Investors Attracted to Weak Environmental Regulations? Evaluating the Evidence from China," World Bank Policy Research Working Paper 3505, February 2005, available at http://www.ssrn.com; Robert J. R. Elliott and Kenichi Shimamoto, "Are ASEAN

Similarly, organized labor in developed countries often expresses the concern that a country eager to attract foreign investment will lower, or fail to raise, labor standards, offering a low wage and compliant labor force as a competitive advantage for investments locating in its territory. The result, in theory, would be that investment will flow from countries with high labor standards to those with low standards, reducing employment in countries that have high labor standards and forcing labor in those countries to accept weaker standards in order to preserve their jobs. The fear is that developed and developing countries alike will engage in competitive rounds of reductions in wages and in the quality of working conditions, that is, in another race to the bottom. Similar concerns are echoed by human rights groups who believe that labor rights should be among the internationally protected human rights.[138] This concern is sometimes expressed as a critique that BITs protect property rights, but not worker rights or human rights.

Once again, however, the evidence calls into question whether a race to the bottom exists.[139] Studies also have demonstrated that foreign investors in developing countries tend to pay higher wages than domestic investors,[140] if for no other reason than the fact that, as foreign investors, they are under greater scrutiny. Foreign direct investment is rarely attracted to the lowest wage economies, because investors prefer an abundant supply of educated labor.[141]

Indeed, governments in many developing countries regard developed country concerns about a race to the bottom in environmental or labor standards as a disguise for economic protectionism. They fear, for example, that such standards, especially in free trade agreements, will provide a pretext for protectionists seeking to impose sanctions on developing countries.[142] In this view, groups that oppose investment liberalization in the name of protecting the environment or labor in fact are only impeding economic development, which over the long term will produce better labor and environmental standards in developing countries as it has in developed countries.

Apart from general concerns about a race to the bottom, critics of a liberal investment policy have argued more specifically that foreign direct investment promotes

---

Countries Havens for Japanese Pollution-Intensive Industry?" 31 *World Economy* 236 (2008); Frankel, *supra* note 133, at 129 (2005).

138 *See generally* Hans-Michael Wolffgang and Wolfram Feuerhake, "Core Labour Standards in World Trade Law," 36 *Journal of World Trade* 883, 889 (2002). For example, the International Labor Organization's 1998 "Declaration on Fundamental Principles and Rights at Work" affirmed that all members have an obligation to promote freedom of association and the right to bargain collectively, freedom from forced labor, freedom from child labor, and freedom from discrimination.

139 *See* Kimberly Ann Elliott, "Labor Standards and the Free Trade Area of the Americas," at 6, available at http://www.ssrn.com (noting the complexity of the issue and the difficulty of generalizing).

140 Navaretti and Venables, *supra* note 14, at 44. They term the evidence "overwhelming" on this point.

141 *Id.* at 29.

142 For a discussion of the uses of environmental regulations as protectionist measures, *see* Nita Ghei, "Evaluating the WTO's Two Step Test for Environmental Measures Under Article XX," 18 *Colorado Journal of International Environmental Law* 117 (2007).

child labor. The theory is that foreign investors, by offering employment, induce parents to send their children to work. One can scarcely doubt that this occurs. Yet, there are reasons to believe that foreign investment also may contribute to reducing the extent of child labor, at least over time. First, the effect of foreign investment in a low wage country should be to increase the income of those in the unskilled, low wage labor force, thereby reducing the need to send their children to work. This effect would be increased to the extent that foreign investment promotes the growth of the economy as a whole. Second, as has been noted, foreign investments often are subjected to more intense scrutiny than other companies and may avoid employing children in order to protect their reputations in their home countries. Multinational companies sometimes implement firm wide policies that prohibit child labor in their subsidiaries.[143] Of course, some foreign direct investment occurs as a result of the acquisition of an existing company by a foreign investor. Such an existing company may already have been employing child labor at the time of the acquisition. For the reasons just described, the company may be less likely to continue to employ children than it was prior to the acquisition.

Once again, theory is ambiguous: plausible accounts predict both increases and decreases in child labor associated with foreign investment. One recent study, after reviewing the theoretical arguments discussed above, found empirically that increases in foreign direct investment are associated with decreases in child labor.[144] A subsequent study by different analysts found the same result and determined that the effect of foreign direct investment in reducing child labor was attributable to increases in income.[145] That is, foreign direct investment is more likely to reduce child labor where the investment employs more workers and pays higher wages.

Another labor concern is that the establishment of foreign subsidiaries may result in job losses in the home country. Economic theory on this issue is ambiguous as well. Outward foreign investment could act as a substitute for domestic employment, in which case it would destroy jobs in the home economy, or as a complement, in which case it would create jobs in the home economy. In general, horizontal foreign direct investment appears to act as a substitute, while vertical foreign direct investment acts as a complement.[146]

Efforts to measure the effects of employment on outflows of foreign direct investment are hampered by limitations on the data, which are available from only a few countries, such as the United States.[147] In any event, data from "mass layoffs" in the United States during 2004 and 2005 indicate that only 1.6 percent of job separations in

143 Raymond Vernon, *In the Hurricane's Eye* 25 (1998).

144 Eric Neumayer and Indra De Soysa, "Trade Openness, Foreign Direct Investment and Child Labor," 33 *World Development* 43 (2005).

145 Ronald B. Davies and Annie Voy, "The Effect of FDI on Child Labor," IIIS Discussion Paper No. 215, February 2007, available at http://www.ssrn.com.

146 Navaretti and Venables, *supra* note 14, at 44.

147 P.S. Andersen and P. Hainaut, "Foreign Direct Investment and Employment in the Industrial Countries," BIS Working Papers, No. 68, November 1998.

"mass layoffs" were the result of job relocations to foreign countries.[148] One study found that the establishment of overseas subsidiaries has resulted in job creation in the United States that more than offsets the job losses.[149] For example, the outsourcing of computer programming jobs may be associated with the creation of higher level software engineer jobs in the United States.[150] A subsequent study, however, found that U.S. direct investment in developing countries does result in a loss of manufacturing jobs in the United States.[151] Both studies concurred that shifting jobs to a low-wage country increases the competitiveness of U.S. companies and thus their ability to survive. In other words, not investing abroad might have caused the United States even greater job losses in the long run because, had companies not been able to shift production to a lower cost environment, they might have failed entirely.

To the extent that a race to the bottom exists, it is not attributable to the BITs. No part of a BIT encourages a race to the bottom. Where a race occurs, it could be attributable instead to the host state's policy of seeking foreign investment, the same policy that may have prompted the host state to conclude a BIT. That is, the race to the bottom and the race to negotiate BITs would be jointly caused by a pro-investment policy.

While BITs do not cause a race to the bottom, the concern nevertheless exists that they may impede efforts to raise standards. For example, some have expressed the fear that environmental regulations would be found by tribunals to constitute a regulatory expropriation. Experience to date, however, has not validated that concern. Tribunals have rejected the vast majority of regulatory expropriation claims, including those involving environmental measures. Yet, BITs may impede efforts to raise environmental and labor standards in another way. Specifically, host states often induce foreign investors to invest by entering into investment agreements in which the state promises to exempt the foreign investment from new legislation, such as environmental or labor legislation.[152] The host state's failure to honor these commitments may violate any of several BIT obligations, including the fair and equitable treatment standard, the observance of obligations provision, and the expropriation provision. In such a case, however, to the extent that a legitimate objection to the situation exists, the problem lies not in the host state's having committed itself to the rule of law, but in its having committed itself to an exemption for the foreign investment. That is, BITs are likely to impede efforts to raise environmental or labor standards principally in the situation where the host state has voluntarily committed itself, apart from the BIT, not to raise standards, or at least not to apply heightened standards to a covered investment.

---

148 N. Gregory Mankiw and Phillip Swagel, "The Politics and Economics of Offshore Outsourcing," March 2006, available at http://www.ssrn.com.

149 *Id.*

150 *Id.*

151 Ann E. Harrison and Margaret S. McMillan, "Dispelling Some Myths about Offshoring," available at http://www.ssrn.com.

152 *See* International Finance Corporation, "Stabilization Clauses and Human Rights," March 11, 2008, available at http://www.ifc.org.

3.5 THE ROLE OF BITS

3.5.1 Promoting a Liberal Investment Regime

BITs profess to be instruments of a liberal investment policy and, in fact, they were created by developed countries at a time when the developed world was seeking to create a liberal investment regime.[153] Yet, BITs are only limited instruments of a liberal investment policy.

A liberal investment policy rests on principles of investment neutrality, investment security, and market facilitation.[154] Of these three, most BITs promote principally investment security. They have limited investment neutrality provisions and virtually no provisions on market facilitation.

Most of the provisions of a typical BIT further the liberal principle of investment security. First, BITs usually contain a broad provision guaranteeing that covered investment receive fair and equitable treatment[155] and, less often, full protection and security.[156] The former has been interpreted to protect the investor's legitimate expectations arising from promises or assurances from the host state, while the latter imposes on the host state a duty to exercise reasonable care to protect investment against at least certain types of harm. Second, BITs uniformly impose conditions on the right of the host state to expropriate covered investment, including in particular the condition that compensation be paid.[157] Third, most BITs include a provision guaranteeing the right of investors to transfer payments related to an investment into a freely convertible currency.[158] Fourth, some BITs require the host state to observe any commitments into which it has entered with respect to investments. Fifth, some BITs require the host state to compensate foreign investors for losses attributable to host state requisitioning or destruction of investment during war or civil disturbance.

The investment security provisions of the BIT protect covered investment against the most important sources of political risk facing foreign investment, specifically expropriation, currency exchange controls, and war and civil disturbances.[159] They also stabilize host state commitments to foreign investment. These provisions, taken together, provide protection for both property and contract rights against host state

---

153 *See* Section 2.2.

154 *See* Section 3.1.

155 *See* Section 5.2.

156 *See* Section 6.3.

157 *See* Section 6.5.

158 *See* Section 6.7.

159 Some measure of the importance of these three types of risk is suggested by the fact that they are the risks typically covered by investment insurance programs, such as that offered by the Overseas Private Investment Corporation or the Multilateral Investment Guarantee Agency. *See* Maura B. Perry, "A Model for Efficient Foreign Aid: The Case for the Political Risk Insurance Activity of the Overseas Private Investment Corporation," 36 *Virginia Journal of International Law* 511 (1996); George T. Ellinidu, "Foreign Direct Investment in Developing and Newly Liberalized Nations," 4 *Detroit College of Law Journal of International Law and Practice* 299 (1995); Ibrahim I.F. Shihata, *MIGA and Foreign Investment: Origins, Operations, Policies and Basic Documents of the Multilateral Investment Guarantee Agency* (1988).

interference and, in some cases, against private party interference as well. These protections are strengthened by the investor-state[160] and state-state disputes provisions[161] that have become virtually universal in BITs, as well as by BIT provisions that protect the investor against a denial of justice.[162] The prohibition on denial of justice is important because it provides a basis for protecting investment against private interference with property and contract rights under host state law, a matter not addressed by most of a typical BIT's substantive provisions.

To promote investment neutrality, BITs should have provisions ensuring that the host and home states will permit investment to cross borders (the BIT principle of access) and will not discriminate among investments on grounds unrelated to legitimate host state regulatory policies (the BIT principle of nondiscrimination). With respect to access, the typical BIT provides that each party shall admit investment by investors of the other party, but subject to the laws of the first party.[163] In effect, local law rather than the BIT determines whether a particular foreign investment may be established. Neither do most BITs require the host state to permit entry of technical or managerial personnel needed in connection with the operation of the investment.[164] The typical BIT also imposes no requirement of any kind on home states to permit outward investment flows.

BITs generally do provide several guarantees of nondiscriminatory treatment of investment, once established. First, most BITs include a guarantee of national treatment and of MFN treatment,[165] as well as separate national and MFN treatment requirements with respect to the payment of compensation for damage to investment caused by war or civil disturbance.[166] In addition, the great majority of BITs include a provision requiring fair and equitable treatment of investment, which has been interpreted to prohibit unreasonable discriminations, [167]and some BITs also include an explicit prohibition on unreasonable or discriminatory measures, which has a similar effect.[168] Although the national and MFN treatment provisions may have exceptions for concessions involving taxes[169] and those made to other states as part of an agreement establishing an economic integration organization, such as a customs union or free trade area,[170] the other nondiscrimination provisions typically do not.

Given the content of these provisions, the BITs are limited instruments of investment neutrality. Most of them guarantee no right of access for capital or persons to the

---

160 *See* Section 10.2.

161 *See* Section 10.3.

162 *See* Section 10.4

163 Typical is article 2(1) of the Germany-Dominica BIT, which provides that "Each Contracting Party shall in its territory promote as far as possible investments by nationals or companies of the other Contacting Party and admit such investments in accordance with its legislation."

164 *See* Section 9.7.

165 *See* Section 7.2.

166 *See* Section 6.6.

167 *See* Section 7.5.

168 *See* Section 7.4.

169 *See* Section 7.2.1.

170 *See* Section 7.2.1.

host state, they leave the home state with unlimited discretion to prohibit or regulate outward investment flows, and the obligation of the host state not to discriminate applies only after investment is established. Further, because BIT protections typically apply only to foreign investment, the BIT investment protection provisions in some respects are inconsistent with the nondiscrimination principle.[171] For example, the nondiscrimination provisions of the BITs do not prohibit the host state from offering special concessions to foreign investors and, in the event that the investment climate in the host state deteriorates, only foreign investors will be protected by a BIT.[172]

BITs have few provisions promoting the liberal principle of market facilitation. Those that do exist address the problem of lack of information, which is a pervasive problem in developing countries,[173] and thus rest primarily on the BIT principle of transparency. The fair and equitable treatment provision, which appears in most BITs, has been interpreted to require transparency in the host state's treatment of foreign investment, although the precise scope of this requirement remains unclear.[174] A few BITs have provisions requiring specific forms of transparency, such as the publication of laws relating to investment.[175]

The typical BIT, however, beyond the problem of transparency, addresses few market failures,[176] which can be especially prevalent in developing states.[177] For example, one important market imperfection is anticompetitive behavior. In general, the process of globalization usually weakens monopolies.[178] Foreign investment can encourage competition not only in the sector in which it is established, but in other

---

171 The preference for foreign investors created by BITs will be of practical significance in only very limited circumstances. Host state investors have natural advantages that, all else being equal, will usually give them a competitive advantage that foreign investors must offset through greater efficiency. The preference is not without significance, however. In Colombia, for example, successful legal action was taken to invalidate a portion of the Colombia-United Kingdom BIT on the ground that the treaty granted special treatment to foreign investors. "Court rejects treaty clause," *Financial Times* (USA Edition), August 16, 1996, page 5.

172 Developing countries, for example, often offer special incentives to foreign investors not available to domestic competitors. *See* World Bank, *supra* note 16, at 228–231.

173 On the problem of lack of information, *see* Meier, *supra* note 11; Richard Grabowski & Michael P. Shields, *Development Economics* 270–271 (1996); World Bank, *The East Asian Miracle* 90–91 (1993).

174 *See* Section 8.5.

175 *See* Sections 8.2–8.4. The United States inserted a particularly strong transparency provision at Article 11 of its 2004 model, but the provision is not within the scope of the investor-state disputes provision.

176 Enterprises, particularly those that are vertically integrated, often deal with various market imperfections, such as lack of information, by acquiring foreign subsidiaries and thereby creating an internal market. Sodersten & Reed, *supra* note 27, at 472, Salvatore, *supra* note 17, at 379. In this sense, merely facilitating foreign direct investment can reduce the effect of market imperfections. At the same time, however, foreign direct investment, especially that involving horizontal integration, can reduce competition, thereby creating a market failure.

177 UNTCMD, *supra* note 12, at 48, at 51; Poulson, *supra* note 10, at 87, 588–9.

178 World Bank, *Globalization, Growth, and Poverty* 16 (2002).

sectors as well. As an illustration, the fact that foreign investment has access to foreign capital may encourage local banks to reduce the cost of services.

Yet, the process of globalization sometimes clears the way for a firm to obtain a global monopoly, which poses a severe challenge for national enforcement authorities.[179] Moreover, the small size of local markets renders developing countries particularly susceptible to anticompetitive practices.[180] Anticompetitive practices are rife in developing countries[181] and often such practices are not attributable to multinational enterprises.[182] One estimate is that in 1997 alone the value of cartel effects in developing countries was $51.1 billion, more than the amount of foreign aid to those countries in that year.[183] Yet many developing countries have few if any laws relating to anticompetitive behavior and little capacity to enforce such laws.[184] International agreements may provide a means of addressing some problems of enforcement,[185] but the problem of anticompetitive behavior remains outside the scope of any BIT.[186]

Similarly, negative externalities, particularly in the form of environmental degradation, are also an important form of market failure. Environmental groups have been concerned that BITs actually would aggravate this problem by limiting the discretion of host states to regulate to protect the environment or by promoting pro-investment policies that would lead to a race to the bottom in environmental standards. The race to the bottom, however, seems not to have occurred[187] and environmental regulations have rarely been the cause of an award in favor of the investor in an investor-state arbitration.[188] Developing countries, by contrast, have feared that environmental

---

179 *Id.*

180 United Nations Conference on Trade and Development & World Bank, *Liberalizing International Transactions in Services: A Handbook* 47 (1994). Indeed, foreign investment involving horizontal integration often reduces competition because the transnational enterprise proceeds by acquiring its local competition. Sodersten & Reed, *supra* note 27, at 469.

181 See Eleanor M. Fox, "Economic Development, Poverty and Antitrust: The Other Path," 13 *Southwestern Journal of Law and Trade in the Americas* 211 (2007).

182 Julian L. Clarke, Simon J. Evenett, and Krista Lucenti, "Anti-Competitive Practices and Liberalizing Markets in Latin America and the Caribbean," May 2005, available at http://www.ssrn.com.

183 D. Daniel Sokol, "Monopolists Without Borders: The Institutional Challenge of International Trust in a Global Gilded Age," 4 *Berkeley Business Law Journal* 36, 54 (2007).

184 Approximately 100 nations of the world have enacted antitrust laws. *See* Eleanor M. Fox, "Economic Development, Poverty and Antitrust: The Other Path," 13 Southwestern Journal of Law and Trade in the Americas 211 (2007).

185 The danger of leaving regulation of monopolies solely to host state discretion is that it may be used as a facade for economically nationalist activity or the regulatory process may be captured by host state producers. *See* UNCTAD & World Bank, *supra* note 178, at 42–44, 47.

186 Not only do BIT provisions not explicitly address anticompetitive practices, but a tribunal applying the international minimum standard codified in Article 1105 of the NAFTA has held that no rule of customary international law prohibits anticompetitive practices. *See UPS v. Canada*, Award, paras. 71–99.

187 *See* Section 3.4.3.

188 The tribunal found an expropriation in *Metalclad v. Mexico*, where a state governor issued an environmental decree declaring land on which a foreign investor had built a hazardous waste

provisions in investment-related agreements would serve as a pretext for protectionism. In any event, the problem of externalities necessitates international agreements on environmental standards.[189] Environmental measures, however, largely have remained outside the scope of BITs. A few BITs do include provisions under which the parties should not derogate or shall strive not to derogate from environmental measures to encourage investment,[190] language that imposes a weaker obligation than the typical BIT language. Even this limited obligation occasionally is excluded from the scope of the investor-state and state-state disputes provisions.[191]

Other market failures are prevalent in developing countries. For example, they often lack public goods,[192] such as physical infrastructure. In short, while the liberal model suggests that the market will guide investments to the territories in which they will find their most efficient use, BITs do not ensure that a properly functioning market is in place.

BITs nevertheless are economically liberalizing documents. They prohibit much post establishment discrimination among investors and they protect important property and contract rights. They establish conditions necessary, if not sufficient, for a properly functioning market. For example, an effective competition policy requires an effective rule of law.[193] At least in the case of developing countries, conclusion and implementation of a BIT almost certainly results in a more liberal investment regime than would otherwise exist. This may be less true in the case of developed countries, which in drafting the models on which BITs typically are based may have been careful not to prohibit any of their existing policies. Indeed, because BIT obligations fall on host countries, conclusion of a BIT actually represents a greater commitment to liberalism by the capital importing country than by the capital exporting country.

---

facility to be an ecological preserve. Federal officials, who had responsibility for environmental protection had found the facility to be consistent with Mexico's environmental laws and had issued all the necessary environmental permits. The action of the governor seemed to be a response to opposition from the local community, which objected to the site of the facility. The tribunal in *S.D. Myers v. Canada* found a ban on the export of a hazardous chemical to violate the NAFTA because it was enacted for discriminatory reasons, to preserve the market for remediation of the chemicals for Canadian companies. In neither case, however, was an award issued in favor of a claimant as a result of the enactment of general, nondiscriminatory environmental regulations.

189 Nafziger, *supra* note 10, at 338.

190 *See, e.g.*, 2003 Canadian model BIT, Art. 11 ("should"); United States-Uruguay BIT, Art. 12(1) ("shall strive" rather than "should"); BLEU-Sudan BIT, Art. 5(2)("shall strive").

191 *See, e.g.*, United States-Uruguay BIT, Arts. 24(1) and 37(5).

192 A public good is an activity that benefits all individuals simultaneously and the enjoyment of which by one person is in no way diminished by that of another. Todraro, *supra* note 17, at 698. Because everyone enjoys a public good, specific individuals may try to utilize public goods produced by others rather than expending their own resources to contribute to production of the public good, the problem of the so-called "free rider." Thus, an unregulated market may not produce an adequate quantity of public goods. Richard Grabowski and Michael P. Shields, *Development Economics* 47 (1996).

193 Francisco Marcos, "Do Developing Countries Need Competition Laws and Policy," Sept. 2006, available at http://www.ssrn.com.

3.5.2 Promoting the Rule of Law

BITs are also instruments of liberal legalism.[194] They promote the rule of law.

Empirical evidence suggests that establishing the rule of law contributes to economic development. In general, improvements in the quality of governance, which includes establishment of the rule of law, have been found to attract greater quantities of foreign direct investment.[195] For example, uncertainty regarding the tax consequences of certain behavior has been found to deter foreign investment,[196] reflecting the importance of transparency. Good governance also has been shown to have a positive effect not only on the quantity of foreign direct investment, but on economic growth.[197] Moreover, foreign direct investment has its strongest impact in countries with developed institutional frameworks.[198] Policies of opening the capital account[199] and privatizing state enterprises[200] both have been shown more likely to promote growth where legal frameworks are developed. One study by Professor Dani Rodrik in 1997 found that an index of institutional quality predicted the exact rank ordering of economic growth among East Asian countries. The institutional quality index took into account the quality of the bureaucracy and a number of more specific characteristics addressed explicitly by BITs, specifically, the rule of law, the risk of expropriation, and the risk of contract repudiation by governments.[201]

The evidence is that countries with more efficient regulatory regimes grow faster.[202] Thus, promoting growth in many cases is a matter of improving regulations, rather than simply eliminating them. In fact, too little market regulation has been found to inhibit growth, although too much leads to inefficiency.[203] Excessive regulation inhibits

---

194 *See* Section 1.1.

195 Sviatoslav. A. Moskalev, "Governance and Foreign Direct Investment," February 2007, available at http://www.ssrn.com. Empirical measures of the quality of governance taken into account a number of factors, including the rule of law, the existence of human rights, political stability, government effectiveness, regulatory burden, and lack of corruption. *Id.* at 8. *See generally* Daniel Kaufmann, Aart Kraay, and Massimo Mastruzzi, "Governance Matters VII: Aggregate and Individual Governance Indicators 1996–2007, World Bank Policy Research Working Paper 4654, June 2008, available at http://www.ssrn.com.

196 Kelly Edmiston, Shannon Mudd, and Neven Valev, "Tax Structures and FDI: The Deterrent Effects of Complexity and Uncertainty," William Davidson Working Paper Number 558, April 2003, available at http://www.ssrn.com.

197 The literature is summarized in Mark Gradstein, "Governance and Growth," available at http://www.ssrn.com.

198 *See* Section 3.4.1.1.

199 *See* Section 9.2.

200 *See* Section 3.4.1.1.

201 Dani Rodrik, TFPG Controversies, Institutions, and Economic Performance in East Asia," NBER Working Paper No. 5914, February 1997. Rodrik's paper is summarized in Meier, *supra* note 11, at 137–138.

202 Simeon Djankov, Caralee McLiesh, and Rita Ramalho, "Regulations and Growth," March 17, 2006, available at http://www.ssrn.com.

203 Sambit Bhattacharyya, "Which Institutions Matter Most for Growth?" available at http://www.ssrn.com.

growth, however, only in the most regulated economies.[204] Indeed, even regulations intended to ameliorate the consequences of the market, such as social insurance, have been found not to impede economic growth.[205]

Much attention has been paid to one specific aspect of the rule of law, the protection of property rights and, in particular, intellectual property rights. In general, improvements in intellectual property rights protection are associated with higher levels of economic growth, at least in high- and low- (as opposed to middle-income) countries.[206] The explanation offered is that in high-income countries the increased protection spurs domestic innovation while in low-income countries it attracts inward foreign direct investment and technology transfer. Indeed, stronger intellectual property rights protection does appear to attract foreign direct investment in some cases, but the effect depends upon host country and industry characteristics.[207] It also appears that stronger intellectual property rights protection results in greater technology transfer. One study found that increased intellectual property protection is associated with increases in royalty payments,[208] although it has been observed that this finding may have been influenced by increases in the price charged for technology as well as by an increase in the quantity of licenses granted.[209] The same study found that increased intellectual property protection is also associated with increased research and development expenditures of affiliates of U.S. multinationals in developing countries,[210] but no correlation was found in a subsequent study in which developed countries were included.[211]

In any event, the empirical evidence, taken as a whole, repeatedly has demonstrated that foreign investment is more likely to contribute to economic growth where the host country has strong institutions and, in particular, a commitment to the rule of law.[212] By promoting rule of law principles such as security, reasonableness, nondiscrimination, transparency, and due process, BITs help establish the institutional framework necessary for a modern, developed economy able to benefit from economic globalization.

---

204 Matthias Busse and Jose Luis Groizard, "FDI, Regulations and Growth," HWWA Discussion Paper 342, 2006, available at http://www.ssrn.com.

205 Bhattacharyya, *supra* note 203.

206 Rod Falvey, Neil Foster, and David Greenaway, "Intellectual Property Rights and Economic Growth," University of Nottingham Research Paper 2004/12, 10 *Review of Development Economics* 700 (2006).

207 Peter Nunnenkamp and Julius Spatz, "Intellectual Property Rights and Foreign Direct Investment: The Role of Industry and Host-Country Characteristics," Kiel Working Paper No. 1167, June 2003, available at http://www.ssrn.com.

208 Lee G. Branstetter, Raymond Fisman, and C. Fritz Foley, "Do Strong Intellectual Property Rights Increate International Technology Transfer? Empirical Evidence from U. S. Firm-Level Panel Data," 121 *The Quarterly Journal of Economics* 321 (2006).

209 Sunil Kanwar, "Intellectual Property Protection and Technology Transfer: Evidence from US Multinationals," available at http://www.ssrn.com.

210 Branstetter, Fishman, and Foley, *supra* note 208, at 321.

211 Kanwar, *supra* note 209.

212 In addition to the research cited in this section, *see also* Section 3.6, summarizing research demonstrating that BITs are most effective in attracting foreign investment when host states have strong legal institutions.

3.6 THE EFFECTIVENESS OF BITS

BITs originally were proposed by developing countries to protect their investment abroad. They do so by bringing such investment within the protection of the rule of law and by promoting a liberal investment regime in which host states abjure interference with private property and contract rights except under certain conditions.

Clearly, BITs have improved the level of protection available to covered investment in many cases. By the end of 2008, some 318 treaty-based claims had been submitted to investor-state arbitration. Of the 109 claims that had been concluded by that date, about half resulted in awards to the claimants, in some cases of very substantial amounts.[213] A study of awards made public as of June 1, 2006, found that the average amount awarded, however, was approximately $25.6.million and the amount awarded exceeded $10 million in only about a fifth of the cases.[214]

These awards have developed a body of jurisprudence that is more protective of foreign investment in some respects than earlier cases involving injury to aliens. For example, tribunals have agreed that international law continues to evolve and that it provides greater protection for foreign investment than did early twentieth-century cases such as *Neer v. Mexico*.[215] The reasonableness[216] and transparency[217] principles have appeared in international arbitral practice largely because of the BITs, while the security principle has expanded to protect investor reliance on host state assurances not embodied in formal contracts.[218]

Further, the success of an investment agreement in protecting foreign investment can be measured by more than just the number and monetary value of favorable arbitral awards. Investors who have disputes with host states may use the existence of the treaty and the possibility of arbitration as leverage to negotiate a satisfactory resolution of the dispute. In such a case, the treaty undeniably has contributed to the protection of foreign investment, even if no arbitration occurred. Moreover, the expectation is that the conclusion of multiple BITs committing the host state to certain principles in its treatment of covered investment will promote adherence to those principles generally, so that even investment not covered by a BIT will operate in a more favorable environment.

Developing countries conclude BITs in the hope of attracting foreign investment. As has been noted,[219] investors seek to increase their return and to minimize their risk. BITs are believed to potentially promote foreign investment flows by reducing risk to

---

213 For example, the awards in *Siemens v. Argentina*, a case arising under the Germany-Argentina BIT, and *CME v. Czech Republic*, a case arising under the Netherlands-Czech Republic BIT, exceeded $200 million.

214 Susan D. Franck, "Empirically Evaluating Claims About Investment Treaty Arbitration," 86 *North Carolina Law Review* 1, 60 (2007). These data are based on the awards in which the claimant was successful. If all awards are included, the average amount awarded drops to $10.4 million, with fewer than 10 percent of the awards exceeding $10 million. *Id.* at 58.

215 *See* Section 5.4.

216 *See* Sections 5.2.3, 5.3.3, and 5.4.

217 *See* Section 8.5.

218 *See* Sections 6.3.3 and 6.4.3.

219 *See* Section 3.1.2.

foreign investors. First, they require a host state to provide an investment climate characterized by BIT principles of security, reasonableness, nondiscrimination, transparency, access, and due process. Second, they stabilize this more favorable climate by incorporating BIT principles into an international agreement that provides for binding dispute resolution. BITs may also promote foreign investment by signaling the existence of this more favorable investment climate. Yet, perhaps no one contends that the conclusion of BITs alone will result in increased investment flows.[220] BITs are considered simply one factor among many necessary to create a favorable investment climate.[221]

Several studies have sought to determine whether BITs do increase international investment flows, with inconsistent results. Most studies, however, have found a positive correlation between the conclusion of BITs and an increase in foreign investment flows.

The first study, published by UNCTAD in 1998, found a weak positive correlation. Specifically, UNCTAD concluded that "following the signing of a BIT, it is more likely than not that the host country will marginally increase its share in the outward FDI [Foreign Direct Investment] of the home country . . . The effect, however, is usually small."[222] UNCTAD concluded that BITs play a "minor and secondary role" in attracting foreign direct investment.[223]

In 2003, Mary Hallward-Driemeir published her study for the World Bank of foreign direct investment flows of 537 country pairs from 20 OECD countries to 31 developing countries, during the period 1980 to 2000.[224] In most regressions, she found that the association between BITs and foreign direct investment was negative and not significant. She found that BITs were more likely to be effective where the host state has better established legal institutions.[225]

The next year saw the publication of no fewer than four studies, all of which found evidence that the conclusion of BITs increases foreign direct investment. A study by Eric Neumayer and Laura Spess, involving 119 countries and examining data from 1970 to 2002, found that negotiating additional BITs does increase a host state's share of foreign direct investment.[226] For example, a one standard deviation increase in the number of BITs signed by a country (the statistical equivalent of 4.5 treaties) increased

220 U.S. negotiators generally have been very candid with potential BIT partners in noting that there was no evidence to prove that concluding a BIT would increase investment flows. Kenneth J. Vandevelde, *U.S. International Investment Agreements* 110 (2009).

221 UNCTAD, *Bilateral Investment Treaties in the Mid-1990s* 6 (1998).

222 *Id.* at 122.

223 *Id.*

224 Mary Hallward-Driemeier, "Do Bilateral Investment Treaties Attract FDI? Only a Bit . . . And They Could Bite," World Bank, Working Paper No. 3121, June 2003.

225 *Id.* at 21.

226 Eric Neumayer and Laura Spess, "Do Bilateral Investment Treaties Increase Foreign Direct Investment in Developing Countries?" 33 *World Development* 1567 (2005).

foreign direct investment inflows by .47 to .80 percent.[227] The magnitude of the impact was found to depend upon overall institutional quality.[228]

A study by Tim Buthe and Helen V. Milner of investment flows to 122 developing countries with a population in excess of one million persons over a period of from 1970 to 2000 found "a positive, statistically and substantively significant correlation between BITs and subsequent inward FDI into developing countries."[229]

A study by Peter Egger and Michael Pfaffermayr examined investment flows between 10 home and 54 host countries between 1982 and 1997. They found that "BITs exert a positive and significant effect on real stocks of outward FDI. . . ."[230]

A study by Jeswald W. Salacuse and Nicholas Sullivan focused on the effect of U.S. BITs on investment flows by examining foreign direct investment flows to more than 100 developing countries during 1998–2000 and U.S. foreign direct investment flows to 31 countries over a 10-year period. They found that BITs concluded by the United States are more likely than not to exert a "strong and positive role" in promoting both U.S. investment and overall investment and that U.S. BITs are likely to have a greater impact than BITs concluded by other states in the Organization for Economic Cooperation and Development.[231]

The next year, Deborah Swenson published a study of countries signing BITs during the 1990s and concluded that "BIT signing did help developing countries attract a larger volume of foreign investment."[232]

A few studies after 2004 have focused on particular regions. All of these have found a positive correlation between BITs and increases in foreign investment. Robert Grosse and Len J. Trevino found in a 2005 study that BITs do stimulate foreign direct investment flows into Central and Eastern European countries.[233] Tom Coupé, Irina Orlova, and Alexandre Skiba similarly found "strong evidence" of a positive effect of BITs on foreign direct investment in transitional economies.[234] Their data indicated that BITs

---

227 *Id.* at 21.

228 *Id.* at 19.

229 Tim Buthe and Helen V. Milner, "Bilateral Investment Treaties and Foreign Direct Investment: A Political Analysis," in *The Effect of Treaties on Foreign Direct Investment* 213 (Karl P. Sauvant and Lisa E. Sachs, eds. 2009).

230 Petter Egger and Michael Pfaffermayr, "The Impact of Bilateral Investment Treaties on Foreign Direct Investment," 32 *Journal of Comparative Economics* 788 (2004), reprinted in Sauvant and Sachs, *supra* note 229, at 253, 268.

231 Jeswald W. Salacuse and Nicholas P. Sullivan, "Do BITs Really Work? An Evaluation of Bilateral Investment Treaties and Their Grand Bargain," 46 *Harvard International Law Journal* 67, 111 (2005).

232 Deborah L. Swenson, "Why Do Developing Countries Sign BITs?" 12 *U.C. Davis Journal of International Law & Policy* 131 (2005), *reprinted in* Sauvant and Sachs, *supra* note 229, at 437, 457.

233 Robert Grosse and Len J. Trevino, "New Institutional Economics and FDI Location in Central and Eastern Europe," 45 *Management International Review*123 (2005) *reprinted in* Sauvant and Sachs, *supra* note 229, at 273.

234 Tom Coupé, Irina Orlova, and Alexandre Skiba, "The Effect of Tax and Investment Treaties on Bilateral FDI Flows to Transition Economies," in Sauvant and Sachs, *supra* note 229, at 687, 689.

had a greater impact where institutional quality was weak, suggesting that BITs were a substitute for institutional quality. Kevin P. Gallagher and Melissa B. L. Birch examined FDI flows in Latin America and found in a 2006 study that the total number of BITs that a country has signed has "an independent and positive effect on FDI flows."[235] Kim Sokchea surveyed ten Asian countries and found "evidence that BITs play a significant role in stimulating the inflows of investment."[236] Further, the effect was stronger for high-risk countries, again suggesting that BITs are a substitute for institutional quality.

Three more recent studies, however, have failed to confirm the positive correlation found in the eight studies published between 2004 and 2006. In a 2005 study, Jennifer Tobin and Susan Rose-Ackerman, examining 62 countries and using data dating back to 1984, found a very weak positive relationship between BITs and foreign direct investment.[237] Jason Yackee in a paper published in 2009 attempted to replicate the results found by Neumayer and Spess and "found no evidence that BITs and FDI share the kind of conditional relationship theorized (and identified) by Neumayer and Spess."[238] Emma Aisbett in another paper published in 2009 found a positive correlation between BITs and foreign direct investment, but the finding was not robust. Further, she suggested that the positive impact found by Neumayer and Spess and by Salacuse and Sullivan were due to misspecification and insufficient attention to endogeneity.[239]

Those studies finding little or no correlation between BITs and investment flows may be underestimating the impact of BITs. First, it may be that certain BITs are more effective than others[240] or that BITs are more effective in some circumstances than in others[241] and that these positive results are obscured when all BITs are aggregated together. Those countries that have the least attractive investment climates may

---

235 Kevin P. Gallagher and Melissa B. L. Birch, "Do Investment Agreements Attract Investment? Evidence from Latin America," 7 *Journal of World Investment and Trade* 961 (2006), *reprinted in* Sauvant and Sachs, *supra* note 229, at 295, 305.

236 Kim Sokchea, "Bilateral Investment Treaties, Political Risk, and Foreign Direct Investment," International University of Japan International Development Program 2006, page 30, available at http://www.ssrn.com.

237 Jennifer Tobin and Susan Rose-Ackerman, *Foreign Direct Investment and the Business Environment in Developing Countries: the Impact of Bilateral Investment Treaties* (2005).

238 Jason Yackee, "Do BITs Really Work? Revisiting the Empirical Link Between Investment Treaties and Foreign Direct Investment," in Sauvant and Sachs, *supra* note 229, at 378, 391.

239 Emma Aisbett, "Bilateral Investment Treaties and Foreign Direct Investment: Correlation Versus Causation," in Sauvant and Sachs, *supra* note 229, at 395.

240 That was the implication of the Salacuse and Sullivan study, which found U.S. BITs, which are among the most rigorous of the BITs, to be more likely to attract foreign direct investment than other BITs. Jason Yackee notes that studies of the correlation between BITs and inward investment flows typically do not distinguish among BITs that have different levels of rigor, such as those with investor-state disputes provisions and those without. *See* Jason W. Yackee, "Conceptual Difficulties in the Empirical Study of Bilateral Investment Treaties," 33 *Brooklyn Journal of International Law* 405 (2008).

241 As noted in the text, several of the studies found the effects of BITs to vary depending upon institutional quality, although the studies were not consistent with each other.

negotiate large numbers of BITs in an effort to compensate,[242] while those countries with more attractive investment climates may see less need for a BIT, with the result that BITs would be negatively correlated with the quality of the investment climate, an effect that would obscure any positive impact of the BITs. Further, significant time may be required for BIT principles to be adopted as a matter of practice in some countries and thereby to have a genuine positive influence on the investment climate. Time also may be required for investors to recognize the value of the BITs.[243] For example, more well-publicized arbitral awards in favor of investors may be necessary before potential investors take greater notice of the BITs. Some of the positive impact of the BITs on investment flows may yet lie in the future.

As was noted in Chapter 1, however, a capital importing country may not define the success of a BIT program solely in terms of the increase in inward foreign investment flows. To the extent that BITs promote the rule of law, they may serve to commit host countries to principles that have intrinsic worth and that will strengthen liberal democracy within those countries, apart from any immediate contribution to increasing foreign investment flows. An arbitral award against a particular state may be regarded by some in the state as a defeat, but may be regarded by others as a victory for the rule of law.[244]

The same arbitral awards in favor of investors that may convince investors of the value of the treaties, of course, also may cause host states to conclude that the BITs are too costly. This especially could be true to the extent that BITs over time are not perceived as attracting increased investment flows. Developing countries may come to see the BITs as poor bargains in which states surrender portions of their regulatory discretion and subject themselves to costly arbitrations with investors, without having gained appreciable new investments in return. The result could be a decision to cease negotiating more BITs or at least to diminish some of the investment protections afforded by the treaties in order to decrease the cost of implementing them. They may

---

242 For example, in the 1960s and 1970s, the countries of sub-Saharan Africa were especially active in concluding BITs. It has been theorized that one of the reasons that developing countries conclude BITs is simply that other developing countries already have and countries fear being placed at a competitive disadvantage in attracting foreign investment if they have not concluded as many BITs as neighboring countries. The inducement to conclude the treaties may not be that the treaties attract investment, but rather that their absence will discourage it. *See* Zachary Elkins, Andrew T. Guzman, and Beth Simmons, "Competing for Capital: The Diffusion of Bilateral Investment Treaties 1996–2000," available at http://www.ssrn.com.

243 Jason Yackee offers evidence that investors remain largely unaware of the existence of BITs. *See* Jason W. Yackee, "Conceptual Difficulties in the Empirical Study of Bilateral Investment Treaties," 33 *Brooklyn Journal of International Law* 405 (2008).

244 Officials in developing countries occasionally concede in private conversations that their country deserved to lose a particular arbitration. The government had behaved in an unacceptable manner toward foreign investment, but had learned from its mistake. This is not to suggest, however, that every tribunal reaches the right result. Nevertheless, the rule of law triumphs when sovereign governments commit themselves to legal processes and honor those processes, notwithstanding that errors inevitably do occur.

also seek to amend those that already have been concluded.[245] As noted in Section 2.3, the impulse to weaken BITs may come from the developed countries as well as the developing countries. BITs someday could be victims of their own success.

245 At least 85 BITs already have been renegotiated, though not necessarily to reduce the protections provided. In fact, a typical purpose has been to strengthen old agreements. UNCTAD identified 2608 BITs as of the end of 2007. *See* UNCTAD, "Recent developments in international investment agreements (2007–June 2008)," *IIA Monitor* No. 2, at 6–7 (2008), available at http://www.unctad.org. Some BITs were renegotiated because the prior agreement expired or because one of the parties had joined the European Union, necessitating that BIT obligations be harmonized with EU obligations.

Chapter 4

Scope

4.1 INTRODUCTION

The substantive provisions of a BIT typically apply to assets that fall within the definition of investment and that are located within the territory of one of the BIT parties.[1] Thus, the term "investment" is critical to defining the scope of application of a BIT and a definition of the term virtually always appears in a BIT. This term will be discussed in Section 4.2.

The term "territory," by contrast, is not always defined. BITs are not the instruments by which territorial boundaries are established. Rather, the typical definition, where it appears, provides that the term "territory" refers to all of the state's land territory as well as the areas of the sea over which it exercises jurisdiction.[2] The chief significance of the definition is that it ensures that the BIT applies to sea-based investment, such as offshore mineral extraction. Investment disputes arising under a BIT rarely, if ever, involve the issue of the location of a boundary, but sometimes do involve the issue of whether an intangible asset is located within the territory of the putative host state. This issue is discussed in Section 4.2.3.3.

In nearly every case, a BIT applies to investment only if the investment is owned or controlled by nationals or companies (sometimes referred to collectively as "investors") of the other BIT party, although a few BITs impose some obligations with respect to all investments in the territory of the host state.[3] Thus the definition of investor, national, and company also are critical to defining the scope of BIT application. These terms are discussed in Section 4.3. For the sake of brevity, the term "investor" often will be used in this book to refer, collectively, to nationals and companies that have made, or are seeking to make, an investment.

---

1 Parts of this chapter are based on a study I performed for UNCTAD in 1997. The study in turn formed the basis for UNCTAD's 1999 publication, *Scope and Definition*, which was part of the UNCTAD Series on Issues in International Investment Agreements. I have borrowed freely from my 1997 study.

2 *See, e.g.*, United Kingdom-Bosnia-Herzegovina BIT, Art. I(e).

3 *See* Section 9.5.

The term "investor" is important not only because it identifies those investments to which the BIT applies, but for two other reasons as well. First, the substantive provisions of a BIT sometimes apply to certain activities by investors of a party. That is, the investor, like the investment, may be a beneficiary of BIT protection. In such cases, host-state conduct may violate a BIT not because of its effect on an investment, but because of its effect on an investor. Indeed, in many BITs, only the investor, and not the investment, has standing to submit claims to arbitration.

Second, the term "investor" in some cases establishes the substantive content of BIT protections. For example, the national treatment provision of a BIT requires that the host state provide the investment of investors of the other party treatment no less favorable than that which it provides to the investment of its own investors. Thus, the definitions of investment and investor establish the standard against which the treatment of covered investment is to be judged.

4.2 THE DEFINITION OF INVESTMENT

4.2.1 Structure and Policy

Within the realm of economics, the concept of investment refers to an increase in capital stock, that is, an increase in the productive capacity of an economy. More specifically, the term generally refers to the acquisition or creation of an asset that will generate a return over an extended period of time.

The legal definition of investment as it appears in the BITs is not necessarily coextensive with the economic definition. Most BITs define the term "investment" to include "every kind of asset" and accompany this definition with an illustrative list of assets that fall within the definition.[4] Because the list is illustrative, an asset need not be included in the list to be considered an investment. A synonymous and not uncommon formulation is "any kind of asset," followed by an illustrative list.[5]

The definition of investment is both broad and open-ended. Its breadth is indicated both by the words "every kind" or "any kind" and by the scope of the illustrative list of assets, which will be discussed further below. To say that the definition is open-ended means that the list is only illustrative and that assets of a type not in existence at the time the BIT is concluded nevertheless may fall within the definition at such time as they are created.

Both aspects of the definition, its breadth and its open-endedness, sometimes have been controversial. The reasons for the breadth and open-endedness of the definition

---

4 *See, e.g.*, United Kingdom-Bosnia-Herzegovina BIT, Art. I(a); Netherlands-Ethiopia BIT, Art. I(a) Austria-Armenia BIT, Art. 1(1)(a); Australia-India BIT, Art. 1(c). Egypt-Zambia BIT, Art. 1(1)(a). On the definition of investment, *see generally* Engela C. Schlemmer, "Investment, Investor, Nationality, and Shareholders," in *The Oxford Handbook of International Investment Law* (Peter Muchlinski, Frederico Ortino, and Christoph Schreuer, eds. 2008).

5 *See, e.g.*, Indonesia-Algeria BIT, Art. I(1)(a); BLEU-Sudan BIT, Art. 1(2); Italy-Nicaragua BIT, Art. I(1).

are easy to discern. BITs were drafted by capital-exporting countries to protect their assets abroad. A broad and open-ended definition thus was in their interest because it expanded the range of assets protected by the BITs. At the same time, because the BITs imposed very few obligations on a state in its capacity as a capital exporter, these states had little reason to fear a broad and open-ended definition. Such a definition, however, also furthers the BITs' purpose of promoting the rule of law with respect to foreign investment. The BITs are intended to create protection for covered investment as a matter of principle and a definition that arbitrarily excludes assets undermines the principled nature of the protection. A broad and open-ended definition furthers as well a BIT's purpose in promoting a liberal investment regime. A liberal investment regime requires that the state treat investment in a neutral fashion.[6] A definition that arbitrarily favors some investments over others with respect to treaty protection violates that neutrality. A liberal investment regime also requires that property and contract rights be protected and thus the exclusion of some assets from the definition undermines that protection.

Critics of a broad definition have argued that BITs should exclude certain forms of investment that may not have the desired macroeconomic effects, such as an increase in productivity, and may have adverse macroeconomic effects, such as contributing to a currency crisis. The type of investment that such critics most commonly seek to exclude is portfolio investment. They argue that portfolio investment does not bring technology or managerial expertise to an economy and thus may not contribute to economic development. Further, they argue, portfolio investment does not represent a long-term commitment and may be withdrawn quickly should investors experience a sudden increase in perceived risk or decrease in anticipated return, thus triggering or exacerbating a currency crisis. Portfolio investment, it is said, is more volatile than direct investment, which in its nature usually reflects a long term commitment to the enterprise.

Critics also may be concerned about the interaction of a broad definition of investment with certain of the substantive provisions of the BIT. For example, a broad definition of investment that included assets associated with current as well as capital transactions could preclude the host state from imposing exchange controls on current transactions, even where such controls are permitted under the IMF Articles of Agreement. Similarly, a broad definition of investment that included trade transactions could result in the submission of trade as well as investment disputes to the BIT's investor-state disputes provision, creating a potential conflict with the WTO dispute resolution process.

The response to these concerns has been fourfold. First, a broad definition may be in the interests of capital importing states because all forms of investment potentially can contribute to development. For example, portfolio investment can contribute to capital formation and bring foreign exchange into the economy, without surrendering control over host-state enterprises to foreign investors. Most studies have found that

---

6 *See* Section 3.1.

portfolio equity flows have a significant positive impact on growth.[7] Portfolio investment has been found to enhance access to capital for small firms.[8] Indeed, portfolio investment in the form of bank loans, although among the most volatile forms of investment, may be the principal form of foreign capital available to some developing countries, particularly those with poor investment climates.[9] An influx of portfolio investment also helps the host state to develop financial institutions necessary for a modern economy.[10] While no guarantee exists that any particular instance of portfolio investment will contribute to development, the same is true of any particulate instance of direct investment. Other forms of investment also can contribute to economic development. Management contracts, for example, may bring valuable expertise that is not available locally. Excluding certain assets from the definition risks excluding assets needed for development.

Second, crafting an appropriate definition to exclude certain assets is difficult in practice and results in purely arbitrary distinctions. For example, equity investment is often treated for statistical purposes as direct investment if it constitutes 10 percent or more of the equity in the company. Yet, the mere size of an investment in an enterprise does not necessarily establish either that the investor has control of the enterprise or that the investment is long term. Ten percent may be sufficient to control the company in some cases and insufficient in others. Similarly, an investor may have acquired a relatively small percentage of stock in an enterprise as the first step in a long term strategy to gain a much greater interest. Thus, the small size of the investment in that case would not suggest the absence of a long term commitment. At the same time, an investor may choose to hold a small amount of stock for a lengthy period, again indicating that size is not a proxy for duration. Institutional investors sometimes hold large quantities of stock for relatively short periods of time. Businesses sometimes use short term instruments for long term financing, particularly in developing countries where short term bank loans may be the only foreign capital available. Alternatively, a longer term instrument may be used for short-term financing, such as in the case of forward sales of currencies.

Third, excluding certain assets indicates that the host state is not committed to the protection of investment as a matter of principle, which undermines the purpose of the BIT in promoting the rule of law with respect to foreign investment and in creating a liberal investment regime. It suggests that the host state is willing to protect selected investments only as a short term expedient, to obtain expected benefits, which in turn raises the specter of the obsolescing bargain.[11] This suggestion undermines the BIT's

---

7 The literature is surveyed in M. Ayhan Kose, Eswar Prasad, Kenneth Rogoff and Shang-Jin Wei, "Financial Globalization: A Reappraisal," IMF Working Paper WP/06/189, August 2006, available at http://www.ssrn.com.

8 April M. Knill, "Can Portfolio Investment Bridge the Small Firm Financing Gap Around the World?" World Bank Policy Research Working Paper 3796, December 2005, available at http://www.ssrn.com.

9 Kose *et al., supra* note 7.

10 *See* Section 3.1.2.

11 The concept of an "obsolescing bargain" refers to the phenomenon in which a host state offers favorable treatment to an investment in order to attract the investment, but once the investment has been made and cannot easily be withdrawn, the host state withdraws the favorable treatment.

effect as a signaling device to attract foreign investment. Even apart from the signal, an investor may be deterred by a narrow definition of investment because of a concern that only certain of the investor's assets will be protected in the host state and that the scope of protection available may be dependent on technicalities in the definition or on an unpredictable tribunal interpretation. A narrow definition of uncertain scope provides less security and less transparency and is potentially discriminatory. That is, a narrow definition is less effective in promoting core BIT principles.

Finally, concerns about the effects of particular investments may be addressed by reserving sufficient discretion to the host country in the substantive provisions of the BITs to control those investments, rather than incorporating arbitrary distinctions into the definitions provisions. For example, host states may reserve the right to exclude certain investments and, in fact, only a small number of BITs grant a right of establishment that is not subordinate to local law.[12] Similarly, concerns about the volatility of portfolio investment might be addressed by including exceptions to the transfers provision for balance of payments difficulties or the stability of the financial system. Concerns about the interaction of a broad definition of investment with certain substantive provisions can be addressed through careful drafting of the substantive provisions.

Nevertheless, a few BITs do exclude portfolio investment from their definition of investment. For example, article 1(1)(b) of the Denmark-Poland BIT provides that the term "investment" shall refer to "all investment in companies made for the purpose of establishing lasting economic relations between the investor and the company and giving the investor the possibility of exercising significant influence on the management of the company concerned."

Alternatively, a BIT may adopt an enterprise-based definition of investment, such as that included in the NAFTA. For example, Canada employed such a definition in Article 1 of its 2003 model BIT. That provision defines an investment in terms of an exhaustive list of assets, most of which are related to an enterprise. Thus, investment includes an enterprise, an equity or debt security of an enterprise, a loan to an enterprise, and an interest in an enterprise that entitles the owner to share in income or profits of the enterprise or the assets of the enterprise upon dissolution. It also includes real estate or other property acquired or used for economic benefit or other business purposes and interests arising from the commitment of capital or other resources to economic activity. This exhaustive list is subject to a number of exceptions and exclusions. The enterprise-based definition thus defines investment essentially as an interest in an enterprise, although such definitions typically include at least some other assets as well. In short, such definitions generally are not solely enterprise-based.

Definitions that exclude certain forms of investment, however, remain very much the exception. A broad, asset-based definition is typical in BITs.

The argument against an open-ended definition of investment is simply that a treaty should not apply to assets that cannot possibly be within the contemplation of the parties. This argument, however, largely assumes its own conclusion. The intent of the parties can be defined at different levels of generality and nothing precludes the parties

---

12 *See* Section 9.3.1.

from intending the BIT to apply to types of assets that cannot be specifically identified when the BIT is concluded. Perhaps the genuine basis of the objection is risk aversion: the concern that the BIT may someday be interpreted to apply to an asset to which a party will not wish it to apply at that time. For this reason, a few BITs limit the definition of investment to the assets identified in the list. That is, in these BITs, the list is not illustrative, but exhaustive. An open-ended definition, however, appears in the great majority of BITs.

An open-ended definition is defended on the ground that economies evolve and new forms of investment are created and acquire economic importance over time. For example, in the eighteenth century, foreign-owned property in the host state consisted primarily of vessels, land, buildings, household effects, and merchandise for trade. In the nineteenth century, with the emergence of large enterprises for the purpose of manufacturing, transportation, mineral extraction, and the distribution of power, entrepreneurs needed financing from foreign investors, with the result that portfolio investment in companies, principally in the form of bonds, became the most important form of foreign investment. As improvements in communication and transportation permitted foreign investors to manage their investments from afar, direct investment gained importance and eventually surpassed portfolio investment. In the twentieth century, products incorporating advanced technology and branded products that are perceived as having unique value have become of great economic significance, resulting in demands for the protection of intellectual property, such as patents and trademarks. In the latter half of the twentieth century, many developed economies shifted their production from manufacturing to services; continued improvements in communications and transportation have made it possible to provide services across borders, thus greatly increasing the significance of service contracts as a form of investment. Bank lending in many cases has displaced bonds as the principal form of debt financing.

To exclude assets merely because they were created after a particular date is arbitrary. The arguments against arbitrary limitations on investment are the same as were discussed above in connection with the quality of breadth in the definition. Further, in the absence of an open-ended definition, the parties may need to amend the BIT to include new forms of investment as they emerge, lest those investment be unprotected. Moreover, to limit the definition to specific categories of assets identified in the BIT may create uncertainty about the scope of BIT protection because the categories themselves may be of uncertain scope. Certain assets may be inadvertently omitted. As in the case of a narrow definition of investment, a closed-ended definition of investment is inconsistent with the BIT principles of security, nondiscrimination, and transparency. Thus, the closed list approach has been adopted in only a few BITs.

The illustrative list typically includes five categories of assets that fall within the definition of investment. A sixth category appears in some BITs. As the discussion below indicates, the list includes not only those assets that an economist would consider to be an investment, that is, an addition to the capital stock, but potentially a number of other assets as well. The list is often redundant in places, with some assets belonging in more than one category.

The first category typically included is movable and immovable property. Thus, land, facilities, and equipment, among other forms of property, are included. Interests in property, such as mortgages, liens, pledges, and leases are also included and are often explicitly mentioned.[13] The reference to movable property is broad enough potentially to include ordinary commercial merchandise. That is, while investment as an economic concept generally is regarded as an asset that will generate a long-term return, the typical BIT definition appears broad enough to apply to property that is in the territory of the host state for purposes of earning a short-term return through exchange. As was seen in Section 2.1.1, the earliest property protection provisions of FCNs typically were intended to protect precisely these kinds of assets, that is, the real property and personal effects of foreign nationals and their merchandise. Some BITs include in this first category an explicit reference to tangible and intangible property. Like the reference to movable and immovable property, it is meant to include all forms of property.

The second category comprises companies and interests in companies. The language typically refers explicitly to both debt and equity interests in companies and rarely requires that the interest be a controlling one. Some BITs mention explicitly that the interest may be a minority one,[14] but in most BITs this is implicit. Thus, the language nearly always is broad enough to include direct and portfolio investment.

The third category comprises intellectual property rights, such as patents, copyrights, trademarks, and trade secrets. Some BITs also explicitly include goodwill in this category.[15] Many BITs include "know-how" in the definition,[16] indicating that even knowledge not legally protected as property may be considered an investment. As discussed in Section 3.1.2, intellectual property is one of the principal benefits that host countries hope to obtain from foreign direct investment and thus protection for intellectual property rights is particularly important. Intellectual property rights, of course, typically would be embraced within the first category as well, because they are a form of property. The redundancy is useful, however, because it emphasizes the protection accorded to this form of property, enhancing the signaling effect of the BIT and reassuring investors.

The fourth category includes claims. Typically, the language refers to claims to money as well as claims to performance having an economic value.[17] This category demonstrates that the definition includes not only property rights, but contract rights as well. Contracts are an important form of investment. Management contracts, for example, allow the host state to take advantage of the managerial expertise of a foreign investor, while retaining ultimate ownership of the asset. Indeed, in some cases, expropriated investors subsequently have been asked to operate the investment under a

---

13 *See, e.g.*, United Kingdom-Bosnia-Herzegovina BIT, Art. I(1)(a); BLEU-Sudan BIT, Art. 1(2)(a); Germany-Timor-Leste BIT, Art. 1(1)(a); Austria-Armenia BIT, Art. I(2)(g); Sweden-Kazakhstan BIT, Art. 1(1)(a); Finland-Armenia BIT, Art. 1(1)(a).

14 *See, e.g.*, BLEU-Sudan BIT, Art. 1(2)(b); Netherlands-Ethiopia BIT, Art. 1(a)(iv); Germany-Timor-Leste BIT, Art. 1(1)(d); Switzerland-Algeria BIT, Art. 1(2)(d); Italy-Nicaragua BIT, Art. I(1)(d).

15 *See, e.g.*, BLEU-Sudan BIT, Art. 1(2)(d); Netherlands-Ethiopia BIT, Art. 1(a)(iv); Germany-Timor-Leste BIT, Art. 1(1)(d); Switzerland-Algeria BIT, Art. 1(2)(d); Italy-Nicaragua BIT, Art. I(1)(d).

16 *See, e.g.*, United Kingdom-Bosnia-Herzegovina BIT, Art. I(1)(a)(iv).

17 *See, e.g.*, BLEU-Sudan BIT, Art. 1(2)(c); Austria-Armenia BIT, Art. 1(1)(e).

management contract.[18] As discussed in Section 3.1.2, expertise is one of the benefits host countries seek to obtain through foreign investment. For the investor, such contracts represent a way to earn a return on its investment in expertise, while reducing its risk.[19] The language of the definition does not require that the contracts be of any particular duration, thus avoiding arbitrary limitations. A few BITs seek to exclude ordinary commercial contracts. For example, the Egypt-Zambia BIT provides that "[i]nvestment does not mean claims to money that arise solely from . . . [c]ommercial contracts for the sale of goods or services . . . [or the] extension of credit in connection with a commercial transaction."[20]

The fifth category is concessions, a particular form of contract rights. A concession generally is a contract between the state and a private party, the concessionaire, in which the concessionaire agrees to perform work in consideration of a remuneration paid by a charge on those who benefit from the work.[21] For example, the private party may have a concession to operate a water distribution system, under which it is paid monthly by the customers. The concession generally is defined by state legislation, which specifies the rights of the concessionaire and frequently provides for payment of a fee by the concessionaire to the state. This category is redundant of the fourth category, but given the great importance of concession agreements to international investment flows during certain periods of history and the role that the expropriation of these agreements had in promoting the negotiation of BITs,[22] investors would want an explicit assurance that such agreements are protected.

The sixth category is licenses and permits,[23] although this category appears explicitly in a much smaller number of BITs than the first five. Traditional forms of property typically are acquired through transfer among private parties in accordance with property laws of general application. This category indicates that investment may include rights transferred by the state to private parties through special legislative or administrative action. This category also is redundant with the first, but its presence eliminates any doubt concerning whether entitlements granted by the state directly to the investor are embraced within the definition of investment.

These categories, with the exception of the sixth, are mentioned explicitly in most BITs. Although variations in the language appear, the variations, at least in theory, are of no significance because the list is only illustrative. An interest that does not fall within one of the categories is nevertheless an investment if it falls within the chapeau of the definition, which typically reads "every kind" or "any kind" of asset. That said, differences in the list may be of some practical significance because a tribunal, faced with having to determine whether a particular interest constitutes an investment, is

---

18 Charles Lipson, *Standing Guard: Protecting Foreign Capital in the Nineteenth and Twentieth Centuries* 121–122, 125 (1983).

19 *Id.* at 129–131.

20 *See also* Mexico-Iceland BIT, Art. 1(2)(i).

21 B.A. Wortley, *Expropriation in Public International Law* 55 (1959).

22 *See* Section 2.2.

23 *See, e.g.*, Egypt-Zambia BIT, Art. 1(1)(E).

likely to decide in the affirmative without much difficulty if the interest appears in the list. Thus, a more inclusive list does confer practical advantages on investors.

As these categories demonstrate, the typical definition of investment is not limited to assets that satisfy an economic definition of the term. For example, an investment may not have added to the productive capacity of the host state because it may have been the result merely of a foreign acquisition of an existing enterprise. Neither does the definition require that the asset have furthered any of the goals of the host state in seeking to attract investment.

In fact, the typical BIT imposes only one condition for an asset to gain treaty protection: the asset must be foreign-owned or controlled. In the crudest sense, BITs promote the movement of control over capital, rather than the movement of the capital itself.

Yet, the typical definition can be defended on policy grounds. Liberal economics asserts that productivity is increased by the allocation of resources through competitive markets. That is, productivity is enhanced through the creation of a system that over time will favor the enterprises that most efficiently provide the goods and services desired by consumers. Some enterprises will be ill-conceived, but the opportunity whereby entrepreneurs or investors may freely enter the market and compete, even if they are fated to lose the competition, is indispensable to the market. In that sense, every enterprise contributes to increased productivity and economic development because every enterprise contributes to the process whereby the most efficient enterprises are identified and spurred through competition to greater efficiency. Further, insofar as BITs are instruments for the promotion of the rule of law, they must protect investment as a matter of principle and not only because the investment has proven itself over time to generate particular economic benefits. Moreover, many definitions of investment assume that the concept of an investment entails the assumption of risk.[24] By definition, then, an investment may fail, but the fact that it failed does not make it less of an investment. Its potential to fail, according to some definitions, is precisely what makes it an investment. The host state's goal of providing a favorable investment climate—one characterized by principles such as security, nondiscrimination, and transparency—is hardly furthered by a policy of protecting against government interference only those investments that are eventually judged successful.

The U.S. BITs differ from the typical BIT in that they limit the definition of investment to assets that have the economic character of an investment. The first U.S. models, dating from the early 1980s, defined investment as "every kind of investment," a definition that was criticized as tautological, but that indicated that the legal definition was intended to incorporate the economic definition. In its 2004 model, the United States made this intention explicit. That model defines an investment to mean "every asset . . . that has the characteristics of an investment." The definition specifies that such characteristics include "the commitment of capital or other resources, the expectation of gain or profit, or the assumption of risk."

24 For a discussion of tribunal awards holding that the concept of investment entails risk, *see* Section 4.2.3.1. As discussed in the next paragraph, the definition of "investment" in the 2004 U.S. model BIT explicitly links the concept of investment to the assumption of risk.

Many BITs provide explicitly that the treaty's provisions apply to investments in existence prior to its entry into force, as well as those that are established subsequent to entry into force.[25] Where the BIT is silent, however, its application to previously existing investment is presumed. Thus, a BIT should be interpreted not to apply to investment established prior to its entry into force only if it explicitly so states. The application of the BIT to existing investment is desirable on several grounds. Excluding existing investments would place certain investors at a permanent state-created disadvantage, which could be unfair to those investors and inefficient for the economy as a whole. It also may generate opposition to the BIT from those who are disadvantaged and call into question the host state's commitment to a favorable investment climate as a matter of principle. Such an exclusion would be inconsistent with the nondiscrimination principle of the BITs.

Many BITs provide that they apply to investment only if it is established in accordance with local law.[26] Occasionally, a BIT contemplates that such approval shall be in writing. [27]

Such a clause may be defended on multiple grounds. First, countries typically restrict the sectors in which foreign investment may be established. As already noted, a country might agree to extend BIT protections to investment within its territory precisely because it has retained the right to determine which investments shall be permitted in its territory. Extending protection to investment that the host state did not admit in accordance with its law disrupts the balance of commitments that the parties assumed in the BIT. On equitable grounds, one might argue that an investment established contrary to law should not be permitted to invoke the law for its protection. It also has been argued that investors sometimes resort to bribery to obtain permission to establish investments unlawfully and that protecting investments in that situation promotes corruption.

This type of clause, however, raises important potential concerns. Foreign investments operate in an environment that is, by definition, alien to them. Especially in developing countries, local laws can be notoriously nontransparent. Even in a country where the text of laws is easily obtainable, the wide range of national, regional, and local laws applicable to a major enterprise creates numerous opportunities for a foreign investment to violate unwittingly some applicable requirement. The danger, then, is

25 *See, e.g.*, Netherlands-Ethiopia BIT, Art. 10; Denmark-Ethiopia, Art. 12; Thailand-Argentina BIT, Art. 2(2); Chile-Indonesia BIT, Art. II(3); Sweden-Kazakhstan BIT, Art. 10(1); Finland-Armenia BIT, Art. 13(1); Australia-India BIT, Art. 2(1); Egypt-Zambia BIT, Art.10; Chile-Lebanon BIT, Art. II; United Kingdom-Bosnia-Herzegovina BIT, Art. 1(a); Italy-Nicaragua BIT, Art. I(1); France-Uganda BIT, Art. 1(1).

26 *See, e.g.*, Cambodia-Vietnam BIT, Art. I(1); Lebanon-Chile BIT, Art. I(2); Indonesia-Algeria BIT, Art. I(1); Italy-Nicaragua BIT, Art. I(1); Finland-Armenia BIT, Art. 1(1); Sweden-Kazakhstan BIT, Art. 1(1); Australia-India BIT, Art. 1(c); Cambodia-Vietnam BIT, Art. X; Chile-Indonesia BIT, Art. II; Germany-Timor-Leste BIT, Art. 9 (BIT applies to prior investment consistent with host state legislation); Chile-Lebanon BIT, Art. II; Australia-India BIT, Art. 14.

27 *See, e.g.*, Thailand-Argentina BIT, Art. 2(1).

that the failure of an investment to comply with an obscure or poorly understood regulation could result in a forfeiture of treaty protection, on the ground that the investment was not established in accordance with host-state law. These clauses never provide for repose of any kind and thus an investment that was in place for decades in theory could be denied treaty protection based on an infraction that occurred at the investment's inception. Indeed, such a clause creates an incentive to limit transparency so as to provide opportunities for legal errors by foreign investments that can supply a basis for a denial of treaty protection, should the host state wish in its discretion to deny protection later. This is precisely the kind of investment climate the BITs are intended to prevent.

Host states have the power to prescribe and enforce civil and criminal penalties on foreign investments and investors who operate contrary to domestic laws. Bribery, for example, can be prosecuted as a criminal offense. Thus, host states even without this clause have the means to prevent or discourage the unlawful establishment of investments. Further, assuming that a BIT applies to investments regardless of their compliance with local law, the fact that an investment was established contrary to local law would undercut some claims to BIT protections on the merits.[28] In short, the better policy is to rely on penalties under local law to enforce local legal restrictions on investment, rather than to threaten forfeiture of all BIT protections.

In any event, giving effect to the purposes of the BITs requires that such clauses be interpreted so as to deny treaty protection only for substantial violations of host-state law addressing the right to establish an investment, such as where the investment is prohibited by host-state law, rather than violations of host-state law addressing the routine operation of the investment. Such an interpretation is entirely consistent with the language of these kinds of clauses, which typically require that the investment have been established in accordance with local law.

Many BITs state that any change in the form of an investment shall not affect its character as investment.[29] Thus, for example, a change in the organizational form or corporate structure of an investment would not affect its character as an investment. A few BITs specify that the investment retains treaty protection only if the alteration is in accordance with local law.[30] This specification raises the same concern as the more general clause conditioning treaty protection on establishment in accordance with local law and, like that more general clause, this specification should be interpreted so that only substantial violations of laws relating to the establishment of investment result in loss of treaty protection.

---

28 For example, in *International Thunderbird v. Mexico*, Mexico's prosecution of an investment that conducted illegal gaming activities was held not to violate the investment chapter of the NAFTA. *See* Sections 6.2 and 6.5.3.1.

29 *See, e.g.*, United Kingdom-Bosnia-Herzegovina BIT, Art. 1(a); BLEU-Sudan BIT, Art. 1(2); Germany-Timor-Lest BIT, Art. 1(1); Switzerland-Algeria BIT, Art. 1(2); Italy-Nicaragua BIT, Art. I(1); Finland-Armenia BIT, Art. 1(1).

30 *See, e.g.*, Austria-Armenia BIT, Art. 2(2)

4.2.2 Origins

The first BIT, the 1959 BIT between Germany and Pakistan, essentially defined investment as capital. It provided that "[t]he term 'investment' shall comprise capital brought into the territory of the other Party for investment in various forms in the shape of assets such as foreign exchange, goods, property rights, patents and technical knowledge. The term 'investment' shall also include the returns derived from and ploughed back into such 'investment'."[31] The definition further provided that "[a]ny partnerships, companies or assets of similar kind, created by the utilisation of the above mentioned assets shall be regarded as 'investment'." Thus, the very first definition was broad and open-ended. It included capital, returns, and companies, and some examples of these were included in a non-exhaustive list.

German BIT practice, however, quickly moved toward the contemporary form of the definition. Germany's 1961 BIT with Togo defined investment as every kind of asset and then included a non-exhaustive list of assets that fell within the definition.[32] These are the five categories common to BITs in 2009, including movable and immovable property, interests in companies, claims to money or to performance having an economic value, intellectual property rights, and concessions under public law. The definition provided that changes in the form of an investment do not affect its nature as an investment.

Other countries did not immediately adopt the German definition or any definition of investment. The first Swiss BIT, concluded with Tunisia in 1961, did not define the term. Neither did the first Dutch BIT, concluded with Tunisia in 1963, the first Belgium-Luxembourg Economic Union (BLEU) BIT, concluded with Tunisia in 1964, the first Italian BIT, concluded with Guinea in 1964, the first Swedish BIT, concluded with the Ivory Coast, in 1965, or the first Danish BIT, concluded with Madagascar in 1965.

Kuwait included a definition in its first BIT, which was with Iraq and which was concluded in 1964. The definition in that BIT, however, simply provided an exhaustive list that included movable and immovable property, company shares, copyright and industrial ownership rights, and technical operations.[33].

By 1970, however, the German definition was entering the treaty practice of other countries. Switzerland had begun to use the definition by 1965.[34] The Netherlands introduced the German definition into its treaty practice in 1970 when it concluded a BIT with Sudan.[35] The BLEU introduced a modified version of the German definition into its BIT practice when it concluded its 1970 BIT with Indonesia. Specifically, the BLEU definition applied only to assets in the sectors of agriculture, industry, mining, forestry, communications, and tourism. These qualifications were abandoned in 1976, however, when the BLEU concluded its BIT with the D.R. Congo.[36] The French had

31 Germany-Pakistan BIT, Art. 8(1)(a).
32 Germany-Pakistan BIT, Art. 8(1).
33 Kuwait-Iraq BIT, Art. 1.
34 *See, e.g.*, Switzerland-Tanzania BIT, Art. 4(1); Switzerland-Costa Rica BIT, Art. 6(3).
35 Netherlands-Sudan BIT, Art. XV(3).
36 BLEU-D.R. Congo BIT, Art. 1.

adopted the German definition by 1972.[37] The United Kingdom inaugurated its BIT program in 1975 by concluding a BIT with Egypt, which included at Article 1 the typical definition, based on the German definition. The Swedish BIT program went into a hiatus in the late 1960s, but, when Sweden resumed its BIT program in 1978 by concluding a BIT with Egypt, the definition that had become typical among BITs was included.[38] The Danish BIT program also went into hiatus in the late 1960s, only to resume in 1980, at which time a modified version of the German definition appeared.[39] Denmark's next BIT, concluded with China in 1985, included a more typical version of the definition.[40] Thus, by the mid 1970s, the definition introduced by Germany was in wide use among countries that were actively negotiating BITs.

The United States signed its first BIT in 1982, with Egypt, at which time it introduced a subtle innovation into the definition. Specifically, the U.S BITs defined investment as "every kind of investment," rather than "every kind of asset."[41] This seemingly tautological definition was intended to clarify that an asset constituted investment only if it had the character of an investment. The U.S. definition also included licenses and permits as an additional category of assets in the non-exhaustive list.

4.2.3 Arbitral Practice

4.2.3.1 The Definition of Investment Under the ICSID Convention Because ICSID has jurisdiction only over legal disputes arising directly out of an investment, where a claim under a BIT is brought before an ICSID tribunal the claimant must demonstrate that the case concerns an investment both within the meaning of the BIT and within the meaning of the ICSID convention. This section discusses the definition of investment within the meaning of the ICSID convention, while the next section discusses the definition of investment within the meaning of the BITs. Because many awards discuss both definitions, to avoid needless repetition, a portion of the discussion of the definition of investment under the ICSID convention is deferred to the next section.

The ICSID convention does not define the term "investment," the drafters having thought that states should have broad discretion to define the term for purposes of their consent to ICSID jurisdiction. Tribunals have considered whether the ICSID convention limits the discretion that the parties have in defining the term "investment." In *Aucoven v. Venezuela*, a case not involving a BIT, the tribunal held that the parties have the "greatest latitude" to define the term "investment," provided that the criteria are reasonable and not totally inconsistent with the purposes of the ICSID convention.[42]

37 *See, e.g.*, France-D.R. Congo BIT, Art. 1; France-Mauritius BIT, Art. 1.

38 Sweden-Egypt BIT, Art. 1.

39 Denmark-Romania BIT, Art. 2(1).

40 Denmark-China BIT, Art. I(1)(a).

41 United States-Egypt BIT, Art. I(1)(c).

42 Decision on Jurisdiction, para. 97. *See also Enron v. Argentina*, Decision on Jurisdiction, para. 42 (definition may not be "something absurd or entirely incompatible with its object and purpose").

In that case, the investor and the host state had agreed that a contract to build and maintain roads was an investment. The tribunal found this to be a reasonable application of the ICSID convention given that performance of the contract would require the expenditure of substantial resources over a significant period of time.[43]

Some tribunals have sought to adopt a definition of investment within the meaning of the ICSID convention that arguably is narrower than the definition in many BITs. The effect of such a definition would be to limit the discretion that the BIT parties have in defining the term "investment." In determining whether a dispute arises out of an investment within the meaning of the convention, tribunals often examine whether the asset entails a contribution of capital for an extended period of time that is placed at risk in the expectation of periodic return. Some cases have also considered as an additional criterion whether the asset contributes to economic development.[44] These criteria collectively are sometimes identified as the *Salini* criteria, referring to one of the early awards in which these criteria were enunciated.[45]

Although the presence of capital and an expected return would seem to be core elements of an investment, it is by no means clear that treaty protection should be limited to investments that can demonstrate a contribution to economic development. If all that is required is a potential contribution to development, then the criterion adds nothing because every asset will satisfy it. If the inquiry is whether the investment actually does contribute to development in some significant way, then the existence of treaty protection would depend upon the success of a particular investment. As discussed in Section 4.2.1, to accord treaty coverage only to successful investments is inconsistent with the purposes of the BITs. If all the criterion requires is an insignificant contribution to development, then it serves no practical purpose. For reasons such as these, some tribunals have questioned whether this criterion should be included.[46]

Nevertheless, the criterion of a contribution to economic development has been dispositive in at least one case. In the annulment proceeding in *Patrick Mitchell v. D.R. Congo*, a case arising under the United States-D.R. Congo BIT, the committee noted that the BIT did not actually define the term "investment," except as "every kind of investment." The committee then observed that ICSID awards had enunciated four characteristics of investment—commitment, duration, risk, and contribution to economic development. The committee also noted that the preamble to the BIT at issue stated that "agreement upon the treatment to be accorded such investment will stimulate the flow of private capital and the economic development of both Parties."[47] Perhaps recognizing the problematic nature of the economic development criterion, the committee said that the contribution to development need not always be sizable or

---

43 Decision on Jurisdiction, para. 101[it is from Aucoven].

44 *See, e.g.*, *Salini v. Morocco* (Italy-Morocco BIT); *Fedax v. Venezuela* (Netherlands-Venezuela BIT); *CSOB v. Czech Republic* (Slovak Republic-Czech Republic BIT).

45 The case is *Salini v. Morocco* (Italy-Morocco BIT). The criteria already had been identified in an earlier award in *Fedax v. Venezuela* (Netherlands-Venezuela BIT).

46 *Saipem v. Bangladesh*, (Italy-Bangladesh BIT) Decision on Jurisdiction, para. 99; *LESI v, Algeria* (Italy-Algeria BIT), Decision on Jurisdiction, para. 72.

47 *Patrick Mitchell v. D.R. Congo*, Decision on the Application for Annulment of the Award, para. 32.

successful and that the concept was "extremely broad but also variable depending on the case."[48] Turning to the facts of the case, the committee observed that the award had identified as elements of the investment the movable property of the claimant's law firm as well as his know-how, goodwill, and right to practice law and that each of these fell within one of the illustrative categories of assets included within the definition. The committee found, however, that the claimant was required to demonstrate that his entire operation, not just certain assets used by his law firm, was an investment. The committee also found that, notwithstanding references in the award to the effect that the law firm had provided legal advice to U.S. investors in the D.R. Congo, the award had failed to explain in what way a law firm contributed to economic development. For that reason, the committee annulled the award.

More generally, the question has been posed whether all the *Salini* criteria must be satisfied in order to find that an asset is an investment or whether the criteria are merely factors to be considered together, such that the presence of some criteria to a greater degree might compensate for the absence of others. This question was discussed extensively by the sole arbitrator in *Malaysian Historical Salvors v. Malaysia*, a case arising under the United Kingdom-Malaysia BIT. The sole arbitrator found that other tribunals had split over the question and suggested that tribunals might be more inclined to treat the criteria as necessary when the evidence in favor of their existence or nonexistence was strong, but to treat them as factors where the evidence was less conclusive. In that case, the arbitrator found a contract to salvage a sunken ship not to be an investment. The arbitrator found no regularity of profit, but regarded that factor as not critical. He found that the investor had made a contribution, although more comparable in size to that associated with a commercial salvage contract than to that associated with investments in other cases. The duration of the original contract was only 18 months, but it had been extended subsequently to 4 years. The extensions had been fortuitous and unrelated to developmental concerns and thus the arbitrator was unwilling to consider them as part of the duration of the investment. As a result, the duration criterion was not satisfied. The arbitrator, however, was performing a "holistic" assessment of the putative investment and thus this factor was not dispositive. The risks were those associated with a normal commercial transaction. The arbitrator found, finally, that the contribution to development must be "significant" because to find otherwise, as a practical matter, would eliminate this requirement. A contract to salvage items of cultural significance provided some employment and know-how, but this was the kind of contribution made by a typical service contract. Based on these considerations, the arbitrator found that the contract did not constitute an investment within the meaning of the ICSID convention, which obviated the need to discuss whether it constituted an investment within the meaning of the BIT.

This award subsequently was annulled. The annulment committee noted that the contract clearly was an investment under the BIT because it fell within the categories of assets explicitly mentioned in the definition.[49] Turning to the definition of "investment" within the meaning of the ICSID convention, the committee reviewed the history

48 *Id.* at 33.

49 *Malaysian Historical Salvors v. Malaysia*, Decision on Annulment, para. 61.

of the convention and found that the drafters deliberately omitted a definition of the term in order to permit the parties, through their consent, to determine the kinds of disputes that would be considered disputes arising directly out of an investment. Indeed, the committee noted, the drafters affirmatively rejected as criteria for a definition of investment both a minimum value and a minimum duration. Thus, the failure of the arbitrator to apply the definition of investment as it appeared in the BIT was a failure to exercise jurisdiction, amounting to a manifest exceeding of the arbitrator's powers.[50] Judge Mohamed Shahabuddeen dissented.

In *Biwater v. Tanzania*, a case arising under the United Kingdom-Tanzania BIT, the tribunal observed that

> there is no basis for a rote, or overly strict, application of the *Salini* criteria in every case. These criteria are not fixed or mandatory as a matter of law. They do not appear in the ICSID Convention. On the contrary, it is clear from the *travaux preparatoire* of the Convention that several attempts to incorporate a definition of "investment" were made, but ultimately did not succeed. In the end the term was left intentionally undefined, with the expectation (inter alia) that a definition could be the subject of agreement as between Contracting Parties.[51]

The tribunal also noted that the *Salini* criteria might contradict the explicit terms of a BIT, implying that to permit a set of criteria developed through arbitral awards to prevail over the express agreement of the parties would be inconsistent with the intent of the ICSID convention in allowing the parties to employ their own definition. The tribunal observed that, moreover, the definition could be inconsistent not only with the terms of a particular BIT, but with a definition in wide use throughout the BIT network reflecting an international consensus that was not consistent with the *Salini* criteria.[52] The tribunal therefore considered that a "flexible and pragmatic approach" to the meaning of "investment" was appropriate.[53] That is, "even if the Republic could demonstrate that any, or all, of the *Salini* criteria are not satisfied in this case, this would not necessary be sufficient—in and of itself—to deny jurisdiction."[54] Turning to the facts before it, which involved a contract between Tanzania and the claimant's company to provide water and sewerage services for Dar es Salaam, the tribunal found that the claimant had made an investment. The claimant intended the project to be profitable, although with a low rate of return. Substantial amounts of equity were invested (in excess of $2 million when the contract was terminated), a substantial performance bond was posted, and a loan of $1 million was advanced to the company, with other support and funds. The claimant supplied the company with key personnel, technology and know-how. Tanzania argued that the project was not intended to be profitable and was a "loss leader." The tribunal observed that, even if this were true, the project nevertheless could be an investment. In such a case, the project still yields benefits to the investor, although perhaps long-term and indirect. Further, the tribunal

---

50 Decision on Annulment, para. 80.
51 Award, para. 321.
52 Award, para. 314.
53 Award, para. 316.
54 Award, para. 318.

wished to avoid a difficult inquiry at the jurisdictional stage into the motives of an investment and its place in the investor's business strategy.[55]

4.2.3.2 The Definition of Investment Under the BITs

In determining whether an asset is an investment within the meaning of a BIT, tribunals apply the language of the definition. For example, the tribunal noted in *Azurix v. Argentina*, a case arising under the United States-Argentina BIT, that the definition of a recoverable investment under a concession contract does not determine what constitutes an investment within the meaning of the BIT.

The decision on jurisdiction in *Enron v. Argentina*, another case arising under the United States-Argentina BIT, summarizes what has been the consensus view among tribunals applying the definition of the term "investment." First, tribunals are in agreement that the definition is a broad one.[56] Further, a tribunal should examine the "general unity of an investment."[57] That is, an investment is often a complex process and may include many components that, standing alone, do not constitute an investment. Thus, the tribunal should consider the economic character of the investor's entire operation in determining whether the investor has made an investment. In *Duke Energy v. Peru*, a case arising under contracts between the disputing parties rather than a BIT, the tribunal found an investment to exist by virtue of a web of agreements, although the claimant could rely in the merits phase only on the single agreement with respect to which Peru had consented to arbitration. In *Tokios Tokeles v. Ukraine*, a case involving the Lithuania-Ukraine BIT, the tribunal held that money spent to modify, maintain or improve an investment is also an investment.[58] The BITs do not distinguish between investment made by the investor or acquired from a predecessor.[59]

Often, the investment is a local company and, because a company and shares in a company are explicitly included within the definition of investment, the tribunal has little difficulty concluding that an investment exists. For example, in *Plama v. Bulgaria*, a case arising under the Energy Charter Treaty, the investor owned 96.78 percent of the local company in which it had invested. In *Siemens v. Argentina*, a case arising under the Germany-Argentina BIT, the claimant wholly owned the local company in which it had invested. In *Continental Casualty v. Argentina*, a case arising under the United States-Argentina BIT, the claimant owned 99.995 percent of the local company in which it had invested. In all of these cases, the existence of an investment was easily established.

As the text of the BITs generally makes clear, the investor need not be a majority owner of the company to have an investment in the company. For example, in *GAMI Investments v. Mexico*, a case arising under the NAFTA, the tribunal held that a

---

55 Award, para. 321.

56 *See, e.g., MCI Power v. Ecuador* (United States-Ecuador BIT).

57 *See also Holiday Inns v. Morocco* (not involving a BIT); *Fedax v. Venezuela* (Netherlands-Venezuela BIT); *Saipem v. Bangladesh* (Italy-Bangladesh BIT), Decision on Jurisdiction, 2007, para. 110 (the tribunal will consider the "entire operation").

58 Award, para. 100.

59 *CME v. Czech Republic* (Netherlands-Czech Republic BIT), Partial Award, para. 384.

14.18 percent equity interest in a company was an investment. The claimant argued that Mexico had expropriated five sugar mills owned by the company, which were substantially all of the company's assets, thereby renderings its shares virtually worthless. Although the tribunal ultimately rejected GAMI's claim on the merits, it concluded that GAMI's shares did constitute an investment and that GAMI could assert a claim for injury to the value of the shares. In *CME v. Czech Republic*, a case arising under the Netherlands-Czech Republic BIT, the tribunal similarly held that it had jurisdiction over the investor's claim that the host state's expropriation of the assets of a local company in which the investor had invested "eviscerated" the value of the investor's shares in the company.[60]

In *Lanco v. Argentina*, a case arising under the United States- Argentina BIT, the claimant was a minority shareholder in an Argentine company that had been awarded a concession contract. The tribunal observed that the treaty "says nothing indicating that the investor in the capital stock has to have control over the administration of the company, or a majority share; thus the fact that [the claimant] holds an equity share of 18.3% in the capital stock of the Grantee allows one to conclude that it is an investor. . . ."[61] As it happened, the investor was a party to the concession contract under which the dispute arose and thus the contract also could be considered an investment in which the claimant was an investor.

In *CMS Gas Transmission v. Argentina*, another case arising under the United States-Argentina BIT, a U.S. investor owned 29.42 percent of an Argentine company that had a license from the state for the distribution of natural gas. The tribunal held that the investor's shares in the company constituted an investment. The fact that the investor was not also a party to the license was immaterial. This holding was followed by the tribunal in *LG&E v. Argentina*, another case involving the United States-Argentina BIT; in *Total v. Argentina*, a case involving the France-Argentina BIT; in *Suez & Vivendi v. Argentina*, a case arising under the France-Argentina BIT, the Spain-Argentina BIT, and the United Kingdom-Argentina BIT; and in *Suez & InterAguas v. Argentina*, a case arising under the France-Argentina BIT and the Spain-Argentina BIT. In *ADC v. Hungary*, a case arising under the Cyprus-Hungary BIT, the tribunal found that the investor's 34 percent holding in a local company constituted an investment. In *Camuzzi International v. Argentina*, a case arising under the BLEU-Argentina BIT, the tribunal found that the investor's ownership of approximately 49 percent of one local company and 51 percent of another local company constituted an investment.

In *Yaung Chi Oo Trading v. Myanmar*, a case arising under the 1987 ASEAN Agreement for the Promotion and Protection of Investment, the investment was in the form of a capital contribution to a joint venture. The joint venture had purchased equipment and supplies from the resources provided by the investor. The tribunal found that "a substantial inward direct investment" had been made by the investor.[62]

In *Eureko v. Poland*, a case arising under the Netherlands-Poland BIT, the investor had entered into a share purchase agreement to acquire a 30 percent interest in an

60 Partial Award, para. 392.

61 Preliminary Decision on Jurisdiction, para.10.

62 Award, para. 45.

insurance company undergoing privatization. The agreement conferred upon the investor the ability to exercise substantial influence over the management and operation of the company beyond that implied by the 30 percent shareholding. The tribunal held that these corporate governance rights constituted an investment, as long as they had economic value. It explained that

> since the grant to Eureko of corporate governance rights markedly more extensive than those that followed from its shareholding was a key element of the investment, without which it appears that there would have been no investment at all, the Tribunal concludes that those rights have some economic value and are entitled to protection under the Treaty.[63]

A few awards have addressed the issue whether indirect ownership of shares in a company constitutes an investment, where the BIT does not explicitly provide that investment may be indirectly owned. Most awards have answered this question in the affirmative. For example, in *Siemens v. Argentina*, a case arising under the Germany-Argentina BIT, the claimant owned a company through an intermediary company. Argentina argued that the claimant could not bring a claim because the investment was owned indirectly and the BIT did not explicitly authorize claims by investors who held their investments indirectly. The tribunal rejected that argument, holding that "[t]he Treaty does not require that there be no interposed companies between the investment and the ultimate owner of the company."[64]

In *Kardassopoulos v. Georgia*, a case arising under the Greece-Georgia BIT and the Energy Charter Treaty, the BIT similarly was silent regarding whether shares in a company would constitute investment if indirectly owned. Citing *Siemens v. Argentina*, the tribunal held that indirectly owned shares constitute an investment.[65] The tribunal also addressed whether the claimant's activities with respect to a joint venture to develop oil and gas resources constituted an investment with the meaning of the ICSID convention. Citing the *Salini* factors, the tribunal held that an investment existed. The respondent had not challenged the existence of a financial contribution. The joint venture agreement was for an initial term of 25 years, while the concession agreement was for a period of 30 years. The project had been underway for three years. The tribunal found it unquestionable that the project contributed to Georgia's economic development and the risk element was satisfied in light of the political and economic climate during the period of the investment.

In *Sedelmeyer v. Russia*, a case arising under the Germany-Russia BIT, the BIT did not explicitly provide that investment indirectly owned by an investor was covered. Nevertheless, the tribunal held that investments made by the claimant through an intermediary company of U.S. nationality constituted an investment. The tribunal rested its decision on language in the protocol under which an investor is entitled to compensation if the host country interferes with the economic activities of an enterprise in which it is participating, which the tribunal took to be an acknowledgement of the possibility

---

63 Partial Award, para. 145.

64 Decision on Jurisdiction, para. 137.

65 Decision on Jurisdiction, paras. 123–124.

of indirect investment. The tribunal also relied on the BIT's purpose of promoting investment as far as possible.[66]

Yet, the view that silence implies that a BIT applies to indirectly owned investment is not unanimous. In *Berschader v. Russia*, a case arising under the Belgium-Luxembourg Economic Union-Russia BIT, the claimants were Belgian nationals who owned shares in a Belgian company that had invested in Russia. The Belgian company was in bankruptcy and thus the shareholders brought a claim for damage to their investments in Russia held through the bankrupt company. The tribunal observed that the BIT, unlike some others, did not expressly include indirect investment. The BIT did refer to indirect investments owned through an intermediary company in a third state. The claimants argued that this demonstrated that indirect investments were included in the definition of investment and that only investments through third-country intermediaries were mentioned because the drafters took for granted that indirect investments through companies in the home or host state were included. The tribunal, however, adopted the opposite interpretation: that indirect investments were covered only if held through third-country intermediaries. The tribunal hypothesized that investments held through third-country intermediaries might otherwise be completely unprotected, if the third-country had concluded no BIT with the host state. Protection for investment indirectly held through a company of one BIT party in the territory of the other BIT party was unnecessary because the company itself was a protected investor. As it happened, in this case, the shareholders could not rely upon their company to bring the claim because the company itself was bankrupt. This unfortunate circumstance, in the opinion of the tribunal, did not justify expanding the scope of the BIT to apply to cover indirect investment. Arbitrator Todd Weiler dissented.

Investment may be held indirectly through multiple layers of intermediate companies. In *Société Générale v. Dominican Republic*, a case arising under the France-Dominican Republic BIT, the tribunal explained that "there may be one or several layers of intermediate companies or interests intervening between the claimant and the investment."[67] In that case, six layers existed between the claimant and the investment. The elaborate structure was intended to minimize the claimant's risk in an enterprise that already had suffered heavy losses.

The typical definition of investment also makes clear that nonequity interests constitute an investment as well. As the tribunal observed in *Link-Trading v. Moldova*, a case involving the United States-Moldova BIT, the host state's change in tax policies destroyed its business of importing goods duty-free and reselling them. The tribunal held that "the fact that an investment consists of debt financing does not appear to affect its characterization as an investment under the BIT."[68] Similarly, in *Berschader v. Russia*, a case arising under the Belgium-Luxembourg Economic Union-Russia BIT, the tribunal held that credit extended to Russia constituted an asset.[69] Article 1.2.2 of

---

66 Award, para. 2.1.5.

67 Award, para. 51.

68 Award on Jurisdiction, page 8.

69 Award, para. 119. The asset, however, was not a protected investment because it was indirectly owned and the tribunal held that indirectly owned assets were not investments.

the treaty explicitly included in the illustrative list of assets that constitute investment "financial credits, as well as shares, and other forms of participation in companies and enterprise, and related debts." In *CSOB v. Slovak Republic*, a case arising under the Czech Republic-Slovak Republic BIT, the tribunal held that a loan constituted an investment.

The tribunal held that a financial investor in an electricity distribution company was an investor in *Société Générale v. Dominican Republic*, a case arising under the France-Dominican Republic BIT. The tribunal found that the distribution of electricity played an important role in the economy. Although the claimant had purchased its investment for a nominal price, the tribunal did not consider that a disqualifying circumstance, nothing that "[t]he purchase of property for a nominal price is a normal kind of transaction the world over when there are other interests and. risks entailed in the business. To the extent that the purchase price might include a discounted value and hence entail a form of compensation for the distressed state of a company, this is something that might be discussed at the merits stage of a dispute. . . ."[70] The investment involved risk, given that the business already had suffered heavy losses.

Tangible property has been held to constitute an investment. In *ADF Group v. United States*, a case arising under the NAFTA, the tribunal held that U.S. origin steel purchased by the investor for use in a construction project in the United States constituted an investment in the territory of the United States. The tribunal noted in particular the definition of investment in the NAFTA, which includes "property, tangible or intangible acquired in the expectation or used for the purpose of economic benefit or other business purposes."[71] In *Tradex Hellas v. Albania*, a case not arising under any BIT but under an Albanian foreign investment law very similar substantively to a typical BIT, the tribunal held that equipment valued at US $432,803 supplied by the investor constituted an investment within the meaning of the Albanian foreign investment law.

In *Sedelmayer v. Russia*, a case arising under the Germany-Russia BIT, the tribunal observed that, while the definition of investment was broad, an investment was one made within the frame of a commercial activity and aimed at creating a further economic value.[72] The tribunal treated office equipment, furniture, and vehicles contributed by the claimant for use in his business in Russia as an investment. Vehicles allegedly acquired by the claimant for use in his business in Russia, but never actually transported to Russia, however, were not investments in Russia. In addition, personal household items contributed by the claimant for use in a building that served as both his residence and his place of business were not an investment. Improvements in the premises constituted an investment, although certain deductions from the value were made because the premises also were used as the claimant's private residence.

Interests in property have been held to constitute an investment. In *Berschader v. Russia*, a case arising under the Belgium-Luxembourg Economic Union-Russia BIT, the tribunal held that a right pursuant to Russian law to retain ownership of a construction site until payment for construction services had been made in full was an asset because

70 Decision on Jurisdiction, para. 36.

71 Award of January 9, 2003, para.152.

72 Award, para. 2.1.4.

it "entails an economic value."[73] In *Bayview v. Mexico*, a case arising under the NAFTA, the tribunal held that water rights were an investment.

A common form of investment is a contract. For example, in *Azurix v. Argentina*, a case arising under the United States-Argentina BIT, the tribunal held that a concession agreement qualifies as an investment, noting that it falls within the category of "any right conferred by law or contract."[74] Further, where the concession agreement is held by a local company, the agreement is an investment of the foreign investor if the foreign investor can establish ownership or control of the local company. The tribunal noted that the investor is the real party in interest and that the purpose of the definition of investment in the BITs is to protect the party with the real interest. In that case, the U.S. claimant owned 90 percent of an Argentine company that was a party to the concession agreement upon which the dispute was based. Thus, the dispute arose out of a contract to which the claimant was not a party. The tribunal nevertheless held that the dispute arose out of the claimant's investment.

A concession agreement also was held to be an investment in *PSEG v. Turkey*, a case arising under the United States-Turkey BIT. In that case, the agreement was to build and operate a lignite-fired electric power plant. Turkey's jurisdictional objection was that the agreement was not valid and binding, but the tribunal concluded that the parties had in fact reached an agreement. In *Occidental v. Ecuador*, a case arising under the United States-Ecuador BIT, the respondent conceded that the concession agreement for hydrocarbon exploration and exploitation was an investment.

The contract need not be a concession agreement to be considered an investment. In *Fedax v. Venezuela*, a case arising under the Netherlands-Venezuela BIT, the tribunal held that a promissory note was an investment because it fell within the category of "titles to money." In addition to applying the plain language of the BIT, the tribunal also considered whether the note had the character of an investment. It found that the note represented a substantial amount of capital placed at risk for use in the public interest for a long period of time with an expectation of a periodic return. The tribunal noted that the promissory notes were issued pursuant to a law on public credit that was enacted specifically to authorize financing for projects in the national interest. Accordingly, the note had the character of an investment. In *ADC v. Hungary*, a case arising under the Cyprus-Hungary BIT, the tribunal held that the entitlement to an income stream from an agreement to manage an airport constituted an investment. In *Duke Energy v. Ecuador*, a case arising under the United States-Ecuador BIT, the tribunal held that payment trust agreements under which the Ministry of Finance guaranteed payment obligations under electrical power purchase agreements were an investment. In *Berschader v. Russia*, a case arising under the Belgium-Luxembourg Economic Union-Russia BIT, the tribunal held that a contract to construct new court facilities was an investment.[75]

---

73 Award, para. 118. The asset, however, was not a protected investment because it was indirectly owned and the tribunal held that indirectly owned assets were not investments.

74 *Accord Vivendi v. Argentina* (France-Argentina BIT) (water service concession was investment).

75 Award, para.117. The asset, however, was not a protected investment because it was indirectly owned and the tribunal held that indirectly owned assets were not investments.

In *Salini v. Morocco*, a case arising under the Italy-Morocco BIT, the tribunal found that a highway construction contract met the definition of an investment under the BIT because it was a "contract benefit having economic value" or a "right of an economic nature conferred by contract" and thus explicitly within the definition.[76] The contract also met the definition of investment under the ICSID convention. The tribunal found that the term "investment" implies "contributions, a certain duration of performance of the contract and a participation in the risks of the transaction."[77] Taking into account the preamble to the ICSID convention, which states, "Considering the need for international cooperation for economic development, and the role of private international investment therein," the tribunal noted that "one might add the contribution to the economic development of the host State of the investment as an additional condition."[78] The investor's contributions included know-how, providing equipment and personnel, and assistance in obtaining financing, including the issuance of bank guarantees. The contract was for 36 months, which was of sufficient duration. The tribunal believed that two to five years was the minimum required to constitute an investment. Risks were associated with performance and the highways clearly contributed to economic development.

In *Helnan v. Egypt*, a case arising under the Denmark-Egypt BIT, the tribunal held that a contract to manage a hotel constituted an investment. It fell within the definition of investment in the BIT, including in particular "concessions or other rights conferred by law or under contract" and a "contract having an economic value." It also met the criteria of duration, return, risk, commitment, and contribution to development. The duration was 26 years, regular remuneration was expected, the project risked not succeeding commercially, the money necessary to achieve the goal qualified as a substantial commitment, and the importance of tourism to Egyptian economic development was obvious.

In *Jan de Nul v. Egypt*, a case arising under the 1977 and 2002 Belgium-Luxembourg Economic Union-Egypt BITs, the tribunal held that a contract to widen and deepen portions of the Suez Canal was an investment. Specifically, it found that the claimants had made a "contribution in . . . services" within the meaning of the 2002 BIT. The tribunal adopted the same factors as the tribunal in *Salini* to determine whether the contract was an investment within the meaning of the ICSID convention. An operation of that magnitude and complexity represented a substantial contribution and a risk and the Suez Canal was of paramount importance to Egypt's economic development. Although the contract period was about a year and eleven months, counting the prequalification period, when funds were first expended, the duration of the project was approximately three years, which the tribunal found to be sufficient. The tribunal found that the claimants had made a contribution of capital or other assets in the communications sector and thus had established an investment within the meaning of the 1977 BIT.

---

76 Decision on Jurisdiction, para. 45.

77 *Id.* at para. 52.

78 *Id.*

In *SGS v. Pakistan*, a case arising under the Switzerland-Pakistan BIT, the tribunal found that a contract to perform pre-shipment customs inspection services constituted an investment. The contract fell within the categories of "claims to money," "concessions under public law," and "rights given by law" and "by contract."[79] Expenditures made by the investor pursuant to the agreement also constituted an investment. The tribunal noted that the investor, in facilitating the raising of revenue, was performing a public function. In *SGS v. Philippines*, a case arising under the Switzerland-Philippines BIT and also involving a pre-shipment customs inspection services contract, the tribunal similarly found the contract to fall within the category of "claims to money or to any performance having an economic value."[80]

In *Petrobart v. Kyrgyz Republic*, a case arising under the Energy Charter Treaty, citing *Fedax v. Venzuela, Salini v. Morocco*, and *SGS v. Pakistan*, the tribunal observed that "[i]t is thus not unusual that claims to money, even if not based on any long-term involvement in a business in another country, are included in treaties within the concept of 'investment'."[81] In that case, the treaty defined an investment to include "any right conferred by law or contract or by virtue of any licenses or permits pursuant to law" to undertake activity in the energy sector.[82] The tribunal found that Petrobart's right to payment under a contract to deliver two hundred thousand tons of gas condensate over a period of twelve months constituted an investment.

In *Chevron v. Ecuador*, a case arising under the United States-Ecuador BIT, the investor had liquidated its investment in the form of oil concession agreements, but retained claims for payment of money for services under the agreements. The tribunal held these claims to constitute investment.[83]

In *Saipem v. Bangladesh*, a case arising under the Italy-Bangladesh BIT, the tribunal held that a contract to construct a gas pipe line constituted "property," the term used in the BIT in lieu of "investment." It fell within the concept of "credit for sums of money . . . connected with investments." Applying the *Salini* criteria, the tribunal held that the contract also was an investment within the meaning of the ICSID convention. The tribunal rejected the argument that the duration of the contract should be limited to the actual time of construction, which was less than a year, observing that the risk during periods when work is suspended may be greater than during periods when work was being performed. Bangladesh objected that, because construction had been financed by funds advanced by the government, the investor had neither imported capital nor assumed an investment risk. The tribunal rejected both arguments, holding that the source of the funds is irrelevant and that risk was associated with the project.

Where the investment is composed of contract rights, the claimant need not be a party to the contract under which the claim arises, if it owns or controls a party to the contract. In *Azurix v. Argentina*, a case arising under the United States-Argentina BIT, the U.S. claimant owned 90 percent of an Argentine company, which was a party to the

---

79 Decision on Jurisdiction, para.135.

80 Decision on Jurisdiction, para. 33.

81 Award, page. 72.

82 Award, page 72.

83 Interim Award, para. 211.

concession agreement upon which the dispute was based.[84] Based on those facts, the tribunal held that the claimant had an investment.[85]

A permit, license, or other government grant may be an investment, provided that an entitlement has been created. In *Middle East Cement v. Egypt*, a case arising under Greece-Egypt BIT, the tribunal held that a license to import cement was an investment, relying on an explicit reference to business concessions conferred by law or under contract in the definition of investment in the BIT. In *Tradex Hellas v. Albania*, a case arising under the Albanian foreign investment law rather than a BIT, the tribunal held that the right to use land could qualify as an investment, although it found in that case that the investor did not possess such a right. In *BG Group v. Argentina*, a case arising under the United Kingdom-Argentina BIT, the tribunal held that a 35year exclusive license to distribute natural gas in Buenos Aires constituted an investment. In *MCI Power v. Ecuador*, a case arising under the United States-Ecuador BIT, the tribunal held that accounts receivable and an operating permit could constitute an investment.

In *Generation Ukraine v. Ukraine*, a case involving the United States-Ukraine BIT, the tribunal found that a resolution on land allocation that was not yet legally binding, a Protocol of Intentions that created no enforceable rights, and a Registration Certificate recording planned contributions not yet made all failed to meet the definition of an investment. None of these created legally enforceable rights. An Order of Land Allocation, however, did grant to the claimant the right to obtain leases and therefore met the definition of investment, which included "any right conferred by law or contract, and any licenses and permits pursuant to law."[86] The same was true of the claimant's construction permits. Leases and a Foundation Agreement fell within several categories of the definition of an investment.

Although tribunals commonly examine whether an asset claimed to be an investment falls within one of the categories in the illustrative list of assets that accompanies most definitions of "investment," obviously an asset need not fall within one of the illustrative categories in order to fall within the definition of "investment." For example, in *AES v. Argentina*, a case arising under the United States-Argentina BIT, the tribunal noted that the definition of investment in that treaty, which was "every kind of investment," was a "very wide one" and left no doubt that the investor's majority ownership of certain energy companies fell within the definition.[87] The tribunal did not seek to place the investment within one of the illustrative categories.

Similarly, in *Bayindir v. Pakistan*, a case arising under the Turkey-Pakistan BIT, investment was defined as "every kind of asset," following which the treaty included an illustrative listing of five categories of assets. The tribunal noted that such a definition is "very broad."[88] The tribunal held that the investor's contribution of know-how, equipment, and personnel to a road construction project constituted an investment.

---

84 Decision on Jurisdiction, para. 65.

85 *Accord: Parkering-Compagniets v. Lithuania* (Norway-Lithuania BIT); *Telenor v. Hungary* (Norway-Hungary BIT).

86 Award, para. 18.22.

87 Decision on Jurisdiction, para, 88.

88 Decision on Jurisdiction, para. 113.

It also held that the investor's financial contribution, which took the form of providing bank guarantees and incurring bank commission charges in excess of $11 million constituted an investment. The tribunal held that these various contributions were assets within the meaning of the definition of investment, without discussing whether they fell within one of the illustrative categories. The tribunal considered separately whether the investor had established an investment within the meaning of the ICSID convention. Applying the *Salini* criteria, the tribunal found that the investor made an investment within the meaning of the convention. The investor's contribution of know-how, equipment, personnel, and financing was substantial. The contract had a duration of three years, followed by a defect liability period of one year, followed by a maintenance period of four years, which the tribunal found to be sufficient. The tribunal found a significant risk for the investor, comprising both the inherent risk in long-term contracts and the risks associated with the defect liability period and the maintenance period. Finally, although citing *LESI v. Algeria*, a case arising under the Italy-Algeria BIT, for the proposition that the additional condition that a project contribute to development is often implicit in the first three conditions, the tribunal went on to note that Pakistan itself had declared in the past that the roads were important for development. The tribunal noted that *Aucoven v. Venezuela* had held that a highway construction project is an investment within the meaning of the convention and that Pakistan had not questioned in *Impregilo v. Pakistan* that a dam construction project constituted an investment under the convention. The tribunal observed in any event that these factors "may be closely interrelated, should be examined in their totality, and will normally depend on the circumstances of each case."[89]

In *Micula v. Romania*, a case arising under the Sweden-Romania BIT, the tribunal held without extensive discussion that plants for the production of food and related services were investments within the meaning of the BIT.[90] It also found them to be investments within the meaning of the ICSID convention because they involved a substantial commitment of resources over a significant period of time.[91]

While in the great majority of cases submitted to investor-state arbitration under a BIT the dispute was found to arise out of an investment, tribunals have held in a few cases that the dispute did not arise out of an investment. In *Mihaly v. Sri Lanka*, a case arising under the United States-Sri Lanka BIT, the claimant made expenditures in an effort to obtain a contract to construct and operate a power generation facility in Sri Lanka. Ultimately, however, the parties never concluded a contract. The tribunal held that, since no agreement had been reached, no investment within the meaning of the ICSID convention had come into existence. Accordingly, the tribunal had no jurisdiction over the claim. The tribunal observed that the claimant had not made reference to the definition of investment in the U.S. BIT and declined to discuss the definition in the BIT.[92]

---

89 Decision on Jurisdiction, para. 130.
90 Decision on Jurisdiction, para. 126.
91 Decision on Jurisdiction, para. 125.
92 Award of March 15, 2002, para. 61.

In *Nagel v. Czech Republic*, a case arising under the United Kingdom-Czech Republic BIT, the claimant had entered into a cooperation agreement with a state-owned enterprise for the purpose of obtaining a license to operation a telecommunications business. Ultimately, the effort was unsuccessful. The tribunal held that "a claim can be accepted as an 'asset' if it has a financial value. A claim normally has a financial value, however, only if it appears to be well-founded or at the very least creates a legitimate expectation of performance in the future."[93]

The tribunal found that the cooperation agreement contained no guarantee that a license would be received. Although the claimant might have been encouraged by various comments made by government officials, this was not sufficient to create a legitimate expectation that a license would be obtained.[94] Accordingly, the claimant's rights under the cooperation agreement were not an investment.

In *PSEG v. Turkey*, a case arising under the United States-Turkey BIT, the tribunal held that a memorandum of understanding conferring on a U.S. company the option to acquire ownership interests in the investment in Turkey by means of a shareholders' agreement to be negotiated later was not an investment. That is, the tribunal found that, under the specific circumstances of that case, an option was not an investment.

In *Joy Mining Machinery v. Egypt*, a case arising under the United Kingdom-Egypt BIT, the claimant had sold mining equipment to an Egyptian government agency and had supplied letters of guarantee for the performance of the equipment. When the Egyptian government agency refused to release the guarantees, the claimant submitted the dispute to arbitration. The tribunal held that a bank guarantee put in place by the claimant was a contingent liability and therefore not an investment within the meaning of the BIT. The tribunal also found that the guarantee was not an investment within the meaning of the ICSID convention. To be an investment under the convention, a project "should have a certain duration, a regularity of profit and return, an element of risk, a substantial commitment and . . . it should constitute a significant contribution to the host State's development."[95] Here, the bank guarantee was related to the purchase of equipment, which the tribunal regarded as an ordinary commercial transaction. The transaction was not of long duration. The entire purchase price was paid early and thus there was no return over a long period of time. The risk was that associated with a normal commercial contract. The tribunal did find the amount of the contribution to be relatively substantial, but did not believe that the project could be considered an economic development contract or a concession agreement. The tribunal distinguished this case from *Fedax* on the ground that, unlike the notes in *Fedax* that financed the state budget and that were given in exchange for something of value, the bank guarantees provided no benefit to Egypt. Egypt had not drawn down against the guarantees and therefore had not benefited from them.

In *Occidental v. Ecuador*, a case arising under the United States-Ecuador BIT, the tribunal rejected the claimant's argument that a claim for a tax refund is an investment. The only explanation offered by the tribunal was that "it would be quite extraordinary

---

93 Award, 1 Stockholm Arbitration Report 141, 158 (2004).

94 *Id.* at page 164.

95 Award on Jurisdiction, para.53.

for a company to invest in a refund claim."[96] The tribunal found, however, that even if the refund claim were considered a "claim for money," which the BIT explicitly listed as a category of investment, the claim had not been expropriated. Thus, the tribunal did not so much find the claim not to be an investment as to decide that the claimant had failed to persuade the tribunal that it was an investment. The tribunal avoided a clear finding that the claim was not an investment by noting that no expropriation of the claim had occurred in any event and thus the issue of whether it was an investment effectively need not be decided.

In *Genin v. Estonia*, a case arising under the United States-Estonia BIT, the tribunal doubted that an amount to buy a claim could be an investment. The tribunal did not have to decide the issue, however, because the claimant also had interests in a company that qualified as an investment under language in the BIT defining "investment" to include "shares of stock or other interests in a company."[97]

4.2.3.3 Identifying the Location of the Investment Several cases have involved disputes concerning whether the investment was located in the territory of the host state. In *Fedax v. Venezuela*, a case arising under the Netherlands-Venezuela BIT, the investment consisted of six promissory notes issued by Venezuela that eventually were purchased by an investor outside Venezuela. Venezuela had failed to make payments due under the notes. The tribunal found that, even though no funds had been physically transferred by the claimant into Venezuela, nevertheless the funds made available through the notes were utilized to finance the government's needs. The notes were not part of an ordinary commercial transaction, but involved the public interest. Accordingly, the notes constituted an investment in the territory of Venezuela.

In *Tradex Hellas v. Albania*, a case arising under the Albanian investment code, which in many respects resembles a BIT textually, a Greek company had entered into a joint venture with an Albanian state-owned company to undertake engineering, industrial, and agricultural investments in Albania. The tribunal held that investments made by the claimant outside the host state of Albania allegedly for the benefit of the joint venture could constitute investments in the territory of Albania, but only if they were debited to the joint venture. In *CME v. Czech Republic*, a case involving the Netherlands-Czech Republic BIT, the tribunal, citing *Tradex Hellas*, observed that the BIT "does not require that the assets or funds be imported from abroad or specifically from [the territory of the other BIT party] or have been contributed by the investor itself."[98]

In *SGS v. Pakistan*, a case arising under the Switzerland-Pakistan BIT, the claimant entered into a contract to perform customs inspection services outside the territory of Pakistan and at Pakistani points of entry. The tribunal found that the claimant had made certain expenditures in the territory of Pakistan, albeit small, and that these expenditures included the establishment of offices in Pakistan. The tribunal also took note of Pakistan's argument in domestic court proceedings that the claimant was

96 Final Award, para. 86.
97 Award, para. 324.
98 Partial Award, para. 418.

entrusted with the sovereign power of collecting revenue. For these reasons, the tribunal found that the claimant had made an investment in the territory of Pakistan.

A second case, *SGS v. Philippines*, which arose under the Switzerland-Philippines BIT, involved a similar contract with the Philippines. The tribunal again noted that the claimant had established a substantial office in the Philippines. Further, the inspections conducted abroad were not conducted for their own sake, but as part of a process culminating in the issuance of a certificate in the Philippines. Thus, the tribunal refused to segregate the services performed abroad from those performed in the host state. Inasmuch as services were provided in the Philippines, the cost incurred to perform those services amounted to an investment in the Philippines. The tribunal disregarded the fact that the services were treated for tax purposes as performed abroad, since that determination was governed by local law, which has criteria distinct from those of the BIT.

In *CSOB v. Slovak Republic*, a case arising under the Czech Republic-Slovak Republic BIT, the tribunal considered whether a loan made by CSOB constituted an investment in the Slovak Republic, even though it did not result in the outlay of any resources in the Slovak Republic. The loan, however, was part of a related group of transactions to restructure CSOB. The banking activities of CSOB would involve an outlay of resources and contribute to economic development. Thus, the entire process of which the loan was a part could be considered an investment in the Slovak Republic. As the tribunal explained,

> a dispute that is brought before [ICSID] must be deemed to arise directly out of an investment even when it is based on a transaction which, standing alone, would not qualify as an investment under the [ICSID] Convention, provided that the particular transaction forms an integral part of an overall operation that qualifies as an investment.[99]

Citing *Fedax*, the tribunal found that "a transaction can qualify as an investment even in the absence of a physical transfer of funds."[100] CSOB's undertaking "involved a significant contribution by CSOB to the economic development of the Slovak Republic; it qualifie[d] CSOB as an investor and the entire process as an investment in the Slovak Republic within the meaning of the [ICSID] Convention."[101] Interestingly, the tribunal commented that while CSOB's activities "were designed to produce a benefit and to offer CSOB a return in the future, subject to an element of risk . . . [,] these elements . . . are not a formal prerequisite for the finding that a transaction constitutes an investment as that concept is understood in the Convention."[102] Thus, the tribunal seemed to focus on whether the arrangement contributed to economic development, rather than the more traditional elements of whether the transaction involved placing resources at risk in the expectation of gain, an approach that is not consistent with that of most tribunals. As for whether CSOB had established an investment within the meaning of the BIT, the tribunal observed that the consolidation agreement on

---

99 Decision on Jurisdiction, para.72.

100 *Id.* at para. 78.

101 *Id.* at para. 88.

102 *Id.* at para. 90.

which the claim was based explicitly referenced the BIT, thus reflecting the parties' recognition that the contract constituted an investment. This was confirmed by the language of the BIT, which included as an investment "movable and immovable property and any other encumbrances, including any mortgages, liens, guarantees, and similar rights"

In *Bayview v. Mexico*, a case arising under the NAFTA, the claimants were U.S. nationals who owned land in the United States. They alleged that Mexico had wrongfully curtailed the amount of river water flowing into U.S. territory and thereby deprived them of water to which they were legally entitled. The tribunal held that that the claimants' water rights arose under U.S. law. While finding that water rights were an investment protected by the NAFTA, such rights were created by U.S. law and therefore were not an investment in Mexico. More generally, the tribunal explained that the NAFTA protects "foreign" investment and that, to be "foreign," an investment must be regulated by the law of a state other than that of the investor.

In *Ethyl Corporation v. Canada*, a case arising under the NAFTA, the issue arose concerning the significance of the fact that some losses were incurred outside the territory of the host state, but the issue was not resolved at the jurisdictional stage and the case was settled before the tribunal reached the merits. Similarly, in *Gruslin v. Malaysia*, a case arising under the Belgium-Luxembourg Economic Union-Malaysia BIT, the issue of the location of the investment was raised but not decided.[103]

In *Berschader v. Russia*, a case arising under the Belgium-Luxembourg Economic Union-Russia BIT, the claimants owned shares in a Belgian company, which in turn owned assets in Russia. The tribunal held that shares in a Belgian company could not constitute an investment in Russia. As discussed in Section 4.2.3.2, the tribunal also held that the BIT did not protect indirect investment and thus the claimants owned no investment in Russia indirectly.

4.2.3.4 Relevance of the Source of Financing Host states sometimes have argued that a claimant has not made an investment because the claimant was not the source of the financing. In *Tradex Hellas v. Albania*, a case arising under the Albanian investment law rather than a BIT, the tribunal held that the source of financing was irrelevant to whether the claimant owned or controlled an investment. The tribunal observed that the definition of investment "nowhere requires that the foreign investor has to finance the investment from his own resources."[104] In *Olguin v. Paraguay*, a case arising under the Peru-Paraguay BIT, the Peruvian claimant brought U.S. dollars into Paraguay, where he invested them. The tribunal held that the location where the funds originated was irrelevant.[105]

In *Tokios Tokeles v. Ukraine*, a case arising under the Lithuania-Ukraine BIT, the financing originated in the host country. That is, Ukrainian nationals had incorporated a company under the laws of Lithuania and the Lithuanian company in turn had

103 Award, para. 16. The sole arbitrator found that he had no jurisdiction on the ground that the investment was not an "approved project," which was a condition of treaty coverage.

104 Award, para. 109.

105 Award, para. 66.

invested in Ukraine. When the Lithuanian company submitted a claim against Ukraine to investor-state arbitration under the Lithuania-Ukraine BIT, Ukraine objected that the claimant had not made an investment in Ukraine because the capital originated in Ukraine. The tribunal held that the BIT does not require that the capital have originated outside the host country.[106] The claimant had caused an expenditure of money and effort from which it expected a return in Ukraine. Put another way, investment capital under the claimant's control had been deployed in Ukraine and thus the claimant had an investment in Ukraine, notwithstanding that the capital had originated in Ukraine. The tribunal considered whether the equitable doctrine of "veil piercing" should "override the terms" of the BIT and cause the tribunal to deny jurisdiction.[107] Without deciding under which circumstances, if any, such a result might be justified, the tribunal found no evidence of fraud or abuse of legal personality and declined to apply the doctrine.[108]

The award in *Tokios Tokeles* was followed by the tribunal in *Siag and Vecchi v. Egypt*, a case arising under the Italy-Egypt BIT. In that case, the host state, Egypt, argued that both claimants were in fact Egyptian nationals and that the investment had its origins in Egypt. The tribunal ultimately found that both claimants were Italian nationals.[109] Citing the award in *Tokios Tokeles* with approval, the tribunal dismissed Egypt's argument, noting that "[t]he terms of the BIT do not impose any 'origin of capital' requirement."[110]

The award was followed as well in *ADC v. Hungary*, a case arising under the Cyprus-Hungary BIT. The claimant was incorporated in Cyprus, paid taxes in Cyprus, used Cypriot auditors, and received payment from Hungary in Cyprus. Thus, the claimant was a Cypriot investor. Under the terms of the BIT, the fact that the claimant was controlled by Canadians and received funds from Canadians was irrelevant.[111] The tribunal observed that "the majority opinion in *Tokios Tokeles* still represents good international law. . . ."[112] The tribunal acknowledged that some domestic legal systems recognize the principle of "piercing the corporate veil," but declined to do so. Such a principle would be inapplicable in this case, the tribunal said, because it is limited to situations where corporate formalities are fraudulently misused. As the tribunal explained, "Hungary was fully aware of the use of Cypriot entities and manifestly approved it."[113] The tribunal also rejected Hungary's argument that the BIT required a "genuine link" between the investor and its state of nationality, noting that the parties had not included such a requirement in the BIT.[114] Nor was it relevant that the

---

106 *Accord: Siag & Vecchi v. Egypt* (Italy-Egypt BIT); *Saipem v. Bangladesh* (Italy-Bangladesh BIT). The decision in *Tokios Tokeles* was not unanimous. Professor Prosper Weil strongly dissented.

107 Decision on Jurisdiction, para. 53.

108 Decision on Jurisdiction, para. 56.

109 Professor Francisco Orrego Vicuna dissented with respect to one of the claimants.

110 Decision on Jurisdiction, para. 210.

111 Award, paras. 355–357.

112 Award, para. 360.

113 Award, para. 358.

114 Award, para. 359.

Canadian investors had sought the assistance of the Canadian government in resolving the dispute.[115]

The tribunal agreed in *Rompetrol v. Romania*, a case arising under the Netherlands-Romania BIT. In that case, Romania argued that Romanian investors had established a shell corporation in the Netherlands through which they owned their investment in Romania and thus the claim brought by the Dutch company should be treated as a claim by Romanian investors against Romania, over which the tribunal would have no jurisdiction. The tribunal held, however, that the BIT used a place of incorporation test and thus the nationality of the corporation's owners, the location of its seat and the origin of its capital were irrelevant to determining its nationality.[116]

The same approach was taken by the tribunal in *Saluka Investments v. Czech Republic*, a case arising under the Netherlands-Czech Republic BIT. A group of Japanese companies established the claimant company in the Netherlands for the sole purpose of holding shares in a Czech Republic company. The respondent alleged that the claimant was a mere shell that should not be entitled to the status of an investor. The tribunal rejected that argument, noting that the claimant was incorporated in the Netherlands and, therefore, an investor within the meaning of the BIT.[117] The Czech Republic argued that the tribunal should pierce the corporate veil to prevent fraud or malfeasance, but the tribunal found insufficient evidence of either. While the Japanese investors had not fully disclosed their ultimate objectives in acquiring their investment in the Czech Republic, they were under no duty to do so. The tribunal noted that it had "some sympathy for the argument that a company which has no real connection with a State party to a BIT, and which is in reality a mere shell company . . . should not be entitled to invoke the protections of that treaty. Such a possibility lends itself to abuses of the arbitral procedure, and to practices of 'treaty shopping' which can share many of the disadvantages of the widely criticized practice of 'forum shopping.'"[118] The tribunal concluded, however, that it must decide in accordance with the terms of the BIT, under which the claimant qualified as an investor. The tribunal noted that the Czech authorities had been aware that the Japanese investors would be establishing "a special-purpose vehicle" to hold the investment and thus "no violence [was] done to the positions knowingly adopted by the parties at all relevant times."[119]

4.2.3.5 Consistency of the Investment with Local Law Many BITs limit treaty protection to investment established in accordance with local law.[120] In *Salini v. Morocco*, a case arising under the Italy-Morocco BIT, the host state argued that such language meant that the term "investment" was to be defined by local law. The tribunal rejected that argument, holding that the purpose of the BIT provision is to prevent the BIT "from protecting investments that should not be protected, particularly because

115 Award, para. 361.
116 Decision on Jurisdiction, para. 110.
117 Award, para. 229.
118 Award, para. 240.
119 Award, para. 242.
120 *See* Section 4.2.1.

they would be illegal."[121] The tribunal found no indication that the claimants had violated Moroccan law. Similarly, in *L.E.S.I. v. Algeria*, a case arising under the Italy-Algeria BIT, the tribunal held that the requirement of conformity with local law is not intended to define investment in terms of local law, but rather to exclude from treaty protection "investments that have been made in violation of the fundamental principles that apply."[122]

Occasionally, a host state argues that an investment is not protected by a BIT because the investment was not established in accordance with local law. These claims sometimes have failed. Tribunals have refused to allow minor violations of local law to divest an investment of protection, but have denied treaty protection where the investment was established through fraud.

For example, in *Tokios Tokeles v. Ukraine*, a case arising under the Lithuania-Ukraine BIT, the host state argued that the investment was not protected because its registered name referred to itself as a "subsidiary enterprise" rather than a "subsidiary private enterprise," which was the recognized legal form under Ukrainian law. Other defects in the corporate documents also were alleged, such as documents relating to asset procurement and transfer, including the absence of necessary signatures or notarizations. The tribunal began its discussion of this issue by concurring with the *Salini* award about the purpose of the language regarding local law. Then, noting the object and purpose of the BITs to provide broad protection for investors and their investments, the tribunal rejected Ukraine's argument. The tribunal found that the claimant's business activity, which was advertising, printing, and publishing, was not illegal *per se*. Further, the government had registered the investment as a valid enterprise in 1994. The alleged defects were based on minute details of administrative procedures under Ukrainian law and to exclude an investment "on the basis of such minor errors would be inconsistent with the object and purpose of the Treaty."[123] The tribunal also noted the absence of a denial of benefits clause, reasoning that if the parties had wished to exclude investments from treaty protection such a clause would provide a means of so doing. The parties had elected not to include such a clause and the tribunal would not impose limits on its jurisdiction not found in the text.[124]

In *Desert Line v. Yemen*, a case arising under the Oman-Yemen BIT, the BIT required not only that the investment be accepted by the host state as an investment according to its laws and regulations, but that an investment certificate be issued. The tribunal first held that the phrase "according to its laws and regulations" excludes investments made in breach of fundamental principles of the host state's law. The fact that Yemen had accepted the investment was demonstrated by the dealings between

---

121 Decision on Jurisdiction, para. 84, quoting *Salini v. Morocco*, Decision on Jurisdiction, para. 46. *Accord Bayindir v. Pakistan* (Turkey-Pakistan BIT), Decision on Jurisdiction, para. 110. *See also Saipem v. Bangladesh* (Italy-Bangladesh BIT), Decision on Jurisdiction, para. 79 (Parties agree that the clause refers to the mode, not the definition, of investment).

122 Award, para. 24 (unofficial translation from French).

123 Decision on Jurisdiction, para. 86.

124 Decision on Jurisdiction, para. 36. For a discussion of the denial of benefits clause, see Sections 4.3.1 and 4.3.3.1.

the claimant and the highest levels of government, including the president, prime minister, minister of finance, and minister of public works. The tribunal held that the requirement of a certificate should not be interpreted in a formalistic manner, lest it constitute an "artificial trap depriving investors of the very protection the BIT was intended to provide."[125] The tribunal noted that the BIT does not identify any particular document that must be provided and thus an acceptance of the investment in substance was all that was required. Noting that the project had been encouraged and welcomed by the president and prime minister, the tribunal refused to conclude that that some further technical approval was necessary for the project to receive BIT protection.

In *Kardassopolous v. Georgia*, a case arising under the Greece-Georgia BIT and the Energy Charter Treaty, the violations of local law were committed not by the investor or the investment, but by state-owned enterprises that had exceeded their authority in approving a concession agreement. The tribunal held that the requirement that investment be established in accordance with local law was intended to apply where the investor violated local law. Georgia had not alleged any violation of local law by the investor and thus the investment was entitled to BIT protection.[126]

In *Sedelmayer v. Russia*, a case arising under the Germany-Russia BIT, the tribunal found evidence in the form of registration certificates that the investment was established in accordance with Russian law. The tribunal also noted that the investment, which provided training to police in St. Petersburg, operated openly and elicited no objections from the Russia authorities. Although the police department may have violated the law in its participation in a joint venture with the claimant, the tribunal declined to treat any such violation as an illegality with respect to the establishment of the claimant's investment.[127] As in *Kardassapolous*, the tribunal limited its inquiry to illegality by the investor, not the host state.

In *Plama v. Bulgaria*, a case arising under the Energy Charter Treaty, the tribunal found that the claimant had obtained approval of its investment by misrepresenting the nature of its ownership. More specifically, the claimant had induced Bulgaria to believe that it was a consortium of substantial investors, rather than an entity owned by a single individual without the resources to operate the refinery that it had agreed to operate. Accordingly, the tribunal held that the claimant was not entitled to the protection of the treaty.

In *Inceysa v. El Salvador*, a case arising under the Spain-El Salvador BIT, the tribunal noted that the determination of illegality rested with the tribunal rather than the host-state courts.[128] Otherwise, a host state through its courts could modify unilaterally the scope of BIT protection. Because under Salvadoran laws international treaties are considered the law of the republic, the relevant law in determining the legality of the investment was the BIT. The BIT contained a choice of law clause that included generally recognized principles of international law. One supreme principle was that of good faith, which means the absence of deceit. The tribunal found that the

125 Award, para. 106.

126 Decision on Jurisdiction, para. 184.

127 Award, para. 2.2.4.

128 Award, para. 213. *Accord Fraport v. Philippines* (Germany-Philippines BIT), Award, para. 391.

claimant had violated the principle of good faith by submitting false information during the process of bidding for the contract that was the basis of the dispute. Another general principle provides that no one may profit from his own wrong. To permit the claimant to obtain treaty protection for a contract obtained fraudulently would violate that principle[129] as well as international public policy[130] and the principle that prohibits unjust enrichment.[131]

In *Fraport v. Philippines*, a case arising under the Germany-Philippines BIT, the tribunal suggested that legal violations made by the investment or investor in good faith, such as where the law was not clear or the legal violation was not central to the profitability of the investment, should not result in a loss of treaty protection.[132] In that case, however, the investor deliberately and secretly structured the investment in a way that violated host-state law. Because the investment was established in violation of local law, it did not fall within the BIT's definition of investment and the tribunal lacked jurisdiction over its claim.[133]

In *TSA v. Argentina*, a case arising under the Netherlands-Argentina BIT, the tribunal found insufficient evidence that the claimant had obtained the concession agreement illegally, although criminal investigations in Argentina were continuing. Because the tribunal found that it lacked jurisdiction on other grounds, the tribunal did not need to resolve the issues related to Argentina's objection that the investment was established illegally.

In *Siemens v. Argentina*, a case arising under the Germany-Argentina BIT, more than a year after the tribunal awarded $217 million to the claimant, Siemens admitted that its Argentine subsidiary had procured the contract that was the subject of the arbitration through bribery of local officials. As this book went to press, Argentina was seeking revision of the award on the basis of the admission.

In *Berschader v. Russia*, a case arising under the Belgium-Luxembourg Economic Union-Russia BIT, the tribunal held that the issue of the lawfulness of the investment is a substantive issue related to the merits of the claim, rather than the jurisdiction of the tribunal. The tribunal therefore declined to consider the issue at the jurisdictional stage.[134] The tribunal subsequently dismissed the claim for lack of jurisdiction on other grounds.

The limitation of BIT protection to investments established in accordance with the laws of the host state, although typically included in the definition of investment, may be expressed in other parts of the BIT. In *Inceysa v. El Salvador*, the Spain-El Salvador BIT included a provision requiring each party to admit investment in accordance with its laws. During negotiations, El Salvador had proposed that the definition of investment in the negotiating text be modified so that it would include only investment established in accordance with host-state law. Spain replied that the modification was

129 Award, para. 244.
130 Award, para. 252.
131 Award, para. 256.
132 Award, para. 396.
133 Award, para. 401.
134 Award, para. 5.4.2.

unnecessary in light of the language on admission. Thus, the tribunal concluded, based on this negotiating history, that the BIT protected only investment made in accordance with host-state law. The tribunal noted that two other provisions of the BIT provided that BIT protections applied to investment made in accordance with host-state law, confirming its interpretation of the BIT.

In *Saluka Investments v. Czech Republic*, a case arising under the Netherlands-Czech Republic BIT, the tribunal found that a requirement that each party shall admit investments in accordance with its law implicitly limits treaty protection to investments established in accordance with local law.[135] Unlike the tribunal in *Inceysa*, the tribunal in *Saluka Investments* did not rely on the negotiating history for its interpretation of the provision on admissions. That interpretation seems questionable, however, because the purpose of the admissions provision is to liberalize investment flows, not to diminish their protection. That is, the admissions provision is in furtherance of the access principle and should not be read as imposing an implied limitation on the security principle. The implication of the tribunal's interpretation is that a BIT that contains an admission provision offers less protection than one that does not. In any event, the tribunal found no violation of law in the establishment of the investment.

The tribunal observed in *Fraport v. Philippines*, a case arising under the Germany-Philippines BIT, that the references to local law in the definition and admissions provisions pertain only to the establishment of investment. An investment that was established in accordance with host-state law, but then operated in ways that violated local law, would be protected by the BIT, although the violations might serve as defenses to claims of substantive violations of the BIT by the host state.[136] The observation was *dictum*, however, because the tribunal noted that the contention before it dealt with the legality of the establishment of the investment.

One objection to conditioning BIT protection on compliance with local law is that it may create an incentive for the host state to ignore violations of law by the investment, knowing that these later can be raised as a defense to treaty protection in the event that the investment or investor submits a claim to arbitration. The tribunal also addressed this issue in *Fraport.* The tribunal observed that a host state that knowingly overlooked violations of local law by the investment or investor would be estopped from raising those violations as a jurisdictional defense.[137] In that case, however, the tribunal found no evidence that the host state knew, should have known or could have known of any illegality.

In some cases, establishment of an investment in accordance with local law requires formal approval. For example, in *Gruslin v. Malaysia*, a case arising under the Belgium-Luxembourg Economic Union-Malaysia BIT, the tribunal dismissed the claim for lack of jurisdiction because the claim was not an "approved project," which was a condition of treaty coverage under the BIT.[138] In particular, an approval for the listing of shares on the stock exchange that had been granted was not the approval required. The mere

135 Award, para. 204.
136 Award, para. 345.
137 Award, para. 346.
138 Award, paras. 25.5–25.6.

fact that a BIT conditions protection of investment on compliance with local law, however, is not read to require approval of the investment where no such approval is required by local law.[139] Where the BIT expressly limits its protection to approved investments, that normally refers to the approval required by local law and not some additional approval process under the treaty,[140] unless the treaty specifies a separate approval process.[141]

4.3 THE DEFINITION OF INVESTOR

4.3.1 Structure and Policy

Many BITs apply to investment of nationals and companies of one party in the territory of the other party.[142] Some BITs protect investment of investors of one party in the territory of the other, but then define the term "investor" simply to mean nationals and companies.[143] In this book, the term "investor" is used to refer to nationals and companies collectively.

The term "investor" raises two broad issues. The first is the type of person who may be considered an investor. The second is the method by which the nationality of the investor is to be determined.

The most common definition of a national is a person who is a national under the domestic law of a party. Customary international law permits a state to confer nationality upon a person only if there is a "genuine link" between that person and the state of nationality.[144] The BITs do not impose any limit on a host state's ascription of nationality. Thus, under the typical BIT, a person is a national of a state if the domestic law of that state so provides. A few BITs require a greater link than nationality, such as that the person reside or be domiciled in the state of nationality.[145] Other BITs, by contrast, treat permanent residents of a state as covered investors even if they are not nationals under that state's domestic law.[146]

Most BITs do not address the issue of whether a person who has the nationality of more than one country may claim the nationality of either for purposes of the BIT.

---

139 *See Middle East Cement v. Egypt* (Greece-Egypt BIT), Award, para. 137.

140 *See Yaung Chi Oo v. Myanmar* (1987 ASEAN Agreement on Promotion and Protection of Investment), Award, paras. 58–59.

141 *Id.*, paras 60–62.

142 *See, e.g.*, United Kingdom-Bosnia-Herzegovina BIT; France-Uganda BIT. *See generally* Engela C. Schlemmer, "Investment, Investor, Nationality, and Shareholders," in *The Oxford Handbook of International Investment Law* (Peter Muchlinski, Frederico Ortino, and Christoph Schreuer, eds. 2008).

143 *See, e.g.*, BLEU-Sudan BIT; Germany-Timor-Leste BIT, Art. 1(3); Italy-Nicaragua BIT, Art. 1(2); Austria-Armenia BIT, Art. 1(1); Sweden-Kazakhstan BIT, Art. 1(2); Denmark-Ethiopia BIT, Art. 1(3); Chile-Indonesia BIT, Art. 1(1); Australia-India BIT, Art. 1(d); Thailand-Argentina BIT, Art. 1(1); Lebanon-Chile BIT, Art. 1(1); Mexico-Iceland BIT, Art. 1(1).

144 *See The Nottebohm Case* (Liechtenstein v. Guatemala), 1955 I.C.J. 4.

145 *See, e.g.*, Germany-Israel BIT, Art. 1(3)(b) (requiring permanent residence).

146 *See, e.g.*, Australia-India BIT, Art. 1(d)(ii); Canada-Argentina BIT, Art. I(b).

The rule under customary international law is that such a person shall be treated as a national of the country of his or her "dominant and effective" nationality.[147] This issue is addressed in a few BITs. For example, the 2004 U.S. model BIT provides that "a natural person who is a dual national shall be deemed to be exclusively a national of the State of his or her dominant and effective nationality."[148]

BITs generally do not limit significantly the kinds of entities that can qualify as a covered investor. The typical definition lists a wide range of entities and includes a residual phrase, such as "and similar organizations," "other organization,"[149] "other entity,"[150] or "legally recognized entity"[151] to indicate that the list is not exhaustive. The list often includes companies, partnerships, and associations.[152] Sometimes language appears making explicit that entities that are within the definition include those that are operated for profit and those that are not,[153] but often this is left implicit. Some BITs state explicitly that such entities may include those that have limited liability as well as those that do not,[154] but again this is often only implicit. Language also sometimes appears stating explicitly that entities within the definition include those that are governmentally owned as well as those that are privately owned.[155] Where such language does not appear, the definition nevertheless may be phrased in terms broad enough to include implicitly both governmental and private entities. Some BITs, rather than listing the types of entities included, adopt a different approach. They use a generic term, such as "legal person" or "juridical person."[156] Still other BITs use the generic term, coupled with an illustrative list.[157]

The definition of companies in the BITs typically is broad and open-ended, much like the definition of investment. The arguments for such a definition are the same in the case of companies as they are in the case of investments. First, new forms of organizations are continually being created and an open ended definition ensures that the

---

147 *See Esphahanian v. Bank Tejarat*, 2 *Iran-US Claims Tribunal Reporter* 157 (1983).

148 2004 U.S. Model BIT, Art. 1.

149 *See, e.g.*, Switzerland-Algeria BIT, Art. 1(1).

150 *See, e.g.*, Lebanon-Chile BIT, Art. 1(1).

151 *See, e.g.*, Australia-India BIT, Art. 1(a).

152 *See, e.g.*, Italy-Nicaragua BIT, Art. 1(4); Austria-Armenia BIT, Art. 1(3); Finland-Armenia BIT, Art. 1(3)(b); Canada-Uruguay BIT, Art. 1(a).

153 *See, e.g.*, Germany-Timor-Leste BIT, Art. 1(3)(a).; Austria-Armenia BIT, Art. 1(3). Finland-Armenia BIT, Art. 1(3)(b); Australia-India BIT, Art. 1(a); Thailand-Argentina BIT, Art. 1(b); Canada-Uruguay BIT, Art. 1(a).

154 *See, e.g.*, Finland-Armenia BIT, Art. 1(3)(b); Australia-India BIT, Art. 1(a); Thailand-Argentina BIT, Art. 1(b).

155 *See, e.g.*, Italy-Nicaragua BIT, Art. 1(4); Austria-Armenia BIT, Art. 1(3); Australia-India BIT, Art. 1(a); Egypt-Zambia BIT, Art. 1(3)(B); Canada-Uruguay BIT, Art. 1(a); Japan-Vietnam BIT, Art. 1(1)(b).

156 *See, e.g.*, BLEU-Sudan BIT, Art. 1(1)(b); Germany-Timor-Leste BIT, Art. 1 (3)(b); Sweden-Kazakhstan BIT, Art. 1(2)(b) and (c); France-Uganda BIT, Art. 1(3); Cambodia-Vietnam BIT, Art. 1(2).

157 *See, e.g.*, Austria-Armenia BIT, Art. 1(1); Finland-Armenia BIT, Art. 1(3)(b); Denmark-Ethiopia BIT, Art. 1(3)(b); Chile-Indonesia BIT, Art. 1(1)(b); India-Indonesia BIT, Art. 2(b); Mexico-Iceland BIT, Art. 1(1)(b); Canada-Uruguay BIT, Art. 1(a).

BIT continues to protect investors regardless of the particular form of organizational structure they choose. Second, a broad definition demonstrates the host state's commitment to investment protection as a matter of principle. The exclusion of certain types of entities almost inevitably leads to arbitrary distinctions that are the antithesis of the principled investment climate that the BIT seeks to create. Where a host state excludes some entities from the definition, the inference is that the host is promising to protect certain investors as a matter of expediency rather than principle, which calls into question the genuineness and permanence of the host state's commitment to a favorable investment climate. A broad definition of companies also complements the broad definition of investment in that certain types of investments are more likely to be owned by certain types of investors. For example, investors whose investments provide professional services often operate in the form of a partnership. To exclude certain categories of entities from coverage as investors effectively would exclude the investments they establish from coverage as well.

The range of entities embraced within the term "company" or "investor" is important not only to defining the scope of treaty coverage, but in some cases the content of treaty coverage as well. For example, the national treatment provision guarantees to covered investment treatment no less favorable than that accorded to investment of nationals and companies of the host state. Thus, the term "company" limits the investments that serve as the comparators for purposes of establishing the content of the national treatment standard. For example, if the term "company" includes governmentally owned entities, then state enterprises are potential comparators for purposes of establishing the national treatment standard. If the term "company" excludes governmentally owned entities, then state enterprises would not be potential comparators and a host state may provide better treatment to state enterprises than to covered investments without violating the national treatment standard.

The BIT generally applies to an entity's investments in the territory of one party only if the entity has the nationality of the other party. Generally, three tests exist for ascribing corporate nationality. Virtually all BITs use one, or some combination,[158] of these three tests.

The most commonly used test is the place of incorporation. This test ascribes the nationality of the company to the state under the laws of which it is organized.[159] This test is the most easily administered because rarely will there be doubt about the place where a company is organized. In the event of a dispute, corporate nationality can be proven quickly. The place of incorporation test, however, also requires the least substantial link between an entity and its country of nationality. A company may claim

---

158 *See, e.g.*, Finland-Armenia BIT, Art.1(3)(b); Mexico-Iceland BIT, Art. 1(1)(b) Egypt-Zambia BIT, Art. 1(3)(B) (incorporation and "permanent residence"); Denmark-Ethiopia BIT, Art. 1(3)(b) (requiring economic activities as well as the seat and incorporation); Chile-Indonesia BIT, Art. 1(1)(b) (same); Lebanon-Chile BIT, Art. 1(1)(b) (same).

159 *See, e.g.*, United Kingdom-Bosnia-Herzegovina BIT, Art. 1(c); Cambodia-Vietnam BIT, Art. 1(2)(ii); Sweden-Kazakhstan BIT, Art. 1(2)(b) (used as an alternative to place of ownership test); Australia-India BIT, Art. 1(a) (used as an alternative to place of ownership test); Indonesia-India BIT, Art. 2(b); Canada-Uruguay BIT, Art, 1.

the nationality of a country and yet have no assets or employees in that country and its owners all may be nationals and residents of other countries. In a sense, the place of incorporation test is the most liberal of the three tests. Because of the ease of establishing corporate nationality, a country's embrace of this test reflects a commitment to investment protection as a matter of principle. Adoption of this test means that the host state is willing to confer protection on virtually any investor, as long as that investor establishes a modest link with the other BIT party. At the same time, the home country is willing to treat as its own investor a company that may have virtually no economic link to its territory.

An investor that has the nationality of one BIT party is entitled to protection only of investment in the territory of the other BIT party that it owns or controls. Many BITs do not explicitly refer to ownership or control, but may simply require that the investment be "of" an investor. These BITs nevertheless are universally understood to require ownership or control of the investment by the investor as a condition of protection.[160]

A few BITs define the term "control." The test to determine control may be qualitative or quantitative. A typical qualitative test defines control to mean the ability to exercise decisive influence over the management and operation of the investment.[161] A typical quantitative test defines control to mean ownership of a specified percentage of stock, such as at least 51 percent, or the ability to select a majority of the members of the board of directors.[162] A BIT may provide that control may be established through either of these tests.[163]

Some BITs state explicitly that ownership or control may be direct or indirect.[164] That is, the investment may be owned through one or more intermediary companies. Where such language does not appear explicitly, the principle that investment may be owned or controlled indirectly is usually presumed to be implicit.

Nothing in the BITs requires that ownership or control be ultimate. That is, if an investor of one BIT party owns or controls an investment in the territory of the other BIT party, the investment is covered investment, even if the investor is itself owned or controlled by another investor, who does not have the nationality of the first BIT party.

The fact that ownership or control may be direct or indirect, but need not be ultimate, yields two propositions: First, an investment does not lose its treaty protection by virtue of the nationality of intermediary companies in the chain of ownership. Second, an investment may gain treaty protection by virtue of the nationality of intermediary companies in the chain of ownership.[165]

---

160 A few BITs extended limited protection to all investment, regardless of the identity of the investor, and thus in these BITs the relationship between the investment and investor is irrelevant for some purposes. An example is certain U.S. BITs that prohibit certain performance requirements imposed on any investment. *See* Section 9.5.

161 *See, e.g.*, Australia-India BIT, Art. 1(h).

162 *See, e.g.*, Australia-India BIT, Art. 1(h).

163 *See, e.g.*, Australia-India BIT, Art. 1(h).

164 *See, e.g.*, United States-Argentina BIT, Art. I(1)(a); Austria-Armenia BIT, Art. I(2); Japan-Vietnam BIT, Art. I(2).

165 For a summary of the arbitral awards discussing these points, *see* Section 10.2.3.1.2.

Accordingly, an investor of a BIT party who owns investment in the territory of the other BIT party generally is entitled to protection under the BIT even if the investment is owned through multiple intermediary companies of different nationalities. The nationality of these intermediaries will not cause the investment to lose treaty protection. At the same time, any of these intermediaries, because it owns or controls the investment, may be treated as the investor and thus may claim the protection of a BIT between its state of nationality and the host state. The existence of ultimate owners or controllers of a different nationality does not divest the intermediary of BIT protection. In effect, if Company A owns Company B, which owns Company C, which owns the investment in State D and, if Companies A, B, and C are nationals of States A, B, and C, respectively, the investment in State D potentially is protected by any BIT between State D and States A, B, or C. That is, the investment potentially is protected by any of the three BITs. The insertion of Companies B and C into the chain of ownership did not divest the investment of protection under the BIT between State D and State A. Rather, it created protection for investment under the BITs between State D and State B and the BIT between State D and State C.

Thus, virtually any potential investor can obtain protection under any BIT that utilizes the place of incorporation test. Investors who wish to protect their investment in the territory of a BIT party need only incorporate a company in the territory of the other BIT party and vest ownership of its investment in this company. This company will be regarded under the BIT as an investor that is entitled to treaty protection of the investment that it owns. In the event that the host state wrongfully injures the investment, the company may submit a claim to investor-state arbitration on behalf of its investment. The beneficial owners of the investment, of course, will be the third-country investors who created the company, but that fact is irrelevant under the place of incorporation test.

A country that concludes a BIT using the place of incorporation test may have in effect a BIT with the entire world. Any investor anywhere can obtain treaty protection of its investment in that country's territory by placing ownership of the investment in a company organized under the laws of the other BIT party. Yet, that country's own investment abroad will not reciprocally be protected in every other country. That is, the country will be extending protection to investors in states that do not protect its own investment abroad. The country, of course, can remedy this situation in some cases by encouraging its own investors to take advantage of the place of incorporation test and to obtain protection for their investments abroad by incorporating subsidiaries in states that have BITs with the host states where those investments are located. In effect, the place of incorporation test allows all investors equally to take advantage of its liberality.

Many investors are well aware of this feature of the place of incorporation test. Thus, investors seeking BIT protection for their foreign investment do sometimes insert in the chain of ownership a company that is incorporated under the laws of a country that has a BIT in force with the host state (assuming that the BIT uses the place of incorporation test). In fact, the investor could insert into the chain of ownership multiple companies of different nationalities, each of which is incorporated under the laws of a different state that has a BIT in force with the host state. In the event that the host state wrongfully injures the investment, these investors can select the company in the chain of ownership that will submit a claim to investor-state arbitration on behalf of the investor and thereby choose the BIT that will apply to the dispute. The process of structuring investments so as to take advantage of the protection of a particular BIT has become known as "treaty shopping."[166]

The practice of "treaty shopping" sometimes has been criticized. Some tribunals have contemplated disregarding mere shell corporations inserted into the chain of ownership to obtain treaty protection, but the disputes that have arisen thus far typically have involved intermediary companies that are not mere shells.[167] In any event, the awards issued to date generally have not sought to deter treaty shopping.

The significance of the fact that an investment may be protected by more than one BIT to which the host state is a party is lessened by the existence of an MFN provision in most BITs. Under the MFN provision, an investment covered by one BIT concluded by the host state is entitled to the treatment accorded under any other BIT concluded by the host state. The MFN provision, in effect, generalizes treaty provisions and thereby eliminates substantive differences among BITs.[168] Each BIT concluded by a host state is as strong as all the other BITs concluded by that host state. Thus, the potential applicability of multiple BITs described above broadens the range of entities that can submit claims as an investor, but the substantive protections accorded under any of the BITs, as a result of the MFN treatment provisions in these BITs, should differ little. Exceptions are the provisions relating to the scope of the treaty and to dispute resolution, as opposed to substantive protections, which may not necessarily be generalized by the MFN provision.[169] Thus, the protection accorded by one BIT concluded by a host country may be superior in some respects to the protection accorded by another BIT, notwithstanding the MFN treatment provision..In any event, treaty shopping is often used not to obtain the protection of a different BIT than otherwise would apply, but simply to obtain the protection of a BIT for otherwise unprotected investment. In one sense, the place of incorporation test and the MFN treatment provision function complementarily to spread and harmonize BIT protections. One facilitates obtaining BIT protection while the other reduces the significance of obtaining the protection of one BIT as opposed to another.

The investors who may take advantage of the place of incorporation test to obtain BIT protection are not limited to those in the third states. Host-state investors potentially may take advantage of the test to obtain BIT protection for their investment in their own country. These investors may incorporate a company under the laws of the other BIT party and place ownership of their domestic investment in that company. In the event that their government wrongfully injures their investment, they can direct the

166 *See generally* Anthony C. Sinclair, "The Substance of Nationality Requirements in Investment Treaty Arbitration," 20 *ICSID Review—Foreign Investment Law Journal* 357 (2005).

167 *See* Section 10.2.3.1.2.

168 *See* Section 7.2.1.

169 *See* Section 7.2.3.

company of the other BIT party that owns the investment to submit a claim to investor-state arbitration against their own government for a violation of the BIT.[170]

To limit the practice of treaty shopping, some BITs that use the place of incorporation test include a denial of benefits clause.[171] Although the content of these clauses varies, this clause typically allows the host country to deny the benefits of the BIT to a company of the home country if third-country nationals own or control the company, unless the company conducts substantial business activities in the territory of the home country. An important variation of this clause authorizes the denial of benefits where the host country's nationals own or control the company, which limits the ability of domestic investors to obtain treaty protection against their own country merely by incorporating a company in the territory of the other BIT party and vesting ownership of their investment in that company. Some denial of benefits clauses also allow the denial of benefits to a company if it is owned or controlled by nationals of a third country with whom the host state does not have diplomatic or normal economic relations.[172] This variation obviously is not directed at treaty shopping in itself, but is a means of furthering certain foreign policy goals of the host state by denying treaty benefits to investors of certain specific states.

The denial of benefits clause does not entirely prevent treaty shopping. A third country investor may still insert a company into the chain of ownership in order to gain treaty protection, but the typical denial of benefits clause effectively requires as a condition of obtaining treaty protection that the company be not a mere shell, but that it have substantial business activities in the territory of its place of incorporation. Treaty shopping thus becomes somewhat more difficult, but is not precluded.

The second test for corporate nationality ascribes nationality to the state where the company has its seat, also known as the principal place of business or *siège social.*[173] This test obviously requires a stronger link between a company and its state of nationality than the place of incorporation test. The company must have its headquarters or perhaps its most important production facilities in the territory of that state. The test, however, may not be as easily applied as the place of incorporation test. In the case of a company with facilities in multiple countries, a dispute may arise as to which is its seat. Such an issue may arise, for example, in the case of a joint venture composed of companies of different nationalities.

The seat test is subject to the same kinds of treaty shopping as the place of incorporation test. Investors who wish to obtain treaty protection for investment in the territory of a BIT party may insert into the chain of ownership a company that has its seat in the territory of the other BIT party. Nothing requires that the company be a large one. The test merely requires that the seat of the corporation be in the state of its nationality. If the sole function of the company is to own the investment, then the seat may consist

---

170 *See* Section 4.2.3.4.

171 *See, e.g.*, United States-Argentina BIT, Art. I(2); Austria-Armenia BIT, Art. 10.

172 *See, e.g.*, United States-Argentina BIT, Art. I(2) (normal economic relations); United States-Uruguay BIT, Art. 17(1)(a).

173 *See, e.g.*, Germany-Timor-Leste BIT, Art. 1(3)(a); Switzerland-Algeria BIT, Art. 1(1); Thailand-Argentina BIT, Art. 1(b).

of little more than a small office. This may require more of an economic link than mere incorporation, but not always a great deal more.

The third test is the place of ownership or control test. This test is most commonly found in combination with one of the other two, rather than alone. It ascribes to a company the nationality of those who own or control the company.[174] This test also requires a more significant economic link between the company and its state of nationality than the place of incorporation test. The problem with the place of ownership test, however, is that it may not be easily administered. Where the stock of a company is publicly traded, determining the nationality of ownership or control may be difficult. Further, while the place of incorporation only rarely changes and the seat may change with only slightly more frequency, the place of ownership or control is potentially subject to frequent change, with little advance notice. An investment may lose or gain treaty protection numerous times during the term of a BIT as stock trades change the nationality of the principal investors. An investor may forfeit the ability to submit a claim to investor-state arbitration because it happened not to have the nationality of a BIT party at the time when nationality must be established to create tribunal jurisdiction.[175]

The place of ownership or control test, however, does prevent treaty shopping. If investors establish a company in which ownership of the investment will be vested, that company will have the same nationality as the investors because it is owned or controlled by them. If the investors already had the nationality required to gain BIT protection, then creating the intermediate company accomplishes nothing. If they do not have the requisite nationality, then again nothing is gained by creating yet another company with their nationality.

4.3.2 Origins

The first BIT, that concluded between Germany and Pakistan in 1959, used the terms "nationals" and "companies." The nationality of individuals was to be determined by the law of the state the nationality of which they claimed.[176] Thus, for example, a German national is a German within the meaning of German law. This established the universal practice in BITs.

The term "company" was broadly defined, in the case of German companies, to include "any juridical person, any commercial company or any other company or association, with or without legal personality . . . irrespective of whether the liability of its partners, associates or members is limited or unlimited and whether or not its activities are directed to pecuniary gain."[177] Thus, from the beginning the definition was not restricted to any particular legal form and included both for profit and nonprofit entities and entities with limited and unlimited liability. Interestingly, the breadth of the

174 *See, e.g.*, Netherlands-Ethiopia BIT, Art. 1(b)(iii); Switzerland-Algeria BIT, Art. 1(1)(c); Sweden-Kazakhstan BIT, Art. 1(2)(c); Australia-India, Art. 1(a)(ii).

175 *See* Section 10.2.3.1.5.

176 Germany-Pakistan BIT, Art. 8(3).

177 Germany-Pakistan BIT, Art. 8(4)(a).

term "company" with respect to Pakistan was not explicitly so broad. It was defined to mean "any juridical person or any company or association."[178]

The two parties chose different methods of ascribing nationality to companies. A company was a German company if it had its seat in Germany and lawfully existed in accordance with German law.[179] A company was a Pakistani company if it was incorporated in the territory of Pakistan and lawfully existed in accordance with Pakistani law.[180]

Kuwait became the second country to inaugurate a BIT program in the 1960s and to include a definition of these terms. Its 1964 BIT with Iraq defined "legal persons" for Kuwait to include any legal persons constituted under Kuwaiti law, as well as commercial firms in accordance with the Kuwaiti Commercial Companies Law.[181] Iraq also used the place of incorporation test, but specified that its definition applied regardless of whether the company had limited or unlimited liability.[182] The definition of "natural persons" followed the approach of the definition of "nationals" under the German BITs.[183]

Although Switzerland began its BIT program in 1961, it did not begin to define the terms "national" and "company" until 1965. With respect to individuals, the Swiss BITs followed the German practice.[184] In the Switzerland-Tanzania BIT, the term "company" in the case of Switzerland refers to companies, with or without legal personality, in which Swiss nationals own, directly or indirectly, a preponderant interest.[185] In the case of Tanzania, the term company refers to companies constituted under the laws of Tanzania.[186] In the Switzerland-Costa Rica BIT, concluded that same year, Switzerland adopted the place of incorporation test as an alternative to the place of ownership test. That is, a company could establish Swiss nationality under either test.[187] Costa Rica also adopted both tests.[188] Other Swiss BITs followed this approach,[189] but often the place of ownership test alone was used[190] and sometimes no definition appeared.[191]

The Netherlands launched its BIT program in 1963 and, like Switzerland, did not initially define the terms "national" and "company."[192] In 1968, in its BIT with

---

178 Germany-Pakistan BIT, Art. 8(4)(b).

179 *Id.*, Art. 8(4)(a).

180 *Id.*, Art. 8(4)(b).

181 *See* Kuwait-Iraq BIT, Art. 1(4)(b).

182 *Id.*, Art. 1(4)(a).

183 *Id.*, Art. 1(3).

184 Switzerland-Tanzania BIT, Art. 4(3).

185 Switzerland-Tanzania BIT, Art. 4(4)(a).

186 *Id.*, Art. 4(4)(b).

187 Switzerland-Costa Rica BIT, Art. 6(b)(1).

188 Switzerland-Costa Rica BIT, Art. 6(b)(2).

189 *See, e.g.*, Switzerland-Republic of Korea BIT, Art. 7(b)(1) (place of incorporation or place of ownership); Switzerland-Ecuador BIT, Art. 6(b).

190 *See, e.g.*, Switzerland-Uganda BIT, Art. 1(2)(b); Switzerland-Zaire BIT, Art. 1; Switzerland-Egypt BIT, Art. 1(2).

191 *See, e.g.*, Switzerland-Gabon BIT; Switzerland-Central African Republic BIT.

192 *See* Netherlands-Tunisia BIT.

Indonesia, the Netherlands adopted the place of incorporation test, although the term actually used was "nationals" rather than "companies" and the definition applied only to the taxation provisions of the treaty.[193] In 1970, in its BIT with Tanzania, the Netherlands applied the definition to the entire treaty.[194] The early Dutch BITs typically were not explicit about the kinds entities that fell within the definition, focusing principally on the ascription of nationality, but a 1970 BIT with Uganda did specify that the term "national" included "a company, partnership, association, society, or other body of persons, irrespective of whether the liability of its members is limited or unlimited and of whether or not its activities are directed to the making of profit."[195] The Dutch BITs continue to follow the early practice of using the place of incorporation test and the term "nationals."[196]

The Belgium-Luxembourg Economic Union (BLEU) inaugurated its BIT program in 1964 and, like Switzerland and the Netherlands, did not initially define the terms "national" or "company."[197] The BLEU adopted definitions in its 1974 BIT with Republic of Korea. The term "nationals" was defined as in other BITs.[198] The term "companies" was defined for the BLEU as "any juridical person as well as any commercial company" which had its seat in the territory of a party and was legally constituted under the laws of that party.[199] Republic of Korea applied the place of incorporation test, but required that Korean nationals have a substantial interest in the company.[200] The BLEU BITs continue to use the place of incorporation test combined with the seat test and define companies to include "any legal person."[201]

France similarly adopted definitions in 1974. The term "national" was defined as in other BITs.[202] A company had the nationality of a party if it was constituted under the laws of that party and had its seat in the territory of that party was well.[203] The following year, the France-Malaysia BIT added the requirement that the company, to be French, be controlled directly or indirectly by French nationals,[204] but this additional requirement did not consistently appear thereafter.[205]

Italy inaugurated its BIT program in 1964[206] and concluded five BITs in the 1960s, none of which defined the terms. When Italy revived its BIT program in the 1980s, the BITs included a definition that required an Italian company to have its seat and to be

193 Netherlands-Indonesia BIT, Art. 12.
194 Netherlands-Tanzania BIT, Art. XIII.
195 Netherlands-Uganda BIT, Art. XIV(a).
196 *See, e.g.*, Netherlands-Ethiopia BIT, Art. 1.
197 *See* BLEU-Tunisia BIT.
198 BLEU-Republic of Korea BIT, Art. 3(2)(a).
199 *Id.*, Art. 3(2)(b)(2).
200 *Id.*, Art. 3(2)(b)(2).
201 *See, e.g.*, BLEU-Sudan BIT, Art. 1(1).
202 *See, e.g.*, France-Egypt BIT, Art. 1(2).
203 *Id.*, Art. 1(3). *See also* France-Singapore BIT, Art. 1(3)(a) (same test for France; place of incorporation test for Singapore).
204 France-Malaysia BIT, Art. 1(2)(b).
205 *See, e.g.*, France-Romania BIT, Art. 2(2)(b); France-Malta BIT, Art. 1(3). France-Republic of Korea BIT, Art.2(2)(B)(a).
206 *See* Italy-Guinea BIT.

incorporated in Italy.[207] although Italy was not entirely consistent with respect to whether it required only that the company have its seat in Italy or whether it also required that the company be incorporated under Italian law. The term included within its scope "any legal entity" that met the nationality criterion. The definition of "national" adopted the approach common in other BITs.[208]

Sweden began its BIT program in the 1965, [209] but concluded only three BITs in the 1960s. These 1960s BITs did not define the terms "national" and "company." When Sweden concluded its fourth BIT, with Egypt in 1978, the BIT included definitions of those terms. With respect to Sweden, a company was any legal person with its seat in Sweden or with a predominating Swedish interest.[210] For Egypt, the definition was the same *mutatis mutandis*. The definition of national was the usual definition.[211] Since the 1990s, Sweden has used the place of incorporation test in lieu of the seat test.[212]

Denmark inaugurated its BIT program in 1965,[213] but concluded only four BITs before the program was suspended. When it was revived in 1980, the Danish BITs included a definition of investors under which Denmark used the place of incorporation test for its companies.[214]

When the United Kingdom concluded its first BIT, with Egypt in 1975, the BIT included a definition of national and company. The definition of national, as in other BITs, referred to the national law of the parties.[215] The definition of company adopted the place of incorporation test.[216] The definition with respect to the United Kingdom included "corporations, firms or associations."[217] That for Egypt applied to "any juridical person as well as any commercial, industrial or other company, association or organization with or without legal personality."[218] The U.K. BITs continue to use the place of incorporation test.[219]

When Austria concluded its first BIT, with Romania in 1976, it included a definition of company that required satisfaction of both the place of incorporation test and the seat test.[220] With respect to Austrian companies, the definition also specified that the term included juridical persons with limited or unlimited liability and operated for profit or not for profit. It also included state-operated economic enterprises.

The United States concluded its first BIT, with Egypt, in 1982. The U.S. BITs consistently used the place of incorporation test. The definition gave a broad scope to

---

207 *See, e.g.*, Italy-Egypt BIT, Art. VIII(4); Italy-Tunisia BIT, Art. 1(3)(b).

208 *See, e.g.*, Italy-Egypt BIT, Art. VIII(3).

209 *See* Sweden-Ivory Coast BIT.

210 Sweden-Egypt BIT, Art. 1(3)(a).

211 *Id.*, Art. 1(2).

212 *See, e.g.*, Sweden-Republic of Korea BIT, Art. 1(3)(b) (place of incorporation only); Sweden-Kazakhstan BIT, Art. 1(2) (place of incorporation or place of ownership).

213 *See* Denmark-Madagascar BIT.

214 *See* Denmark-Romania BIT, Art. 2(3)(b).

215 United Kingdom-Egypt BIT, Art. 1(c).

216 *Id.*, Art. 1(d).

217 *Id.*, Art. I(d)(i).

218 *Id.*, Art, 1(d)(ii).

219 *See* United Kingdom-Bosnia-Herzegovina BIT, Art. 1(d).

220 Austria-Romania BIT, Art. 1(3)-(4).

the term, specifying that it included any juridical entity regardless of whether the entity is organized for pecuniary gain, privately or governmentally owned, or organized with limited or unlimited liability.[221] They differed from other BITs typical of that period in that they included a denial of benefits clause. This clause permitted the parties to deny treaty protection to a company that was incorporated under the laws of a party, but that was owned or controlled by nationals of a third party and did not engage in substantial business activities in the territory of the host state.

A few minor innovations have appeared in BIT practice since the early 1980s. For example, a few BITs address the issue of dual nationality.[222] Some BITs also treat as a national of a state an individual who is domiciled or a long term resident of that state.[223]

As this survey indicates, the three principal tests of corporate nationality already were in use in the BIT by the early 1960s. The practice of using more than one test also was in place by the early 1960s as well. Most countries in the early years of BIT programs, however, did not appear to recognize the need to define the terms "national" and "company." Definitions of these terms became common only in the 1970s, although when definitions were adopted they generally followed patterns already established in the 1960s. Early BITs also were less likely to include detailed definitions indicating the kinds of entities included in the definition of company. This kind of definition has become more common since the 1980s.

4.3.3 Arbitral Practice

4.3.3.1 Ascribing Nationality to a Company BITs routinely include a test for ascribing nationality to a company that purports to be a covered investor. For purposes of determining whether a company is a covered investor, the BIT test rather than local law applies. For example, in *Bogdanov v. Moldova*, a case arising under the Russia-Moldova BIT, the sole arbitrator held that a local company was not a foreign investor because it did not fall within the definition of that term in the BIT, even though the company was a foreign investor with the meaning of local law.[224]

In *Micula v. Romania*, a case arising under the Sweden-Romania BIT, the tribunal questioned whether customary international law principles relating to nationality, such as the genuine link requirement of *Nottebohm*, apply to the BITs. The tribunal held that it should apply the nationality standard of the BIT, under which the Swedish nationality of an individual is determined by Swedish law.[225] The tribunal also noted that, in any

221 United States-Egypt BIT, Art. 1(1)(a).

222 *See, e.g.*, United States-Uruguay BIT, Art. 1.

223 *See, e.g.*, Australia-India BIT, Art. 1(d)(ii); Canada-Argentina BIT, Art. I(b).

224 Award, para. 2.2.1.

225 Decision on Jurisdiction, para. 101. On the continuing vitality of *Nottebohm*, see Campbell McLachlan, Laurence Shore, and Matthew Weiniger, *International Investment Arbitration: Substantive Principles* 134–135 (2007).

event, the claimants maintained certain links with Sweden and intended to retire there. Thus, the tribunal would treat them as Swedish nationals.

In *Rompetrol v. Romania*, a case arising under the Netherlands-Romania BIT, the tribunal agreed that international law did not preclude the BIT parties from prescribing the place and law of incorporation upon which they wished to rely to determine corporate nationality for purposes of the BIT.[226] Thus, a corporation incorporated in the Netherlands would be treated as a Dutch corporation, without regard to the nationality of those who controlled it, the location of its effective seat or the source of its capital.

In *ADC v. Hungary*, a case arising under the Cyprus-Hungary BIT, the tribunal observed that the BIT contained no "genuine link" requirement. A company incorporated under the laws of Cyprus and that paid taxes in Cyprus, that was audited by Cypriot auditors and that received payment in Cyprus could claim Cypriot nationality, notwithstanding that it was controlled and funded by Canadians.[227]

Where an investor seeks to submit a claim to ICSID arbitration, the investor must have the nationality of an ICSID member as well as the nationality of a BIT party. In *Tokios Tokeles v. Ukraine*, a case arising under the Lithuania-Ukraine BIT, the tribunal noted that the ICSID convention does not prescribe the method by which states shall ascribe nationality and that states are allowed the widest possible latitude in this regard, as long as the criteria used are reasonable. In that case, the test adopted was state of incorporation, which the tribunal noted was not only a reasonable test, but the most commonly used test. In *Aucoven v. Venezuela*, a case not involving a BIT, the tribunal held that under the ICSID convention the parties have the "greatest latitude" to define the term "nationality," provided that the criteria are reasonable and not totally inconsistent with the purposes of that convention.[228] In that case, the tribunal found that ascribing nationality based on majority ownership was reasonable.

Most BITs ascribe to a company the nationality of its state of incorporation, which, as has been noted, is a well-established basis for corporate nationality.[229] Where this is the test, the nationality of the investor is often easily proven and requires little discussion by the tribunal.[230]

In some cases, however, such as where the investor is owned by host state nationals, respondent states have argued that the investor's place of incorporation should be disregarded for purposes of ascribing nationality. These cases are discussed in Section 4.2.3.4.

Some BITS ascribe nationality to the state where the investor's seat is located. The 1987 ASEAN Agreement for the Promotion and Protection of Investment requires that both this test and the place of incorporation test be satisfied. Specifically, Article I(2) of the agreement defines a company as "a corporation, partnership or

---

226 Decision on Jurisdiction, paras. 92–93.

227 Award, paras. 353–359.

228 Decision on Jurisdiction, September 27, 2001, para. 97. *Accord Tokios Tokeles v. Ukraine* (Lithuania-Ukraine BIT), Decision on Jurisdiction, para. 25. *See also Enron v. Argentina* (United States-Argentina BIT), Decision on Jurisdiction, para. 42 (definition may not be "something absurd or entirely incompatible with its object and purpose").

229 *See Tokios Tokeles v. Ukraine* (Lithuania-Ukraine BIT).

230 *See. e.g., Plama v. Bulgaria* (Energy Charter Treaty); *ADF Group v. United States* (NAFTA); *Petrobart v. Kyrgyz Republic* (Energy Charter Treaty).

business association, incorporated or constituted under the laws in force in the territory of any Contracting Party wherein the place of effective management is situation." The meaning of the term "effective management" was at issue in *Yaung Chi Oo v. Myanmar*. In that case, one Madame Win Win Nu had incorporated a company in Singapore and established an office there, from which she managed the company. All parties agreed that at that time the place of effective management was in Singapore. Subsequently, she relocated to Myanmar, from which she continued to manage the company by sending directions to her youngest sister, who served as the company's resident director in Singapore. The company was engaged in the business of procuring supplies for its investment in Myanmar. The company's accounts were audited annually in Singapore, as required by local law. The tribunal began its analysis by noting that the purpose of the "effective management" requirement was to prevent treaty shopping, i.e., the incorporation of a shell company in the territory of a treaty party in order to obtain treaty protection. No one suggested that treaty shopping had occurred in this case. The tribunal then rejected Myanmar's argument that effective management had changed from Singapore to Myanmar. The tribunal held that there is a presumption that effective management, once established, is not readily lost, because the result is a loss of treaty protection. The company continued to have a resident director in Singapore, continued to engage in procurement operations there, and continued to meet other legal requirements of incorporation in Singapore. While meeting these legal requirements was not necessarily sufficient in itself to establish effective management, neither should such requirements be ignored. The tribunal noted that Madame Win Win Nu had relocated to Myanmar for the purpose of operating the investment, which had been contemplated by the joint venture agreement establishing the investment. Further, a small company investing in another ASEAN country may be required to make significant changes in management. Thus, to require her to remain in Singapore would have disfavored her company as a small investor. The ASEAN Agreement, however, was intended to protect investors of all sizes. The tribunal found, accordingly, that Singapore remained the place of effective management of the corporation.

BIT protection is not conditioned upon the host state's knowledge of the investor's identity or nationality. In *Waste Management v. Mexico*, a case arising under the NAFTA, the city of Acapulco entered into a concession agreement with a Mexican company to provide waste disposal services. When the U.S. investor that owned the Mexican company brought a claim, Mexico objected that it had been unaware that the investment was owned by that investor. The tribunal held that "it is no defense for the Respondent State to argue that it was not aware of the investor's identity or national character."[231] The tribunal noted, in any event, that the city was aware that U.S. interests were involved in the concession agreement.

Some BITs contain denial of benefits clause under which a party may deny the benefits of the treaty to a company that is incorporated under the laws of a party, but owned or controlled by nationals of a third country.[232] In *Plama v. Bulgaria*, a case arising under the Energy Charter Treaty, the tribunal held that the clause applies only

231 Award, para. 79.

232 *See* Section 4.3.1.

to the substantive provisions of the treaty. Were it to apply to the disputes provisions, a host country could use the clause to deny unilaterally the investor's right to investor-state arbitration, in effect allowing the host state to be the judge of its own cause.[233] The tribunal held, moreover, that the denial of benefits clause operates only prospectively. That is, the clause excludes an investor from treaty protection only after the host state exercises its right to deny benefits, generally by providing the investor with reasonable notice that the right has been exercised.[234] Any other interpretation would prevent the investor from making long-term plans in reliance upon treaty protection, a situation that the tribunal found to be inconsistent with the treaty's purpose.[235]

This reading of the denial of benefits clause is questionable. Host states are not necessarily in a position to know whether third country nationals own or control an investment. Further, the fact may be of no significance until a dispute arises and an investor suddenly claims the benefit of a treaty, at which point under the *Plama* analysis it is too late for the host state to investigate the facts and, if appropriate, invoke the denial of benefits clause. That is, unless the host state continually monitors the ownership of all investors potentially covered by a treaty, it may never be in a position to invoke the clause. A better approach is to put the investor on notice that if it chooses to structure its investment so that ownership or control is through a shell corporation, it is at risk of losing treaty protection through the denial of benefits clause. The investor is in a better position to know the true facts concerning ownership and control and to structure the investment so as to ensure treaty protection, where treaty protection legitimately is available.

Benefits generally may not be denied under a denial of benefits clause if the investor has substantial business activities in the state of nationality. In *Plama*, the claimant conceded that it did not have substantial business activities in Cyprus, its state of incorporation.

The tribunal in *Plama* also addressed the meaning of the terms "own" or "control" within the meaning of the denial of benefits clause of the Energy Charter Treaty. The tribunal opined that ownership includes indirect and beneficial ownership, while control includes control in fact, including an ability to exercise substantial influence over the entity's management and operation.[236] The tribunal, however, did not need to decide the issue of whether that test was met in the case before it.

In *LLC AMTO v. Ukraine*, another case arising under the Energy Charter Treaty, in applying the denial of benefits clause the tribunal examined who had ultimate control of the investor. The tribunal explained that "AMTO is incorporated in Latvia and wholly owned by Five Key Invest and Assets Limited Holding JSC, a company incorporated in Liechtenstein. This company is in turn wholly owned by the Foundation."[237] Although the foundation had no owners, the tribunal found that one of the beneficiaries

233 Decision on Jurisdiction, paras. 150–151.

234 Decision on Jurisdiction, paras. 155–157, 161.

235 Decision on Jurisdiction, paras. 161–165.

236 Decision on Jurisdiction, para. 170.

237 Award, para. 66.

of the foundation, a Russian national who also served as one of only two persons on the board of Five Key, was the person who controlled AMTO.[238]

In *Generation Ukraine v. Ukraine*, a case arising under the United States-Ukraine BIT, the tribunal noted that the respondent invoking the denial of benefits clause has the burden of proving third-country control. In that case, the claimant, which was incorporated under U.S. law, was 100 percent owned by a U.S. national.[239] The tribunal rejected the respondent's argument that Canadian control was demonstrated by the fact that the Canadian ambassador to Ukraine provided assistance to the claimant on one occasion, that a Canadian national served as president of the claimant for a time and rendered architectural services to the claimant, and that the claimant established an office in Toronto and a Canadian bank account.

A couple of awards have considered whether the investor's business activities in the state of nationality were substantial. In *Petrobart v. Kyrgyz Republic*, yet another case arising under the Energy Charter Treaty, the tribunal found that the investor had its principal office in the United Kingdom, the state of nationality, and that this office handled many of its strategic and administrative matters.[240] Thus, the test was met.

In *LLC AMTO v Ukraine*, the tribunal found that the word "substantial" in the denial of benefits clause meant "of substance, and not merely of form" rather than "large."[241] The tribunal found that the claimant had substantial business activities in Latvia based on the employment of two permanent staff members in Latvia and the conduct of investment-related activities from its rented office in Riga.

4.3.3.2 The Nationality of an Intermediary Corporation The question has arisen whether the nationality of the intermediary companies matters for purposes of determining whether the investor of the home country owns or controls an investment indirectly. In *Waste Management v. Mexico*, a case arising under the NAFTA, the claimant, a U.S. company, owned a Caymanian company, which owned a second Caymanian company, which owned the investment. When the U.S. claimant submitted a claim against Mexico under the NAFTA, the tribunal held that it had jurisdiction. It explained that the claimant had the requisite nationality and owned or controlled the investment, albeit through intermediaries. Nothing in the text of the NAFTA required the intermediaries to have the nationality of a NAFTA party.

In *Siag and Vecchi v. Egypt*, a case arising under the Italy-Egypt BIT, the claimants were Italian nationals who had made investments in Egypt. The tribunal held that its jurisdiction was not affected by the fact that the claimants "managed their investment through the medium of companies incorporated under Egyptian law. . . ."[242]

4.3.3.3 Ascribing Nationality to an Individual The nationality of individual investors has been at issue in only a few cases. In *Feldman v. Mexico*, a case arising

238 Award, para. 67.
239 Award, paras. 15.8–15.9.
240 Award, page 63.
241 Award, para. 69.
242 Decision on Jurisdiction, para. 207.

under the NAFTA, the tribunal confirmed that nationality refers to citizenship rather than residency. Thus, a U.S. citizen could institute arbitration against Mexico, notwithstanding that he was a resident of Mexico.

Only rarely is a claim dismissed because the claimant lacks the nationality of a BIT party. One such case is *Soufraki v. United Arab Emirates*, a case arising under the Italy-United Arab Emirates BIT. In that case, the claimant was born Italian, but unwittingly lost his Italian nationality by operation of Italian law when he relocated to Canada and acquired Canadian nationality. The claimant submitted to the tribunal several certificates of nationality issued by Italian officials, but the tribunal found no evidence that any of the officials had investigated the circumstances before issuing the certificates and the claimant admitted that he had not informed the officials of his loss of nationality, not believing that he had lost it. Thus, the certificates did not conclusively establish his Italian nationality. All parties agreed that the claimant could have reacquired his Italian nationality by residing in Italy for a year, but the tribunal found that he had not done so. Accordingly, the claimant was not a national of a BIT party and not entitled to submit a claim under the BIT.

More common is the problem of dual nationality, which was before the tribunal in *Champion Trading v. Egypt*, a case arising under the United States-Egypt BIT. The tribunal found that Article 25 of the ICSID convention precluded individuals who possessed both U.S. and Egyptian nationality from submitting a claim against Egypt to ICSID arbitration.[243] A company incorporated under U.S. law, however, would be regarded as a U.S. national in a claim against Egypt, notwithstanding that it was owned by individuals with dual U.S. and Egyptian nationality. This result is consistent with the language of that BIT, which employs the place of incorporation test.

In *Siag & Vecchi v. Egypt*, a case arising under the Italy-Egypt BIT, claimant Siag was born an Egyptian national, but later forfeited his Egyptian nationality after becoming a Lebanese national and then, as a result of marriage, an Italian national. Claimant Vecchi was born an Italian national, lost her Italian nationality when she married an Egyptian and became an Egyptian national, but then reacquired her Italian nationality upon the death of her husband. Egypt argued that both claimants had greater links with Egypt and that, in fact, neither claimant had a genuine or effective link to Italy. The tribunal held, however, that because neither claimant was a dual national, it need not determine whether claimants' "dominant and effective" nationality was that of Egypt or Italy. Both claimants were Italian nationals and therefore entitled to submit a claim. The tribunal also observed that, in any event, the ICSID convention "does not leave room for a test of dominant or effective nationality."[244]

In *Micula v. Romania*, a case arising under the Sweden-Romania BIT, the tribunal agreed that the ICSID convention leaves no room for the dominant and effective nationality test. The claimant must demonstrate only that it is a national of one party and not a national of another party against which it is asserting a claim. The fact that

243 Decision on Jurisdiction, para. 3.4.1.

244 Decision on Jurisdiction, para. 198.

the claimant may hold other nationalities is irrelevant for purposes of the ICSID convention.[245]

In *Olguin v. Paraguay*, a case arising under the Peru-Paraguay BIT, the tribunal held that the claimant could asset a claim as a Paraguayan national, notwithstanding that he also possessed U.S. nationality. Further, it was irrelevant that under Peruvian law that, for purposes of diplomatic protection, the place of residency was determinative of nationality for dual nationals because the purpose of the ICSID convention was to permit a claim to proceed without diplomatic protection.[246]

4.3.3.4 Ownership or Control of an Investment A few awards have addressed the issue of whether an investment was owned or controlled by a particular investor. The tribunal recognized in *Mondev v. United States*, a case arising under the NAFTA, that the phrase "owned or controlled" was adopted by the United States to circumvent the barriers to shareholder standing created by the *Barcelona Traction*[247] decision, which had held that diplomatic protection could be exercised on behalf of a corporation only by the state of incorporation, not by the state of the corporation's owners. Thus, the tribunal noted that NAFTA is not to be interpreted as consistent with *Barcelona Traction*.

The meaning of ownership and control as used in the NAFTA was addressed in *International Thunderbird v. Mexico*, another case arising under the NAFTA. The tribunal found that "control" means effective control or "de facto" control. In deciding whether International Thunderbird controlled the investment, the tribunal noted that Thunderbird had the ability to exercise a significant influence on decision making and that it was the consistent driving force behind the investment's business endeavors in Mexico. More specifically, the tribunal noted the interlocking key officers between Thunderbird and the investment and observed that the initial expenditures, know-how, and selection of suppliers were determined by Thunderbird.

The prevailing rule is that ownership or control may be indirect. The awards addressing this issue are discussed in Section 4.2.3.2.

In determining whether investment is owned or controlled by an investor, a tribunal may rely upon the fact that ownership or control may be indirect. For example, in *S.D. Myers v. Canada*, a case arising under the NAFTA, the claimant was S.D. Myers International, a U.S. company. The investment was Myers Canada, a separate Canadian company. S.D. Myers International did not own or control Myers Canada. Rather, the same family members owned or controlled both companies. Relying on treaty language to the effect that ownership or control may be "indirect," the tribunal held that S.D. Myers International could be considered an investor that owned or controlled an investment in Canada. The tribunal said that the choice of corporate form should not be a critical consideration and that it would look at the underlying economic reality,

---

245 Decision on Jurisdiction, para. 100.

246 Award, para. 62.

247 *Barcelona Traction, Light and Power Co. Ltd.* (Belgium v. Spain), 1970 I.C.J. Rep. 3. *Mondev* Award, para. 78.

which was that the same people who controlled S.D. Myers International also controlled Myers Canada.

4.4 THE TEMPORAL APPLICATION OF A BIT

In general, BITs apply only to events that occurred subsequent to their entry into force.[248] This merely reflects a rule of customary international law that has been codified in Article 28 of the Vienna Convention on the Law of Treaties. Accordingly, as indicated in Article 13 of the International Law Commission (ILC)'s Articles on Responsibility of States for Internationally Wrongful Act, the duties imposed by a BIT may be breached only by conduct that occurred subsequent to the BIT's entry into force. As a result, it sometimes is said that a BIT does not apply retroactively.

BITs often provide that they apply to investment established prior to their entry into force.[249] Where such language does not appear, the application of a BIT to investment existing at the time of its entry into force is presumed. In general, application of a BIT to investment existing when the agreement enters into force is not considered retroactive application.[250]

Although BIT obligations bind the parties only prospectively, that does not necessarily mean that a dispute that arose prior to a BIT's entry into force is outside the jurisdiction of an investor-state arbitral tribunal. In principle, two states could agree to create a tribunal to arbitrate previously existing claims. Indeed, as noted in Section 2.1, until the beginning of the twentieth century, states typically agreed to arbitrate only previously existing disputes. Nevertheless, as will be explained, tribunals typically hold that they do not have jurisdiction over disputes that arose prior to a BIT's entry into force.

Some BITs state explicitly that the provisions of the BIT are not applicable to claims or disputes arising out of events that occurred prior to the BIT's entry into force.[251] Even where such language does not appear, tribunals generally have refused to apply BIT obligations to conduct occurring before the treaty entered into force.[252]

For example, in *Mondev v United States*, a case arising under the NAFTA, the tribunal held that conduct prior to entry into force of NAFTA cannot violate that agreement. Under the NAFTA, a claim may be submitted to arbitration only if it alleges a breach

248 For a discussion of the temporal scope of BITs, *see* Nick Gallus, *The Temporal Scope of Investment Protection Treaties* (2008).

249 *See* Section 4.2.1.

250 *See Yaun Chi Oo v. Myanmar* (applying the 1998 Framework Agreement on the ASEAN Investment Area).

251 *See, e.g.*, Netherlands-Ethiopia BIT, Art. 10; Denmark-Ethiopia, Art. 12; Thailand-Argentina BIT, Art. 2(2); Cambodia-Vietnam BIT, Art. X; Chile-Indonesia BIT, Art. II(3); Sweden-Kazakhstan BIT, Art. 10(1); Finland-Armenia BIT, Art. 13(1); Egypt-Zambia BIT, Art.10; Chile-Lebanon BIT, Art. II.

252 *See, e.g.*, *MCI Power v. Ecuador* (United States-Ecuador BIT), Award, paras. 186–190; *Kardassopoulos v. Georgia* (Greece-Georgia BIT), Decision on Jurisdiction, para. 255.

of the NAFTA.[253] Thus, a claim may be submitted to investor-state arbitration only if the breach occurred after the NAFTA entered into force. This rule applies even where some facts critical to the claim occurred before the BIT entered into force. The tribunal in *Tecmed v. Mexico*, a case arising under the Spain-Mexico BIT, elaborated upon this rule by noting that a tribunal may consider events that occurred prior to entry into force of the agreement as aggravating or mitigating factors.[254]

The holding in *Mondev* is widely accepted.[255] In *Mondev*, the claimant alleged a denial of justice in state court proceedings that occurred after the NAFTA entered into force and thus the claim was properly before the tribunal, even though the dispute that gave rise to the state court litigation arose before the NAFTA entered into force.

In some cases, the claim may not be based on a breach that occurred at a single moment in time, but rather a continuous course of conduct. This situation occurred in *Feldman v. Mexico*, another case arising under the NAFTA. The tribunal noted that it had no jurisdiction over acts committed prior to the date when the NAFTA entered into force, although a continuous course of conduct that began before entry into force and that continued after entry into force could become a breach as of the date of entry into force.[256]

Some claimants have argued that an unremedied wrong constitutes a continuous wrong. For example, in *Mondev*, the claimant argued that an uncompensated expropriation was a continuous wrong. Thus, where investment was expropriated prior to the entry into force of the BIT, but compensation had not been paid as of the date of entry into force, the continuing failure to pay compensation was a continuous wrong that could give rise to a claim under the BIT. The tribunal relied upon the ILC's Articles on the Responsibility of States for Internationally Wrongful Acts in assessing the effect of a continuous course of conduct that began before entry into force of the agreement and continued afterward.[257] Applying these rules, the tribunal rejected the claimant's argument and held that the NAFTA did not effect a "remedial resurrection" of a claim of expropriation contrary to customary international law, where that claim arose before the NAFTA entered into force.

In *MCI Power v. Ecuador*, a case arising under the United States-Ecuador BIT, the tribunal applied customary international law, which it found to be codified in Articles 13, 14, and 15 of the ILC's Articles on the Responsibility of States for Internationally

253 NAFTA, Arts. 1116–1117; *Tradex Hellas v. Albania* (Greece-Albania BIT), Decision on Jurisdiction, para. 44.

254 Award, para. 68.

255 *Generation Ukraine v. Ukraine* (United States-Ukraine BIT), Award, para. 11.2 (not citing *Mondev*); *PSEG v. Turkey* (United States-Turkey BIT), Decision on Jurisdiction, para. 186 (citing *Mondev*); *SGS v. Philippines* (Switzerland-Philippines BIT), Decision on Jurisdiction, para. 166 (citing *Mondev*); *Tecmed v. Mexico* (Spain-Mexico BIT), Award, paras.66–68 (citing *Mondev*); *Chevron v. Ecuador* (United States-Ecuador BIT), Interim Award, para. 282 (citing *Mondev*); *Société Générale v. Dominican Republic* (France-Dominican Republic BIT), Decision on Jurisdiction, para. 87 (citing *Mondev*); *African Holding v. D.R. Congo* (United States-D.R. Congo BIT), Decision on Jurisdiction.

256 Decision on Jurisdiction, para. 62. *See also Société Générale v. Dominican Republic* (France-Dominican Republic BIT), Decision on Jurisdiction, para. 94.

257 Award, para. 58.

Wrongful Acts. The result was that claims based on contract disputes that arose prior to the BIT's entry into force were outside the tribunal's jurisdiction.

In *Chevron v. Ecuador*, a case arising under the United States-Ecuador BIT, the tribunal found that, distinct from disputes relating to contract breaches that occurred prior to entry into force of the BIT, the claimants were asserting claims for denial of justice arising out of the manner in which the local courts addressed those contract breaches. These denial of justice claims arose after the BIT entered into force.[258] Further, because the denial of justice claims involved lengthy continuing delays, the claims rested on an allegation of continuing conduct, such as was discussed in *Feldman*.[259] Like the tribunal in *MCI*, the tribunal in *Chevron* relied extensively on the ILC articles to determine when the breach occurred.

Many BITs, however, do not limit the jurisdiction of investor-state arbitral tribunals to claims alleging a violation of the BIT. Rather, the more common practice is to confer jurisdiction over any dispute concerning an investment.[260] Thus, in these cases, tribunals often have considered the relevant date to be not the date on which a breach of the BIT occurred, but rather the date on which the dispute arose.

For example, in *Maffezini v. Spain*, Article II(2) of the Argentina-Spain BIT provided that the "agreement shall not apply to disputes or claims originating before its entry into force." This language necessitated an inquiry into the meaning of the word "dispute."[261] The tribunal found that while the parties had disagreed as early as 1989, the disagreement did not become a dispute until 1994, the same year that the BIT entered into force. Accordingly, the claim was within the tribunal's jurisdiction.

In *Helnan v. Egypt*, the Denmark-Egypt BIT provided that it was not applicable to "divergences or disputes" that arose prior to its entry into force. The tribunal concluded that the words "divergences" and "disputes" should be given different meanings, inasmuch as the latter implies a greater degree of animosity than the former and in light of the presumption in favor of giving every word of a treaty independent effect. The tribunal found that a divergence exists when parties are mutually aware of their disagreement and that a divergence "crystallizes" as a dispute when a party decides to resolve it.[262] In that case, the claimant was awarded a contract to manage a state-owned hotel. After the hotel was inspected and its quality rating lowered, the government terminated the contract with the claimant. The tribunal found that divergences existed between the parties dating back to 1993, prior to the entry into force of the BIT in 2000. The tribunal found, however, that the divergences changed in 2002, when the contract was amended in connection with a privatization process. These divergences, which were related to the privatization process, became the dispute before the tribunal. Because both the relevant divergences and the dispute arose after the treaty entered into force, the tribunal had jurisdiction over the claim.

---

258 Interim Award, para. 270.

259 Interim Award, para. 298.

260 *See* Section 10.2.1.

261 For a discussion of the meaning of the word "dispute," *see* Section 10.2.3.1.4.

262 Decision on Jurisdiction, para. 52.

In *Empresas Lucchetti v. Peru*, Article 2 of the Chile-Peru BIT provided that the BIT shall not "apply to differences or disputes that arose prior to its entry into force." In that case, prior to the entry into force of the BIT, the claimant had challenged in local courts an environmental decree that affected the operation of its pasta factory, which was located near an environmental reserve. After the BIT's entry into force, additional decrees established an environmental regulatory framework and revoked the claimant's operating license. The government justified the new decrees as part of its continuing effort to ensure that the claimant's factory operated in an environmentally sound manner and alleged that the claimant's successful local court action had been the result of corruption. The tribunal held that the later decrees merely continued a dispute that existed prior to the treaty's entry into force.[263] Because the dispute arose prior to the BIT's entry into force, the tribunal had no jurisdiction over the claim.

In *Jan de Nul v. Egypt*, Article 12 of the 2002 BLEU-Egypt BIT provided that the BIT shall "not be applicable to disputes having arisen prior to its entry into force." The claimants had been awarded a contract to dredge the Suez Canal. After disputes arose concerning the contract, the claimants brought claims in local courts. While the disputes were pending, the BIT entered into force. When the local court issued a decision that was adverse to the claimants in certain respects, the claimants submitted a claim to investor-state arbitration. The tribunal held that the dispute submitted to local courts was based on allegations of breach of contract and thus was a different dispute than that submitted to arbitration, which was based on allegations of BIT violations.[264] The dispute before the tribunal arose only after the local court rendered its judgment.[265] The tribunal distinguished the award in *Lucchetti*. It explained that *Lucchetti* involved repeated efforts by a municipality to protect an environmental reserve and these efforts by the municipality could be regarded as part of a single, continuing dispute, while in the case before it the action of the local courts constituted the intervention of a new actor, which gave rise to a new dispute.[266]

4.5 EXCEPTIONS

An exception in one sense can be the most important provision of a BIT because it has the potential to render a practical nullity any other provision of the BIT. A measure that falls within an exception may be lawful, notwithstanding its inconsistency with every other provision of the BIT. Whereas treaty interpretation normally requires that provisions be read harmoniously and to give effect to each, exceptions may be read so as to give no effect to other provisions of the BIT, to the extent of the exception. Exceptions, like all BIT provisions, must be interpreted in light of the object and purpose of the BIT, but they may define an area within which the other operative provisions of the BIT create no rights or duties.

263 Award, para. 53.
264 Decision on Jurisdiction, para. 117.
265 Decision on Jurisdiction, para. 121.
266 Decision on Jurisdiction, para. 123.

For this reason, clarity with respect to the content of an exception is especially desirable. Uncertainty about the scope of a single exception creates uncertainty about the scope of every other provision to which the exception applies.

Yet, exceptions in some cases actually may serve to strengthen the operative provisions of the BIT. States often face circumstances that offer perhaps compelling reasons to derogate from BIT obligations. For example, low levels of foreign exchange reserves may tempt a state to disregard its obligations under the transfers provision. States rarely concede that they are in violation of treaty obligations and thus a state is likely to offer an interpretation of the obligation that would render the state's conduct consistent with its BIT obligations. Typically, the interpretation will be one that narrows the factual situation to which the provision applies or the nature of the right or duty created by the provision. This interpretation establishes a precedent that may tend to erode the strength of the obligation in other circumstances. An exception might have allowed the state to take the same action, while leaving the obligation fully intact, apart from the carefully drawn exception. That is, an exception creates an area in which the state may operate unrestrained by BIT obligations, but leaves the obligations fully in effect where the exception does not apply. Exceptions thus may tend to further BIT principles of security and transparency by informing potential investors that the state regards certain types of conduct to be outside BIT obligations, which is preferable to *ad hoc* narrowing interpretations adopted after the investment has been established. An exception also can be crafted to preserve other BIT principles. For example, an exception may allow a state to derogate from some obligation of security, but require that any derogation be on a nondiscriminatory basis and notified to the other party, thus preserving principles of nondiscrimination and transparency. Similarly, an exception to a nondiscrimination obligation may require that any such exception apply only to investments not already established, thereby preserving the principle of security.

Exceptions thus may serve to vitiate BIT principles, but also may serve to preserve them. An investor clearly would prefer that a BIT include no exceptions. Certainly, a large number of exceptions or even one very broad exception may undermine much or all of the benefit that otherwise would have been gained from concluding a BIT. Yet, BITs are instruments that reflect compromises among competing policies and in some cases a host state's policy choices compel it to limit the scope of application of BIT principles. Where such is the case, a carefully crafted exception that preserves adherence to at least some BIT principles may be preferable to tempting the state to adopt a corrosive, narrowing interpretation of BIT obligations.

This section considers the two most common exceptions: that for protection of a party's essential security interests and that for measures relating to taxation.

4.5.1 The Essential Security Interests Exception

Some BITs include an exception for measures necessary to preserve a party's essential security interests.[267] Such provisions may contain limitations, such that any measures

267 *See, e.g.*, Finland-Armenia BIT, Art. 14(1); Australia-India BIT, Art. 15; India-Indonesia BIT, Art. 12(2); United States-Argentina BIT, Art. XI.

be reasonable and nondiscriminatory[268] or that the exception shall not apply to the expropriation or war and civil disturbance provisions.[269]

Such an exception appeared in the GATT,[270] although with language that made clear that each party is the judge of which measures are necessary to preserve such interests. Specifically, the GATT language provides that a party may take "any action which [the party] considers necessary for the protection of its essential security interests."[271] This language is sometimes described as "self-judging" because each state judges for itself whether a measure is within the exception. The United States included an essential security interests exception in its post-war FCNs, although without the self-judging language. It also included the exception in its BITs, although the self-judging language has been included in only a small number of the U.S. BITs.[272] Even where the self-judging language appears, the invocation of the exception should be subject to an obligation of good faith.[273]

In the *Case Concerning Military and Paramilitary Activities In and Against Nicaragua* (Nicaragua v. United States),[274] Nicaragua brought a claim in the International Court of Justice against the United States, alleging that U.S. support for paramilitary forces, known as the *contras*, who were seeking to overthrow the Nicaraguan government violated the post-war FCN between the United States and Nicaragua. The United States argued that its support for the *contras* was necessary to protect its essential security interests and therefore not a violation of the FCN. The United States argued, further, that the essential security interests exception of the FCN is "self-judging," by which it meant that a party's invocation of that exception is conclusive upon any tribunal and renders nonjusticiable any claim with respect to which the exception has been invoked. Accordingly, the United States contended, the court was without jurisdiction to adjudicate Nicaragua's claim. The court, however, in its Judgment on the Merits, dated June 27, 1986, rejected this position. In reaching its decision, the court relied in particular on the difference between the GATT provision, which expressly declares itself to be self-judging, and the FCN language, which does not. Even Justice Stephen Schwebel, the American member of the court, concluded that the court had jurisdiction to interpret the meaning of "essential security interests" for the purpose at least of determining if it had jurisdiction to adjudicate the merits. The court affirmed its *Nicaragua* holding in the *Case Concerning Oil Platforms*,[275] submitted by Iran against the United States on November 2, 1992, under the post-war FCN between those two countries. In that case, the United States did not argue that the essential security interests exception was self-judging, but only that it granted to each

268 *See, e.g.*, Australia-India BIT, Art. 15; India-Indonesia BIT, Art. 12(2).

269 *See, e.g.*, Finland-Armenia BIT, Art. 14(1).

270 General Agreement on Tariffs and Trade, Art. XX(b), T.I.A.S. No. 1700, 55 U.N.T.S. 188.

271 *Id.* Art. XXI(b).

272 *See* Kenneth J. Vandevelde, *U.S. International Investment Agreements* 206–216.(2009).

273 *See* Kenneth J. Vandevelde, "Of Politics and Markets: The Shifting Ideology of the BITs," 11 *International Tax and Business Lawyer* 159 (1993).

274 1984 I.C.J. Rep. 392.

275 (Iran v. United States), 2003 I.C.J. Rep. 161.

party wide discretion to determine, according to its own best judgment of the circumstances, the measures necessary to protect such interests.

One issue that has arisen is the relationship between the essential security interests exception and the plea of necessity codified in Article 25 of the ILC's Articles on Responsibility of States for Internationally Wrongful Acts. Under Article 25, necessity may not be invoked by a state as a ground for precluding the wrongfulness of an act not in conformity with an international obligation of that state unless the act (1) is the only way for the state to safeguard an essential security interest against a grave and imminent peril and (2) does not seriously impair an essential interest of the state or states toward which the obligation exists or of the international community as a whole. Further, necessity may not be invoked in any case if the international obligation excludes the possibility of invoking necessity or the state has contributed to the situation of necessity. Under Article 27, a plea of necessity is without prejudice to the question of compensation owed for any material loss caused by the act.

The essential security interests exception generally is a limitation on the scope of the obligations in the BIT. That is, host state conduct that falls within the essential security interests exception does not violate the BIT. Such conduct is not wrongful and does not result in liability for compensation. The plea of necessity, by contrast, is raised with respect to host state conduct that is otherwise wrongful, i.e., that is not authorized by the essential security interests exception. As noted by the official commentary to the ILC articles, the plea of necessity "arises where there is an irreconcilable conflict between an essential interest on the one hand and an obligation of the state invoking necessity on the other."[276] The essential security interests exception, however, does not arise in the case of an irreconcilable conflict. Where the exception applies, by the express terms of the treaty it prevails over the obligations of the BIT. Further, as Article 27 indicates, the plea of necessity, in contrast to the essential security interests exception, does not necessarily excuse the host state's obligation to pay compensation. As will be seen, tribunals have not always recognized the difference between the treaty exception for essential security interests and the customary international legal doctrine of necessity.

The essential security interests exception has been invoked by Argentina in a number of cases arising under the United States-Argentina BIT and involving measures taken by Argentina to address an economic crisis that occurred in 2001 and 2002. Awards have been rendered thus far in five of these cases.

In *CMS Gas Transmission Company v. Argentina*, the tribunal began its discussion of this provision by considering whether Argentina could justify its conduct under the customary international law plea of necessity, codified in Article 25 of the ILC's articles on state responsibility. The tribunal concluded that Argentina's circumstances were not sufficient to impair an essential interest of the state and therefore the customary law plea of necessity was inapplicable.[277]

---

276 Commentary on International Law Commission's Articles on Responsibility of States for Internationally Wrongful Acts, Article 25, para. 2.

277 On the state of necessity generally, *see* Andrea K. Bjorklund, "Emergency Exceptions: State of Necessity and *Force Majeure,*" in *The Oxford Handbook of International Investment Law*

The tribunal next turned to the essential security interests exception of the BIT. It held that the essential security interests exception is not self-judging, reasoning that, where states wish to create a unilateral right to determine the legitimacy of extraordinary measures, states do so explicitly, as in the case of the GATT and in some U.S. BITs, such as that with Russia. In support of this view, the tribunal cited the decisions of the International Court of Justice in the *Nicaragua* and *Oil Platforms* cases, where the court found a similarly worded exception in the Nicaragua and Iran FCNs not to be self-judging, as well as the court's decision in the *Case Concerning the Gabcikovo-Nagymaros Project*,[278] where the court observed that the plea of necessity under customary law is subject to judicial review. Accordingly, the tribunal's review of Argentina's invocation of the exception was not limited merely to whether the exception was invoked in good faith. The tribunal also found that the essential security interests exception could apply to a major economic crisis. With these comments, the tribunal concluded its discussion of the exception, apparently believing that if the circumstances did not warrant application of the customary international law plea of necessity, *ipso facto* they did not justify application of the essential security interests exception. The tribunal observed that, even if the plea of necessity had been accepted, the plea would excuse only conduct occurring while the necessity existed and that the obligation to comply with treaty requirements would resume when the necessity ended.

Finally, the tribunal held that article 27 of the ILC articles stated the customary law applicable to the exception. That is, the tribunal held that, even if the plea of necessity were applicable, the host state nevertheless would be required to pay compensation for injury to the claimant. Otherwise, the cost of the necessity would be paid by the claimant rather than by the state.

The ad hoc committee on the application for annulment of the *CMS* award found that the tribunal had erred in its treatment of the relationship between the essential security interests exception and Article 25 of the ILC articles. The committee noted that the effect of the essential security interests exception, where it applies, is that host-state conduct does not breach the BIT. In such a case, Article 25 has no application. Where the essential security interests exception does not apply, then host state conduct may violate the BIT, in which case the tribunal must consider whether Article 25 may be invoked to preclude state responsibility for its conduct. Nevertheless, the ad hoc committee noted, it did not function as a court of appeal and an error of law was not a sufficient basis on which to annul the award.

In *LG&E v. Argentina*, the tribunal found that the United States did not adopt the self-judging interpretation of the essential security interests exception until June 1992, when it signed the Russia BIT and issued a July 1992 description of its 1992 model negotiating text as self-judging. Argentina had argued that both the United States and

---

(Peter Muchlinski, Frederico Ortino, and Christoph Schreuer, eds., 2008). On state of necessity in the *CMS* case and in *LG&E*, discussed below, *see* August Reinisch, "Necessity in International Investment Arbitration—An Unnecessary Split of Opinions in Recent ICSID Cases?" 8 *Journal of World Investment and Trade* 191 (2007).

278 (Hungary v. Slovakia), 1997 I.C.J. Rep. 7.

Argentina intended the exception to be self-judging, although it did not argue, as the United States had in *Nicaragua*, that its invocation of the exception rendered the dispute nonjusticiable. Rather, Argentina argued that its invocation of the exception was subject to a good faith limitation. The tribunal observed that, even if it were to determine that the exception was self-judging, the exception would be subject, as Argentina contended, to a good faith exception. The tribunal went on to say that its application of the exception as a non-self-judging provision would not differ significantly from its application of the exception as a self-judging provision, subject to an obligation of good faith.

Turning to the application of the standard, the tribunal found that between December 1, 2001, and April 26, 2003, Argentina was in a period of crisis during which it was necessary to enact measures to maintain public order and protect its essential security interests. The tribunal observed that this period was not one merely of economic problems or business cycle fluctuations, but of an extremely severe crisis in the economic, political, and social sectors that threatened the total collapse of the government and the Argentine state.

In finding the exception to apply to some of the measures taken by Argentina, the tribunal rejected the claim that the essential security interests exception applies only to military action and war and found that a severe economic crisis could threaten an essential security interest. The tribunal observed that, "[w]hen a State's economic foundation is under siege, the severity of the problem can equal that of any military invasion."[279]

Although the claimants had argued that Argentina's measures were not justified because they were not the only way to respond to the crisis, the tribunal found them to be a "necessary and legitimate measure" on the part of the Argentine government, noting that time was of the essence and that the measures taken by Argentina were taken "across-the-board" in a setting in which it was not possible to make individual assessments.[280]

The tribunal then alluded to the war and civil disturbance provision of the BIT and, noting that it applied to a state of national emergency, concluded that the parties contemplated that state of emergency was a separate category of exceptional circumstances that could be invoked to excuse measures otherwise inconsistent with the treaty.[281] Reiterating that the text of the essential security interests exception was applicable and excused Argentina's measures, the tribunal went on to explain that these same measures could be excused under the customary international law state of necessity doctrine, codified in Article 25 of the ILC articles.

In *Enron v. Argentina*, the tribunal began its analysis by considering the applicability of Article 25 of the ILC articles. According to the tribunal, Article 25 excuses noncompliance with an obligation if it is the only way to safeguard an essential interest against a grave and imminent peril. The tribunal found that, while Argentina was in a

279 Award, para. 238.

280 *Id.* at para. 241.

281 The war and civil disturbance provision, of course, only imposes obligations on the host state. It has no relevance to the issue of whether the essential security interests exception applies or to the scope of that exception.

severe crisis, the existence of the state was not threatened and, therefore, the peril was not sufficient. The tribunal also found that the measures adopted were not the only way to protect the state's interest. Further, under Article 25, the state is excused only if it did not contribute to the peril, but in this case Argentina had played a role in causing the crisis. For all these reasons, Article 25 did not excuse Argentina's compliance with its BIT obligations.

Turning to the essential security interests exception, the tribunal held that the exception must be restrictively applied to economic situations, lest the BIT's purpose of providing stability be defeated. The tribunal, as had the tribunals in *CMS* and *LG&E*, found that the essential security interests exception of the United States-Argentina BIT is not self-judging, noting again the holdings of the International Court of Justice in the *Nicaragua, Oil Platforms*, and *Gabcikovo-Nagymaros* cases. The unilateral claim of the United States that the exception is self-judging was not sufficient to establish the self-judging nature of the exception. The claim by the United States and Argentina today that the provision is self-judging also was insufficient to establish that the parties so intended in 1991 when the treaty was concluded.

The tribunal next considered whether the essential security interests exception applied to Argentina's conduct. Finding the terms of the exception undefined by the treaty, the tribunal looked to the similar language of Article 25 of the ILC articles for guidance. Having concluded that Article 25 was not satisfied, the tribunal held that the essential security interests exception, accordingly, was not satisfied either. The tribunal concluded by noting, in *obiter dictum*, that even had the exception applied, Article 27 of the ILC articles may require that compensation be paid.

In *Sempra Energy v. Argentina*, the tribunal considered first whether the wrongfulness of Argentina's conduct was precluded by the defense of necessity under customary international law, which the tribunal found had been codified in Article 25 of the ILC articles. On the evidence, the tribunal was unpersuaded that the defense was available. It did not believe that the existence or independence of the state was threatened by the economic circumstances or that the measures adopted were the "only way" to safeguard its essential interests. Further, the state had contributed to the situation.

Turning to the essential security interests exception, the tribunal observed that, while the exception could apply to economic emergencies, the object and purpose of the United States-Argentina BIT was to apply during times of economic difficulty and thus "any interpretation resulting in an escape route from the defined obligations cannot be easily reconciled with that object and purpose."[282] For that reason, the tribunal held that the exception should be interpreted restrictively. Like the first three tribunals, it rejected Argentina's argument that the exception is self-judging, holding in light of the *Nicaragua* and *Oil Platforms* judgments that express language is necessary for an exception to be self-judging and noting that to interpret the exception as self-judging would deprive the BIT of any "substantive meaning."[283] Because the BIT did

---

282 Award, para. 373.

283 *Id.* at para. 374. *See* Kenneth J. Vandevelde, "Of Politics and Markets: The Shifting Ideology of the BITs," 11 *International Tax and Business Lawyer* (now *Berkeley Journal of International Law*) 159 (1993).

not define the term "essential security interests," the tribunal referred to Article 25 of the ILC articles for guidance as to the meaning of that term and as to the meaning of the concept of necessity. Having found that Argentina's economic crisis did not meet the requirements of Article 25, the tribunal concluded that, for the same reasons, the essential security interests exception did not justify the measures taken by Argentina.

In *Continental Casualty v. Argentina*, the tribunal agreed that essential security interests could include economic security.[284] The application of the exception did not require the total collapse of the country. Rather, the severity of the economic emergency in Argentina was sufficient for Argentina to rely upon the exception. The tribunal also agreed that the essential security interests exception was not self-judging, noting the ICJ's rejection of that interpretation on two occasions, the inconclusive evidence of whether the United States had conveyed to Argentina its view that the exception was self-judging or that Argentina had accepted such an interpretation, and the fact that to interpret the exception as self-judging would conflict with the principle of compulsory arbitration embraced in the BIT.[285] Looking to GATT jurisprudence for guidance,[286] the tribunal found that the word "necessary" did not mean "indispensable" or "inevitable." Rather, necessity should be determined by assessing the relative importance of interests further by the challenged measures, the contribution of the measure to promoting these interests, and the restrictive impact of the measure.[287] A measure, however, would not be considered necessary if an alternative less inconsistent with the BIT was available.[288] The tribunal reviewed the various measures undertaken by Argentina and found most, but not all, of them to be necessary. The tribunal acknowledged that a measure might not qualify as necessary if the host state had contributed to the circumstances that endangered its essential security interests, because a different policy would have avoided the danger and thereby avoided the necessity to adopt the measure. The tribunal observed that a country might be said always to be responsible ultimately for its economic policy, but legal responsibility was measured by a different standard. In this case, Argentina's policies had been praised by international observers for many years and the tribunal did not believe that it should impose liability on Argentina for adopting policies that, at the time, were widely regarded by qualified observers as sound policies.[289]

The essential security interests exception of the United States-D.R. Congo BIT was discussed by the annulment committee in *Patrick Mitchell v. D.R. Congo.* The committee noted there that application of the exception does not necessarily preclude an obligation to pay compensation, although the D. R. Congo had not raised the exception as a defense in the arbitration and thus that exception could not be considered as a basis

284 Award, para. 175.

285 Award, para. 187.

286 *See generally* Frederico Ortino, "The principle of non-discrimination and its exception in GATS: Selected Legal Issues," April 2006, available at http://www.ssrn.com.

287 Award, para. 194.

288 Award, para. 195.

289 Award, paras. 234–236.

for annulling the award. The committee, however, did annul the award on grounds unrelated to the exception.

In a couple of cases involving Argentina's emergency measures, the relevant BIT did not include an essential security interests exception and thus Argentina argued that its measures were justified under Article 25 of the ILC articles on state responsibility. In *BG Group v. Argentina*, a case arising under the United Kingdom-Argentina BIT, the tribunal observed that Article 25 may apply only to obligations between sovereign states and, if so, it would not disentitle a private investor from compensation under the BIT.[290] The tribunal also noted that the defense of necessity under Article 25 is unavailable where the international obligation in question explicitly or implicitly excludes reliance on necessity and that, arguably, a BIT implicitly excludes reliance. In this view, while Argentina was entitled to adopt the measures it adopted, Argentina would remain obligated to pay compensation.[291] Finally, the tribunal noted that the defense was an exceptional one subject to very strict conditions and that Argentina did not satisfy them in this case.[292] Thus, whether Article 25 applied or not, the result would be the same.[293]

In *National Grid v. Argentina*, another case arising under the United Kingdom-Argentina BIT, the tribunal held that Article 25 codified customary international law and thus Argentina was entitled to raise it as a defense. In so holding, the tribunal rejected an argument that the defense was unavailable because the United Kingdom was a persistent objector to the doctrine. The tribunal noted that the defense was an exceptional one subject to strict conditions. The tribunal found that Argentina's policies had contributed to the state of necessity and therefore Argentina could not invoke the defense.[294]

4.5.2 The Taxation Exception

Many BITs include an exception to the MFN and national treatment provisions for tax matters. This exception is discussed in Section 7.2.1.

Other BITs, however, apply their taxation exception to all the provisions of the BIT, not only the national and MFN treatment provisions.[295]

Still other BITs exempt taxation measures from most, but not all, of the BIT's provisions. For example, the Austria-Romania BIT provides that the BIT does not apply to taxation measures except for the articles dealing with Articles 4 and 5.[296] Similarly, the

290 Award, para. 408.
291 Award, para. 409.
292 Award, para. 411.
293 Award, para. 412.
294 Award, para. 260.
295 *See, e.g.*, Canada-Uruguay BIT, Art. XI. On taxation exceptions generally, *see* Thomas W. Walde and Abba Kolo, "Coverage of Taxation Under Modern Investment Treaties," in *The Oxford Handbook of International Investment Law* (Peter Muchlinski, Frederico Ortino, and Christoph Schreuer, eds. 2008).
296 Austria-Romania BIT, Art. 9.

U.S. BITs generally have applied only selected provisions to measures of taxation, although the selection has varied over time. Initially, the expropriation, currency transfers, and disputes provisions applied to matters of taxation, but in the 1994 model negotiating text the transfers provision no longer applied, while the 2004 model applied parts of the performance requirements provision to matters of taxation.[297] The 2003 Canadian model BIT authorizes investor-state arbitration of claims with respect to taxation measures only if the claim is either that the measure breaches an agreement between the investor and the host state or that the measure constitutes an expropriation.[298]

A few BITs grant to the taxation authorities of the two parties the power to decide whether certain measures violate the BIT. For example, the Canada-Uruguay BIT provides that a tax measure shall not be considered to contravene an agreement between the investor and the host state or to constitute an expropriation if the taxation authorities jointly so determine.[299] Many U.S. BITs provide that a tax measure shall not be considered an expropriation if the taxation authorities of the two parties jointly so decide.[300]

A few tribunals have addressed the scope of the taxation exception. In *Occidental v. Ecuador*, a case arising under the United States-Ecuador BIT, the claimant argued that the tax exception applies only to direct taxes. The tribunal, however, rejected this argument. In *Encana v. Ecuador*, a case arising under the Canada-Ecuador BIT, the tribunal held that the term "taxation measure" should be given its normal meaning. A taxation measure is one "which imposes a liability on a class of persons to pay money to the State for public purposes."[301] The term was not limited to direct taxation and included a value-added tax exemption.[302] In *Link Trading v. Moldova*, a case arising under the United States-Moldova BIT, the tribunal held that the term "taxation" is broad enough to include customs duties and other forms of raising revenue within the state's power. The tribunal in *Duke Energy v. Ecuador*, a case arising under the United States-Ecuador BIT, adopted the definition employed in *Encana*. Consistent with the award in *Link Trading*, the tribunal held that an exemption for customs duties was a matter relating to taxation.

---

297 Kenneth J. Vandevelde, *U.S. International Investment Agreements* 442–449 (2009).

298 2003 Canadian Model BIT, Art. 16.

299 Canada-Uruguay BIT, Art. XVI(3)–(4).

300 *See, e.g.*, United States-Georgia BIT, Art. XIII(2); United States-Albania BIT, Art. XIII(2).

301 Award, para. 142.

302 Award, para. 142.

Chapter 5

Reasonableness

5.1 INTRODUCTION

The reasonableness principle requires in essence that host-state treatment of foreign investment be reasonably related to a legitimate host-state regulatory objective. Thus, it prohibits treatment that is arbitrary or motivated by political or discriminatory considerations.

The reasonableness principle emerged as an explicit element in investment treaty practice only in the Cold War Era. The post-war U.S. FCNs prohibited "unreasonable or discriminatory measures" that impaired certain legally acquired rights, including rights in enterprises or in capital or technology. Those FCNs also required that covered property receive fair and equitable treatment, although that standard had as yet no clearly defined meaning.

The 1959 Abs-Shawcross convention similarly guaranteed fair and equitable treatment for foreign investment and prohibited unreasonable or discriminatory measures that impaired in any way the management, use, or enjoyment of covered property. In a comment they published on the convention, the authors explained that the fair and equitable treatment standard was drawn from U.S. treaty practice. They then explained that the prohibition on unreasonable conduct

> merely gives clear expression to a concept inherent in any system of law and which, in the sphere of international law, has been affirmed in general terms by the International Court of Justice in, for example, the advisory opinion on *Conditions of Admission of a State to Membership in the United Nations.*[1] The prohibition of measures of discrimination is in close accord with the principle laid down by the Permanent Court of International Justice in the *Case of Certain German Interests in Polish Upper Silesia.*[2]

1 Advisory Opinion of May 28, 1948, [1948] I.C.J. Rep. 57 [footnote in original].

2 Hermann Abs and Lord Shawcross, "The Proposed Convention to Protect Private Foreign Investment: A Round Table: Comments on the Draft Convention by its Authors," 9 *Journal of Public Law* 116 (1960). The citation for the *Upper Silesia* case is P.C.I.J. Ser. A, No. 7 (1926).

Thus, it was in the prohibition on unreasonable or discriminatory measures that the reasonableness principle explicitly entered investment treaty practice. Yet, as will be seen, investor-state arbitral tribunals have treated the reasonableness principle as an element of the fair and equitable treatment standard as well.

The reasonableness principle has become a widely applicable restriction on host-state treatment of foreign investment. Indeed, at times it has threatened to subsume, at least in part, the longer established principles of nondiscrimination and security.

First, as will be seen in Section 7.1, the nondiscrimination principle generally is violated only by unreasonable discriminations. Because an unreasonable discrimination by definition would violate the reasonableness principle, the nondiscrimination principle might seem to have been subsumed within the reasonableness principle. Yet, the nondiscrimination principle does retain some independent force. As discussed in Section 7.1, the nondiscrimination principle makes clear that discrimination is not a legitimate policy objective. Thus, the nondiscrimination principle establishes a minimum content to the reasonableness principle: certain host state conduct is per se unreasonable.

Second, as will be seen in Section 6.5.3.1, a very few tribunals have held that, in determining whether regulatory activity constitutes an expropriation, a tribunal must determine whether the impact on the investment was proportional to the public interest served. This proportionality analysis suggests that an investment may be destroyed without compensation by the host state provided that a sufficient public interest exists. Under this approach, the security principle behind the expropriation provision would be collapsed into the reasonableness principle. This approach, however, remains a distinctly minority approach that has been implicitly rejected by most tribunals.

5.2 FAIR AND EQUITABLE TREATMENT

5.2.1 Structure and Policy

The fair a..d equitable treatment standard defines the nature of the relationship between the host state and covered investment.[3] It establishes a set of norms applicable to every instance of host-state treatment of covered investment.[4] It is the most common general absolute standard of treatment in the BITs.

---

3 As discussed in Section 5.2.2, the Havana Charter, which inspired (at least in part) the inclusion of the fair and equitable treatment standard as a regular element of post-war treaty practice, would have authorized the International Trade Organization to make recommendations for and promote bilateral and multilateral agreements on measures designed "to assure just and equitable treatment for the enterprise, skills, capital, arts and technology brought from one Member country to another." Art. 11(2)(a). That was the only characterization of the agreements. Thus, "just and equitable treatment" or its equivalent, "fair and equitable treatment," was understood from the beginning as a standard that characterized the entire relationship between the host state and foreign investment.

4 On the fair and equitable treatment standard generally, *see* Ioana Tudor, *The Fair and Equitable Treatment Standard in the International Law of Foreign Investment* (2007); Rudolf Dolzer,

The most typical formulation requires that the host-state accord covered investment fair and equitable treatment.[5] Sometimes the standard appears alone in a sentence and sometimes it appears in the same sentence as one or both of two other general absolute standards of protection: the full protection and security standard[6] and the prohibition on unreasonable or discriminatory measures.[7] This juxtaposition is more than casual. These other standards explicitly articulate principles of security, reasonableness, and non-discrimination that are among those at the core of the fair and equitable treatment standard.

Some BITs refer to fair and equitable treatment in conjunction with national or MFN treatment. The most common formulation requires fair and equitable treatment which in no case shall be less than national or MFN treatment.[8] That is, national and MFN treatment establish a minimum standard below which fair and equitable treatment may not fall, although fair and equitable treatment may require more than national or MFN treatment. Thus, some BITs explicitly link fair and equitable treatment with the principle of non-discrimination, although in a way that suggests that fair and equitable treatment requires more than non-discrimination.

Alternatively, some BITs refer to fair and equitable treatment in conjunction with customary international law. This formulation requires each party to provide covered investment with fair and equitable treatment that in no case shall be less than that required by customary international law.[9] Thus, in this formulation, international law establishes a minimum standard below which fair and equitable treatment may not fall, although fair and equitable treatment may require more than customary law. As the tribunal observed in *Azurix v. Argentina*, a case arising under the United States-Argentina BIT, which employs this formulation, "[t]he clause, as drafted, permits to interpret fair and equitable treatment and full protection and security as higher standards than required by international law. The purpose of the third sentence is to set a

---

"Fair and Equitable Treatment: A Key Standard in Investment Treaties," 39 *International Lawyer* 87 (2005); Christoph Schreuer, "Fair and Equitable Treatment in Arbitral Practice," *Journal of World Investment and Trade* 357 (2005); Katia Yannaca-Small, "Fair and Equitable Treatment Standard: Recent Developments," in *Standards of Investment Protection* (August Reinisch, ed. 2008); Barnali Choudhury, "Evolution or Devolution? Defining Fair and Equitable Treatment in International Investment Law," 6 *Journal of World Investment and Trade* 297 (2005).

5 *See, e.g.*, BLEU-Sudan BIT, Art. 3(1); Italy-Nicaragua BIT, Art. (3) ("just and fair"); Australia-India BIT, Art. 3(2); Indonesia-India BIT, Art. 3(2). *But see* Article 4(1) where fair and equitable treatment shall be not less favorable than MFN treatment; Chile-Lebanon BIT, Art. IV(1).

6 *See, e.g.*, United Kingdom-Bosnia-Herzegovina BIT, Art. 2(2); Germany-Timor-Leste BIT, Art. 2(2); Switzerland-Algeria BIT, Art. 4(1); Austria-Armenia BIT, Art. 3(1); Finland-Armenia BIT, Art. 2(2); Chile-Indonesia BIT, Art. III(2); Egypt-Zambia BIT, Art. 2(2); Cambodia-Vietnam BIT, Art. II(2).

7 *See, e.g.*, Netherlands-Ethiopia BIT, Art. 3(1); Sweden-Kazakhstan BIT, Art. 2(3); Chile-Indonesia BIT, Art. IV(1); Cambodia-Vietnam BIT, Art. III(1). *But see* Art. III(2), where MFN treatment is set as a floor.

8 *See, e.g.*, Denmark-Ethiopia BIT, Art. 3(1); Thailand-Argentina BIT, Art. 4.

9 *See, e.g.*, Finland-Armenia BIT, Art. 2(2).

floor, not a ceiling, in order to avoid a possible interpretation of these standards below what is required by international law."[10]

Other BITs link the fair and equitable treatment standard to customary international law, but in a way that suggests a different relationship between the standard and customary law. This language originated with Article 1105 of the NAFTA, which requires each party to accord covered investment "treatment in accordance with international law, including fair and equitable treatment and full protection and security." The United States incorporated similar language into its most recent BITs,[11] as have Canada[12] and Mexico.[13] Thus, the three NAFTA parties have taken the position that the fair and equitable treatment standard is an element of customary international law, although they have not defined the content of the standard. The 2004 U.S. model BIT does provide that "'fair and equitable treatment' includes the obligation not to deny justice in criminal, civil, or administrative adjudicatory proceedings in accordance with the principle of due process embodied in the principal legal systems of the world."[14] The use of the word "includes" indicates that the obligation not to deny justice does not exhaust the content of the standard.

Finally, some BITs link fair and equitable treatment with customary international law in a way that leaves the relationship ambiguous. The typical formulation of this type guarantees fair and equitable treatment in accordance with international law.[15] This language could be interpreted to mean either that fair and equitable treatment is required by customary international law[16] or that fair and equitable treatment must be consistent with customary international law.

Many of the earliest cases involving the fair and equitable treatment standard happened to arise under the NAFTA, in which the fair and equitable treatment standard is identified as an element of customary international law. Thus, several of the earliest awards discussed the relationship between the fair and equitable treatment standard and the international minimum standard.

The consequences of linking the fair and equitable treatment standard and the international minimum standard depend upon the assumptions one makes about the meaning of the international minimum standard in the absence of a link. Because of the debates in the mid-twentieth century about the existence and content of an international minimum standard, some believed that the international minimum standard might offer weak protection for foreign investment, such as in *Neer v. Mexico*,[17] where the tribunal

---

10 Award, para. 361. *Accord Duke Energy v. Ecuador* (United States-Ecuador BIT), Award, para. 336.

11 *See, e.g.*, United States-Uruguay BIT, Art. 5(1).

12 *See* 2003 Canadian Model BIT, Art. 5(1).

13 *See, e.g.*, Mexico-Iceland BIT, Art. 3(1).

14 2004 U.S. Model BIT, Art. 5(2)(a).

15 *See, e.g.*, Mexico-France BIT, Art. 4(1); Canada-Uruguay BIT, Art. II(2(a).

16 *See* Palitha Kohona, "Investment Protection Agreements: An Australian Perspective," 21 *Journal of World Trade Law* 79 (1987).

17 U.S.A. (L.F. Neer) v. United Mexican States, (United States-Mexico), October 15, 1926, 3 *International Law Reports* 213.

held that customary law protects aliens against host-state conduct involving outrage or bad faith. Indeed, one reason for the inclusion of the fair and equitable treatment standard in the post-war U.S. FCNs had been to provide a basis for treaty protection not dependent upon the contested international minimum standard. Where one takes that view of the international minimum standard, treaty language providing that fair and equitable treatment is an element of customary international law could be regarded as strengthening customary international law. For example, Article 1105 of the NAFTA could be regarded as a considerable achievement for the United States and Canada because they had persuaded Mexico, long a Calvo Doctrine country and historically a principal antagonist of the United States on the issue of the content of customary international law, to concede that an international minimum standard exists under customary law and that the standard is breached not only by acts of bad faith, but by any conduct that is not fair and equitable. Even the weakest reading of the terms "fair and equitable" would seem to require more than a mere avoidance of outrage and bad faith. In the absence of the reference to fair and equitable treatment, Article 1105 might have been interpreted to prohibit only outrageous conduct.

Others might take a more robust view of customary international law as an evolving standard that in the late twentieth century prohibited certain conduct even if not outrageous or in bad faith. Where this view is taken, incorporating the fair and equitable treatment standard into customary law might have done little to raise the minimum standard. In this view, the principal effect of the linkage thus might be merely to limit the fair and equitable treatment standard. For example, in *ADF Group v. United States*, a case arising under the NAFTA, the tribunal observed that "any general requirement to accord 'fair and equitable treatment' and 'full protection and security' must be disciplined by being based upon State practice and judicial or arbitral case law or other sources of customary or general international law."[18] In *Mondev v. United States*, another case arising under the NAFTA, the tribunal noted that it "is bound by the minimum standard as established in State practice and in the jurisprudence of arbitral tribunals. It may not simply adopt its own idiosyncratic standard of what is 'fair' or 'equitable' without reference to established sources of law."[19]

Most tribunals, however, have found no need to address the relationship between the two standards. In the great majority of BITs, the fair and equitable treatment standard appears without a reference to customary international law and thus the text of the treaty does not require that the tribunal address the relationship.[20] The U.S. BITs do require both standards. Cases arising under the U.S. BITs nevertheless have often avoided the issue. As the tribunal explained in *Lauder v. Czech Republic*, a case arising under the United States-Czech Republic BIT, tribunals tend to address whether the host state's conduct violates the more specific language of fair and equitable treatment or full protection and security, where such language appears, rather than broader

18 Award, para. 184.

19 Award, para. 119.

20 *See, e.g.*, *MTD Equity v. Chile* (Malaysia-Chile BIT), Award, paras. 109–115.

language referring to the international minimum standard. In some cases, tribunals merely observe that, under the facts before them, they would reach the same decision whether fair and equitable treatment is part of customary international law or a separate, treaty-based standard.[21] In other cases, tribunals have found that the international minimum standard and the fair and equitable treatment standard are substantially the same.[22] In one case, the parties agreed that any violation of the international minimum standard also constitutes a violation of the fair and equitable treatment standard and, because the tribunal found a violation of the international minimum standard, it did not need to decide whether the fair and equitable treatment standard provided greater protection.[23]

Tribunal decisions applying the international minimum standard have made clear that the standard is an evolving one and that it has evolved beyond the language of *Neer*.[24] One might well conclude that the network of more than twenty-six hundred BITs, nearly all requiring fair and equitable treatment, has influenced customary law by suggesting that a standard of outrage or bad faith simply was anachronistic. That is, the fair and equitable treatment standard arguably has been highly successful in raising expectations concerning the level of protection to which investment is entitled under a BIT and, where a BIT refers to customary law, those heightened expectations have informed the interpretation of the international minimum standard under customary law. Thus, the international community appears to have moved past the situation where associating the fair and equitable treatment standard with customary law is necessary to raise the level of protection under customary law. Nor has associating the fair and equitable treatment standard with customary law served in most cases to limit the scope of the fair and equitable treatment standard. In general, tribunals have declined to distinguish carefully between the two standards and both have been interpreted to provide protection well beyond that of the *Neer* standard. The precise scope of protection is addressed in this and subsequent chapters.

Although the context in which the fair and equitable treatment standard appears varies, those differences have had little impact on the interpretation of the standard. International arbitral awards have been uniform in their interpretation of the standard, regardless of the context in which it appears, whether alone, combined with other general absolute standards of treatment, linked with non-discrimination standards, or linked with customary international law.[25]

---

21 *See, e.g.*, *Occidental v. Ecuador* (United States-Ecuador BIT), Award, para. 190; *Azurix v. Argentina* (U.S.-Argentina BIT), Award, para. 361; *CMS v. Argentina* (United States-Argentina BIT), Award, paras. 282–284.

22 *Azurix v. Argentina* (United States-Argentina BIT), Award, para. 364; *Duke Energy v. Ecuador* (United States-Ecuador BIT), Award, para. 337; *Biwater Gauff v. Tanzania* (United Kingdom-Tanzania BIT), Award, para. 592; *Saluka Investments v. Czech Republic* (Netherlands-Czech Republic BIT), Award, para. 291.

23 *See BG Group v. Argentina* (United Kingdom-Argentina BIT), Award, para. 290–291

24 *See, e.g.*, *International Thunderbird v. Mexico* (NAFTA), Award, para. 194; *BG Group v. Argentina* (United Kingdom-Argentina BIT), Award, para. 302.

25 *See* Section 5.2.3.

In occasional instances, BITs require fair and equitable treatment in a specific context. For example, the 1980 Belgium-Luxembourg Economic Union-Cameroon BIT requires at Article 6(3) that the exchange rate used for transfers related to an investment be fair and equitable. Some U.S. BITs provide that each party "should strive to accord fairness and equity" with respect to its tax policies.[26] These special applications have not contributed significantly to the process of elucidating the meaning of the standard.

The fair and equitable treatment standard has been interpreted by tribunals to require adherence to five of the six core BIT principles: those of reasonableness, security, non-discrimination, transparency, and due process.[27] As I have argued elsewhere,[28] these five principles are related in that all are elements of the rule of law. Thus, the fair and equitable treatment standard instantiates the role of the BITs in promoting the rule of law.

5.2.2 Origins

Variations in the context in which the fair and equitable treatment standard appears have been a feature of the standard since the first BITs. The standard occasionally appeared in FCN practice prior to the 1940s, but was not consistently present in FCNs prior to the war.[29]

The 1948 Havana Charter for the establishment of the International Trade Organization, however, contemplated that the new organization would be authorized to make recommendations for international agreements on measures designed "to assure just and equitable treatment for the enterprise, skills, capital, arts and technology brought from one Member country to another. . . ."[30] The Havana Charter did not further define the standard of just and equitable treatment.

That same year, the Organization of American States adopted the Economic Agreement of Bogota.[31] Article 22 of the agreement provided that "Foreign capital shall receive equitable treatment. The States therefore agree not to take unjustified, unreasonable or discriminatory measures that would impair the legally-acquired rights or interests of nationals of other countries in the enterprises, capital, skills, arts or technology they have supplied." By the use of the word "therefore," the OAS agreement seemed to associate fair and equitable treatment with reasonable and non-discriminatory treatment. The agreement, however, never received a sufficient number of ratifications to enter into force.

---

26 *See, e.g.*, United States-Egypt BIT, Art. XI.

27 *See, e.g.*, *Biwater v. Tanzania* (United Kingdom-Tanzania BIT), where the tribunal found that fair and equitable treatment includes protection of legitimate expectations, good faith, transparency, consistency and nondiscrimination. Award, para. 602.

28 *See* Kenneth J. Vandevelde, "A Unified Theory of Fair and Equitable Treatment," (forthcoming).

29 *See* Section 2.1.

30 Havana Charter, Article 11(2). For an excellent discussion of the history of the fair and equitable treatment standard, *see* Stephen Vascianne, "The Fair and Equitable Treatment Standard in International Investment Law and Practice," 70 *British Yearbook of International Law* 99 (1999).

31 Available at http://www.oas.org.

The fair and equitable treatment standard quickly was incorporated into the FCN treaties then being negotiated by the United States. For example, Article V of the U.S. FCN with Ireland, concluded in 1950, provided that "Each Party shall at all times accord equitable treatment to the capital of nationals and companies of the other Party." By the early 1950s, the United States was sometimes using the equivalent formulation "fair and equitable treatment." For example, Article I(1) of the U.S. FCN concluded with Germany in 1954 provided that "Each Party shall at all times accord fair and equitable treatment to the nationals and companies of the other Party, and to their property, enterprises and other interests."

In 1959, Hermann J. Abs and Lord Shawcross, acting at the behest of a group of European attorneys and business leaders, prepared a Draft Convention on Investments Abroad. Article 1 of the convention provided that "Each Party shall at all times ensure fair and equitable treatment to the property of nationals of the other Parties."[32] Article 1 also required that property receive the most constant protection and security and prohibited the impairment of the maintenance, use and enjoyment of property by unreasonable or discriminatory measures. The imposition of these three standards in a common article established a pattern widely followed in future BITs. In a commentary published with the draft convention, the authors explained that these three standards were based on U.S. FCN practice.[33]

That same year, when Germany signed the first BIT, with Pakistan, the fair and equitable treatment standard did not appear, despite the fact that the standard was known to Germany as a result of its FCN with the United States, which was signed in 1954 and entered into force in 1956. In its 1960 BIT with Malaysia, Germany required in its transfers provision, at Article 7(3), that a "fair and equitable" rate of exchange be used. The BIT with Pakistan, at Article 6(3), had read "just and reasonable". By 1961, however, Germany had adopted the fair and equitable treatment standard. Its BIT with Thailand, for example, provides at Article 2(3) that "[e]ach Contracting Party shall in its territory in any case accord such investments by investors of the other Contracting Party and their returns fair and equitable treatment and full protection." Germany's 1962 BIT with Turkey provided at article 1(1) that "In all cases the Contracting Parties shall accord these investments fair and equitable treatment."

When Switzerland inaugurated its BIT program in 1961, it employed the standard as well. Its first BIT, with Tunisia, required at Article 1 that each party accord investment "just and equitable" treatment, not less favorable than that accorded by that party to its own nationals. Thus, the Swiss language seemed to link the standard to national treatment, although national treatment appeared to set a minimum standard below which fair and equitable treatment could not fall. The following year, Switzerland added MFN treatment to the link.[34] Although this linkage continued into the 1970s

32 Hermann Abs and Lord Shawcross, "The Proposed Convention to Protect Private Foreign Investment: A Round Table: Comments on the Draft Convention by its Authors," 9 *Journal of Public Law* 116 (1960).

33 *Id.* at 119.

34 Switzerland-Guinea BIT, Art. 7.

in Swiss commerce, investment, and technical cooperation agreements, Swiss treaties limited solely to investment sometimes omitted the reference to national or MFN treatment and instead guaranteed fair and equitable treatment, conforming to international law.[35] By the early 1970s, that linkage also had disappeared and the Swiss BITs guaranteed fair and equitable treatment without further elaboration.[36] Yet, the fair and equitable treatment standard could sometimes be found in the same paragraph as the MFN and national treatment standards, reflecting Switzerland's continued association of the of fair and equitable treatment standard with the nondiscrimination principle.[37]

The Netherlands launched its BIT program in 1963, also with Tunisia. Article 1 of the Netherlands-Tunisia BIT required that investment receive treatment that was "just and nondiscriminatory" and that was no less favorable than that accorded to the host party's own nationals. By the mid-1980s, however, the Netherlands no longer linked the standard to national treatment, but rather included it with the full protection and security standard or the prohibition on unreasonable or discriminatory measures. For example, Article 4(1) of the 1984 Netherlands-Sri Lanka BIT provided that investments "shall at all times be accorded fair and equitable treatment and shall enjoy full protection and security. . . ." Article 3(1) of the 1985 Netherlands-Yemen Arab Republic BIT provided that "Each Contracting Party shall ensure fair and equitable treatment to the investments of nationals of the other Contracting Party and shall not impair, by unjustified or discriminatory measures, the operation, management, maintenance, use, enjoyment or disposal thereof. . . ."

In 1964, the Belgium-Luxembourg Economic Union (BLEU) inaugurated its BIT program, also with Tunisia. Article 1 required "fair and equitable treatment" of investment, a standard that remained in the BLEU BITs more than forty years later.[38] The first BLEU BIT further provided in the next paragraph that, "to that end," investment shall receive the same security and protection as investment of host-state nationals and nationals of any third country, suggesting that nondiscrimination was an element of fair and equitable treatment. The language quickly evolved, however, to suggest that MFN treatment was merely a floor below which fair and equitable treatment could not fall[39] and that international law provided a different such floor.[40]

Kuwait also commenced its BIT program in 1964, concluding a treaty with Iraq. Article 2 guaranteed to investments "just and equitable treatment as well as full protection in accordance with the provisions" of the treaty. Kuwait's BITs continue typically to require fair and equitable treatment.[41] The standard sometimes appears in the

---

35 *See, e.g.*, Switzerland-Tanzania BIT, Art. 1(1); Switzerland-Chad BIT, Art. 4(1).

36 *See, e.g.*, Switzerland-Egypt BIT, July 25, 1973, Art. 3(1); Switzerland-D.R. Congo BIT, March 10, 1972, Art. 2; Switzerland-Sudan BIT Feb. 17, 1974, Art. 3.

37 *See, e.g.*, Switzerland-Jordan BIT, Nov, 11, 1976, Art. 2(2); Switzerland-Syria BIT, June 22, 1977, Art. 2(2); Switzerland-Mali BIT, March 8, 1978, Art. 2(2).

38 *See, e.g.*, Belgium-Nicaragua BIT, Art. 3(1).

39 *See, e.g.*, Belgium-Indonesia BIT, Art. 1(1).

40 *See, e.g.*, BLEU-Republic of Korea BIT, Art. 2(3).

41 *See, e.g.*, Kuwait-Hungary BIT, Art. 2(3); Kuwait-Jordan BIT, Art. 4(1); Kuwait-Pakistan BIT, Art. 2(2); Kuwait-China BIT, Art. 2(2); Kuwait-Ethiopia BIT, Art. 4(1); Kuwait-Croatia BIT, Art. 4(1); Kuwait-Bulgaria BIT, Art. 3(2).

same paragraph as the prohibition on unreasonable or discriminatory measures[42] and sometimes with national or MFN treatment.[43]

Italy commenced a BIT program in 1964 as well, but did not include the standard in its BITs until 1985. The standard initially appeared alone in a paragraph,[44] but Italy soon included the standard in the same paragraph as the prohibition on unreasonable or discriminatory measures.[45]

Sweden's BIT program, which began in 1965 with a BIT with the Ivory Coast, linked fair and equitable treatment to international law as well as national treatment. Article VI provided that investments shall receive fair and equitable treatment, in accordance with international law and the domestic law of the parties and no less favorable than that accorded by each party to its own nationals or nationals of any third country. After concluding three BITs, Sweden suspended its BIT program. When the program resumed in 1978, the fair and equitable treatment standard no longer was linked with any other standard.[46] As the Swedish BITs added other absolute standards of treatment, these were included in the same paragraph as fair and equitable treatment.[47]

Denmark began its BIT program in 1965 by concluding a BIT with Madagascar. Article 6 of that BIT required fair and equitable treatment, no less favorable than that provided by the host state to its own nationals or to nationals of the most favored nation. The fair and equitable treatment standard disappeared from the Danish BITs in 1968,[48] only to reappear in 1980 in the Denmark-China BIT, where it was included in the same paragraph as the full protection and security provision and the observance of obligations provision.[49] By 1988, the prohibition on unreasonable or discriminatory measures appeared in the same paragraph as well.[50] In some of its more recent BITs, however, Denmark has placed the standard in a separate paragraph that requires fair and equitable treatment that in no case shall be less than national and MFN treatment.[51] In some cases, a second clause requires fair and equitable treatment with respect to the management, maintenance, use, enjoyment or disposal of investment.[52]

---

42 *See, e.g.*, Kuwait-Hungary BIT, Art. 2(3); Kuwait-China BIT, Art. 2(2).

43 *See, e.g.*, Kuwait-Jordan BIT, Art. 4(1); Kuwait-Ethiopia BIT, Art. 4(1); Kuwait-Croatia BIT, Art. 4(1); Kuwait-Bulgaria BIT, Art. 3(2).

44 *See, e.g.*, Italy-China BIT, Art. 1; Italy-Tunisia BIT, Art. 2(2).

45 *See, e.g.*, Italy-Hungary BIT, Art. 2(2); Italy-USSR BIT, Art. 2(2); Italy-Czechoslovakia BIT, Art. 2(2); Italy-Venezuela BIT, Art. 2(2); Italy-Nicaragua BIT, Art. II(3).

46 *See, e.g.*, France-Serbia and Montenegro BIT, Art. 2(1); Sweden-Egypt BIT, Art. 2(1).

47 *See, e.g.*, Sweden-Bosnia-Herzegovina BIT, Art. 2(1); Sweden-India BIT, Art. 3(1); Sweden-Ecuador BIT, Art. 2(3). Sweden-Kazakhstan BIT, Art. 2(3).

48 *See* Denmark-Indonesia BIT.

49 Denmark-China BIT, Art. 3(1). The standard was phrased as "equitable and reasonable treatment," while the full protection and security standard did not include the word "full".

50 *See, e.g.*, Denmark-Republic of Korea BIT, Art. 3(1).

51 *See, e.g.*, Denmark-Croatia BIT, Art. 3(1); Denmark-Kyrgyz Republic BIT, Art. 3(1); Denmark-Ethiopia BIT, Art. 3(1).

52 *See, e.g.*, Denmark-Croatia BIT, Art. 3(2); Denmark-Croatia BIT, Art. 3(2).

In 1967, the OECD adopted its Draft Convention on the Protection of Foreign Property. All of the OECD countries that were involved actively in BIT negotiations in the mid-1960s had adopted the fair and equitable treatment standard in their BITs and thus, not surprisingly, the draft convention included the standard. Article 1(a) of the convention provided that "Each Party shall at all times ensure fair and equitable treatment to the property of the nationals of the other Parties," language that was almost identical to that of the Abs-Shawcross convention. The same article also required the most constant protection and security for investment and prohibited unreasonable or discriminatory measures that would impair foreign property, again the same approach used in the Abs-Shawcross convention.

Note 1 to the OECD draft convention asserted that there is "a well-established general principle of international law that a State is bound to respect and protect the property of nationals of other States" and that "[f]rom this basic principle flow the *three rules* contained" in Article 1(a). That is, all three of the U.S. FCN standards, fair and equitable treatment; most constant protection and security; and the prohibition on unreasonable or discriminatory measures, were part of the international minimum standard. At the same time, however, these three FCN standards did not exhaust the content of customary law. As Note 1(b) to Article 3 made clear, for example, customary law also imposes limitations on the right of a state to expropriate foreign owned property.

The OECD draft convention was not very illuminating with respect to the meaning of the phrase "fair and equitable treatment." Note 4(a) to Article 1 stated that the phrase

> indicates the standard set by international law for the treatment due by each State with regard to the property of foreign nationals. The standard requires that . . . protection afforded under the Convention shall be that generally accorded by the Party concerned to its own nationals, but, being set by international law, the standard may be more exacting where rules of national law or national administrative practices fall short of the requirements of international law. The standard required conforms in effect to the "minimum standard" which forms part of customary international law.

Note 7 observed that "[i]n many cases," a measure that violated the prohibition on unreasonable measures "will also violate the standard of 'fair and equitable treatment.'" Thus, the OECD draft convention indicated explicitly that the fair and equitable treatment standard incorporates principles of nondiscrimination and reasonableness as well as other principles embraced within customary law, which, given other provisions of the convention, such as that on most constant protection and security, would have included at least the security principle as well. The draft convention, in any event, was never opened for signature.

In the 1970s, several more developed counties inaugurated BIT programs. France had commenced a BIT program in 1960, signing BITs with Chad, the Central African Republic, and Congo over a five-day period in August 1960, but none of these ever entered into force. Although France's first BIT in the 1970s, with Tunisia, did not require fair and equitable treatment, its next BIT, with the D.R. Congo, did impose such a requirement at Article 2. Thus, the standard initially appeared in only some French BITs. By the late 1970s, the provision required fair and equitable treatment, conforming with the principles of international law.[53] Although some variations have appeared over the years, [54]that remains the approach used today.[55]

The United Kingdom concluded its first BIT, with Egypt, in 1975. Article 2(2) provided that "Investments of nationals or companies of either Contracting Party shall at all times be accorded fair and equitable treatment and shall enjoy full protection and security. . . ." This remains essentially the language used in the U.K. BITs today.[56]

Austria's first BIT, concluded with Romania in 1976, employed the fair and equitable treatment standard as part of the MFN obligation.[57] That is, it required that each party provide to covered investment the fair and equitable treatment that it provided to investment of the most favored nation. Austria, however, subsequently adopted fair and equitable treatment as an independent standard.[58] In its more recent BITs, Austria couples the fair and equitable treatment standard with the full protection and security standard, which is phrased as "full and constant protection and security".[59]

Finland concluded its first BIT, with Egypt, in 1980. Article 2(1) of that BIT required fair and equitable treatment, but the obligation was subject to each party's laws and regulations. In the early 1990s, the subordination to local law was removed and the standard began to appear in a variety of contexts, sometimes accompanied by MFN or national treatment as a floor,[60] sometimes linked with a prohibition on unreasonable or discriminatory treatment,[61] and sometimes accompanied by the full protection and security standard.[62] In Finland's more recent BITs, the fair and equitable treatment standard typically appears accompanied by the full protection and security standard.[63]

The United States inaugurated a BIT program in 1977, but did not conclude its first BIT, with Egypt, until 1982. The Egypt BIT did not include a general requirement of fair and equitable treatment, although Article XI provided that each party "should strive to accord fairness and equity" with respect to its tax policies. The second U.S.

---

53 *See, e.g.*, France-Jordan BIT, Art. 3; France-Sudan BIT, Art. 3; France-Liberia BIT, Art. 3; France-Equatorial Guinea BIT, Art. 3.

54 *See, e.g.*, France-Hungary BIT, Art. 3 (fair and equitable treatment linked with the prohibition on unjustified or discriminatory measures rather than international law); France-Czechoslovakia BIT, Art. 3 (fair and equitable treatment linked to both international law and the prohibition on unjustified or discriminatory measures); France-Uruguay BIT, Art. 3 (fair and equitable treatment standard not linked to any other standard).

55 *See, e.g.*, France-Tajikstan BIT, Art. 4; France-Bahrain BIT, Art. 3; France-Bosnia-Herzegovina BIT, Art. 4.

56 *See, e.g.*, United Kingdom-Vietnam BIT, Art. 2(1); UK-Bosnia and Herzegovina BIT, Art. 2(1).

57 Austria-Romania BIT, Art. 3(1).

58 *See, e.g.*, Austria-Malaysia BIT, Art, 3(2); Austria-Chile BIT, Art. 3(1); Austria-India BIT, Art. 2(1).

59 *See, e.g.*, Austria-Bosnia-Herzegovina BIT, Art. 3(1); Austria-Armenia BIT, Art. 3(1); Austria-Jordan BIT, Art. 3(1); Austria-Libya BIT, Art. 3(1).

60 *See, e.g.*, Finland-Chile BIT, Art. 3(1).

61 *See, e.g.*, Finland-Turkey BIT, Art. 3; Finland-Vietnam BIT, Art. 2(2); Finland-Argentina BIT, Art. 2(2).

62 *See, e.g.*, Finland-Republic of Korea BIT, Art. 2(2).

63 *See, e.g.*, Finland-Algeria BIT, Art. 2(2); Finland-Armenia BIT, Art. 2(2); Finland-Azerbaijan BIT, Art. 2(2); Finland-Belarus BIT, Art. 2(2).

BIT, however, signed one month later with Panama, required at Article II(2) that investment "shall at all times be accorded fair and equitable treatment and shall enjoy full protection and security in the territory of the other Party." A subsequent sentence required treatment in accordance with national law and international law. That language appeared in the U.S. BITs until the preparation of the 1984 model negotiating text, when the reference to national law was omitted. With the omission of the reference to national law, the United States shortened the text by adding the requirement of compliance with international law to the sentence requiring fair and equitable treatment and full protection and security. The new language thus read, "Investments shall at all times be accorded fair and equitable treatment, shall enjoy full protection and security and shall in no case be accorded treatment less than that required by international law."[64] The U.S. language remained unchanged until the 1994 model, when some stylistic changes were made.[65]

Thus, by the early 1980s, the fair and equitable treatment standard was widely employed in BITs, although some BITs associated it with nondiscrimination while other BITs associated it with references to the international minimum standard. Typically, though, the language of these BITs tended to use nondiscrimination or the international minimum standard as setting a minimum level of treatment below which fair and equitable treatment could not fall. The OECD draft convention had suggested in 1967 that fair and equitable treatment was an element of the international minimum standard and that in some cases it required more than nondiscriminatory treatment and would be violated by unreasonable treatment. In 1984, the OECD's Committee on International Investment and Multinational Enterprises issued a report that briefly addressed the meaning of "fair and equitable treatment." The precise issue addressed by the report was whether the fair and equitable treatment standard added a substantive obligation or merely affirmed other obligations in the BIT, such as the nondiscrimination obligation. As the United States explained in its counter-memorial in *Loewen v. United States*, all member countries that commented on this point believed that "fair and equitable treatment introduced a substantive legal standard referring to general principles of international law. . . ."[66] The report thus seemed to link the standard not to "international custom" within the meaning of article 38(2) of the Statute of the International Court of Justice, but to "general principles of law recognized by civilized nations" within the meaning of article 38(3) of the statute.[67] The report did not indicate, however, whether the standard incorporated all such general principles or only some and, if so, which. The committee's report also did not indicate how many of the OECD countries commented on this point. The report, however, did answer the question that it had posed and concluded that fair and equitable treatment is an independent substantive obligation and not a mere reference to other treaty obligations.

---

64 *See, e.g.*, United States-Grenada BIT, Art. II(2).

65 *See, e.g.*, United States-Georgia BIT, Art. 2(3)(a).

66 Counter-Memorial of the United States of America, page 172, note 89.

67 *See* Katia Yannaca-Small, "Fair and Equitable Treatment Standard in International Law," in Organisation for Economic Co-operation and Development, *International Investment Law: A Changing Landscape* 97 (2005).

Meanwhile, in 1992, Canada, Mexico, and the United States concluded the North American Free Trade Agreement (NAFTA), which entered into force in 1994. Article 1105 of that agreement requires that each party accord to covered investment "treatment in accordance with international law, including fair and equitable treatment and full protection and security." The NAFTA thus adopted the position taken in the 1967 OECD draft convention, under which international law requires fair and equitable treatment. The language of the U.S. BITs, however, was not modified at that time to conform to the NAFTA language. Beginning in 1995, the United States asserted in its public explanation of its BITs that customary international law requires fair and equitable treatment. In 2004, the United States modified its model BIT language to conform closely to the NAFTA language.[68] Article 5(1) of the United States-Uruguay BIT, for example, provides that "'fair and equitable treatment' includes the obligation not to deny justice in criminal, civil, or administrative adjudicatory proceedings in accordance with the principle of due process embodied in the principal legal systems of the world."

The principal ways in which the fair and equitable treatment standard would appear in BITs thus were not established until the early 1990s. The standard appears in the vast majority of BITs. Typically, it appears as a free-standing obligation, although some BITs link it with international law and others with non-discrimination. These linkages may imply that fair and equitable treatment duplicates in some ways, but is not precisely coextensive with, either non-discrimination or the customary international law minimum standard of treatment or they may imply that non-discrimination or the international minimum standard set a floor below which treatment under the fair and equitable treatment standard may not fall. The requirement of fair and equitable treatment is normally considered an absolute standard, which is not dependent on how other investment is treated, and thus non-discrimination could not exhaust the requirements of fair and equitable treatment, although it could be a component of it. Some BITs place the fair and equitable treatment standard in the same paragraph as other general absolute standards, such as the full protection and security standard or the prohibition on unreasonable or discriminatory measures, suggesting a relationship between the fair and equitable treatment and the principles of security, reasonableness and non-discrimination embraced in these other standards. A small number of BITs explicitly provide that fair and equitable treatment is an element of customary international law. The U.S. BITs from 2004 and later are unusual in attempting to define the standard, although even the U.S. definition is not exhaustive, but merely indicates one component of the standard, essentially the principle of due process.

5.2.3 Arbitral Practice

Tribunals applying the fair and equitable treatment standard have held that the standard embraces principles of reasonableness, consistency (in effect, the security of

68 Language virtually identical to that which appeared in the U.S. BITs in 2004 previously had appeared in the investment chapters of the U.S. FTAs beginning in 2002. *See* Kenneth J. Vandevelde, *U.S. International Investment Agreements* 315–320 (2009).

legitimate expectations), non-discrimination, transparency, and due process. This section will discuss arbitral awards in which the fair and equitable treatment standards has been held to incorporate the principle of reasonableness. Arbitral awards holding that the standard incorporates other principles will be discussed in the chapters addressing those principles.

The fair and equitable treatment standard is the standard most often invoked by investors in investor-state arbitrations. This is largely attributable to the ubiquity, generality, and vagueness of the standard. The standard appears in the great majority of BITs and thus is nearly always available as a basis for a claim. Because the language by its terms can apply to virtually any instance of host-state conduct, it is potentially a basis for recovery in any situation. Further, because the meaning of the standard historically was uncertain, few claims could be categorically excluded from its scope. Thus, claimants' counsel, in the exercise of their professional responsibility as zealous advocates, could scarcely avoid alleging a violation of the standard. At the same time, where a tribunal concluded that the host state's conduct was sufficiently unacceptable to merit an award of compensation, such conduct likely could be characterized as unfair or inequitable. Unless the conduct fell within one of the more specific standards, such as in the case of an expropriation or the imposition of exchange controls, the fair and equitable treatment standard offered a malleable basis for an award in favor of the claimants.

One consequence of the broad applicability of the fair and equitable treatment standard is that it may displace some of the other standards in important ways. For example, the national and MFN treatment standards often include exceptions for commitments under regional economic integration agreements or taxation agreements. Yet, such exceptions usually do not apply to the fair and equitable treatment standard, with the result that the fair and equitable treatment standard may provide a basis for compensation for discriminatory treatment where the national or MFN treatment provisions would not have. Of course, the same result could occur under the standard prohibiting unreasonable or discriminatory measures and thus the seeming inconsistency in prohibiting under one standard the very conduct that is permitted under another is not solely attributable to the breadth of the fair and equitable treatment standard in those BITs where the prohibition on unreasonable or discriminatory measures appears.

As noted in Section 5.2.1, tribunals generally have placed little significance on the varied contexts in which the fair and equitable treatment standard appears. That is, they have not given the standard a different meaning depending upon the context in which the standard appears, such as whether it appears in isolation, with other general absolute standards, linked with non-discrimination, or linked with customary international law. For example, in *Bogdanov v. Moldova*, the text of the Russia-Moldova BIT linked the fair and equitable treatment standard with nondiscrimination, which the sole arbitrator found not to exist in that case. The sole arbitrator held, however, that the standard also prohibited conduct that violated principles of reasonableness, transparency, and security.[69]

---

69 Award, para. 4.2.4.

Nor have differences in the wording of the standard been treated as significant. For example, in *Parkerings-Compagniet v. Lithuania*, a case arising under the Norway-Lithuania BIT, the tribunal held that "equitable and reasonable" has the same meaning as "fair and equitable."[70]

In cases applying the reasonableness principle, tribunals generally consider whether the action of the host state was reasonably related to legitimate policy objectives. As the tribunal explained in *Saluka Investments v. Czech Republic*, a case arising under the Netherlands-Czech Republic BIT, reasonableness requires that the host state's conduct "bear[] a reasonable relationship to some rational policy. . . ."[71] Thus, a purely arbitrary act, that is, one not related to legitimate policy objectives, would violate the standard. Tribunals have been reluctant to conclude that host-state conduct was unreasonable, unless it was motivated by political or discriminatory considerations. Where it appears that host-state action was based on legitimate policy concerns, tribunals have tended to find the conduct to be reasonable, even if the host state acted unwisely or incompetently.

The tribunal in *S.D. Myers v. Canada*, a case arising under the NAFTA, averred that its duty was to interpret the fair and equitable treatment standard "in light of the high measure of deference that international law generally extends to domestic authorities to regulate matters within their own borders."[72] Thus, in determining whether the act of the host state is reasonable, a tribunal does not examine the action of the host state for errors of judgment, but for acts that are arbitrary or that are based on political or discriminatory motives. In many cases, the tribunal has found the host-state conduct to be reasonably related to a legitimate policy objective and thus reasonable.

For example, in *ADF Group Inc. v. United States*, another case arising under the NAFTA, the tribunal found that a domestic content regulation for steel used in highway construction did not violate the fair and equitable treatment standard. First, such a regulation could hardly be considered per se a violation of international law given that all three NAFTA parties as well as many other states impose domestic content requirements. Thus, these requirements could not be considered "idiosyncratic or aberrant and arbitrary."[73] Over time, the U.S. Congress had modified the statutes applicable to the program and thus the failure of the U.S. government to adhere to court decisions applying the predecessor statute was not "grossly unfair or unreasonable."[74]

The claimant complained that the U.S. Federal Highway Administration had acted *ultra vires* in its administration of the highway program, but any such violation of national law did not necessarily violate Article 1105. In an oft-quoted remark, the tribunal noted that "something more than simple illegality or lack of authority under the domestic law of a State is necessary to render an act or measure inconsistent"

---

70 Award, para. 276.

71 Award, para. 460. *See also* para. 309.

72 Award, para. 263.

73 Award, para. 188.

74 Award, para. 189.

with Article 1105.[75] The tribunal did not explain what the something more was, but found that the claimant had not shown it.

In *Noble Ventures v. Romania*, a case arising under the United States-Romania BIT, the tribunal found the fair and equitable treatment standard "to be a more general standard which finds its specific application in *inter alia* the duty to provide full protection and security, the prohibition of arbitrary and discriminatory measures and the obligation to observe contractual obligations towards the investor."[76] The tribunal noted that it already had found that none of these other provisions had been breached, but then noted that "this in itself cannot lead to the conclusion that the more general fair and equitable treatment standard has not been breached."[77] The tribunal next considered whether Romania violated the standard by seeking judicial reorganization of the claimant's company, which the claimant alleged had been undertaken not for commercial purposes but in order to effect a rescission of Romania's privatization agreement with the claimant and to regain control of the company. The tribunal found that the decision to initiate the proceedings was not arbitrary, but seemingly the only solution to the company's insolvency and its inability to pay its four thousand employees. Further, the proceedings were conducted in accordance with Romanian law. Because the decision was not arbitrary, it did not violate the fair and equitable treatment standard.

In *Continental Casualty v. Argentina*, a case arising under the United States-Argentina BIT, Argentina adopted a policy that converted dollar denominated assets into pesos at a rate of 1.4 pesos to the dollar, as opposed to the prior rate of one to one, resulting in a nominal gain in the peso value of the assets, although the real value of the assets in fact declined. Argentina nevertheless imposed a capital gains tax on the increase in nominal value. The tribunal held that the tax was consistent with common tax accounting principles and thus did not violate the fair and equitable treatment standard.[78]

In *Tokios Tokeles v. Ukraine*, a case arising under the Lithuania-Ukraine BIT, the tribunal held that retaliation against a covered investment for supporting a political candidate would violate the fair and equitable treatment standard, although the evidence of retaliation in that case was insufficient. In *MCI Power v. Ecuador*, a case arising under the United States-Ecuador BIT, the tribunal found that the host state's conduct toward the claimant, which included threatening a tax audit, investigating its legal representative, and instituting litigation against it, constituted legitimate regulatory acts, rather than harassment.

In *Parkerings-Compagniet v. Lithuania*, a case arising under the Norway-Lithuania BIT, the tribunal found no arbitrariness in Lithuania's failure to disclose information available to the public. Lithuania had obtained a legal opinion that the claimant could have obtained from any qualified law firm. The claimant also alleged that the Lithuania had acted arbitrarily when its courts refused to accept *force majeure* as grounds for excusing the investment's obligation to pay a fee due under a parking concession agreement.

---

75 Award, para. 190.

76 Award, para.182.

77 *Id.*

78 Award, paras. 269–270.

The tribunal held that an erroneous judgment by a court would not violate the treaty in the absence of a denial of justice.

In *Genin v. Estonia*, a case arising under the United States-Estonia BIT, Estonia had revoked a license held by the investor's bank, thus forcing the bank out of business. The tribunal observed that, to violate the fair and equitable treatment standard, state conduct must reflect "a willful neglect of duty, an insufficiency of action falling far below international standards, or even subjective bad faith."[79] The principal ground for revocation was the fact that corporate documents listed "Eurocapital Group Limited" as a major shareholder, when the entity authorized to acquire a qualified shareholding was the "Eurocapital Group Company." The tribunal found this ground to be "exceedingly formalistic" and "extremely technical" because the similarity of the names of the two entities and the fact that they were listed as having identical shareholdings suggested that the two entities were actually the same.[80] The tribunal concluded nevertheless that Estonia was at least arguably justified in concluding that a major shareholder had not received a permit to acquire its holding, which meant that the bank did not meet capitalization requirements. The tribunal found that the decision was a reasonable regulatory decision that reflected the Estonian government's legitimate concerns about the management and financial soundness of the bank. More generally, the decision occurred in the context of a newly independent state seeking to regulate modern financial institutions, a context in which the claimant knowingly chose to invest. Thus, the tribunal found no violation of the fair and equitable treatment standard.

The *Genin* award seemed to suggest that bad faith might be necessary to violate the standard. Yet, Estonia's conduct was found consistent with the standard not simply because Estonia lacked bad faith, but because Estonia acted pursuant to legitimate regulatory concerns. In any event, the clear consensus now is that bad faith is not required to find a violation of the fair and equitable treatment standard.

In *Pope & Talbot v. Canada*, a case arising under the NAFTA, in an effort to address a trade dispute with the United States over Canadian exports of softwood lumber, Canada had allocated quotas of softwood lumber exports from certain provinces. The effect was to limit the amount of lumber that the claimant could export and the amount diminished over time as the quotas were adjusted. Despite the explicit language of the NAFTA, the tribunal concluded that the fair and equitable treatment standard was not encompassed within the international minimum standard under customary law, but was additive to it.[81] In a very lengthy discussion, the tribunal held that the various aspects of the quota system were reasonable responses to Canada's trade dispute with the United States.[82]

---

79 Award, para. 367.

80 Award, paras. 359–361.

81 Award, para. 113. The NAFTA Free Trade Commission subsequently issued an interpretation of the relevant NAFTA provision, Article 1105, declaring that the fair and equitable treatment standard is not additive to the international minimum standard, with the result that the tribunal was required to reexamine its initial decision. The FTC interpretation and the tribunal's reexamination are discussed in Section 5.4.

82 Award, paras. 121, 123, 125, 128.

Nevertheless, the tribunal did find a violation. After the claimant had notified the Canadian government that it was submitting the dispute concerning the quotas to investor-state arbitration under the NAFTA, Canada responded with a series of actions that the tribunal regarded as retaliation. The Canadian government imposed unnecessary and onerous reporting requirements on the company and refused to cooperate to find less burdensome alternatives. The government also threatened the company with criminal prosecution for noncompliance with these requirements and wrote internal memoranda in which it mischaracterized the situation, thereby injuring the reputation of the company. The tribunal found that this conduct, taken together, violated the requirement of fair and equitable treatment,[83] citing the lack of a reasonable basis for the conduct[84] as well as a lack of forthrightness.[85]

Conduct motivated by political (or discriminatory) considerations also was found to violate the reasonableness principle in several other cases. For example, in *Eureko v. Poland*, a case arising under the Netherlands-Poland BIT, the claimant had acquired a 30 percent interest in a state-owned insurance company in the process of being privatized, relying upon Poland's commitment to sell the remaining stock, which would enable the claimant to acquire a majority interest. The privatization, however, became politically controversial and Poland decided not to complete it. The tribunal found that Poland had violated the fair and equitable treatment standard because it had refused to honor its commitment for "purely arbitrary reasons linked to the interplay of Polish politics and nationalistic reasons of a discriminatory character."[86] Initially, it would seem that Poland's misdeed in *Eureko* was inconsistent conduct: it promised to privatize the company, but then failed to do so. The tribunal, however, appeared willing to excuse the inconsistency if there were a sufficient justification. The tribunal never explained what kind of justification would be necessary, but regarded the justification in that case as "arbitrary." Poland's decision was not a reasoned judgment, but based on political opposition to foreign investment.

In *Azurix Corp. v. Argentina*, a case arising under the United States-Argentina BIT, the claimant's investment had obtained a concession to operate a water distribution system in Buenos Aires. Subsequently, however, disputes arose over the tariffs that could be charged. When, partly as a result of the provincial government's misfeasance, an algae bloom affected adversely the appearance and taste of the water, the province refused to accept any responsibility, blamed the foreign investment, and urged consumers not to pay their bills. At that point, the investment made what the tribunal regarded as a reasonable request to terminate the concession by mutual agreement, but the province refused and insisted on terminating the concession on the grounds of abandonment by the foreign investment.[87] Noting the refusal of this reasonable request and the fact that Argentina had allowed the tariff regime to become politicized,[88] the

---

83 Award, para. 181.
84 Award, paras. 173–174.
85 Award, paras. 177–179.
86 Award, para. 233.
87 Award, para. 374.
88 Award, para. 375.

tribunal found that the fair and equitable treatment standard had been violated. The tribunal also found a violation in the government's urging of customers not to pay their water bill, another politically motivated act.

In *Biwater v. Tanzania*, a case arising under the United Kingdom-Tanzania BIT, the claimant's investment was awarded a contract to operate the water and sewerage service for the city of Dar es Salaam. After disputes arose concerning performance under the contract, the Minister of Water and Livestock Development, who was campaigning for the office of prime minister, called a press conference at which he announced that the contract was terminated and then four days later he held a political rally and confirmed that the contract was terminated. The tribunal found this conduct to be "an unreasonable disruption of the contractual mechanisms . . . and motivated by political considerations."[89] Such conduct inflamed the situation and polarized public opinion so that it was impossible thereafter to follow prescribed procedures under the contract.[90] A week later, Tanzania unilaterally withdrew a value-added tax exemption, an act that the tribunal found to be unreasonable and unjustified.[91] The government then occupied the water company's offices, took control of the operation and deported the senior management. There being no emergency, the tribunal found this action to be "unreasonable and arbitrary, unjustified by any public purpose. . . ."[92] All of these unreasonable acts violated the fair and equitable treatment standard.[93] The tribunal also found that the appointment of the same minister as regulator of the utility, rather than "an independent, impartial regulator insulated from political influence," constituted a further violation of the standard.[94] As it happened, however, the tribunal held that none of these actions caused compensable damage to the claimant because the position of the investment already was such that contract termination was inevitable.

In *Eastern Sugar v. Czech Republic*, a case arising under the Netherlands-Czech Republic BIT, the Czech Republic, as part of the process of joining the European Union, issued two sugar decrees to regulate the sugar market by, in particular, reducing imports and allocating quotas among domestic producers. One of the decrees was later held unconstitutional. Both were ineffectively implemented. Moreover, they allowed new producers to obtain quotas, a decision that the tribunal found to be illogical in light of the decrees' avowed purpose and that the tribunal believed to have been politically motivated. The tribunal nevertheless found no violation, holding that the host state is entitled to some measure of interest balancing, inefficiency, trial and error, and imperfection. After the European Union reduced the Czech Republic's country sugar quota, however, the government reduced the claimant's quota by more than the entire reduction in the country quota, thus forcing one company to bear the entire effect of the country quota reduction. The disproportionate reduction appeared to have been in retaliation for the claimant's politically unpopular decision to close a plant.

---

89 Award, para. 500.
90 Award, para. 627.
91 Award, para. 502.
92 Award, para. 503.
93 Award, para. 605.
94 Award, para. 615.

The tribunal found the reduction to be unreasonable and discriminatory and, therefore, a violation of the fair and equitable treatment standard.

In *Vivendi v. Argentina*, a case arising under the France-Argentina BIT, the claimants' investment had obtained a concession to operate a water distribution system undergoing privatization. The tribunal found that, after sharp rate increases and a temporary but harmless discoloration of the water had stirred local opposition, local officials had engaged in a campaign to force the investment to accept new terms, such as by encouraging customers not to pay their bills. Further, after the investment sought to terminate the agreement and to institute arbitration under the BIT, Argentina enacted legislation to prevent the investment from pursuing collection lawsuits or enforcing debts, measures that the tribunal found to constitute "a vindictive exercise of sovereign power aimed at punishing" the investment in violation of the fair and equitable treatment standard.[95]

In a few instances, tribunals have discussed the concept of good faith in finding a violation of fair and equitable treatment. Yet, it is rare that the concept adds anything to the principle of reasonableness or the other principles embraced within the fair and equitable treatment standard. Indeed, the tribunal in *ADF Group v. United States*, a case arising under the NAFTA, observed that the concept of good faith was of "negligible assistance" in interpreting the standard of fair and equitable treatment. Indeed, no award in favor of the claimant seems to rest solely on a good faith principle.

In *Tecmed v. Mexico*, a case arising under the Spain-Mexico BIT, Mexico denied to the claimant's investment the renewal of a permit necessary to operate its solid waste disposal facility. The reason for the denial appeared to be pressure from the community to eliminate the facility. The tribunal found that the denial of the permit was either a coercive attempt to force relocation of the facility or a nontransparent attempt to achieve some other undisclosed objective. The tribunal held that the denial violated the obligation of good faith, which, it said, requires reasonableness, consistency, and transparency. That is, "in light of the good faith principle," the fair and equitable treatment standard requires the host state

> [t]o provide to international investments treatment that does not affect the basic expectations that were taken into account by the foreign investor to make the investment. The foreign investor expects the host State to act in a consistent manner, free from ambiguity and totally transparently in its relations with the foreign investor, so that it may know beforehand any and all rules and regulations that will govern its investments, as well as the goals of the relevant policies and administrative practices or directives, to be able to plant its investment and comply with such regulations. Any and all State actions conforming to such criterion should relate not only to the guidelines, directives or requirements issued, or the resolutions approved there under, but also to the goals underlying such regulations. The foreign investor also expects the host State to act consistently, i.e., without arbitrarily revoking any preexisting decisions or permits issued by the State that were relied upon by the investor to assume its commitments as well as to plan and launch its commercial

95 Award, para. 7.4.45. This is the award in what is often referred to as *Vivendi II*. The award of the first *Vivendi* tribunal was annulled.

> and business activities. The investor also expects the State to use the legal instruments that govern the actions of the investor or the investment in conformity with the function usually assigned to such instruments, and not to deprive the investor of its investment without the required compensation.[96]

Thus, in Tecmed the obligation of good faith, as the ADF Group tribunal predicted, seems to add little. Rather, the term was used as an umbrella for other principles that are embraced within the fair and equitable treatment standard, notably reasonableness, transparency, and consistency (security of legitimate expectations).

The reference to coercion in the *Tecmed* award is potentially misleading. States are by their nature coercive institutions. The law is coercive and the concept of the rule of law means that individuals are forced to abide by the law. Thus, a host state does not violate the fair and equitable treatment standard merely by coercing an investor or an investment. The rule of law, however, while it coerces individuals, also restrains the power of the state. The state must use its power to advance its legitimate regulatory objectives and in accordance with the law. Accordingly, the violation occurs where the coercion is not related to a legitimate state regulatory objective, in effect, where it is an abuse of power. Similarly, in *Pope & Talbot v. Canada*, a NAFTA case discussed above, the tribunal found a violation where Canada had engaged in a campaign of harassment against the claimant. The campaign included burdensome demands for information and threats of criminal prosecution. Host states may legitimately require investors to provide information and they may pose the threat of criminal sanctions. The violation occurred, however, because these actions were taken for retaliatory purposes rather than to further legitimate regulatory objectives.

The tribunal also relied on the principle of good faith in *Siemens v. Argentina*, a case arising under the Germany-Argentina BIT. In that case, the tribunal observed that

> when a government awards a contract, which includes among its critical provisions an undertaking of that government to conclude agreements with its provinces, the same government cannot argue that the structure of the State does not permit it to fulfill such undertaking. This runs counter to the principle of good faith underlying fair and equitable treatment.[97]

While Argentina's conduct in failing to conclude agreements necessary to fulfill its commitment to the investor would seem quite clearly to violate a principle of good faith, other BIT principles could be invoked to justify finding a violation of the fair and equitable treatment standard. Agreeing to do that which cannot be done would also seem to violate the principle of reasonableness. Alternatively, failing to do that which Argentina had promised to do would violate the principle of consistency, or security of legitimate expectations. The concept of good faith provides an appropriate explanation for the award, but is not essential to it.

In a few awards, the tribunal seemed to believe that the fair and equitable treatment standard included a good faith principle, but found no violation of the principle under the facts of those disputes. For example, in *Waste Management v. Mexico*, a case

---

96 Award, para. 154.

97 Award, para. 308.

arising under the NAFTA, the tribunal observed that a conspiracy by government agencies "without justification to defeat the purposes of an investment agreement" would violate the obligation under Article 1105 of the NAFTA 'to act in good faith.'"[98] The claimant had failed to prove the existence of any such conspiracy, however.[99]

In *MCI Power v. Ecuador*, a case arising under the United States-Ecuador BIT, the tribunal held that Ecuador had not acted in bad faith in refusing to sign an arbitration agreement. Ecuador was under no obligation to agree to arbitrate. Neither did Ecuador's refusal to accept the investor's position in a dispute constitute bad faith. Again, Ecuador was under no obligation to agree with the investor.

Although tribunals occasionally have suggested that bad faith would violate the fair and equitable treatment standard, the overwhelming weight of authority is that a violation of the standard does not require bad faith.[100]

In a number of cases, tribunals have equated the fair and equitable treatment standard with other standards in a BIT, without attempting to articulate any independent content for the fair and equitable treatment standard. For example, in *ADC v. Hungary*, a case arising under the Cyprus-Hungary BIT, the tribunal found with little discussion that under the facts before it the host state's expropriation of claimant's investment in a way that violated the expropriation provision of the treaty also violated the fair and equitable treatment standard. In *Wena Hotels v. Egypt*, a case arising under the United Kingdom-Egypt BIT, the tribunal found that Egypt had known of an attempt by certain government officials to seize possession of the claimant's hotels, but took no action to prevent the takeover, to restore the hotels promptly to the claimant, or to impose a substantial punishment on those responsible for the seizure. Egypt's failure to exercise reasonable care to protect foreign investment would constitute a classic example of a violation of the obligation of full protection and security and, in fact, the tribunal began its discussion by noting that it was addressing claimant's allegation that Egypt had violated exactly that obligation.[101] Following its discussion of the facts, however, the tribunal concluded that Egypt had violated both the obligation to provide full protection and security and the obligation to provide fair and equitable treatment, without discussing the content of either standard or the relationship between the two. The only cases cited by the tribunal were *American Manufacturing & Trading, Inc. v. Zaire* and *AAPL v. Sri Lanka*, both of which involved physical destruction of property and neither of which relied upon the fair and equitable treatment standard.[102]

In *Petrobart v. Kyrgyz Republic*, a case arising under the Energy Charter Treaty, the claimant was a creditor of a state-owned company that produced oil and gas. The host state had stripped assets from the company to the detriment of its creditors and had

---

98 Award, para. 138.

99 Award, para. 139.

100 *See, e.g., Duke Energy v. Ecuador* (United States-Ecuador BIT), Award, para. 341; *Jan de Nul v. Egypt* (BLEU-Egypt BIT), Award, para. 185; *LG&E v. Argentina* (United States-Argentina BIT), Award, para. 129; *Azurix v. Argentina* (United States-Argentina BIT), Award, para. 372; *CMS Gas Transmission v. Argentina* (United States-Argentina BIT), Award, para. 280; *Siemens v. Argentina* (Germany-Argentina BIT), Award, para. 300.

101 Award, para. 83.

102 Both cases are discussed in Section 6.3.3.

intervened in a judicial proceeding to stay execution of a judgment against the company. The claimant alleged that this conduct violated each sentence of Article 10(1) of the treaty, which provides that

> Each Contracting Party shall, in accordance with the provisions of this Treaty, encourage and create stable, equitable, favourable and transparent conditions for Investors of other Contracting Parties to make Investments in its Area. Such conditions shall include a commitment to accord at all times to Investments of Investors of other Contracting Parties fair and equitable treatment. Such Investments shall also enjoy the most constant protection and security and no Contracting Party shall in any way impair by unreasonable or discriminatory measures their management, maintenance, use, enjoyment or disposal. In no case shall such Investments be accorded treatment less favourable than that required by international law, including treaty obligations. Each Contracting Party shall observe any obligations it has entered into with an Investor or an Investment of an Investor of any other Contracting Party.

The tribunal declined to analyze the Kyrgyz Republic's actions in relation to each individual element of Article 10(1), but noted that "this paragraph in its entirety is intended to ensure a fair and equitable treatment of investments."[103] The tribunal concluded that the actions of the Kyrgyz Republic "failed to accord Petrobart a fair and equitable treatment of its investment to which it was entitled under Article 10(1) of the Treaty."[104] The tribunal thus treated fair and equitable treatment as an umbrella term for a number of more specific obligations and did not specify which, if any, of those more specific obligations had been violated by the actions of the host state.

The tribunal proceeded in a similar manner in *LLC AMTO v. Ukraine*, another case arising under the Energy Charter Treaty. The claimant alleged that the host state violated the treaty by instituting a bankruptcy proceeding in order to collect back taxes from the investment. The tribunal found "no evidence arising from the tax inspection and related bankruptcy proceedings of any unreasonable, disproportionate, arbitrary, or discriminatory conduct, or any breach of [the claimant's] legitimate expectations. There was no unfair or inequitable treatment, or any other breach of Article 10(1) ECT."[105]

5.3 UNREASONABLE OR DISCRIMINATORY MEASURES

5.3.1 Structure and Policy

The first BIT provision to incorporate the reasonableness principle explicitly was the prohibition on unreasonable or discriminatory measures. The typical provision prohibits impairment of the management, maintenance, use, enjoyment or disposal of

103 Award, page 76.
104 Award, page 76.
105 Award, para. 99.

investment by unreasonable or discriminatory measures.[106] As the fair and equitable treatment standard has been interpreted, the prohibition on unreasonable or discriminatory measures may add little or nothing to the fair and equitable treatment standard.

One issue presented by the prohibition on unreasonable or discriminatory measures is whether it prohibits every host-state measure that discriminates among investments and that impairs the operation or disposal of covered investment. Such an interpretation seems almost certainly too broad. Governments enact countless laws that impose duties on some enterprises and not others. Because these laws do not apply to every enterprise within the jurisdiction of the state, all of them are discriminatory. Yet, it cannot be that every law must apply to every enterprise. Companies that manufacture computer hardware, that process food, or that deliver parcels all perform quite different functions and legitimately are subject to quite different regulations. To treat them differently for reasons related to the nature of their function is not inconsistent with any purpose underlying the BIT, but to require uniform treatment would be an unwarranted imposition on the regulatory discretion of the host state. Thus, the prohibition on non-discriminatory measures must be read as a prohibition on measures that discriminate unreasonably. If the discrimination is reasonably related to a legitimate host-state regulatory objective, it should not be regarded as a violation of the BIT standard.

This interpretation accounts for the pairing of unreasonable measures and discriminatory measures in this standard. They are paired because, despite the use of the disjunctive "or," in fact unreasonableness is the unifying feature of measures that violate this standard.[107] Such measures impair covered investment through unreasonable discrimination or other unreasonable treatment. The term "unreasonable" always appears first in this standard because of its centrality to the standard, but the standard also refers to discriminatory measures, which indicates that all discriminatory measures will be scrutinized to ensure that the discrimination is reasonable. Further, as will be seen, the principal ground on which measures thus far have been found to be unreasonable is that they are based on a discriminatory motive rather than a legitimate policy objective. Thus, unreasonable measures often are discriminatory measures.

Another issue that may arise is whether this provision applies to any discrimination or only those discriminations that are based on nationality. Nothing in the language suggests that it is limited to discriminations based on nationality. Further, one of the purposes of the BIT is to ensure that investors are not placed at a competitive disadvantage relative to other investors. Although the most common competitive disadvantages imposed on foreign investments may be nationality-based, a competitive disadvantage imposed on some other basis may be just as detrimental to the investment.

---

106 *See, e.g.*, United Kingdom-Bosnia-Herzegovina BIT, Art. 2(2); Germany-Timore-Leste BIT, Art. 2(3); Austria-Armenia BIT, Art. 3(2); Sweden-Kazakhstan BIT, Art 2(3); Denmark-Ethiopia BIT, Art.2(2); Chile-Indonesia BIT, Art. IV(1); Egypt-Zambia BIT, Art. 2(2) (*but see* Article 3, where MFN treatment is set as a minimum standard for fair and equitable treatment); Chile-Lebanon BIT, Art. III(2); Cambodia-Vietnam BIT, Art. III(1). On the unreasonable or discriminatory measures provision generally, see Veijo Heiskanen, "Arbitrary and Unreasonable Measures," in *Standards of Investment Protection* (August Reinisch, ed. 2008).

107 Thus, the standard is introduced in this chapter rather than in Chapter 7, on the nondiscrimination principle.

Thus, the language of the provision and the purpose of the BIT both militate in favor of interpreting this provision potentially to apply to any discrimination. As will be seen, the tribunals have not been entirely consistent with respect to this issue.[108]

Some BITs use the conjunction "and" rather than "or." In these BITs, the standard is narrower because it prohibits only those measures that are both discriminatory and unreasonable. That is, an unreasonable measure that did not discriminate would not violate the standard. Measures that are unreasonable but not discriminatory, as has been noted, however, likely would violate the fair and equitable treatment standard.[109] The use of the conjunction reinforces the conclusion above that a discriminatory measure violates the standard only if it is also unreasonable. The alternative is to read the "or" standard as radically different from the "and" standard. In this alternativc view, any non-discriminatory measure would violate the "or" standard, while only an unreasonable, nondiscriminatory measure would violate the "and" standard. That is, the two formulations would reflect fundamentally different concepts of the types of discriminatory conduct that violates the standard. The interpretation advanced here, however, suggests that both formulations prohibit exactly the same types of discriminatory measures, although the "or" formulation also prohibits unreasonable non-discriminatory measures while the "and" formulation does not. That is, the use of a different conjunction has consequences, but those consequences do not include changing the nature of the prohibited discrimination. As has been noted already, measures held to be unreasonable typically are also discriminatory. Thus, to date, there has been little practical difference in the application of the "and" and the "or" versions of the standard.

Some BITs use the word "arbitrary" in lieu of "unreasonable."[110] These words should be regarded as synonymous. Occasionally, the word "unjustified" or "unjust" appears in lieu of "unreasonable."[111] These too should be regarded as synonymous with "unreasonable." Occasionally the word "discriminatory" does not appear.[112]

The list of protected investment activities also varies. Some BITs add the word "operation,"[113] but it is doubtful that the additional word broadens the scope of the provision. Some BITs include "sale" and "liquidation" instead of the more generic term "disposal."[114] This change similarly seems unlikely to have any substantive impact.

One quite significant variation, however, adds "acquisition" and "expansion" to the list of covered investment activities.[115] This language is significant because it grants to investors rights with respect to the establishment of investment. In some BITs, the list

108 *See* Section 7.3.

109 *See* Sections 5.2.1 and 5.2.3.

110 *See, e.g.*, Germany-Timor-Leste BIET, Art. 2(3).

111 *See, e.g.*, Switzerland-Algeria BIT, Art. 4(1); Italy-Nicaragua BIT, Art. II(3); BLEU-Sudan BIT, Art. 3(2).

112 *See, e.g.*, Finland-Armenia BIT, Art. 2(2) (prohibition on "unreasonable or arbitrary" measures).

113 *See, e.g.*, Austria-Armenia BIT, Art. 3(2); Indonesia-Chile BIT, Art. IV(1).

114 *See, e.g.*, Austria-Armenia BIT, Art. 3(2); Chile-Lebanon BIT, Art. III(2).

115 *See, e.g.*, Finland-Armenia BIT, Art. 2(2).

of covered investment activities includes the "extension" of investment, but not its acquisition.[116]

Given that unreasonable or discriminatory measures would seem to violate the fair and equitable treatment standard, the question arises as to whether this standard serves any purpose. The standard, of course, was introduced into BITs at a time when the meaning of the fair and equitable treatment standard had not yet been elucidated by arbitral practice. Its frequent appearance in BITs reflects the consensus that the kind of investment climate that BITs are intended to produce is one in which unreasonable or discriminatory measures are prohibited. This reinforces the view that such measures would violate the fair and equitable treatment standard, which defines the basic relationship between the investment and the host state. As the meaning of the fair and equitable treatment standard is interpreted today, however, the prohibition on unreasonable or discriminatory measures would seem superfluous in any BIT with a fair and equitable treatment standard. An exception might exist in those BITs where (1) the unreasonable or discriminatory measures provision applies to the establishment of investment and (2) the fair and equitable treatment standard protects only investment once established. In such a BIT, the unreasonable or discriminatory measures provision would ensure that the reasonableness and non-discrimination principles apply to the establishment of investment as well as to its treatment after establishment.

As already noted, the standard is violated in most BITs only if the measure impairs the management, maintenance, use, enjoyment, or disposal of the investment. One effect of this limitation is to indicate that measures that have no significant impact on an investment do not violate the standard, even if they are unreasonable or discriminatory. The fair and equitable treatment standard typically has no similar limitation. Similar limitations appear in the national and MFN treatment provisions of some BITs.

Tribunals generally have not addressed the relationship between this provision and customary international law. One reason may be that the unreasonable or discriminatory measures provision, unlike the fair and equitable treatment provision, is not designated by the NAFTA as an element of customary law. Further, this provision, again in contrast to the fair and equitable treatment provision, rarely appears in BITs in the same sentence as a reference to customary law. Yet, authority exists for the proposition that this standard is part of customary international law. The OECD so indicated in the notes to its 1967 Draft Convention on the Protection of Foreign Property.[117] The United States has taken this position as well.[118] Given that this provision seems to be subsumed within the fair and equitable treatment provision, suggestions that the latter provision is an element of customary law would seem to apply to the former provision as well.

5.3.2 Origins

The prohibition on unreasonable or discriminatory measures originated with the 1948 Havana Charter, Article 11(1)(b) of which provided that "No Member shall take

116 *See, e.g.*, Chile-Lebanon BIT, Art. III(2).

117 *See* Section 5.3.2.

118 *See* Kenneth J. Vandevelde, *U.S. International Investment Agreements* 266–267 (2009).

unreasonable or unjustifiable action within its territory injurious to the rights or interests of nationals or other Members in the enterprise, skills, capital, arts or technology which they have supplied." Thus, the language of the Havana Charter prohibited unreasonable conduct, but did not refer to discrimination.

The Economic Agreement of Bogota, which was adopted that same year by the OAS but never entered into force, added a reference to discriminatory measures. Article 22 of the agreement provided that "Foreign capital shall receive equitable treatment. The States therefore agree not to take unjustified, unreasonable or discriminatory measures that would impair the legally-acquired rights or interests of nationals of other countries in the enterprises, capital, skills, arts or technology they have supplied."

The International Law Association (ILA)'s Draft Statute of the Arbitral Tribunal for Foreign Investment and its Draft Statute of the Foreign Investments Court, also produced in 1948, shortened the language by removing the reference to unjustified measures. Both statutes declared one purpose of these respective entities to be the resolution of any dispute "arising out of any unreasonable or discriminatory impairment within the territory of any Contracting Party of the property of nationals of the other Parties."[119]

The United States incorporated a modified version of the OAS language into its post-war FCNs. These treaties typically provided that "Neither Party shall take unreasonable or discriminatory measures that would impair the legally acquired rights or interests within its territories of nationals and companies of the other Party in the enterprises which they have established or in the capital, skills, arts or technology which they have supplied. . . ." [120] Consistent with the ILA draft statute, however, the U.S. FCNs omitted the word "unjustified."

The standard was adopted as well in the 1959 Abs-Shawcross convention, which further modified the language. Article I of the convention provided that "the management, use, and enjoyment [of covered property] shall not in any way be impaired by unreasonable or discriminatory measures." As noted above,[121] the drafters stated explicitly that they regarded this standard as reflecting a principle of reasonableness that is inherent in any system of law. They traced its origin to the U.S. FCNs.[122]

A prohibition on unreasonable or discriminatory measures also appeared in the earliest BITs and the standard language that appears in contemporary BITs emerged in those early BITs. The 1959 BIT between Germany and Pakistan prohibited either party from subjecting to discriminatory treatment any activities "carried on in connection with investments, including the effective management, use or enjoyment of such investments" unless specifically permitted in the "documents of admission" of

---

119 The quoted language appeared in Article 1 of both instruments. The other purpose was to resolve disputes concerning the observance or interpretation of any undertaking which a party may have given in relation to investments.

120 *See, e.g.*, Luxembourg-United States FCN, *supra* chapter 2, note 178, Art. IV(2); Pakistan-United States FCN, *supra* chapter 2, note 188, Art. VI(3); Japan-United States FCN, *supra* chap. 2, note 194, Art. V(1); Ireland-United States FCN, *supra* chapter 2, note 178, Art. V.

121 *See* Section 5.1.

122 Hermann Abs and Sir Hartley Shawcross, "Comment on the Draft Convention By Its Authors," 9 *Journal of Public Law* 119 (1960).

the investment.[123] Thus, the German BITs adopted the practice, also employed in the Abs-Shawcross convention, of applying the prohibition to measures affecting certain activities. This established the pattern followed by nearly all BITs.

The first Dutch BIT, concluded with Tunisia in 1963, guaranteed to covered investments, at Article 1, "just and non-discriminatory treatment," which shall not be less than national treatment. By 1968, the Dutch BITs prohibited unjustified or discriminatory measures that impair the management, maintenance, use, enjoyment, or disposal of covered investments.[124]

The first Belgium-Luxembourg Economic Union (BLEU) BIT, concluded with Tunisia in 1964, required each party "to take steps to ensure that the exercise of the right so recognized is not impeded by unjust or discriminatory measures."[125] Only in the 1970s would the BLEU BITs adopt the more familiar structure of the provision, like that in the German BITs.

The unreasonable or discriminatory measures provision was introduced into Swiss treaty practice in the mid 1960s. For example, Article 1 of the 1965 Swiss BIT with Costa Rica prohibited unjust or discriminatory measures that impaired the management, maintenance, utilization, enjoyment, expansion, or liquidation of the investment.[126] Having appeared in both the Abs-Shawcross convention and in the earliest BITs, the standard also was incorporated in the 1967 OECD Draft Convention on the Protection of Foreign Property. Article 1 of the convention provided that a party "shall not in any way impair the management, maintenance, use, enjoyment or disposal [of covered property] by unreasonable or discriminatory measures." The OECD language thus was shaped by the Abs-Shawcross Convention and early BIT practice. Note 1(a) to Article 1 of the draft convention stated that this rule was one of three in Article 1 that flowed from the "well-established general principle of international law that a State is bound to respect and protect the property of nationals of other States." The other two were the fair and equitable treatment standard and the full protection and security standard, which, in the OECD draft convention, was phrased as "most constant protection and security." Thus, the notes to the OECD draft convention considered the unreasonable or discriminatory measures provision to reflect customary law. Note 7(c) made clear that unreasonable measures include those that are arbitrary or involve an abuse of right. Note 8(d) explained that the prohibition on discriminatory measures applied to those that were "not justified by legitimate considerations." That is, it applied to unreasonable discriminations.

The first U.K. BIT, that concluded with Egypt in 1975, followed the pattern established in the earlier BITs, but used the term "unreasonable" rather than "unjust" or "unjustified." Article 2(2) of that BIT provided that "[e]ach Contracting Party shall ensure that the management, maintenance, use, enjoyment or disposal of investments in its territory of nationals or companies of the other Contracting Party is not in any way impaired by unreasonable or discriminatory measures." This remains in substance

123 Germany-Pakistan BIT, Art. 2(1).

124 *See, e.g.*, Netherlands-Indonesia BIT, Art. 5(1).

125 BLEU-Tanzania BIT, Art. I.

126 *See also* Switzerland-Ecuador BIT, Art. 1.

the language used by the United Kingdom, although the provision is now phrased as a prohibition on such measures rather than an obligation to prevent such measures. The new language is preferable because it makes clear that the provision applies to state impairments.

By the 1980s, the prohibition on unreasonable or discriminatory measures was becoming much more common in BITs, although variations existed in the language, particularly whether the first word of the dyad was "unreasonable," "unjustified," "unjust," or "arbitrary."

For example, although Kuwait inaugurated its BIT program in 1964, a prohibition on unreasonable or discriminatory measures seems to have appeared for the first time in its 1985 BIT with China.[127] Thereafter, the provision commonly appeared in Kuwaiti BITs.[128] Denmark, which began its BIT program in 1965, added a prohibition on "unreasonable or discriminatory" measures that impair the management, maintenance, use, enjoyment, or disposal of investments to its BITs in the late 1980s[129] and the provision remains in its BITs.[130] Austria, which began its BIT program in 1976, included a prohibition on "unjustified or discriminatory measures" in its 1985 BIT with Malaysia BIT,[131] although it was omitted from many later BITs.[132] The provision, phrased as a prohibition on "unreasonable or discriminatory measures," became increasingly common in the BITs concluded by Austria in 2000 and later.[133] Italy, which began its BIT program in 1964, began to include a prohibition on unjustified or discriminatory measures in 1987.[134] The German BITs also had adopted the more typical language by the mid-1980s.[135] Although Sweden began its BIT program in 1965, it did not include a prohibition on impairment of investment by "unreasonable" measures until 1983.[136] In 1991, Sweden modified the language to refer to unreasonable "or discriminatory" measures.[137] That is the formulation still in use.[138] Finland, which

127 Kuwait-China BIT, Art. 2(2).

128 *See, e.g.*, Kuwait-Hungary BIT, Art. 2(3); Kuwait-Ethiopia BIT, Art. 3(1); Kuwait-Czech Republic BIT, Art. 3(1); Kuwait-Croatia BIT, Art. 3(1); Kuwait-Netherlands BIT, Art. 3(1); Kuwait-Denmark BIT, Art. 3(6).

129 *See, e.g.*, Denmark-Republic of Korea BIT, Art. 3(1).

130 *See, e.g.*, Denmark-Kuwait BIT, Art. 3(6); Denmark-Kyrgyz Republic BIT, Art. 2(2); Denmark-Ethiopia BIT, Art. 2(2); Denmark-Croatia BIT, Art. 2(2).

131 *See, e.g.*, Austria-Malaysia BIT, Art. 3(1).

132 *See, e.g.*, Austria-Cape Verde BIT; Austria-Croatia BIT; Austria-India BIT.

133 *See, e.g.*, Austria-Bosnia-Herzegovina BIT, Art. 32); Austria-Armenia BIT, Art. 3(2); Austria-Jordan BIT, Art. 3(2); Austria-Lebanon BIT, Art. 2(2); Austria-Libya BIT, Art. 3(2).

134 *See* Italy-Hungary BIT, Art. 2(2).

135 *See, e.g.*, Germany-Bolivia BIT, Art. 2(2) (prohibition on arbitrary or discriminatory measures that impair the management, maintenance, use, or enjoyment of covered investment).

136 *See, e.g.*, Sweden-Yemen BIT, Art. 2(2); Sweden-Hungary BIT; Sweden-Poland BIT, Art. 2(1); Sweden-Bolivia BIT, Art. 2(1). The provision does not appear in Sweden's BIT with Tunisia, but otherwise appeared regularly in Sweden's BITs concluded in 1983 and thereafter.

137 *See, e.g.*, Sweden-Argentina BIT, Art. 2(2) (unjustified or discriminatory measures); Sweden-Latvia BIT, Art. 2(2) (unreasonable or discriminatory measures); Sweden-Lithuania BIT, Art. 2(2) (unreasonable or discriminatory measures); Sweden-Estonia BIT, March 31, 1992, Art. 2(2) (unreasonable or discriminatory measures).

138 *See, e.g.*, Sweden-Bosnia-Herzegovina BIT, Art.2(2); Sweden-Kazakhstan BIT, Art. 2(3).

began its BIT program in 1980, introduced the provision in its BITs in the early 1990s, paired with the fair and equitable treatment standard[139] or the full protection and security standard.[140]

The United States concluded its first BITs in 1982, at which time it introduced the last innovations to appear in the unreasonable or discriminatory measures provision: application of the provision to the establishment or acquisition of investment.[141] The U.S. approach has been followed by a few other countries.[142] The United States also used the conjunction "and" rather than "or" in the standard.

In summary, the prohibition on unreasonable or discriminatory measures can be traced to the very first BIT, where it applied only to discriminatory treatment of activities in connection with an investment. In the early 1960s, the provision was broadened to apply to unjust or discriminatory measures and the familiar formulation of activities to which the provision applies—the management, maintenance, use, enjoyment, or disposal of investment—emerged. By the late 1960s, the term "unjustified" sometimes appeared rather than "unjust." Many BITs, however, did not yet include the provision. In the 1970s, the term "unreasonable" began to displace "unjust" or "unjustified," a trend that continued in the 1980s. By the 1980s, the use of the dyad "unreasonable or discriminatory" had become the dominant practice and the provision itself had become common in BITs. During the 1980s as well, the United States introduced the practice of applying the provision to the establishment of investment and of using the conjunction "and" rather than "or." The provision continues to be common in BITs, but is by no means present in all BITs, and in most cases it takes the form that had begun to appear in the BITs in the 1970s.

5.3.3 Arbitral Practice

Tribunals generally have treated "unreasonable" and "discriminatory" as distinct terms to be defined individually. This contrasts with the standards of "fair and equitable treatment" and "full protection and security," where the conjoined terms usually are treated as if they create a single standard. As the tribunal noted in *Lauder v. Czech Republic*, a case arising under the United States-Czech Republic BIT, the plain wording of the provision (in the case before it) requires that the measure be both arbitrary (the word appearing in the United States-Czech Republic BIT) and discriminatory.[143] At the same time, in *Azurix v. Argentina*, a case arising under the United States-Argentina BIT, one of the few U.S. BITs using the conjunction "or" in the standard,

139 *See, e.g.*, Finland-Turkey BIT, Art. 3; Finland-Vietnam BIT, Art. 2(2); Finland-Argentina BIT, Art. 2(2).

140 *See, e.g.*, Finland-Chile BIT, Art. 2(2); Finland-Brazil BIT, Art. 2(2).

141 *See* United States-Panama BIT, Art. 2(2).

142 *See, e.g.*, Finland-Armenia BIT, Art. 2(3); Finland-Belarus BIT, Art. 2(3); Finland-Algeria BIT, Art. 3(2) (prohibiting "unreasonable or arbitrary" measures).

143 Award, para. 219.

the tribunal held that an arbitrary measure would violate the standard even if it were not discriminatory. Both awards assume, however, that the concepts are distinct.

Tribunals in most cases have found host-state conduct not to be arbitrary within the meaning of this provision. In most cases where conduct has been found arbitrary, typically the conduct was directed at the investor because of its foreign nationality or was politically motivated. In a few cases, however, the tribunal has found host-state conduct to violate the standard simply because it lacked a rational basis in policy.

Because both unreasonableness and discrimination generally are held to violate the fair and equitable treatment standard, tribunals do not always discuss the unreasonable or discriminatory treatment standard separately. In some cases, they address claims under this standard as part of a broader discussion of fair and equitable treatment.[144] As noted above, tribunals applying the unreasonable or discriminatory measures standard sometimes attempt to develop separate definitions of the concepts of reasonableness and nondiscrimination, while tribunals applying these concepts as part of a broader fair and equitable treatment standard may not. Yet, the substance of the concepts appears to be the same under both standards. That is, conduct held to be unreasonable or discriminatory under one standard generally will be found unreasonable or discriminatory under the other standard. As the tribunal said concerning the unreasonable or discriminatory measures provision in *Saluka Investments v. Czech Republic*, a case arising under the Netherlands-Czech Republic BIT,

> The standard of "reasonableness" has no different meaning in this context than in the context of the "fair and equitable treatment" standard with which it is associated; and the same is true with regard to the standard of "non-discrimination".[145]

The tribunal explained that

> a violation of the non-impairment requirement does not therefore differ substantially from a violation of the "fair and equitable treatment" standard. The non-impairment requirement merely identifies more specific effects of any such violation, namely with regard to the operation, management, maintenance, use, enjoyment or disposal of the investment by the investor.[146]

Tribunals tend to define the term "arbitrary" by reference to legal dictionaries. In *CMS Gas Transmission v. Argentina*, a case arising under the United States-Argentina BIT, the tribunal referred to the definition of that term found in *Black's Law Dictionary*. Based on that source, the tribunal found that the term means "depending on individual discretion founded on prejudice or preference rather than on reason or fact."[147] As this suggests, the prohibition on "arbitrary" measures duplicates the protection afforded by

---

144 *See, e.g., PSEG v. Turkey* (United States-Turkey BIT); *MCI Power v. Ecuador* (United States-Ecuador BIT). The tribunal in *Plama Consortium v. Bulgaria*, a case arising under the Energy Charter Treaty, did not discuss the unreasonableness element of the standard, but may have regarded its discussion of the fair and equitable treatment standard as subsuming that element, having noted the overlap between the two standards. Award, para. 184.

145 Award, para. 460.

146 Award, para. 461.

147 Award, para. 291.

the reasonableness principle of the fair and equitable treatment standard. Indeed, the tribunal declined to analyze whether the emergency measures taken by Argentina in response to its financial crisis of 2001–2002 violated the arbitrary and discriminatory treatment standard, commenting that to the extent that any arbitrariness or discrimination could be found, it should be treated as a factor in assessing whether Argentina had violated the fair and equitable treatment standard. The tribunal went on to observe that arbitrary and discriminatory conduct necessarily violates the fair and equitable treatment standard.

The tribunal in *National Grid v. Argentina*, a case arising under the United Kingdom-Argentina BIT, cited *Black's Law Dictionary* for the definitions of both "arbitrary" and "unreasonable" and found the two terms to be substantially the same in meaning.[148] It found that the emergency measures taken by Argentina to address its economic crisis of 2001–2002 were reasonable. Each measure was taken pursuant to an articulated policy.

The same definition was employed in *LG&E v. Argentina*, another case arising under the United States-Argentina BIT and involving Argentina's response to the 2001–2002 crisis. The tribunal observed that the parties to the BIT sought to prohibit measures affecting investment that were implemented without "a rational decision-making process."[149] Such a process would include a balance of the interests of the state with the burden of the measure on investment. The tribunal found that the measures were the result of reasoned judgment rather than disregard of the rule of law. Accordingly, they were not arbitrary. The tribunal did hold that Argentina had violated the fair and equitable treatment standard through its inconsistent conduct, which contravened the security principle.[150] This case thus illustrates the broader scope of the fair and equitable treatment standard relative to the prohibition on unreasonable or discriminatory measures.

The Black's definition was adopted as well by the tribunal in *Lauder v. Czech Republic*, a case arising under the United States-Czech Republic BIT. In that case, the claimant had entered into a joint venture with a Czech company to operate a television station. The Czech government approved the structure of the venture, but later required a restructuring on the ground that the existing structure allowed the claimant to broadcast without a license. The restructuring allowed the Czech company to force the claimant out of the venture. The tribunal found that the conduct of the Czech government in requiring the restructuring of the joint venture did not violate the standard because it was based on legitimate regulatory concerns. The tribunal also found, however, that a decision of the Czech government prohibiting the claimant from participating in the business except as part of a joint venture, despite having previously announced that the claimant would be permitted to participate as an equity shareholder in the Czech company, violated the standard because it was founded not on reason or fact, but on mere fear reflecting a preference for national ownership of broadcast licenses.

148 Award, para. 197.

149 Award, para.158.

150 *See* Section 6.2.

The tribunal nevertheless held that the claimant was not entitled to compensation because the conduct of the Czech company was a superseding cause of harm.

The same facts were before a different tribunal in *CME v. Czech Republic*, where the tribunal was charged with applying the Netherlands-Czech Republic BIT. The tribunal found that the actions of the Czech government were unreasonable in that they were motivated by an intent to collude with the local company in order to deprive a foreign investor of its investment, although it did not seek to define further the word "unreasonable." The tribunal noted that the conduct of the Czech government "smacks of discrimination" as well.[151]

The definition from *Black's Law Dictionary* also was adopted in *Occidental v. Ecuador*, a case arising under the United States-Ecuador BIT. In this case, the tribunal found host-state conduct to be arbitrary, although not motivated by political or discriminatory considerations. Ecuador had changed its practice of granting the claimant a refund of the value added tax (VAT) it paid in connection with its oil production business. The tribunal found that Ecuador's actions were not founded on prejudice or preference as opposed to reason or fact. Ecuador simply had been trying to resolve the confusion arising from a variety of practices, regulations, and rules relating to VAT refunds. Yet, the tribunal found that this confusion and lack of clarity had resulted in "some form of arbitrariness," although it never defined the form of arbitrariness that had occurred.[152] In any event, no violation of the provision was found because the tribunal was not persuaded that the management, operation, maintenance, use, enjoyment, acquisition, expansion, or disposal of the investment had been impaired by the measures. The claimant continued to enjoy its rights with respect to its property.[153]

The definition from *Black's Law Dictionary* also was adopted by the tribunal in *Plama Consortium v. Bulgaria*, a case arising under the Energy Charter Treaty. The tribunal, however, in applying the unreasonable or discriminatory measures provision, discussed only the element of discrimination.

A second definition of "arbitrary" that appears in the cases, although less commonly, is based on language used by the International Court of Justice in the *Elettronica Sicula (ELSI)* case.[154] In that case, the Court defined arbitrariness as "not so much something opposed to a rule of law, as something opposed to the rule of law. . . . It is a willful disregard of due process of law, an act which shocks, or at least surprises, a sense of judicial propriety."[155] This definition was cited by the tribunal in *LG&E v. Argentina*, discussed above. The tribunal found that the measures in that case did not reflect a disregard of the rule of law, but rather were the result of reasoned judgment. As noted above, the tribunal in that case also employed a definition drawn from *Black's Law Dictionary*.

The tribunal adopted the *ELSI* definition as well in *Duke Energy v. Ecuador*, a case arising under the United States-Ecuador BIT. The tribunal held that, although the host

---

151 Partial Award, para. 612.

152 Award, para. 163.

153 Award, para. 161.

154 *Case concerning Elettronica Sicula* (United States v. Italy), 1989 I.C.J. Rep. 15.

155 *Id.* at 76.

state breached its power purchase agreements with the claimant's investment, contract breaches do not in themselves constitute arbitrary conduct.[156] The conduct of the Minister of Energy and Mines and of the Attorney General in contesting the legality of local arbitration of the investment's claims for payment "complied with local law and can thus not be regarded as arbitrary."[157]

In *Noble Ventures v. Romania*, a case arising under the United States-Romania BIT, the tribunal also adopted the *ELSI* definition.[158] The tribunal found that, in light of the desperate financial circumstances of the claimant's investment, the institution of judicial reorganization proceedings with respect to the investment could not be regarded as arbitrary.[159] Further, because such proceedings are provided by all legal systems, they cannot be regarded as opposed to the rule of law.[160] The proceedings in this case were conducted in accordance with local law. The tribunal observed that its holding might have been different if it had concluded that the host state was responsible under international law for the economic difficulties of the claimant's investment.[161]

In a couple of awards applying this definition, tribunals did find host-state conduct to be arbitrary. In *Azurix v. Argentina*, a case arising under the United States-Argentina BIT, the tribunal cited the definition from *Black's Law Dictionary*, but then held that the *ELSI* definition is "close to the ordinary meaning of arbitrary since it emphasizes the element of willful disregard of the law."[162] The tribunal found that Argentina's actions in encouraging customers of the claimant's water company not to pay their bills, threatening officials who allowed the company to bill its customers, refusing to honor the tariff arrangement in the concession agreement, and refusing access to documents on the basis of which the company was sanctioned were arbitrary actions without basis in law or the concession agreement.

Similar to the award in *Azurix* is that in *Siemens v. Argentina*, a case arising under the Germany-Argentina BIT. After citing the definition from Black's Law Dictionary, the tribunal also found the *ELSI* definition to be "close to the ordinary meaning of the term emphasizing the willful disregard of the law."[163] In that case, the tribunal found that Argentina acted arbitrarily in suspending the contract that it had issued to the claimant's investment to produce national identity cards. Argentina had failed to offer a satisfactory explanation of the decision and thus it "did not seem to be based on reason."[164]

---

156 *See Impregilo v. Pakistan*, a case arising under the Italy-Pakistan BIT, where the tribunal held that matters of contract performance do not involve *puissance publique* and thus do not violate the prohibition on unreasonable or discriminatory measures. Decision on Jurisdiction, para. 260.

157 Award, para. 382.

158 Award, para. 176.

159 Award, para. 177.

160 Award, para. 178.

161 Award, para. 179.

162 Award, para. 392.

163 Award, para. 318. The similarity in language between the two awards is perhaps attributable to the fact that the same arbitrator served as president of both tribunals.

164 *Id.*

At least one case has adopted a definition drawn from *Neer v. Mexico*.[165] In *Genin v. Estonia*, a case arising under the United States-Estonia BIT, Estonia had revoked the license of the claimant's bank without following generally accepted banking and regulatory practices, such as providing formal notice of the intended revocation, inviting the bank to send a representative to the revocation proceeding, or providing the bank with an opportunity to challenge the revocation in court prior to its public announcement. In order to amount to a violation of the BIT, however, the tribunal found that such irregularities would need to amount to "bad faith, a wilful disregard of due process of law or an extreme insufficiency of action."[166] The tribunal found that the host state's conduct was not arbitrary because it was taken for regulatory reasons justified by the economic circumstances at the time, including in particular the difficulties associated with Estonia's transition to a market economy and its efforts to build a private financial sector. In support of its conclusion, the tribunal also cited the *ELSI* definition. As noted in Section 5.2.3, other tribunals have not followed *Genin* in suggesting that bad faith might be necessary to constitute a violation of the standard.

Not every tribunal relies on the dictionary definition of the terms. As already noted, the tribunal in *Saluka Investments v. Czech Republic*, a case arising under the Netherlands-Czech Republic, relied on the fact that reasonableness principle has the same content under both the fair and equitable treatment standard and the unreasonable or discriminatory measures standard. It held that the reasonableness principle requires "a showing that the State's conduct bears a reasonable relationship to some rational policy. . . ."[167]

One tribunal adopted a unique approach. In *BG Group v. Argentina*, a case arising under the United Kingdom-Argentina BIT, the tribunal distinguished between the terms "arbitrary" and "unreasonable," the only tribunal to do so. It defined arbitrary in accordance with the *ELSI* definition. It held that reasonableness, however, "should be measured against the expectations of the parties" to the BIT.[168] That is, reasonable conduct was that which would be "appropriate behavior in light of the goals of the Treaty."[169] The tribunal then found that Argentina's withdrawal of undertakings and assurances given to investors as an inducement to investment was by definition unreasonable. A change in policy, however, arguably could be a reasonable response to a change in circumstances. Thus, the true ground of the decision may have been that Argentina's change in policy, contrary to its prior assurances, violated the security principle of the BITs rather than the reasonableness principle.

Tribunals do not always define the term "arbitrary" or "unreasonable." One such case was *CME*, discussed above. Similarly, in *MTD Equity v. Chile*, a case arising

---

165 *U.S.A. (L.F. Neer) v. United Mexican States*, (United States-Mexico), October 15, 1926, 3 *International Law Reports* 213.

166 Award, para. 371.

167 Award, para. 460.

168 Award, para. 342.

169 Award, para. 342 (citing *CME v. Czech Republic*, Partial Award, para. 158).

under the Malaysia-Chile BIT, the tribunal in a very brief discussion found that Chile's encouragement of a foreign investor to invest in a land development project that was contrary to local zoning law was unreasonable. In *Enron v. Argentina*, a case arising under the United States-Argentina BIT, the tribunal held that emergency measures adopted by Argentina during its 2001–2002 financial crisis were not arbitrary because they "were what the Government believed and understood was the best response to the unfolding crisis."[170] Four months later, the tribunal in *Sempra Energy v. Argentina*, another case arising under the United States-Argentina BIT, agreed that the measures were not arbitrary. Echoing the language from Enron,[171] the tribunal found that, although Argentina's emergency measures were unlawful, "[t]hey were not . . . arbitrary in that they responded to what the Government believed and understood to be the best response to the unfolding crisis."[172] In *ADC v. Hungary*, a case arising under the Cyprus-Hungary BIT, the tribunal found with little discussion that under the facts before it the host state's expropriation of the claimant's investment in a way that violated the expropriation provision of the treaty also violated the prohibition on unreasonable or discriminatory measures.[173]

Tribunals rarely discuss the meaning of the word "discriminatory" in this provision. The few relevant cases are discussed in Section 7.3.

Tribunals do not always distinguish between unreasonable and discriminatory treatment. In *Eastern Sugar v. Czech Republic*, a case arising under the Netherlands-Czech Republic BIT, the European Union reduced the country sugar quota for the Czech Republic, which in turn reduced the quota allocated to a covered investment. The amount of the investment's quota, however, was reduced by more than the amount of the entire country quota reduction. That is, a single producer was required to bear the entire burden of the country's quota reduction. At the same time, the quota system had been revised to permit new entrants into the system. The tribunal believed that the covered investment, which had done nothing illegal, had been targeted in retaliation for its politically controversial decision to close a plant. The tribunal found, however, that even if the intent was not to punish the foreign investment, the decision to favor new entrants was an unreasonable or discriminatory measure.

In *LLC AMTO v. Ukraine*, a case arising under the Energy Charter Treaty, the tribunal found that the efforts by the tax authorities through a bankruptcy proceeding to collect taxes owed by the claimant's investment were based on nonpayment of taxes dating back to a time before the claimant acquired the investment. Other creditors also participated in the proceeding, which was conducted in accordance with local law. The tribunal found no arbitrary, unreasonable, or discriminatory conduct.[174]

---

170 Award, para. 281.

171 The similarity in language presumably is attributable to the fact that the same arbitrator served as president of both tribunals.

172 Award, para. 318.

173 Award, para. 445.

174 Award, para. 99.

5.4 THE INTERNATIONAL MINIMUM STANDARD

Some BITs require that the host state provide covered investment with treatment no less favorable than that required by customary international law.[175] Illustrative of these provisions is the language of the Finland-Armenia BIT, which provides that "[i]n any case a Contracting Party shall not accord treatment less favourable than that required by international law." Such a provision performs at least three functions.

First, it incorporates into a BIT all the obligations with respect to covered investment or investors imposed on host states by customary international law. Thus, where this provision appears, a breach of customary international law also violates the BIT. In a sense, this provision is analogous to the observance of obligations provision in that it incorporates a separate set of norms into the BIT, in one case the norms of customary law and in the other case the norms created by the terms of the obligation assumed by the host state. The benefit to the investor of the incorporation into the BIT of the international minimum standard is that it ensures that violations of that standard may be the basis of a claim under the investor-state or state-state disputes provisions. Some BITs confer on investor-state arbitral tribunals jurisdiction over an investment dispute only if it violates the BIT (or perhaps another instrument, such as an investment agreement)[176] and the existence of this provision ensures that a violation of the international minimum standard will satisfy that jurisdictional requirement. Other BITs, however, confer on investor-state arbitral tribunals jurisdiction over any dispute concerning an investment[177] and, in such a case, an investor's claim that the host state's treatment of investment violated customary international law may be within a tribunal's jurisdiction, even in the absence of this provision. In any event, the state-state disputes provision in nearly every case applies only to disputes concerning the interpretation or application of the BIT and thus this provision at a minimum facilitates enforcement of customary law under the state-state disputes provision. The usefulness of including a reference to the international minimum standard, however, is diminished by the fact that other provisions, such as the fair and equitable treatment provision, the unreasonable or discriminatory measures provision, the full protection and security provision, the expropriation provision, the observance of obligations provision, and the war and civil disturbance provision, taken together, incorporate much, if not all, of the international minimum standard.

A second function of this provision is that it serves as a choice of law clause for any dispute under the BIT. Because this provision requires the host state to comply with customary law in its treatment of covered investment, international law governs any dispute arising under the BIT. The usefulness of this function is also diminished to the extent that the requirements of customary international law are separately required by other provisions of the BIT.

175 *See, e.g.*, Finland-Armenia BIT, Art. 2(2); Sweden-Kazakhstan BIT, Art 2(4); Mexico-Iceland BIT, Art. 3(1); Austria-Malaysia BIT, Art. 3(2); United States-Georgia BIT, Art. 2(3)(a).

176 *See* Section 10.2.1.1.

177 *See* Section 10.2.1.1.

A third function of this provision is that it provides a general guide to the interpretation of the other provisions of the BIT. Because the provision requires the host state to comply with customary international law in its treatment of covered investment or investors, every provision of the BIT must be interpreted so as not to derogate from the protection provided by customary law. Customary law, of course, provides only a minimum standard. Where the language of a BIT requires more than customary international law requires, the host state must comply with the more rigorous BIT standard as well as the international minimum standard imposed by the BIT. This again is an example of the cumulative nature of BIT obligations.[178] The fair and equitable treatment standard performs a similar role in providing a guide to interpretation of the other provisions of the BIT.[179]

Many of the tribunal awards rendered to date applying this provision arose under BITs that also included requirements of fair and equitable treatment and full protection and security. In such cases, the tribunals often prefer to address whether the host state's conduct violated the somewhat more specific standard of fair and equitable treatment or full protection and security. For example, in *Lauder v. Czech Republic*, a case arising under the United States-Czech Republic BIT, the BIT guaranteed fair and equitable treatment, full protection and security, and treatment in no case less than that required by customary law. The tribunal noted that the claimant had not identified any specific obligation under international law that would provide more protection than the other BIT provisions on which he relied. Thus, the tribunal did not engage in an analysis of whether customary law was violated apart from its analysis of the other general absolute treatment standards alleged to have been violated.

Several tribunals have discussed the meaning of customary international law in the course of arbitrating claims under the NAFTA. Article 1105 of the NAFTA requires that covered investment be treated in accordance with customary international law, which under that article includes the obligations of fair and equitable treatment and full protection and security. As a result, these tribunals have not been required to distinguish carefully between the international minimum standard under customary law and the specific obligations of fair and equitable treatment and full protection and security.

A number of awards, however, have discussed in general terms what is required by customary international law. They are uniform in concluding that customary international law continues to evolve and that the treaty standard refers to customary international law as it exists today.[180]

The international minimum standard clearly incorporates the security principle. This principle is reflected in particular in the obligation of due diligence codified in the full protection and security standard. Awards discussing this standard are discussed in Section 6.3.3. It is reflected as well in the requirement that expropriations meet certain conditions, including payment of compensation. Awards discussing this requirement are discussed in Section 6.5.3. It is also reflected in the rule that unilateral repudiation

178 *See* Section 1.2.

179 *See* Section 5.2.1.

180 *See, e.g., Tecmed v. Mexico* (Spain-Mexico BIT), Award, para. 116; *ADF Group v. United States* (NAFTA), Award, para. 113.

of contracts is unlawful. Awards discussing this rule are discussed in Section 6.4.3. The international minimum standard also incorporates the due process principle, particularly through the prohibition on a denial of justice. Awards discussing the denial of justice doctrine are discussed in Section 10.4.

The international minimum standard incorporates as well the nondiscrimination principle. Awards discussing whether customary law includes a general prohibition on discriminatory treatment of foreign investment are discussed in Section 7.4. Some of the awards that have sought to define the provision requiring compliance with the international minimum standard have equated that provision with the reasonableness principle. As will be seen, the reasonableness principle as reflected in this provision operates the same way as under the fair and equitable treatment provision and the prohibition on unreasonable or discriminatory measures.

For example, in *S.D. Myers v. Canada*, a case arising under the NAFTA, Canada imposed a ban on the export of polychlorinated biphenyls (PCBs). The claimant sought to export the chemicals to the United States for processing at its plant in Ohio and, as a result of the ban, lost that business opportunity. The tribunal held that a breach of customary international law

> occurs only when it is shown that an investor has been treated in such an unjust or arbitrary manner that the treatment rises to the level that is unacceptable from the international perspective. That determination must be made in the light of the high measure of deference that international law generally extends to the rights of domestic authorities to regulate matters within their own borders.[181]

Thus, the tribunal seemed initially to equate a violation of the standard with unreasonable conduct. The tribunal then found that Canada's ban was adopted for the purpose of excluding American companies from the market for PCB disposal and therefore violated the national treatment standard of the NAFTA. It concluded that, under the circumstances of that case, a violation of national treatment also constituted a violation of customary international law, although it acknowledged that a violation of national treatment may not violate customary law in every case. In short, the violation in *S.D. Myers* consisted of an unjustified or unreasonable discrimination.

In *Pope & Talbot v Canada*, another case arising under the NAFTA, the tribunal initially held in its award on the merits that the requirement of fair and equitable treatment was additive to the requirement of treatment in accordance with customary international law in NAFTA Article 1105. A few weeks after that award, on July 31, 2001, the NAFTA parties issued a joint interpretation stating that Article 1105 guarantees only the treatment required by customary international law and that fair and equitable treatment is a component of the international minimum standard under customary law. Accordingly, in its subsequent award on damages, the tribunal undertook to reinterpret Article 1105. Canada had argued that the international minimum standard was the standard adopted in *Neer v. Mexico*. The *Neer* tribunal had required that, for a breach to be found, the treatment "should amount to an outrage, to bad faith, to wilful neglect of duty, or to an insufficiency of government action so far short of international

181 Partial Award, para. 263.

standards that every reasonable and impartial man would readily recognize its insufficiency."[182] The tribunal found, however, that international law had evolved since the *Neer* case was decided in 1926 and that Article 1105 required application of the evolving standard, not the standard as it existed in the 1920s. The tribunal then noted the definition of arbitrariness adopted by the International Court of Justice in the *ELSI* case:

> Arbitrariness is not so much something opposed to a rule of law, as something opposed to the rule of law. . . . It is a willful disregard of due process of law, an act which shocks, or at least surprises, a sense of judicial propriety.[183]

Thus, a tribunal again appeared to equate a violation of customary international law with a violation of the reasonableness principle. The tribunal concluded that the *ELSI* case had lowered the international minimum standard from one of outrage to one of surprise. The tribunal then held, however, that it need not decide the precise formulation of the contemporary international minimum standard because Canada's conduct had met even the higher standard proposed by Canada and would "shock and outrage every reasonable person."[184] Such conduct included imposing very burdensome demands for documents, threats of criminal investigations, and misrepresentations of the facts concerning the investment's situation in internal government memoranda.

In *Mondev v. United States*, yet another case arising under the NAFTA, the tribunal noted that *Neer* and similar cases involved the physical security of aliens and there was insufficient cause to conclude that its standard of outrageous treatment also applied to the treatment of foreign investment. In any event, the tribunal went on to find that international law had evolved since the 1920s. As the tribunal explained,

> there can be no doubt that, by interpreting Article 1105(1) to prescribe the customary international law minimum standard of treatment of aliens as the minimum standard of treatment to be afforded to investments of investors of another Party under NAFTA, the term "customary international law" refers to customary international law as it stood no earlier than the time at which NAFTA came into force. It is not limited to the international law of the 19th century or even of the first half of the 20th century, although decisions from that period remain relevant. In holding that Article 1105(1) refers to customary international law, the FTC interpretations incorporate current international law, whose content is shaped by the conclusion of more than two thousand bilateral investment treaties and many treaties of friendship and commerce. Those treaties largely and concordantly provide for "fair and equitable" treatment of, and for "full protection and security" for, the foreign investor and its investments.[185]

In ascertaining the minimum standard, the tribunal found that it was "bound by the minimum standard as established in State practice and in the jurisprudence of

---

182 *U.S.A. (L.F. Neer) v. United Mexican States*, (United States-Mexico), October 15, 1926, 3 International Law Reports. 213.

183 *Case concerning Elettronica Sicula* (United States v. Italy), 1989 I.C.J. Rep. 15.

184 Award, para. 68.

185 Award, para. 125.

arbitral tribunals."[186] The claim in *Mondev* for a violation of customary international law arose from an alleged denial of justice. The tribunal's assessment of that claim is discussed in Section 10.4.

The tribunal in *Mondev* noted that the law to be applied is the law as it stood "no earlier than" the time at which the NAFTA entered into force.[187] As this language seems to indicate, where customary law continues to evolve after a treaty enters into force, a BIT provision guaranteeing treatment in accordance with customary international law requires treatment in accordance with the standard in its contemporary state, not as it existed at the date of entry into force.[188]

In *ADF Group v. United States*, still another case arising under the NAFTA, the tribunal concurred that the customary international law standard continues to evolve and noted that all three NAFTA parties agreed that Article 1105(1) refers to customary international law "as it exists today."[189] The tribunal then quoted with approval the discussion of *Neer* in *Mondev*. Thus, the tribunal concluded, "[t]here appears no logical necessity and no concordant state practice to support the view that the *Neer* formulation is automatically extendible to the contemporary context of treatment of foreign investors and their investments by a host or recipient state."[190] The tribunal then went on to examine the claimant's argument that a U.S. requirement that steel used in federally funding highway construction projects be manufactured in the United States violated the fair and equitable treatment element of Article 1105(1). As discussed above, the tribunal found that the claimant had not sustained its burden of proof in that regard because it had not demonstrated the unreasonableness of the requirement.

In *Waste Management v. Mexico*, again a case arising under the NAFTA, the claimant concluded a contract with the city of Acapulco under which it would collect and dispose of solid waste. Members of the public, however, opposed the collection program because they were unwilling to pay the fees assessed to finance the program. Eventually, as a result of this opposition, the city ceased to honor its obligations under the contract, including the payments owed to the investment. In determining the applicable standard under Article 1105 the tribunal surveyed several of the awards rendered to date.[191] The tribunal noted that, despite certain differences of emphasis,

> the minimum standard of treatment of fair and equitable treatment is infringed by conduct attributable to the State and harmful to the claimant if the conduct is arbitrary, grossly unfair, unjust or idiosyncratic, is discriminatory and exposes the claimant to sectional or racial prejudice, or involves a lack of due process leading to an outcome which offends judicial propriety—as might be the case with a manifest failure of natural justice in judicial proceedings or a complete lack of transparency and candour in an administrative process. In applying this standard it

---

186 *Id.* at para. 119.

187 *Id.*

188 *Tecmed v. Mexico* (Spain-Mexico BIT), Award, para. 116; *UPS v. Canada* (NAFTA), Award on Jurisdiction, para. 84.

189 Award, para. 179.

190 *Id.* at para. 181.

191 These were the awards in *S.D. Myers v. Canada, Mondev v. United States, ADF v. United States*, and *Loewen v. United States*, all of which involved disputes under the NAFTA.

> is relevant that the treatment is in breach of representations made by the host State which were reasonably relied on by the claimant.[192]

The tribunal observed that the standard "is to some extent a flexible one which must be adapted to the circumstances of each case."[193] As the quoted language indicates, the tribunal did not carefully distinguish between the international minimum standard required by Article 1105(1) and the fair and equitable treatment standard, which Article 1105(1) treats as merely one element of the international minimum standard. Thus, the award has been cited both as evidence of the content of Article 1105(1) and evidence of the content of the fair and equitable treatment standard.

In any event, the claimant alleged that the development bank, Banobras, breached Article 1105(1) in its failure to adhere to a line of credit agreement that would have guaranteed the payments due to claimant's investment. The tribunal found, however, that it need not determine whether Banobras complied because a remedy was available in Mexican courts and, for reasons discussed in Section 10.4, there had been no denial of justice before those courts. Apart from the agreement, Banobras was under no duty to provide a line of credit and therefore did not breach the standard in refusing to grant the claimant a line of credit.

The tribunal did find that the city had failed to fulfill its contractual obligations.[194] The tribunal held, however, that no violation of Article 1105(1) had occurred. The city's conduct was not "wholly arbitrary or grossly unfair."[195] The city's failure of payment was based on a financial crisis it faced and not on any sectoral or local prejudice. The tribunal also observed that nonpayment of a debt would not violate Article 1105, "provided that it does not amount to an outright and unjustified repudiation of the transaction and provided that some remedy is open to the creditor to address the problem."[196] Again, the tribunal associated a violation of the international minimum standard with unreasonable conduct.[197]

In *GAMI Investments v. Mexico*, also a case arising under the NAFTA, the tribunal considered whether Mexico's administration of its regime for regulating sugar production, exports, and prices violated customary international law. The claimant, which owned sugar mills, contended that Mexico's maladministration of the regime, including in particular its failure to enforce its own laws, had injured the claimant's investment. The tribunal quoted language from *S.D. Myers v. Canada*, which stated:

> When interpreting and applying the "minimum standard," a [tribunal formed under the investment chapter of NAFTA] does not have an open-ended mandate to second-guess government decision-making. Governments have to make many potentially controversial choices. In doing so, they may appear to have made mistakes, to have misjudged the facts, proceeded on the basis of a misguided economic

---

192 Award, para. 98.

193 *Id.* at 99.

194 Award, para. 109.

195 *Id.* at para. 115.

196 *Id.*

197 The reference to "unjustified repudiation of the transaction" appears to be a reference to the security principle as well.

> or sociological theory, placed too much emphasis on some social values over others and adopted solutions that are ultimately ineffective or counterproductive. The ordinary remedy, if there were one, for errors in modern governments is through internal political and legal processes, including elections.[198]

The tribunal noted that the failure of a government program to achieve its objectives does not necessarily constitute a violation of international law nor is a failure to follow national law ipso facto a violation of international law. Rather, something more than mere illegality is required, such as an "outright and unjustified repudiation" of the regulations.[199] The tribunal found that, while Mexico had poorly administered the sugar regime, its conduct did not violate international law. The regime had not worked as planned and the evidence did not support the conclusion that Mexico had deliberately sought to undermine the regime. As this suggests, Mexico's conduct did not violate the standard because it was reasonable, even if flawed.[200]

In *CME v. Czech Republic*, a case arising under the Netherlands-Czech Republic BIT, the tribunal did not discuss the meaning of the international minimum standard. It held simply that

> the intentional undermining of the Claimant's investment protection, the expropriation of the value of that investment, its unfair and inequitable treatment, the Media Council's unreasonable actions, the destruction of the Claimant's investment security and protection, are together a violation of the principles of international law. . . .[201]

Because certain of these acts, such as an uncompensated expropriation, even alone would have violated customary international law, finding that the acts collectively violate customary law provides little guidance concerning the standard required under that law. The language suggests, however, that the wrongfulness of the Czech Republic's conduct rested on its violation of principles of reasonableness and security.

---

198 Award, para. 93, quoting *S.D. Myers v. Canada*, First Partial Award of 13 November 2000, para. 260.

199 Award, para.103.

200 In any event, the success of the regime depended upon the conduct of multiple actors and it was not shown that claimant's losses were attributable to the actions of Mexico. As suggested in note 197 *supra*, the reference to repudiation suggests that the tribunal considered the security principle as well.

201 Partial Award, para. 614.

Chapter 6

Security

6.1 INTRODUCTION

Security is perhaps the oldest of the BIT principles to be found in investment treaty practice. As noted in Section 2.1, provisions for the return of property seized in time of war can be found in fourteenth-century treaties. Gradually, provisions on the seizure of property in time of war were expanded to apply in time of peace, although these expanded provisions generally allowed expropriation of foreign-owned property if compensation was paid.

By the 1820s, when the process that would lead to the first era of globalization was beginning, the principle of security was reflected in FCN treaty provisions applicable in two situations. The first was the expropriation of property, for which compensation was owed.[1] The second was the admission of aliens, who were to be protected in their persons and property.[2] By the beginning of the twentieth century, the repudiation of debts had become a third concern, although this was rarely addressed in FCN treaties.[3] The right to payment of the debt was expressed in bond documents and few doubted the obligation of the debtor to pay, although creditor and debtor countries divided over the right of creditor countries to use military force to collect the debts.[4] By the mid-twentieth century, however, the consensus regarding the security principle had begun to collapse, as communist and developing countries repudiated concession agreements and expropriated foreign-owned property while disputing their obligation to pay full or perhaps even any compensation.

Security is the preeminent concern of BITs. Security provisions were present in the first BITs and are universally present in contemporary BITs. These security provisions do not provide investment with security against all events, but rather against particular kinds of host state conduct. Two provisions that are universal in BITs protect investment against exchange controls or wrongful expropriations. An observance of obligations

---

1 *See* Section 2.1.1.

2 *See* Section 2.1.1.

3 *See* Section 2.1.1.

4 *See* Section 2.1.1.

provision that appears in some BITs preserves the security of obligations with respect to investments. A fair and equitable treatment standard, present in the vast majority of BITs, provides security with respect to the investor's legitimate expectations, that is promises or assurances on which the investor has relied. A full protection and security standard requires the host state to exercise due diligence to protect investment against physical harm and, according to some tribunals, at least certain kinds of non-physical harm as well. A provision present in some BITs provides protection against certain confiscations or destructions of property during periods of armed conflict or civil disturbance. These various reflections of the security principle have emerged over time in response to particular instances of host state conduct that impaired the security of investment.

6.2 FAIR AND EQUITABLE TREATMENT

The fair and equitable treatment standard, which was introduced in Section 5.2, has been interpreted by investor-state arbitral tribunals to provide a form of security to covered investment. More particularly, the standard requires that host states act in a way that is consistent. Tribunals have made clear that the standard does not impose on host states a general obligation always to act consistently over time. Host states generally have the discretion to change policies. A violation occurs, however, where the host state has promised to act in a certain way or has offered assurances to the investor (or investment) on which it has reasonably relied. That is, the security principle entitles the covered investment or investor to the protection of its legitimate expectations based on such promises or assurances. Failure of the host state to act in a way that is consistent with its promises and assurances violates the security principle.

Some tribunals have said that such promises or assurances must have been made at the time the investor decided to invest.[5] For example, in *Duke Energy v. Ecuador*, a case arising under the United States-Ecuador BIT, the tribunal refused to find a violation of the fair and equitable treatment standard where the host state was alleged to have violated arbitration agreements entered into two years after the investment was made.[6] Tribunals have said that the reasonableness of the investor's reliance must be evaluated in light of the political, socioeconomic, cultural, and historical conditions prevailing in the host state.[7] More generally, tribunals limit protection to expectations reasonable under the circumstances.[8]

---

5 *Duke Energy v. Ecuador* (United States-Ecuador BIT), Award, para. 340; *LG&E v. Argentina* (United States-Argentina BIT), Award, para. 130; *Jan de Nul v. Egypt* (BLEU-Egypt BIT), Award, para. 265; *BG Group v. Argentina* (United Kingdom-Argentina BIT), Award, para. 298; *National Grid v. Argentina* (United Kingdom-Argentina BIT), Award, para. 173.

6 Award, paras. 365–366.

7 *Duke Energy v. Ecuador* (United States-Ecuador BIT), Award, para. 340.

8 *See, e.g.*, *Saluka v. Czech Republic* (Netherlands-Czech Republic BIT), Award, para. 304; *National Grid v. Argentina* (United Kingdom-Argentina BIT), Award, para. 175.

As already noted, some tribunals have referred to these situations as ones in which the investor or investment has a "legitimate expectation" of certain host-state conduct. To the extent that the phrase "legitimate expectations" refers to expectations created by host state promises or assurances, the phrase does not exhaust the meaning of the fair and equitable treatment standard. As noted in Section 5.2.1, the fair and equitable treatment standard embraces principles other than the security of expectations, specifically, reasonableness, nondiscrimination, transparency, and due process. Some tribunals have suggested that the legitimate expectations doctrine may provide a basis for establishing the scope of the fair and equitable treatment standard generally.[9] To the extent that the phrase "legitimate expectations" is intended to summarize the entire fair and equitable treatment standard, it provides an inadequate theory of the standard because it does not answer the question of when legitimate expectations exist in situations where no promises or assurances have been made.[10] Used in that wider sense, the phrase is little more than a label attached to a conclusion reached on other grounds. That is, once a tribunal has concluded that host-state conduct violated the standard, the tribunal merely declares that the investor had a legitimate expectation that such conduct would not occur. Such an approach, however, obscures the true grounds of the award. Thus, the legitimate expectations doctrine is best understood as referring to the situation where the security principle is breached by host-state conduct inconsistent with prior promises or assurances on which the investor relied, rather than as a complete theory of the fair and equitable treatment standard.

A clear violation of the security principle under the fair and equitable treatment standard exists where the host state enters into a contract with the investor or investment and then repudiates the contract. In *Bayindir v. Pakistan*, a case arising under the Turkey-Pakistan BIT, Pakistan terminated the claimant's contract to construct a highway, allegedly because of delays in completion. The claimant, however, argued that

---

9 *See, e.g.*, *Tecmed v. Mexico* (Spain-Mexico BIT), Award, para. 154.

10 For example, the tribunal in *Plama v. Bulgaria* used the legitimate expectations doctrine to explain the fair and equitable treatment standard. It found that investors have a legitimate expectation of good faith, due process, nondiscrimination, a stable investment framework, and transparency. Award, paras. 176–178. This summary in substance is quite similar to the contention made here that the standard embraces principles of reasonableness (which includes good faith), security, nondiscrimination, due process, and transparency. The contention here, however, is that these principles are linked because they are elements of the rule of law and thus incorporating each of them into the fair and equitable treatment standard brings coherence to the standard. Used in the manner of the *Plama* award, the legitimate expectations doctrine does not explain on what basis these principles are legitimate expectations, but simply declares them to be so. To that extent, the legitimate expectations doctrine provides greater flexibility for tribunals because it permits them to add new legitimate expectations at any time. Yet, because it functions as nothing more than a *post hoc* explanation of the award, it adds nothing to the justification for the award. For different approaches to developing a theory of legitimate expectations, see Todd J. Grierson-Weiler and Ian A. Laird, "Standards of Treatment," in., *The Oxford Handbook of International Investment Law* (Peter Muchlinski, Frederico Ortino, and Christoph Schreuer, eds. 2008) and Elizabeth Snodgrass, "Protecting Investors' Legitimate Expectations—Recognizing and Delimiting a General Principle," 21 *ICSID Review—Foreign Investment Law Journal* 1 (2006).

the true reason for the termination was the desire to save money and to utilize a local contractor. In its decision on jurisdiction, the tribunal noted that, an "alleged change in its general policy toward Bayindir's investment is capable of constituting a breach of Pakistan's obligations to accord fair and equitable treatment."[11] The determination whether Pakistan in fact had violated the obligation was deferred to the merits stage.

The tribunal did find a violation of the contract in *Occidental v. Ecuador*, a case arising under the United States-Ecuador BIT. In that case, the claimant had entered into a participation contract with a state enterprise to undertake oil exploration and production. The claimant regularly applied for, and received, reimbursement of the value-added tax paid by the company. Two years later, however, Ecuador suddenly denied all further reimbursements on the ground that the reimbursement already was accounted for in the participation formula in the contract. The tribunal found, however, contrary to Ecuador's interpretation that the contract did not account for the reimbursement.[12] In changing the tax policy on which the claimant had relied in negotiating the contract, Ecuador had failed to provide the claimant with security. Rather, the effect of Ecuador's change in tax policy was to modify the terms of the participation contract into which it had entered with the claimant. The tribunal held that "the stability of the legal and business framework is . . . an essential element of fair and equitable treatment."[13] Thus, Ecuador had violated the fair and equitable treatment standard.[14]

Ecuador's change in tax policy resulted in a second claim, *EnCana v. Ecuador*, a case arising under the Canada-Ecuador BIT. In that case, the tribunal noted that, under the fair and equitable treatment standard, "the State must act with reasonable consistency and without arbitrariness in its treatment of investments. One arm of the State cannot finally affirm what another arm denies to the detriment of the investor."[15] Thus, consistency again was found to be an element of the fair and equitable treatment standard. Encana, however, had not made this argument and, therefore, the tribunal did not need to discus it further.

Some tribunals have treated a host state's breach of contract as a violation of the fair and equitable treatment standard only where the breach involves the exercise of sovereign power or *puissance publique*.[16] For example, in *Duke Energy v. Ecuador*, a case arising under the United States-Ecuador-BIT, the tribunal held that breaches of power purchase agreements by a state-owned enterprise, including nonpayment and the improper imposition of penalties and fines, were breaches of the type that an ordinary party to a contract might commit, rather than acts of sovereign power and thus did not violate the fair and equitable treatment standard.[17] The tribunal also held, however,

11 Decision on Jurisdiction, para.241

12 Award, para. 110

13 Award, para. 184. Accord: *LG&E v. Argentina* (United States-Argentina BIT), Award, para. 125; *Duke Energy v. Ecuador* (United States-Ecuador BIT), Award, para. 339

14 Award, para. 186.

15 Award, para. 158.

16 *RFCC v. Morocco* (Italy-Morocco BIT), Award, para. 51; *Impregilo v. Pakistan*, (Italy-Pakistan BIT), Decision on Jurisdiction, para. 268; *Duke Energy v. Ecuador* (United States-Ecuador BIT), Award, paras. 342–343.

17 Award, paras. 348, 354, 358.

that where the Ministry of Finance intervened to provide a payment guarantee, the power of the state was engaged and the breach of this guarantee violated the fair and equitable treatment standard.[18]

Tribunals sometimes find no violation where the host state breaches a contract, but provides a remedy in its local courts. For example, in *Waste Management v. Mexico*, a case arising under the NAFTA, the claimant had concluded a contract with the city of Acapulco under which it would collect and dispose of solid waste. Members of the public, however, had opposed the collection program because they were unwilling to pay the fees assessed to finance the program. Eventually, as a result of this opposition, the city ceased to honor its obligations under the contract, including the payments owed to the investment. The tribunal found that the city had failed to fulfill its contractual obligations.[19] The tribunal held, however, that no violation of the fair and equitable treatment standard had occurred. The city's conduct was not "wholly arbitrary or grossly unfair."[20] The city's failure of payment was based on a financial crisis it faced and not on any sectoral or local prejudice.[21] The tribunal also observed that nonpayment of a debt would not violate NAFTA Article 1105,[22] "provided that it does not amount to an outright and unjustified repudiation of the transaction and provided that some remedy is open to the creditor to address the problem."[23] Thus, the tribunal found no violation for breach of contract where the host state provided a remedy for the breach. The tribunal also considered an allegation by the claimant that the development bank Banobras had failed to provide a guarantee of the investment's monthly income. The tribunal found, however, that Banobras had never agreed to provide any such guarantee.

Similarly, in *Biwater v. Tanzania*, a case arising under the United Kingdom-Tanzania BIT, the claimant's investment was awarded a contract to provide water and sewerage services for the city of Dar es Salaam. Although various government agencies were in arrears on their payments, the tribunal noted that this was insufficient to violate the fair and equitable treatment standard. The investment could have brought collection actions in the local courts or even disconnected water service, which had proven effective in at least some cases when it was done.[24] The contract did not include any provisions that would have created a legitimate expectation on the part of the investment that special arrangements would be available to ensure payment of government agency bills. The claimant also alleged that Tanzania failed to adjust the terms of the contract to address changing conditions, but the tribunal found that nothing had created a legitimate expectation of a renegotiation or review of the contract.[25]

---

18 Award, paras. 359–360, 364.

19 Award, para. 115.

20 Award, para. 115.

21 Thus, the tribunal began by finding no violation of the reasonableness principle before turning to the security principle.

22 Article 1105 of the NAFTA requires treatment in accordance with customary international law, which it defines to include fair and equitable treatment.

23 Award, para. 115.

24 Award, paras. 635–636.

25 Award, para. 640.

Again, in *Parkerings-Compagniet v. Lithuania*, a case arising under the Norway-Lithuania BIT, the claimant alleged that the city of Vilnius had unilaterally terminated the parking concession agreement between the city and the claimant's investment. The tribunal noted that "not every breach of an agreement or of domestic law amounts to a violation of the treaty."[26] It did acknowledge that "[u]nder certain limited circumstances, a substantial breach of a contract could constitute a violation of a treaty."[27] In most such cases, however, a determination by local courts whether the contract was breached is necessary.[28] Should the claim then be submitted to arbitration under a BIT, the issue would be whether the conduct of the local courts violated the BIT rather than whether the alleged breach violated the BIT.

In that same case, the tribunal also addressed a claim of inconsistency based on a change in local law. The tribunal held that a state has the right to enact, modify, or repeal a law. It then qualified this general rule by noting that a state may not legislate in a way that is inconsistent with a prior agreement, such as a stabilization clause, or that is unreasonable, unfair, or inequitable. The tribunal went on to note more specifically that an investor has a right to the protection of legitimate expectations that were reasonable in light of the circumstances. In that case, Lithuania had not given any assurances or acted in any other way to create a reasonable expectation that the law would remain unchanged. At the time, Lithuania was in transition from its status as a part of the Soviet Union to a new status as a candidate for membership in the European Union. Legislative changes thus were likely. Any expectation that the laws would remain unchanged was not legitimate. The tribunal added that the legislative changes, moreover, were not unfair, unreasonable, or inequitable.

The tribunal addressed as well an argument that, by failing to disclose the existence of proposals to change the applicable law, Lithuania frustrated the claimant's legitimate expectations that it would protect the integrity of the parking concession agreement. Again, however, the tribunal found that the legal environment was unpredictable and that claimant should have known that change might occur. The record did not indicate that the city was aware of the substance of the proposed modification and, in any event, the claimant through counsel could have obtained information about the amendment process. The tribunal did seem to acknowledge that Lithuania's conduct may have violated its duty of good faith under the contract and that its failure to disclose might have breached the contract, but the expectation of contract compliance is not necessarily an expectation protected by the fair and equitable treatment standard. The standard does not convert to a treaty violation "each and every" breach of contract for which the claimant has a remedy under local law.[29]

---

26 Award, para. 315.

27 *Id.* at 316.

28 The tribunal cited *Generation Ukraine v. Ukraine*, a case arising under the United States-Ukraine BIT. In that award, however, the tribunal observed that a claimant's failure to seek redress from national authorities may be deemed to disqualify a claim of an indirect expropriation through maladministration by the state, not because of a requirement that local remedies be exhausted, but because such a claim is doubtful in the absence of a reasonable effort by the investor to obtain correction. Award, at para. 20.30.

29 Award, para. 344.

Just as an obligation of consistency may arise from a formal contract, it also may arise from host-state assurances on which the investor is induced reasonably to rely. For example, in *CMS Gas Transmission Company v. Argentina*, a case arising under the United States-Argentina BIT, a U.S. company had invested in an Argentine gas transmission company in the process of being privatized. The U.S. investor was induced to invest by an offer memo describing the tariff regime that would apply to the company. The regime included calculation of the tariffs in dollars and certain future adjustments in the tariff amounts. As a result of a financial crisis, however, Argentina modified the tariff regime. It froze the level of the tariffs and ceased calculating them in dollars. Looking at the object and purpose of the treaty, the tribunal held that "fair and equitable treatment is inseparable from stability and predictability."[30] The tribunal explained that "[i]t is not a question of whether the legal framework might need to be frozen as it can always evolve and be adapted to changing circumstances, but neither is it a question of whether the framework can be dispensed with altogether when specific commitments to the contrary have been made."[31] Accordingly, the tribunal found that the change in the tariff regime contrary to commitments in the offer memo violated the fair and equitable treatment standard.[32] The tribunal concluded by noting that, in the case before it, the question whether fair and equitable treatment was equivalent to the international minimum standard or a higher treaty standard was irrelevant because the treaty standard with its "required stability and predictability of the business environment, founded on solemn legal and contractual commitments, is not different from the international law minimum standard and its evolution under customary law."[33]

Essentially the same facts appeared in *Enron v. Argentina*, another case arising under the United States-Argentina BIT. Citing *CMS*, the tribunal observed that the legal framework for investment may evolve, but may not be dispensed with. Thus, Argentina's failure to honor its commitments with respect to the tariff regime violated fair and equitable treatment. These facts also underlay the claim in *LG&E v. Argentina*, a case arising under the same BIT, where the tribunal also found Argentina's violation of its commitments with respect to the tariff regime to violate fair and equitable treatment. The tribunal reached the same result as well in *BG Group v. Argentina*, a case arising under the United Kingdom-Argentina BIT.

In *National Grid v. Argentina*, another case arising under the United Kingdom-Argentina BIT, the tribunal adopted a unique approach and held that it must take into account the economic crisis that was occurring at the time Argentina adopted the measures of which the claimant complained. In light of those circumstances, the tribunal held that Argentina's breach occurred not when the measures were taken, but at the time that the claimant was required to renounce its legal remedies for those measures.[34] In effect, the tribunal seemed to allow the host state a limited privilege to modify its

30 Award, para. 276.

31 Award, para. 277.

32 Award, para. 281.

33 Award, para. 284.

34 Award, para. 180.

commitments in light of changes in economic circumstances, a conception of the fair and equitable treatment standard that no other tribunal appears to have adopted.

In *CME v. Czech Republic*, a case arising under the Netherlands-Czech Republic BIT, the claimant had entered into a joint venture with a Czech company to operate a television station known as "TV Nova" in the Czech Republic. The Czech company possessed the broadcast license, while the claimant brought capital and expertise to the venture. The Czech government initially approved the arrangement. Subsequently, however, after the television station had become successful, the government asserted that the claimant was broadcasting without a license and demanded that the joint venture arrangement be restructured. The restructuring allowed the Czech company to force the claimant out of the venture. The tribunal held that to eviscerate the arrangement upon which the claimant was induced to invest was a violation of the fair and equitable treatment standard. The Czech government had approved the original structure of the joint venture and could not reverse that approval without violating the fair and equitable treatment standard.

In *Lauder v. Czech Republic*, the owner of CME submitted a claim arising out of the same facts to investor-state arbitration under the United States-Czech Republic BIT. The *Lauder* tribunal began its discussion of the fair and equitable treatment standard by noting that it already had concluded that the host state's conduct had not violated the prohibition on arbitrary and discriminatory conduct in the BIT.[35] More specifically, the actions of the host state had not been part of an effort to target a foreign investor, but had been based on legitimate regulatory concerns that TV Nova was operating in violation of the media law.[36] Having addressed the reasonableness principle, the tribunal next considered whether the conduct of the Czech Republic had been inconsistent. It noted that "[t]here can not be any inconsistent conduct in a regulatory body taking the necessary actions to enforce the law, absent any specific undertaking that it will refrain from doing so."[37] No such undertaking had been given in that case. Thus, both tribunals were willing to find liability for violation of a prior commitment, but the *CME* tribunal found a sufficient prior commitment in the approval of the arrangement, while the *Lauder* tribunal did not.

As in *Lauder*, tribunals in other cases also have found that the host state made no promises or assurances that were later violated. In *Plama v. Bulgaria*, a case arising under the Energy Charter Treaty, Bulgaria had amended its environmental laws, but the tribunal found that no promises or assurances had been made that such laws would not be amended.[38] Similarly, the claimant could not complain about Bulgaria's tax treatment of certain transactions because that treatment was consistent with existing law. Bulgaria had not created any legitimate expectation that the claimant's investment would be treated differently.[39]

---

35 Award, paras. 293–294.
36 Award, paras. 263–264, 270, 285.
37 Award, para. 297.
38 Award, para. 219.
39 Award, para. 267.

Similarly, in *Jan de Nul v. Egypt*, a case arising under the Belgium-Luxembourg Economic Union-Egypt BIT, the claimant alleged that the Egyptian prime minister had failed to remedy the allegedly improper behavior of the Suez Canal Authority. The tribunal found, however, that no representations had been made regarding the conduct of the prime minister.

In *Saluka Investments v. Czech Republic*, a case arising under the Netherlands-Czech Republic BIT, in anticipation of joining the European Union, the Czech Republic modified its banking regulations to bring them into conformity with EU standards. One effect was to increase the difficulty of meeting capital requirements. The investor, however, had been aware at the time that the investment was made that the Czech Republic intended to join the EU and that changes in banking regulations would be necessary. Nothing indicated that the Czech Republic had committed itself not to change its regulations and, under the circumstances, the investor could not reasonably rely on the regulations' remaining unchanged.

In that same case, the claimant alleged that the Czech government had issued contradictory declarations of policy with respect to whether state aid would be given to banks undergoing privatization. The Minister of Finance had stated expressly that no state aid would be provided, although subsequently the Czech government had provided aid to three major banks in the process of privatization, but not to the claimant's bank. The claimant conceded, however, that the Minister of Finance could not bind future governments. The tribunal held, accordingly, that the claimant could not reasonably rely on any such assurances and that the Czech Government's failure to adhere to those assurances did not violate the claimant's treaty rights.

The claimant also complained about the Czech Republic's failure to remedy deficiencies in its regulations. The investor, however, had been aware of the deficiencies when it invested and the record revealed no basis for implying a commitment on the part of the Czech Republic to remedy the deficiencies by a particular date.

In addition, the claimant complained that the Czech government had made inconsistent statements in dealing with the claimant's efforts to save the bank. Here, the tribunal found a violation of the fair and equitable treatment standard. Like Chile in the *MTD Equity* case, discussed below, the host state had taken inconsistent positions simultaneously.

The tribunal also found an absence of assurances on which the claimant reasonably could have relied in *Continental Casualty v. Argentina*, a case arising under the United States-Argentina BIT. In that case, the tribunal noted that the dispute differed from many of those generated by Argentina's economic crisis of 2001–2002. Unlike in those cases, the claimant had not been induced to invest by specific commitments made directly to the claimant. The tribunal identified a series of factors to be considered in determining when the host state's conduct gives rise to a claim that "reasonable legitimate expectations" have been defeated.[40] For example, specific undertakings were more likely to generate such expectations than general legislative statements. Unilateral modifications of contracts, when such modifications are aimed at obtaining

40 Award, para. 261.

financial resources, should be carefully scrutinized. The fact that conduct is nondiscriminatory and related to the public interest should be taken into account. Applying these factors, the tribunal found that, for the most part, the claimant had no legitimate expectations that were frustrated by Argentina. Argentina's restructuring of certain government guaranteed loans might have violated the standard, but the restructuring fell within the defense of necessity. The restructuring of certain treasury bills, however, did not fall within that defense and this restructuring did violate the standard. The tribunal also noted that the restructuring was unreasonable at the time it was undertaken. Thus, this conduct apparently violated both the security and the reasonableness principles.

In *MCI Power v. Ecuador*, a case arising under United States-Ecuador BIT, the tribunal found that the revocation of an operating permit did not violate the standard. The permit authorized the operation of an electrical generation plant, which the investment no longer owned or operated. Thus, the host state's change in revoking the permit did not defeat any entitlement.

Cases may arise where the host state gives assurances, but the investor may not reasonably rely upon them. For example, in *International Thunderbird v. Mexico*, a case arising under the NAFTA, the claimant alleged that Mexico was enforcing its anti-gambling laws against its gambling operation despite having given the claimant a legal opinion that the claimant's operation was lawful. In effect, the claimant alleged that Mexico had behaved inconsistently. The tribunal found, however, that the government's opinion was based on the claimant's misrepresentations about the nature of the games it operated. Thus, the claimant could not reasonably rely on the government's opinion.

Thus, the awards recognize the right of a host state to change its law, in the absence of undertakings to the contrary. Yet, circumstances may arise where changes in the law may violate the fair and equitable treatment standard even in the absence of a promise or assurance to the contrary. In *PSEG v. Turkey*, a case arising under the United States-Turkey BIT, the tribunal found that Turkey had violated the fair and equitable treatment standard by abusing its authority. The specific conduct, however, consisted of various acts involving a change of position by the host state. Turkey had demanded that agreements be renegotiated and issues already settled be reopened. Administrative agencies had ignored rights granted by law. The tribunal also found a violation in what it termed "roller coaster" changes in the law.[41] This award perhaps is best explained as holding implicitly that investors have a right to rely on reasonable consistency in the law. A host state may change its policy over time, but "roller coaster" changes violate the security principle.

The security principle also may be violated not by changes in the law over time, but by taking inconsistent positions simultaneously. In *MTD Equity v. Chile*, a case arising under the Malaysia-Chile BIT, Chile had induced a Malaysian company to invest in building a planned community. Subsequently, the Malaysian company learned that construction of the community would violate local zoning laws and thus the work

41 Award, para. 250.

could not be performed. The tribunal held that "approval of an investment by the [Chilean Foreign Investment Commission] for a project that is against the urban policy of the Government is a breach of the obligation to treat an investor fairly and equitably."[42] As the tribunal explained, Chile has "an obligation to act coherently and apply its policies consistently. . . ."[43] *MTD Equity* differs from the cases already discussed[44] because it did not reflect a change in policy. Rather, Chile had adopted two inconsistent policies simultaneously—encouraging an investment at the national level that it simultaneously forbade at the local level.

In *SGS v. Philippines*, the tribunal observed, in its decision on jurisdiction, that "an unjustified refusal to pay sums admittedly payable under an award or a contract at least raises arguable issues under" the fair and equitable treatment standard. The potential inconsistency there was in acknowledging a debt, but declining to pay it. As in *MTD Equity*, the host state was taking two inconsistent positions simultaneously. Alternatively, the case can be conceptualized as involving a change in position contrary to prior assurances. The host state incurred a debt obligation upon which the claimant relied, but subsequently refused to act consistently with the promise of payment. The claimant had a legitimate expectation based on host-state assurances that the host state would pay its debt.

6.3 FULL PROTECTION AND SECURITY

6.3.1 Structure and Policy

Many BITs require that investment receive "full protection and security,"[45] although the standard appears in BITs less commonly than the fair and equitable treatment standard. The requirement of full protection and security is an established standard of customary international law that requires the host state to exercise due diligence or reasonable care to prevent injury to the property (and persons) of foreign nationals. The BITs that incorporate this standard thus make explicit that the standard applies to covered investment, although it would apply through customary law even if it were not included in the treaty. Its inclusion, however, ensures that the standard as applied to covered investment is enforceable through the investor-state and state-state disputes provisions.

Two aspects of the standard are important in establishing its content. First, the standard does not impose strict liability on the host state. The host state's obligation is met

42 Award, para. 166.

43 Award, para. 165.

44 With the exception of one aspect of *Saluka Investments v. Czech Republic*, discussed above.

45 *See, e.g.*, United Kingdom-Bosnia-Herzegovina BIT, Art. 2(2); Denmark-Ethiopia BIT, Art.2(2); Mexico-Iceland BIT, Art. 3(1); Canada-Uruguay BIT, Art. II(2)(b); Germany-Timore-Leste BIT, Art. 4(1). On the full protection and security standard generally, *see* Giuditta Cordero Moss, "Full Protection and Security," in *Standards of Investment Protection* (August Reinisch, ed. 2008).

when the state takes action that is reasonable under the circumstances to protect investment, even if the action is unsuccessful in preventing injury to the investment. Second, the standard requires host-state action to prevent injury by private parties as well as by state actors. Thus, for example, the standard would require that law enforcement authorities exercise due diligence to protect covered investment against damage by rioters or looters. Although very few BITs elaborate upon the meaning of this standard, BITs based on the U.S. 2004 model negotiating text provide that the full protection and security standard "requires each Party to provide the level of police protection required under customary international law."[46]

The language of the standard varies among BITs. Other formulations include, but are not limited to, "most constant protection and security."[47] "full security and protection"[48] "full protection,"[49] "full and constant protection and security,"[50] "protection and security,"[51] and "adequate protection and security."[52] These different formulations, however, generally have not been treated as creating any substantive difference in the standard of care required of the host country.

As discussed in Section 6.3.3, an emerging issue raised by this standard is whether it imposes liability for nonphysical harm to investment. Some tribunals have observed that the standard traditionally applied to physical damage to investment and that to broaden the standard to apply to nonphysical harms would tend to eliminate the distinction between this standard and the fair and equitable treatment standard. Other tribunals have held that the standard does apply to nonphysical harms, in light of the absence of a textual limitation to physical harms. Thus far, however, no tribunal seems to have awarded compensation for nonphysical harm to investment based solely on the full protection and security standard. Some BITs incorporate language intended to address this issue. For example, the 2003 Netherlands-Malawi BIT guarantees to investment "full physical security and protection,"[53] making clear that the standard does not apply to nonphysical harm.

6.3.2 Origins

The full protection and security standard was well-established in early FCN treaty practice. The phrasing of the standard in the FCNs varied considerably,[54] as it does in the BITs. This standard provided the basic guarantee of security for investment in

---

46 *See, e.g.*, United States-Uruguay BIT, Art. 5(2)(b).

47 *See, e.g.*, Thailand-Argentina BIT, Art. 3(2); Japan-Egypt BIT, Art. 5(1).

48 *See, e.g.*, Ethiopia-Netherlands BIT, Art. 3(1).

49 *See, e.g.*, Germany-Timore-Leste BIT, Art. 2(2).

50 *See, e.g.*, Austria-Armenia BIT, Art. 3(1); Finland-Armenia BIT, Art. 2(2).

51 *See, e.g.*, Australia-India BIT, Art. 3(3) "and shall not impair the management, maintenance, use, enjoyment or disposal of investments."

52 *See, e.g.*, Chile-Indonesia BIT, Art. III(2); Egypt-Zambia BIT, Art. 2(2); Cambodia-Vietnam, Arts. II(2) and III(1).

53 *See, e.g.*, Netherlands-Malawi BIT, Art. 3(1).

54 *See* Section 2.1.1.

these treaties, although it was supplemented by provisions requiring compensation for expropriation.

The 1959 Abs-Shawcross Draft Convention on Investments Abroad required, at Article I, that covered property "be accorded the most constant protection and security." A commentary prepared by the authors observed that this standard was based on U.S. post-war FCN practice.[55]

The full protection and security standard appeared in the very first BIT. Article 3(1) of the Germany-Pakistan BIT, concluded in 1959, provided that "[i]nvestments by nationals or companies of either Party shall enjoy protection and security in the territory of the other Party." The language quickly became "full protection and security,"[56] which is the most common phrasing in BITs today.

The standard also was adopted by the Dutch, Swiss, and Kuwaitis in their BITs of the 1960s. The first BIT concluded by the Netherlands, that with Tunisia in 1963, provided at article 3(1) that "[e]ach Contracting Party shall accord to such investments full security and protection" and the standard remains part of Dutch BIT practice.[57] A guarantee of full protection and security had begun to appear in Swiss BITs by 1965,[58] although not in the Swiss commerce, investment, and technical cooperation agreements that were being concluded in the 1960s and early 1970s.[59] The Kuwaiti BITs adopted the standard in 1964. The 1964 Kuwait-Iraq BIT required "just and equitable treatment as well as full protection in accordance with the provisions of this Protocol."[60] The standard continued to appear in Kuwait BITs,[61] in some cases qualified by the language "in a manner consistent with international law and the provisions of this Agreement."[62]

The full protection and security standard also appeared in the 1967 OECD Draft Convention on the Protection of Foreign Property. Article 1 required each party to "accord within its territory the most constant protection and security" to covered property. Note 1(a) to Article 1 characterized this standard as one of three rules that flow from the "well-established general principle of international law that a State is bound to respect and protect the property of nationals of other States." Note 5 to Article 1 observed that the standard was based on language appearing in U.S. post-war FCNs and that it "indicates the obligation of each Party to exercise due diligence as regards actions by public authorities as well as others in relation to [covered] property."

---

55 Hermann Abs and Sir Hartley Shawcross, "Comment on the Draft Convention By Its Authors," 9 *Journal of Public Law* 115, 119 (1960).

56 *See, e.g.*, Germany-Liberia BIT, *signed*, Dec. 14, 1961, Art. 3(1).

57 *See, e.g.*, Netherlands-Malawi BIT, Art. 3(1)("full physical security and protection").

58 *See, e.g.*, Switzerland-Tanzania BIT, Art. 3(1).

59 *See* Section 2.2.

60 Kuwait-Iraq BIT, Art. 2.

61 *See, e.g.*, Kuwait-Hungary BIT, Art. 2(2); Kuwait-Jordan BIT, Art. 3(1)("complete protection and safety"); Kuwait-Ethiopia BIT, Art. 3(1); Kuwait-Czech Republic BIT, Art. 3(1); Kuwait-Croatia BIT, Art. 2(1); Kuwait-Bulgaria BIT, Art. 3(1).

62 *See, e.g.*, Kuwait-Czech Republic BIT, Art. 3(1); Kuwait-Ethiopia BIT, Art. 3(1) ("recognized" principles of international law); Kuwait-Croatia BIT, Art. 2(1); Kuwait-Bulgaria BIT, Art. 3(1) ("in a manner consistent with the provisions of this Agreement").

Italy's practice was more ambivalent than that of other European countries inaugurating BIT programs in the early 1960s. Italy did not include the standard in its first BITs,[63] but included it in its BIT with the Ivory Coast in 1969.[64] Italy's practice immediately thereafter was not consistent, however. It sometimes used the term "adequate protection"[65] or "full protection,"[66] and eventually it removed the standard from its BITs.[67]

Although the Belgium-Luxembourg Economic Union (BLEU) BIT program began in 1964, the full protection and security standard did not appear in the BLEU BITs until the 1970s. The 1976 BLEU-Republic of Korea BIT guaranteed to investments "continuous protection and security, excluding all unjustified or discriminatory measures which would 'de jure' or 'de facto' hinder their management, maintenance, utilization, enjoyment or liquidation."[68] A different clause cited MFN treatment and international law as minimum standards below which this protection could not fall.[69] This provision remains in the contemporary BLEU BITs, virtually without change, except that it now excludes measures to maintain public order.[70]

Some countries that inaugurated BIT programs in the 1970s also included the standard. The 1975 United Kingdom-Egypt BIT provided that "Investments of nationals or companies of either Contracting Party shall at all times be accorded fair and equitable treatment and shall enjoy full protection and security in the territory of the other Contracting Party."[71] This remains essentially the language used in the UK BITs today.[72] Japan's first BIT, concluded with Egypt in 1977, required that investment and returns receive the most constant protection and security.[73] The full protection and security standard appeared in the French BITs in 1977,[74] but it did not consistently appear in BITs thereafter.[75]

Some countries did not adopt the standard until the 1980s. Although Denmark concluded its first BIT in 1965, the Danish BITs adopted the full protection and security

---

63 *See, e.g.*, Italy-Guinea BIT; Italy-Malta BIT, July 28, 1967.

64 *See* Italy-Ivory Coast BIT, Art. 4(1).

65 *See, e.g.*, Italy-Tunisia BIT, Art. 4(1) Italy-China BIT, Art. 4(1).

66 *See, e.g.*, Italy-Egypt BIT, Art. III(1).

67 *See, e.g.*, Italy-Bolivia-BIT; Italy-Czechoslovakia BIT; Italy-Bangladesh BIT, March 20, 1990; Italy-Jordan BIT, Italy-Nicaragua BIT.

68 BLEU-Republic of Korea BIT, Art. 2(2)

69 BLEU-Republic of Korea BIT, Art. 13.

70 *See, e.g.*, BLEU-Sudan BIT, Art. 3(2); BLEU-Nicaragua BIT, Art. 3(2).

71 United Kingdom-Egypt BIT, Art. 2(2).

72 *See, e.g.*, United Kingdom-Vietnam BIT, Art. 2(1); United Kingdom-Bosnia-Herzegovina BIT, Art. 2(1).

73 Japan-Egypt BIT, Art. 5(1).

74 *See, e.g.*, France-Republic of Korea BIT, Art. 3(1); France-Syria BIT, Art. 3(1). The France-Singapore BIT, concluded on September 8, 1975, required "protection and security" at Article 2(1), presumably the equivalent of "full protection and security." The language of the France-Singapore BIT, however, was not typical of other French BITs of that period.

75 *See, e.g.*, France-Paraguay BIT; France-Sudan BIT; France-Liberia BIT.

standard only in the latter half of the 1980s.[76] The standard remains in the Danish BITs.[77] Sweden similarly began its BIT program in 1965, but the full protection and security standard first appeared in the Swedish BITs in 1983[78] and did not commonly appear[79] until 2000.[80]

The first U.S. BITs were concluded in 1982 and the standard typically appeared in the early U.S. BITs. For example, the 1982 United States-Panama BIT provided that covered investment "shall enjoy full protection and security in the territory of the other Party."[81] In 2004, however, the United States modified the language of its model negotiation text to require treatment in accordance with customary international law, including full protection and security.[82]

The full protection and security standard appeared in the Finnish BITs for the first time in 1984.[83] The standard disappeared from most Finnish BITs in the 1980s, but began to reappear at the very end of the decade, most often with MFN treatment as a floor.[84] Occasionally, however, it was linked with the prohibition on unreasonable or discriminatory measures[85] or the fair and equitable treatment standard,[86] if it was not omitted entirely.[87] In Finland's most recent BITs, the standard generally appears paired with the fair and equitable treatment standard, although the standard in some recent BITs is phrased as "full and constant protection."[88]

In summary, by the 1980s, the full protection and security standard was widespread among BITs. Some countries, however, remained slow to include it, if they included it at all. For example, the Austrian BITs, which date from the 1970s, typically did not include the full protection and security standard[89] until after 2000, when they routinely required "full and constant protection and security."[90] In very recent years, a few states

76 *See, e.g.*, Denmark-China BIT, Art. 3(1) (guaranteeing "protection and security"); Denmark-Republic of Korea BIT, Art. 3(1).

77 *See, e.g.*, Denmark-Ethiopia BIT, Art. 2(2); Denmark-Kuwait BIT, June 1, 2001; Denmark-Kyrgyz Republic BIT, Art. 2(2); Denmark-Croatia BIT, Art. 2(2).

78 *See* Sweden-Yemen BIT, Art. 3(1).

79 *See, e.g.*, Sweden-Tunisia BIT, Sweden-Hungary BIT, April 21, 1987.

80 *See, e.g.*, Sweden-India BIT, Art. 3(2); Sweden-Croatia BIT, Art. 3(1). Sweden-Bosnia-Herzegovina BIT, Art. 2(2).

81 United States-Panama BIT, Art. II(2).

82 *See* United States-Uruguay BIT, Art. 5(1).

83 *See, e.g.*, Finland-Bulgaria BIT, Art.3 ("protection and security"); Finland-Malaysia BIT, April 15, 1985, Art. 2 ("full protection and security").

84 *See, e.g.*, Finland-USSR BIT, Art. 4(1) ("full protection"); Finland-Czechoslovakia BIT, Art. 4(1); Finland-Latvia BIT, Art. 4(1); Finland-Latvia BIT, Art. 4(1); Finland-Turkey BIT, Art. 4(1).

85 *See, e.g.*, Finland-Brazil BIT, Art. 2(2).

86 *See, e.g.*, Finland-Republic of Korea BIT, Art. 2(2); Finland-Peru BIT, Art. 2(4).

87 *See, e.g.*, Finland-Argentina BIT; Finland-Vietnam BIT.

88 Finland-Algeria BIT, Art. 2(2); Finland-Armenia BIT, Art. 2(2); Finland-Azerbaijan BIT, Art. 2(2); Finland-Belarus BIT, Art. 2(2).

89 *But see* Austria-Malaysia BIT, Art. 3(1) ("full protection").

90 *See, e.g.*, Austria-Bosnia-Herzegovina BIT, Art. 3(1); Austria-Armenia BIT, Art. 3(1); Austria-Jordan BIT, Art. 3(1); Austria-Libya BIT, Art. 3(1).

have sought to clarify the meaning of the standard, by defining it in terms of police protection[91] or physical security.[92]

6.3.3 Arbitral Practice

In *AAPL v. Sri Lanka*, a case arising under the United Kingdom-Sri Lanka BIT, the tribunal described the full protection and security standard as requiring the "reasonable measures of protection which a well-administered government could be expected to exercise under similar circumstances."[93] In that case, the tribunal found that the conduct of the host state was not reasonable. The Sri Lankan military had occupied the claimant's shrimp farm while carrying out operations against local rebel forces. During the occupation, the farm sustained damage. The claimant failed to establish that government forces caused the destruction, but the tribunal found that the government failed to use peaceful means to remove suspected rebels from the area. Having failed to take a course of action that might have prevented the harm to the property, Sri Lanka violated its obligation to provide full protection and security. Arbitrator Samuel K.B. Asante dissented.

In *American Manufacturing and Trading v. Zaire*, a case arising under the United States-D.R. Congo BIT, the claimant's investment was damaged during a period of severe civil disturbance. In fact, the investment had been looted by members of the military in uniform and using weapons issued by the government. The tribunal found that the government of the D.R. Congo had taken no action at all to protect the investment. Accordingly, the host state had violated the obligation to provide full protection and security.

In *Wena Hotels v Egypt*, a case arising under the United Kingdom-Egypt BIT, the tribunal found that Egypt's failure to protect hotels from seizure by a state controlled enterprise violated its obligation to provide full protection and security. The issue of whether reasonable care had been exercised was easily addressed because the Egyptian government knew of the planned seizure and yet took no action to prevent it or immediately to restore the hotels to the owners.

By contrast, in *Tecmed v Mexico*, a case arising under the Spain-Mexico BIT, the tribunal found that Mexico did not bear responsibility under the full protection and security provision for damage to the claimant's solid waste disposal facility caused by protestors. The tribunal found that the evidence presented by the claimant was not sufficient to show that the Mexican authorities at any level had "encouraged, fostered, or contributed their support" to the protestors.[94] Nor was there sufficient evidence that Mexican authorities had failed to act reasonably in response to the protests. Similarly, in *Noble Ventures v. Romania*, a case arising under the United States-Romania BIT, the claimant alleged that Romania had failed to take adequate measures to prevent the

---

91 *See, e.g.*, United States-Uruguay BIT, Art. 5(2)(b).

92 *See, e.g.*, Netherlands-Malawi BIT, Art. 3(1).

93 Award, para.77 (quoting Professor Alwyn V. Freemon).

94 Award, para. 76.

occupation of its facilities, acts of intimidation, and forcible detention and beatings of its management, all occurring as a result of labor unrest. The tribunal observed that the judgment of the International Court of Justice in the *ELSI*[95] case indicated that violations of the standard of full protection and security "are not easily to be established."[96] In any event, the tribunal found that it could not identify any specific failure by Romania to exercise due diligence or that the alleged injuries and losses could have been prevented by the exercise of due diligence.

In *Parkerings-Compagniet v. Lithuania*, a case arising under the Norway-Lithuania BIT, the claimant alleged damage as a result of vandalism. The tribunal found no violation, however, noting that the claimant had failed to show that the vandalism would have been prevented if the authorities had acted differently. It was conceded that the authorities had investigated the crime, although they never found the perpetrators.

A more difficult question that has arisen is whether the provision should be interpreted to protect the investment against nonphysical harm. Several tribunals have answered this question in the affirmative, relying on the absence of any explicit textual basis for limiting the application of the provision to physical harm, the use of the word "full" to describe the level of protection provided, and the general purpose of the BITs in protecting covered investment against harm. For example, in *Maffezini v. Spain*, a case arising under the Argentina-Spain BIT, the tribunal held that the action of an official in transferring funds out of the claimant's bank account without the claimant's prior knowledge or approval violated the obligation of full protection and security.

The tribunal held in *Biwater v. Tanzania*, a case arising under the United Kingdom-Tanzania BIT, that "full" protection and security implies more than physical security and that a limitation to physical security would be artificial. Rather, the term implies a secure physical, commercial, and legal environment.[97] The standard imposes an obligation of due diligence to protect investment against acts by the state as well as third parties. In that case, the host state had seized the premises of the investment and removed the management, acts that the tribunal found to be unnecessary and abusive. Such acts therefore violated the standard, although the tribunal also found that the acts caused no quantifiable financial or commercial loss.[98]

In *National Grid v. Argentina*, a case arising under the United Kingdom-Argentina BIT, the tribunal found that the language of the standard, in that case "protection and constant security," did not imply any limitation to physical security and that the placement of the standard in the same article as the fair and equitable treatment standard reinforced that interpretation. Thus, the tribunal found that Argentina's dismantling of the regulatory framework that it agreed to provide at the time the investor decided to invest violated the standard.[99]

---

95 *Case concerning Elettronica Sicula* (United States v. Italy), 1989 I.C.J. Rep. 15.

96 Award, para.165.

97 Award, para. 729. In so holding, the tribunal was following the award in *Azurix v. Argentina*, discussed below. Unlike in *Azurix*, however, the tribunal in *Biwater* did not hold that violations of fair and equitable treatment ipso facto violate the full protection and security standard.

98 Award, para. 731.

99 Award, para. 189.

The tribunal also applied the standard to nonphysical harm in *Siemens v. Argentina*, a case arising under the Germany-Argentina BIT. The tribunal observed that "[a]s a general matter and based on the definition of investment, which includes tangible and intangible assets, the Tribunal considers that the obligation to provide full protection and security is wider than 'physical' protection and security. It is difficult to understand how the physical security of an intangible asset would be achieved."[100] The tribunal's interpretation was aided, however, by the fact that the language of the treaty referred to full protection and "legal security." The tribunal concluded that Argentina's renegotiation of its contract with the claimant's investment "for the sole purpose of reducing its costs, unsupported by any declaration of public interest, affected the legal security of Siemens' investment."[101]

In *CME v. Czech Republic*, a case arising under the Netherlands-Czech Republic BIT, the Czech government initially approved an arrangement whereby the claimant entered into a joint venture with a domestic company possessing a broadcast license for the purpose of operating a television station. Subsequently, the government accused the claimant of broadcasting without a license and required the parties to restructure the arrangement. Later, the Czech company terminated the arrangement, destroying the claimant's business. The tribunal held that "[t]he host State is obligated to ensure that neither by amendment of its laws nor by actions of its administrative bodies is the agreed and approved security and protection of the foreign investor's investment withdrawn or devalued."[102] Accordingly, the respondent had breached the obligation.

The principal owner of CME presented virtually the identical claim to a different tribunal applying the United States-Czech Republic BIT in *Lauder v. Czech Republic*. The tribunal held that the full protection and security provision requires the parties "to exercise such due diligence in the protection of foreign investment as reasonable under the circumstances."[103] The tribunal found that the action of the host state was the result of legitimate regulatory concerns and thus was reasonable. Further, any damage to the investor was caused by the decision of a private company to terminate a business relationship, not by the action of the government. With respect to the dispute between the claimant and other private parties, the host state had met its obligations by making its judicial system available to the claimant and deciding the dispute in accordance with domestic and international law. No allegation had been made that the Czech Republic had failed in that regard. Accordingly, no violation of the full protection and security standard had occurred.

In *Parkerings-Compagniet v. Lithuania*, a case arising under the Norway-Lithuania BIT, the claimant alleged that a violation of the standard occurred when the national government failed to prevent the city of Vilnius from violating its parking concession agreement with the investor. The tribunal found that the claimant failed "to demonstrate a negligence of the Prime Minister that could amount to a breach of the BIT."[104]

---

100 Award, para. 303.
101 Award, para. 308.
102 Partial Award, para. 613.
103 Award, para. 308.
104 Award, para. 358.

The tribunal also held that the standard applied to nonphysical harm in *Vivendi v. Argentina*, a case arising under the France-Argentina BIT. In that case, Article 5(1) of the BIT guaranteed that ". . . investments . . . shall enjoy . . . protection and full security in accordance with the principle of fair and equitable treatment. . . ." The tribunal held that the text included no express limitation to physical interference, although in light of the language of the BIT a violation would occur only if the state's conduct was unfair and inequitable. Thus, the tribunal's application of the standard merged into its discussion of whether the state's conduct violated the obligation of fair and equitable treatment.

Some tribunals have avoided the issue of whether the standard extends to nonphysical harm. In *Plama v. Bulgaria*, a case arising under the Energy Charter Treaty, the tribunal observed that some tribunals had extended the standard to include more than physical security. The tribunal declined to decide whether the standard should be so extended, but held that, even if it were extended, it would not have been violated. First, Bulgaria had amended its environmental laws in a way that allegedly imposed liability on the investment for damage caused prior to its acquisition by the investor. Yet, the facts suggested that the investment might already have been liable even prior to the amendment. The amendment had been publicly debated and the claimant knew or should have known of its potential liability for past damage at the time it invested. Under the circumstances, the tribunal found no lack of due diligence on the part of Bulgaria. Similarly, the tribunal found no lack of due diligence in Bulgaria's tax treatment of the investment. The claimant was advised by a leading tax advisory firm, Ernst & Young, and knew or should have known of its potential tax liability for the transactions in which it was engaged. Ultimately, Bulgaria amended its tax laws to exempt the investment from the taxes at issue. The tribunal thus found that Bulgaria's conduct was "beyond reproach."[105]

In *Jan de Nul v Egypt*, a case arising under the Belgium-Luxembourg Economic Union-Egypt BIT, the claimant alleged that Egypt's breach of a dredging contract violated the full protection and security standard. The tribunal held that no breach occurred and thus the standard was not violated, "irrespective of [its] precise scope."[106] The tribunal noted that the standard requires due diligence by the state and was to be distinguished from the fair and equitable treatment standard, although the two "can overlap."[107]

Other tribunals have refused, or at least expressed reluctance, to apply the standard to nonphysical harm. For example, in *PSEG v. Turkey*, a case arising under the United States-Turkey BIT, the tribunal observed that the standard had developed to promote physical security and that it should be given broader scope only in exceptional situations. In that case, the tribunal held that claimant's concerns could be addressed under the fair and equitable treatment standard. Similarly, in *Sempra Energy v. Argentina*, a case arising under the United States-Argentina BIT, the tribunal held that "historically this particular standard has been developed in the context of physical

105 Award, para. 271,
106 Award, para. 271.
107 Award, para. 269.

protection and the security of a company's officials, employees and facilities."[108] The tribunal declined to exclude as a matter of principle the possibility of a broader application, but suggested that such a situation would constitute an exception to the traditional understanding of the standard. In that case, the claimant had not developed its argument under this standard and the tribunal did not consider it.

The tribunal refused to extend the standard to nonphysical harm in *BG Group v. Argentina*, a case arising under the United Kingdom-Argentina BIT. The tribunal declined to depart from the "originally understood" meaning of the standard.[109] The claimant had not alleged physical violence or damage and thus the standard could not have been breached.[110]

The standard was limited to physical harm by third parties in *Eastern Sugar v. Czech Republic*, a case arising under the Netherlands-Czech Republic BIT. The tribunal said that the standard

> concerns the obligations of the host state to protect the investor from *third* parties, in the cases cited by the Parties, mobs, insurgents, rented thugs and others engaged in physical violence against the investor in violation of the state monopoly of physical force. Thus, where a host state fails to grant full protection and security, it fails to act to prevent actions by third parties that it is required to prevent.[111]

This reading, however, clearly is too narrow. In fact, tribunals in cases such as *American Manufacturing and Trading* and *Wena Hotels* have held that physical harm inflicted by the host state itself violates the standard. As the tribunal said in *Parkerings-Compagniet v. Lithuania*, a case arising under the Norway-Lithuania BIT, a violation of the standard "could be committed by the host State, or by its agencies or by an individual."[112] The purpose of this standard is to protect the investment, not to protect the host state's monopoly on the use of force. Indeed, for purposes of investment protection, the situation where the state itself attacks the investment may be more worrisome than where the attacks come from private third parties, precisely because the state does have a monopoly on the use of force. Private parties are in some measure deterred from physical assaults on foreign investment by the knowledge that they would be acting outside the law. If the state itself undertakes to destroy the physical security of an investment, no countervailing force exists to deter it. Investment security is not promoted by a rule that simply reserves to the state the power to undermine the security of foreign investment.

The tribunal in *Enron v. Argentina*, a case arising under the United States-Argentina BIT, expressed the concern that extending the full protection and security standard beyond its traditional role of protecting physical security could tend to eliminate the distinction between that standard and fair and equitable treatment. In *Enron*, however, the claimant had not alleged a failure to provide full protection and security to the

---

108 Award, para. 323.

109 Award. para. 326.

110 Award, paras. 327–328.

111 Award, para. 203. Emphasis in original.

112 Award, para. 355.

employees or property of the investment and no argument about a lack of protection and security in the overall legal framework for investment had been developed or proven by the claimant. Thus, the tribunal found no violation of the standard.

In *Saluka Investments v. Czech Republic*, a case arising under the Netherlands-Czech Republic BIT, the tribunal expressed doubt about whether the standard should be applied to nonphysical harms. The tribunal found that arbitral practice indicated that the standard was intended to protect "the physical integrity of an investment against interference by use of force."[113] The tribunal then addressed whether the Czech Republic's injunction imposing a suspension of trading in shares of claimant's investment violated the full protection and security standard. Without deciding whether such an action could fall within the standard, the tribunal found that the suspension was justifiable on regulatory grounds and thus would not violate the standard in any event. It was, in other words, not an unreasonable act and therefore not a violation of the duty to exercise reasonable care. The tribunal thus interpreted the standard in the same way as the *Lauder* tribunal, that is, to mean that reasonable regulatory acts do not violate the standard. The tribunal next addressed the question of whether the Czech Republic's order freezing the claimant's shareholding in its investment violated the standard. Again without deciding whether such an action could fall within the standard, the tribunal found no violation because the order was appealed and quashed. Although that decision was itself appealed and reversed, the tribunal found no denial of justice. The tribunal turned finally to the claim that an office search and the seizure of certain documents violated the standard. The tribunal found no violation because the claimant had successfully obtained relief in local courts.

Although the language of the full protection and security standard seems unqualified, no tribunal has held that the full protection and security standard prohibits all state action injurious to investment. Such an interpretation would vitiate the state's legitimate regulatory power. The difference among tribunals is the way in which they limit the scope of the standard.

As has already been indicated, many tribunals limit the standard to the kinds of physical harms that gave rise to the customary obligation. Host state actions that inflict nonphysical harms would be subject to other BIT provisions, such as the fair and equitable treatment standard or the prohibition on unreasonable or discriminatory measures. The virtue of this approach is that it is consistent with the historical origins of the standard and it distinguishes the standard from the fair and equitable treatment standard and the prohibition on unreasonable or discriminatory measures.

Those awards that have applied the standard to nonphysical harm and found a violation have rested the finding on the state's having modified the regulatory framework upon which the investor had relied.[114] As discussed in Section 6.2, such conduct by the host state also has been held to violate the security principle of the fair and equitable treatment standard. Thus, this particular extension of the full protection and security standard does not expand the obligations of the host state beyond those imposed by the fair and equitable treatment standard.

---

113 Award, para. 484.

114 These awards include those in *National Grid, Siemens*, and *CME*, all discussed above.

An alternative approach was suggested by the awards in *Lauder* and *Saluka Investments*, neither of which found a violation of the full protection and security standard. These awards suggested that the standard may prohibit unreasonable regulatory conduct. In effect, the standard would be collapsed into the prohibition on unreasonable or discriminatory measures and the fair and equitable treatment standard. It would prohibit only unreasonable conduct that impaired investment, both of which are separately prohibited by the other two provisions. Such an interpretation, however, profoundly changes the very nature of the standard and not merely the type of harm to which it applies. The standard historically was one that protected the security of investment. The *Lauder/Saluka* approach converts it into a standard that furthers not the principle of security, but the principle of reasonableness. The tribunals in *Lauder* and *Saluka Investments* purported merely to be applying the standard as it traditionally existed, although potentially to a new type of harm. That is, the standard traditionally required reasonable care to protect investment and the tribunals found no violation because the host-state conduct was a reasonable regulatory act and therefore not a breach of the duty of reasonable care. In fact, however, the reasoning rests on a play on words. The word "reasonable" has more than one sense. Under the traditional standard, it referred to the level of effort exerted by the host state. It judged whether the host state had made sufficient effort to secure property. As used in *Lauder* and *Saluka Investments*, however, it refers to the instrumental connection between the means employed by the state and the state's legitimate regulatory interests. To use a mathematical analogy, the former sense of the term refers to the magnitude of the vector, while the latter sense refers to its direction. The fact that the term "reasonable" has been used to refer both to the intensity of the state's effort and the purpose of that effort should not obscure the essential difference between the principles of security and reasonableness. Under the traditional standard, the host state was required to protect the security of investment. Legitimate public interests no more excused the obligation than they excused the obligation to pay compensation for expropriation. That was the security guaranteed to the investor. The host state's responsibility was discharged, however, once it had exercised due diligence. The investor was entitled to protection, but only to a certain quantity of protection. Under the approach suggested in *Lauder* and *Saluka Investments*, the host state may diminish the value of investment as long as the impairment is in the public interest. Thus, the language in *Lauder* and *Saluka Investments* did not so much extend the scope of the provision as to transform its very nature.

In general, the awards that seek to extend the full protection and security standard beyond physical harms reflect a dearth of theorizing about the scope of the standard. Because the full protection and security provision rarely appears in a treaty that does not also include the fair and equitable treatment provision, although the latter frequently appears without the former, tribunals often address the full protection and security standard only after they have addressed the fair and equitable treatment standard.[115] Thus, the fair and equitable treatment standard has been the subject of

115 In *Encana v. Ecuador*, Article II of the Canada-Ecuador BIT required each party to encourage the creation of favorable conditions for investment and to accord investment fair and equitable

much more theoretical discussion. Often, a finding of liability under that standard moots the need for a detailed application of the full protection and security standard.

Tribunals sometimes have avoided developing a theory of full protection and security by holding either that, under the facts of the case, the violation of fair and equitable treatment also violates full protection and security or that a violation of fair and equitable treatment always violates full protection and security. For example, in *Occidental v. Ecuador*, a case arising under the United States-Ecuador BIT, the tribunal held that "a treatment that is not fair and equitable automatically entails an absence of full protection and security of the investment."[116] In *Azurix v. Argentina*, a case arising under the United States-Argentina BIT, the tribunal observed that "the stability afforded by a secure investment environment is as important" as physical security,[117] noted the absence of any qualifying language that would limit the scope of the provision to physical security, and held that Argentina's failure to provide fair and equitable treatment also breached the standard of full protection and security. In *ADC v Hungary*, a case arising under the Cyprus-Hungary BIT, the tribunal noted in a very brief discussion that Hungary's expropriation of the claimant's investment through its abrogation of a concession agreement, under the specific circumstances of the case, violated the full protection and treatment standard, as well as the fair and equitable treatment standard and the prohibition on unreasonable or discriminatory measures.

In short, tribunals that have applied the standard to nonphysical harm generally have declined to articulate a distinctive content for the full protection and security standard that would distinguish it from the fair and equitable treatment standard.[118] In any event, no case appears to rely exclusively upon the full protection and security standard as a basis for liability for nonphysical harm.

The distinction between physical and nonphysical harm may not always be a sharp one. In *Eureko v. Poland*, a case arising under the Netherlands-Poland BIT, the tribunal observed that harassment of the claimant's management could constitute a violation of the standard. Harassment, by its nature, may involve actions that cause related

---

treatment and full protection and security. The claimant alleged violations of only the first two of these three standards and not the standard of full protection and security. The tribunal observed that "[u]nder standards such as those in Article II of the BIT the State must act with reasonable consistency and without arbitrariness in its treatment of investments. One arm of the State cannot finally affirm what another arm denies to the detriment of a foreign investor." Award, para. 158. The claimant, however, had not alleged a treaty violation on this ground and the tribunal in any event found such a claim unsustainable on the facts before it. The tribunal's seeming willingness to treat the fair and equitable treatment standard and the full protection and security standard as at least in some respects indistinguishable is not unusual, although one could argue that, inasmuch as the claimant had alleged a violation of every part of Article II except the full protection and security standard, the tribunal was not addressing that standard at all, despite its general reference to "standards such as those in Article II."

116 Award, para.187.

117 Award, para. 408.

118 In *Wena Hotels v. Egypt*, the tribunal held that Egypt's conduct in failing to prevent a seizure of the claimant's hotels violated both standards. The tribunal began the discussion with an explanation of the full protection and security standard and thus, in that case, it was the fair and equitable treatment standard for which distinctive content was not articulated.

physical and nonphysical harms. The award, unfortunately, does not specify the nature of the harassment. In any event, the tribunal found that there was insufficient evidence to attribute the harassment to the Polish government and thus did not need to decide whether the harassment was sufficiently grave to violate the treaty. The tribunal also held that, even if the Polish government were not the instigator of the harassment, it would be responsible for a failure to prevent the harassment if the actions of harassment were repeated and sustained.

In a few awards, tribunals have discussed the effect of variations in the language of the standard. In *Parkerings-Compagniet v. Lithuania*, a case arising under the Norway-Lithuania BIT, the tribunal held that the single word "protection" referred to the full protection and security standard. By contrast, in *Siemens v. Argentina*, a case arising under the Germany-Argentina BIT, the tribunal noted that the word "security" was qualified by the word "legal" and questioned whether the standard applied to physical harm, although it did not need to decide the issue because the harm in that case was economic.

BITs occasionally use language that might seem to refer to the full protection and security standard, but does not. For example, in *Bogdanov v. Moldova*, the sole arbitrator observed that article 2(2) of the Russia-Moldova BIT requires the host state to provide "in accordance with its own legislation, full and unconditional legal protection" of covered investment. While the phrase "full and unconditional legal protection" in the abstract could be regarded as one of the many formulations of the full protection and security standard, the reference to national law was held to indicate that such is not the case in that BIT. The arbitrator found that "the full protection principle is not to be considered as a corrective of the host state's legislation, but is to be applied in accordance with the host country's law."[119] That is, the arbitrator found that the language of the treaty incorporated not the customary international law standard, but a requirement that national law be observed. The arbitrator held that Moldova's conduct had been consistent with its laws and, therefore, the treaty standard was not violated.

6.4 OBSERVANCE OF OBLIGATIONS

6.4.1 Structure and Policy

The protection of contract rights long has been an important element in creating security for both direct and portfolio investment. In fact, the failure of host states to comply with contractual obligations has concerned investors for at least two centuries. For example, in the nineteenth century, bond defaults were a major source of insecurity for foreign investors,[120] but host state governments sometimes annulled or interfered with

119 Award, para. 4.2.3.

120 *See* Section 2.1.1.

other contracts as well.[121] In the mid-twentieth century, many major foreign investments in the form of concession agreements were abrogated by host states.[122] In more recent years, some host states have come to regret the terms on which they privatized particular industries and have sought to modify those terms after a foreign investor has invested in the privatized industry. In all of these instances, the security of the investment could be destroyed by the failure of the host state to honor its commitments.

The rule that had emerged by the nineteenth century was that contracts are obligations created by domestic law and thus are enforceable to the extent provided by the law applicable to the contract, typically host-state law.[123] Where a host state law breached a contract with a foreign investor, the investor's remedy was through a contract action in local courts. A mere breach alone did not violate any rule of customary law, provided that the investor was able to obtain compensation for the breach through the local courts. The failure of the host state to provide a remedy, however, could constitute a denial of justice, which was wrongful under customary law. In addition, annulment of the contract might constitute an expropriation.[124] By the mid-twentieth century, some contended that at least certain contracts could create obligations founded on international law and that a breach of these contracts would violate customary law.[125]

Many BITs explicitly address the enforceability of contractual obligations of the host state to an investor. They include a provision requiring each party to observe any obligation into which it has entered into with respect to an investment.[126] This provision, however, is not as common as the fair and equitable treatment or full protection and security standards or the expropriation, transfers, or war and civil disturbance provisions. It sometimes is referred to as the "umbrella clause," because it brings contractual commitments within the coverage, or umbrella, of the BIT.

---

121 *See* Harvard Research in International Law, "Responsibility of States for Damage Done in Their Territory to the Persons or Property of Foreigners," 23 *American Journal of International Law Special Supplement* 133, 169–173 (1929) (describing nineteenth-century state practice).

122 *See* Section 2.2.

123 The state practice on which this paragraph is based is described in Harvard Research in International Law, "Responsibility of States for Damage Done in Their Territory to the Persons or Property of Foreigners," 23 *American Journal of International Law Special Supplement* 133, 169–173 (1929). *See also* F.A. Mann, "State Contracts and State Responsibility," 54 *American Journal of International Law* 572 (1960).

124 The circumstances under which an annulment would constitute an expropriation were disputed. *See* R. Y. Jennings, "State Contracts in International Law," 37 *British Yearbook of International Law* 156, 157 (1961).

125 *See Id.* Many argued, for example, that long-term economic agreements were enforceable under international law, rather than merely domestic law. *Id.* at 177. Such contracts were said to be "internationalized."

126 *See generally* Christoph Schreuer, "Traveling the BIT Route: Of Waiting Periods, Umbrella Clauses and Forks in the Road," 5 *Journal of World Investment and Trade* 231 (2004); Thomas W. Walde, "The 'Umbrella Clause' in Investment Arbitration—A Comment on Original Intentions and Recent Cases," 6 *Journal of World Investment and Trade* 183 (2005); Bjorn Kunoy, "Singing in the Rain: Developments in the Interpretation of Umbrella Clauses," 7 *Journal of World Investment and Trade* 275 (2006).

The language of the observance of obligations provision is virtually identical in most of the BITs in which it appears. The typical language requires each party to "observe any obligation it may have entered into" with respect to investments.[127] That is, the scope of the obligations is not qualified, except that the obligation must relate to investments. An alternative formulation requires each party to "observe any obligation it has entered into with investors of the other [party] with regard to their investment."[128] The obligations protected by this provision may be created by a contract between the host state and the investor or the investment, but they also may be unilaterally assumed by the host state, such as through the enactment of legislation. The obligation, however, must be related to investment. As will be seen in Section 6.4.2, some BITs include language intended to define more precisely the sense in which an obligation must relate to investment. Tribunals have addressed this issue as well.[129]

Although customary international law now treats the repudiation of a contract as an expropriation,[130] the literal language of the observance of obligations provision applies to breaches that do not constitute a repudiation of the contract. If the language of the provisions is given its ordinary meaning, a breach of a contract with respect to an investment constitutes a breach of the BIT.[131]

One notable variation that occasionally appears is language that seems to guarantee a legal framework within which obligations are preserved. An example is language requiring each party to "create and maintain in its territory a legal framework capable of guaranteeing investors the continuity of legal treatment, including compliance in good faith with undertakings entered upon by each individual investor."[132]

One interesting, but unusual, variation of this provision appears in the Mexico-Iceland BIT, which requires each party to observe any other obligation it has assumed in writing with regard to covered investments, but specifies that disputes arising from such obligations shall be settled only under the terms of the contracts underlying such obligations.[133]

The presence of the observance of obligations provision can be justified from at least four different perspectives. First, host-state abrogation of contracts with foreign

127 *See, e.g.*, United Kingdom-Bosnia-Herzegovina BIT, Art. 2(2); Denmark-Ethiopia BIT, Art. 2(3); Thailand-Argentina BIT, Art. 4(2); Austria-Armenia BIT, Art. 9(1); Finland-Armenia BIT, Art. 12(1) ("any obligation it may have with regard to a specific investment").

128 *See, e.g.*, Sweden-Kazakhstan BIT, Art 2(4); BLEU-Sudan BIT, Art.11(2) ("the commitments it has entered into vis-a-vis investors" of the other party); Germany-Timor-Leste BIT, Art. 8(2) ("any other obligation it has assumed with regard to investments"); Switzerland-Algeria BIT, Art. 10(2).

129 *See* Section 6.4.3.

130 *See* Section 2.2.

131 *See* F.A. Mann, "British Treaties for the Promotion and Protection of Investments," 52 *British Yearbook of International Law* 241 (1981); Rudolf Dolzer and Margrete Stevens, *Bilateral Investment Treaties* 81–82 (1995); Christoph Schreuer, "Traveling the BIT Route: Of Waiting Periods, Umbrella Clauses and Forks in the Road," 5 *Journal of World Investment and Trade 231 (2004); Stanimir A. Alexandrov, "Breaches of Contract and Breaches of Treaty," 5 Journal of World Investment and Trade* 555 (2004).

132 *See, e.g.*, Italy-Nicaragua BIT, Art. II(4)

133 Mexico-Iceland BIT, Art. 8.

investors in the past has been a common way in which host-state conduct impaired foreign investment. Thus, this provision is an important element of a favorable investment climate. Second, the enforcement of contracts, along with the protection of property rights, is a core function of the state in a liberal economic system. Liberal economics prescribes a system in which existing entitlements are protected and changes in entitlements are the results of bargaining. A contract, then, is the legal manifestation of a market transaction. Markets cannot function without the enforcement of contracts. A host state must provide access to courts where investors and investments can enforce private contracts, but also must observe the obligations into which it has entered with respect to investments. Third, the enforcement of obligations into which the state has entered is consistent with the rule of law. To permit the host state to dispense with obligations it has voluntarily assumed would convert those obligations from legal commitments to the objects of political power. Fourth, the protection of contracts is particularly important for foreign investors, who stand outside the political community of the host state. In the event of an adverse change in economic circumstances, host state revision or abrogation of contracts with foreign investors is likely to impose minimal political costs on the government. Contracts, by their nature, embody rights and duties among only a relatively few parties and thus host state measures easily can be directed specifically at the interests of foreign investors. Thus, normal domestic political pressures that might prevent host states from complying with their obligations may not exist where the obligations are to foreign investors.

The observance of obligations provision is but a special application of the customary international law norm of *pacta sunt servanda*. Moreover, the fair and equitable treatment standard, as it has been interpreted, requires consistent conduct by the host state with respect to investment, an obligation that in particular prohibits the violation of commitments made with respect to an investment.[134] Some tribunals have interpreted the full protection and security standard to have a similar effect.[135] Further, it long has been recognized that the repudiation of contract rights may constitute an expropriation in violation of international law.[136] Even ordinary breaches of contracts may result in a violation of customary law where the host state provides no remedy and thus commits a denial of justice.[137] Thus, the duty imposed by the observance of obligations provision at least in part may be independently imposed by customary international law and by other treaty provisions, such as the fair and equitable treatment standard or the expropriation provision. Yet, the observance of obligations provision perhaps may impose a greater obligation than at least some of these other treaty provisions to the extent that it is violated by mere breaches of contract not constituting a repudiation of the contract or a denial of justice.

---

134 *See* Section 6.2.

135 *See* Section 6.3.3.

136 For a discussion of U.S. practice suggesting that the repudiation of contracts violates customary law, *see* Kenneth J. Vandevelde, *U.S. International Investment Agreements* 261 (2009).

137 *Azinian v. Mexico* (NAFTA), Award, paras. 102–103. On denial of justice generally, see Section 10.4.1.

The observance of obligations provision can be of great practical significance. Major foreign investments in developing countries often are established under the terms of an investment agreement, sometimes in the form of a concession agreement, concluded by the host state and the investor. Such agreements typically grant to investors special rights and privileges, such as tax exemptions, and may include stabilization clauses under which the investment is exempt from at least certain changes in the law, such as changes in environmental laws.[138] Such rights and privileges may be a critical factor upon which the investor relies in deciding to invest. To the extent that the investment is beneficial to the host state, an investment agreement that makes the investment possible may be beneficial to the host state as well. The effect of the observance of obligations provision is to ensure that these agreements are enforceable through the investor-state and state-state disputes provisions, although of course the investment agreement itself also may include an investor-state disputes provision.

While requiring host states to honor their commitments to investments, as has been noted, can be justified on multiple grounds, the practical consequence is that host-state efforts to raise environmental or labor standards could be impeded. Further, as noted in Section 2.2, the twentieth century witnessed the negotiation of many concession agreements by corrupt or inept host state governments that granted highly favorable terms to foreign investors over long periods of time and the adverse consequences of such agreements for the host state and its people could be staggering. That is, to say that an investment agreement may be a necessary condition for the establishment of an investment is not to say that all the terms of a particular investment agreement were a necessary condition. Particular terms may reflect little more than rent-seeking behavior by investors.

In any event, ensuring the enforceability of investment agreements long has been of great importance to the investor community, while the belief on the part of some that these investment agreements are often poor bargains for the host state has been a major complaint against efforts to ensure the security of host state obligations. Many of the most controversial and notorious expropriations of the twentieth century were repudiations of concession agreements between an investor and a host state. The security of investment agreements thus is potentially both of great value to the investor and of great cost to the host state. The security of investment agreements, given the special rights and privileges that they often confer on investors, also represents another example of the way in which the principle of investment security can conflict with the principle of nondiscrimination.[139]

6.4.2 Origins

The observance of obligations provision was not a feature of FCN practice. In 1948, the International Law Association prepared its Draft Statute of the Arbitral Tribunal

---

138 *See* International Finance Corporation, "Stabilization Clauses and Human Rights," March 11, 2008, available at http://www.ifc.org.

139 *See* Section 7.1.

for Foreign Investment and its Draft Statute of the Foreign Investments Court.[140] Both statutes stated that one purpose of the respective entities that they would create was to resolve disputes "concerning the observance or interpretation of any undertaking which a Party may have given in relation to investments made by nationals of any other Party."[141]

The 1959 Abs-Shawcross convention also included a provision on observance of undertakings.[142] Specifically, Article II provided that "Each Party shall at all times ensure the observance of any undertakings, which it may have given in relations to investments made by nationals of any other Party." Thus, the Abs-Shawcross convention followed closely the language of the 1948 ILA draft statutes, although as a substantive provision rather than a jurisdictional clause it referred only to the observance of undertakings and not to their interpretation.

Later that year, when Germany concluded the first BIT, with Pakistan, an observance of obligations provision was in the treaty. Article 7 provided that "Either Party shall observe any other obligation it may have entered into with regard to investments by nationals or companies of the other Party." This language, which owes much to the 1948 ILA draft statutes and the Abs-Shawcross convention, remains typical of that employed in a large number of BITs fifty years later.

In the early German BITs, the observance of obligations provision was in the same article as the preservation of rights provision.[143] Thus, Article 7 also provided that the BIT shall not derogate from any favorable treatment guaranteed to investment by any legislation or international obligation. A preservation of rights provision also appeared in the Abs-Shawcross convention, but not in the same article as the observance of obligations provision.

The observance of obligations and preservation of rights provisions are related in the sense that both pertain to agreements with respect to investment, but their effects are different. The preservation of rights provision ensures that the BIT does not displace such agreements, but does not strengthen them in any way. The observance of obligations provision requires that such agreements be observed and allows claims arising out of breaches of such agreements to be submitted to arbitration under the BIT's disputes provisions.

The 1967 OECD Draft Convention on the Protection of Foreign Property included an observance of obligations provision as well. Article 2, which was headed "Observance of Undertakings," provided that "[e]ach Party shall at all times ensure the observance of undertakings given by it in relation to property of nationals of any other Party." Note 1 stated that this article represented "an application of the general principle of

---

140 Reprinted in United Nations Conference on Trade and Development, *3 International Investment Instruments: A Compendium* 259 (1996).

141 The quoted language appeared in Article 1 of both instruments. The other purpose was to resolve disputes arising out of any unreasonable or discriminatory impairment of covered property.

142 *See* Anthony C. Sinclair, "The Origins of the Umbrella Clause in the International Law of Investment Protection," 20 *Arbitration International* 411 (2004).

143 *See* Section 6.8.

pacta sunt servanda—the maintenance of the pledged word." Note 3 commented that such undertakings could be consensual or they could represent a unilateral engagement on the part of the host state. Further, such an undertaking must relate to the property, meaning either that it identified the property or party that was the beneficiary of the undertaking or that, where the undertaking was a general one, the circumstances were such that the host state had created "a legitimate expectation of the continuance of a particular state of affairs."

Despite its presence in the German BITs, the Abs Shawcross convention, and the OECD draft convention, the observance of obligations provision generally did not appear in the BITs of most countries in the 1960s or even the 1970s. The provision did appear in the U.K. BITs in the 1970s. For example, the 1975 United Kingdom-Egypt BIT provided that "Each Contracting Party shall observe any obligation it may have entered into with regard to investments of nationals of companies of the other Contracting Party."[144] This phrasing, which is quite similar to that of the German BITs, remains the language used in the U.K. BITs.[145] Although Austria included an observance of obligations provision in its first BIT,[146] with Romania in 1976, the provision typically is not a feature of the Austrian BITs.

The provision became more prevalent in the 1980s. Denmark included an observance of obligations provision for the first time in its 1980 BIT with Romania, which required at Article 3(5) that parties observe "all other obligations" entered into with regard to investors, their investments and returns. In Denmark's next BIT, concluded five years later with China, the provision applied to "any obligation . . . with regard to approved investment contracts."[147] By 1988, however, Denmark had adopted the language "any obligation . . . with regard to investments"[148] and that remains the language typically used in the Danish BITs.[149] The Denmark-Kuwait BIT applies the provision to "any obligation . . . with regard to any particular investment."[150]

The provision also appears in the Dutch BITs beginning in the 1980s. For example, the 1986 Netherlands-Turkey BIT provides that "[e]ach Contracting Party shall observe any obligations it may have entered into with regard to investments."[151] The 1985 Netherlands-Philippines BIT provides that "Each Contracting Party shall observe any obligations arising from a particular commitment it may have entered into with regard to a specific investment of nationals of the other Contracting Party."[152]

Although Sweden launched its BIT program in 1965, the observance of obligations provision did not appear at that time. It first appeared in a Swedish BIT in 1983,[153]

---

144 United Kingdom-Egypt BIT, Art. 2(2)

145 *See, e.g.*, United Kingdom-Vietnam BIT, Art. 2(1); United Kingdom-Bosnia-Herzegovina BIT, Art. 2(1).

146 *See* Austria-Romania BIT, Art. 3(3).

147 Denmark-China BIT Art. 3(1).

148 *See, e.g.*, Denmark-Republic of Korea BIT, Art. 3(1).

149 *See, e.g.*, Denmark-Croatia BIT, Art. 2(3); Denmark-Kyrgyz Republic BIT, Art. 2(3).

150 Denmark-Kuwait BIT, Art. 3(2).

151 Netherlands-Turkey BIT, Art. 3(3).

152 Netherlands-Philippines BIT, Art. 3(3).

153 Sweden-Yemen BIT, Art. 2(2).

where the language required each party to observe "any obligation . . . with regard to investments." The provision, however, has appeared principally in Swedish BITs concluded in 2000 or later, where it requires each party to "observe any obligation it has entered into with the investors of the other Contracting Party with regard to their investments."[154]

Kuwait launched its BIT program in 1964, but the observance of obligations provision seems[155] to have first appeared in its 1985 BIT with China,[156] although the provision in that BIT was narrowly worded to apply only to investment authorizations and investment contracts. Kuwait's later BITs, on those occasions when the observance of obligations provision appeared, generally used the more typical language.[157]

The United States concluded its first BIT in 1982, with Egypt, although the provision did not appear in that BIT. The provision was present in the second U.S. BIT, that with Panama, concluded in 1982 as well.[158] The provision remained in the U.S. BITs until 1994, when it was deleted from the U.S. model negotiating text, although the U.S. BITs continue to authorize the enforcement of investment agreements and investment authorizations through the investor-state disputes provision.[159]

Finland launched its BIT program in 1980, but the provision did not appear in its BITs until the 1990s.[160] The provision applied to "any obligation . . . with regard to investments." Although the provision still occasionally appeared in the 1990s,[161] it is not a regular feature of Finland's more recent BITs.[162]

In summary, the observance of obligations provision was slow to gain widespread acceptance and became prevalent only in the 1980s. Many countries continue not to include it in their BITs. Among those that do, however, the language has become relatively standard, requiring observance of any obligations entered into with regard to investments, language that already was in use by 1959.

6.4.3 Arbitral Practice

The first case to apply the observance of obligations provision was *Fedax v. Venezuela*, a case arising under the Netherlands-Venezuela BIT. Venezuela had failed to make

154 *See, e.g.*, Sweden-Bosnia-Herzegovina BIT, Art. 2(2); Sweden-Kazakhstan BIT, Art. 2(4); Sweden-Ecuador BIT, Art. 2)(4).

155 Several early Kuwaiti BITs never entered into force and are not readily available.

156 Kuwait-China BIT, Art. 2(2).

157 *See, e.g.*, Kuwait-Hungary BIT, Art. 2(10); Kuwait-Ethiopia BIT, Art. 3(3); Kuwait-Croatia BIT, Art. 3(1) ("any obligation or undertaking"); Kuwait-Netherlands BIT, Art. 3(4).

158 United States-Panama BIT, Art. II(2).

159 *See* Vandevelde, *supra* note 135, at 261.

160 *See, e.g.*, Finland-Czechoslovakia BIT, Art. 4(1); Finland-Estonia BIT, Art. 4(1); Finland-Latvia BIT, Art. 4(1); Finland-Turkey BIT, Art. 4(1).

161 *See, e.g.*, Finland-Croatia BIT, Art. 3 (applying to "any other obligation . . . with regard to specific investments").

162 *See, e.g.*, Finland-Armenia BIT; Finland-Belarus BIT; Finland-Azerbaijan BIT; Finland-Algeria BIT.

payments under promissory notes held by the claimant. Article 3 of the BIT provided that "[e]ach Contracting Party shall observe any obligation it may have entered into with regard to the treatment of investments of nationals of the other Contracting Party." The tribunal found that Venezuela was required by the BIT to honor the promissory notes.[163]

A number of tribunals have expressed a concern that the ordinary meaning of the clause is too broad and they have sought to interpret it narrowly. The second case to apply the observance of obligations provision and the first to discuss its meaning in any detail was *SGS v. Pakistan*, which arose under the Switzerland-Pakistan BIT.[164] Article 11 of that BIT provided that "[e]ither Contracting Party shall constantly guarantee the observance of the commitments it has entered into with respect to the investments of the investors of the other Contracting Party." The tribunal, however, declined to interpret the clause in accordance with its ordinary meaning. Rather, the tribunal noted that the text of the obligations clause, if read literally, suggests that it applies to any commitment by the state or any entity the conduct of which is attributable to the state. Such a sweeping effect, in the view of the tribunal, should not be given to a clause in the absence of clear and convincing evidence that such an effect was intended. That is, the tribunal reversed the usual presumption in favor of interpreting treaty language in accordance with its ordinary meaning. Noting that the observance of obligations provision in that treaty was located not with other substantive obligations but at the end of the treaty just prior to its final provisions, the tribunal held that the provision was not intended to impose a substantive obligation. In reaction to the award, on October 1, 2003, the Swiss Government sent a letter to ICSID stating that it was "alarmed about the very narrow interpretation" given to the provision by the tribunal, which was contrary to Switzerland's intention in concluding the treaty.[165]

The approach in *SGS v. Pakistan* was rejected by the tribunal in *SGS v. Philippines*, which arose under the Switzerland-Philippines BIT. In that case, SGS had entered into a contract to provide inspection services similar to the contract in the Pakistan case. The observance of obligations provision of the Switzerland-Philippines BIT, however, was worded differently than that in the Pakistan case. Article X(2) of the treaty provided that "[e]ach Contracting Party shall observe any obligation it has assumed with regard to specific investments in its territory by investors of the other Contracting Party." In the Philippines case, the tribunal read the observance of

---

163 Award, para. 29.

164 As the first BIT case to analyze such a provision in detail, the tribunal's award reflects the early struggle among competing metaphors by which to refer to the provision. Counsel invoked the metaphor of an "elevator," because the provision elevates contract violations to the level of treaty obligations, the metaphor of a "mirror," because the provision in effect incorporates into the BIT a mirror image of the contract, and the metaphor of an "umbrella," because the BIT creates an umbrella under which is brought the obligations of contracts. As indicated in the text, the consensus among those who like to assign metaphorical names to international legal obligations has favored the last of the terms and the observance of obligations provision is now often called "the umbrella clause."

165 The letter is quoted in the Partial Award of August 19, 2005, in *Eureko v. Poland*, at para. 254.

obligations provision as granting "assurances to foreign investors with regard to the performance of obligations assumed by the host State under its own law with respect to specific investments—in effect, to help secure the rule of law in relation to investment protection."[166] The obligations "must have been assumed vis-à-vis the specific investment—not as a matter of the application of some legal obligation of a general character."[167] The tribunal in the Philippines case criticized the tribunal in the Pakistan case for creating a presumption against the ordinary meaning of the provision and then requiring clear and convincing evidence to overcome the presumption. It also criticized the tribunal in the Pakistan case for placing so much weight on the location of the clause in the treaty. Accordingly, the tribunal found that the Philippines' refusal to pay sums admittedly payable raised a claim under the observance of obligations provision, although the tribunal stayed the arbitration pending a decision of the local courts, applying local contract law, concerning the amount that was payable.[168]

The majority of tribunals to address the issue essentially have followed the approach of the *SGS v. Philippines* tribunal in seeking to give the provision its ordinary meaning, rejecting the holding in *SGS v. Pakistan* that the ordinary meaning applies only if supported by clear and convincing evidence. Tribunals, however, have not followed the *SGS v. Philippines* tribunal in staying the arbitration to permit resolution of the contract claim in local courts.[169]

In *Eureko v. Poland*, a case arising under the Netherlands-Poland BIT, the text of the observance of obligations provision, at Article 3.5 of the BIT, provided that "[e]ach party shall observe any obligations it may have entered into with regard to investments of investors of the other Contracting Party." The tribunal held that the language of the provision, in accordance with Article 31 of the Vienna Convention on the Law of Treaties, should be given its "ordinary meaning." It found that the phrase "shall observe" was imperative and categorical, while the word "any" was capacious and meant "all." The tribunal thus agreed with the tribunal in *SGS v. Philippines* that the obligations provision "means what it says."[170] The tribunal found that Poland's failure to honor its commitment to complete the privatization of an insurance company in which the claimant had invested violated the observance of obligations provision.

In *Noble Ventures v. Romania*, Article II(2)(c) of the United States-Romania BIT provided that "[e]ach Party shall observe any obligation it may have entered into with regard to investments." The tribunal sought to give the provision its ordinary meaning and found that the provision in the United States-Romania BIT was "even more general and straightforward" than that in the Switzerland-Philippines BIT addressed in

---

166 Award, para. 126.

167 *Id.* at para. 121.

168 Decision on Jurisdiction, para. 171. The stay was lifted in December 2007. *See* Order of the Tribunal on Further Proceedings, December 17, 2007. On the reasoning of these two awards, *see* Stanimir A. Alexandrov, "Breaches of Contract and Breaches of Treaty," 5 *Journal of World Investment and Trade* 555 (2004).

169 *See* Andrew Newcombe and Lluís Paradell, *Law and Practice of Investment Treaties: Standards of Treatment* 473–475 (2009).

170 Partial Award, paras. 256–257.

SGS v. Philippines.[171] The tribunal raised the question of whether some limitation on the scope of the provision should be imposed. As it happened, however, the tribunal found that Romania had not breached any obligations to the claimant with regard to an investment. Noting that the issue of the existence of any limitations on the scope of the provision was mooted by that conclusion, the tribunal proceeded on the assumption that the parties intended "to equate contractual obligations governed by municipal law to international treaty obligations as established in their BIT."[172]

In *Duke Energy v. Ecuador*, a case arising under the United States-Ecuador BIT, a claim was brought by the investor and its investment against Ecuador for breach of various power purchase agreements entered into with the investment by an Ecuadoran state-owned enterprise. The tribunal found the breaches of these agreements to violate the observance of obligations provision.[173]

In *MTD Equity v. Chile*, a case arising under the Malaysia-Chile BIT, the tribunal appeared to be prepared to give the observance of obligations provision its ordinary meaning. The tribunal found, however, that the investor's project had not yet become fully approved. Thus, the host state's ultimate refusal to permit the project did not violate any obligation.

In some cases, the obligation is created not through a bilateral contract, but by the unilateral action of the host state, typically by the enactment of a statute. The tribunal in *SGS v. Pakistan* explicitly acknowledged that the obligations to which the provision applies could be those arising from legislation rather than contracts,[174] although the obligation at issue in that case was a contract.

Unilateral undertakings through legislation were at issue in several cases involving the United States-Argentina BIT, which contains an observance of obligations provision identical to that in the United States-Romania BIT, quoted above. For example, in *LG&E v. Argentina*, the tribunal held that Argentina's gas law and regulations establishing the tariff regime that ensured the value of claimant's investment in a privatized gas distribution company and that were advertised in order to induce investors to participate in the privatization program were not obligations of a general nature, but were specific in relation to that investment. Because the gas law and its regulations targeted foreign investors, they were obligations within the meaning of the observance of obligations provision.

Similarly, in *Enron v. Argentina*, the tribunal adopted the ordinary meaning of the provision and held that the phrase "any obligation" means any obligation regardless of its nature. The tribunal found that Argentina's gas law, the same one that was at issue in *LG&E*, was an obligation. Dismantling the tariff regime therefore violated the observance of obligations provision. The tribunal also found that the terms of a license approved by a government decree were an obligation and that violations of those terms constituted a separate violation of the observance of obligations provision.

---

171 Award, para.60.

172 *Id.* at para. 61.

173 Award, para. 325.

174 Decision on Jurisdiction, para. 166.

In *CMS Gas Transmission Company v. Argentina*, the tribunal also found that the measures undertaken by Argentina with respect to its gas law violated the observance of obligations provision. The tribunal did comment that "[p]urely commercial aspects of a contract might not be protected by the treaty in some situations, but the protection is likely to be available when there is significant interference by government or public agencies with the rights of the investor."[175] The language was *dictum*, however, inasmuch as the tribunal found that none of the measures on which the claim was based could be "described as a commercial question," but rather all "related to government decisions"[176] that breached treaty standards. As is noted below, the tribunal's finding with respect to the observance of obligations provision was annulled on other grounds.

In *Continental Casualty v. Argentina*, the tribunal held that covered obligations were not limited to those based on contract, but that they must address investments with some degree of specificity in order to be considered obligations "with regard to" investment. For example, unilateral commitments in legislation "regulating a particular business sector and addressed specifically to foreign investors in relation to their investments therein" could fall within the observance of obligations provision.[177] The tribunal also noted that the undertaking could be entered into with the investor or with its investment. In that case, however, several of the statutes at issue were addressed to the public generally or a wide range of depositors and subscribers and thus were not obligations with regard to covered investments. Any breach of Argentina's obligations with respect to certain government-guaranteed loans fell within its defense of necessity. Argentina's restructuring of certain treasury bills already had been held to violate the fair and equitable treatment provision and thus did not need to be considered under the observance of obligations provision.

In *Plama v. Bulgaria*, a case arising under the Energy Charter Treaty, the tribunal said that the term "any obligation" seemed to suggest statutory or contractual obligations, although it noted that the annulment committee in *CMS v. Argentina* commented that it should include only consensual obligations.[178] In any event, the obligations at issue in *Plama* were contractual. The tribunal noted that such obligations were embraced within the provision only if assumed by the host state with the investor. The tribunal found that legislation enacted by Bulgaria amending its environmental laws had not breached its privatization agreement with the investor.

Not every award, however, rendered after that in *SGS v. Philippines* has given the provision its ordinary meaning. For example, in *Joy Mining Machinery v. Egypt*, a case arising under the United Kingdom-Egypt BIT, the claimant had entered into a contract to sell mining equipment to an agency of the Egyptian government. The claimant supplied letters of guarantee for the performance of the equipment. Although the claimant was paid in full, disputes arose concerning the performance of the equipment and the Egyptian government agency refused to release the guarantees. The claimant

175 Award, para. 299.
176 Award, para. 301.
177 Award, para. 301.
178 Award, para. 186.

submitted the dispute to arbitration, seeking compensation and the release of the guarantees. The tribunal held that the observance of obligations provision does not transform a contract dispute into an investment dispute unless there is a violation of other treaty rights or a violation of contract rights "of such a magnitude to trigger the Treaty protection."[179] The tribunal found that the dispute was purely a commercial one and therefore lacked a connection to the treaty. The holding in *Joy Mining*, however, seemed to be that the observance of obligations provision may be violated when the host state acts as a sovereign, but not when it acts in a proprietary capacity.

A state's repudiation of a contract obligation in its capacity as sovereign, as opposed to a mere breach such as that in which any private party might engage, is generally held to constitute an expropriation of the contract.[180] Thus, under the *Joy Mining* interpretation, the observance of obligations provision would seem to add little or nothing to the expropriation provision. That interpretation, in other words, seems to deprive the observance of obligations of any independent effect.

In *El Paso Energy v. Argentina*, a case arising under the United States-Argentina BIT, the tribunal after reviewing the reasoning in *SGS v. Pakistan* and *SGS v. Philippines* concluded that it preferred the interpretation adopted in the *Pakistan* case. Citing *Joy Mining*, the tribunal held that it had jurisdiction only if the host state was alleged to have breached an obligation in such a way as to violate one of the other provisions of the BIT. The tribunal also observed, correctly, that under Article VII(1) of the United States-Argentina BIT, a breach of a contract that met the definition of an "investment agreement"[181] would violate the BIT. Thus, the practical effect of the tribunal's decision was to enforce obligations set forth in an investment agreement, but to follow *Joy Mining* with respect to all other obligations.[182]

Three months later, the tribunal in *Pan American Energy v. Argentina*, another case arising under the United States-Argentina BIT, issued its Decision on Preliminary Objections, addressing a claim very similar to that in *El Paso Energy*. As it happened, two[183] of the three arbitrators on the *El Paso* tribunal also were members of the *Pan American Energy* tribunal. Not surprisingly, the *Pan American Energy* tribunal reasoned in the same way as the *El Paso* tribunal, in some instances repeating the language from the earlier decision verbatim, and reached the same conclusion as had the *El Paso* tribunal.

Both awards misinterpreted the U.S. BITs. The observance of obligations provision clearly was intended to have an effect beyond merely the enforcement of investment agreements.[184] U.S. BIT negotiators deliberately chose the broader term "obligations" rather than "investment agreements" so that the clause would apply to obligations that

---

179 Award, para.81.

180 *See* Section 6.5.3.2.

181 The term "investment agreement" is a term of art in the U.S. BIT practice. The United States-Argentina BIT defines it as an agreement between the investor and the host state. For a more detailed discussion, *see* Vandevelde, *supra* note 135, at 173–178.

182 Decision on Jurisdiction, para. 79.

183 The arbitrators that sat on both tribunals were Lucius Caflisch and Brigitte Stern.

184 *See* Vandevelde, *supra* note 135, at 258.

were not in the narrower category of investment agreements.[185] Further, both awards relied on the 2004 U.S. model negotiating text as an interpretive guide to the U.S.-Argentina BIT, but in fact that BIT was based on an earlier, 1991 model negotiating text.[186] A tribunal explicitly rejected distinctions among different types of agreements in *Siemens v. Argentina*, a case arising under the Germany-Argentina BIT.[187]

In *Sempra Energy v. Argentina*, another case arising under the United States-Argentina BIT, the tribunal held that the observance of obligations provision is violated only where the breach of the obligation is committed by the host state acting in its sovereign capacity rather than as an ordinary party to a contract. The tribunal noted that this distinction may be difficult to draw in some cases, but not in the case before it. Argentina had adopted major regulatory changes that violated specific obligations not to freeze tariffs or subject them to price controls and not to amend a license without the licensee's consent and thus violated the observance of obligations provision.

A different formulation of the observance of obligations provision was at issue in *Salini v. Jordan*, which arose under the Italy-Jordan BIT. Article 2(4) of that BIT provided that "[e]ach Contracting Party shall create and maintain in its territory a legal framework apt to guarantee the investors the continuity of legal treatment, including compliance, in good faith, of all undertakings assumed with regard to each specific investor." The tribunal held that the provision requires the host state to create a legal framework in which contracts are observed, but did not require the host state to observe an obligation that it previously had entered into with respect to investments. Thus, the breach of a particular contract did not constitute a violation of the treaty provision. As the tribunal explained, "Only the State, in the exercise of its sovereign authority, and not as a contracting party, has assumed obligations under the bilateral agreement."[188]

In a few awards, no breach of an obligation between the claimant and the host state was found. In these cases, the obligation typically was entered into by some entity other than the national government and the tribunal declined to hold the host state responsible for the obligation. That is, the tribunal declined to apply the usual rules of state attribution to the assumption of the contractual obligation.

For example, in *Azurix v. Argentina*, a case arising under United States-Argentina BIT, the tribunal held the observance of obligations provision inapplicable because Argentina had not entered into any contract with the claimant. Rather, the contract was between an Azurix subsidiary and the province of Buenos Aires.[189] Because the claimant owned 90 percent of the shares in the subsidiary, it should have been entitled to assert a claim on behalf of the subsidiary. Thus, the award must have rested on the fact that the contract was with the province rather than the central government.

In *LLC AMTO v. Ukraine*, a case arising under the Energy Charter Treaty, the tribunal held the observance of obligations provision inapplicable because the contract with the investment was entered into by a state-owned entity, rather than by the state itself.

---

185 *Id.* at 259.

186 *Id.* at 295.

187 Award, para. 206.

188 Award, para. 155.

189 Award, para. 384.

In *Impregilo v. Pakistan*, a case arising under the Italy-Pakistan BIT, the tribunal held that an observance of obligations provision would not apply to the contracts in that case because the contracts were entered into by the Pakistan Water and Power Development Authority rather than with Pakistan itself.[190]

Most tribunals, however, apply the ordinary rules of state attribution.[191] For example, in *Noble Ventures v. Romania*, a case arising under the United States-Romania BIT, the tribunal applied the observance of obligations provision to a contract between the claimant and a State Ownership Fund, an entity to which governmental authority had been delegated.[192] In *Eureko v. Poland*, a case arising under the Netherlands-Poland BIT, the observance of obligations provision was applied even though the obligations were entered into by the Treasury Department, which possessed independent legal personality.[193] In *Duke Energy v. Ecuador*, a case arising under the United States-Ecuador BIT, the provision was applied to contracts entered into by a state enterprise. In *Nykomb v. Latvia*, a case arising under the Energy Charter Treaty, the contract was entered into by a state-owned enterprise the conduct of which was attributable to the state for purposes of the observance of obligations and other provisions of the BIT,[194] although the tribunal found it unnecessary to decide whether Latvia violated the observance of obligations provision. Indeed, even the tribunal in *SGS v. Pakistan* had commented that the commitments to which the observance of obligations provision applies "may, without imposing excessive violence on the text itself, be commitments of the State itself as a legal person, or of any office, entity or subdivision (local government units) or legal representative thereof whose acts are, under the law on state responsibility, attributable to the State itself."[195]

Where the claimant is neither the obligee nor the controlling investor in the obligee, the claimant will not easily be able to enforce the obligation through the observance of obligations provision. For example, as noted above, in *CMS v. Argentina*, a case arising under the United States-Argentina BIT, the tribunal found that Argentina violated the observance of obligations provision. The *ad hoc* committee on annulment, however, annulled this finding on the ground that the tribunal failed to explain how CMS, which was a minority shareholder in the investment, could enforce the obligations of Argentina to the investment.[196]

Even where the claimant is the controlling investor in the obligee, a very few tribunals have declined to apply the observance of obligations provision if the claimant itself was not a party to the contract. The tribunal did so in *Siemens v. Argentina*,

---

190 Decision on Jurisdiction, para. 223.

191 On the problem of attribution in this context, see Kaj Hober, "State Responsibility and Attribution," in *The Oxford Handbook of International Investment Law* (Peter Muchlinski, Frederico Ortino, and Christoph Schreuer, eds. 2008).

192 Award, paras. 82–86.

193 Partial Award, paras. 115–134.

194 Award, paras. 109–115.

195 Decision on Jurisdiction, para. 166.

196 Decision on Annulment, para. 96.

a case arising under the Germany-Argentina BIT.[197] As already noted, the tribunal may also have declined to apply the provision for the same reason in *Azurix v. Argentina*, a case arising under the United States-Argentina BIT. The prevailing rule, however, is that a controlling investor may submit a claim for violation of the observance of obligations provision with respect to an obligation entered into with the investment.[198]

Finally, in *PSEG v. Turkey*, a case arising under the United States-Turkey BIT, the host state's only breach of a contractual obligation was noncompliance with a schedule, a term that the tribunal found to be nonessential. Accordingly, no breach of the BIT obligation occurred.

6.5 EXPROPRIATION

6.5.1 Structure and Policy

The sovereign power of a state over its internal affairs includes a number of distinct powers, such as the power of eminent domain, the power to regulate for the health, safety, welfare, and morals of the people (sometimes referred to as "the police power"), and the power to tax. Traditionally, the exercise of the power of eminent domain, *i.e.*, the power to take title and possession of property, was regarded as an expropriation, for which compensation was owed.

An expropriation is the single greatest impairment of the security of an investment. It is an act that eliminates all or substantially all of the value of the investment to the investor. The threat of expropriation was a principal motivating factor in the origin of the BITs. Accordingly, BITs universally include a provision restricting the right of the host state to expropriate covered investment. Indeed, in a few BITs, the investor-state arbitration provision applies only to disputes involving an expropriation.[199]

BIT expropriation provisions always acknowledge the power of the host state to expropriate covered investment, but they impose conditions on the exercise of that power. Four conditions are very often imposed, although not every condition appears in every BIT. These conditions are that the expropriation be for a public purpose,[200]

---

197 Award, para. 204.

198 *See, e.g., Continental Casualty v. Argentina* (United States-Argentina BIT), Award, para. 98.

199 *See, e.g.*, Italy-Bangladesh BIT, Art. 9; Italy-Pakistan BIT, Art. 9; Austria-Romania BIT, Art. 5.

200 *See, e.g.*, United Kingdom-Bosnia-Herzegovina BIT, Art. 5(1); BLEU-Sudan BIT, Art. 7(2); Netherlands-Ethiopia, Art. 6; Germany-Timore-Leste BIT, Art. 4(2); Switzerland-Algeria BIT, Art. 6(1); Austria-Armenia BIT, Art. 5(1); Finland-Armenia BIT, Art. 5(1); Sweden-Kazakhstan, Art. 4; Denmark-Ethiopia, Art. 5(1); Chile-Indonesia BIT, Art. VI(1); Australia-India BIT, Art. 7 (1); Thailand-Argentina BIT, Art. 6(1); Cambodia-Vietnam BIT, Art. IV; Mexico-Iceland BIT, Art. 4(1); Canada-Uruguay BIT, Art. VIII(1).

nondiscriminatory,[201] in accordance with due process of law,[202] and accompanied by full compensation. Less often, the BITs impose a fifth condition, that the expropriation not be inconsistent with any prior commitment.[203] The requirement of compensation always appears. In most cases, the provision requires payment of prompt, adequate, and effective compensation,[204] although those precise words often do not appear.[205] The expropriation provision has been treated as a codification of the relevant principles of customary international law.[206] The 2004 U.S. model BIT states explicitly that the language establishing the conditions for an expropriation "is intended to reflect customary international law concerning the obligation of States with respect to expropriation."[207]

The requirement of a public purpose, often phrased as a requirement that the expropriation be in the "public interest," is one with respect to which the host state is given considerable discretion. The requirement serves a simple goal: to prohibit expropriations undertaken only for private benefit. The classic example is that of an expropriation that merely transfers title to property from one private party to another, without benefit to the public. The distinction between public and private ends may not always been a clear one. In liberal economic systems, private parties engage in economic activity that is for the public benefit and thus an expropriation may benefit private parties while also serving public purposes. The inquiry ultimately is whether the measure is intended to benefit the public, even if benefits were conferred on private parties as well. Another example of an expropriation that violates the public purpose requirement is an expropriation effected as an act of retaliation, rather than in pursuit of legitimate public objectives.[208] The requirement that expropriatory conduct be in furtherance of legitimate state objectives reflects the reasonableness principle that

---

201 *See, e.g.*, United Kingdom-Bosnia-Herzegovina BIT, Art. 5(1); BLEU-Sudan BIT, Art. 7(1); Netherlands-Ethiopia, Art. 6; Switzerland-Algeria BIT, Art. 6(1); Austria-Armenia BIT, Art. 5(1); Finland-Armenia BIT, Art. 5(1); Sweden-Kazakhstan, Art. 4; Denmark-Ethiopia, Art. 5(1); Chile-Indonesia BIT, Art. VI(1); Australia-India BIT, Art. 7 (1); Thailand-Argentina BIT, Art. 6(1); Cambodia-Vietnam BIT, Art. IV; Mexico-Iceland BIT, Art. 4; Canada-Uruguay BIT, Art. VIII(1).

202 *See, e.g.*, BLEU-Sudan BIT, Art. 7(2); Netherlands-Ethiopia, Art. 6; Austria-Armenia BIT, Art. 5(1); Finland-Armenia BIT, Art. 5(1); Sweden-Kazakhstan, Art. 4; Thailand-Argentina BIT, Art. 6; Cambodia-Vietnam BIT, Art. IV; Mexico-Iceland BIT, Art. 4(1); Canada-Uruguay BIT, Art. VIII(1).

203 *See, e.g.*, BLEU-Sudan BIT, Art. 7(2); Denmark-Ethiopia, Art. 5(1).

204 *See, e.g.*, United Kingdom-Bosnia-Herzegovina BIT, Art. 5(1); Netherlands-Ethiopia, Art. 6; Austria-Armenia BIT, Art. 5(1); Finland-Armenia BIT, Art. 5(1); Sweden-Kazakhstan, Art. 4; Denmark-Ethiopia, Art. 5(1); Chile-Indonesia BIT, Art. VI(1); Thailand-Argentina BIT, Art. 6(1); Cambodia-Vietnam BIT, Art. IV; Canada-Uruguay BIT, Art. VIII(1).

205 *See, e.g.*, BLEU-Sudan BIT, Art. 7(2)–(3)("adequate and effective compensation . . . without undue delay"); Switzerland-Algeria BIT, Art. 6(1) (effective and adequate compensation . . . without delay"); Mexico-Iceland BIT, Art. 4(2) (compensation must be the fair market value of the investment, be paid without delay and be freely transferable)

206 *See Generation Ukraine v. Ukraine* (United States-Ukraine BIT), Award, para. 11.3.

207 Annex B, para. 1.

208 *See British Petroleum Exploration Company (Libya) Limited v. Government of the Libyan Arab Republic*, 53 International Law Reports 297, 329 (1979).

pervades the BITs, particularly in the fair and equitable treatment standard and in the prohibition on unreasonable or discriminatory measures.

The condition that expropriation be in accordance with due process of law essentially requires that the host state provide the investor an adequate opportunity to challenge the legality under host-state law of the expropriation and the amount of any compensation.[209] This condition also requires that the expropriation conform to national law[210] and prohibits a denial of justice with respect to judicial review of an expropriation. Some BITs include a separate provision independently requiring that the investor have the right to obtain a review in local courts of the legality of the compensation and of the amount of any attendant compensation.[211] The requirement that the host state not deny justice to a covered investment or investor reflects the due process principle that is found throughout the BITs, including in the fair and equitable treatment standard,[212] in any provision requiring treatment in accordance with international law,[213] and in the judicial access provisions of some BITs.[214]

The condition that expropriation be nondiscriminatory prohibits expropriations that are of particular investments selected for reasons unrelated to the host state's legitimate regulatory objectives. For example, a measure that expropriates foreign investment solely because it is foreign-owned would violate this condition. Similarly, an expropriation of an investment because of animosity between host-state officials and the investor or in retaliation for lawful, but politically unpopular, conduct by the investment would violate this condition. The requirement that the expropriation not be discriminatory reflects the nondiscrimination principle found throughout the BIT, such as in the prohibition on unreasonable or discriminatory measures, the requirement of national and MFN treatment, and the requirement of fair and equitable treatment.

The condition that an expropriation not violate any prior undertaking prohibits expropriations that are inconsistent with a prior commitment by the host state. This condition reflects the norm of *pacta sunt servanda, i.e.*, the norm that commitments are to be performed. The preservation of contractual commitments is an important element of the security principle that pervades the BITs and is reflected most explicitly in the observance of obligations provision, but also in, for example, the fair and equitable treatment standard.[215]

The condition always found in a BIT is that expropriation be accompanied by compensation, described in the great majority of BITs as prompt, adequate, and effective compensation, either in those precise words or in words to the same effect. Because the

---

209 *See, e.g.*, Austria-Georgia BIT, Art. 5(3).

210 *See, e.g.*, Switzerland-Algeria BIT, Art. 6(1); Chile-Indonesia BIT, Art. VI(1); Australia-India BIT, Art. 7 (1).

211 *See, e.g.*, United Kingdom-Bosnia-Herzegovina BIT, Art. 5(1); Germany-Timore-Leste BIT, Art. 4(2); Austria-Armenia BIT, Art. 5(2); Finland-Armenia BIT, Art. 5(6); Denmark-Ethiopia, Art. 5(4); Chile-Indonesia BIT, Art. VI(3); Australia-India BIT, Art. 7(4); Canada-Uruguay BIT, Art. VIII(2).

212 *See* Section 10.4.2.

213 *See* Section 10.4.2.

214 *See* Section 10.4.1.

215 *See* Section 6.2.

requirement of compensation is so important, most BITs elaborate in some way upon the compensation requirement.

The requirement of promptness usually is described as requiring payment without delay[216] or without undue delay.[217] Those BITs that attempt to define the requirement of promptness more precisely generally state that provision for payment shall be made at or prior to the time at which the expropriation occurs.[218]

The reference to adequate compensation generally means the full value of the investment, that is, the fair market value of the investment. Some BITs use the terms "just" compensation or "full" compensation, rather than "adequate," but these are synonymous. BITs often elaborate upon these terms by providing that compensation shall be the genuine value[219] or actual value[220] of the investment. Some BITs state explicitly that fair market value must be paid,[221] although often this is implicit in the other terms of the provision.

The problem in determining fair market value is that a market in the expropriated investment may not exist and thus it becomes necessary to estimate the value of the investment. Most BITs do not address in explicit terms the way in which fair market value shall be determined. A number of valuation methods exist.[222] Where the investment is an operating enterprise, an investment should be valued as a going concern. A widely accepted method for valuing a going concern is the discounted cash flow method, in which the value of the investment is the sum of the future income of the investment, discounted by the projected rate of inflation, the time value of money, and the risk that the income will not be received.[223] Where the enterprise does not yet have a record on which estimates of future profitability may be based or where the investment is not an enterprise, another method of valuation must be used, such as the replacement value or the book value of the investment. Book value in particular,

---

216 *See, e.g.*, Thailand-Argentina BIT, Art. 6(1); Mexico-Iceland BIT, Art. 4(2); Canada-Uruguay BIT, Art. VIII(1).

217 *See, e.g.*, BLEU-Sudan BIT, Art. 7(3).

218 *See, e.g.*, Germany-Timore-Leste BIT, Art. 4(2).

219 *See, e.g.*, United Kingdom-Bosnia-Herzegovina BIT, Art. 5(1).

220 *See, e.g.*, BLEU-Sudan BIT, Art. 7(3).

221 *See, e.g.*, Netherlands-Ethiopia, Art. 6; Austria-Armenia BIT, Art. 5(2); Sweden-Kazakhstan, Art. 4(2); Chile-Indonesia BIT, Art. VI(1); Cambodia-Vietnam BIT, Art. IV; Mexico-Iceland BIT, Art. 4(2); Canada-Uruguay BIT, Art. VIII(1); Australia-India BIT, Art. 7(2) ("market value"); Thailand-Argentina BIT, Art. 6(1) ("market value").

222 *See generally* Mark Kantor, *Valuation for Arbitration* (2008); Sergey Ripinsky and Kevin Williams, *Damages in International Investment Law* (2008); Thomas W. Walde and Borzu Sabahi, "Compensation, Damages, and Valuation," in *The Oxford Handbook of International Investment Law* (Peter Muchlinski, Frederico Ortino, and Christoph Schreuer, eds. 2008); Abby Cohen Smutny, "Some Observations on the Principles Relating to Compensation in the Investment Treaty Context," 22 *ICSID Review—Foreign Investment Law Journal* 1 (2007); Irmgard Marboe, "Compensation and Damages in International Law: The Limits of 'Fair Market Value,'" 7 *Journal of World Investment and Trade* 723 (2006).

223 The use of the discounted cash flow method by chief financial officers of firms in their routine capital budgeting decisions has grown considerably over the past thirty years. *See* William L. Megginson and Scott B. Smart, *Introduction to Corporate Finance* 350–351 (2d ed. 2008).

however, tends to greatly understate the worth of an investment.[224] Some BITs do address the method of valuation, often by referring the tribunal to recognized principles of valuation. For example, the Chile-Indonesia BIT specifies that market value "shall be determined in accordance with internationally acknowledged practices or methods."[225] Rather than referring to recognized principles, some BITs explicitly identify some of the available methods. The Mexico-Iceland BIT, for example, provides that "[t]he valuation criteria shall include the going concern value, asset value, including declared tax value of tangible property, and other criteria, as appropriate, to determine the fair market value."[226]

BITs often prescribe the time at which expropriated investment shall be valued. The general rule is that investment must be valued so as to exclude any diminution in value attributable to the expropriation itself. This rule prevents the host state from using the intended expropriation to reduce the value of investment prior to expropriating it, thereby reducing its compensation obligation. Thus, some BITs provide that investment shall be valued as of the moment immediately before the expropriation occurred.[227] Other BITs, taking into account that the value of an investment may be affected by the announcement of an intended expropriation, provide that the investment shall be valued before the expropriation occurred or became known.[228] Some refer only to the date when the expropriation became known.[229] Some French BITs require valuation as of the time prior to the threat of expropriation.[230] The principle is the same, however: the investment shall be valued as if the expropriation had never occurred.

Recognizing that some delay in payment is virtually inevitable, some BITs explicitly require interest from the date of expropriation until the date of payment. Often these BITs also specify the rate of interest.[231] Where BITs do not explicitly require interest, the virtually universal practice of arbitral tribunals is to award interest.

---

224 *See* Charles R. Hulten and Xioahui Hao, "What is a Company Really Worth? Intangible Capital and the 'Market to Book Value' Puzzle," NBER Working Paper w 14548, December 2008, available at http://www.ssrn.com. Book value is the cost of an asset minus any accumulated depreciation. Thus, an asset that is generating an income stream and therefore clearly of economic value to the owner may have a book value of zero.

225 Chile-Indonesia BIT, Art. VI(2). *See also* Cambodia-Vietnam BIT, Art. IV.

226 Mexico-Iceland BIT, Art. 4(3). *See also* Canada-Uruguay BIT, Art. VIII(1).

227 *See, e.g.*, Mexico-Iceland BIT, Art. 4(2)(b).

228 *See, e.g.*, United Kingdom-Bosnia-Herzegovina BIT, Art. 5(1); BLEU-Sudan BIT, Art. 7(3); Switzerland-Algeria BIT, Art. 6(1); Austria-Armenia BIT, Art. 5(1); Finland-Armenia BIT, Art. 5(2); Mexico-Iceland BIT, Art. 4(2)–(3); Canada-Uruguay BIT, Art. VIII(1).

229 *See, e.g.*, Netherlands-Ethiopia, Art. 6; Germany-Timore-Leste BIT, Art. 4(2); Sweden-Kazakhstan, Art. 4(2); Denmark-Ethiopia, Art. 5(2); Chile-Indonesia BIT, Art. VI(2); Australia-India BIT, Art. 7 (2); Cambodia-Vietnam BIT, Art. IV.

230 *See, e.g.*, France-Costa Rica BIT, Art. 5(2); France-Peru BIT, Art. 5(2).

231 *See, e.g.*, United Kingdom-Bosnia-Herzegovina BIT, Art. 5(1)("normal commercial rate"); BLEU-Sudan BIT, Art. 7(3) ("market prevailing rate of return"); Netherlands-Ethiopia, Art. 6 ("normal banking commercial rate"); Germany-Timore-Leste BIT, Art. 4(2) ("usual bank interest"); Switzerland-Algeria BIT, Art. 6(1) ("commercial rate"); Austria-Armenia BIT, Art. 5(2) ("normal commercial rate"); Finland-Armenia BIT, Art. 5(1)(3) ("commercial rate"); Sweden-Kazakhstan, Art. 4(2) ("commercial rate"); Denmark-Ethiopia, Art. 5(3) ("commercial rate"); Chile-Indonesia BIT, Art. VI(2) ("appropriate market rate of interest");

The requirement of interest must be regarded as an element of full compensation, lest the value of the compensation be significantly eroded by the delay in payment such that the investor does not receive the equivalent of the investment expropriated.

The requirement of effective compensation is intended to ensure that the investor realizes, that is, is able to make use of, the benefit of the compensation. Most commonly, BITs require that the compensation be paid in a freely convertible currency,[232] meaning a currency that is exchanged on the principal foreign exchange markets of the world. Some BITs use the term "freely usable currency,"[233] which is a term used by the International Monetary Fund. Under article XXX(f) of the IMF Articles of Agreement, the term refers to "a member's currency that the Fund determines . . . is, in fact, widely used to make payments for international transactions, and . . . is widely traded in the principal exchange markets." At present, four currencies are considered freely usable: the U.S. dollar, the euro, the British pound, and the Japanese yen. Occasionally, a BIT will specify some other currency, such as the currency in which the investment was made unless the investor and host state agree on a different currency.[234]

In further elaboration upon the concept of effective compensation, BITs sometimes require that compensation be "freely transferable"[235] or "effectively realizable."[236] The former term assumes a monetary payment and requires that the investor have the right to exchange the payment amount for a freely convertible currency. It replicates to a large extent the protection accorded by the transfers provision, although the transfers provision usually describes the obligation of free transferability in greater detail[237] and, as discussed below, may designate a different exchange rate. The phrase "effectively realizable" has essentially the same meaning as "effective." It requires that the investor have the ability to enjoy the benefit of the compensation immediately. Paying compensation in a freely convertible currency generally satisfies the requirement that compensation be effectively realizable.

Most BITs do not explicitly address the exchange rate in the expropriation provision. Compensation for expropriation, however, typically is a payment covered by the transfers provision, which often does address the exchange rate. As discussed in Section 6.7.1, the transfers provision generally requires the use of the exchange rate on

---

Australia-India BIT, Art. 7(3) ("normal market rate"); Canada-Uruguay BIT, Art. VIII(1) ("normal commercial rate").

232 *See, e.g.*, BLEU-Sudan BIT, Art. 7(3); Netherlands-Ethiopia, Art. 6; Austria-Armenia BIT, Art. 5(1) (if accepted by claimants); Sweden-Kazakhstan, Art. 4(1); Denmark-Ethiopia, Art. 5(3); Australia-India BIT, Art. 7 (3) (payable in the currency in which the investment was made unless the investor requests a freely convertible currency).

233 *See, e.g.*, Cambodia-Vietnam BIT, Art. IV.

234 *See, e.g.*, Switzerland-Algeria BIT, Art. 6(1).

235 *See, e.g.*, BLEU-Sudan BIT, Art. 7(3); United Kingdom-Bosnia-Herzegovina BIT, Art. 5(1): Germany-Timore-Leste BIT, Art. 4(2); Austria-Armenia BIT, Art. 5(2); Thailand-Argentina BIT, Art. 6(1); Cambodia-Vietnam BIT, Art. IV; Mexico-Iceland BIT, Art. 4(2); Canada-Uruguay BIT, Art. VIII(1).

236 *See, e.g.*, United Kingdom-Bosnia-Herzegovina BIT, Art. 5(1); Germany-Timore-Leste BIT, Art. 4(2); Thailand-Argentina BIT, Art. 6(1); Mexico-Iceland BIT, Art. 4(2); Canada-Uruguay BIT, Art. VIII(1).

237 *See* Section 6.7.1.

the date of transfer, while the expropriation provision may require the use of the exchange rate on the date of expropriation, so that the expropriating state bears any exchange risk associated with the delay in payment of compensation. The United States, in its 1994 model BIT, adopted a detailed clause on this subject. This clause is noteworthy because it takes account of the fact that compensation may be calculated in a currency that is not freely transferable, which creates a greater exchange risk for the investor than if it is calculated in a currency that is freely transferable. Article III(3) of that model provides that, if the fair market value is denominated in a freely usable currency, the compensation must be no less than the fair market value on the date of expropriation, plus interest at a commercially reasonable rate for that currency, accrued from the date of expropriation until the date of payment. Article III(4) provides that, if the fair market value is denominated in a currency that is not freely usable, the compensation shall be no less than the fair market value on the date of expropriation, converted into a freely usable currency at the market rate of exchange prevailing on that date, plus interest at a commercially reasonable rate for that freely usable currency, accrued from the date of expropriation to the date of payment, with the entire amount converted into the currency of payment at the market rate of exchange prevailing on the date of payment. In general, the principle underlying prompt, adequate, and effective compensation is that the host state should bear the risk of exchange loss during the delay between the occurrence of the expropriation and the payment of compensation.[238]

Expropriation provisions very commonly apply to both direct and indirect expropriations.[239] A direct expropriation occurs where the host state takes title to, or possession of, the investment, either for its own use or for the use of a third party. An indirect expropriation occurs where the host state deprives the investor of the economic benefit of the investment.[240] In the case of an indirect expropriation, the investor

---

238 *See* Austria-Armenia BIT, Art. 5(2)(a).

239 *See, e.g.*, Germany-Timore-Leste BIT, Art. 4(2); United Kingdom-Bosnia-Herzegovina BIT, Art. 5(1) (expropriation or measures having equivalent effect); BLEU-Sudan BIT, Art. 7(1); Netherlands-Ethiopia BIT, Art. 6 (expropriation or any measures having the same nature or the same effect); Switzerland-Algeria BIT, Art. 6(1); Austria-Armenia BIT, Art. 5(1) (expropriation or any other measure which has similar effects); Finland-Armenia BIT, Art. 5(1); Sweden-Kazakhstan, Art. 4(1); Denmark-Ethiopia, Art. 5(1) (expropriation or measure having equivalent effect); Chile-Indonesia BIT, Art. VI(1); Australia-India BIT, Art. 7(1) (expropriation or measures having equivalent effect); Thailand-Argentina BIT, Art. 6(1); Cambodia-Vietnam BIT, Art. IV (expropriation or any other dispossession having effect equivalent to expropriation); Mexico-Iceland BIT, Art. 4; Canada-Uruguay BIT, Art. VIII(1) (expropriation or measures having an equivalent effect).

240 On indirect expropriations, *see* Anne K. Hoffman, "Indirect Expropriation," in *Standards of Investment Protection* (August Reinisch, ed. 2008); August Reinisch, "Expropriation," in *The Oxford Handbook of International Investment Law* (Peter Muchlinski, Frederico Ortino, and Christoph Schreuer, eds. 2008); Ursula Kriebaum, "Regulatory Takings: Balancing the Interests of the Investors and the State," 8 *Journal of World Investment and Trade* 717 (2007); Andrew Newcombe, "The Boundaries of Regulatory Expropriation in International Law," 20 *ICSID Review—Foreign Investment Law Journal* 1 (2005); L. Yves Fotier and Stephen L. Dymer, "Indirect Expropriation in the Law of International Investment: I Know It When I

may continue to have title to and possession of the investment, but the value of the investment to the investor has been destroyed, often as the result of regulatory activity by the host state. For this reason, indirect expropriations sometimes have been described as "regulatory expropriations" or "regulatory takings," although an indirect expropriation may occur through actions that, strictly speaking, may not be considered regulatory actions. Some BITs refer to measures "tantamount"[241] or "equivalent"[242] to expropriation to describe indirect expropriations.

The principle essentially is that the existence of an expropriation is not determined solely by which of the host state's powers is exercised. That is, a host state may expropriate through the exercise of its power of eminent domain, but it also may expropriate through, for example, the exercise of its regulatory power or its power to tax. Thus, the means adopted by the state to achieve its objective are not necessarily dispositive in determining whether an expropriation has occurred. Neither is the host state's characterization of its conduct. Rarely does a state characterize a regulation as an expropriation, although the measure may be expropriatory nonetheless.

A few recent BITs have authorized the two BIT parties by mutual agreement to determine that a particular taxation measure does not constitute an expropriation. For example, the Canada-Uruguay BIT provides that the expropriation provision applies to taxation measures unless, within six months of notification by the investor that it disputes a taxation measure, the taxation authorities of the two parties jointly determine that the measure is not an expropriation.[243] As this indicates, the provision specifies that the determination shall be made by the taxation authorities of each party.

An expropriation may be effected by a single action or a series of actions. An expropriation that occurs through a series of actions over a period of time often is described as a "creeping expropriation."[244] The legal consequences of an expropriation are the same whether it occurs instantaneously or over a long period of time. The principal issue raised by the fact that an expropriation is "creeping" is to determine the points at which the process of expropriation began and ended. Identifying the point at which the

---

See It, or *Caveat Investor*," 19 *ICSID Review—Foreign Investment Law Journal 293* (2004); Rudolf Dolzer, "Indirect Expropriation: New Developments," 11 *New York University Environmental Law Journal* 64 (2002); Thomas Waelde and Abba Kolo, "Environmental Regulation, Investment Protection and 'Regulatory Taking' in International Law," 50 *International and Comparative Law Quarterly* 811 (2001); G.C. Christie, "What Constitutes a Taking of Property Under International Law?" 38 *British Yearbook of International Law* 307 (1962).

241 *See, e.g.*, Germany-China BIT, Protocol, para. 4; United States-Argentina BIT, Art. IV(1).

242 *See, e.g.*, Germany-Timore-Leste BIT, Art. 4(2); United Kingdom-Bosnia-Herzegovina BIT, Art. 5(1) (expropriation or measures having equivalent effect); Denmark-Ethiopia, Art. 5(1) (expropriation or measure having equivalent effect); Australia-India BIT, Art. 7(1) (expropriation or measures having equivalent effect); Cambodia-Vietnam BIT, Art. IV (expropriation or any other dispossession having effect equivalent to expropriation); Canada-Uruguay BIT, Art. VIII(1) (expropriation or measures having an equivalent effect).

243 Canada-Uruguay BIT, Art. VIII(3). *See also* United States-Uruguay BIT, Art. 21(3). .

244 *Generation Ukraine v. Ukraine* (United States-Ukraine BIT), Award, para. 20.22. *See also* American Law Institute, Third Restatement of the Foreign Relations Law of the United States, Section 712, Comment g (1987).

expropriation began may be important for purposes of determining the amount of compensation, because the investment should be valued as of a date prior to when the expropriation occurred. The host state should not be permitted to base the amount of compensation on the value of the investment after the state has diminished it through a series of acts culminating in the expropriation. Identifying the point at which the expropriation was completed may be necessary for purposes of determining the date when interest shall commence and, in some BITs, whether a claim has been submitted to investor-state arbitration too soon or too late.

Indirect expropriations, particularly regulatory expropriations, pose a conceptual problem. Many regulations diminish the value of property by limiting the ways in which it may be enjoyed. If every regulation diminishing the value of an investment were an expropriation requiring compensation, the state likely would be unable to afford to regulate. Limitations on the power of the state to engage in the extraordinary act of taking private property for public use would have been extended to apply to the power of the state to engage in the ordinary act of regulating the use of property still in private ownership. No state is prepared to surrender its power to regulate or to commit to the payment of compensation each time it exercises that power. Yet, to the owner of an investment, an ordinary regulation may have the same consequences as a seizure of an investment by the state and, in principle, the state should not be able to accomplish indirectly through regulation that which it could not accomplish directly through seizure. The conceptual problem thus is to distinguish between those regulatory acts that, because of the extent of their consequences, should be treated as an indirect expropriation and those that should not.

Very few BITs have suggested criteria for drawing this distinction, other than to specify that measures that are equivalent or tantamount to an expropriation are to be treated as an expropriation. In its 2004 model BIT, however, the United States included an Annex B that did identify criteria to be used to determine whether an indirect expropriation had occurred. First, Paragraph 2 of Annex B provides that "An action or series of actions by a Party cannot constitute an expropriation unless it interferes with a tangible or intangible property right or property interest in an investment." This sentence applies equally to direct and indirect expropriations. The sentence makes clear that the inquiry concerning whether an expropriation has occurred begins with a determination of what was taken.

Second, Paragraph 4 of Annex B provides:

> (a) The determination of whether an action or series of actions by a Party, in a specific fact situation, constitutes an indirect expropriation, requires a case-by-case, fact-based inquiry that considers, among other factors:
>
> > (i) the economic impact of the government action, although the fact that an action or series of actions by a Party has an adverse effect on the economic value of an investment, standing alone, does not establish that an indirect expropriation has occurred;
> >
> > (ii) the extent to which the government action interferes with distinct, reasonable investment-backed expectations; and
> >
> > (iii) the character of the government action.

> (b) Except in rare circumstances, non-discriminatory regulatory actions by a Party that are designed and applied to protect legitimate public welfare objectives, such as public health, safety, and the environment, do not constitute indirect expropriations.

Thus, according to the United States, determining whether an indirect expropriation has occurred requires a case-by-case determination, taking into account, among other things, the economic impact of the government action, the extent of interference with reasonable expectations, and the character of the government action. These factors are based upon the language of *Penn Central Transportation Company v. New York City*,[245] a 1978 U.S. Supreme Court case discussing factors to be considered in determining whether a regulation constitutes an expropriation. The annex acknowledges, at Paragraph 4(b), that nondiscriminatory regulations may constitute an indirect expropriation, but asserts that such will be the case only in rare circumstances. The 2003 Canadian model BIT, at Annex B.13, contains language similar to that which appears in Annex B of the 2004 U.S. model BIT.

Another conceptual difficulty is to define the nature of the interest that must be taken for an expropriation to occur.[246] This problem arises in part because the definition of investment includes assets that are grouped at different levels of generality. For example, a company is an investment, but so are shares in a company, and so are intangible property rights. Thus, rights in a share of stock may be an investment, the entire share of stock may be an investment, or the entire company in which the share is held may be an investment. Similarly, land is an investment, but so are rights in land.

The latter example illustrates the problem very simply. A zoning regulation may prohibit an investor from using its land in a certain way, while permitting a wide variety of other economically beneficial uses. If the investment is the land, then the value of the investment has been only slightly diminished and no expropriation has occurred. If the right to use the land in a certain way is the investment, then the investment has been expropriated because the right has been completely extinguished. As this example suggests, defining the investment in narrow terms results in converting many routine regulations into expropriations. In order to avoid this result, tribunals often decline to disaggregate an investment into individual rights and to treat each as a separate investment. Rather, they often examine the effect of the host state's action on the entirety of the investment owned by the investor. That is, these tribunals characterize the investment at the highest level of generality at which the investor's assets can be described.

Yet, it cannot be true that an expropriation never occurs unless the investor's entire investment has been taken. For example, where the investor owns a large tract of land and the host state takes half the land, that action must be considered an expropriation of half the land. That is, in this case the investment must be disaggregated into

---

245 438 U.S. 104 (1978).

246 *See generally* Ursula Kriebaum, "Partial Expropriation," 8 *Journal of World Investment and Trade* 69 (2007).

two parcels, one taken and one not. Otherwise, the seizure of a parcel would not be an expropriation if the investor happened to own other land, but would be an expropriation if the investor did not, an absurd result.

These two examples, in which consideration of the land as a unitary whole seems required in the first instance, but not in the second, can be explained by a rule that the investor may not disaggregate the rights it has in an investment for purposes of claiming an expropriation, but may subdivide the asset into identical units. In this view, if only certain rights in the asset are taken, but other economically beneficial rights are retained by the investor, then no expropriation has occurred. If all the rights in a portion of the asset have been taken, however, then that portion of the asset has been expropriated. Thus, the host state may expropriate part of the investor's land, some of the investors shares in a corporation or a portion of its bank account, even though other parcels of land, other shares or other funds deposited in the account are left unaffected.

Further, where the asset consists of tangible property, treating each thing with a distinct physical existence as a separate investment is intuitively appealing. For example, if the investor owns a fleet of automobiles, seizure of any of them would be considered an expropriation of those automobiles, even if many others were left to the investor. The example of land, where the seizure of any part is an expropriation, also may be explained on the basis of the physicality of the land. Cases such as these may not be regarded as involving disaggregation at all. Rather, those interests taken may seem intuitively to be distinct assets.

In some cases, however, disaggregation has been permitted. For example, an investor may have rights in an asset that were disaggregated by the process through which the rights were created or conveyed to the investor. Thus, where a company enters into a contract with the host state and the host state repudiates the contract, the contract may be treated as a distinct investment that has been expropriated. Or, where the government issues a license or permit which is later revoked, the individual license or permit may be treated as a distinct investment that has been expropriated.

Allowing any kind of disaggregation potentially converts many kinds of regulations into expropriations if they destroy a single right possessed by the investor. Yet, most regulations will not constitute an expropriation because the test of whether an expropriation exists depends on the nature of what was taken as well as the extent of the deprivation. To say that an interest has been destroyed is not to say that it has been expropriated. Annex B to the 2004 U.S. model BIT provides useful guidance. First, the interest must be a property interest or it cannot be expropriated. Second, even assuming that the interest is a property interest, under Annex B the determination of whether an indirect expropriation has occurred requires examination of whether the interest constitutes a distinct, reasonable expectation. The investor's reasonable expectations must take account of the state's regulatory power. Many kinds of regulations enacted by a host state are to be expected and an investor whose investment is affected by such a regulation has no reasonable expectation that the regulation will not be imposed. For example, property that has been smuggled may be seized without payment of compensation because the owner has no reasonable expectation that the state will allow smuggling. As the 2004 U.S. model BIT language indicates, the determination of whether an indirect expropriation exists requires the exercise of judgment under the circumstances of each case.

6.5.2 Origins

Treaty protection against expropriation has existed for hundreds of years, although the earliest instances involved restitution of property seized during war.[247] By the early nineteenth century, however, the FCN treaties contained a variety of provisions on seizure of property.[248] These provisions differed from their early antecedents in three respects. First, the provisions were prospective, rather than retrospective. That is, they applied to expropriations that had not yet occurred when the provisions entered into force, a much broader limitation on sovereignty than an agreement to return property already taken. Second, they sometimes applied regardless of whether the expropriation occurred during hostilities, although until the twentieth century seizures were unlikely to occur except during time of war or civil disturbance. Third, in some cases they did not seek to reverse the seizures, but validated them as long as compensation was paid. In other cases, being prospective, treaty provisions simply prohibited the seizures entirely, a practice that eventually was displaced by treaties permitting seizures with compensation. Expropriation provisions eventually would include additional conditions, although in practice the requirement of compensation would be the most significant limitation on expropriation. Later expropriation provisions also would elaborate more specifically on the nature of the compensation owed. Nevertheless, the nineteenth-century FCNs already had established the basic structure for the modern expropriation provision: a prospective prohibition on any expropriation of foreign property unless full compensation is paid.

Conditions beyond the payment of compensation began to find their way into treaty practice in the period after 1920. For example, U.S. FCNs negotiated during the inter-war decades provided that covered property "shall not be taken without due process of law and without payment of just compensation." [249]As this indicates, the U.S. treaties required both compensation and compliance with the requirements of due process.

---

247 *See* Section 2.1.

248 *See* Section 2.1.1

249 *See, e.g.*, Treaty of Friendship, Commerce and Consular Rights, United States-Germany, December 8, 1923, Art. XII, 44 Stat. 2132, T.S. No. 725; Treaty of Friendship, Commerce and Consular Rights, United States-El Salvador, February 22, 1926, ("1926 El Salvador FCN") Art. XII, 46 Stat. 2817, T.S. No. 827; Treaty of Friendship, Commerce and Consular Rights, United States-Estonia, December 23, 1925, ("(1925 Estonia FCN") Art. XII, 44 Stat. 2379, T.S. No. 736; Treaty of Friendship, Commerce and Consular Rights, United States-Austria, June 19, 1928, Art. IX, 47 Stat. 1876, T.S. No. 838; Treaty of Friendship, Commerce and Consular Rights, United States-Norway, June 5, 1928, Art. XII, 47 Stat. 2135, T.S. No. 852; Treaty of Friendship, Commerce and Consular Rights, United States-Finland, February 13, 1934, Art. XVI, 49 Stat. 2659, T.S. No. 868.

A series of early twentieth-century disputes produced a body of jurisprudence supporting the requirement of compensation under customary law.[250] For example, in the *Norwegian Shipowners Claim*,[251] the United States had taken control of American shipyards in order to prosecute World War I, but did not perform contracts entered into by those shipyards with the Norwegian claimants prior to the war or return progress payments made by the claimants. The tribunal noted that the Fifth Amendment to the U.S. Constitution requires that "just compensation" be paid for the taking of property and found that "the public law of the Parties is in complete accord with the international public law of all civilized countries."[252] Accordingly, the United States was ordered to pay compensation.

In 1928, the Permanent Court of International Justice issued its highly influential judgment in the *Chorzow Factory*[253] case. In that case, Poland had taken properties owned by German companies in its territory that were transferred to Poland under the peace treaties concluded after World War I. Germany sought reparations from Poland for these properties. The court held that "reparations must, as far as possible, wipe out all consequences of the illegal act and reestablish the situation which would, in all probability, have existed if the act had not been committed."[254] This holding has become the definitive statement of the principle on which the requirement of compensation for an unlawful expropriation is based.

In the 1930s, Mexico explicitly denied any obligation to pay compensation at least where the expropriation was nondiscriminatory. As early as 1915, Mexico had begun to expropriate agrarian property, including some foreign-owned property. This process continued into the 1930s. On March 18, 1938, Mexico expropriated the assets of 17 foreign oil companies. Faced with a demand for compensation from the United States, Mexico contended in a diplomatic note dated August 3, 1938, that

> There does not exist, in international law, any principle universally accepted by countries, nor by the writers of treatises on this subject, that would render obligatory the giving of adequate compensation for expropriations of a general and impersonal character.[255]

Mexico also argued that foreign investors were not entitled to better treatment with respect to compensation than host state nationals and that, to demand more, would constitute discrimination:

> The jurisdiction of the States within the limits of the national territory, is applicable to all the inhabitants. Nationals and foreigners who are under the same protection

---

250 *See, e.g., Shufeldt Case* (United States v. Guatemala), 2 Report of International Arbitral Awards 1080 (1929); *Cape Horn Pigeon Case* (United States v. Russia), 9 Report of International Arbitral Awards 63 (1902).

251 (Norway v. United States), 1 Report of International Arbitral Awards 307 (1922).

252 *Id.* at 332.

253 *Chorzow Factory* (Germany v. Poland), 1928 P.C.I.J. (Ser. A) No. 17.

254 *Id.* at 47.

255 Mexican Note to the United States of America, dated August 3, 1938, III Green Hackworth, *Digest of International Law* 658 (1942).

of the national legislation and authorities the foreigners cannot claim rights different from or more extensive than nationals.

The demand for unequal treatment is implicitly included in your Government's note for while it is true that it does not so state clearly, it does require the payment to its nationals, independently of what Mexico may decide to do with regard to her citizens, and as your Government is not unaware that our Government finds itself unable immediately to pay the indemnity to all affected by the agrarian reform, by insisting on payment to American landholders, it demands, in reality, a special privileged treatment which no one is receiving in Mexico.[256]

On August 22, 1938, U.S. Secretary of State Cordell Hull sent a note to the Mexican government articulating what became the definitive formulation of the developed country view of the standard of compensation required under customary international law in the event of an expropriation. He stated that "no government is entitled to expropriate private property, for whatever purpose, without provision for prompt, adequate, and effective payment therefor."[257] In that same note, Secretary Hull denied that the principle of nondiscrimination justified uncompensated expropriations:

The doctrine of equality of treatment, like that of just compensation, is of ancient origin. It appears in many constitutions, bills of rights and documents of international validity. The word has invariably referred to equality in lawful rights. There is now announced by your Government the astonishing theory that this treasured and cherished principle of equality, designed to protect both human and property rights, is to be invoked, not in the protection of personal rights and liberties, but as a chief ground of depriving and stripping individuals of their conceded rights. It is contended, in a word, that it is wholly justifiable to deprive an individual of his rights if all other persons are equally deprived, and if no victim is allowed to escape.[258]

In short, Secretary Hull regarded the nondiscrimination principle as a means of extending protection, not diminishing it. That is, nondiscrimination complemented, rather than derogated from, security.

The United States soon incorporated the Hull formula into its treaty practice. The FCNs that it negotiated from the mid-1940s to the mid-1960s required that an expropriating state make "prompt payment of just compensation . . . in an effectively realizable form."[259] Although the language was slightly different, the treaty standard was in substance identical to the Hull formula. It elaborated upon the concept of promptness by requiring that adequate provision for payment shall have been made at or prior to the time of taking. These treaties also required that the expropriation be for a public purpose.

The first BIT, concluded in 1959 between Germany and Pakistan, was substantively equivalent to the U.S. post-war FCNs, except that, as discussed below, it imposed one

256 Quoted in B.A. Wortley, *Expropriation in Public International Law* 121 (1977).

257 Green Hackworth, *Digest of International Law* vol. 3, 658–659 (1942).

258 *Id.* at 659.

259 *See, e.g.*, Netherlands-United States FCN, *supra* chap. 2, note 179, Art. VI(4); Pakistan-United States FCN, *supra* chap. 2, note 188, Art. VI(4).

additional condition on expropriation. It required, at Article 3(1), that any expropriation be for the "public benefit." The expropriating state was required to pay compensation that represented the "equivalent" of the investments affected. The compensation was to be "actually realizable and freely transferable in the currency of the other Party without undue delay." The expropriating state also was required to make adequate provision at or prior to the time of expropriation for the determination and payment of compensation. Paragraph 3 of the Protocol stated that the term "expropriation" shall "also pertain to acts of sovereign power which are tantamount to expropriation, as well as measures of nationalization." The Germany-Pakistan FCN added a requirement that the legality of any such expropriation and the amount of compensation "shall be subject to review by due process of law." The requirement of due process had appeared in the inter-war U.S. FCNs, but not in the expropriation provision of the typical post-war U.S. FCNs, although these latter FCNs did have a general provisions on judicial access.[260] The Germany-Pakistan BIT did not use the phrase "prompt, adequate, and effective," but the language was the equivalent. Indeed, the very next year, Germany concluded a BIT with Malaysia, which provided that covered investments shall not be expropriated "except for a public purpose, nor shall they be expropriated without prompt, adequate and effective compensation which shall be freely transferable. . . ."[261]

The 1959 Abs-Shawcross convention, at Article III, differed from the contemporaneous German treaty practice in that it imposed two additional conditions on an expropriation. Specifically, the expropriation must not be discriminatory or contrary to undertakings given by the expropriating party. Like the U.S. FCNs and the German BITs, the convention required prompt, adequate, and effective compensation, although without using those words. Like the German BITs, the convention required that any expropriation be under due process of law. The Abs-Shawcross convention differed from the German and U.S. treaties, however, in that it did not require that the expropriation be for a public purpose. Like the German BITs, the Abs-Shawcross convention also explicitly recognized the distinction between a direct and an indirect expropriation. It referred to measures tantamount to an expropriation as an indirect expropriation.

The concept of an indirect expropriation in these early instruments quickly gained recognition in general BIT practice. The first Swiss BIT, signed with Tunisia in 1961, applied to expropriations or measures having a similar effect. The following year, the Swiss BITs explicitly referred to direct and indirect expropriation using those terms.[262]

All of the conditions imposed on expropriation reflected in the U.S. FCNs, the German BITs, and the Abs-Shawcross Convention also soon appeared in other BITs. For example, the Swiss-Tunisia BIT required that any expropriation be in the public interest, in accordance with the requirements of law, nondiscriminatory and

---

260 *See* Pakistan-United States FCN, *supra* chap. 2, note 188, Art. V(1); Netherlands-United States FCN, *supra* chap. 2, note 179, Art. V(1).

261 Germany-Malaysia BIT, Art. 4(1).

262 *See, e.g.*, Switzerland-Guinea BIT, Art. 7; Switzerland-Niger BIT, Art. 7.

accompanied by prompt, adequate, and effective compensation. That treaty further provided that the expropriation must be valued as of the moment the expropriation occurred.

Two years later, the Netherlands signed its first BIT, also with Tunisia. Article 3 explicitly applied to measures of expropriation that were direct or indirect and required that the measure be neither discriminatory nor contrary to a specific commitment. Within five years, the Netherlands had begun to include the requirements that the expropriation be for a public purpose and in accordance with due process.[263] This established the typical Dutch practice for the next quarter century or more.[264] In the mid-1980s, the Netherlands added a further provision granting to investors the right to judicial review of the expropriation.[265]

The first BIT concluded by the Belgium-Luxembourg Economic Union (BLEU), with Tunisia in 1964, applied to direct and indirect expropriations. Article 3 required payment of "effective and adequate" compensation, the amount of which was to be fixed at the time of expropriation and transferred without delay. Such measures were not permitted to be discriminatory or contrary to a specific agreement. By 1970, the BLEU treaties included the requirements that the expropriation be in the public interest and under due process in accordance with international law [266] Compensation sometimes was described as prompt, adequate, and effective,[267] but most typically those precise terms were not used. In its 1980 BIT with Cameroon, the BLEU adopted a novel approach in which under Article 4(1) the parties agree not to expropriate covered investments. Article 4(2) provides, however, that expropriations may be permitted where called for by exigencies of a "public or national interest or security," provided that the measures shall follow a legal procedure, be not discriminatory or contrary to a specific commitment, and include provision for payment of adequate compensation. Thus, the conditions remained the same, although due process no longer was defined in terms of international law. Although this new approach was not uniformly adopted in other BLEU BITs at that time, it has become typical of the BLEU's more recent BITs.

Italy's first BIT, signed with Guinea in 1964, required at Article IV that any expropriation be in the public interest and accompanied by compensation equal to the value of the property expropriated. The compensation was to be paid without delay in a freely convertible currency that could be transferred immediately. The term "expropriation" was defined to include any measures having the effect of an expropriation.

Kuwait inaugurated its BIT program that same year by concluding a BIT with Iraq. Article 4 of that BIT required that any expropriation be in the public interest and accompanied by just and immediate compensation, with the value of the compensation being equal to that of the expropriated investments at the time of expropriation. Compensation must be paid as soon as the value of the investment has

---

263 *See, e.g.*, Netherlands-Indonesia BIT, Art. 7.

264 *See, e.g.*, Netherlands-Malawi BIT, Art. 6.

265 *See, e.g.*, Netherlands-Sri Lanka BIT, Art. 6(1); Netherlands-Philippines BIT, Art. 5.

266 *See, e.g.* BLEU-Indonesia BIT, Art. 5.

267 *See, e.g.*, BLEU-Singapore BIT, Art. 4(1).

been established, which shall occur within a year. The compensation shall be transferred in the same currencies as those in which the investment was established. Under Article 5, the exchange rate shall be determined in accordance with the IMF official rate. If no such rate is available, the rate of exchange for gold, dollars, or any convertible currency shall be used. An unusual provision at Article 7 required the two parties, following payment of compensation, to acknowledge the transfer of ownership. Later Kuwaiti BITs made clear that the expropriation provision applied to direct and indirect expropriations[268] and added in various combinations other conditions commonly imposed by the BITs on expropriation, including nondiscrimination,[269] adherence to due process,[270] and consistency with prior undertakings.[271] They also adopted explicitly the "prompt, adequate and effective" formulation.[272]

Sweden's first BIT, with Ivory Coast in 1965, also applied its expropriation provision to direct and indirect expropriations. Article VI of that BIT required adequate and effective compensation, conforming to the law of nations. The expropriation could be neither discriminatory nor contrary to any specific commitment. Denmark's first BIT, with Madagascar, concluded the same year, was similar, at Article 6, to the Sweden-Ivory Coast BIT in all these respects. The Sweden-Ivory Coast BIT required that any deprivation be for a public purpose, while the Denmark-Madagascar BIT specified that the compensation must be paid in a transferable currency, without unjustified delay.

The 1967 OECD Draft Convention on the Protection of Foreign Property incorporated all of the elements that had become common treaty practice after 1959. Article 3 of the OECD draft convention applied to measures that expropriate property directly or indirectly. The measures must be taken in the public interest and under due process of law, must not be discriminatory, and must be accompanied by "just compensation" which shall be paid without "undue delay" and which "shall be transferable to the extent necessary to make it effective for the national entitled thereto." Note 1 to Article 3 referred to these as conditions imposed by "recognized rules of international law." Article 3 did not explicitly require that the expropriation be consistent with any prior commitment. Article 2 of the OECD draft convention, however, required that each party "at all times ensure the observance of undertakings given by it in relation to property of nationals of any other Party." Further, Note 2 to Article 3 commented that nothing in Article 3 relieves a party from the obligation imposed by Article 2.

BIT practice over the past half century largely has conformed to the principles established in these early agreements. The classic elements of a BIT expropriation provision all had been identified by the end of the 1950s and had become prevalent in BIT practice by the mid 1960s. The classic provision applies to direct and indirect

268 *See, e.g.*, Kuwait-Ethiopia BIT, Art. 6(1); Kuwait-Hungary BIT, Art. 7(1); Kuwait-Czech Republic BIT, Art. 6(1); Kuwait-Croatia BIT, Art. 6(1).

269 *See, e.g.*, Kuwait-Ethiopia BIT, Art. 6(1); Kuwait-Hungary BIT, Art. 7(1); Kuwait-Czech Republic BIT, Art. 6(1); Kuwait-Croatia BIT, Art. 6(1); Kuwait-Bulgaria BIT, Art. 7(1).

270 *See, e.g.*, Kuwait-Ethiopia BIT, Art. 6(1); Kuwait-Czech Republic BIT, Art. 6(1); Kuwait-Croatia BIT, Art. 6(1).

271 *See, e.g.*, Kuwait-Hungary BIT, Art. 7(1); Kuwait-Bulgaria BIT, Art. 7(1).

272 *See, e.g.*, Kuwait-Ethiopia BIT, Art. 6(1); Kuwait-Hungary BIT, Art. 7(1); Kuwait-Czech Republic BIT, Art. 6(1); Kuwait-Croatia BIT, Art. 6(1); Kuwait-Bulgaria BIT, Art. 7(1).

expropriation and requires that expropriation be for a public purpose, nondiscriminatory, in accordance with due process, accompanied by prompt, adequate, and effective compensation, and not inconsistent with any prior undertaking. Not all of these conditions appear in every BIT and the last one appears in significantly fewer BITs than the others, but all are commonly found.

For example, when the United Kingdom inaugurated its BIT program in the 1970s, its BITs required that expropriation be for a public purpose and against prompt, adequate, and effective compensation.[273] Today, the U.K. BITs also require that the expropriation be nondiscriminatory.[274] The French BITs concluded in the early 1970s also applied to direct and indirect expropriation and required that the expropriation be for a public purpose, nondiscriminatory, not contrary to any specific commitment, and accompanied by just compensation.[275] Recent French BITs impose the same conditions, although they refer to "prompt and adequate" rather than "just" compensation and specify that the payment must be effectively realizable.[276] The Swedish BIT program, when it was revived in 1978 after an eleven-year hiatus, required that any expropriation be in the public interest, consistent with due process, nondiscriminatory, and accompanied by prompt, adequate, and effective compensation,[277] essentially the same conditions imposed by the Swedish BITs today.[278] The Finnish BITs, from Finland's first BIT, concluded in 1980, applied the expropriation provision to direct and indirect expropriations and required that the measure be in the public interest, under due process, nondiscriminatory, and accompanied by prompt, adequate, and effective compensation,[279] the same approach that appears in the Finnish BITs a quarter-century later.[280] After some evolution in language, the more recent Austrian BITs generally apply to direct and indirect expropriation and require that the expropriation be for a purpose in the public interest, nondiscriminatory, under due process of law, and accompanied by the payment of prompt, adequate, and effective compensation.[281]

Most developments in BIT practice since the mid-1960s have involved elaborating upon or refining these classic elements. For example, when the United States concluded its first BIT, with Egypt in 1982, that agreement required payments for delay.[282] The United States-Panama BIT, concluded a month later, was more explicit, requiring

---

273 *See* United Kingdom-Egypt BIT, Art. 5(1).

274 *See, e.g.*, United Kingdom-Bosnia-Herzegovina BIT, Art. 5(1).

275 *See, e.g.*, France-D.R. Congo BIT, Art. 3; France-Mauritius BIT, Art. 3.

276 *See, e.g.*, France-Tajikstan BIT, Art. 6; France-Uganda BIT, Art. 5; France-Bahrain BIT, Art. 5.

277 *See, e.g.*, Sweden-Egypt BIT, Art.3; Egypt-Yugoslavia BIT, Art. 3.

278 *See, e.g.*, Sweden-Bosnia-Herzegovina BIT, Art. 4; Sweden-Kazakhstan BIT, Art. 4; Sweden-Ecuador BIT, Art. 4; Sweden-Croatia BIT, Art. 5.

279 *See* Finland-Egypt BIT, Art. 3.

280 *See, e.g.*, Finland-Belarus BIT, Art. 4; Finland-Algeria BIT, Art. 4.

281 *See, e.g.*, Austria-Lebanon BIT, Art. 5; Austria-Libya BIT, Art. 4; Austria-Jordan BIT, Art. 5; Austria-Bosnia-Herzegovina BIT, Art. 5.

282 United States-Egypt BIT, Art. III(1).

"payment of interest at a commercially reasonable rate."[283] The 2004 U.S. model BIT includes an annex that elaborates upon the meaning of an indirect expropriation.

6.5.3 Arbitral Practice

Although the expropriation provision was inserted into the BITs primarily to establish the conditions applicable to expropriation, especially the requirement of compensation, cases rarely arise in which the only issue under the expropriation provision is the amount of compensation due for an admitted expropriation. The principle that full value, meaning fair market value, must be paid under the BITs is now widely accepted. The investor and the host state invariably disagree about the value of the investment, but they usually do not disagree about the basic principles to be applied. Apart from the valuation of the investment, the issue that is most likely to arise in an expropriation claim is whether an expropriation, in fact, has occurred.

6.5.3.1 Expropriation of Property Rights The clearest example of an expropriation occurs where the host state takes title to the investment. For example, in *Santa Elena v. Costa Rica*, a case submitted to arbitration by agreement of the parties and involving no BIT, Costa Rica issued a decree stating that land owned by the claimant was expropriated and directing the Attorney General to register the land in the name of the state. So clear was the existence of an expropriation that Costa Rica conceded that the land had been expropriated. The principal issue before the tribunal thus was the value of the land.

In *Sedelmayer v. Russia*, a case arising under the Germany-Russia BIT, the tribunal held that a presidential decree requiring that certain premises leased by the claimant be transferred to the procurement department of the Russian government constituted an expropriation.[284] The tribunal also held, however, that the seizure of the claimant's automobiles by the customs authority did not constitute an expropriation, a holding that seemed to rest on evidence in the record that the seizure was related to customs violations by the claimant.[285]

A direct expropriation also occurs where the host state leaves the investor with title to the investment, but takes possession of it. Tribunals have divided over the issue of whether a temporary dispossession can constitute an expropriation. For example, in *LG&E v. Argentina*, a case arising under the United States-Argentina BIT, the tribunal observed that a dispossession must be permanent to constitute an expropriation.

Yet, other tribunals have held that a temporary dispossession can constitute an expropriation. For example, in *Wena Hotels v. Egypt*, a case arising under the United Kingdom-Egypt BIT, officials of an Egyptian state enterprise took possession of two hotels owned by the claimant. After a period of almost a year, the Egyptian government admitted that the seizure of the hotels was wrongful and returned possession of

283 United States-Panama BIT, Art. IV(1).

284 Award, para. 2.3.4

285 Award, para. 3.2.4

the hotels to the owner. Before the tribunal, Egypt contended that no expropriation had taken place because the occupation of the hotels was temporary. The tribunal held that an expropriation exists where the investor suffers a "non-ephemeral" deprivation of a fundamental right of ownership. It concluded that interference with the owner's possession of the hotels for nearly a year was more than an ephemeral interference and, therefore, constituted an expropriation.[286]

These two conflicting views were reconciled to some degree by the tribunal in *S.D. Myers v. Canada*, a case arising under the NAFTA. The tribunal there said that "[a]n expropriation usually amounts to a lasting removal of the ability of an owner to make use of its economic rights although it may be that, in some contexts and circumstances, it would be appropriate to view a deprivation as amounting to an expropriation, even if it were partial or temporary."[287] That is, the tribunal believed that the general rule requires a permanent deprivation, but under some circumstances a non-ephemeral deprivation is sufficient. The *S.D. Myers* award, however, does not define the circumstances under which a temporary deprivation is sufficient to constitute an expropriation. In that case, the measure was repealed after 16 months and thus the tribunal held that it did not constitute an expropriation. Indeed, the tribunal in *Azurix v. Argentina*, a case arising under the United States-Argentina BIT, suggested that "there is no mathematical formula to reach a mechanical result. How much time is needed must be judged by the specific circumstances of each case."[288]

The holding in *Wena Hotels* that an interference with possession lasting less than a year is an expropriation might seem questionable at first glance. The test announced in that award, that the deprivation be non-ephemeral, is potentially too broad. The term "ephemeral" is derived from a Greek word meaning, literally, lasting only one day. Although the word in common usage is not limited to events of that brevity, it does suggest a very short duration. The tribunal, in any event, may have been influenced by the fact that the hotels were seriously damaged during the period when they were under government control and, by the time the dispute reached the tribunal, the claimant's efforts to obtain compensation in local courts for violation of the lease agreements had resulted in loss of ownership of both hotels. Thus, while the government's physical occupation of the hotels was temporary, the investor ultimately lost its investment. In short, the result in the case seems sound taking into account all the circumstances.

---

286 *Wena Hotels* may be contrasted with *Tradex Hellas v. Albania*, a case that arose not under a BIT, but under the Albanian investment law, the provisions of which included a prohibition on uncompensated expropriation very similar to that which appears in many BITs. In that case, the claimant had entered into a joint venture with a state company to create an agricultural development. The land was provided by the state company. After inhabitants of the region occupied the lands, causing damage to them, the parties to the joint venture decided, in light of the lack of security, to dissolve the joint venture. Although the occupation of the lands caused the claimant to lose its investment, the tribunal was not persuaded that the actions leading to the loss were attributable to the Albanian government.

287 Award, para. 283.

288 Award, para. 313.

Further, the *Wena Hotels* case involved a physical seizure of the hotels, while *LG&E* and *S.D. Myers* involved regulatory acts. Thus, it could be inferred that tribunals are more likely to find a temporary measure to constitute an expropriation where it involves a taking of title or possession, rather than a regulation that diminishes the value of the investment.

Most claims of expropriation of property in violation of a BIT are based on conduct involving the exercise of the state's regulatory power. Host states rarely concede that a regulation constitutes an expropriation and thus they do not offer compensation. For this reason, in nearly every expropriation claim before an investor-state arbitral tribunal, the tribunal must decide whether an expropriation has occurred and, if so, the value of the expropriated investment.

As the tribunal noted in *Saluka v. Czech Republic*, a case arising under the Netherlands-Czech Republic BIT,

> international law has yet to identify in a comprehensive and definitive fashion precisely what regulations are considered "permissible" and "commonly accepted" as falling within the police or regulatory power of States and, thus, noncompensable. In other words, it has yet to draw a bright and easily distinguishable line between non-compensable regulations on the one hand and, on the other, measures that have the effect of depriving foreign investors of their investment and are thus unlawful and compensable in international law.
>
> . . . It thus inevitably falls to the *adjudicator* to determine whether particular conduct by a state "crosses the line" that separates valid regulatory activity from expropriation. Faced with the question of *when, how and at what point an otherwise valid regulation becomes, in fact and effect, an unlawful expropriation*, international tribunals must consider the circumstances in which the question arises.[289]

In that case, the Czech National Bank, acting as the banking regulator of the host state, had assumed control over a bank in which the claimant had invested. Armed police had entered the bank and forcibly removed all bank managers from the premises. The tribunal found that no expropriation had occurred because the forced administration of the bank had been a permissible regulatory action based on the bank's failure to maintain sufficient liquidity.

In determining whether an expropriation has occurred, tribunals focus on the consequences of the regulation. The consequences are evaluated both qualitatively and quantitatively. First, qualitatively, the investor must have lost a property right. Second, quantitatively, the investor must have lost substantially all of the investment. As will be seen in this section, the great majority of claims of indirect expropriation of property rights have been unsuccessful. Most commonly, the tribunal holds that the claimant's investment has not been diminished sufficiently for the host state action to be considered an expropriation. As will be seen in Section 6.5.3.2, indirect expropriations have been found in a number of cases involving the repudiation of contracts, because in such cases the contract is extinguished in its entirety. An expropriation

289 Award, paras. 263–264. Emphasis in original.

may occur, even if the host state did not intend to expropriate the investment,[290] although the host state's intent to expropriate an investment will militate in favor of a finding that an expropriation did occur.[291]

With respect to the qualitative inquiry, tribunals have held that no expropriation occurs unless the investor has been deprived of an essential attribute of property. A wide variety of interests may fall within this definition. For example, in *Saipem v. Bangladesh*, a case arising under the Italy-Bangladesh BIT, the tribunal held that rights under a judicial decision are property rights that may be expropriated.

In a number of cases, tribunals have held that no expropriation occurred because the investor had no entitlement to that which was lost. This lack of entitlement is often phrased as the absence of a legitimate expectation of retaining that which was lost. For example, in *Methanex v. United States*, a case arising under the NAFTA, the state of California banned the use of a chemical known as methyl tertiary-butyl ether (MTBE) in gasoline because of concerns about the adverse environmental impact of the chemical. Methanex, a Canadian company, manufactured methanol, which is an ingredient in MTBE. The ban on MTBE, in effect, destroyed the market for methanol in California. The tribunal observed that Methanex was well aware that California regulated potentially hazardous substances and could not reasonably expect that its product would be immune from regulation. Thus, Methanex had not lost its reasonably-to-be-expected economic benefit.

Similarly, in *MTD Equity v. Chile*, a case arising under the Malaysia-Chile BIT, the government of Chile initially had encouraged the claimant to invest in a project to construct a planned community and granted approval for the establishment of the investment. As it happened, however, the project was contrary to local zoning laws. The claimant was unable to persuade local officials to change the zoning and thus the project could not be developed. The tribunal held that the refusal to modify the law to allow an investment was not an expropriation. The principle, again, was that the investor had no reasonable expectation of receiving an economic benefit from a project that was unlawful. No investor has a right to a modification of the laws of the host country.[292]

In *Generation Ukraine v. Ukraine*, a case arising under the United States-Ukraine BIT, the claimant was a U.S. company that had encountered numerous bureaucratic problems in attempting to develop its construction projects in Kyiv, ultimately resulting in the abandonment of the project. For example, the Kyiv city administration failed to produce revised land-lease agreements accurately reflecting the territory on which the project would be constructed. Such agreements were needed to satisfy

---

290 *See Siemens v. Argentina* (Germany-Argentina BIT), Award, para. 270 (the BIT refers to measures that have the effect of an expropriation, rather than the intent to expropriate); *Vivendi v. Argentina* (France-Argentina BIT), Award, para. 7.5.20 (the effect, not the intent, is the critical factor); *Tecmed v. Mexico* (Spain-Mexico BIT), Award, para. 116 (Intent is less important than the effects of the measure).

291 *Vivendi v. Argentina* (France-Argentina BIT), Award, para. 7.5.20.

292 The tribunal did find Chile's conduct, however, to violate the fair and equitable treatment standard. *See* Sections 5.2.3 and 10.4.2.

land code requirements. The tribunal noted that while the claimant had "experienced frustration and delay caused by bureaucratic incompetence and recalcitrance in various forms," the claimant nevertheless "had managed to secure a 49-year leasehold over prime commercial property in the centre of Kyiv without having participated in a competitive tender and without having made any substantial payment to the Ukrainian authorities."[293] Under the circumstances, the tribunal found no expropriation. The lease purportedly had been cancelled, but the action of cancellation was beyond the power of the officials who performed the action and thus of no legal effect. The city authorities also had failed to assist the claimant in obtaining the right to use an adjoining property as a staging area, but the claimant had not demonstrated any legal right to the land. The tribunal held that there cannot be an expropriation of something to which the claimant had no legitimate claim.

In *International Thunderbird v. Mexico*, a case arising under the NAFTA, the claimant alleged that Mexico's decision to prohibit its investment from conducting a gambling operation, after having previously issued an opinion approving the operation, constituted an expropriation. The tribunal observed that gambling of the type in which the claimant's investment engaged was illegal in Mexico and that the Mexican government had issued its opinion in reliance upon misrepresentations by the investment about the nature of the operation. It held that, in light of the legal prohibition, the claimant could not have had a legitimate expectation that its investment would be permitted to conduct the business.

In *Noble Ventures v. Romania*, a case arising under the United States-Romania BIT, the claimant alleged that the forced judicial reorganization of its investment constituted an expropriation. The tribunal found, however, that at the time of the judicial reorganization the claimant no longer had a valuable company or valuable assets to be expropriated. Accordingly, the judicial reorganization could not be regarded as an expropriation.

In *MCI Power v. Ecuador*, a case arising under the United States-Ecuador BIT, the tribunal held that the revocation of a permit was not an expropriation. The permit was to be used to operate an electrical plant, but the claimant no longer operated or owned a plant. Further, by not seeking administrative review of the revocation, the claimant's investment acquiesced in that decision.

A temporary permit may be a sufficient property interest. In *Tecmed v. Mexico*, a case arising under the Spain-Mexico BIT, Mexico had declined to renew a permit allowing the claimant's investment, Cytar, to operate a landfill. In finding an expropriation, the tribunal observed,

> There is no doubt that, even if Cytar did not have an indefinite permit but a permit renewable every year, the Claimant's expectation was that of a long-term investment relying on the recovery of its investment and the estimated return through the operation of the Landfill during its entire useful life. [294]

---

293 Award, para. 20.37.

294 Award, para.149.

In *Middle East Cement Shipping v. Egypt*, a case arising under the Greece-Egypt BIT, Egypt suspended an export license approximately four years before its expiration date. The suspension continued for the duration of the term of the license and the tribunal held that the suspension measure constituted an expropriation.

In *Tecmed* and *Middle East Cement*, the effect of the putatively expropriatory measure necessarily was temporary, because the right taken was temporary. Yet, where the right was of sufficient duration or there was a legitimate expectation of a renewal, the tribunals have treated the extermination of the right as an expropriation.

Turning to the quantitative inquiry, assuming that host-state conduct has deprived the investor of an essential attribute of property, the conduct nevertheless will not constitute an expropriation if the value retained by the investor is sufficient. Tribunals assessing quantitatively the extent of the investor's loss have used different formulations of the test to be applied. One formulation asks whether the regulation "substantially deprives" the investor of the economic value of the investment.[295] Another asks whether the regulation "effectively neutralizes" the value of the investment to the investor.[296] The principle in some BITs is explicitly stated in language that describes an indirect expropriation as consisting of measures "tantamount" [297]or "equivalent"[298] to an expropriation, meaning essentially that the measure must have the same effect as a direct expropriation. Several awards have said that an expropriation occurs where the investor is deprived in "significant part" of the value of its investment.[299]

In deciding whether this test is met, the tribunal must determine the scope of the investment that has been diminished. For example, in *Occidental v. Ecuador*, a case arising under the United States-Ecuador BIT, the host state denied a tax refund to the claimant, who contended that its right to the refund had been expropriated. The tribunal questioned whether there could be an investment in a claim to a refund, although it conceded that such a claim seemed to fall literally within the definition of "investment." In any event, the tribunal found no expropriation because the refund was not a sufficient part of the claimant's investment. That is, the tribunal declined to treat the refund as the investment, but rather treated the investor's entire enterprise as the investment.

---

295 *See, e.g., Telenor Mobile Communications v. Hungary* (Norway-Hungary BIT), Award, para.63; *Eastern Sugar v. Czech Republic* (Netherlands-Czech Republic BIT), para. 210; *Tokios Tokeles v. Ukraine* (Lithuania-Ukraine BIT), Award, para. 120; *MCI Power v. Ecuador* (United States-Ecuador BIT), Award, para. 300.

296 *See, e.g., CME v. Czech Republic* (Netherlands-Czech Republic BIT) Award, para. 604; *LG&E v. Argentina* (United States-Argentina BIT), Award, para. 188.

297 *See, e.g.*, Germany-China BIT, Protocol, para. 4; United States-Argentina BIT, Art. IV(1).

298 *See, e.g.*, Germany-Timore-Leste BIT, Art. 4(2); United Kingdom-Bosnia-Herzegovina BIT, Art. 5(1) (expropriation or measures having equivalent effect); Denmark-Ethiopia, Art. 5(1) (expropriation or measure having equivalent effect); Australia-India BIT, Art. 7(1) (expropriation or measures having equivalent effect); Cambodia-Vietnam BIT, Art. IV (expropriation or any other dispossession having effect equivalent to expropriation); Canada-Uruguay BIT, Art. VIII(1) (expropriation or measures having an equivalent effect).

299 *See, e.g., Bayinderi Insaat v. Pakistan* (Decision on Jurisdiction); *Encana v. Ecuador; Metalclad v. Mexico* (NAFTA), *para. 103; S.D. Myers v. Canada* (NAFTA), paras. 282–283.

Yet, tribunals have recognized that specific rights may be characterized as an investment and treated as expropriated, even though the investor owns other rights that are undisturbed by the host state's conduct. For example, in *Waste Management v. Mexico*, a case arising under the NAFTA, the tribunal observed that it needed to determine "whether the enterprise as a whole was subject to conduct in breach of Article 1110 [the expropriation provision of the NAFTA], and finally whether (even if there was no wholesale expropriation of the enterprise as such) the facts establish a partial expropriation."[300] Similarly, in *GAMI v. Mexico*, another case arising under the NAFTA, the tribunal commented that "The taking of 50 acres of a farm is equally expropriatory whether that is the whole farm or just a fraction. The notion must be understood as this: *the affected property* must be impaired to such an extent that it must be seen as 'taken.'"[301]

Cases where regulatory expropriations have been found typically have arisen in situations where the regulation prevents the continued operation of the investment, even though the investor may still retain assets. For example, in *Metalclad v. Mexico*, a case arising under the NAFTA, a Mexican state issued a decree that declared a landfill owned by the claimant to be an environmental preserve. Although the investor continued to own and possess the land, the decree rendered the investment worthless. The tribunal found that the decree constituted an expropriation of the land. [302]As this tribunal explained,

> Expropriation under the NAFTA includes not only open, deliberate and acknowledged takings of property, such as outright seizure or formal or obligatory transfer of title in favour of the host state, but also covert or incidental interference with the use of property which has the effect of depriving the owner, in whole or in significant part, of the use or reasonably-to-be expected economic benefit of property even if not necessarily to the obvious benefit of the host state.[303]

In *CME v. Czech Republic*, a case arising under the Netherlands-Czech Republic BIT, the claimant participated in a joint venture with a Czech company to operate a television station. The Czech company possessed the broadcast license, while the claimant possessed the capital and the expertise. The Czech government initially approved the arrangement, but subsequently accused the claimant of broadcasting without a license and demanded that the arrangement be restructured. The restructuring permitted the Czech company to terminate its arrangement with the claimant, thereby destroying the claimant's business. The tribunal found that the Czech government's role in destroying the claimant's business constituted an expropriation.

This same claim was presented by CME's principal owner, Ronald Lauder, to a different tribunal in *Lauder v. Czech Republic*, relying on the United States-Czech

300 Award, para. 141.

301 Award, para. 126. Emphasis in original.

302 The tribunal in *Metalclad* also rested its finding of an expropriation on a separate and independent ground, which related in part to the nontransparent way in which Mexican officials had dealt with the claimant. This portion of the award, however, was set aside by the Supreme Court of British Columbia.

303 Award, para. 103.

Republic BIT. In *Lauder*, the tribunal agreed that the claimant's business was destroyed, but attributed the destruction to the action of the Czech company in terminating its arrangement with claimant. The tribunal, in other words, refused to attribute the destruction to the state.

The tribunal further held that the complicit conduct of the host state in facilitating the action of the Czech company was not an expropriation because it did not benefit the state and was not for a public purpose. This aspect of the Lauder decision seems clearly wrong. The text of the United States-Czech Republic BIT, like that of most other BITs, makes clear that an expropriation must be for a public purpose to be lawful. An expropriation for a private purpose is unlawful in every case. The *Lauder* tribunal misinterpreted the BIT language to mean that a private purpose precludes a finding of an expropriation, when in fact it precludes a finding of a lawful expropriation.

In *Tecmed v. Mexico*, a case arising under the Spain-Mexico BIT, Mexico denied the renewal of a permit that had allowed the claimant's investment to operate a landfill. Because the land was not usable for any other purpose, the investment had lost the use of the land. The tribunal held that non-renewal of the permit constituted an expropriation.

The tribunal in *Tecmed*, however, did not rest its decision solely on the loss of the value of the land to the investment. Rather, the tribunal said that, to determine whether an expropriation had occurred, it must consider whether the public benefit from the revocation was proportional to the injury inflicted. In that case, although the state had sought to justify the revocation of the permit on the ground that the landfill had been operated unlawfully, the true motive for the revocation was to respond to community protests. The tribunal found this public benefit insufficient to justify the complete neutralization of the value of the land. The approach in *Tecmed* reduces the security offered by the expropriation provision in that it potentially allows the host state to engage in uncompensated expropriations where the public benefit from the deprivation is sufficiently great. The purpose of the expropriation provision, of course, is to prevent the state from shifting the burden of achieving a public benefit onto a few investors and thus the existence of even a very large public benefit should not excuse the obligation to pay compensation for what is otherwise an expropriation. Further, a rule that allows the host state to escape the obligation of compensation where the public benefit is sufficiently great may encourage the host state to engage in more sweeping regulatory actions in order to bolster the state's claim of a large public benefit, while more modest reforms might be eschewed as conferring insufficient benefit on the public to allow the state to escape the obligation to compensate. Thus, the award in *Tecmed* potentially undermines the security afforded by the expropriation provision. Indeed, the *Tecmed* approach seems to collapse the principle of security into the principle of reasonableness. That is, if the host state's taking of the investment sufficiently further the state's legitimate interests, then the state need not pay compensation. Under this approach, the principle of security ceases to have much independent significance. In any event, most tribunals thus far have declined to follow the approach adopted in *Tecmed*.

One exception, however, is *LG&E v. Argentina*, a case arising under the United States-Argentina BIT, where the tribunal, citing *Tecmed*, observed that a regulation having a social or general welfare purpose should not require compensation unless the means were disproportionate to the need being addressed.[304] The tribunal ultimately concluded that no expropriation existed, but the proportionality analysis did not seem to affect the result. As discussed below, the tribunal found that Argentina's measures had an insufficient impact on the value of the investment.[305] The tribunal in *Azurix v. Argentina*, another case arising under the United States-Argentina BIT, referred to the *Tecmed* approach as offering "useful guidance," but then did not actually apply it.[306] Rather, as will be seen below, no expropriation was found to exist because the impact on the investment was insufficient.[307]

In the majority of regulatory expropriation cases arising under BITs, tribunals have found that the diminution in the value of the investment attributable to the host state's regulatory action was insufficient to constitute an expropriation. In a typical case, the claimant continues to operate the investment, although perhaps at reduced profits, and the tribunal finds therefore that no expropriation has occurred.

For example, in *Pope & Talbot v. Canada*, a case arising under the NAFTA, the claimant's investment exported softwood lumber from Canada to the United States. In order to resolve a trade dispute with the United States, Canada imposed restrictions on the amount of such exports, which the claimant alleged to have expropriated its market share. The tribunal found that the restrictions did not constitute an expropriation. As the tribunal explained,

> the Investor remains in control of the Investment, it directs the day-to-day operations of the Investments, and no officers or employees of the Investment have been detained by virtue of the Regime. Canada does not supervise the work of the officers or employees of the Investment, does not take any of the proceeds of company sales (apart from taxation), does not interfere with management or shareholders' activities, does not prevent the Investment from paying dividends to its shareholders, does not interfere with the appointment of directors or management and does not take any other actions ousting the Investors from full ownership and control of the Investment. . . . it continues to export substantial quantities of softwood lumber to the U.S. and to earn substantial profits on those sales.[308]

Similarly, in *Azurix v. Argentina*, a case arising under the United States-Argentina BIT, Argentina granted to the claimant's company a concession to provide water services, but then as a result of political considerations failed to honor the terms of the agreement including those with respect to the tariffs to be charged. When an algae bloom attributable in part to the conduct of the province caused a deterioration in the quality and appearance of the water, the province both prohibited the billing of customers and encouraged customers not to pay those bills that they did receive. The tribunal found, however, that the impact on the investment attributable to the actions of the province was not sufficient to constitute an expropriation. The claimant continued

304 Award, para. 195.
305 Award, para. 200.
306 Award, para. 312.
307 Award, para. 322.
308 Interim Award, paras. 100–101.

to own and control its investment. Although the management of the investment was affected, the extent was not sufficient to constitute an expropriation.

In *CMS Gas Transmission Company v. Argentina*, another case arising under the United States-Argentina BIT, the government of Argentina, in response to a serious economic crisis, modified the tariff structure applicable to the claimant's investment in a gas transmission company, with the result that claimant suffered substantial losses. The claimant, however, continued to own and control its business. That is, the value of the investment had not been "effectively neutralized."[309] Thus, the tribunal found no expropriation.

Other cases involving Argentina's response to the crisis and decided under the United States-Argentina BIT have held similarly. In *LG&E v. Argentina*, the tribunal found that the host state's measures may have caused the value of the claimant's shares to fluctuate and may have reduced earnings, but the claimant never lost control of the shares or the ability to direct the investment and the asset base in fact had rebounded since the end of the crisis. In other words, no "permanent, severe deprivation of [the claimant's] rights or almost complete deprivation of the value of [the claimant's] investment" had occurred and thus the circumstances did not amount to an expropriation.[310] In *Enron v. Argentina*, the tribunal found no substantial deprivation, noting that the claimant's interests in the companies affected by Argentina's measures subsequently had been freely sold and included in complex transactions. In *Sempra Energy v Argentina*, the tribunal held that finding an indirect expropriation would require that "the investor no longer be in control of its business operation, or that the value of the business have been virtually annihilated."[311] Although measures taken by Argentina during the economic crisis had "a very adverse effect" on the investment, the test for an indirect expropriation was not met.[312]

Tribunals also have reached the same result in cases arising under the United Kingdom-Argentina BIT and involving Argentina's emergency measures. In *National Grid v. Argentina*, the tribunal found that the value of the investment was diminished by the emergency measures, but that the investment was not worthless and thus no expropriation had occurred. In *BG Group v. Argentina*, the tribunal observed that Argentina's measures had caused a fluctuation in the value of the investment, but the investment continued to operate. Accordingly, the investment had not been expropriated.

In *Continental Casualty v. Argentina*, the last of the cases to be considered here that involved Argentina's emergency measures and a case arising under the United States-Argentina BIT, the tribunal held that a state's setting of its exchange rate, its establishment of mechanisms for exchanging currency, and its setting of conditions on accounts denominated in a foreign currency do not render that state liable for losses, provided that such conduct is not discriminatory or unfair.[313] Further, "[m]inor losses

309 Award, paras. 262–263

310 Decision on Liability, para. 300.

311 Award, para. 286.

312 *Id.* at para. 285.

313 Award, para. 278.

that are an incidental consequence to a general regulation of the economy adopted in the public interest are not considered to be expropriation. . . ."[314] In that case, some of the claimant's losses were attributable to exchange rate policies and thus were not expropriatory. Some fell within the defense of necessity. The remaining losses already had been held compensable under the fair and equitable treatment standard and thus the tribunal did not need to decide whether they constituted an expropriation.

In *Telenor Mobile Communications v. Hungary*, a case arising under the Norway-Hungary BIT, the claimant's investment operated a mobile telephone service in Hungary. It suffered losses when the Hungarian government imposed a levy on all telecommunications service providers to be used to create a fund that would reimburse fixed line service providers for the unrecovered costs of providing universal service. Mobile telephone service providers were excluded from the opportunity to participate in the universal service arrangement. The government also imposed price controls on service providers. The tribunal held that whether government measures constitute an expropriation depends upon "the intensity and duration of the economic deprivation" suffered as a result.[315] It noted that the company remained a highly profitable company whose net income and asset value increased annually. The management of the company remained in the hands of its board and the company had access to all of its resources.

In *Plama v. Bulgaria*, a case arising under the Energy Charter Treaty, Bulgaria had amended its environmental laws in ways that allegedly required the claimant's investment to pay for past environmental damage. The tribunal found no evidence, however, that the claimant or its investment actually had incurred any costs. In the absence of proof of any loss, the tribunal could not find that an expropriation had occurred. The claimant also alleged that Bulgaria's tax policies had prevented the claimant's investment from obtaining the necessary financing, but the tribunal found evidence that the lack of financing in fact was attributable to the investment's poor credit rating. Thus, the claimant had not proved that Bulgaria's conduct had deprived the claimant of the economic benefit of its investment and thus had not proved the existence of an expropriation.

In *GAMI Investments v. Mexico*, a case arising under the NAFTA, Mexico expropriated several sugar mills owned by the claimant's company, although it was in the process of either returning them or paying compensation for them. Because the claimant was the investor in the company, not the company itself, the question before the tribunal was whether any reduction in the value of claimant's shares in the company, attributable to the actions of the Mexican government, constituted an expropriation. The tribunal found that the claimant did not have a claim for an expropriation. The claimant remained in control of the company. Although the company's principal assets had been taken, Mexican law was providing a remedy for the taking.

In *Tokios Tokeles v. Ukraine*, a case arising under the Lithuania-Ukraine BIT, the tribunal found no showing that the claimant could not operate its business. The Ukrainian government had issued press announcements falsely stating that the investment,

314 Award, para. 284.

315 Award, para. 70.

a publishing company, was under a criminal investigation. The claimant had not shown that these announcements damaged the investment's reputation to the point where it could not obtain new customers. The investment also had been subject to police raids, but these had not significantly impaired its ability to operate.

In *Bogdanov v. Moldova*, a case arising under the Russia-Moldova BIT, Moldova required a privatized company to transfer certain assets to the state in exchange for shares in certain state owned companies, but such shares effectively were of no value. The sole arbitrator found nevertheless that no expropriation had occurred because the transferred shares corresponded to less than seven percent of the value of the privatized company.

In *S.D. Myers v. Canada*, a case arising under the NAFTA, the claimant not only was left in control of its company, but such interference as had occurred with the operation of the company was temporary. In that case, the claimant operated a facility in the United States for the safe disposal of toxic substances known as polychlorinated biphenyls (PCBs) and had sought to obtain contracts in Canada for the disposal of PCBs. The Canadian government, however, imposed a ban on the export of PCBs, thus preventing the claimant from pursuing its business in Canada. Subsequently, the Canadian government repealed the export ban, thereby allowing the claimant to resume its business in Canada. The tribunal began its analysis by noting that regulatory action is unlikely to constitute an expropriation, though it did not "rule out that possibility."[316] It then observed that

> [a]n expropriation usually amounts to a lasting removal of the ability of an owner to make use of its economic rights although it may be that, in some contexts and circumstances, it would be appropriate to view a deprivation as amount to an expropriation, even if it were partial or temporary.[317]

The tribunal found that the claimant's entry into the Canadian market was postponed for approximately eighteen months. Further, no property or benefit was transferred directly to others. The tribunal held that this temporary interference with the claimant's business did not constitute an expropriation. Although the delay may have reduced the claimant's competitive advantage, such costs could be compensated as a part of the damages for Canada's violation of other provisions of the NAFTA.

In some cases, the regulation may have neither the qualitative nor the quantitative characteristics of an indirect expropriation. For example, in *Feldman v. Mexico*, a case arising under the NAFTA, the Mexican government refused to rebate the excise taxes paid by the claimant's company in connection with the export of cigarettes. Without the rebates, the export of the cigarettes was economically infeasible. Based on several factors, the tribunal found that the regulation did not constitute an expropriation. One was that international law does not require a country to permit the claimant's company to engage in the type of business in which it sought to engage and indeed states have legitimate grounds on which to prohibit it. Another was that the relevant tax regulations had been in place before the claimant sought to export the cigarettes, but had not

---

316 Partial Award, para. 281.

317 Award, para. 283.

been enforced. All that had changed was that the regulations now were being enforced. Thus the claimant had no right to expect that the law would not be enforced. In short, the loss of this opportunity did not deprive the investor of any reasonable economic expectation. Beyond that, the tribunal also noted that, although the claimant had lost the value of the opportunity to export cigarettes, the claimant continued to own and be in full possession of his business and could continue to export products other than cigarettes. Thus, the claimant still retained too much for an expropriation to have occurred.

The tribunal observed in one case that an expropriation cannot occur through omission. In *Olguin v. Paraguay*, a case arising under the Peru-Paraguay BIT, the claimant lost its funds when a bank became insolvent. The tribunal held that the government's omission to prevent the insolvency or to fully ensure all bank accounts did not constitute an expropriation of the claimant's account. That is, an omission could not constitute an expropriation.[318] By contrast, the tribunal in *CME v. Czech Republic*, a case arising under the Netherlands-Czech Republic BIT, observed that "it makes no difference whether the deprivation was caused by actions or by inactions."[319] As already noted above, the tribunal found that the claimant's investment was expropriated and attributed the expropriation to the Czech Republic's "actions and inactions."[320]

The tribunal in *Olguin* also observed that an expropriation exists only if the state acquires the benefit of the expropriated property.[321] This latter statement, however, seems clearly inconsistent with the great weight of authority. In determining whether an expropriation has occurred, tribunals rarely examine the extent of benefit to the state. Rather, they consider the loss to the investor.

A very few tribunals have included *dictum* in their awards that questioned whether a nondiscriminatory regulation ever constitutes an expropriation. For example, in *Methanex v. United States*, a case arising under the NAFTA, the tribunal held that, "as a matter of general international law, a non-discriminatory regulation for a public purpose, which is enacted in accordance with due process and, which affects, inter alios, a foreign investor or investment is not deemed expropriatory and compensable unless specific commitments had been given by the regulating government to the then putative foreign investor contemplating investment that the government would refrain from such regulation."[322]

This language expresses a distinctly minority view and ample grounds exist for questioning its correctness. The dispute in *Methanex* arose out of an agreement to which the United States is a party and, in fact, was a claim against the United States. Clearly, the United States recognizes the possibility of a regulatory expropriation[323] and all of its BITs as well as the NAFTA are intended to guarantee compensation for

318 Award, para. 84.

319 Partial Award, para. 605.

320 Partial Award, paras.607, 609.

321 Award, para. 84.

322 Award, Part IV.D., para. 7.

323 *See* text *supra* at note 246.

regulatory expropriations. To the extent that the tribunal in *Methanex* expressed a contrary view, it misconstrued the language of the NAFTA. Further, virtually all BITs recognize the concept of an indirect expropriation, often described as measures equivalent to expropriation, and require that any such expropriation be for a public purpose and nondiscriminatory. That is, these BITs explicitly recognize that nondiscriminatory measures in pursuit of the state's public policy objectives may still constitute an expropriation. To take all nondiscriminatory regulations for a public purpose outside the scope of the expropriation provision, including those that have effects equivalent to an expropriation, would seem contrary to the clear text of the expropriation provision as it appears in most BITs. In principle, the fact that host-state action takes the form of a nondiscriminatory regulation should not foreclose the possibility that it could constitute an expropriation and the great majority of tribunals to have addressed the issue have so held. To quote the tribunal in *Feldman v. Mexico*, a case arising under the NAFTA, "No one can seriously doubt that in some circumstances governmental regulatory activity can be a violation of Article 1110 [imposing conditions on expropriation]."[324] As the tribunal explained in *Pope & Talbot v. Canada*, another case arising under the NAFTA, "a blanket exception for regulatory measures would create a gaping hole in international protection against expropriation."[325]

Although, as noted above, indirect expropriations usually arise from the exercise of the state's police power, a few cases have considered whether an exercise of the state's power to tax constituted an indirect expropriation. In *Encana v. Ecuador*, a case arising under the Canada-Ecuador BIT, the tribunal held that Ecuador's denial of value-added tax (VAT) refunds in the amount of ten percent of transactions associated with the claimant's oil production and export business did not deny the claimant in whole or significant part of the benefits of its investment. The tribunal observed that taxation should be treated as a separate category and that "only if a tax law is extraordinary, punitive in amount or arbitrary in its incidences" could it constitute an indirect expropriation.[326] Taxes always directly diminish the value of an investment. The mere fact that a tax diminishes the value of an investment does not in itself mean that the tax is expropriatory. Ecuador's policy also resulted in an expropriation claim in *Occidental v. Ecuador*, a case arising under the United States-Ecuador BIT. For reasons explained above, the tribunal found no expropriation in that case as well.

In *Link-Trading v. Moldova*, a case arising under the United States-Moldova BIT, the claimant alleged that the repeal of certain tax exemptions constituted an expropriation, particularly in that it violated stabilization commitments given by the government. The tribunal held that, as a general matter, fiscal measures become expropriatory only when they are abusive. An abuse exists, according to the tribunal, where the state has acted unfairly or inequitably toward the investment, where it has adopted measures that are arbitrary or discriminatory in their character or in their implementation, or where the measures violate an obligation undertaken by the state in regard to investment. None of these factors was present in that case. The state had

324 Award, para. 110.
325 Award, para. 99.
326 Award, para. 177.

merely applied general tax measures to the claimant. Indeed, the repeal only placed the claimant on the same footing as other businesses. The stabilization commitment on which the claimant rested its allegation of an expropriation did not apply to the taxes at issue. The tribunal considered finally whether a claim of expropriation might rest on the fact that the taxation measures substantially interfered with the claimant's business. In other words, the tribunal inquired into whether the tax was sufficiently burdensome to constitute an expropriation. Although the claimant's business declined following the loss of the tax exemption, the tribunal found insufficient evidence that the decline was attributable to the loss of the tax exemption as opposed to the devaluation of the Moldovan currency,[327] which caused a loss in the purchasing power of the claimant's customers.

6.5.3.2 Expropriation of Contract Rights The general rule is that the repudiation of a contract by the host state constitutes an expropriation, while a mere breach of contract does not.[328] In the former case, the host state effectively declares the obligation not to exist, while in the latter case the host state violates the obligation but provides the investor with a remedy in local courts. The distinction is based on the division between the sovereign and proprietary capacities of a government. Where the host state effectively repudiates the contract, it acts in a way that only a sovereign can. That is, only a sovereign can eliminate the legal obligation of a contract. By contrast, where the host state leaves the contract in effect, but violates it, the host state acts in much the same way as any private party, who may violate its contractual obligations, although it will be liable for compensation. Thus, where the state breaches, but does not repudiate, the contract, the remedy for the claimant lies in local courts.[329]

In *Southern Pacific Property v. Egypt*, a case arising under the Egyptian investment law rather than a BIT, the claimant had entered into a contract with the government of Egypt to build tourist complexes near Cairo and on the Mediterranean coast. After political opposition to the Cairo project emerged, based on a concern that it jeopardized undiscovered antiquities, the Egyptian government cancelled the Cairo project and declared the land on which the project was based to be public property. The tribunal found that the cancellation of the Cairo project constituted an expropriation of the claimant's contract rights. Although the project on the coast was never cancelled, the tribunal found that development of that project alone was not economically feasible. The tribunal rejected Egypt's argument that contract rights could not be expropriated. It also rejected Egypt's argument that no expropriation had occurred because the claimant retained rights with respect to the coastal project. Finally, it rejected Egypt's

---

327 Devaluation of a currency does not violate customary international law. *See National Grid v. Argentina* (United Kingdom-Argentina BIT), Award, para. 96.

328 *Consortium R.F.C.C. v. Royaume du Maroc* (Italy-Morocco BIT), Award, para. 65; *Impregilo v Pakistan* (Italy-Pakistan BIT), Decision on Jurisdiction, para. 260; Siemens v. Argentina (Germany-Argentina BIT), Award, para. 248–253. *See generally* B. Wortley, *Expropriation in Public International Law* 57 (1977).

329 *See, e.g., Waste Management v. Mexico* (NAFTA), Award, para. 174; *Parkerings-Compagniet v. Lithuania* (Norway-Lithuania BIT), Award, para. 448.

argument that no expropriation had occurred on the ground that the claimant had been offered an alternative site for the project because the evidence was that the alternative site was unsuitable for development.

In *Siemens v. Argentina*, a case arising under the Germany-Argentina BIT, the tribunal held that contract rights may be expropriated, although only through conduct amounting to an exercise of sovereign authority, such as a repudiation of a contact, as opposed to a mere breach that can be remedied in local courts.[330] In that case, Argentina, during an economic crisis, had issued an emergency decree terminating the contract. Even before the crisis arose, Argentina had exercised its sovereign power to require changes in the contract. Further, Argentina failed to enter into agreements with its provincial governments, which were necessary for the performance of the contract, and justified this failure on the political structure of the state. Argentina also suspended the contract and refused to pay compensation, relying on arguments that went beyond its rights as a contracting party. Accordingly, Argentina had expropriated the contract.[331]

In *Vivendi v. Argentina*, a case arising under the France-Argentina BIT, the claimant's investment had a concession to operate water services undergoing privatization. After sharp rate increases and a couple of episodes in which the water was colored by harmless mineral deposits, local officials commenced a campaign to destroy the credibility of the concessionaire and to persuade customers not to pay their bills. The tribunal found this conduct to be sovereign rather than commercial in nature and, in light of its devastating effect on the economic viability of the concession, to constitute an expropriation.

In *Eureko v. Poland*, a case arising under the Netherlands-Poland BIT, the claimant entered into a share purchase agreement with the Polish government under which the claimant would purchase 20 percent of the shares of a state insurance company and then, through an initial public offering, be permitted to acquire majority control of the company. Subsequently, when the proposed public offering became politically controversial, Polish officials undertook to have the share purchase agreement voided in court and in other ways breached the agreement. No public offering ever occurred. The tribunal held that the deprivation of claimant's contract rights constituted an expropriation of those rights.[332]

By contrast, no expropriation was found in *SGS v. Philippines*, a case arising under the Switzerland-Philippines BIT. In that case, the claimant had entered into a contract with the government of the Philippines to provide pre-shipment customs inspection services in countries of export. In connection with the implementation of the WTO valuation system, which made the claimant's services less useful, the government decided against a further extension of the duration of the contract. SGS alleged that the government of the Philippines owed it certain payments under the contract. When the government refused to pay, the claimant instituted arbitration. The tribunal found that the refusal to pay the debt was not an expropriation. The government had not cancelled the debt. The debt still existed and the investor possessed remedies under the law of the

---

330 Award, paras. 248, 253.

331 Award, para. 260.

332 Award, para. 240.

Philippines for collecting the debt. Again, the Philippines, in refusing to pay its debt, had done nothing more than a private party might do in refusing to meet a contractual obligation. The underlying obligation had not been cancelled, annulled, or repudiated. The contractual right continued to exist, although the Philippines had failed to honor the obligation.

The decision in *Waste Management v. Mexico*, a case arising under the NAFTA, is similar. In that case, the claimant's company had entered into a concession agreement with the city of Acapulco to collect and dispose of waste. The concession agreement, however, was unpopular with the local population, which objected to the amount that they were expected to pay for the service. In the face of popular opposition, the city failed to observe its obligations under the contract. For example, the city failed to enforce the exclusivity provisions in the agreement and failed to make available land promised for a disposal site. The tribunal held, however, that a breach of contract is not an expropriation in the absence of an "effective repudiation" of the contract that is "unredressed by any remedies available to the Claimant. . . ."[333] The claimant's company at all times retained the use of its property and was able to serve its customers and collect fees from them. Failure to provide land could not constitute an expropriation. Although the conduct of the city had the effect of depriving the claimant's company of its reasonably-to-be-expected economic benefit with respect to the monthly fees due from the city, this was merely an incident of any breach of contract.

The tribunal compared the situation to an ordinary commercial venture in which there is always a risk that the business will not succeed. In this case, in attempting to offer a service at a higher price than the customers were willing to pay, the claimant's company had relied on a bad business plan. Mexico's treaty obligation not to engage in uncompensated expropriations was not insurance against bad business judgment. In other words, the fact that the business partner of the claimant's company was the city, rather than a private party, did not provide the company with the right to compensation in the event that the business failed.

In *Encana v. Ecuador*, a case arising under the Canada-Ecuador BIT, the claimant alleged an expropriation based on the refusal of Ecuadoran authorities to honor certificates entitling the claimant's companies to VAT refunds. Citing *Waste Management*, the tribunal held that nonperformance of a contractual obligation is not an expropriation unless it amounts to a repudiation of the contract, leaving the private contracting party without a remedy. The tribunal observed that an executive agency of a state does not repudiate an obligation merely by contesting its existence, as long as the agency, in good faith, submits its actions to judicial review and honors the decisions of the courts in performing that review.[334] The tribunal found that these conditions were met and thus the refusal to pay the certificates was not an expropriation.

In *Petrobart v. Kyrgyz Republic*, a case arising under the Energy Charter Treaty, the claimant had entered into contracts with a state energy company to supply gas condensate. Subsequently, the host state stripped the state company of its assets, interfered in the claimant's efforts to seek judicial relief, and then placed the state company

---

333 Award, para. 175.

334 Award, paras. 192–194.

in bankruptcy, conduct that in the view of the claimant rendered its contracts worthless. The tribunal held, however, that the state's conduct did not constitute an expropriation because the claimant still retained claims in the bankruptcy proceeding.

In *Parkerings-Compagniet v. Lithuania*, a case arising under the Norway-Lithuania BIT, the city of Vilnius terminated its contract with the investment to build a parking facility on the basis of an alleged material breach by the investment. The tribunal held that, in terminating a contract for breach, the city acted not in a sovereign capacity but as any other contracting party would. The remedy for the claimant was to initiate proceedings in local court.[335]

In *Azinian v. Mexico*, a case arising under the NAFTA, the Mexican city of Naucalpan de Juarez had terminated its concession contract with the claimant's company for the collection and disposal of waste. The claimant's company challenged the termination in the Mexican courts, which upheld the termination. The tribunal observed that a government cannot be faulted for acting in a manner validated by its courts unless the courts themselves have acted wrongfully, a statement that might be correct in the context of a breach of contract claim, but not perhaps in other contexts. The tribunal found that the termination was justified under the Mexican law of contracts and that there had been no denial of justice. Thus, termination of the contract, although it completely extinguished the claimant's rights under the contract, did not constitute an expropriation.

Occasionally, the tribunal finds no contract rights to expropriate. For example, in *PSEG v. Turkey*, a case arising under the United States-Turkey BIT, the tribunal held that no expropriation had occurred because the claimant's contract rights were not yet complete.

In some cases, a dispute may arise as to whether the rights expropriated were contract rights or property rights. In *ADC v. Hungary*, a case arising under the Cyprus-Hungary BIT, Hungary cancelled the claimants' concession contract to operate a state-owned airport, after which it privatized the airport. Hungary argued that it had cancelled the contract for the purpose of harmonizing Hungary's transportation laws with European Union law, but the tribunal found that claim unsubstantiated. In fact, in light of the subsequent privatization of the airport, the tribunal found no public interest in support of the contract termination. Hungary argued that no expropriation had occurred because the claimants still had their contract claims. The tribunal held, however, that the investment consisted of claimants' equity contribution of $16.765 million at the inception of the project and thus the dispute was not of a contractual nature.

6.5.3.3 Expropriation by the Judicial Branch Most claims of expropriation are based on conduct by the political branches of government—the executive or legislative authorities. Investors, however, may also assert that the action of the judicial branch constitutes an expropriation. Such was the case in *Loewen v. United States*, a case arising under the NAFTA. In that case, the Canadian investor had been sued by a U.S. competitor in a U.S. court. During the trial before a jury, the Canadian investor

---

335 Award, para. 448.

was the subject of numerous comments by the U.S. plaintiff concerning the investor's foreign nationality and the jury ultimately rendered a verdict for $500,000,000 against the Canadian investor. The Canadian investor claimed that the decision of the court amounted to an expropriation. The tribunal held, however, that an act by the judicial branch may constitute an expropriation only where there is a denial of justice. In this case, for reasons discussed in Section 10.4, no denial of justice occurred and thus there was no expropriation.

6.5.3.4 Grounds for Wrongfulness BITs universally permit expropriations, provided that certain conditions are met. As indicated by the discussion in Sections 6.5.3.1 through 6.5.3.3, expropriations of investment covered by a BIT rarely take the form of a seizure of title or possession of property, a situation where the existence of an expropriation is usually difficult to dispute. Rather, they more commonly involve regulatory action or a repudiation of a contract. Host states typically deny that an expropriation has occurred and therefore do not pay compensation. Thus, in virtually all of the cases discussed above, the expropriations were wrongful in that they were not accompanied by the compensation required by the applicable BIT.[336]

In only a few cases has a tribunal found that an expropriation was wrongful for failure to satisfy one of the other conditions imposed by the BIT. In *ADC v. Hungary*, a case arising under the Cyprus-Hungary BIT, the tribunal found that the expropriation was not for a public purpose. In that case, Hungary issued a decree canceling the claimants' concession contract to operate a state-owned airport, after which it privatized the airport. Hungary argued that it had cancelled the contract for the purpose of harmonizing Hungary's transportation laws with European Union law, but the tribunal found that claim unsubstantiated. In fact, in light of the subsequent privatization of the airport, the tribunal found no public interest in support of the contract termination. Accordingly, the tribunal found the decree to constitute "the clearest possible case of expropriation."[337] The tribunal also questioned the existence of a public purpose behind certain host state conduct leading up to an expropriation in *Siemens v. Argentina*, a case arising under the Germany-Argentina BIT, although the final expropriatory act, a decree that terminated a contract, was for the public purpose of avoiding a fiscal emergency.[338]

While an expropriation must be for a public purpose if it is to be lawful, the fact that it is for a public purpose in no way excuses the obligation to pay compensation. As the tribunal said in *Santa Elena v. Costa Rica*, "Expropriatory environmental measures—no matter how laudable and beneficial to society as a whole—are in this respect, similar to any other expropriatory measures that a state may take in order to implement its policies: where property is expropriated, even for environmental purposes, whether domestic or international, the state's obligation to pay compensation remains."[339]

---

336 On the legality of expropriation generally, *see* August Reinisch, "Legality of Expropriations," in *Standards of Investment Protection* (August Reinisch, ed. 2008).

337 Award, para. 304.

338 Award, para. 273.

339 Award, para. 71.

Similarly, the tribunal in *Vivendi v. Argentina*, a case arising under the France-Argentina BIT, observed that "[i]f public purpose automatically immunizes the measure from being found to be expropriatory, then there would never be a compensable taking for a public purpose."[340]

A few awards have discussed whether an expropriation violated the condition that it be nondiscriminatory, although such discussions have not been particularly illuminating because of their brevity. In *Eureko v. Poland*, a case arising under the Netherlands-Poland BIT, the host state reneged on a commitment to complete the process of privatizing a state-owned insurance company. The investor continued to own the shares of the enterprise that it already had acquired, but it was unable to acquire majority control, which had been the purpose of investing in the company. The tribunal found the breach of the commitment to be an expropriation. Further, because the purpose of failing to complete the privatization was to prevent foreign control of the enterprise, the tribunal found the expropriation to be discriminatory.[341]

In *ADC v. Hungary*, a case arising under the Cyprus-Hungary BIT, the host state had terminated the claimants' contract to operate an airport and transferred control over the airport to a newly created entity, following which the airport was privatized. The host state argued that because the claimants were the only foreign parties involved in the airport, they could not complain of discrimination. The tribunal held, however, that there was discrimination as between foreign investors and the operator appointed by the host state. Thus, the expropriation was discriminatory.[342]

Occasionally, a tribunal addresses an allegation that an expropriation was unlawful because it did not occur in accordance with due process. In *ADC v. Hungary*, the tribunal found that the expropriation occurred without due process of law. The tribunal held that due process in the context of expropriation "demands an actual and substantive legal procedure for a foreign investor to raise its claims against the depriving actions already taken or about to be taken against it. Some basic legal mechanisms, such as reasonable advance notice, a fair hearing, and an unbiased and impartial adjudicator to assess the actions in dispute, are expected to be readily available and accessible to the investor to make such legal procures meaningful. In general, the legal procedure must be of a nature to grant an affected investor a reasonable chance within a reasonable time to claim its legitimate rights and have its claims heard."[343] In that case, the tribunal found that no methods to satisfy this requirement were in place.

In *Middle East Cement v. Egypt*, a case arising under the Greece-Egypt BIT, the host state seized and auctioned the claimant's vessel without prior notice to the claimant. The tribunal found that this taking of the claimant's property was not in accordance with due process of law and thus violated the expropriation provision.[344]

Under most BITs, a state that lawfully expropriates covered investment must pay prompt, adequate, and effective compensation. Where an expropriation is unlawful,

340 Award, para. 7.5.21.
341 Award, para. 242.
342 Award, paras. 442–443.
343 Award, para. 435.
344 Award, para. 143.

however, the standard of compensation is that set by the *Chorzow Factory* case,[345] that is, compensation must eliminate the consequences of the wrongful act.[346] Thus, for example, in *ADC v. Hungary*, the tribunal held that the claimant must be awarded the market value of the expropriated investment as of the date of the award, rather than as of the date of expropriation,[347] thus providing the claimant with the benefit of any appreciation in the value of the investment. Similarly, in *Siemens v. Argentina*, a case arising under the Germany-Argentina BIT, the tribunal adopting the *Chorzow Factory* standard held that the claimant was entitled to any increase in value gained by the investment after its unlawful expropriation as well as any consequential damages.[348]

6.6 WAR AND CIVIL DISTURBANCE

6.6.1 Structure and Policy

Among the earliest treaty provisions protecting foreign property were provisions requiring restitution or compensation with respect to property seized during war.[349] Prior to the twentieth century, host state interference with foreign property typically occurred, if at all, during periods of war or civil disturbance. The first half of the twentieth century witnessed two world wars, both of which resulted in the destruction or loss of foreign property. Those who drafted the earliest BITs in the period after World War II included a provision that addressed specifically the problem of losses attributable to war and civil disturbance.

The most common provision requires the host state to grant both MFN and national treatment with respect to any compensation paid for losses occurring as a result of such events.[350] Some BITs that require both MFN and national treatment specify that the treatment to be accorded is that which is more favorable.[351] Even where this language does not appear, however, requiring that both be accorded implicitly requires that the investor receive the benefit of the more favorable treatment. Some BITs require only MFN treatment with respect to any such compensation.[352] The nondiscrimination provision, whether it guarantees national and MFN treatment or only MFN treatment,

345 *Chorzow Factory* (Germany v. Poland), 1928 P.C.I.J. (Ser. A) No. 17.

346 *See* Thomas Walde and Borzu Sabahi, *supra* note 221; Abby Cohen Smutny, *supra* note 221, at 1; Irmgard Marboe, *supra* note 221, at 723.

347 Award, para. 499.

348 Award, para. 352. *See also Vivendi v. Argentina* (France-Argentina BIT), Award, para. 8.2.3.

349 *See* Section 2.1.

350 *See, e.g.*, United Kingdom-Bosnia-Herzegovina BIT, Art. 5(1); Netherlands-Ethiopia BIT, Art. 7; Germany-Timor-Leste BIT, Art. 5(3)-(4); Switzerland-Algeria BIT, Art. 6(2); Austria-Armenia BIT, Art. 6(1); Finland-Armenia BIT, Art. 6(1); Sweden-Kazakhstan BIT, Art. 5(1); Denmark-Ethiopia, Art. 6; Chile-Indonesia BIT, Art. VII; Australia-India BIT, Art. 8; Argentina-Thailand BIT, Art. 6(3); Cambodia-Vietnam BIT, Art. V; Mexico-Iceland BIT, Art. 5; Canada-Uruguay BIT, Art. VII; India-Indonesia BIT, Art. 6.

351 *See, e.g.*, Denmark-Ethiopia BIT, Art. 6; Finland-Armenia BIT, Art. 6(1); Chile-Indonesia BIT, Art. VII; Cambodia-Vietnam BIT, Art. V.

352 *See, e.g.*, BLEU-Sudan BIT, Art. 7(4); Egypt-Zambia BIT, Art. 4.

does not require that compensation be paid. If, however, the host state elects to pay compensation, the payment must be on a nondiscriminatory basis. Some BITs provide that any payment shall be freely transferable.[353]

This nondiscrimination provision may be seen as a special application of the more general MFN and national treatment obligation. It is compared to the general MFN and national treatment provisions in Section 7.4.

Losses are covered by this provision only if they are the result of war or civil disturbance. The terms "war" and "civil disturbance" are used here as generic terms. BITs that include this provision generally include a list of the kinds of events to which the provision applies. The reference to war may be supplemented or supplanted by a reference to armed conflict. The term "armed conflict" may have a broader connotation, making clear that the provision applies to all military hostilities, whether or not the antagonists are of the same nationality and whether or not a formal state of war exists. The term "war" is used in this book as a generic term for war and armed conflict for the sake of brevity. The term "civil disturbance" generally is supplemented or supplanted by a number of other terms, including revolution, insurrection, riot, and national emergency. Some BITs include a residual term, such as "similar events," to make clear that the list is not exhaustive.[354] Occasionally, BITs include acts of God or *force majeure* as well.[355]

A second, less common, provision requires that the host state pay compensation for any losses arising during war or civil disturbance from host-state requisitioning of investment or destruction of investment by government forces or authorities not caused by combat or military necessity.[356] This provision, which reflects the principle of security rather than nondiscrimination, essentially codifies customary international law.[357] Like the nondiscrimination provision, the security provision applies only to losses attributable to war or civil disturbance. Unlike the nondiscrimination provision, the security provision applies only where the losses are caused by the action of the host state. Typically, it specifies that it applies to the requisitioning or destruction of all or part of an investment. Many BITs omit the reference to combat action.[358]

Further, unlike the nondiscrimination provision, the security provision requires payment of compensation, often described in the provision as adequate compensation.[359] In some cases, a BIT explicitly requires that the host state pay prompt, adequate, and effective compensation for such losses.[360] This provision may require no more

---

353 *See, e.g.*, Germany-Timor-Leste BIT, Art. 5(3); Sweden-Kazakhstan BIT, Art. 5(1); Egypt-Zambia BIT, Art. 4; India-Indonesia BIT, Art. 6.

354 *See, e.g.*, Austria-Armenia BIT, Art. 6(1).

355 *See, e.g.*, Austria-Armenia BIT, Art. 6(1); Canada-Uruguay BIT, Art. VII ("natural disaster").

356 *See, e.g.*, United Kingdom-Bosnia-Herzegovina BIT, Art. 4(2).

357 The Austria-Armenia BIT, at Art. 6, notes that, "for avoidance of doubt," each party shall observe its obligations under customary international law.

358 *See, e.g.*, Austria-Armenia BIT, Art. 6(2); Finland-Armenia BIT, Art. 6(2); Sweden-Kazakhstan BIT, Art. 5(2)

359 *See, e.g.*, United Kingdom-Bosnia-Herzegovina BIT, Art. 4(2); Austria-Armenia BIT, Art. 6(2).

360 *See, e.g.*, Finland-Armenia BIT, Art. 6(2); Sweden-Kazakhstan BIT, Art. 5(2).

protection than is already provided by the expropriation provision. To the extent that the provision addresses the transferability of compensation payments, it may replicate protection otherwise accorded by the transfers provision.

6.6.2 Origins

Treaty provisions creating a remedy for foreign property losses during time of war have existed for hundreds of years.[361] The earliest provisions required restitution of property seized during war, but gradually payment of compensation was accepted as an alternative.[362]

Early nineteenth-century FCNs required compensation for foreign property taken during hostilities. As they broadened their property protection provisions to apply to any seizures, the FCNs no longer contained provisions specifically applicable to war losses.[363]

From the beginning, the BITs included both a provision dealing with expropriation generally and a provision dealing with losses during time of war or civil disturbance. The new war and civil disturbance provisions addressed seizures as well as destruction of property.

A provision addressing compensation due in the event of losses attributable to war or other civil disturbance dates from the first BIT, although it was not common in the early BITs. The 1959 BIT between Germany and Pakistan merely required national and MFN treatment with respect to any remedy provided for losses attributable to war or other armed conflict, revolution or revolt in the territory of the host state.[364] It also required national and MFN treatment with respect to the transfer of any such payments.[365] Germany, of course, had lost its overseas investment as a result of the World War II and thus the problem of war losses was particularly salient to German investors.

The other country to adopt such a provision by the early 1960s was Germany's wartime ally, Italy. The first Italian BIT, concluded with Guinea in 1964, provided at Article IV that the same compensation owed under the expropriation provision must be paid in the event of loss caused by war. In 1969, in the Italy-Ivory Coast BIT, this provision was broadened to apply to war or other armed conflict, revolution, or state of national emergency[366] and obligations of national and MFN treatment with respect to compensation were added.[367] The obligation that the payment be freely transferable also was made explicit. The Italian BIT program then went into a hiatus and Italy did not resume BIT negotiations until the mid 1980s. The Italy-Ivory Coast BIT

361 *See* Section 2.1.
362 *See* Section 2.1.
363 *See* Section 2.1.1.
364 Germany-Pakistan BIT, Art. 3(3).
365 Germany-Pakistan BIT, Art. 3(3).
366 Italy-Ivory Coast BIT, Art. 4(3)
367 *Id.* at Art. 4(3)–(4).

nevertheless established the policy that Italy followed in a number of its subsequent BITs, although the list of events was rephrased to apply to war, armed conflict, state of emergency and "similar events."[368]

A war and civil disturbance provision was not immediately included by other countries in their BITs. It did not appear, for example, in the first BITs concluded by Switzerland, the Netherlands, the Belgium-Luxembourg Economic Union (BLEU), Sweden, Denmark, Finland, or France. Neither was there such a provision in the 1959 Abs-Shawcross convention or the 1967 OECD Draft Convention on the Protection of Foreign Property.

Denmark did include a commitment to provide national and MFN treatment with respect to compensation for losses attributable to armed conflict, revolution, state of national emergency, or revolt beginning with its 1968 BIT with Indonesia.[369] The provision also required that any payments be freely transferable.

When the United Kingdom inaugurated its BIT program in 1975, its BITs included a provision headed "Compensation for Losses" that comprised both a nondiscrimination and a security provision. The nondiscrimination provision, at Article 4(1), was similar to that which appeared in the German BITs. It required national and MFN treatment with respect to any remedies provided for losses to investments owing to war or other armed conflict, revolution, a state of national emergency, revolt, insurrection, or riot. This language has remained virtually unchanged in the U.K. BITs, although a sentence has been added requiring that payments be freely transferable.[370]

The security provision, at article 4(2), was an innovation in BIT practice. Although the Italy-Ivory Coast BIT had included a security provision requiring adequate compensation, the U.K. language was more elaborate and nuanced. It required that adequate and freely transferable compensation be paid to nationals and companies of a party who in any of the situations referenced in Article 4(1) suffered losses in the territory of the other party resulting from the requisitioning of property by the host state's forces or authorities or destruction of property by the host state's forces or authorities that was not caused in combat or required by the necessity of the situation. Thus, the security provision applied to losses to property, as opposed to investment. Article 4(2) was explicitly "without prejudice" to Article 4(1), meaning that the obligation to pay compensation for destruction or requisitioning did not diminish the obligation not to discriminate with respect to any compensation paid for losses arising from war or civil disturbance. This language, which was intended to codify customary law,[371] has remained largely unchanged in the U.K. BITs.[372]

---

368 *See, e.g.*, Italy-Bangladesh BIT, Art. 4; Italy-Pakistan BIT, Art. 4; Italy-Nicaragua BIT, Art. IV.

369 Denmark-Indonesia BIT, Art. V.

370 *See, e.g.*, United Kingdom-Vietnam BIT, Art. 4(1); United Kingdom-Bosnia-Herzegovina BIT, Art. 4(1).

371 Denza & Brooks, "Investment Protection Treaties: United Kingdom Experience," 36 *International and Comparative Law Quarterly* 908, 911–912 (1987).

372 *See, e.g.*, United Kingdom-Vietnam BIT, Art. 4(2); United Kingdom-Bosnia- Herzegovina BIT, Art. 4(2).

The U.K. provision set a precedent that soon was followed by a number of other countries. For example, the next year, Austria signed its first BIT, with Romania, and included language requiring that compensation be paid for losses due to armed conflict and requiring nondiscriminatory treatment with respect to such losses,[373] although Austria soon abandoned the language. The provision subsequently was restored and expanded in Austria's BITs so that it not only requires MFN and national treatment with respect to any compensation paid, but (with some variations among agreements) also requires prompt, adequate, and effective compensation for losses due to requisitioning by the forces or authorities of the host state or destruction by such forces or authorities not caused by necessity.[374]

At the beginning of the 1980s, France included a guarantee of national treatment with respect to losses due to war, armed conflict, revolution, national emergency, or revolt.[375] Other French BITs concluded in the 1980s required in addition the payment of appropriate compensation for such losses resulting from a requisition by the forces or authorities of the host state or destruction by the forces or authorities not resulting from combat or necessity.[376]

The first U.S. BITs, concluded with Egypt and Panama in 1982, included only the nondiscrimination provision. Within a year both a nondiscrimination and a security provision similar to that in the U.K. BITs appeared.[377] The security provision was eliminated from the U.S. model negotiating text in 1984, but was restored in the 1994 model.[378] One distinctive feature in the 1994 model was that it applied to requisitioning or destruction of investments, as opposed to property, as in the U.K. BITs. Such a provision remains in the U.S. BITs[379]

Although its BIT program dated from 1965, Sweden first included a war and civil disturbance provision in its BITs in 1983. Article 4 of the Sweden-Yemen BIT required national and MFN treatment with respect to compensation for losses suffered as well as adequate compensation for losses attributable to requisitioning by host-state forces or authorities or destruction by host-state forces or authorities not caused by combat or necessity. Sweden's practice since 1983 has not been entirely consistent, with some BITs omitting the provision,[380] some requiring only MFN treatment,[381] some requiring MFN and national treatment,[382] and some adopting language similar to that which

---

373 Austria-Romania BIT, Art. 4(3)-(4).

374 *See, e.g.*, Austria-Bosnia-Herzegovina BIT, Art. 6; Austria-Armenia BIT, Art. 6; Austria-Egypt BIT, Art. 5; Austria-Jordan BIT, Art. 6; Austria-Lebanon BIT, Art. 6; Austria-Libya BIT, Art. 5.

375 *See, e.g.*, France-Sri Lanka BIT, Art. 7(3).

376 *See, e.g.*, France-Equatorial Guinea BIT, Art.5(3)–(4).

377 *See* U.S.-Haiti BIT, signed Dec. 13, 1983, Art. IV.

378 Kenneth J. Vandevelde, *U.S. International Investment Agreements* 433–434 (2009)

379 *See, e.g.*, United States-Uruguay BIT, Art. 5(4)–(5).

380 *See, e.g.*, Sweden-Tunisia BIT; Sweden-Czechoslovakia BIT,

381 *See, e.g.*, Sweden-Morocco, Art. 4(2); Sweden-Hungary, Art. 6; Sweden-Poland, Art. 4(2); Sweden-Bolivia, Art. 4(3); Sweden-Argentina, Art. 4(3).

382 *See, e.g.*, Sweden-Republic of Korea, Art. 4; Sweden-Ecuador, Art. 4(4); Sweden-Albania BIT, Art. 4(3).

appeared in the Sweden-Yemen BIT, although sometimes without the reference to combat.[383]

The Netherlands added a nondiscrimination provision in the mid-1980s.[384] The Dutch BITs continue to include a provision guaranteeing national and MFN treatment with respect to losses for war and civil disturbance.[385]

As already noted, Denmark has included a nondiscrimination provision with respect to compensation for war and civil disturbance losses since the 1960s. In the late 1980s, Denmark added a second clause to the provision requiring adequate compensation or restitution for such losses resulting from requisitioning of property by the host state's authorities or forces or destruction of property by host state authorities or forces not caused by necessity.[386] This new clause appeared in most,[387] but not all,[388] subsequent Danish BITs, although in the 1990s language was added stating explicitly that compensation must be prompt, adequate, and effective.

Kuwait had included no war and civil disturbance provision in its first BIT, concluded in 1964 with Iraq, but by the 1980s Kuwait was incorporating in its BITs a provision with both clauses, that is, requiring MFN and national treatment with respect to compensation and requiring prompt, adequate, and effective compensation for requisitioned property or destruction not caused by combat action or necessity.[389]

Finland had no provision on war and civil disturbance in its first BIT, concluded in 1980, but included such a provision in its second BIT, concluded with Bulgaria in 1984.[390] The provision required MFN treatment with respect to compensation. Beginning in the mid 1990s, some Finnish BITs also included a right to national treatment with respect to compensation.[391] During this same period, the first Finnish BITs providing for a right to compensation for such losses appeared, limited initially to requisitioning and then expanded to include destruction not caused by combat or, later, necessity.[392] The most recent Finnish BITs include all of these clauses.[393]

---

383 *See, e.g.*, Sweden-Croatia BIT, Art. 6; Sweden-Bosnia-Herzegovina, Art.5; Sweden-Kazakhstan, Art. 5; Sweden-India, Art. 6.

384 *See, e.g.*, Netherlands-Turkey BIT, Art. 6 (national and MFN treatment); Netherlands-Hungary BIT, Art. 4(2) (MFN treatment).

385 *See, e.g.*, Netherlands-Ethiopia BIT, Art. 7.

386 *See, e.g.*, Denmark-Republic of Korea BIT, Art. 5(2).

387 *See, e.g.*, Denmark-Mongolia BIT, Art. 6; Denmark-Poland BIT, May 1, 1990; Art. 4; Denmark-India BIT, Art. 6 (fair and equitable compensation required); Denmark-Croatia BIT, Art. 5; Denmark-Cuba BIT, Art. 7; Denmark-Kyrgyz Republic BIT, Art. 6; Denmark-Kuwait BIT, June 1, 2001, Art. 5 (just and adequate compensation required).

388 *See, e.g.*, Denmark-Peru BIT, Nov. 23, 1994, Art. 6; Denmark-Venezuela BIT, Nov. 28, 1994, Art. 6; Denmark-Nicaragua BIT, Art. 6; Denmark-Ethiopia BIT, Art. 6.

389 *See, e.g.*, Kuwait-China BIT, Art. 4; Kuwait-Hungary BIT, Art. 5; Kuwait-Ethiopia BIT, Art. 5; Kuwait-Czech Republic BIT, Art. 5; Kuwait-Croatia BIT, Art. 5.

390 Finland-Bulgaria BIT, Art. 3(3).

391 *See, e.g.*, Finland-Republic of Korea BIT, Art. 4; Finland-Thailand BIT, Art. 4(3); Finland-Brazil BIT, Art. 6.

392 *See, e.g.*, Finland-Chile BIT, Art. 6; Finland-Vietnam BIT, Art. 5; Finland-Brazil BIT, Art. 6; Finland-Azerbaijan BIT, Art. 7; Finland-Armenia BIT, Art. 6.

393 *See, e.g.*, Finland-Belarus BIT, Art. 6; Finland-Algeria BIT, Art. 5.

As this discussion indicates, the British innovation was widely accepted by the mid-1980s. No important innovations in the war and civil disturbance provision have appeared subsequently.

6.6.3 Arbitral Practice

Only a few awards have applied the war and civil disturbance provision. The first such case was *AAPL v. Sri Lanka*, a case arising under the United Kingdom-Sri Lanka BIT. In that case, the claimant sought compensation for damage to its shrimp farm caused by hostilities between government troops and Tamil rebels. The tribunal found that the claimant was unable to prove that the damage was caused by the government forces or that it was not caused by military necessity. Thus, Sri Lanka had not violated the provision.

In *American Manufacturing and Trading v. Zaire*, a case arising under the United States-D.R. Congo BIT, the claimant sought compensation for damage caused by a civil disturbance in which the participants included soldiers in uniform. The tribunal held that the reference to "the forces" of the host state meant organized forces, not soldiers acting individually.[394] Arbitrator Heribert Golsong dissented on this point.

A few cases have discussed the war and civil disturbance nondiscrimination provision. In *CMS Gas Transmission Company v. Argentina*, a case arising under the United States-Argentina BIT. Argentina addressed a serious economic crisis in 2001–2002 by adopting a series of measures that adversely affected the claimant's business providing gas transmission services. In a very brief discussion, the tribunal found that Argentina's measures had been nondiscriminatory as among similarly situated individuals or entities and thus could not have violated the provision. To the extent that Argentina had drawn some distinctions among various businesses that could not be justified by the economic emergency, these were more appropriately seen as violations of the fair and equitable treatment standard.

Those same measures also were the basis of a claim in *LG&E v. Argentina*, another case arising under the United States-Argentina BIT. The tribunal again found no violation on the ground that the measures taken by Argentina were "across the board."[395]

In both *CMS* and *LG&E*, Argentina argued that the war and civil disturbance provision indicated that national emergencies generally were not covered by the BIT. That is, Argentina suggested that the provision was intended to excuse, rather than impose, liability. The tribunal rejected this argument in both cases. It also rejected the same argument in cases involving the United Kingdom-Argentina BIT.[396]

---

394 Award, paras. 7.07–7.09.

395 Decision on Liability, para. 244.

396 *BG Group v. Argentina*, Award, para. 382 (citing *CMS v. Argentina and LG&E v. Argentina)*; *National Grid v. Argentina*, Award, para. 253.

6.7 CURRENCY TRANSFERS

6.7.1 Structure and Policy

An inherent feature of foreign investment is that the investor earns a return in a different country than that of the investor's own nationality. Thus, with only a few exceptions, the returns on the investment are generated in a different currency than that which the investor uses for its transactions in its home country. To realize the benefit of the returns on its investment, the investor must be able to exchange the currency in which the returns are generated for a currency that the investor can use for its other transactions.

In order to exchange the local currency for another currency, the investor must draw upon the host state's foreign exchange reserves. Central banks, however, have finite amounts of foreign currency that serve purposes in addition to providing foreign currency for foreign investors wishing to repatriate their earnings. First, the purchase of imports requires the expenditure of the currency of the country from which the good or service is imported, unless the seller is willing to accept the currency of the importing country. Second, if a country imports more than it exports, then a surplus of its currency may accumulate in foreign markets, which will cause the value of the currency to fall relative to foreign currencies. In order to maintain the value of the currency, the central bank may go into the market and purchase its own currency, thereby reducing the surplus and bidding up its price, *i.e.*, its value. To purchase its own currency, the central bank must use foreign currency, which again is drawn from its finite foreign exchange reserves. Thus, foreign exchange reserves serve vital interests of a country, including the purchase of necessary imports, such as food and fuel, and the maintenance of the value of its currency.

The possibility thus exists that, to conserve its foreign exchange reserves, the host state will impose restrictions on the conversion of local currency into another currency, with the result that the investor will be unable to convert the returns on the investment into a currency that the investor can use for its transactions outside the host country. The practical effect may be the same as if the investor had received no return at all. Further, at the point at which the investor wishes to sell or otherwise liquidate the investment, the proceeds from that disposition also may be denominated in the currency of the host state. If the investor cannot convert the liquidation proceeds into another currency, the practical effect may be the same as if the investment had been expropriated. Moreover, where the investment is part of a global enterprise, it may need to purchase goods or services from its affiliates or other companies abroad. It may need to borrow funds from foreign lenders that require payment of the debt service in a foreign currency. That is, the daily operation of the investment may require the ability to obtain foreign currency. Currency exchange controls thus pose a potentially serious risk to the security of both the investment and the returns on the investment. Finally, the efficient operation of the investment may necessitate that the investor inject new capital into the investment. Thus, the investor must be able to transfer funds into, as well as out of, the host state.

Customary international law does not require that countries permit foreign investors to transfer currency freely into or out of the host country.[397] The imposition of overly burdensome controls on currency transfers, however, may constitute an expropriation giving rise to an obligation to compensate the investor.[398] Regulations on currency transfers that fall short of a compensable taking nevertheless may cause investors considerable loss. Thus, investors have sought treaty protection against host-state restrictions on the free transfer of currency.[399]

The currency transfers provision of the BITs typically provides that each party shall permit the free transfer of certain payments related to an investment. The provision must identify the transfers to which it applies and define what is meant by free transferability.

The most common practice is that the transfers provision applies to all "transfers" or "payments" related to an investment.[400] Usually, this language is accompanied by an illustrative list of transfers or payments to which the provision applies. These generally fall into one of four categories, although the illustrative list may subdivide or combine these categories.

The first category is the principal amount of the investment. The BIT may refer to this amount in different ways. It may refer to the amount originally invested[401] or it may refer to sale or liquidation proceeds.[402] Often, it refers to both, in different paragraphs. Obviously, the proceeds from the sale or liquidation of the investment may be greater in amount than the original amount invested. Although in most cases the list is only illustrative, the better practice is to refer separately to sale or liquidation proceeds in order to avoid the implication from omission that only the original amount

---

397 *See, e.g., West v. Multilbanco Comermex, S.A.*, 807 F2.d 820 (1987).

398 Marian Whiteman, 8 *Digest of International Law* 981–982 (1967); B. Wortley, *supra note 328, at* 107.

399 Other agreements also may limit the imposition of restrictions on currency transfers. For example, as discussed in Section 6.7.2, the Articles of Agreement of the International Monetary Fund limit the imposition of restrictions on transfers related to current, as opposed to capital, transactions. The General Agreement on Trade in Services limit the imposition of restrictions on transfers related to trade in services, which may entail the establishment of investment. The OECD's Code of Liberalization of Capital Movements and its Code of Liberalization of Current Invisible Operations also limit transfer restrictions by OECD members.

400 *See, e.g.*, Austria-Armenia BIT, Art. 7(1); Netherlands-Ethiopia BIT, Art. 5(1); BLEU-Sudan BIT, Art. 8(1); Italy-Nicaragua BIT, Art. VI(1); Finland-Armenia BIT, Art. 7(1); Denmark-Ethiopia BIT, Art. 7(1); Switzerland-Algeria BIT, Art. 5(1); Australia-India BIT, Art. 9(1); Germany-Timor-Leste BIT, Art. 5; Mexico-Iceland BIT, Art. 6(1); Indonesia-India BIT, Art. 7(1).

401 *See, e.g.*, Austria-Armenia BIT, Art. 7(1); BLEU-Sudan BIT, Art. 8(1); Italy-Nicaragua BIT, Art. VI(1); Finland-Armenia BIT, Art. 7(1); Denmark-Ethiopia BIT, Art. 7(1); Australia-India BIT, Art. 9(1); Germany-Timor-Leste BIT, Art. 5; Indonesia-India BIT, Art. 7(1).

402 *See, e.g.*, Austria-Armenia BIT, Art. 7(1); Netherlands-Ethiopia BIT, Art. 5(1); BLEU-Sudan BIT, Art. 8(1); Sweden-Kazakhstan BIT, Art. 6(1); Italy-Nicaragua BIT, Art. VI(1); Finland-Armenia BIT, Art. 7(1); Denmark-Ethiopia BIT, Art. 7(1); Switzerland-Algeria BIT, Art. 5(1); Germany-Timor-Leste BIT, Art. 5; Mexico-Iceland BIT, Art. 6(1); Indonesia-India BIT, Art. 7(1).

may be transferred. This category includes not only the original investment, but additional contributions to capital.[403]

A second category consists of the returns on the investment.[404] These include, for example, profits and dividends. Many BITs also include earnings of personnel employed in the host state in connection with investment.[405]

A third category comprises payments necessary for the operation of the investment. Such payments may include, for example, royalty payments, management fees, license fees, contract payments, or payment of interest and principal on loans.[406]

A fourth category, included in some but not all BITs, is compensation for expropriation[407] or for losses due to war or civil disturbance,[408] or compensation received pursuant to dispute settlement.[409] Where the compensation is for expropriation, the expropriation provision usually also addresses the transferability of expropriation compensation. The transferability of compensation is sometimes addressed by the provision on war and civil disturbance as well. The transferability of other forms of compensation, however, is rarely addressed apart from in the transfers provision. As will be explained below, the transfers provision may not be consistent with the transfers clause of the expropriation provision.

In some BITs, the transfers provision applies only to the transfers included in the list.[410] Although this was a common practice in the earliest BITs, the trend over time has been toward applying the provision to all transfers related to an investment.

---

403 *See, e.g.*, Austria-Armenia BIT, Art. 7(1); Netherlands-Ethiopia BIT, Art. 5(1); BLEU-Sudan BIT, Art. 8(1); Italy-Nicaragua BIT, Art. VI(1); Finland-Armenia BIT, Art. 7(1); Denmark-Ethiopia BIT, Art. 7(1); Australia-India BIT, Art. 9(1); Germany-Timor-Leste BIT, Art. 5; Indonesia-India BIT, Art. 7(1).

404 *See, e.g.*, Austria-Armenia BIT, Art. 7(1); Netherlands-Ethiopia BIT, Art. 5(1); BLEU-Sudan BIT, Art. 8(1); Sweden-Kazakhstan BIT, Art. 6(1); Italy-Nicaragua BIT, Art. VI(1); Finland-Armenia BIT, Art. 7(1); Denmark-Ethiopia BIT, Art. 7(1); Switzerland-Algeria BIT, Art. 5(1); Australia-India BIT, Art. 9(1); Germany-Timor-Leste BIT, Art. 5; Mexico-Iceland BIT, Art. 6(1); Indonesia-India BIT, Art. 7(1).

405 *See, e.g.*, Austria-Armenia BIT, Art. 7; Netherlands-Ethiopia BIT, Art. 5(1); BLEU-Sudan BIT, Art. 8(2); Sweden-Kazakhstan BIT, Art. 6(1); Italy-Nicaragua BIT, Art. VI(1); Finland-Armenia BIT, Art. 7(1); Denmark-Ethiopia BIT, Art. 7(1); Australia-India BIT, Art. 9(1); Indonesia-India BIT, Art. 7(1).

406 *See, e.g.*, Austria-Armenia BIT, Art. 7(1); Netherlands-Ethiopia BIT, Art. 5(1); BLEU-Sudan BIT, Art. 8(1); Sweden-Kazakhstan BIT, Art. 6(1); Italy-Nicaragua BIT, Art. VI(1); Finland-Armenia BIT, Art. 7(1); Denmark-Ethiopia BIT, Art. 7(1); Australia-India BIT, Art. 9(1); Germany-Timor-Leste BIT, Art. 5; Mexico-Iceland BIT, Art. 6(1); Indonesia-India BIT, Art. 7(1).

407 *See, e.g.*, Italy-Nicaragua BIT, Art. VI(1); Finland-Armenia BIT, Art. 7(1); BLEU-Sudan BIT, Art. 8(1); Austria-Armenia BIT, Art. 7(1); Sweden-Kazakhstan BIT, Art. 6(1); Denmark-Ethiopia BIT, Art. 7(1); Germany-Timor-Leste BIT, Art. 5; Mexico-Iceland BIT, Art. 6(1).

408 *See, e.g.*, Finland-Armenia BIT, Art. 7(1); Netherlands-Ethiopia BIT, Art. 5(1); Austria-Armenia BIT, Art. 7(1); Sweden-Kazakhstan BIT, Art. 6(1); Denmark-Ethiopia BIT, Art. 7(1); Australia-India BIT, Art. 9(1).

409 *See, e.g.*, Austria-Armenia BIT, Art. 7; Finland-Armenia BIT, Art. 7(1); Mexico-Iceland BIT, Art. 6(1).

410 *See, e.g.*, France-Uganda BIT, Art. 6.

Clearly, the latter, more common, approach is preferred by the investor for two reasons. First, it offers a broader protection, because it applies to transfers that may not be included in the enumeration. Second, it offers a more transparent protection because the likelihood of a dispute arising over whether a particular transfer falls within the enumeration is reduced. This approach also provides a stronger signal of a favorable investment climate. Applying the transfers provision to all payments related to an investment indicates that free transferability has been adopted as a matter of principle and that the host state believes that it can adhere to the principle. For the same reason, the broader approach imposes a greater obligation on the host state. All that said, the enumeration usually is broad enough that it covers the vast majority of transfers related to an investment and thus any differences in practice between the two approaches is likely to be small.

In some BITs, the transfers provision applies to "capital" (or "investment") and "returns," although these terms may be supplemented by an illustrative list.[411] While this language would seem not to apply payments necessary for the operation of the investment, in some cases the illustrative list explicitly does include some such payments,[412] suggesting that the reference to investment and returns is not to be read literally. Such also has been the case when the transfers provision guarantees free transfer of investments.[413] That is, the illustrative list makes clear that the provision applies to more than the transfer of the principal amount of the investment.

Some BITs state explicitly that the transfers provision applies to transfers into or out of the territory of the host state.[414] Most BITs, however, are silent on this point. Where the provision applies to all transfers related to an investment, it often can be inferred that such transfers include transfers into the territory as well as those out of the territory. Where the provision applies only to certain enumerated transfers, whether the provision applies to transfers into as well as out of the territory will depend upon the language of the enumeration.

In defining what is meant by free transferability, BITs typically address three issues: (1) the amount of time that may elapse before the transfer occurs; (2) the currency into which transfer shall be permitted; and (3) the rate of exchange at which transfer shall be permitted.

Many BITs refer simply to "free" transfer, which implies a requirement of promptness,[415] and some BITs elaborate upon this requirement by stating explicitly

---

411 *See, e.g.*, United Kingdom-Bosnia-Herzegovina BIT, Art. 6; Canada-Uruguay BIT, Art. IX ("investments and returns" supplemented by an illustrative list).

412 *See, e.g.*, Canada-Uruguay BIT, Art. IX; Thailand-Argentina BIT, Art. 7(1).

413 *See, e.g.*, Cambodia-Vietnam BIT, Art. VI(1) (accompanied by broad illustrative list of transfers not limited to the investment itself and any contributions to capital, but including returns and payments for the operation of the investment).

414 *See, e.g.*, Austria-Armenia BIT, Art. 7(1); Italy-Nicaragua BIT, Art. VI(1); Finland-Armenia BIT, Art. 7(1).

415 *See, e.g.*, Austria-Armenia BIT, Art. 7; United Kingdom-Bosnia-Herzegovina BIT, Art. 6 ("unrestricted" transfer); BLEU-Sudan BIT, Art. 8(1); Italy-Nicaragua BIT, Art. VI(1); Thailand-Argentina BIT, Art. 7(1).

that a free transfer is one without delay[416] or, occasionally, without unreasonable delay.[417] Other BITs omit the word "free" and instead require transfer "without delay"[418] or, much less often, "without undue delay."[419] Some BITs define the term "without delay." For example, the Austria-Armenia BIT defines "without delay" to mean "such period as is normally required for the completion of formalities for the transfer of payments." [420]The normal period, however, may not be one that is consistent with the requirement of promptness or transfers without delay. Thus, the normal period should not be conclusively presumed to satisfy the requirement of promptness unless the BIT so specifies. Occasionally, BITs specify a period of time within which the transfer must be permitted, such as thirty days,[421] or sixty days.[422] Where BITs specify the time period in this way, they typically are departing from the ordinary meaning of promptness, seeking to give the host state the discretion to delay transfer for a limited time.

BITs most commonly require that transfer be permitted into a freely convertible currency.[423] A few BITs refer to a freely usable currency rather than a freely convertible currency.[424] The term "freely usable currency" is a defined term in Article XXX(f) of the IMF Articles of Agreement. It refers to "a member's currency that the Fund determines . . . is, in fact, widely used to make payments for international transactions, and . . . is widely traded in the principal exchange markets." At present, the IMF regards four currencies as freely usable. These are the U.S. dollar, the euro, the British pound, and the Japanese yen.

Some BITs require that a transfer be permitted in the currency in which it originally was made or in any currency to which the parties mutually agree.[425] The theory behind this language is that the investor is permitted to transfer out of the host state only the currency that it transferred in, although the amount of the outward transfer may be much larger than the inward transfer. The investor may demand a different currency only if the host state agrees. This language is less desirable from the perspective of the investor because the operation of the investment may require the use of

---

416 *See, e.g.*, Thailand-Argentina BIT, Art. 7(2); Austria-Armenia BIT, Art. 7(1); Finland-Armenia BIT, Art. 7(2); Mexico-Iceland BIT, Art. 6(1); Germany-Timor-Leste BIT, Art. 7(1).

417 *See, e.g.*, Australia-India BIT, Art. 9(1); Indonesia-India BIT, Art. 7(1).

418 *See, e.g.*, United Kingdom-Bosnia-Herzegovina BIT, Art. 6; Netherlands-Ethiopia BIT, Art. 5(1) (without restriction or delay); Sweden-Kazakhstan BIT, Art. 6(1); Denmark-Ethiopia BIT, Art. 7(1); Switzerland-Algeria BIT, Art. 5(1).

419 *See, e.g.*, BLEU-Sudan BIT, Art. 8(4); Cambodia-Vietnam BIT, Art. VI(1) ("without unreasonable delay").

420 *See also* Cambodia-Vietnam BIT, Art. 1(3); Chile-Indonesia BIT, Protocol; Germany-Timor-Leste BIT, Protocol, para. 4.

421 *See, e.g.*, Chile-Indonesia BIT, Protocol; Austria-Armenia BIT, Art. 1(5) (one month).

422 *See, e.g.*, Germany-Timor-Leste BIT, Protocol, para. 4 (two months).

423 *See, e.g.*, Austria-Armenia BIT, Art. 7; Netherlands-Ethiopia BIT, Art. 5(1); BLEU-Sudan BIT, Art. 8(3); Sweden-Kazakhstan BIT, Art. 6(1); Finland-Armenia BIT, Art. 7(2); Denmark-Ethiopia BIT, Art. 7(2); Switzerland-Algeria BIT, Art. 5(1); Thailand-Argentina BIT, Art. 7(2).

424 *See, e.g.*, United States-Argentina BIT, Art. V(2).

425 *See, e.g.*, United Kingdom-Bosnia-Herzegovina BIT, Art. 6; Canada-Uruguay BIT, Art. IX(2) Denmark BITs.

other currencies. Further, this formulation could negate the right of transfer in situations where the investment was locally financed, meaning that no foreign exchange was used to make the investment.

BITs vary in the language that they use to describe the rate of exchange that shall be used. Some refer to the market rate of exchange[426] while others refer to the official rate of exchange.[427] The market rate of exchange generally is preferable to investors because it is less subject to host-state control, but a market rate of exchange may not exist. Some BITs are less specific and refer simply to the exchange rate.[428] Some BITs provide that, in the absence of a market rate of exchange, the most recent exchange rate for conversion of currency into Special Drawing Rights shall be used.[429]

A few BITs specify that the rate shall be that used for spot transactions.[430] A spot transaction is in theory an immediate exchange of currencies, although in practice spot transactions often take place over a period of about 48 hours. A spot transaction is distinguished from a forward transaction, in which the exchange takes place at some specified future date, perhaps in three, six or twelve months. Because exchange rates for forward transactions vary depending upon the date on which the transfer occurs, specifying use of a forward rate without a time period leaves uncertain which rate shall be used. Thus, to ensure some measure of certainty and transparency, consistent with the goals of the BIT, the transfers provision should be interpreted to require use of the rate for spot transactions unless explicit language to the contrary appears.

Exchange rates, of course, change daily and thus some BITs specify that the exchange rate to be used is that applicable on the date of transfer.[431] This presumably is the rate that would be used in the absence of such language. Assuming that transfer occurs promptly, the exchange rate on the date of transfer in most cases will not differ significantly from the exchange rate on the date that transfer was requested. Where the BIT specifies use of the exchange rate on the date of transfer, the investor or the investment making the transfer bears the risk of any adverse change in the exchange rate during the time between the date of application for transfer and the date of transfer.

---

426 *See, e.g.*, Austria-Armenia BIT, Art. 7; Sweden-Kazakhstan BIT, Art. 6(2); Finland-Armenia BIT, Art. 7(2); Denmark-Ethiopia BIT, Art. 7(2); Australia-India BIT, Art. 9(2); Mexico-Iceland BIT, Art. 6(2); Thailand-Argentina BIT, Art. 7(2); Indonesia-India BIT, Art. 7(3); Germany-Timor-Leste BIT, Art. 7(1).

427 *See, e.g.* France-Uganda BIT, Art. 6.

428 *See, e.g.*, United Kingdom-Bosnia-Herzegovina BIT, Art. 6 ("the rate of exchange applicable on the date of transfer pursuant to the exchange regulations in force"); Netherlands-Ethiopia BIT, Art. 5(2); BLEU-Sudan BIT, Art. 8(3); Switzerland-Algeria BIT, Art. 5(2); Canada-Uruguay BIT, Art. IX(2); Vietnam-Cambodia BIT, Art. VI(2)

429 *See, e.g.*, Finland-Armenia BIT, Art. 7(3); Denmark-Ethiopia BIT, Art. 7(2); Austria-Armenia BIT, Art. 7(3); Germany-Timor-Leste BIT, Art. 7(2).

430 *See, e.g.*, BLEU-Sudan BIT, Art. 8(3); Sweden-Kazakhstan BIT, Art. 6(2); Denmark-Ethiopia BIT, Art. 7(2).

431 *See, e.g.*, United Kingdom-Bosnia-Herzegovina BIT, Art. 6; Austria-Armenia BIT, Art. 7(2); BLEU-Sudan BIT, Art. 8(3); Sweden-Kazakhstan BIT, Art. 6(2); Finland-Armenia BIT, Art. 7(2); Denmark-Ethiopia BIT, Art. 7(2); Switzerland-Algeria BIT, Art. 5(2); Australia-India BIT, Art. 9(2); Mexico-Iceland BIT, Art. 6(2); Thailand-Argentina BIT, Art. 7(2); Indonesia-India BIT, Art. 7(3).

If the date of transfer is delayed, however, then the cost to the investor or investment as a result of adverse changes in the exchange rate during the delay could be substantial. Thus, the element of promptness is critical to ensuring the security of the investment. Occasionally BITs provide that interest shall be paid during any delay in the transfer.[432]

In the event of an expropriation, BITs generally require prompt, adequate, and effective compensation. Thus, payment of expropriation compensation also must be prompt. The completion of formalities for payment of expropriation compensation, however, may require far more time than the completion of formalities for an ordinary exchange of currency because of the extraordinary nature of an expropriation. Considerable time may elapse between the date of expropriation and the date of payment, particularly if valuation is complex or contested, and the losses to the investor attributable to changes in the exchange rate could be severe. Accordingly, some BITs specify that the exchange rate to be used for transferring expropriation compensation shall be the rate on the date of expropriation.[433] Under these BITs, the host state bears the risk of any adverse changes in the exchange rate during the delay between the expropriation and the transfer of compensation. For example, the Austria-Armenia BIT, at Article 1(5), reflects the distinction in that it requires that the period available for completion of formalities shall begin in the case of expropriation on the date of expropriation and in the case of transfers on the date on which the request for transfer is submitted. In general, where the expropriation is unlawful, which is the case where compensation is not paid promptly, the compensation awarded by a tribunal must eliminate the consequences of the wrongful act.[434] This may require use of the exchange rate on the date of expropriation.

Some BITs include an exception for certain kinds of ordinary restrictions on the free movement of capital that are unrelated to investment policy. Most common is an exception for restrictions to implement the host state's tax laws. Thus, for example, the U.S. BITs contain an exception for laws imposing withholding taxes,[435] while other BITs specify that taxes must be paid prior to transfer.[436] Other exceptions are for equitable, good faith, nondiscriminatory measures to protect the rights of creditors,[437] to regulate the securities market,[438] to enforce the criminal laws,[439] and to enforce judgments.[440]

Many BITs also provide that transfers shall be in accordance with the exchange regulations in force.[441] This language, if interpreted broadly, could vitiate the basic

---

432 *See, e.g.*, Finland-Armenia BIT, Art. 7(4).

433 *See, e.g.*, United States-Argentina BIT, Art. IV(1).

434 *See* Section 6.5.3.4.

435 *See, e.g.*, United States-Argentina BIT, Art. V(3).

436 *See, e.g.*, Italy-Nicaragua BIT, Art. VI(1)-(2); Switzerland-Algeria BIT, Art. 5(3).

437 *See, e.g.*, Austria-Armenia BIT, Art. 7(3); Mexico-Iceland BIT, Art. 6(3).

438 *See, e.g.*, Austria-Armenia BIT, Art. 7(3); Mexico-Iceland BIT, Art. 6(3).

439 *See, e.g.*, Austria-Armenia BIT, Art. 7(3); Mexico-Iceland BIT, Art. 6(3).

440 *See, e.g.*, Austria-Armenia BIT, Art. 7(3); Mexico-Iceland BIT, Art. 6(3).

441 *See, e.g.*, United Kingdom-Bosnia-Herzegovina BIT, Art. 6; Netherlands-Ethiopia BIT, Art. 5(2); Denmark-Ethiopia BIT, Art. 7(2) ("pursuant to the exchange regulations in force . . .

guarantees provided by the transfers provisions, such as where the exchange regulations include extensive exchange controls. Whether such a result is intended ultimately must be determined by the specific language of each provision. BITs often do not include explicit language indicating that this clause prevails over the rest of the provision, but some BITs do.[442] Other BITs state explicitly that the exchange regulations shall not impair the right of free transfer.[443] Some BITs impose restrictions on the fees that can be charged.[444]

Where an investor seeks to transfer a large amount, the host state may not have enough foreign currency to supply the investor's request, while also continuing to satisfy other needs for foreign exchange. Accordingly, some BITs include an exception allowing a host state to derogate from its obligation of free transfer in such circumstances. This exception typically is subject to certain conditions. Thus, the exception must identify the circumstances in which it applies and the conditions that govern its application.

Several different formulations are used to identify the circumstances in which the exception applies. Various BITs apply the exception, for example, when the host state experiences "serious balance of payments difficulties or the threat thereof"[445] or when foreign exchange reserves are at "very low levels."[446] Another formulation triggers the exception where capital movements "cause or threaten to cause serious difficulties for macroeconomic management, in particular, monetary and exchange rate policies."[447]

The applicable conditions also vary, but certain conditions are typical. First, the host state sometimes is required to notify promptly the other party of the restriction.[448] Second, the duration of the permitted delay is usually specified,[449] although the specification may be only that the exceptional measures shall be discontinued as soon as conditions permit.[450] Some BITs also require that a portion of the amount be transferable at intervals during the delay. For example, if a delay is permitted for a period of

---

in conformity with paragraph 1 and 2 of this Article"); Switzerland-Algeria BIT, Art. 5(2); Thailand-Argentina BIT, Art. 7(2).

442 *But see* Cambodia-Vietnam BIT, Art. VI(1) (right of transfer is "subject to" local law); Chile-Indonesia BIT, Art. V(1) (right of transfers is "within the scope of [each party's] laws and regulations").

443 Thailand-Argentina BIT, Art. 7(2). *See also* Denmark-Ethiopia BIT, Art. 7(2) ("pursuant to the exchange regulations in force . . . in conformity with paragraph 1 and 2 of this Article").

444 *See, e.g.*, BLEU-Sudan BIT, Art. 8(4) ("usual banking costs"); Austria-Armenia BIT, Art. 7(2) ("fair and equitable").

445 *See, e.g.*, Mexico-Iceland BIT, Art. 6(4). *See also* France-Uganda BIT, Art. 6 ("serious balance of payments difficulties and external financial difficulties or the threat thereof"); Japan-Vietnam BIT, Art. 16(1)(a) (same as France-Uganda's); Italy-Nicaragua BIT, Art. VI(4) ("serious balance of payments difficulties"); Singapore-Jordan BIT, Art. 10 ("serious balance of payments and external financial difficulties or threat thereof").

446 *See, e.g.*, United States-Egypt BIT, Protocol, Para. 10; United States-Bangladesh BIT, Protocol, para. 4.

447 Japan-Vietnam BIT, Art. 16(1)(b).

448 *See, e.g.*, France-Uganda BIT, Art. 6.

449 *See, e.g.*, France-Uganda BIT, Art. 6 (six months)

450 *See, e.g.*, Japan-Vietnam BIT, Art. 16(2)(c).

five years, then the BIT may require that transfer of 20 percent of the amount be permitted during each of the five years. [451] Another typical provision is that the delay be on a nondiscriminatory basis.[452] That is, covered investment may not be required to bear a disproportionate share of the burden of the delay. Some BITs require that the host state, during the period of delay, make available to the investor an opportunity to invest the amount sought to be transferred in a way that preserves its value free of exchange risk.[453] Some BITs require that the restrictions be consistent with the IMF Articles of Agreement.[454]

Other exceptions sometimes appear. Some Chilean BITs provide that capital may not be transferred until one year after it has entered the territory of Chile, a provision intended to reduce the volatility of investment.[455]

An exception to the obligation of free transferability may be of little value to a host state unless the host state includes such an exception in every BIT that it concludes. Under the MFN provision of a country's BITs, covered investments are entitled to the protection accorded to investment under any other BIT into which that country enters. If any of a country's BITs guarantees free transfer without exception, then investments covered by other BITs to which that country is a party will be entitled to the same right of transfer without exception.

6.7.2 Origins

In the late nineteenth century, in the period when stocks of foreign investment began to be significant, the need to exchange one currency for another posed few problems for investors. By that time, most of the developed world adhered to the gold standard, under which currencies could be freely exchanged for gold at a specified rate. Thus, the value of a currency was assured and, because all currencies could be exchanged for gold, in effect all currencies were fully convertible into other currencies. Countries did not impose exchange controls.

Thus, only on rare occasions in the nineteenth century did bilateral agreements address issues related to transfers. For example, an 1881 FCN treaty between the United States and Serbia guaranteed the right to "export proceeds of the sale of property" without paying higher duties than nationals of the host state or any third state.[456]

---

451 *See, e.g.*, United Kingdom-Paraguay BIT, Art. 6; United Kingdom-China BIT, Art. 6; United Kingdom-Haiti BIT, Art. 6; United Kingdom-Malta BIT, Art. 6(1); United States-Bangladesh BIT, Protocol, para. 4; United States-Sri Lanka BIT, Protocol, para. 6; United States-Jamaica BIT, Protocol, para. 3.

452 *See, e.g.*, France-Uganda BIT, Art. 6; Italy-Nicaragua BIT, Art. VI(4); Mexico-Iceland BIT, Art. 6(4); Singapore-Jordan BIT, Art. 10. .

453 *See, e.g.*, United States-Egypt BIT, Protocol, Para. 10; United States-Bangladesh BIT, Protocol, Para. 4.

454 *See, e.g.*, France-Uganda BIT, Art. 6; Japan-Vietnam BIT, Art.16(2)(a); Singapore-Jordan BIT, Art. 10.

455 *See, e.g.*, Chile-Indonesia BIT, Protocol; Chile-Lebanon BIT, Protocol.

456 Treaty of Commerce, United States-Serbia, Oct. 14, 1881, Art. II, 22 Stat. 963, T.S. No. 319.

The disadvantage of the gold system was that it required a state to adopt macroeconomic policies that would ensure that its stocks of gold could be maintained at sufficient levels. World War I destroyed the gold standard system because the system's rigidities would have prevented countries from making the expenditures necessary to wage war. After the war, countries adopted highly nationalistic economic policies. Restrictions on trade were accompanied by limitations on inward investment and by exchange controls.[457]

Exchange controls led to the development of black markets in currency and other forms of evasion and thus were often ineffective, particularly in the early years before governments gained experience with enforcement. They also were sometimes counterproductive, as the prospect of exchange controls would prompt capital flight or discourage lending from foreign sources, thus aggravating the problems that they were intended to address.

Nevertheless, belief in the necessity of regulating capital movements remained strong after 1914. The rise of the Great Depression in the early 1930s only reinforced that view, as many policymakers regarded excessive capital mobility as one of the causes of the depression. Thus, in the period after 1914, while protection against capital controls would have been desirable from the perspective of investors, treaty protection was not yet widespread, although some provisions on the subject could be found. For example, a 1938 FCN between the United States and Liberia guaranteed MFN treatment with respect to certain currency transfers.[458]

After the World War II, the developed countries led an effort to rebuild a global economy. Forty-four allied nations met at Bretton Woods, New Hampshire, and created a system of fixed, but adjustable, exchange rates. Floating exchange rates were regarded as conducive to macroeconomic instability. The International Monetary Fund (IMF) was created to lend convertible currency to countries with low foreign exchange reserves to assist them in maintaining their exchange rate.[459] If a country's balance of payments difficulties appeared to be long-term, then the solution was to adjust the exchange rate with IMF approval.

The architects of the new post-war economic system sought free trade. Thus, the General Agreement on Tariffs and Trade began to lower barriers to trade, while the IMF Articles of Agreement[460] sought to eliminate exchange controls on current, that is, trade-related, transactions. Specifically, Article VIII(2) of the agreement prohibited an IMF member from imposing transfer restrictions on current transactions unless it obtained the prior approval of the IMF. Further, under Article VIII(3), a member was

457 *See* Section 2.1.2.

458 Treaty of Friendship, Commerce, and Navigation, United States-Liberia, August 8, 1938, Art. X, 94 Stat. 1739, T.S. No. 956.

459 As explained in Section 6.7.1, countries experiencing a declining exchange rate for their currency can use foreign currency to purchase their own currency and thereby bid up the exchange rate.

460 60 Stat. 1401, T.I.A.S. No. 1501, 2 U.N.T.S. 39, *entered into force* December 27, 1945. For a good general discussion of the IMF Agreement, *see* Kenneth Dam, *The Rules of the Game* (1982).

permitted to engage in discriminatory currency arrangements or multiple currency practices only with such approval.

The architects of the post-war international economic system were more wary of capital mobility and thus restrictions on capital transfers were slower to disappear. Article VI of the IMF Articles of Agreement explicitly authorized countries to impose new controls on capital transactions. Apart from a general wariness about complete capital mobility, many countries lacked sufficient foreign exchange reserves to permit free transfer of payments related to an investment. In recognition of the fact that many members had low foreign exchange reserves, Article XIV permitted members to elect certain "transitional arrangements" that exempted them from the Article VIII obligation of free transfers with respect to current transactions. Members who elected these transitional arrangements could "maintain and adapt" the restrictions that were in force on the date they joined the IMF and, initially, a large portion of the IMF's members availed themselves of the Article XIV exception. In fact, as of 1957, only ten members had accepted the restrictions of Article VIII. The number has continued to grow, however, and today all but approximately twenty of the IMF's members have subjected themselves to the obligations of Article VIII.

As this suggests, in the period after World War II, most countries were unable to guarantee the free transfer of capital and exchange controls were widely used. Indeed, bilateral agreements sometimes called for controlling, rather than liberalizing, capital transfers. For example, a 1949 agreement on commercial and financial relations between Norway and Argentina, at Article 30(c), obligated the parties to consult to control capital transfers and "to prevent transfers that would serve no useful economic purpose."[461] A 1949 agreement on financial relations between Norway and the Netherlands, at Article 4(a), required the parties to agree upon measures to avoid the transfer of gold or U.S. dollars.[462]

The United States, by contrast, sought to use its post-war FCN treaties to restrict the parties' prerogative to impose exchange controls. These FCNs required each party to accord national and MFN treatment to nationals and companies of the other party with respect to currency transfers.[463] In addition, the parties were prohibited from imposing exchange controls that unnecessarily harmed or arbitrarily discriminated against the investment of nationals and companies of the other party.[464] Finally, these FCNs regulated the circumstances under which even nondiscriminatory restrictions on currency transfers could be imposed. The language used, however, was not uniform. One formulation prohibited each party from imposing exchange restrictions except "to the extent necessary to prevent its monetary reserves from falling to a very low level or to

461 Signed August 9, 1949, 42 U.N.T.S. 154.

462 Protocol concerning financial relations and exchange of goods, February 26, 1949, 29 U.N.T.S. 33.

463 *See, e.g.*, Pakistan FCN, *supra* chap. 2, note 188, Art. XII(1); Japan FCN, *supra* chap. 2, note 194, Art. XII(1); Netherlands FCN, *supra* chap. 2, note 179, Art. XII(1).

464 *See, e.g.*, Pakistan FCN, *supra* chap. 2, note 188, Art. XII(4); Japan FCN, *supra* chap. 2, note 194, Art. XII(4); Netherlands FCN, *supra* chap. 2, note 179, Art. XII(4).

effect a moderate increase in very low monetary reserves."[465] Another formulation prohibited exchange restrictions except "to the extent necessary to maintain or restore adequately [a party's] monetary reserves."[466]

Where a party adopted nondiscriminatory exchange controls pursuant to the authorization set forth in either formulation, the post-war U.S. FCNs imposed limitations on the nature and duration of these authorized controls. After assuring the availability of foreign currency sufficient to obtain the goods and services essential to the health and welfare of its people, the party adopting the controls was required to make "reasonable provisions" for the withdrawal, in the currency of the other party, of compensation for expropriation, earnings, and amounts for amortization of loans, depreciation of direct investments and capital transfers, giving consideration to special needs for other transactions. In the event that more than one rate was available, the withdrawals were to be at a rate approved by the IMF. If there was no IMF-approved rate, the parties were to use an "effective rate" that was "just and reasonable."[467]

By their terms, the provisions of the post-war U.S. FCNs relating to exchange controls were subordinate to the IMF Agreement.[468] Thus, a party to a post-war U.S. FCN may impose transfer restrictions approved by the IMF, notwithstanding the provisions described above.

The first BIT, concluded in 1959 between Germany and Pakistan, included a transfers provision. Article 4 required each party to guarantee to nationals and companies of the other party the transfer of the invested capital, of the returns therefrom and, in the event of liquidation, the proceeds of such liquidation. Article 6 further provided that such transfers shall be made "without undue delay and at rates of exchange applicable to current transactions on the date the transfer is made." This rate was to be based on the par value agreed with the IMF. If no such rate existed, then a rate that was just and reasonable was to be used. Germany, in fact, led the movement in Europe toward free convertibility.

No provision on transfers appeared in the Abs-Shawcross convention, which appeared that same year. The International Chamber of Commerce had published an International Code of Fair Treatment for Foreign Investments[469] exactly one decade earlier and its code had contained a provision, at Article 9, requiring free transfer of certain payments related to an investment, but this language does not appear to have influenced the German or other early BITs.

Italy's first BIT, with Guinea, concluded in 1964, guaranteed transfer into a convertible currency of certain returns, as well as the capital deriving from expansions of

---

465 *See, e.g.*, Pakistan FCN, *supra* chap. 2, note 188, Art. XII(2); Japan FCN, *supra* chap. 2, note 194, Art. XII(2).

466 *See, e.g.*, Luxembourg FCN, *supra* chap. 2, note 178, Art. XI(2); Netherlands FCN, *supra* chap. 2, note 179, Art. XII(2).

467 *See, e.g.*, Pakistan FCN, *supra* chap. 2, note 188, Art. XII(3); Netherlands FCN, *supra* chap. 2, note 179, Art. XII(3).

468 *See, e.g.*, Pakistan FCN, *supra* chap. 2, note 188, Art. XII(2); Japan FCN, *supra* chap. 2, note 194, Art. XII(1); Netherlands FCN, *supra* chap. 2, note 179, Art. XII(1).

469 Reprinted in United Nations Conference for Trade and Development, III *International Investment Instruments: A Compendium* 273 (1996).

the original enterprise.[470] The provision applied, however, only to investments established in a convertible currency. A novel clause provided that investments in the form of machinery could be transferred in the form of convertible currency after a period of two years. Within five years, however, the qualification that the investment have been made in a freely convertible currency disappeared.[471] By the mid-1970s, Italy began to describe the list of covered transfers in more precise detail.[472] In that same period, Italy also introduced an exception allowing each party to exercise equitably, in good faith, and in a nondiscriminatory manner the powers conferred by its laws,[473] an exception that appeared in some of its later BITs as well, although limited to situations of balance of payments difficulties and generally accompanied by other conditions.[474] In the mid-1980s, Italy began to include a guarantee of MFN treatment with respect to transfers,[475] which became a common clause in its BITs.[476] Italy also introduced in the late 1980s a clause providing that the right of free transfer applies after the investor has satisfied all its fiscal obligations,[477] which also became a common element in subsequent Italian BITs.[478] Although the transfers provision of the Italian BITs from the beginning typically applied only to an exhaustive list of transfers, in some Italian BITs the provision applies to all transfers relating to an investment.[479]

Denmark, in its first BIT, signed with Madagascar in 1965, guaranteed free transfer of capital as well as the product of the capital and any liquidation proceeds.[480] In 1968, the language was modified to specify the covered transfers more precisely.[481] At the beginning of the 1980s, the provision was qualified by the right of each party to exercise equitably in good faith and on a nondiscriminatory basis the powers conferred by its laws,[482] but this qualification largely disappeared from the provision in the 1990s.[483] In its more recent BITs, Denmark has added language stating explicitly that the right of free transfer extends to payments into and out of the host state's territory.[484]

---

470 Italy-Guinea BIT, Art. 3.

471 *See, e.g.*, Italy-Ivory Coast BIT, Art. 3.

472 *See, e.g.*, Italy-Egypt BIT, Art. IV.

473 *See, e.g.*, Italy-Romania BIT, Art. 5.

474 *See, e.g.*, Italy-Argentina BIT, Art. 6; Italy-Nicaragua BIT, Art. VI.

475 *See, e.g.*, Italy-Tunisia BIT, Art. 5.

476 *See, e.g.*, Italy-Hungary BIT, Art. 6; Italy-Bangladesh BIT, Art. 6. Italy-Vietnam BIT, Art. 6; Italy-Pakistan BIT, Art. 6; Italy-Lebanon BIT, Art. 5.; Italy-Jordan BIT, Art. 6; Italy-Nicaragua BIT, Art. VI.

477 *See, e.g.*, Italy-Hungary BIT, Art. 6; Italy-Bangladesh BIT, Art. 6.

478 *See, e.g.*, Italy-Vietnam BIT, Art. 6; Italy-Venezuela BIT, Italy-Argentina BIT, Art. 6; Italy-Pakistan BIT, Art. 6; Italy-Lebanon BIT, Art. 5; Italy-Nicaragua BIT, Art. VI.

479 *See, e.g.*, Italy-Lebanon BIT, Art. 5; Italy-Croatia BIT, Art. 6; Italy-Nicaragua BIT, Art. VI.

480 Denmark-Madagascar BIT, Art. 6.

481 *See, e.g.*, Denmark-Indonesia BIT, Art. II

482 *See, e.g.*, Denmark-Romania BIT, Art. 5; Denmark-China BIT, Art. 6; Denmark-Republic of Korea BIT, Art. 6.

483 *See, e.g.*, Denmark-Peru BIT, Art. 7; Denmark-Mongolia BIT, Art. 7; Denmark-India BIT, Art. 7; Denmark-Venezuela BIT, Art. 7. *But see, e.g.*, Denmark-Kuwait BIT, Art. 8.

484 *See, e.g.*, Denmark-Croatia BIT, Art. 6; Denmark-Cuba BIT, Art. 8; Denmark-Kyrgyz Republic BIT, Art. 9.

In at least one BIT, Denmark has abandoned the exhaustive list approach and guaranteed free transfer of all payments in connection with an investment, although the provision includes an illustrative list of such payments.[485]

The first Swedish BIT, also concluded in 1965, guaranteed free transfer of capital, returns on capital, and liquidation proceeds.[486] The same provision appeared in the other two BITs concluded by Sweden in the 1960s.[487] When Sweden resumed its BIT program in the late 1970s, however, the right of free transfer was subject to each party's laws.[488] Each party also guaranteed MFN treatment with respect to covered transfers. In the late 1990s, the transfers provision was broadened to apply to any transfers in connection with investment, rather than to an exhaustive list of transfers, and the MFN clause was eliminated.[489] More recent Swedish BITs sometimes state explicitly that the transfers provision applies to transfers into and out of the host state's territory.[490]

The first BITs concluded by Switzerland, the Netherlands, the Belgium-Luxembourg Economic Union (BLEU), and Kuwait in the 1960s required that the host state authorize transfers in accordance with its own laws. In 1967, when the OECD adopted its Draft Convention on the Protection of Foreign Property, the convention contained only a recommendation on transfers. Under Article 4, each party recognized the principle of free transfer of current income and liquidation proceeds. Article 4 explicitly provided that it created no obligation, but did state that each party "will endeavor to grant the necessary authorization" for such transfers.

As this discussion indicates, BITs in the 1960s did not always guarantee free transfer of capital or returns on investment. In the 1970s, however, with the collapse of the Bretton Woods system, many developed countries moved to a system of floating exchange rates, accompanied by the gradual elimination of capital controls. Thus, in the 1970s, more countries began to incorporate an obligation to permit free transfer into the BITs. For example, the 1970 Netherlands-Tanzania BIT required the parties to permit the transfer of liquidation proceeds, without subordinating the right to local law.[491]

Similarly, France in many of its BITs in the 1970s also guaranteed free transfer of capital, returns and expropriation compensation.[492] The French BITs continue to apply generally to an exhaustive list of transfers, although the list has expanded over time.[493] Recent French BITs include a balance of payments exception, permitting equitable,

---

485 *See, e.g.*, Denmark-Ethiopia BIT, Art. 7.

486 *See* Sweden-Ivory Coast BIT, Art. IV.

487 *See, e.g.*, Sweden-Madagascar BIT, Art. 8; Sweden-Senegal BIT, Art. 12.

488 *See, e.g.*, Sweden-Malaysia BIT, Art. 4; Sweden-Yugoslavia BIT, Art. 4; Sweden-Egypt BIT, Art. 4.

489 *See, e.g.*, Sweden-Macedonia BIT, Art. 5; Sweden-South Africa BIT, Art. 5.

490 *See, e.g.*, Sweden-Bosnia-Herzegovina BIT, Art. 6; Sweden-Ecuador BIT, Art. 5; Sweden-Croatia BIT, Art. 5.

491 Netherlands-Tanzania BIT, Art. VIII(1).

492 *See, e.g.*, France-D.R. Congo BIT, Art. 4; France-Malaysia BIT, Art. 4.

493 *See, e.g.*, France-Bosnia-Herzegovina BIT, Art. 7; France-Uganda BIT, Art. 6; France-Bahrain BIT, Art. 6; France-Tajikstan BIT, Art. 7.

nondiscriminatory and good faith restrictions on transfers not to exceed six months and subject to certain other restrictions.[494]

The 1970 BLEU-Indonesia BIT required each party to issue the authorizations necessary to ensure that certain transfers, such as returns, loan payments, and liquidation proceeds, could be effected without delay and on an MFN basis,[495] but it also specified that the exchange shall be pursuant to the exchange regulations in force on the date of transfer.[496] It prohibited any fees other than the usual bank chargers.[497] In the early 1980s, the BLEU transfers provision was broadened to apply to transfers generally, with the list of covered transfers becoming merely illustrative.[498] The BLEU BITs sometimes included an exception allowing a party to exercise equitably and in good faith its powers conferred by law in case of balance of payment difficulties.[499] In concept, the transfers provision of the BLEU BITs has changed little since the 1980s. It applies to "all payments relating to an investment," although the right is defined more clearly as a right to transfer "in a freely convertible currency at the rate applicable on the date transfers are made to spot transactions in the currency used."[500]

The first U.K. BIT, concluded with Egypt in 1975, required each party to guarantee the free transfer of returns from investment, subject to the right of each "in exceptional financial or economic circumstances to exercise equitable and in good faith powers conferred by its laws."[501] A further exception was added to a few BITs, beginning in 1978, allowing the host state to require that transfer of "large amounts" of expropriation compensation be paid in "reasonable installments,"[502] but this exception did not appear widely in the U.K. BITs. The following year, however, the original exception was limited in some BITs to the host state's powers under existing law[503] and a limit of five years was sometimes imposed,[504] accompanied in some instances by a requirement that at least 20 percent of the amount be transferred each year.[505] By the early 1980s, the U.K. BITs sometimes specified that transfer be effected without delay in the convertible currency in which the investment was originally constituted or in any other convertible currency accepted by the investor.[506] Unless otherwise agreed by the investor, transfers were to be made at the rate of exchange applicable on the date

494 *See, e.g.*, France-Bosnia-Herzegovina BIT, Art. 7(3); France-Uganda BIT, Art. 6; France-Bahrain BIT, Art. 6; France-Tajikstan BIT, Art. 7.

495 BLEU-Indonesia BIT, Art. 4.

496 BLEU-Indonesia BIT, Art. 7.

497 BLEU-Indonesia BIT, Art. 4.

498 *See, e.g.*, BLEU-Singapore BIT, Art. 5(1); BLEU- Cameroon BIT, Art. 5(1).

499 *See, e.g.*, BLEU-Bangladesh BIT, Art. 5(1); BLEU-Sri Lanka BIT, Art. 5(1).

500 *See, e.g.*, BLEU-Sudan BIT, Art. 8.

501 United Kingdom-Egypt BIT, Art. 6.

502 *See, e.g.*, United Kingdom-Thailand BIT, Art. 7(2); United Kingdom-Philippines BIT, Art. VII(3); United Kingdom-Sierra Leone BIT, Art. 6(2).

503 *See, e.g.*, United Kingdom-Jordan BIT, Art. 5; United Kingdom-Senegal BIT, Art. 6.

504 *See, e.g.*, United Kingdom-Belize BIT, Art. 6; United Kingdom-St. Lucia BIT, Art. 6.

505 *See, e.g.*, United Kingdom-Paraguay BIT, Art. 6; United Kingdom-China BIT, Art. 6; United Kingdom-Haiti BIT, Art. 6; United Kingdom-Malta BIT, Art. 6(1).

506 *See, e.g.*, United Kingdom-Paraguay BIT, Art. 6; United Kingdom-Costa Rica BIT, Art. VI.

of transfer pursuant to exchange regulations in force.[507] By the end of the 1980s, however, the United Kingdom began to conclude BITs without the clause addressing exceptional circumstances,[508] and the U.K. BIT transfers provision has remained little changed since that time.[509]

The transfers provision of the earliest Austrian BITs in the 1970s and 1980s subordinated the right of free transfer to local law and applied only to an exhaustive list of transfers.[510] By the 1990s, however, Austrian BITs provided for free transfer of all payments in connection with an investment.[511] More recent Austrian BITs specify that such transfers include transfers into and out of the host state's territory.[512]

Finland's earliest BITs in the 1980s included a transfers provision under which the right of free transfer applied to an exhaustive list of transfers and was subject to host-state law,[513] but in some cases with a right of MFN treatment with respect to transfers.[514] Finnish practice began to vary at the end of the decade and in the early 1990s, with some BITs omitting the subordination to local law[515] and some BITs applying to any transfers relating to an investment,[516] in some cases specifying that covered transfers included those into and out of the host state's territory.[517] Typically, the MFN clause no longer appeared. All of these features are characteristic of Finland's more recent BITs.[518]

By the 1980s, the Netherlands BITs no longer routinely subordinated the right of free transfer to local law. In some cases, they included an escape clause to allow derogation from the right of free transfer in defined situations. For example, the 1984 Netherlands-Sri Lanka BIT guaranteed the free transfer into a convertible currency of investment and returns, subject to the right of each party in exceptional balance of payments difficulties and for a limited time to exercise equitably and in good faith and in a manner consistent with its IMF obligations, the powers conferred by its laws

507 *See, e.g.*, United Kingdom-Paraguay BIT, Art. 6; United Kingdom-Belize BIT, Art. 6.

508 *See, e.g.*, United Kingdom-Guyana BIT, Art. 6.

509 *See, e.g.*, United Kingdom-Bosnia and Herzegovina BIT, Art. 6.

510 *See, e.g.*, Austria-Romania BIT, Art. 6; Austria-Malaysia BIT, Art. 5.

511 *See, e.g.*, Austria-Republic of Korea BIT, Art. 5; Austria-Cape Verde BIT, Art. 5; Austria-Chile BIT, Art. 4.

512 *See, e.g.*, Austria-Lebanon BIT, Art. 7; Austria-Libya BIT, Art. 6; Austria-Jordan BIT, Art. 7; Austria-Armenia BIT, Art. 7.

513 *See, e.g.*, Finland-Egypt BIT, Art. 4; Finland-Bulgaria BIT, Art. 4; Finland-Malaysia BIT, Art. 6; Finland-Sri Lanka BIT, Art. 7.

514 *See, e.g.*, Finland-Egypt BIT, Art. 4; Art. 4; Finland-Malaysia BIT, Art. 6; Finland-Sri Lanka BIT, Art. 7.

515 *See, e.g.*, Finland-USSR BIT, Art. 5; Finland-Chile BIT, Art. 4; Finland-Vietnam BIT, Art. 6; Finland-Argentina BIT, Art. 6; Finland-Brazil BIT, Art. 7.

516 *See, e.g.*, Finland-Chile BIT, Art. 4; Finland-Vietnam BIT, Art. 6; Finland-Argentina BIT, Art. 6.

517 *See, e.g.*, Finland-Vietnam BIT, Art. 6; Finland-Argentina BIT, Art. 6; Finland-Brazil BIT, Art. 7.

518 *See, e.g.*, Finland-Belarus BIT, Art. 7; Finland-Algeria BIT, Art. 6; Finland-Armenia BIT, Art. 7.

and regulations.[519] Such powers, however, shall not be used to impede the transfers of profits, interests, dividends, royalties, or fees. Increasingly, however, no such clause appeared.[520]

The U.S. BITs included a strong transfers provision from their inception. The typical provision in the early 1980s guaranteed a right to transfer all payments related to an investment and specified that such transfers included those into as well as out of the host state. Transfers in the earliest U.S. BITs were to be permitted in any currency selected by the investor, but in the 1984 model negotiating text this was changed to any freely convertible currency and, in 1987, to any freely usable currency.[521] Transfers were to be effected at the prevailing market rate of exchange with respect to spot transactions. The U.S. BITs from the beginning included an evolving list of exceptions intended not to permit exchange controls, but to allow routine restrictions such as attachments of funds in satisfaction of creditors and stays in connection with bankruptcy proceedings. In the 1980s, the United States on a number of occasions agreed to escape clauses under which a state could impose temporary restrictions on transfers when its balance of payments reached very low levels, but over time became increasingly unwilling to agree to such exceptions. [522]

Kuwait abandoned the subordination to local law in some of its BITs in the 1980s,[523] and by the 1990s the Kuwaiti BITs guaranteed the free transfer of all payments in connection with an investment into and out the host state's territory.[524]

As this suggests, the transfers provision was one of the slowest to emerge in its developed form. Only in the 1970s did the provision become common in BITs and subordination to local law was routine even in BITs drafted by developed countries into the 1980s and 1990s. These provisions also showed significant diversity of language as they evolved, with exhaustive lists more common than in any other provision except the performance requirements provision. The trend, however, has been toward a gradual broadening of the list of transfers to which the provision applies, often with countries eventually applying it to all transfers related to an investment.

6.7.3 Arbitral Practice

The transfers provision of the BITs has been at issue in only a very few arbitrations and, to date, no tribunal has found a violation of the provision. In *Continental Casualty v. Argentina*, a case arising under the United States-Argentina BIT, the claimant's investment had sought to transfer funds out of Argentina in order to protect them against an impending devaluation. The transfer was prevented by an order of the

---

519 Netherlands-Sri Lanka BIT, Art. 7.

520 *See, e.g.*, Netherlands-Hungary BIT, Art. 5; Netherlands-Uruguay BIT, Art. 5; Netherlands-Bulgaria BIT, Art. 5. Netherlands-Pakistan BIT, Art. 7. Netherlands-Ghana BIT, Art. 5.

521 Kenneth J. Vandevelde, *U.S. International Investment Agreements* 527–534 (2009). .

522 *Id.* at 61, 534–535.

523 *See, e.g.*, Kuwait-Pakistan BIT, Art. 5; Kuwait-Hungary BIT, Art. 8.

524 *See, e.g.*, Kuwait-Czech Republic BIT, Art. 7; Kuwait-Ethiopia BIT, Art. 7; Kuwait-Bulgaria BIT, Art. 8; Kuwait-Croatia BIT, Art. 7.

Argentine government. The tribunal held that the proposed transfer was not a transfer related to an investment and, therefore, it was not guaranteed by the transfers provision. The tribunal's decision seemed to rest largely on the fact that the transfer was not identified in the illustrative list of transfers related to an investment set forth in the BIT. Yet, the list is only illustrative. The tribunal noted as well that the proposed transfer was merely intended to be a short-term placement of the funds outside Argentina and thus should not be considered a transfer related to an investment. Yet, one purpose of the provision is to guarantee the security of the claimant's investment. In the absence of this provision, exchange controls imposed by the host state could force the investor to leave its investment and returns in the host state where they might be of little or no practical value to the investor and where they might suffer from an extended period of devaluation or depreciation. The desire of the claimant's investment to transfer funds out of Argentina to protect their value thus fell squarely within the purpose of the transfers provision. In any event, the transfers provision permits the investor to transfer its investment and returns at any time, without limitation as to the motivation for the transfer. For example, the investor may wish to invest the funds elsewhere or to consume them. In this case, it wished to invest them elsewhere, albeit only temporarily. Nothing in the text of the BIT, however, suggests that funds may be transferred out of the host country only if they are to remain outside the country for a specified period of time.[525]

The tribunal no doubt sympathized with Argentina's efforts to prevent capital flight during a time of financial crisis. Many BITs contain exceptions to their transfers provisions for exigent circumstances, such as low foreign currency reserves. The United States-Argentina BIT, however, contains no such exception. A BIT should not be interpreted to include what appears to be an implied exception for transfers for short-term investments of the funds, particularly if the BIT does not contain language that places any significance on the duration of an investment.

In *Metalpar v. Argentina*, a case arising under the Chile-Argentina BIT, the tribunal rejected a claim that Argentina's emergency decree violated the transfers provision. The decree required that the claimant obtain prior approval of the central bank for certain transfers. The tribunal found that the claimant had not sought the necessary approval.[526]

6.8 PRESERVATION OF RIGHTS

One BIT provision is intended not to increase the security of investment, but to ensure that the BIT does not detract from existing investment protection. That is, it ensures

525 In *Saluka Investments v. Czech Republic*, a case arising under the Netherlands-Czech Republic BIT, the tribunal in a different context held that an investor has no duty to disclose its ultimate objectives in making a particular investment. Partial Award, para. 232. The tribunal noted that ultimate objectives may be speculative, subject to change, and not susceptible to precise articulation. As this suggests, BIT protection for an investment should not depend upon the investor's investment strategy.

526 Award, para. 179.

that the BITs do not diminish the security provided by other instruments. Specifically, many BITs include a preservation of rights provision stating that, in the event that investment is entitled to more favorable treatment under another legal instrument, that other instrument shall prevail over the BIT.[527] Thus, the BIT shall not diminish the rights to which covered investment is otherwise entitled.

The preservation of rights provision generally does not incorporate these other obligations into the BIT. Rather, its purpose is to leave these other obligations undisturbed. They continue as if the BIT did not exist.

A preservation of rights provision was included in the 1959 Abs-Shawcross convention. Article VI of the convention provided that "[t]he provisions of this Convention shall not prejudice the application of any present or future treaty or municipal law under which more favourable treatment is accorded to nationals of any of the Parties."

The preservation of rights provision also appeared in the BITs from the very beginning. The first BIT, that concluded in 1959 between Germany and Pakistan, included such a provision, where it appeared with the observance of obligations provision. The link between the two provisions is simply that both deal with the security of host state obligations existing outside the BIT. The preservation of rights provision ensures that such obligations are not diminished by the BIT. The observance of obligations provision goes further and renders obligations with respect to an investment enforceable under the BIT. BITs eventually uncoupled the two provisions, often placing the observance of obligations provision with other absolute standards of treatment, such as fair and equitable treatment and full protection and security, while placing the preservation of rights provision in a separate article.

The preservation of rights provision has been discussed in several awards. In these cases, the tribunals have rejected creative arguments by disputants that ascribed to this provision a meaning different from that evident in its ordinary language. Rather, the tribunals have interpreted the provision in accordance with its clear meaning.

In *SGS v. Philippines*, a case arising under the Switzerland-Philippines BIT, the tribunal noted that the preservation of rights provision merely "provid[es] that legislative provisions or international law rules more favorable to an investor shall to that extent 'prevail over this Agreement'."[528] Thus, the provision did not impose any additional obligations on the host state.

Similarly, in *Yaung Chi Oo Trading v. Myanmar*, a case arising under the 1987 ASEAN Agreement for the Promotion and Protection of Investment, the tribunal rejected the argument that the preservation of rights provision of the 1998 Framework Agreement on the ASEAN Investment Area had the effect of expanding the coverage

---

527 *See, e.g.*, Netherlands-Ethiopia BIT, Art. 3(4); BLEU-Sudan, Art. 10; United Kingdom-Bosnia-Herzegovina BIT, Art. 11; Austria-Armenia BIT, Art. 9(2); Thailand-Argentina BIT, Art. 11; Cambodia-Vietnam BIT, Art. XI; Chile-Indonesia BIT, Art. XI; Sweden-Kazakhstan BIT, Art. 10(2); Finland-Armenia BIT, Art. 12(2); Australia-India BIT, Art. 16; Germany-Timor-Leste BIT, Art. 8; France-Uganda BIT, Art. 9; Chile-Lebanon BIT, Art. XI; India-Indonesia BIT, Art. 13.

528 Decision on Jurisdiction, para. 114.

of the 1987 agreement. Rather, the provision "simply makes clear that in relation to any investment which is covered by both Agreements, the investor is entitled to the benefit of both and thus of the most beneficial treatment afforded by either."[529] Accordingly, the tribunal concluded that the preservation of rights provision of the framework agreement did "not give the Claimant any new rights in relation to the present claim."[530]

In *Salini v. Jordan*, a case arising under the Italy-Jordan BIT, the tribunal cited *SGS* and *Yaung Chi Oo* with approval and held that the preservation of rights provision is "a kind of without prejudice clause."[531] Accordingly, "it could not have the effect of incorporating the commitments it mentions into the BIT."[532]

In *LG&E v. Argentina*, a case arising under the United States-Argentina BIT, Argentina raised the preservation of rights provision as an objection to jurisdiction. In a very brief discussion, the tribunal declared the provision to be irrelevant. The tribunal explained that the provision "is a right addressed to the investor and not the host State."[533]

---

529 Award, para. 82.

530 *Id.*

531 Decision on Jurisdiction, para. 130. The quoted phrase was taken from the paragraph 114 of the decision on jurisdiction in *SGS v. Philippines*, discussed above in the text,

532 *Id.*

533 Decision on Jurisdiction, para. 56.

Chapter 7

Nondiscrimination

7.1 INTRODUCTION

The principle of nondiscrimination is the heart of investment neutrality, one of the key elements of liberal economic theory. Investment flows, under the principle of investment neutrality, should be allocated by market forces rather than by political intervention. In theory, this promotes the most efficient allocation of resources and promotes economic development. A nondiscriminatory investment regime also imposes fewer transaction costs on the host state because its investment regime is necessarily more uniform across different investments and investors.

The principle of nondiscrimination is additionally an important element of a favorable investment climate. At a minimum, it permits the investor to operate free of competitive disadvantages, that is, on a level playing field, to use the metaphor from Chapter 1. In some cases, it may improve the host state's treatment of covered investments or investors because the beneficiary of the protection gains the favorable treatment accorded to host-state investors or investors of favored third countries. That is, the principle of nondiscrimination multiplies the effects of host-state policies favoring particular investments or investors by requiring the extension of those policies to all investments or investors entitled to nondiscrimination.

The principle of nondiscrimination is also a key element of the rule of law. The rule of law contemplates that like cases will be treated in a like manner, that all actors will receive equal justice under the law.

Finally, the principle of nondiscrimination tends to promote other core principles of the BIT—reasonableness, transparency, and security—because the host state's treatment of its own nationals in particular is likely to be rational, visible and relatively stable.

Although nondiscrimination can promote other BIT principles, the relationship is not necessarily reciprocal. Other BIT principles may vitiate to some degree the principle of nondiscrimination because these other principles may provide protection for covered investment that exceeds the protection provided to other investment, including domestic investment. For example, host-state law may not require prompt, adequate, and effective compensation for expropriation or may not guarantee a right of free transfer of payments related to investment, with the result that covered investment has greater security than domestic investment. Even where the host state's laws are strongly protective of the security of all investment, BITs provide covered investors uniquely with the right to investor-state arbitration. While BITs purport through the nondiscrimination principle to level the playing field, the other principles in some respects may tilt the playing field in favor of the covered investor or investment. Although this result may be inconsistent with the principle of nondiscrimination, it is not inconsistent with any of the BIT provisions, which guarantee nondiscriminatory treatment only for covered investments and investors.

The principle of nondiscrimination does not prohibit all differences between the treatment of covered investment and the treatment of other investment. Such a prohibition would eviscerate the host state's legitimate regulatory authority, which necessitates treating differently situated investments dissimilarly. For example, competition policy may require prohibiting the merger of two large investments, but not the merger of two much smaller investments.

Thus, the principle of nondiscrimination prohibits unreasonable discriminations. A discrimination is unreasonable if it is unrelated to a legitimate regulatory interest. For example, in the context of the BITs, preferring one investment over another on the grounds of nationality is not a legitimate regulatory interest.

Tribunals have used two different approaches for distinguishing between permissible and impermissible discriminations. In some cases, they have held explicitly that the nondiscrimination principle prohibits only unreasonable discriminations. This approach is most likely to be used in the case of the fair and equitable treatment provision or the unreasonable or discriminatory measures provision. In other cases, they have held that the nondiscrimination principle prohibits only discriminations between covered investment and certain selected investments, often termed "comparators." This approach is most often used in the case of a national or MFN treatment provision, particularly where the provision requires equivalent treatment of investments "in like circumstances" (or similar language). Thus, the appropriate comparators are those in like circumstances with the covered investment. An investment and a comparator may be considered in like circumstances if there is no legitimate regulatory reason for treating them differently. Either approach, however, may be used with any kind of nondiscrimination provision. Either approach permits the host state to treat investments differently for legitimate regulatory reasons, but not on the basis of their nationality or for other arbitrary reasons.

Ultimately, both approaches pose the same question: whether the host state has a legitimate reason to treat a covered investment differently than another investment. If so, a tribunal may say that the other investment is not in like circumstances with the covered investment or that the discrimination is reasonable. Both characterizations of the situation should rest on the same analysis.

Some tribunals may consider, first, whether the covered investment and the comparator are in like circumstances and then, second, whether any discrimination between them is reasonable. That is, they may employ both approaches. As the discussion indicates, they, in effect, ask the same question twice.

7.2 MOST FAVORED NATION AND NATIONAL TREATMENT

7.2.1 Structure and Policy

The great majority of BITs include guarantees of national and most favored nation (MFN) treatment for covered investments or investors.[1] National treatment provisions appear somewhat less frequently than MFN treatment provisions. National and MFN treatment provisions have parallel structures and thus they will be discussed together to the extent possible.

The national and MFN treatment provisions always comprise at least three components: a beneficiary, a comparator, and an obligation of equivalency. Some provisions include a fourth component defining their scope of application. Most such provisions also contain a fifth component identifying special exceptions to which one or both obligations are subject.

The beneficiary is the person or asset entitled to national or MFN treatment. In BITs, the beneficiary of the MFN and national treatment provisions is usually the investment,[2] but in some provisions it is the investor.[3] The definitions of investment and investor thus are critical to determining which persons or assets are protected. Clearly, a BIT that guarantees nondiscrimination to both the investor and the investment provides a more favorable investment climate.

Where a BIT guarantees a right of establishment, ideally the investor should be named as a beneficiary. Although an entity that qualifies as an investment may seek to establish an investment, often the entity establishing an investment falls within the definition of a covered investor but not of a covered investment. If the investor is not a beneficiary of the standard, then any commitment of MFN (or national) treatment with respect to establishment may be lost as a practical matter. If only an investment is a beneficiary and the host state denies permission to establish the investment, no entity entitled to claim the protection of the national of MFN treatment provision comes into existence. Other situations also may exist where the host state's conduct is directed at the investor rather than the investment and thus naming the investor as a beneficiary could expand the scope of treaty protection.[4]

---

1 On National Treatment generally, *see* Andrea K. Bjorklund, "National Treatment," in *Standards of Investment Protection* (August Reinisch, 2008). On MFN treatment generally, *see* Andreas P. Ziegler, "Most-Favoured-Nation (MFN) Treatment," in *id.* and Pia Acconci, "Most-Favoured-Nation Treatment," in *The Oxford Handbook of International Investment Law* (Peter Muchlinski, Frederico Ortino, and Christoph Schreuer, eds. 2008).

2 *See, e.g.*, United Kingdom-Bosnia-Herzegovina BIT, Art. 3(1); Netherlands-Ethiopia, Art. 3(2); Thailand-Argentina BIT, Art. 4(1); Australia-India, Art. 4(1)–(2); Sweden-Kazakhstan BIT, Art. 3(1); Mexico-Iceland BIT, Art. 3(2); Germany-Timor-Leste, Art. 3(1); Canada-Uruguay BIT, Art. IV(1); Cambodia-Vietnam BIT, Art. III(2); Egypt-Zambia, Art. 3(1); (MFN only); Chile-Indonesia BIT, Art. IV(2).

3 *See, e.g.*, BLEU-Sudan BIT, Art. 4(1); Austria-Armenia BIT, Art. 3(3); Thailand-Argentina BIT, Art. 4(2); Australia-India, Art. 4(3) (MFN only); Mexico-Iceland BIT, Art. 3((3); Germany-Timor-Leste, Art. 3(2); Canada-Uruguay BIT, Art. IV(2); United Kingdom-Bosnia-Herzegovina BIT, Art. 3(2); Egypt-Zambia BIT, Art. 3(2) (MFN only).

4 For an example, *see* the discussion of *RosInvestCo v. Russia* in Section 7.2.3.

The comparator is the person or asset the treatment of which sets the standard that must be met. Once again, the definitions of the terms "investor" and "investment" are critical, but here they are critical for purposes of establishing the content of the standard, rather than the scope of its application. If an entity is not an investor or an investment, then the host state's treatment of that entity is not relevant for purposes of establishing the content of the MFN or national treatment standard. For example, if the term "investor" includes state enterprises, then the host state's treatment of its own state enterprises defines the treatment that must be accorded to a covered investor that is entitled to national treatment. If state enterprises are excluded, however, then the host state may discriminate in favor of its own state enterprises without violating the national treatment provision.

Two general problems arise with respect to identifying the comparator. The first problem is determining whether every potential comparator that falls within the literal language of the provision should be treated as relevant. Thus, for example, it must be determined whether national treatment requires that covered investment be treated as favorably as any investment of the host state or only certain investment of the host state. Some BITs explicitly address this question by providing that the appropriate comparator is one that is "in like situations"[5] or "in like circumstances"[6] with the beneficiary. Such language, however, is absent from most BITs.

Yet, it would seem that the concept of MFN and national treatment assumes that the treatment of covered investment shall be compared only to the treatment of comparable investments. The purpose of national treatment, for example, does not require that covered investment be treated as favorably as every investment in the host state in every respect. For example, a large automobile manufacturing plant located in a major urban area and owned by a covered investor might be required to satisfy various municipal regulations on matters such as land use that would not be applied to a small domestically owned grocery store located in a remote rural area. Read literally, the national treatment standard would seem to be violated in such a case because the covered investment was treated less favorably than a domestic investment. Yet, the different treatment can be justified by the fact that the covered investment and the domestic investment are not in the same situation. They are in different sectors of the economy, they are on different scales, and they are situated in areas of radically different population densities. Nor is the automobile plant being put at a competitive disadvantage. The host state can be allowed the different treatment based on the dissimilar circumstances of the two investments without defeating any of the purposes of the national treatment provision. To apply the national treatment standard literally and to require that the two investments be treated the same would impose a senseless restriction on host-state regulatory discretion. As this example illustrates, the MFN and national treatment standards not only may, but must, be interpreted to require that the treatment of covered investment or investors be evaluated only with respect to the treatment of comparable investments or investors. Even where a phrase such as "in like situations" or "in like

---

5 *See, e.g.*, United States-Argentina BIT, Art. II(1).

6 *See, e.g.*, Mexico-Iceland BIT, Art. 3(2)–(3); Canada-Uruguay BIT, Art. IV; Japan-Vietnam BIT, Art. 2.

circumstances" does not appear in the provision, such a limitation should be treated as implicit.

The BITs provide little guidance concerning the meaning of the phrase "in like situations" or "in like circumstances," which should be treated as synonymous.[7] It has been argued that, in the case of national treatment, for example, the ideal comparator is an investment that is identical to the beneficiary in every respect except nationality. Given that it may not be possible to find such a comparator, this view regards choosing the comparator that is most like the beneficiary as a second-best solution. In other words, the phrase "in like circumstances" would be interpreted as if it read "in the most like circumstances." Obviously, the effect of this interpretation is potentially to weaken the provision by eliminating a large number of comparators. The covered investment may have been treated less favorably than a large number of potential comparators, but if it is treated no less favorably than the closest comparator then no violation of the standard would be found. Further, where a covered investment is comparable to other investments in different ways, the question is of which is the most comparable may not have an obvious solution.

Alternatively, one might treat as a comparator any investment in the same sector of the economy. The argument in favor of this approach is that one purpose of the relative standards is to ensure a level playing field among competitors and this purpose is served by prohibiting discrimination among competitors. Presumably, an investment's competitors are other investments in the same sector of the economy. Equating "like circumstances" with operating in the same sector of the economy, however, presents some potential difficulties. One is that no other investment in the same sector may exist. Another is that sectors can be described at different levels of generality, which allows the test to be manipulated easily.[8] In addition, ensuring competitive equality does not exhaust the purpose of a nondiscrimination provision. For example, a nondiscrimination provision also promotes a favorable investment climate by prohibiting at least some forms of arbitrary treatment and it promotes the rule of law by requiring equal treatment under the law.

A better approach is to consider whether the differences between the beneficiary and the comparator are relevant to the host state's legitimate regulatory objectives. A regulatory objective is legitimate only to the extent that it is consistent with BIT principles. For example, if a covered investment and a comparator were subject to different environmental regulations, one would consider whether the different treatment of the investment and the comparator was based on a legitimate regulatory objective. Environmental preservation would be such an objective, while economic protectionism would not be. If the different treatment was based on environmental preservation, then the beneficiary and the comparator would be regarded as in unlike circumstances and the different treatment would not violate the MFN or national treatment standard. If the different treatment was based on economic protectionist objectives, then the beneficiary and comparator would be regarded as in like circumstances because the

---

7 The two appear interchangeable, for example, in U.S. BIT practice. *See* Kenneth J. Vandevelde, *U.S. International Investment Agreements* 252 (2009).

8 *See* Section 7.2.3.

difference was not related to a legitimate regulatory objective. Treating them differently would violate the national or MFN treatment provision.

As this suggests, where no obvious comparator exists, the covered investment or investor should be permitted to show a violation of the national or MFN treatment provision by demonstrating that its treatment was the result of a discriminatory motive. For example, if an investment was subjected to adverse treatment because it was a foreign investment, then it would seem clear that the investment did not receive national treatment. A discriminatory motive should be provable by circumstantial evidence, such as the inability of the host state to articulate a legitimate nondiscriminatory motive for its treatment of the investment.

The second general problem raised by the identification of the comparator is that the host state may treat some comparators more favorably than others. For example, a host state may discriminate among its own investments. Assuming that all are appropriate comparators, the question arises as to which potential comparator establishes the required standard of treatment: the one receiving the best treatment, the one receiving the worst treatment, or some other comparator, such as one receiving the typical treatment. As a practical matter, this problem may arise infrequently because many of the putative comparators might be found not to be in like circumstances with the beneficiary. Where it does arise, however, BITs rarely provide any explicit guidance.

The solution may turn on the level of generality at which one defines the purpose of the MFN and national treatment standards. At a very low level of generality, the purpose of the MFN and national treatment provisions is to preclude discrimination based on nationality. On that assumption, the most poorly treated comparator would set the standard. As long as the beneficiary were treated no less favorably than a national investment or an investment of the most favored nation, one could not say that the beneficiary had been treated unfavorably on the basis of nationality.

At a higher level of generality, the purpose of the MFN and national treatment provisions, like any nondiscrimination provision, is to establish a level playing field and thereby promote market-based allocations of capital as well as a rules-based investment regime. On that assumption, the most poorly treated comparator would not set the standard because treatment in accordance with that standard would not level the playing field between the beneficiary and other potential comparators.

This is an issue with respect to which clarification in the text of the BIT would be desirable. In fact, a few BITs do provide some clarification with respect to this issue in one context. The context is that of a federal system in which political subdivisions may discriminate against investments from other political subdivisions. For example, in the case of the United States, California might enact a law that provided California corporations with more favorable treatment than corporations of the other 49 states. The U.S. BITs have adopted explicit language providing that, in this situation, the appropriate comparator for purposes of the national treatment provision is investments of the other political subdivisions.[9] Thus, in the example, California would be required to accord covered investment with treatment no less favorable than that which it accords

9 *See, e.g.*, United States-Argentina BIT, Art. II(8).

to investment of any of the other 49 U.S. states, rather than the treatment it accords to California investments. Interestingly, the NAFTA adopts the contrary approach. National treatment under the NAFTA requires treatment no less favorable than the political subdivision provides to its own investments.[10] Thus, California would be required to treat covered investment as favorably as it treats California investment. Under the NAFTA approach, the national treatment standard favors covered investment over some domestic investment.

The third component of a relative standard is the equivalency requirement. This component of the standard identifies the way in which the beneficiary must be treated relative to the comparator. The most common formulation requires that the beneficiary receive treatment "no less favorable" than that accorded to the comparator.[11] This language permits the beneficiary to be treated more favorably than the comparator. It also permits the beneficiary to receive different treatment than the comparator, provided that the different treatment is not less favorable. Cases may arise in which a dispute exists as to whether the different treatment accorded to covered investment is less favorable.

In the case where an MFN provision requires no less favorable treatment and the host state provides more favorable treatment to the covered investment than it accords to investment of other nations, the investment of these other nations can be expected to invoke the MFN provision of BITs applicable to them so as to elevate the treatment they receive. Thus, in a setting where all foreign investment is covered by an MFN treatment provision, an investment of one foreign nationality may be provided more favorable treatment than investment of other foreign nationalities, but to do so will trigger an obligation to elevate the treatment of all other foreign investment. That is, where all investment has the benefit of MFN treatment, it is actually not possible, at least in theory, to treat one investment more favorably than another. Each time the treatment of one investment is raised above the level accorded to other investments, those other investments become entitled to that same treatment.

Some BITs require that the beneficiary receive "the treatment" that the comparator receives.[12] This language does not preclude providing the beneficiary with more favorable treatment. That is, the host state is obligated to provide the same treatment, not prohibited from providing better treatment. This formulation, however, does seem to preclude providing treatment that is different, but equally favorable.[13]

As between these two formulations, the "no less favorable" formulation would seem preferable. First, it provides the host state with the flexibility to make inconsequential

---

10 *See* NAFTA Art. 1102(3).

11 *See, e.g.*, BLEU-Sudan BIT, Art. 4(2); Netherlands-Ethiopia BIT, Art. 3(2); United Kingdom-Bosnia-Herzegovina BIT, Art. 3; Finland-Armenia BIT, Art. 3(1); Austria-Armenia BIT, Art. 3(3); Denmark-Ethiopia BIT, Art. 3; Thailand-Argentina BIT, Art. 4(1); Cambodia-Vietnam BIT, Art. III(2); Chile-Indonesia BIT, Art. IV(2).

12 *See, e.g.*, BLEU-Sudan BIT, Art. 4(1).

13 Compare Article XVII of the General Agreement on Trade in Services, which explicitly provides that treatment no less favorable may include formally identical or formally different treatment, provided that it does not modify the conditions of competition in favor of service suppliers of the member according the treatment.

distinctions, which may serve administrative convenience in some cases. At the same time, the requirement of no less favorable treatment implies the possibility of more favorable treatment, language that may be more appealing to investors than the alternative formulation, which connotes treatment that is neither better nor worse, although, as has been discussed, it permits better treatment. In some cases, however, the "no less favorable treatment" formulation is not politically acceptable to one of the BIT parties, at least in the context of national treatment, precisely because of its connotation that foreign investment may receive better treatment than domestic investment.

An ambiguity exists with respect to the scope of the word "treatment." In one sense, the word could be read narrowly to refer to specific benefits provided to the comparator. In another sense, the word could be read more broadly to refer to the entire relationship between the host state and the comparator.

An example will illustrate the potential significance of this ambiguity. As will be discussed in greater detail below, one function of an MFN treatment provision is to require the host state granting MFN treatment under a BIT to accord to covered investment the same benefits guaranteed by that same host state under any other BIT to which it is a party. Thus, if the treaty containing the MFN treatment provision, sometimes described by commentators as "the basic treaty,"[14] does not include a guarantee of fair and equitable treatment, a covered investment nevertheless would be entitled to fair and equitable treatment if the host state has promised fair and equitable treatment to investments under any other BIT. Where the term "treatment" is given its narrow reading, the benefit of fair and equitable treatment is considered "the treatment" guaranteed by the MFN treatment provision. Yet, the BIT with the fair and equitable treatment standard may include various other provisions that qualify the standard, such as an exception for measures necessary to protect a state's essential security interests. Where th term "treatment" is given its broad reading, the entire relationship between the host country and the investment created by the BIT with fair and equitable treatment standard would be considered "the treatment." Thus, covered investment under the basic treaty would be entitled to fair and equitable treatment qualified by the essential security interests exception.

On purely textual grounds, either reading of the term "treatment" is defensible. The practice of tribunals, however, is to employ the narrow reading of the term.[15] The explanation may be a practical one. The broader the term "treatment" is read, the more difficult it is to determine whether the beneficiary has been denied the treatment to which it is entitled. In the example above, the effect of reading the term "treatment" broadly, taken to its logical conclusion, would be to substitute the entire BIT applicable to the comparator for the BIT applicable to the beneficiary. As a result of the narrow reading of the term "treatment," covered investments may claim specific benefits granted by the host state to other investments, without necessarily being subject to accompanying

---

14 This terminology was employed by the International Court of Justice in the *Case Concerning the Anglo-Iranian Oil Company* (United Kingdom v. Iran), 1952 I.C.J. Rep. 93.

15 *See Siemens v. Argentina* (Germany-Argentina BIT), Decision on Jurisdiction, para. 120, where this problem is discussed explicitly.

detriments to which those other investments are subject. Thus, a promise of no less favorable treatment in practical effect may be a promise of more favorable treatment.

The term "treatment" is ambiguous not only as to its scope, but also as to its content. For example, in the case of the MFN treatment provision, the issue has arisen whether the term refers to the treatment accorded to comparators under the substantive provisions of other BITs or whether it refers to the treatment accorded to comparators under the procedural as well as the substantive provisions of other BITs. On textual grounds, the word "treatment" certainly could include treatment with respect to procedural rights as well as with respect to substantive rights. Indeed, in a positivist conception of law in which rights exist only to the extent that they are enforceable, the distinction between substantive and procedural rights may be of no practical significance and thus a reading of treatment that included one and not the other could be seen as arbitrary. Certainly, the BIT principle of due process, which is reflected in the procedural provisions of the BITs, is as important as other BIT principles, such as security, nondiscrimination, and reasonableness. Thus, reading the MFN treatment provision to apply to rights of security granted by another BIT, but not to rights of due process, also seems arbitrary. Yet, as will be seen in Section 7.2.3, tribunals are divided with respect to the question of whether the term "treatment" includes procedural rights. Some host states have argued that, regardless of the treaty language, they never intended the term "treatment" to refer to procedural rights. Further, as also discussed below and in Section 7.2.3, disputes provisions of a BIT are often complex and thus applying a single clause of the disputes provision of one BIT to a disputes process prescribed by another BIT potentially threatens the coherence of the latter BIT.

A fourth component of the national and MFN treatment provisions that sometimes appears is language establishing the scope of these provisions. Although the provision often simply requires national or MFN "treatment," in some BITs the concept of treatment is qualified by additional language. The most common qualification provides that national and MFN treatment is required with respect to the management, maintenance, operation, use, enjoyment, and sale or other disposal of the investment, or words to similar effect. This qualification may apply either where the beneficiary is the investor,[16] or where it is the investment.[17] One effect of this language, where it applies to the investor, is to clarify that the investor is protected in its capacity as an investor. That is, the investor is entitled to national or MFN treatment only where it is engaged in activities in connection with investment. Another effect of this language may be to exclude dispute resolution provisions from the scope of the MFN treatment provision.[18] Thus, where this language appears, an investor or investment protected under one BIT may not be entitled to the benefit of the investor-state disputes provision in another BIT concluded by the host country.

---

16 *See, e.g.*, BLEU-Sudan BIT, Art. 4(1); Austria-Armenia BIT, Art. 3(3); Thailand-Argentina BIT, Art. 4(2); Australia-India, Art. 4(3) (MFN treatment only); Mexico-Iceland BIT, Art. 3(3); Germany-Timor-Leste, Art. 3(2); Canada-Uruguay BIT, Art. IV(2).

17 Austria-Armenia BIT, Art. 3(3); United Kingdom-Bosnia-Herzegovina BIT, Art. 3(2).

18 *See* Section 7.2.3.

Occasionally, the qualifying language emphasizes the breadth of the provision's scope, such as where the provision applies to "all matters relating to the treatment of investment"[19] Some of the U.K. BITs include language confirming that the treatment includes treatment under certain enumerated articles of the BIT, among which are the articles on dispute resolution.[20]

In some BITs, the qualifying language specifies that the national and MFN treatment obligations apply to the establishment of investment, as well as the treatment of investment once established.[21] Thus, these BITs guarantee to covered investors or investments the right to establish or acquire investment in any case where host state (in the case of national treatment) or third state (in the case of MFN treatment) investors are entitled to establish or acquire investment.

A fifth component of the national and MFN treatment provisions that appears in many BITs comprises a set of exceptions. The MFN and national treatment provisions are more commonly subject to exceptions than other provision of the BITs. Two exceptions appear widely in BITs.

First, these provisions commonly are subject to an exception for matters of taxation. The most common version of this exception provides that the MFN treatment provision does not apply to any advantage granted pursuant to an international agreement relating wholly or mainly to taxation.[22] Many countries have concluded bilateral taxation treaties, especially treaties to prevent double taxation, and the effect of this formulation of the taxation exception is to exclude concessions made in those treaties from the MFN treatment or, in some cases, national treatment, obligation. Indeed, in some cases, the BIT explicitly excludes advantages granted under a double taxation treaty,[23] as opposed to taxation treaties generally. The stipulation that the treaty apply "mainly" to taxation ensures that concessions under a treaty are not excluded from the scope of the MFN treatment provision merely because of a few references to taxation in the treaty. For example, the BITs themselves occasionally allude to matters of taxation, if only to exclude them, and those references do not convert the BITs to agreements dealing with taxation that are outside the scope of BIT MFN provisions. Another common version of this exception is broader and applies not only to advantages conferred by international agreements, but also advantages conferred by domestic legislation relating

---

19 *See, e.g.*, BLEU-Sudan BIT, Art. 4(1).

20 *See, e.g.*, United Kingdom-Bosnia-Herzegovina BIT, Art. 3(3).

21 *See* Section 9.3.1.

22 *See, e.g.*, Denmark-Ethiopia BIT, Art. 4; United Kingdom-Bosnia-Herzegovina BIT, Art. 7; Thailand-Argentina BIT, Art. 5; Sweden-Kazakhstan BIT, Art. 3(3); Indonesia-India, Art. 4(2); Chile-Indonesia BIT, Art. IV(3); Finland-Thailand BIT, Art. 4(2); Germany-Timor-Leste, Art. 3(4) (no qualifying language requiring that the agreement relate wholly or mainly to taxation); Austria-Armenia BIT, Art. 3(4) (no qualifying language requiring that the agreement relate wholly or mainly to taxation).

23 *See, e.g.*, Netherlands-Ethiopia, Art. 4; Australia-India, Art. 4(4); Egypt-Zambia, Art. 3(3); Germany-Timor-Leste, Art. 3(3).

wholly or mainly to taxation.[24] Some BITs simply exclude "tax matters" from the scope of these provisions.[25]

The taxation exception is based on a couple of considerations. One is that the complexity of tax matters may render them unsuitable for the generalizing effect of an MFN provision.[26] As already noted, tax matters are often addressed in separate treaties that are largely limited to taxation. The taxation exception reduces the possibility of duplication or contradiction between the BIT and tax treaties. Further, tax matters generally are the responsibility of a department within the government that is different from the department that is responsible for negotiating BITs. BIT negotiating teams typically do not include members with expertise in tax matters.

The taxation exception also may apply to the national treatment obligation. To the extent that it applies to benefits under domestic legislation relating to taxation, this exception provides an important way in which host states can provide assistance to domestic enterprises without having to extend the same assistance to foreign investments. Subsidies can be provided to domestic enterprises in the form of tax measures, such as reduced tax rates, tax deductions, tax credits, and accelerated depreciation schedules.

A second exception commonly found in national and MFN treatment provisions is one for advantages granted pursuant to an agreement establishing a customs union, free trade area, or other organization for economic integration.[27] Some BITs refer only to customs unions or free trade areas,[28] although it is not clear to what extent this language would be narrower in practice because organizations of economic integration are likely to include a free trade area or customs union and thus presumably would fall within the exception. Occasionally, a BIT includes multilateral agreements on investment in the exception as well.[29] As part of their economic integration into a customs union or free trade area, countries often make deep concessions to other countries in exchange for similarly deep concessions. A BIT party may be unwilling to grant those same concessions to any other country unless that country makes the same concessions that were granted by the other members of the customs union or free trade area. In effect, this exception curtails benefits to the free rider, a country that seeks through a

24 *See, e.g.*, Denmark-Ethiopia BIT, Art. 4; United Kingdom-Bosnia-Herzegovina BIT, Art. 7; Thailand-Argentina BIT, Art. 5; Australia-India, Art. 4(4); Sweden-Kazakhstan BIT, Art. 3(3); Indonesia-India, Art. 4(2); Germany-Timor-Leste BIT, Protocol, Para. 3(b)(tax legislation providing special tax treatment for nationals); Austria-Armenia BIT, Art. 3(4)(no qualifying language requiring that the agreement relate wholly or mainly to taxation).

25 *See, e.g.*, BLEU-Sudan BIT, Art. 4(1); Cambodia-Vietnam BIT, Art. III(4); Mexico-Iceland BIT, Art. 3(5).

26 The "generalizing effect" is discussed in greater detail below and in Section 7.2.3.

27 *See, e.g.*, BLEU-Sudan BIT, Art. 4(1); Denmark-Ethiopia BIT, Art. 4; Austria-Armenia BIT, Art. 3(4); United Kingdom-Bosnia-Herzegovina BIT, Art. 7; Netherlands-Ethiopia, Art. 3(3); Thailand-Argentina BIT, Art. 5; Australia-India, Art. 4(4); Cambodia-Vietnam BIT, Art. III(3);); Egypt-Zambia, Art. 3(3); Mexico-Iceland BIT, Art. 3(4); Indonesia-India, Art. 4(2); Chile-Indonesia BIT, Art. IV(3).

28 *See, e.g.*, Sweden-Kazakhstan BIT, Art. 3(2); Germany-Timor-Leste, Art. 3(3).

29 *See, e.g.*, Austria-Armenia BIT, Art. 3(4).

BIT MFN provision to gain the benefit of concessions made by the other BIT party to other countries without having to grant in exchange the concessions that were given by those other countries.

A few BITs, following an approach first utilized by the United States,[30] allow each party to specify in an annex sectors or matters with respect to which that party reserves the right to deny MFN treatment, national treatment, or both.[31] Typically, this technique is used where the BIT guarantees MFN and national treatment with respect to the right to establish investment and not merely to investment once established. The exceptions may apply to the establishment of investment, the treatment of investment after establishment, or both.

BITs with this exception thus employ national and MFN treatment provisions that are both broader and narrower than those of other BITs. The provisions are broader in that they apply to the right of establishment, a very important feature of these provisions, but are narrower in that they may be riddled with sectoral exceptions. The sectoral exceptions may be seen as the price of applying these provisions to the right of establishment, because few, if any, countries are willing to grant complete national treatment with respect to the right of establishment.[32] Yet the technique allows exceptions to be made to the treatment of investment once established as well.

To promote transparency, the most recent U.S. BITs separate the list of sectors into two annexes.[33] One annex lists existing nonconforming measures that a party reserves the right to maintain. The other annex lists sectors in which a party reserves the right to adopt future nonconforming measures. This approach necessitates including a definition of an existing measure. In these BITs, an existing measure includes a measure in force at the time the BIT was concluded as well as a prompt renewal of any such measure.[34] Thus, a measure that is allowed to lapse for a sufficient period of time ceases to be an existing measure and it may be reenacted only if the host state has reserved the right to adopt future measures in that sector of the economy. A measure that is amended does not cease to be an existing measure provided that the amendment does not increase the measure's nonconformity with the BIT.[35] This latter rule sometimes is referred to as a "one-way ratchet" because it permits a measure to be amended so as to decrease its nonconformity with the BIT, but the measure may not be amended so as to increase its nonconformity.

Other exceptions to the national and MFN treatment provisions sometimes appear. Some BITs exclude concessions made under the World Trade Organization agreements,[36] while other BITs exclude government procurement programs, subsidies

30 *See, e.g.*, United States-Egypt BIT, Art. II(3)(a).

31 *See, e.g.*, Canada-Uruguay BIT, Annex I(1)–(2).

32 *See* Sections 9.1–9.3.

33 *See, e.g.*, United States-Uruguay BIT, Art. 14.

34 *Id.*, at Art. 14(1)(b).

35 *Id.* at Art. 14(1)(c).

36 *See, e.g.*, United States-Ecuador BIT, Art. II(10) (exception future agreements within the framework of the GATT); Canada-Thailand BIT, Art. III(3)(b) (exception for future agreements negotiated within the framework of the GATT or its successor organization and liberalizing trade in services).

and grants.[37] Some BITs have a specific exception to the national and MFN treatment provisions for measures of public security, public order, or public health or morality[38]

Although the national and MFN treatment provisions are similar in structure, their functions are different. The national treatment provision is antiprotectionist. It eliminates state-created competitive advantages for domestic investments and investors and, if it applies to the establishment of investment, opens the economy to foreign investors. As this suggests, the national treatment provision can impose a substantial impediment to certain host state policies. For example, many countries have economic policies that require some forms of state intervention to assist local industries in their development. Often, these policies are based on the infant industry argument, that is, the argument that that some new enterprises can be competitive once they achieve a certain scale or maturity, but are not competitive prior to that. Under this argument, free market principles are not inconsistent with state support for that industry until such time as it becomes competitive. Indeed, such support arguably facilitates the operation of the market and increases its competitiveness because the support permits enterprises that otherwise would be excluded to enter the market. Free entry, of course, is a key premise of market economics. A variation of this argument applies to mature industries, which may have become temporarily uncompetitive, but if sustained for a period of time by state support could again become competitive and contribute to the contestability of the market. Such assistance is inconsistent with the national treatment obligation, unless the same assistance is provided to foreign investments. Yet, providing assistance to competing foreign investments may defeat the purpose of the assistance to the domestic enterprises. Moreover, developing countries can ill afford to provide indiscriminate financial assistance to multinational enterprises from developed countries. If assistance must be provided on a national treatment basis, then the developing country may be best served by providing no assistance at all. Further, many countries believe that domestic enterprises should occupy, perhaps exclusively, certain sectors of the economy. One common justification for this belief is national security: a country should not be dependent upon foreign enterprises for goods or services critical to its national defense. Another justification is cultural: preservation of the national culture may necessitate that domestic enterprises have a presence in sectors of the economy such as news and entertainment. States may want domestic enterprises to have a presence in a particular sector of the economy as a matter of national prestige. States also may want to protect domestic enterprises from foreign competition simply to promote the economic welfare of those involved in the domestic enterprises.

The MFN treatment provision is a generalizing provision. As a result of the MFN treatment provision, every BIT concluded by a country is as strong as the strongest BIT concluded by that country. In fact, every BIT concluded by a country is as strong as a hypothetical BIT composed of the strongest provisions of every other BIT concluded by that country. Thus, the effect of MFN treatment provisions is to render many

---

37 *See, e.g.*, United States-Uruguay BIT, Art. 14(5).

38 *See, e.g.*, Germany-Timor-Leste, Protocol, para. 3(a)

of the differences among BITs concluded by any one country largely irrelevant.[39] If a country has guaranteed a particular kind of treatment to investment in any BIT, then at least in the case of substantive treatment it generally has guaranteed that treatment to investment covered by any BIT with an MFN treatment provision.

Most countries have little reason to discriminate among classes of foreign investors, perhaps except where the host state has entered into an economic integration agreement and wishes to extend special preferences to investments from other members. This problem can be and is addressed through a special exception to the MFN treatment provision, already described.

One difficulty presented by an MFN treatment provision is that it potentially creates the phenomenon of the free rider, already discussed in connection with the customs union exception. The free rider problem can inhibit the deepening of treaty commitments in at least two ways. First, some states may object to offering MFN guarantees because they wish to avoid free riders. Second, some states may refuse to make strong commitments to treaty partners because through the MFN provision they can obtain the benefit of any commitments made by the partner to third countries, without offering the strong commitments in exchange. That is, these states wish to operate as free riders. One way to address the free rider problem, apart from specific exceptions to limit the range of agreements upon which the free rider may ride, is to adopt a conditional MFN treatment provision. Under a conditional MFN treatment provision, a country is entitled to benefits granted by its treaty partner to third countries only if that country grants the same benefits to its treaty partner. Thus, a country cannot free-ride upon commitments made by its partner. It must purchase those concessions by offering the same commitments to its partner. Such a provision, however, reduces to some degree the generalizing effect of an MFN treatment provision. Thus, a conditional MFN treatment provision would not benefit the investment in the circumstance in which BIT MFN treatment provisions most often are invoked. The typical invocation of a BIT MFN treatment provision arises where an investment covered by a BIT claims entitlement to some protection accorded to foreign investment by another BIT concluded by the host state. Under a conditional MFN treatment provision, the investment would be entitled to that protection only if its home state granted that protection to investments of the host state. Yet, the most likely way that the investor could prove that the home state had made such a grant would be to show that the grant was included in the BIT between the home and host states, in which case the investment already would be entitled to the protection and would not need the benefit of the MFN treatment provision. In any event, BITs rarely use conditional MFN treatment provisions.

Another difficulty presented by an MFN treatment provision is that the generalizing effect of the provision impedes efforts to modify a host state's investment policy over time. The provision perhaps presents little problem if a host state wishes to expand the obligations it assumes under its BITs. Each obligation, once assumed with respect to

39 As will be discussed in Section 7.2.3, some tribunals have held that the term "treatment" in the MFN treatment provision does not apply to all BIT provisions. Thus, according to these tribunals, an investor may not claim the benefit of every provision in a BIT concluded by the host country.

one treaty partner, is by virtue of the MFN treatment provision extended to every other treaty partner. The provision presents a more substantial problem if a host state wishes to reduce the obligations it is assuming under its BITs. Although it can eliminate the obligation from future BITs, future BIT partners still will be entitled by the MFN treatment provision in their BITs to the benefit of the obligation as it exists in earlier BITs.

To address this problem, the United States, in some of its BITs, has excluded from its MFN treatment provision any benefit extended under any prior agreement.[40] This allows the parties to diminish the protection extended in later agreements, relative to that guaranteed in earlier agreements. In the absence of such an exclusion, a covered investment in a later BIT could invoke the MFN treatment provision and demand the same level of treatment guaranteed under an earlier BIT. Under the exclusion, investments covered by earlier BITs do receive the benefit of increases in the level of protection in later BITs. In effect, the exclusion operates as a one-way ratchet with respect to investment under any particular BIT, which can gain but not lose protection as a result of later BITs. It allows the treaty program as a whole, however, to move in either direction, raising or lowering the level of protection accorded under the BITs. In the absence of this exclusion, the MFN provision would function as a one-way ratchet with respect to the BIT program as a whole because later BITs would increase the protection guaranteed under earlier BITs, while attempts to decrease protection in later BITs would be prevented by the existence of earlier BITs. In effect, this exclusion eliminates the one-way ratchet in the BIT program as a whole, while retaining it with respect to investment covered under any particular BIT. For this exclusion to be effective, the omitted obligation must be omitted from all subsequent BITs. If it appears in a later BIT, then an exception for obligations in earlier BITs will be futile because the obligation will have been assumed by virtue of its presence in a later BIT, the obligations of which are applicable through the MFN provision.

A third difficulty presented by the MFN treatment provision is that it can render complex provisions incoherent. Where the MFN treatment provision is used to claim the benefit of a simple provision, such as the fair and equitable treatment standard, the consequences for covered investment may be substantial, but adding that obligation to the other obligations of the applicable BIT is not conceptually difficult. Where the MFN provision is used to claim the benefit of a clause in a complex provision, however, determining how this clause shall be integrated into another BIT may be quite difficult conceptually. The best example is the provision that is usually the most complex of any in the BITs, the investor-state disputes provision. This provision sometimes includes an interrelated series of clauses, which may incorporate entire bodies of arbitration rules adopted by organizations such as ICSID or UNCITRAL. The BIT with the MFN provision that has been invoked may include a complex investor-state disputes provision that is quite different from that in the BIT the benefit of which has been claimed. One BIT, for example, may call for ICSID arbitration while the other BIT may call for arbitration under the rules of the United Nations Commission on International Trade Law (UNCITRAL). Integrating a clause designed to operate within

40 *See, e.g.*, United States-Uruguay BIT, Annex II.

one system into a provision that contemplates a different system may threaten the coherency of the latter system. The problem is exacerbated where multiple clauses from different investor-state disputes provisions of different BITs are incorporated into the BIT with the MFN provision. As will be seen, some states have contended that the MFN provision should not be interpreted to apply to dispute resolution provisions and, in fact, the text of some BITs does seem to exclude the investor-state disputes provision from the scope of the MFN provision.[41] Yet, a few BITs make clear that the MFN provision does apply to the dispute resolution provisions.[42] Tribunals have divided over the circumstances in which an MFN provision should be held to apply to investor-state disputes provisions.[43] In any event, claimants to date generally have not sought to use the MFN treatment provision in a way that raised the coherence problem to any significant degree. Thus, the problem of coherence has been largely a hypothetical concern.

Many BITs that guarantee both MFN and national treatment include language indicating that the beneficiary is entitled to the more favorable of the two standards.[44] Often the language is more precise, stating that the treatment to be accorded is that which is more favorable to the investor[45] or more favorable from the investor's point of view.[46] Such language merely makes explicit that which otherwise would be implicit. A guarantee of both MFN and national treatment necessarily requires that the beneficiary receive the benefit of both, including that which is more favorable. More generally, BIT obligations typically are cumulative.[47] That is, the host state is not excused from complying with one provision on the ground that it has complied with a different provision.

7.2.2 MFN Treatment: Origins

As discussed in Section 2.1.1, MFN provisions were common in the early FCNs. Prohibitions on discrimination also appeared in the earliest BITs. Article 1(2) of the first BIT, the 1959 Germany-Pakistan BIT, provided that "capital" in the territory of one party y"shall not be subjected to any discriminatory treatment on the ground that ownership of or influence upon it is vested in nationals or companies" of the other party, although this right to nondiscrimination was subject to existing local law. Further, Article 2(1) prohibited either party from subjecting to discriminatory treatment any activities "carried on in connection with investments, including the effective management, use or enjoyment of such investments" unless specifically permitted in the "documents of admission" of the investment, language that essentially was an early

41 *See* below and Section 7.2.3.
42 *See, e.g.*, United Kingdom-Bosnia-Herzegovina BIT, Art. 3(3).
43 *See* Section 7.2.3.
44 *See, e.g.*, Sweden-Kazakhstan BIT, Art. 3(2).
45 *See, e.g.*, Austria-Armenia BIT, Art. 3(3); Netherlands-Ethiopia, Art. 3(2); Thailand-Argentina BIT, Art. 4(1)–(2); Mexico-Iceland BIT, Art. 3(2)–(3).
46 *See, e.g.*, Denmark-Ethiopia BIT, Art. 3(1)–(2).
47 *See S.D. Myers v. Canada* (NAFTA), Partial Award, paras. 292–294.

form of the prohibition on unreasonable or discriminatory measures that appears in many BITs.[48]

The first Belgium-Luxembourg Economic Union (BLEU) BIT, signed with Tunisia in 1964, required that each party provide to covered investments "at least the same security and protection that it grants to those of its own nationals or to the investments of nationals and companies of third states."[49] This language was similar to that which had appeared in many FCNs.[50] Thus, MFN as well as national treatment were elements of the BLEU BIT practice from the beginning. The reference to national treatment, however, quickly disappeared. For example, the BLEU's third BIT, concluded with Indonesia in 1970, provided, at Article 1(3), that "[t]he protection guaranteed by paragraphs 1 and 2 of this article [guaranteeing admission in accordance with host state law, fair and equitable treatment, and full protection] shall at least be equal to that enjoyed by nationals of any third State and may in no case be less favorable that that recognized by international law." This formulation became typical of the BLEU BITs until the current decade, during which the BLEU BITs more commonly guarantee to covered investors MFN treatment "in all matters relating to the treatment of investments"[51] and "with respect to the operation, management, maintenance, use, enjoyment and sale or other disposal of investments."[52].

The first Italian BIT, concluded with Guinea in 1964, guaranteed MFN treatment to covered investment.[53] This provision did not apply to advantages deriving from a customs union agreement or an agreement to prevent double taxation. This remains Italy's approach today, although the Italian BITs also include an exception for trade agreements even if they do not establish a customs union or free trade area[54] and the Italian BITs sometimes extend MFN treatment to activities in connection with an investment.[55]

The Swiss, Dutch, and Kuwaiti BITs of the 1960s did not initially contain any general, explicit prohibition on discrimination among foreign investors, although they did require fair and equitable treatment. By 1968, however, the Dutch BITs guaranteed to covered investment the same protection as investment of any third state.[56] By the mid-1980s, the Dutch BITs guaranteed MFN "treatment," with exceptions for benefits resulting from economic integration or taxation agreements.[57]

The first Danish BIT, concluded with Madagascar in 1965, included an MFN treatment provision linked to fair and equitable treatment. Article 6 of that treaty required fair and equitable treatment, which in no case was permitted to be less than national or MFN treatment. In 1968, however, Denmark deleted the fair and equitable treatment standard and incorporated instead a general requirement of national and MFN treatment

---

48 *See* Section 5.3.

49 BLEU-Tunisia BIT, Art. 1.

50 *See* Section 2.1.

51 BLEU-Sudan BIT, Art. 4(1); BLEU-D.R. Congo BIT, Art. 4(2).

52 *See, e.g.*, BLEU-Sudan BIT, Art. 4(2); BLEU-D.R. Congo BIT, Art. 4(2).

53 Italy-Guinea BIT, Art. 5.

54 *See, e.g.*, Italy-Nicaragua BIT, Art. III; Italy-Jordan BIT, Art. 3; Italy-Pakistan BIT, Art. 3.

55 *See, e.g.*, Italy-Nicaragua BIT, Art. III; Italy-Pakistan BIT, Art. 3.

56 *See* Netherlands-Indonesia BIT, Art. 5.

57 *See, e.g.*, Netherlands-Sri Lanka BIT, Art. 5; Netherlands-Philippines BIT, Art. 4.

with respect to "any similar enterprise."[58] Denmark did not conclude any more BITs until 1980. When it resumed its program, the national treatment obligation was omitted as was the "similar enterprise" qualification, but an exception for agreements on double taxation was added.[59] In 1988, Denmark modified its practice again It adopted a general MFN and national treatment obligation, with an exception for taxation agreements,[60] while also restoring the fair and equitable treatment standard. In the mid-1990s, Danish practice required fair and equitable treatment, which in no case shall be less than national and MFN treatment, although the national and MFN treatment obligations were subject to exceptions for customs union agreements and matters of taxation [61]

The first Swedish BIT, concluded in 1965 with Ivory Coast,[62] was similar to the early Danish BITs, as was the first Austrian BIT, concluded with Romania in 1976.[63]. Switzerland concluded a BIT with Tanzania in 1965 that guaranteed to covered investment treatment no less favorable than that accorded to any similar investment,[64] but its BITs in the mid-1960s more typically were consistent with the early Danish BITs.[65] Sweden's BIT program went into hiatus in 1967. When the program resumed in 1978, the fair and equitable treatment standard was placed in a separate paragraph from the MFN treatment standard and the MFN treatment standard was made subject to a customs union exception.[66]

Given its omission from several early BIT programs, perhaps not surprisingly the MFN treatment provision did not appear in the 1967 OECD Draft Convention on the Protection of Foreign Property. The convention did include general prohibitions on discrimination. The 1959 Abs–Shawcross Convention also had contained no MFN treatment provision. The International Code of Fair Treatment for Foreign Investment proposed by the International Chamber of Commerce in 1949 contained extensive provisions on nondiscrimination, but these seem not to have influenced the content of the BITs.

The MFN treatment provision became more common in the 1970s, although it still was not universal. For example, an MFN provision became routine in the Swiss BITs beginning in the early 1970s,[67] sometimes with a customs union exception.[68]

58 *See, e.g.*, Denmark-Indonesia BIT, Art. III.

59 *See, e.g.*, Denmark-Romania BIT, Art. 3; Denmark-China BIT, Art. 3.

60 *See, e.g.*, Denmark-Republic of Korea BIT, Art. 3, Denmark-Peru BIT, Art. 3; Denmark-Venezuela BIT, Arts. 3–4.

61 *See, e.g.*, Denmark-Mongolia BIT, Arts. 3(1),4; Denmark-India BIT, Arts. 3(1), 4; Denmark-Nicaragua BIT, Arts. 3–4; Denmark-Ethiopia BIT, Arts. 3–4; Denmark-Croatia BIT, Art. 3; Denmark-Cuba BIT, Arts. 4–5; Denmark-Kyrgyz Republic BIT, Arts. 3–4.

62 Sweden-Ivory Coast BIT, Art. VI.

63 Austria-Romania BIT, Art. 3(1).

64 Switzerland-Tanzania BIT, Art. 1(2).

65 *See, e.g.*, Switzerland-Costa Rica BIT, Art. 1(2); Switzerland-Togo BIT, Art. 7; Switzerland-Malta BIT, Art. 5.

66 *See, e.g.*, Sweden-Egypt BIT, Art.2; Sweden-Yugoslavia BIT, Art. 2.

67 *See, e.g.*, Switzerland-Egypt BIT, Art. 3; Switzerland-Indonesia BIT, Art. 4(3); Switzerland-Sudan BIT, Art. 3.

68 *See, e.g.*, Switzerland-Egypt BIT, Art. 3; Switzerland-Jordan BIT, Art. 2(3).

French BITs concluded in the early 1970s required that each party provide the same security and protection to covered investments that it provides to nationals of any third country.[69] By 1974, the term used was "treatment" rather than "security" and a customs union exception was added.[70] A tax exception appeared by 1980.[71]

The United Kingdom's first BIT, signed with Egypt in 1975, prohibited treatment of investment that was less favorable than that accorded to investment of third states.[72] The United Kingdom-Egypt BIT also guaranteed MFN treatment to investors of the other party with respect to the management, use, enjoyment, or disposal of their investments. These provisions, however, did not apply to treatment extended by virtue of an agreement establishing a customs union or free trade area or an agreement or legislation relating wholly or mainly to taxation.[73]

Austria's first BITs, concluded in the mid-1970s, included a general MFN provision, which provided a floor to the fair and equitable treatment standard.[74] The MFN treatment provision, however, soon was separated from the fair and equitable treatment provision[75] and was made subject to exceptions for customs union agreements, border trade agreements, and taxation agreements.[76] Although the early Austrian BITs varied with respect to whether MFN treatment was owed to investments or investors, by the 1990s the Austrian BITs made clear that it was owed to both.[77] In the more recent Austrian BITs, the MFN obligation applies to treatment with respect to the management, operation, maintenance, use, enjoyment, sale, or liquidation of an investment, as opposed to all treatment generally,[78] and the separate exception for border trade agreements has been eliminated.[79]

Kuwait, which began its BIT program in 1964, did not include general MFN treatment obligations until the 1980s,[80] with customs union and taxation exceptions being typical of these agreements. The MFN treatment provisions often applied to both investments and investors. Some Kuwaiti BITs required that the investments or investors be "in like situations."[81]

The United States' first BIT, with Egypt, signed in 1982, guaranteed MFN treatment to covered investment. The U.S. BITs, however, included three innovations in MFN practice.

69 *See, e.g.*, France-D.R. Congo BIT, Art. 2; France-Indonesia BIT, Art. 3.

70 *See, e.g.*, France-Egypt BIT, Art. 3.

71 *See, e.g.*, France-Sri Lanka BIT, Art. 6.

72 United Kingdom-Egypt BIT, Art. 3(1).

73 *Id.*, Art. 7.

74 *See, e.g.*, Austria-Romania BIT, Art. 3(1); Austria-Malaysia BIT, Art. 3(2).

75 *See, e.g.*, Austria-China BIT, Art. 3(1).

76 *See, e.g.*, Austria-Malaysia BIT, Art. 3(3); Austria-China BIT, Art. 3(3).

77 *See, e.g.*, Austria-Republic of Korea BIT, Art. 3(1); Austria-Cape Verde BIT, Art. 3(1).

78 *See, e.g.*, Austria-Bosnia-Herzegovina BIT, Art (3)(3); Austria-Libya BIT, Art. 3(3); Austria-Jordan BIT, Art. 3(3); Austria-Armenia BIT, Art. 3(3).

79 *See, e.g.*, Austria-Bosnia-Herzegovina BIT, Art (3)(4); Austria-Libya BIT, Art. 3(4); Austria-Jordan BIT, Art. 3(4); Austria-Armenia BIT, Art. 3(4).

80 *See, e.g.*, Kuwait-China BIT, Art. 3; Kuwait-Hungary BIT, Art. 3; Kuwait-Czech Republic BIT, Art. 4; Kuwait- Ethiopia BIT, Art. 4; Kuwait-Croatia BIT, Art. 4.

81 *See, e.g.*, Kuwait-Ethiopia BIT, Art. 4; Kuwait-Croatia BIT, Art. 4.

First, in the U.S. BITs, the obligation of MFN treatment applied not only to the treatment of investments once established, but to the right of investors to establish investments. The U.S. BITs would remain unique in this regard until the conclusion of the NAFTA. A right of national and MFN treatment with respect to the establishment of investment now can be found as well in the Canadian and Japanese BITs.[82]

Second, the U.S. BITs guaranteed MFN (and national) treatment to investments and to certain activities associated with investments. The U.S. BITs abandoned the protection for associated activities in its 1994 model negotiating text.

Third, beginning with the BITs based on its 1991 model negotiating text, the U.S. BITs permitted the parties to specify, in a treaty annex, sectors of the economy to which the MFN treatment obligation does not apply. Prior to that, the U.S. BITs generally allowed sectoral exceptions only to the national treatment obligation.

The U.S. BITs require treatment as favorable as that granted only to investments in like situations with covered investment. As has been noted, some concept of comparability is inherent in any nondiscrimination provision. The U.S. BITs, however, in using the phrase "in like situations" provided a verbal formula for ascertaining which investments shall be compared to the covered investment. As already noted, some earlier Danish BITs had included language guaranteeing MFN treatment to "similar enterprises."[83]

Finland's first BIT, which also was with Egypt, although it was concluded in 1980, at Article 2(2) was similar to article 3(1) of the United Kingdom-Egypt BIT. The Finland-Egypt BIT, however, excepted more favorable treatment granted pursuant to a customs union agreement or granted under a previously existing bilateral agreement. At the beginning of the 1990s, Finland added an exception for taxation agreements.[84] For a time in the early 1990s, MFN treatment was included in the Finnish BITs as a floor for the full protection and security standard or the fair and equitable treatment standard, but that approach was abandoned.[85] Beginning in the mid-1990s, some Finnish BITs guaranteed MFN treatment for investors as well as investments.[86] Recent Finnish BITs continue to guarantee MFN treatment to both investments and investors, although the right of MFN treatment has been modified in two ways in some Finnish BITs. First, the required treatment sometimes applies to the right to establish investment.[87] Second, the required treatment, at least in the case of investor, sometimes was qualified to refer only to treatment with regard to the management, maintenance, use, enjoyment, and disposal of investments,[88] as well as in some cases the establishment of investments.[89]

---

82 *See, e.g.*, Japan-Vietnam BIT, Art. 2; Canada-Uruguay BIT, Art. 3.

83 *See, e.g.*, Denmark-Indonesia BIT, Art. III.

84 *See, e.g.*, Finland-Czechoslovakia BIT, Art. 4(3); Finland-Estonia BIT, Art. 4(3).

85 *See, e.g.*, Finland-Czechoslovakia BIT, Art. 4(1); Finland-Estonia BIT, Art. 4(1); Finland-Chile BIT, Art. 3(1).

86 *See, e.g.*, Finland-Thailand BIT, Art. 4(2); Finland-Brazil BIT, Art. 3(2); Finland-Peru BIT, Art. 3(2).

87 *See, e.g.*, Finland-Belarus BIT, Art. 4; Finland-Armenia BIT, Art. 3; Finland-Algeria BIT, Art. 3.

88 *See, e.g.*, Finland-Croatia BIT, Art. 3; Finland-Azerbaijan BIT, Art. 4.

89 *See, e.g.*, Finland-Belarus BIT, Art. 4; Finland-Armenia BIT, Art. 3; Finland-Algeria BIT, Art. 3.

At the beginning of the 1990s, the United Kingdom added a new paragraph to its investor-state disputes provision specifying that, "[f]or the avoidance of doubt," the treatment provided by the MFN treatment provision shall apply to the provisions of Articles 1 to 11, which constitute the entire BIT except for the articles on territorial extension, entry into force, duration, and termination.[90] More particularly, the new language confirms that the MFN treatment obligation extends to dispute resolution. This provision remains virtually unchanged in the U.K. BITs.[91] A number of U.K. BITs that were concluded beginning in the 1980s include language noting that special incentives granted to stimulate the creation of local industries are considered compatible with this provision, provided that they do not significantly affect the investment and activities of nationals and companies of the other party in connection with an investment.[92]

As this discussion indicates, the MFN treatment provision became common in BITs only in the 1970s. Further, the structure of the provision was the subject of significant variation in the early history of the provision, with some developed countries that were among the first to launch BIT programs continuing to modify their provisions significantly even into the 1990s.

7.2.3 MFN Treatment: Arbitral Practice

Several investment disputes have arisen under the MFN treatment provision of various BITs.[93] In the typical case, the claimant alleges that the host state has denied to a covered investment or investor treatment that is as favorable as that guaranteed by the host state to investments or investors of a third country. For example, the claimant may allege a violation of the MFN treatment provision on the ground that the claimant's investment did not receive fair and equitable treatment, which is guaranteed by the host state to investments of investors of third countries. Or, the claimant may allege a violation of the MFN treatment provision on the ground that it was not permitted to submit a claim to investor-state arbitration on the same terms that would apply to an investor covered by the host state's BIT with a third country. In these cases, tribunals never require that the claimant prove that third-country investments or investors actually have received the guaranteed treatment, but only that they are guaranteed the treatment and that the claimant has not received treatment as favorable as that which is guaranteed to the third-country investments or investors. For example, the claimant is not required to prove that investments or investors of a third country actually receive fair and equitable treatment, but only that they are entitled to it. Further, in these cases,

---

90 *See, e.g.*, United Kingdom-Burundi BIT, Art. 3(1).

91 *See, e.g.*, United Kingdom-Bosnia-Herzegovina BIT, Arts. 3, 7.

92 *See, e.g.*, United Kingdom-Papua New Guinea BIT, Art. 3(3); United Kingdom-Jamaica BIT, Art. 3(3).

93 For additional commentary on the cases, *see* Okezie Chukwumerije, "Interpreting Most-Favoured-Nation Clauses in Investment Treaty Arbitrations," 8 *Journal of World Investment and Trade 597* (2007).

tribunals never consider whether the claimant is in like circumstances with a particular investment or investor covered by the host country's BIT with a third country. Indeed, it may be that no investor or investment covered by the BIT with a third country even exists. Thus, in the typical case, the claimant is relying upon the generalizing effect of an MFN treatment provision and asking the tribunal to treat the claimant or its investment as if it were covered by one or more provisions in the host state's BIT with a third country.

The general MFN treatment provision typically confers a right to no less favorable treatment. Thus, to gain the benefit of the provision, the covered investment or investor must demonstrate that investments or investors of another state have received or have been guaranteed more favorable treatment, a demonstration that may not always be easy. In *AAPL v. Sri Lanka*, a case arising under the United Kingdom-Sri Lanka BIT, the tribunal rejected the claim that Sri Lanka's BIT with Switzerland provided more favorable treatment than its BIT with the United Kingdom.[94] Specifically, the tribunal was unpersuaded that Sri Lanka's BIT with Switzerland imposed a strict liability standard on the parties, as opposed to the due diligence standard imposed by the full protection and security standard of Sri Lanka's BIT with the United Kingdom.

Similarly, in *ADF Group v. United States*, Article 1105 of the NAFTA guaranteed to investment treatment in accordance with international law, including fair and equitable treatment and full protection and security. The claimant argued that the MFN treatment provision of the NAFTA entitled it to rely on the fair and equitable treatment and full protection and security standards of BITs concluded by the United States with Albania and Estonia in which the fair and equitable treatment and full protection and security standards were not characterized as requirements of customary international law, but were guaranteed in terms that implied that they could require greater protection than is required by customary law. The tribunal was not persuaded, however, that the fair and equitable treatment and full protection and security standards as they appeared in these two BITs guaranteed more favorable treatment than the standards as they appeared in the NAFTA.[95]

An early decision that is invoked in many claims involving the MFN treatment provision is the decision on jurisdiction in *Maffezini v. Spain.* In that case, an Argentine claimant submitted a claim to arbitration against Spain under the Argentina-Spain BIT. That BIT provided that an investor could submit a claim to arbitration only if the investor had first submitted the claim to the local courts and 18 months had elapsed since the claim was submitted. The claimant had not satisfied that condition. Spain's BIT with Chile, however, contained no such condition. The claimant argued that the MFN treatment provision of the Argentina-Spain BIT, which guaranteed MFN treatment to covered investments "[i]n all matters subject to this Agreement," required Spain to grant the claimant the same treatment, i.e., the right to submit a claim to arbitration without first submitting the claim to local remedies for a period of 18 months. The tribunal observed that an MFN treatment provision applies only to the subject

94 Award, para. 54.
95 Award, para. 194.

matter of the "basic treaty," that is, the treaty in which appears the MFN treatment provision on which the claimant relies. The tribunal took note of the fact that the MFN treatment provision in the Argentina-Spain BIT guaranteed MFN treatment with respect to "all matters" covered by the treaty. The tribunal found that dispute resolution is inextricably related to the protection of foreign investment, which is the purpose of the BIT, and thus an MFN treatment provision applies to provisions relating to dispute resolution. The tribunal further observed, however, that the MFN treatment provision should not be used to override public policy considerations that the parties might have envisaged as fundamental conditions for their acceptance of the agreement. For example, the MFN treatment provision could not be used to avoid an exhaustion of local remedies requirement, to avoid a provision that resort to local remedies foreclosed resort to international arbitration, or to permit the claimant to choose a different forum than that authorized in the basic treaty. In this case, however, in light of the negotiating history of the treaty between Spain and Argentina and the practice of Spain and Argentina in not consistently including in their other BITs a requirement such as that in the Argentina-Spain BIT, the tribunal did not believe that the requirement to pursue local remedies for a period of 18 months was a fundamental question of public policy. Accordingly, the MFN treatment provision entitled the claimant to the treatment accorded by Spain under the Chile-Spain BIT, meaning that the claimant was entitled to submit its dispute to arbitration without first invoking local remedies.

The *Maffezini* award was instantly controversial. Yet, much could be said in support of the award. Long before *Maffezini* was decided, MFN treatment provisions were understood to generalize treaty benefits, i.e., to extend the benefits accorded by a state in one treaty to all other states with which it has concluded a treaty with an MFN provision applicable to that benefit. The question that elicited the controversy, however, was precisely whether the MFN treatment provision, in fact, is applicable to treatment in the form of remedies. Certainly, in many BITs, including the BIT at issue in *Maffezini*, the language is broad enough to apply to remedies. The treaty in *Maffezini*, for example, applied the MFN treatment provision to "all matters subject to this Agreement" and clearly dispute resolution was a matter subject to the BIT. Further, the distinction between rights and remedies that critics of *Maffezini* asserted that the award had improperly disregarded is a distinction that on principled grounds is difficult to defend. As noted at the beginning of Chapter 10, substantive rights are defined as a practical matter by the extent of their enforcement through disputes provisions. Thus, the host state's consent to investor-state arbitration as a means of enforcing its substantive commitments to covered investment is part of the favorable treatment that the host state provides to covered investment. More generally, the investor-state disputes provision is one of the most important provisions of the BIT and thus ensuring that investors of one nationality receive treatment no less favorable than investors of another nationality generally would require that the former receive the procedural as well as the substantive treatment accorded to the latter. The due process principle of the BITs, embodied in the investor-state disputes provision, is not less important than the principles embodied in other provisions. Further, an investment sometimes is owned by investors of different nationalities. In the event of injury to the investment, claims may be submitted to arbitration by multiple claimants asserting rights under different BITs. Assuming that all of the BITs have an MFN provision, each claimant is likely to be able to claim the benefit of substantive rights granted to any of the claimants, although there is no guarantee that different tribunals will interpret the rights similarly under the facts of the particular dispute. Eliminating differences in remedial provisions may allow claims to be heard contemporaneously either by a single tribunal or by tribunals with overlapping memberships. Such a procedure could advance both efficiency and fairness.

Still, host states when named as respondents in investor-state arbitrations often have objected to the application of the MFN treatment provision to remedial provisions on at least four grounds. One is that they never intended the MFN treatment provision to apply to remedial provisions and thus they have been subjected to the tribunal's jurisdiction in a case not within the scope of their consent to jurisdiction. In many cases, however, it may be more accurate to say that the parties never thought about the issue either way. Host states that raise this objection typically have no *travaux préparatoires* of any kind demonstrating that application of the MFN treatment provision to disputes provisions was contrary to their intent. That said, however, the objection that this result is contrary to the parties' intention, even if it cannot be proven, may well be correct in some or even many cases, especially in the case of BITs concluded after the issuance of the *Maffezini* award, which focused the attention of many governments on this issue. If states do intend to exclude dispute resolution from the scope of the MFN treatment provision, they could ensure this result in at least some cases by adopting language in their future BITs so specifying. The omission to include such language in the face of so many tribunal decisions applying the MFN treatment provision to dispute resolution would cast doubt on the sincerity of at least some claims that MFN treatment provisions are not intended to apply to dispute resolution provisions. A second ground is that as a matter of policy these countries are opposed to granting the remedial rights that are being claimed by virtue of the MFN treatment provision, although they would not be in the position of having to grant such rights to the claimant had they not agreed to grant them to at least some potential claimants under another BIT. Thus, the objection cannot be that the host state does not wish to grant those procedural rights, but only that it does not wish to grant those procedural rights to investors or investments covered by this treaty. That is, the host state is arguing that, notwithstanding the inclusion of a nondiscrimination provision in the BITs, the host state in fact does wish to discriminate among foreign investments in at least some respects related to the BIT. That position is buttressed by the third ground, that every treaty is a unique balance of rights and duties and to pluck rights from another agreement and transport them into this agreement disturbs that balance. Such plucking, however, is precisely the function of the MFN treatment provision. MFN treatment provisions generalize treaty rights and thereby eliminate distinctions in the type of treatment provided to investments or investors of different nationalities, including to investments or investors not contemplated when the right was first granted. The fourth ground is that, as noted above, application of the MFN treatment provision to complex provisions like investor-state disputes provisions potentially can disrupt the coherence of the treaty and create interpretive difficulties, although in the disputes that have arisen to date such a problem has not yet occurred.

Most tribunals have followed the reasoning in *Maffezini*. In *Gas Natural v. Argentina*, a tribunal again had before it a dispute arising under the Spain-Argentina BIT, although in this case the nationalities of the parties were reversed relative to the situation in *Maffezini*. A Spanish claimant sought to avoid the requirement that it submit its claim to local remedies for 18 months on the ground that the MFN treatment provision in the BIT entitled it to rely upon the United States-Argentina BIT, where no such requirement exists. The tribunal noted that investor-state arbitration has been a crucial element in the protection accorded by BITs and that the MFN treatment provision of the Spain-Argentina BIT explicitly applies to "all" matters subject to the BIT. Argentina's argument that to disregard the 18-month requirement would be inconsistent with its public policy was belied by the fact that most of Argentina's BITs lacked any such requirement. Argentina could not rest its argument on the importance of the exhaustion of local remedies requirement, because the 18-month clause did not require exhaustion of local remedies, but only a resort to them for 18 months. Accordingly, the claimant was entitled to avail itself of the more favorable treatment provided by the investor-state disputes provision in the United States-Argentina BIT.[96] Indeed, the tribunal went on to say that

> [u]nless it appears clearly that the state parties to a BIT or the parties to a particular investment agreement settled on a different method for resolution of disputes that may arise, most-favored-nation provisions in BITs should be understood to be applicable to dispute resolution.[97]

In *Suez & Interaguas v. Argentina*, another Spanish investor submitted a claim against Argentina under the Spain-Argentina BIT, this time seeking to avoid the 18-month local remedies requirement on the ground that such a requirement did not appear in the France-Argentina BIT. The tribunal emphasized the breadth of the term "all matters" and the parties' failure to list dispute resolution among the matters excluded from the provision. Regarding the interpretation of the text, the tribunal declined Argentina's invitation to interpret the MFN treatment provision narrowly and held that the ordinary meaning of the language should be adopted. The tribunal noted that, with regard to investment promotion and protection, dispute resolution is as important as other matters governed by the BIT and, therefore, rejected the argument that application of the *ejusdem generis* principle would result in exclusion of dispute resolution from the scope of the provision. The tribunal distinguished the award in *Plama v. Bulgaria*, discussed below, on the basis of differences in the treaty text, evidence from the negotiating history of the BIT at issue in *Plama* that had no counterpart in the Spain-Argentina BIT, and the much more limited effect of applying the MFN treatment provision to dispute resolution in this case than in *Plama*. The tribunal also

---

96 The tribunal noted that its decision did not appear to be inconsistent with the award of any other tribunal, citing *Siemens v. Argentina* and *Maffezini v. Spain*. The tribunal did note the different result in *Salini v. Jordan*, but remarked that the *Salini* tribunal itself had rested its decision on the particular language of the BIT, which differed from that in *Gas Natural*.

97 Decision on Jurisdiction, para. 49.

rejected the assertion in *Plama* that arbitration provisions are subject to stricter rules of interpretation than other provisions of a BIT.

In *Siemens v. Argentina*, article 3 of the Germany-Argentina BIT prohibited a party from according to covered investments, companies, or nationals of the other party "a less favorable treatment of activities related to investments" than it grants to investments, companies, or nationals of any third state. The tribunal noted that the terms "treatment" and "activities" were unqualified and therefore were not limited to transactions of a commercial or economic nature. Article 4(4) additionally required MFN treatment in all matters covered in Article 4, which included a guarantee of full protection and legal security of investments, a requirement of compensation for expropriation, and a requirement of national treatment with respect to compensation for losses due to war or civil disturbance. The tribunal rejected the argument that its interpretation of Article 3 would render Article 4 superfluous. The tribunal noted that Article 4 addressed matters of special importance to the parties, which could account for the inclusion of an additional MFN treatment provision to deal with those matters.[98] The tribunal cited *Maffezini* with approval and conceded that the word "treatment" in the Germany-Argentina BIT was narrower than the phrase "all matters subject to this Agreement" that had been at issue in *Maffezini*, but concluded that the Germany-Argentina BIT language nevertheless was sufficiently broad to include dispute settlement. Accordingly, the German claimant was entitled to invoke the MFN treatment provision to avoid the requirement in the Germany-Argentina BIT that a dispute be submitted to local courts for 18 months prior to its submission to arbitration because such a requirement was not in the Chile-Argentina BIT. The tribunal found insufficient evidence that the requirement of submission to local remedies was a sensitive public policy or essential part of consent, particularly given that it did not consistently appear in contemporaneous treaties concluded by the parties. The tribunal also rejected the argument that the fact that the investor-state dispute provision of the Germany-Argentina BIT departed from the German model agreement proved that it was a specially negotiated provision, the effect of which should not be modified by application of the MFN provision. The tribunal would not speculate as to the reasons for the departure from the model language and believed that the treaty language should be interpreted in accordance with the clearly expressed intention of the parties. Indeed, the tribunal explained, the very purpose of an MFN treatment provision is to generalize treaty protections and thereby negate the effect of specially negotiated provisions. The tribunal also rejected the argument that, if one benefit of the Chile-Argentina BIT was to be claimed, then the Chile-Argentina BIT should be applied in its entirety. Allowing the German claimant to select provisions from the Chile-Argentina BIT of which to claim the benefit did not elevate the German investor over a Chilean investor because a Chilean investor in Argentina, if it was covered by a treaty with an MFN treatment provision, could claim the benefits of the Germany-Argentina BIT.

---

98 In *Wintershall v. Argentina*, discussed below, the tribunal gave a different interpretation to this language.

In *National Grid v. Argentina*, the claim arose under the United Kingdom-Argentina BIT, which also required submission of a claim to local remedies for 18 months prior to submission to international arbitration. The claimant argued that the MFN treatment provision of the United Kingdom-Argentina BIT entitled it to rely on the United States-Argentina BIT, which does not include such a requirement. The MFN treatment provision of the United Kingdom-Argentina BIT on which the claimant relied contained two paragraphs of particular relevance. Article 3(1) provided that neither party shall subject covered investments to "treatment" less favorable than that which it accords to investments of third states. Article 3(2) guaranteed MFN treatment to covered investors "as regards their management, maintenance, use, enjoyment or disposal of their investments." As it happened, the United Kingdom had inserted in the MFN treatment provision of BITs concluded after 1991 a sentence reading, "For the avoidance of doubt it is confirmed that treatment provided in paragraphs (1) and (2) above shall apply to the provisions of Articles 1 to 11 of this Agreement." The articles listed include the investor-state dispute resolution provision. Such language, however, did not appear in the United Kingdom-Argentina BIT. Further, the United Kingdom had exchanged notes with Panama agreeing that the MFN treatment provision in their BIT did not extend to dispute settlement. Even if it were inferred from this practice that the United Kingdom regarded dispute resolution as within the scope of the MFN treatment provision, no evidence existed concerning whether Argentina concurred in this view. Thus, the tribunal found that the external evidence of the parties' intent was inconclusive. The tribunal held that, in light of the context in which the MFN treatment provision was concluded, which included the importance of dispute resolution procedures to investment protection, the term "treatment" includes dispute resolution.

The award in *National Grid* avoided explicitly answering some obvious questions. The first is the question of identifying the paragraph of the MFN treatment provision on which the tribunal relied. The first paragraph guaranteed an unqualified MFN "treatment" and thus was the most obvious choice. The first paragraph, however, guaranteed MFN treatment to the investment. The claimant was not the investment or the owner of the investment, but a minority shareholder in the investment. This leads in turn to a question as to whether the treatment of an investment includes access to dispute resolution for its minority shareholders. Were the first paragraph the full extent of the MFN treatment provision, one reasonably could conclude from the award that treatment of investment does indeed extend to the ability of even minority shareholders to protect their rights in the investment. Yet, the United Kingdom-Argentina BIT had a second provision guaranteeing to MFN treatment to investors, but only as regards their management, maintenance, use, enjoyment, or disposal of their investments. This raises the question of whether the protection accorded to the investor is different from that accorded to the investment or whether the qualifying language was intended not to limit the scope of the word "treatment" but only to indicate that the treatment did indeed have to relate to the investment in some way and was not a right to MFN treatment of an investor in all matters. Of course, even if the language were considered to qualify the word "treatment," the tribunal could conclude that the qualifying language nevertheless is broad enough to include dispute resolution, as indeed at least two tribunals already have.[99] In short, the tribunal's decision clearly can be justified based on the language of the treaty, but that justification might rest on any of several different lines of reasoning and the award does not indicate which of these lines formed the basis of the decision.

In *Suez & Vivendi v. Argentina*, the tribunal addressed explicitly the issues avoided in *National Grid.* In that case, a Spanish claimant sought to assert a claim under the Spain-Argentina BIT, while a British claimant sought to assert a claim under the United Kingdom-Argentina BIT. Both BITs required that disputes be submitted to local remedies for 18 months and both claimants sought to avoid this provision by claiming through the MFN treatment provision of their respective BITs the benefit of the France-Argentina BIT, which had no such requirement. As it happened, the tribunal in *Suez & Vivendi* was composed of the same three arbitrators as the tribunal in *Suez & Interaguas*, discussed above, in which a Spanish claimant made the same argument regarding the MFN treatment provision under the Spain-Argentina BIT as the Spanish claimant in *Suez & Vivendi*. With regard to the claim by the Spanish claimant, the tribunal employed the same reasoning and often the same language that it employed in *Suez & Interaguas,* and reached the same result, i.e., consistent with *Maffezini* the MFN treatment provision could be used to claim the benefit of the remedies provision in the France-Argentina BIT. With regard to the claim by the British claimant, the tribunal faced essentially the same argument as that made by the British claimant under the United Kingdom-Argentina BIT in *National Grid.* The tribunal applied the same reasoning to the United Kingdom-Argentina BIT provision that it applied to the Spain-Argentina BIT provision. The tribunal in *Suez & Vivendi* acknowledged that the language of the United Kingdom-Argentina BIT was different from that in the Spain-Argentina BIT, but, as had the tribunal in *National Grid*, it interpreted the word "treatment" as broad enough to encompass dispute resolution. Although the tribunal in *Suez & Vivendi* did not explicitly identify the paragraph of the MFN treatment provision upon which it was resting its decision, the tribunal did find that dispute resolution is related to investors' "management, maintenance, use, enjoyment or disposal of their investment" and in particular is related to the "maintenance" of an investment.[100] By interpreting the language of Article 3(2), it implied that it was resting its decision on the paragraph applicable to the investor rather than that applicable to the investment, although it may only have been indicating that the additional language did not affect the result.

Reasons exist to question the *Suez & Vivendi* tribunal's interpretation of the phrase "management, maintenance, use, enjoyment, or disposal of investment." Footnote 13 to the draft Free Trade Agreement of the Americas (FTAA), dated November 21, 2003, records that one delegation proposed inclusion in the negotiating history of a footnote in which the parties note the *Maffezini* decision and then record their shared understanding that the MFN article of the FTAA is expressly limited to matters with respect to the establishment, acquisition, expansion, management, conduct, operation, and sale or other dispositions of investments and that this does not encompass international dispute resolution mechanisms and therefore could not reasonably lead to a conclusion

---

99 *See Suez & Vivendi v. Argentina* and *RosInvestCo v. Russia*, discussed below.

100 Award, para. 57.

similar to that of the *Maffezini* case.[101] Language similar to that in Article 3(2) of the United Kingdom-Argentina BIT appears in the U.S. BITs and it is understood in those BITs not to apply to dispute resolution.[102] An explicit statement to that effect appears in a footnote included in the negotiating history of the Central America-Dominican Republic-United States Free Trade Agreement (CAFTA-DR).[103] Thus, in light of these examples of state practice, the tribunal may have interpreted the language too broadly.

Yet, a second award supports the interpretation in *Suez & Vivendi.* In *RosInvestCo v. Russia*, a case arising under the United Kingdom-Russia BIT, the investor-state disputes provision applied only to certain claims involving an expropriation, such as claims concerning the amount of compensation (but not the fact of the expropriation itself). The claimant, wishing to assert a claim that an expropriation had occurred, sought to incorporate through the general MFN treatment provision a broader investor-state disputes provision in the Denmark-Russia BIT, which applied to "any dispute . . . in connection with an investment." The general MFN treatment provision included two clauses. One guaranteed MFN treatment to investment, while the other guaranteed to investors MFN treatment with respect to their management, maintenance, use, enjoyment, or disposal of investments. The tribunal held that the "treatment" of the "investment" did not include the availability of an investor-state disputes provision of another treaty for the purpose of alleging an expropriation.[104] Rather, access to arbitration affected the rights of the investor rather than the investment. The tribunal held, however, that in the second clause, which guaranteed MFN treatment to the investor, the terms "uses" and "enjoyment" did implicate the availability of investor-state arbitration of an expropriation claim. Thus, the tribunal had jurisdiction over the expropriation claim.[105] The tribunal in *RosInvestCo* thus reached the same result as the tribunals in *National Grid* and in *Suez & Vivendi,* applying similar MFN provisions, although it was more explicit about its rationale, answering questions not completely answered by either of those awards. In *RosInvestCo,* the identity of the beneficiary of the MFN provision was crucial. Other tribunals, however, have rejected the argument that the application of the MFN treatment provision depends on whether the MFN treatment is granted to the investment or the investor.[106]

Application of the principle in *Maffezini* does not necessarily mean that the claimant will prevail in its attempt to apply the MFN treatment provision to the disputes provisions of another treaty. For example, in *Yaung Chi Oo v. Myanmar*, the Singaporean claimant submitted a claim against Myanmar to arbitration under the ASEAN Agreement for the Promotion and Protection of Investments, but sought to base the jurisdiction of the tribunal on the provisions of the Myanmar-Philippines BIT, which

---

101 The text is available at http://www.ftaa-alca.org.

102 Kenneth J. Vandevelde, *U.S. International Investment Agreements* 248 (2009).

103 *Id.* at 318.

104 Decision on Jurisdiction, para. 129.

105 Decision on Jurisdiction, para. 133.

106 *See Plama v. Bulgaria* (Cyprus-Bulgaria BIT), Decision on Jurisdiction, para. 190; *Siemens v. Argentina* (Germany-Argentina BIT), Decision on Jurisdiction, para. 92.

the claimant argued should be applied through the MFN treatment provision of the ASEAN agreement. The tribunal rejected this argument because the two treaties called for arbitration before different bodies and utilizing different appointing authorities. In short, the tribunal wished to avoid the coherency problem identified above.

Some tribunals have been critical of the reasoning in *Maffezini*. For example, in *Salini Costruttori v. Jordan*, a case that arose under the Italy-Jordan BIT, the claimant sought to submit to arbitration a dispute involving a contract that contained a choice of forum clause. Article 9(2) of the BIT provided that "In case the investor and an entity of the Contracting Parties have stipulated an investment Agreement, the procedures foreseen in such investment Agreement shall apply." The MFN provision, Article 3(1) of the BIT, provided that the parties shall grant investments "no less favourable treatment" than that accorded to investments of third states. The claimant argued that Jordan's BITs with the United States and the United Kingdom contained no such requirement as that which appeared in Article 9(2) and thus the claimant was entitled to submit its dispute to investor-state arbitration without satisfying such a requirement. The tribunal rejected this argument, however, holding that the MFN treatment provision of the Italy-Jordan BIT did not apply to dispute resolution because, unlike the provision in the *Maffezini* decision, it did not explicitly provide that it applied to "all matters" relating to investment. Further, article 9(2) of the Italy-Jordan BIT requiring recourse to previously-agreed dispute procedures suggested the existence of a policy contrary to the position urged by the claimant. The tribunal in *Salini* was careful to find textual differences between the MFN treatment provision that it was interpreting and the MFN treatment provision applied in *Maffezini*. As a result, the *Salini* award is not inconsistent in principle with the *Maffezini* award. Nevertheless, the *Salini* tribunal expressed concerns about the wisdom of the *Maffezini* decision. In particular, the tribunal feared that the public policy exception "may in practice prove difficult to apply, thereby adding more uncertainties to the risk of 'treaty shopping.'"[107] Whereas the tribunal in *Maffezini* seemed inclined to apply the MFN treatment provision to dispute resolution unless its text precluded application, the *Salini* tribunal seemed inclined not to apply the MFN treatment provision to dispute resolution unless its text explicitly applied to "all matters" related to investment.

In *Plama v. Bulgaria*, Article 4.1 of the Cyprus-Bulgaria BIT provided for ad hoc investor-state arbitration of disputes concerning the amount of compensation for expropriation. The claimant, however, did not rely upon this provision. Rather, the claimant submitted the claim to ICSID arbitration, asserting that the MFN treatment provision of the Cyprus-Bulgaria BIT entitled it to the benefit of Bulgaria's consent to ICSID jurisdiction in other BITs. The MFN treatment provision, Article 3.1, guaranteed to covered investment "a treatment" that is not less favorable than that accorded to investments of investors of third states. Article 3.2 excluded from this treatment privileges that either party accords to third-country investors by virtue of their participation in an economic community, customs union, or free trade area. The tribunal acknowledged that the failure to include dispute resolution in the list of exclusions implied that

107 Decision on Jurisdiction, para. 115.

dispute resolution was included within the term "treatment," but observed that the use of the word "privileges" with equal force could imply that only substantive protections were within the scope of the MFN treatment provision. The tribunal noted that the BIT was intended to provide favorable conditions for investment, but thought that such general statements were not sufficient to establish the intention of the parties to apply the MFN treatment provision to dispute resolution provisions and, citing Sir Ian Sinclair,[108] cautioned that undue emphasis on the object and purpose of a treaty could result in failing to adhere to the intention of the parties. The tribunal observed that BITs concluded by Bulgaria after the 1987 Cyprus-Bulgaria BIT and after the end of the communist regime included dispute resolution provisions authorizing resort to ICSID and that an attempted but unsuccessful renegotiation of the Cyprus-Bulgaria BIT in 1998 sought to revise the dispute resolution provision, from which it could be inferred that the parties themselves did not believe that the MFN treatment provision applied to dispute resolution provisions in other BITs. The tribunal held that a consent to arbitration must be "clear and unambiguous"[109] and that the word "treatment" did not constitute a clear and unambiguous incorporation by reference of dispute resolution procedures. In many cases, it also would be unclear whether a particular dispute resolution provision in another treaty was more favorable and therefore within the scope of an MFN treatment provision. The tribunal questioned whether one could infer from an MFN treatment provision an intent to incorporate "an entirely different mechanism" than that authorized in the BIT.[110] The tribunal also challenged the desirability of incorporating dispute resolution provisions as a matter of policy. Because such a clause allows the investor to select the provisions of another treaty the benefit of which it wishes to claim, applying the MFN treatment provision to dispute resolution could result in the host state's being confronted with a large variety of dispute resolution procedures and undermine efforts to harmonize dispute resolution.

This last point is particularly interesting, because one purpose of an MFN treatment provision is to harmonize treaty practice by allowing all covered investments and investors to claim the same treatment. Where claimants have different perceptions of what is the most favorable treatment, however, the application of an MFN treatment provision to a complex investor-state disputes provision could result in innumerable combinations of provisions, rather than the emergence of a single mechanism constituted of the most favorable clauses of the host state's BITs. As it happens, many of the cases that have addressed the application of the MFN treatment provision to the investor-state disputes provision have involved the claimant's efforts to avoid the same clause, one requiring resort to local remedies for 18 months, a clause that is in only a small number of BITs. To the extent that they were successful, they would have harmonized the host state's treaty practice rather than increased its variety. Other cases, like *Plama*, have involved efforts to avoid an unusually restrictive consent to jurisdiction limited only to certain claims, such as expropriation claims. Thus, in general, claimants have not sought to use the MFN treatment provision to create unique investor-state disputes

---

108 Sir Ian Sinclair, *The Vienna Convention on the Law of Treaties* 130 (2d ed. 1984).

109 Decision on Jurisdiction, para. 198.

110 *Id.* at para. 209.

provisions tailored to their special circumstances, but to avoid unusual clauses that impose atypical restrictions on investor-state dispute resolution. This is not to say that the *Plama* tribunal's concern about disharmony would not arise in the future, but only that experience to date has not confirmed it. As it happens, the majority of the tribunals to address whether the MFN treatment provision could be used to avoid the 18-month requirement have decided in the affirmative, while tribunals addressing whether the MFN treatment provision could be used to avoid unusually restrictive consents to jurisdiction generally have decided in the negative.

The *Plama* tribunal disagreed with the *Maffezini* award because the latter did not require clear and unambiguous evidence that the MFN treatment provision applies to dispute resolution, but, in effect, interpreted the MFN treatment provision in the same way as every other provision of the BIT. The tribunal noted that the public policy exception in *Maffezini* did not appear anywhere in the text of the treaty and reflected a recognition by the *Maffezini* tribunal that applying the MFN treatment provision to dispute resolution could lead to undesirable results. The tribunal suggested that a better approach would be to adopt a rule that an MFN treatment provision does not incorporate dispute resolution provisions, in whole or in part, unless the MFN treatment provision "leaves not doubt" that the parties intended to incorporate them.[111] The tribunal observed that the *Maffezini* award is "perhaps understandable."[112] The 18-month local remedies requirement was "nonsensical" from a practical point of view and the tribunal in that case had sought a way to avoid it.[113] The *Plama* tribunal remarked, however, that the difficult exceptional circumstances of the *Maffezini* case should not form the basis of a general principle that would be applied in future cases not involving exceptional circumstances. The tribunal concluded by noting that its considerations were consistent with the award in *Salini*, although it had not relied on that award because the award had been issued after the parties submitted their pleadings.

In a sense, the tribunals in *Maffezini* and *Plama* were concerned about the same problem. In *Maffezini*, the tribunal was concerned about the potential consequences of applying the MFN treatment provision to dispute resolution provisions and thus created, with no basis in the text of the BIT, a public policy exception to its conclusion that an MFN treatment provision could apply to dispute resolution provisions. The *Plama* tribunal, similarly concerned, again without a basis in the text of the BIT, simply created a rebuttable presumption against the inclusion of investor-state disputes provisions within the scope of the MFN treatment provision, a presumption that could be overcome by clear and convincing evidence, which it defined as evidence that leaves no doubt.

In *Telenor v. Hungary*, the dispute resolution provision of the Norway-Hungary BIT applied only to disputes concerning the expropriation, war and civil disturbance, and transfers provisions. The claimant argued that the MFN treatment provision of the treaty allowed it to invoke the investor-state disputes provisions of other unspecified BITs concluded by Hungary. The MFN treatment provision of the Norway-Hungary BIT, at

111 *Id.* at para. 223.

112 *Id.* at para. 224.

113 *Id.*

Article IV, guaranteed to covered investment "treatment" no less favorable than that accorded to investments of investors of any third state. The tribunal "wholeheartedly endorsed[d]" the reasoning of the *Plama* award.[114] The tribunal found that the ordinary meaning of "treatment" is limited to the investor's substantive rights. To interpret the treaty otherwise, said the tribunal, would expose the host state to "treaty shopping," potentially allowing the investor to claim the benefit of selected clauses from a treaty, while disregarding others. Such an interpretation would invite uncertainty and instability, as it would be unclear whether the language of the treaty or the broader language of another treaty would be operative. In addition, where the parties have expressly limited the categories of disputes that may be submitted to arbitration, that interpretation would subvert their intention to limit the tribunal's jurisdiction. The tribunal held, therefore, that an MFN treatment provision should not be used to expand the jurisdiction of the tribunal to categories of disputes beyond those identified in the BIT itself in that absence of clear language that such is the intent of the parties. In this case, the tribunal noted that this was the only BIT that Norway had concluded with such a limitation, while Hungary's practice varied with respect to whether such a limitation was included. The tribunal inferred from this evidence that the parties had made a deliberate choice to limit arbitration to the categories specified in the BIT.

The tribunal also noted that three factors used by the tribunal in *Suez & Interaguas* to distinguish the *Plama* award militated in favor of distinguishing this case from *Suez & Interaguas*. The MFN treatment provision was more limited in *Telenor*, the prior treaty practice demonstrated the parties' intent not to broaden the scope of treaty rights, and the effect of the MFN treatment application sought by the claimant would go beyond merely removing a condition for invoking dispute resolution to expanding the jurisdiction of the tribunal.

The reasoning of the *Plama* tribunal also was adopted in *Berschader v. Russia*, a case arising under the Belgium-Luxembourg Economic Union-Russia BIT, which limited the investor-state disputes provision only to claims concerning the amount or mode of compensation for expropriation. The tribunal held that an MFN treatment provision would apply to an arbitration provision only if its terms clearly and unambiguously so provided. The tribunal found that the phrase "all matters covered by the present Treaty" did not include dispute resolution. The tribunal noted that the phrase could not be read literally, because it did not apply, for example, to provisions addressing the relationship between the two BIT parties. The tribunal noted that the MFN treatment provision had clarifying language under which it applied "particularly to Articles 4, 5 and 6."[115] The investor-state disputes provision was not among the articles listed. The tribunal observed that, given the uncertainty as to the application of the MFN treatment provision to investor-state arbitration, the BIT parties would have had a strong incentive to include the investor-state disputes provision in the clarifying language if they wished the MFN treatment provision to apply to it. The tribunal noted as well the longstanding policy of the Soviet Union, which had been Russia's predecessor as a party to the BIT, not to consent to arbitration of the issue whether an expropriation

---

114 Award, para. 90.

115 Award, para. 193.

had occurred, thus suggesting that the Soviet Union would not have intended the MFN treatment provision to apply to dispute resolution. For these reasons, the tribunal concluded that the MFN treatment provision did not clearly and unambiguously apply to arbitration clauses.

The tribunal followed the *Plama* award as well in *Wintershall v. Argentina*, a case arising under the Germany-Argentina BIT. In that case, the tribunal held that the term "treatment" did not apply to investor-state dispute resolution because to do so would allow an investor to circumvent the 18-month waiting period that the tribunal considered to be an element of Argentina's consent to arbitration. The tribunal also found support for its decision in Article 4(4) of the BIT, which guaranteed MFN treatment with respect to the matters covered in Article 4, which included the full protection and security provision and the expropriation provision and which were the provisions that underlay the claim in that case. The tribunal found that the special language of Article 4(4) had the effect of excluding matters relating to full protection and security and expropriation from the scope of the general MFN treatment provision, else Article 4(4) would have been superfluous.[116] Thus, the general MFN treatment provision did not apply to the claim at all. The only MFN treatment provision applicable the claim was that in Article 4(4), which applied only to the matters covered in Article 4, which did not include dispute resolution. The tribunal concluded that an MFN treatment provision should be interpreted to apply to dispute resolution only where its language clearly and unambiguously so indicates. Further, even assuming that the *Maffezini* award was followed, the tribunal held that the MFN provision should not be applied to permit the claimant to enjoy the benefit of the investor-state disputes provision in the United States-Argentina BIT, because that BIT provided for a fundamentally different system of arbitration than did the Germany-Argentina BIT. Specifically, the Germany-Argentina BIT required submission of claims to local remedies before their submission to investor-state arbitration, while the United States-Argentina BIT included an election of remedies clause under which submission of a claim to local remedies would preclude investor-state arbitration of that claim. Further, the Germany-Argentina BIT authorized ICSID arbitration, while the United States-Argentina BIT authorized the investor to choose between ICSID arbitration and ad hoc arbitration under the UNCITRAL Rules. Noting that the *Maffezini* award had said that the MFN provision should not be permitted to allow the investor to select a different system of arbitration, the tribunal found that refusing to allow the claimant to invoke the MFN provision to obtain the benefits of the investor-state disputes provision in the United States-Argentina BIT was consistent with *Maffezini*. The tribunal did not address the fact that the claimant was not seeking to utilize the MFN provision to obtain the right to submit

116 As noted above, in *Siemens v. Argentina*, the tribunal interpreted this as language of emphasis rather than language of exclusion. The *Wintershall* tribunal's interpretation is a counter-intuitive one that is justified only by the tribunal's effort to ensure that each provision of the BIT had some independent effect. In fact, however, BITs sometimes do include redundant clauses. The interpretation of the *Siemens* tribunal is likely the correct one, even if it does render a treaty provision superfluous. As the *Siemens* tribunal found, the language of Article 4(4) was likely included for emphasis.

the claim to arbitration under the UNCITRAL Rules, but only to avoid the 18-month local remedies requirements, precisely the use permitted by the *Maffezini* award.

In *Camuzzi v. Argentina*, the Belgium-Luxembourg Economic Union (BLEU)-Argentina BIT required that a claim be submitted to local courts for a period of 18 months prior to their submission to investor-state arbitration. The claimant argued that it should not be required to comply with this requirement because no such requirement appeared in the United States-Argentina BIT. As it happened, Argentina had not argued that the claimant had failed to meet this requirement and thus the tribunal did not need to consider whether it could be avoided through recourse to the MFN treatment provision of the BLEU-Argentina BIT. The tribunal noted that the dispute had been submitted to local courts and that 18 months would have passed without a solution and thus the requirement would have been met in any event.[117]

Some cases have involved efforts to use the MFN treatment provision to apply the substantive provisions, rather than the procedural provisions, of a host-state BIT with a third country. For example, in *MTD Equity v. Chile*, a Malaysian claimant submitted to arbitration a claim against Chile under the Malaysia-Chile BIT. Article 3(1) of that BIT guaranteed to investments "treatment" not less favorable than that received by investments of investors of any third state. The tribunal held that the MFN treatment provision allowed the claimant to rely on the fair and equitable treatment requirement and the prohibition on unreasonable or discriminatory measures in Chile's BIT with Croatia as well as the prohibition on unreasonable or discriminatory measures and the observance of obligations provision in Chile's BIT with Denmark. The tribunal reasoned that the MFN treatment provision should be interpreted in the manner that best protects investments. Further, the MFN treatment provision specified certain exclusions, notably those for tax treatment and benefits extended under regional cooperation agreements, and dispute resolution was not one of the matters expressly excluded.

In reply to: *Bayinder v. Pakistan*, the Turkey-Pakistan BIT did not include a fair and equitable treatment provision. The claimant argued that it was entitled, through the MFN treatment provision of that BIT, to the protection of that standard because it appeared in Pakistan's BITs with France, the Netherlands, China, the United Kingdom, Australia, and Switzerland. The tribunal accepted this argument for purposes of assessing jurisdiction.[118] Similarly, in *L.E.S.I. v. Algeria*, a case arising under the Italy-Algeria BIT, the tribunal permitted the claimant to obtain the benefit of the fair and equitable treatment standard in the BLEU-Algeria BIT, although the tribunal found no violation of the standard. In *CME v. Czech Republic*, the tribunal held that the MFN treatment provision of the Netherlands-Czech Republic BIT entitled the claimant to the benefit of the standard of compensation for expropriation prescribed by the United States-Czech Republic BIT.[119]

Some awards involved unsuccessful efforts to apply the MFN treatment provision to scope provisions, rather than substantive or procedural provisions. In *Tecmed v. Mexico*, a case arising under the Spain-Mexico BIT, the claimant sought to use the

117 Decision on Jurisdiction, para. 121.

118 Decision on Jurisdiction, para. 232.

119 Final Award, para. 500.

MFN treatment provision to obtain more favorable treatment with respect to the retroactive application of the BIT provided by the Austria-Mexico BIT. The tribunal rejected that argument, however, holding that matters relating to the agreement's temporal application, due to their significance and importance, must be specifically negotiated by the parties and cannot be impaired by application of the MFN treatment provision. In reaching this conclusion, the tribunal cited with approval the paragraphs of the *Maffezini* decision on jurisdiction in which it was held that the beneficiary of the MFN treatment provision should not be able to override fundamental public policy considerations.[120] In *MCI Power v. Ecuador*, the claimants argued that the MFN provision of the United States-Ecuador BIT entitled them to the protection of the preservation of rights provision of the Argentina-Ecuador BIT, but the tribunal rejected the argument.[121]

In *Société Générale v. Dominican Republic*, a case arising under the France-Dominican Republic BIT, the tribunal held that the MFN treatment provision could not be used to import a definition of "investment" from the CAFTA-DR.[122] This award seems clearly correct, because an asset must be an investment before the MFN treatment provision can apply at all. To permit an asset to use the MFN treatment provision to qualify itself as an investment entitled to use the MFN treatment provision would rest on circular reasoning.

In one case, the claimant sought unsuccessfully to utilize the MFN treatment provision to rely on the absence of a provision from a BIT between the host state and a third party. In *CMS Gas Transmission Company v Argentina*, the Argentina-United States BIT, on which the claim was based, included a clause that permitted either party to take measures necessary for the maintenance of public order or the protection of its own essential security interests. Argentina sought to invoke this clause to justify its modification of the tariff structure applicable to claimant's investment. The U.S. claimant contended that the clause was rendered inapplicable by the MFN treatment provision of the BIT because Argentina's BITs with other states did not include such a clause and thus the U.S. claimant was entitled to protection undiminished by the presence of the clause. The tribunal, however, rejected this argument. It held that the MFN treatment provision might be used to claim the benefit of a similar, but more favorable, clause in another treaty. It could not be used, however, to claim the benefit of the absence of a clause in another treaty.

In one case, *Parkerings-Compagniet v. Lithuania*, a case arising under the Norway-Lithuania BIT, the claimant did allege that it had been treated less favorably than a third-country investor, a rare case in which the MFN treatment provision is relied upon not for its generalizing effect but as a basis for compensation as a result of preferential treatment of a third-country investor. As discussed in Section 7.2.5, the tribunal found that the Norwegian claimant was not in like circumstances with the Dutch investor who was the beneficiary of the more favorable treatment. Thus, no violation occurred. The Norway-Lithuania BIT did not expressly impose a like circumstances condition

---

120 Award, para. 69, citing *Maffezini v. Spain*, Decision on Jurisdiction, paras. 62–63.

121 Award, para. 128.

122 Decision on Jurisdiction, para. 41.

on the MFN treatment provision, but the tribunal found such a condition to be inherent in the concept of MFN treatment.[123]

7.2.4 National Treatment: Origins

As noted in Section 7.2.2, prohibitions on discrimination appeared in the earliest BITs. Article 1(2) of the first BIT, the 1959 Germany-Pakistan BIT, provided that "capital" in the territory of one party "shall not be subjected to any discriminatory treatment on the ground that ownership of or influence upon it is vested in nationals or companies" of the other party, although this right to nondiscrimination was subject to existing local law. Article 2 set forth an early form of the unreasonable and discriminatory measures provision. Certainly, the references to discrimination were broad enough to include denials of national treatment.

The first Swiss BIT, concluded with Tunisia in 1961, included a national treatment provision linked to fair and equitable treatment. Article 1 of that treaty required fair and equitable treatment, which in no case was permitted to be less than national treatment.

The first Dutch BIT, concluded with Tunisia in 1963, required at Article 1 a "just and nondiscriminatory" treatment, which shall not be less than national treatment. This language quickly evolved to require the same "protection" as host-state nationals received.[124] By the mid-1980s, the Dutch BITs guaranteed national "treatment," with exceptions for benefits accorded under an economic integration or taxation agreement. [125]

The first Belgium-Luxembourg Economic Union (BLEU) BIT, signed with Tunisia in 1964, required that each party provide to covered investments "at least the same security and protection that it grants to those of its own nationals or to the investments of nationals and companies of third states."[126] This language was similar to that which had appeared in many FCNs. Thus, both national treatment and MFN treatment were elements of the BLEU BIT practice from the beginning. That said, however, the BLEU BITs over the next forty years typically contained no national treatment provision. Only in the current decade has the national treatment provision become a regular feature of the BLEU BITs.[127]

The first Danish BIT, concluded with Madagascar in 1965, like the Swiss-Tunisia BIT of four years before, included a national treatment provision linked to fair and equitable treatment. Article 6 of that treaty required fair and equitable treatment, which in no case was permitted to be less than national treatment. Danish practice ever since has, at times, linked fair and equitable treatment with nondiscrimination. In 1968, Denmark deleted the fair and equitable treatment standard and incorporated instead a

123 Award, paras. 368–369.

124 *See, e.g.*, Netherlands-Indonesia BIT, Art. 5.

125 *See, e.g.*, Netherlands-Sri Lanka BIT, Art. 5; Netherlands-Philippines BIT, Art. 4.

126 BLEU-Tunisia BIT, Art. 1.

127 *See, e.g.*, BLEU-Costa Rica BIT, Art. 4; BLEU-Sudan BIT, Art. 4; BLEU-D.R. Congo BIT, Art. 4.

general requirement of national treatment with respect to "any similar enterprise".[128] Denmark did not conclude any more BITs until 1980. When it resumed its program, the national treatment obligation was omitted.[129] In 1988, Denmark modified its practice again. It adopted a general national treatment obligation, with an exception for taxation agreements,[130] while also restoring the fair and equitable treatment standard. In the mid 1990s, Danish practice required fair and equitable treatment, which in no case shall be less than national treatment, although the national treatment obligation was subject to exceptions for customs union agreements and matters of taxation.[131]

The first Swedish BIT, concluded with Ivory Coast also in 1965, was similar[132] to the early Danish BITs. The Swedish BIT program went into a hiatus in 1967. When it resumed in 1978, the reference to national treatment was omitted. A general national treatment provision was inserted into many of the Swedish BITs beginning in the early 1990s[133] and such a provision is now typical.[134]

By the mid-1960s, no form of the national treatment provision was yet typical in the BITs. Perhaps not surprisingly, a national treatment provision did not appear in the 1967 OECD Draft Convention on the Protection of Foreign Property. Neither had one appeared in the 1959 Abs-Shawcross convention. The OECD draft convention did include general prohibitions on discrimination. The International Code of Fair Treatment for Foreign Investment proposed by the International Chamber of Commerce in 1949 contained extensive provisions on nondiscrimination, but these seem not to have influenced the content of the BITs.

State practice continued to be inconsistent in the 1970s. Early French BITs sometimes required that each party provide the same security and protection to covered investments that it provides to its own nationals.[135] Alternatively, they sometimes required fair and equitable treatment, which in no case shall be less than national treatment.[136] Sometimes a national treatment provision did not appear at all.[137] By the early 1980s, however, the French BITs included a general national treatment provision applicable to investments and associated activities.[138]

---

128 *See, e.g.*, Denmark-Indonesia BIT, Art. III.

129 *See, e.g.*, Denmark-Romania BIT, Art. 3; Denmark-China BIT, Art. 3.

130 *See, e.g.*, Denmark-Republic of Korea BIT, Art. 3,Denmark-Peru BIT, Art. 3; Denmark-Venezuela BIT, Arts. 3–4.

131 *See, e.g.*, Denmark-Mongolia BIT, Arts. 3(1),4; Denmark-India BIT, Arts. 3(1),4; Denmark-Nicaragua BIT, Arts. 3-4; Denmark-Ethiopia BIT, Arts. 3-4; Denmark-Croatia BIT, Art. 3; Denmark-Cuba BIT, Arts. 4–5; Denmark-Kyrgyz Republic BIT, Arts. 3–4.

132 Sweden-Ivory Coast BIT, Art. VI.

133 *See, e.g.*, Sweden-Chile BIT, Art. 3(1); Sweden-Bulgaria BIT, Art. 3(1); Sweden-Belarus BIT, Art. 3(1); Sweden-Republic of Korea BIT, Art. 3(1).

134 *See, e.g.*, Sweden-Kazakhstan BIT, Art. 3(1); Sweden-Croatia BIT, Art. 4(1); Sweden-Bosnia-Herzegovina BIT, Art. 3(1); Sweden-Ecuador BIT, Art. 3(1).

135 *See, e.g.*, France-D.R. Congo BIT, Art. 2; France-Indonesia BIT, Art. 3; France-Malaysia BIT, Art. 2.

136 *See, e.g.*, France-Egypt BIT, Art. 3.

137 *See, e.g.*, France-Singapore BIT.

138 *See, e.g.*, France-Equatorial Guinea BIT, Art. 4; France-Panama BIT, Art. 4.

Italy's 1975 BIT with Egypt included a general national treatment provision,[139] although such a provision did not become standard until the late 1980s.[140] Some Italian BITs also guarantee national treatment with respect to activities connected with an investment.[141]

The United Kingdom's BIT program consistently included a national treatment provision from the beginning. The first U.K. BIT, signed with Egypt in 1975, at article 3(2), guaranteed national treatment to covered investors with respect to the management, use, enjoyment, or disposal of their investments. Under Article 7, however, this provision did not apply to treatment extended by virtue of a customs union or free trade area agreement or an agreement or legislation relating wholly or mainly to taxation. A number of U.K. BITs that were concluded beginning in the 1980s included language noting that special incentives granted to stimulate the creation of local industries are considered compatible with the general national treatment provision provided that they do not significantly affect the investment and activities of nationals and companies of the other party in connection with an investment.[142]

The U.S. BIT program also adopted a consistent approach to national treatment from the beginning. Its first BIT, concluded with Egypt in 1982, guaranteed national treatment to covered investment, but brought several innovations to BIT practice.[143] First, in the U.S. BITs, the obligation of national treatment applied not only to the treatment of investments once established, but to the right of investors to establish investments. The U.S. BITs would remain unique in this regard until the conclusion of the NAFTA in 1992. A right of national and MFN treatment with respect to the establishment of investment now can be found as well in the Canadian and Japanese BITs.[144]

Second, the U.S. BITs guaranteed national treatment to investments and to certain activities associated with investments. The U.S. BITs abandoned the protection for associated activities in its 1994 model negotiating text.

Third, the U.S. BITs allowed each party to designate in an annex sectors of the economy in which it reserved the right to deny national treatment. Beginning with the 1991 model negotiating text, the U.S. BITs also authorized the parties to specify sectoral exceptions to the MFN treatment obligation.

The U.S. BITs required treatment as favorable as that granted only to investments in like situations with covered investment. As has been noted, some concept of comparability is inherent in any nondiscrimination provision.[145] The U.S. BITs, however, in using the term "in like situations" provided a verbal formula for ascertaining which

---

139 Italy-Egypt BIT, Art. II(1).

140 *See, e.g.*, Italy-Hungary BIT, Art. 3(1); Italy-Bangladesh BIT, Art. 3(1); Italy-Argentina BIT, Art. 3(1).

141 *See, e.g.*, Italy-Hungary BIT, Art. 3(2); Italy-Bangladesh BIT, Art. 3(2); Italy-Nicaragua BIT, Art. III(1).

142 *See, e.g.*, United Kingdom-Papua New Guinea BIT, Art. 3(3); United Kingdom-Jamaica BIT, Art. 3(3).

143 United States-Egypt BIT, Art. II.

144 *See, e.g.*, Japan-Vietnam BIT, Art. 2; Canada-Uruguay BIT, Art. 3.

145 *See* Section 7.1.

investments shall be compared to the covered investment. Some earlier Danish BITs had included language guaranteeing national treatment to a "similar enterprise."[146]

By the mid-1980s, the main forms of the national treatment provision were established in BIT practice. Yet the provision achieved its current level of prevalence in BIT practice only in the 1990s. Indeed, several countries that were among the first to inaugurate BIT programs adopted the national treatment standard only in the 1990s. For example, Kuwait began its BIT program in 1964, but a general national treatment obligation did not become typical of the Kuwaiti BITs until the 1990s.[147] The provision commonly guaranteed national treatment to both investments and investors. Some Kuwaiti BITs required that the investors or investors be "in like situations."[148]

Austria launched its BIT program in the 1970s, but a general national treatment standard did not regularly appear until the 1990s. The national treatment standard in the 1990s applied to both investors and their investments,[149] although in some cases the national treatment guaranteed to investors was limited to treatment with respect to the management, maintenance, use, enjoyment, operation, sale, and liquidation of investments.[150] In the more recent Austrian BITs, this qualification applies to the national treatment obligation with respect to both investments and investors. [151]

Finland began its BIT program in 1980, but the Finnish BITs began to guarantee national treatment to investments only in the mid-1990s.[152] Soon, national treatment was guaranteed to investors as well as investments.[153] Recent Finnish BITs continue to guarantee national treatment to both investments and investors, although the right of national treatment has been modified in two ways in some Finnish BITs. First, the requirement of national treatment often applies to the right to establish investment.[154] Second, the required treatment, at least in the case of investor, may not be treatment generally, but treatment with regard to the management, maintenance, use, enjoyment, and disposal of investments,[155] as well as in some cases the establishment of investments.[156]

7.2.5 National Treatment: Arbitral Practice

Several arbitrations have considered claims that the host state violated its national treatment obligation. In general, the awards have held that the national treatment

---

146 *See, e.g.*, Denmark-Indonesia BIT, Art. III.

147 *See, e.g.*, Kuwait-Czech Republic BIT, Art. 4; Kuwait-Ethiopia BIT, Art. 4; Kuwait-Croatia BIT, Art. 4.

148 *See, e.g.*, Kuwait-Ethiopia BIT, Art. 4; Kuwait-Croatia BIT, Art. 4.

149 *See, e.g.*, Austria-Cape Verde BIT, Art. 3(1); Austria-Croatia BIT, Art. 3(1).

150 *See, e.g.*, Austria-Republic of Korea BIT, Art. 3(1)-(2); Austria-Chile BIT, Art. 3(1)–(2).

151 *See, e.g.*, Austria-Bosnia-Herzegovina BIT, Art (3)(4); Austria-Libya BIT, Art. 3(4); Austria-Jordan BIT, Art. 3(4); Austria-Armenia BIT, Art. 3(4).

152 *See, e.g.*, Finland-Chile BIT, Art. 3(1).

153 *See, e.g.*, Finland-Republic of Korea BIT, Art. 3; Finland-Thailand BIT, Art. 4; Finland-Brazil BIT, Art. 3; Finland-Peru BIT, Art. 3(2).

154 *See, e.g.*, Finland-Belarus BIT, Art. 4; Finland-Armenia BIT, Art. 3; Finland-Algeria BIT, Art. 3.

155 *See, e.g.*, Finland-Croatia BIT, Art. 3; Finland-Azerbaijan BIT, Art. 4.

156 *See, e.g.*, Finland-Belarus BIT, Art. 4; Finland-Armenia BIT, Art. 3; Finland-Algeria BIT, Art. 3.

provision prohibits discrimination on the basis of nationality. Measures that explicitly treat comparable foreign and domestic investment differently would violate national treatment. Measures that do not explicitly treat foreign and domestic investment differently, but that have a disproportionate adverse impact on foreign investment (sometimes referred to as "*de facto* discrimination") also violate national treatment if the host state's intent was to discriminate against foreign investment. As will be seen, in at least one case a tribunal has held that even unintentional discrimination violates national treatment.

Most cases do not involve discrimination against foreign investment on the face of the measure. Rather, in the typical claim under the national treatment provision, a host-state measure that is textually neutral is alleged to have a discriminatory impact on foreign investment. For example, in *S.D. Myers v. Canada*, a case arising under the NAFTA, the claimant challenged Canada's ban on the export of a hazardous chemical known as PCBs. The claimant wished to export PCBs to the United States, where its facility would dispose of them for a fee. Thus, the effect of the ban was to foreclose S.D. Myers from the business of disposing of PCBs originating in Canada. The ban did not textually discriminate in any way against foreign investments. All companies, Canadian and foreign, were prohibited from exporting PCBs. The tribunal held that discrimination could be demonstrated either by the contents of the measure on its face or by its practical effect in creating a disproportionate benefit for nationals over non-nationals. Although the tribunal conceded that the measure on its face did not favor Canadian nationals over others, it found that the practical effect was to disadvantage the U.S. company, since no Canadian competitor needed to export PCBs in order to enter the market. The tribunal then inquired as to whether this discriminatory effect was the result of an intent to discriminate. It noted statements by Canadian officials to the effect that the ban would preserve the PCB disposal business for Canadian companies and found that the ban therefore violated national treatment. While Canada's desire to strengthen its industry was a legitimate goal, alternative ways consistent with NAFTA obligations were available for achieving that goal. For example, Canada could have granted subsidies to Canadian industry. Indeed, the fact that Canada eventually reopened its border to PCB exports demonstrated that the ban was not necessary to address the situation effectively.

While in *S.D. Myers* the claimant had proof of the host state's discriminatory intent, that is not always the case. In *Pope and Talbot v. Canada*, another case arising under the NAFTA, in an effort to resolve a trade dispute with the United States, Canada limited softwood lumber exports to the United States, assigning an export quota to each producer. The claimant alleged that it had received a less favorable treatment with respect to its quota. As explained below, the tribunal found that most of the Canadian producers with more favorable treatment were not in like circumstances with the claimant and thus were not appropriate comparators for purpose of applying the national treatment provision. Although the claimant apparently was regarded by the tribunal as in like circumstances with certain producers in British Columbia, the tribunal observed that the measures of which the claimant complained adversely affected a large number of Canadian producers. The tribunal thus could find no convincing evidence that the treatment of claimant's investment was based on nationality. Rather, the tribunal found that the manner of allocating quotas was a rational means of avoiding a trade dispute. Accordingly, the tribunal found no violation of national treatment.

Where evidence of a discriminatory motive is absent, a tribunal may be willing to presume discriminatory motive from the evidence of the discriminatory impact. For example, in *Feldman v. Mexico*, another case arising under the NAFTA, Mexico denied a company owned by a U.S. national a tax rebate for cigarettes sold for export, while at least three exporters of Mexican nationality were given the rebates. The tax law did not explicitly discriminate against foreign investment, but the law was applied in such a way that the foreign investment was treated differently than the domestic companies. The tribunal observed that the national treatment provision of the NAFTA, Article 1102, did not explicitly require that a discriminatory motive be shown, but seemed to require only proof of less favorable treatment. The tribunal nevertheless found, citing the U.S. Statement of Administrative Action regarding NAFTA, that Article 1102 prohibits only discrimination by reason of nationality. The tribunal observed that requiring a claimant to prove that discrimination is based on nationality could impose an insurmountable burden on the claimant, because such information may be available only to the government. The tribunal thus was willing to assume that the different treatment was based on claimant's nationality, in the absence of evidence to the contrary. The tribunal went on to find evidence that raised at least a "strong suspicion" that Mexico had acted on the basis of the claimant's nationality.[157] The tribunal accordingly found that Mexico had violated its obligation to provide national treatment.

In *Champion Trading v. Egypt*, a case arising under the United States-Egypt BIT, the claimant alleged that Egypt had violated the national treatment obligation by declining to make reimbursement payments to its investment, a cotton trading company, although such payments had been made to other cotton trading companies owned by Egyptian investors. The tribunal observed that, even assuming that claimant's investment were treated differently than local investment in like situations, "[t]he question would remain whether a difference of treatment in like situations could be permissible based on other objective grounds."[158] That is, the tribunal appeared to recognize that different treatment would not violate the national treatment obligation if it were justified on grounds other than nationality, i.e., if it were not the result of a discriminatory motive. In any event, as discussed below, the tribunal found that none of the companies that received the more favorable treatment were in like situations with the claimant's investment.

In *Occidental v. Ecuador*, a case arising under the United States-Ecuador BIT, the tribunal did not require proof of a discriminatory motive. In that case, Ecuador had administered a value-added tax (VAT) refund system in such a way that the claimant received less favorable treatment than domestic investments in like situations. Specifically, the claimant did not receive a refund of the tax on its exports, while domestic companies did. The tribunal found this difference in treatment to be a violation of the national treatment provision, although it acknowledged that the difference was not the result of an intent to discriminate against foreign investment, but rather the

---

157 Award, para. 182.

158 Award, para. 134.

result of an effort to administer a complex web of regulations. The finding of a violation where the difference in treatment was founded on legitimate regulatory objectives is inconsistent with the majority of the awards.

In some cases, a claim that the national treatment obligation has been violated fails because the claimant does not prove that the host-state measures affected the claimant differently than other investments. In *International Thunderbird v. Mexico*, a case arising under the NAFTA, the claimant alleged that Mexico's enforcement of the gambling laws against its investment violated the national treatment obligation. The tribunal found, however, that the Mexican authorities had sought to close not only claimant's operation, but Mexican gambling facilities as well. The tribunal observed that some facilities had been able to gain temporary injunctive relief in Mexican courts that allowed them to operate, but that the Mexican authorities were appealing those orders. The judicial branch, of course, is bound by BIT obligations just as the political branches are and thus judicial decisions that discriminated on the basis of nationality by allowing Mexican gambling facilities, but not the claimant's facility, to operate would violate the national treatment provision. In the case of the judicial branch, however, tribunals have held that it is the court system as a whole that is to be evaluated against the obligations of the BIT[159] and thus a claim that the judicial branch had violated the national treatment obligation could not arise while appeals were pending. The tribunal also acknowledged that some Mexican facilities were still operating, but found insufficient evidence to establish that Mexico had knowledge of these facilities and had deliberately allowed them to remain open.

The tribunal also engaged in an ambiguous discussion of whether establishing the claim would have required proof a discriminatory motive. The tribunal said,

> It is not expected from Thunderbird that it show *separately* that the less favourable treatment was motivated because of nationality. The text of Article 1102 of the NAFTA does not require such showing. Rather, the text contemplates the case where a foreign investor is treated less favourably than a national investor. That case is to be proven by a foreign investor, and, additionally the reason why there was a less favourable treatment.[160]

Thus, the tribunal seemed to suggest in the first sentence that the claimant need show only less favorable treatment and need not show that the less favorable treatment was motivated by nationality. The last sentence, however, seems to suggest that the claimant must prove the reason for the less favorable treatment, i.e., must show that it was motivated on improper grounds. To deepen the ambiguity, the tribunal cited *S.D. Myers*, where the tribunal found a discriminatory motive; *Pope & Talbot*, where the tribunal rejected the national treatment claim because it did not find a discriminatory motive; *Feldman*, where the existence of a motive was required but presumed; and *Occidental*, where no motive was required. Because the tribunal found no discrimination, however, it did not need to address the issue of a discriminatory motive.

---

159 *See* Section 10.4.

160 Award, para. 177. Emphasis in original. Citations omitted.

The tribunal closed its discussion of the national treatment provision with a *dictum* that seemed to place a public policy limitation on the national treatment obligation. The tribunal observed that even if the claimant had proven that Mexico did not enforce its gambling laws uniformly and, in effect, selectively prosecuted the claimant on the basis of its nationality, "it would be inappropriate for a NAFTA tribunal to allow a party to rely on Article 1102 of the NAFTA to vindicate equality of nonenforcement within the sphere of an activity that a Contracting Party deems illicit."[161] This *dictum* seems questionable. The tribunal appears to say that on grounds of public policy it would decline to apply the national treatment provision to the enforcement of criminal laws. Covered investments are entitled to nondiscriminatory treatment, including in the application of criminal laws. As the tribunal said in *Feldman v. Mexico*, "Mexico is of course entitled to strictly enforce its laws, but it must do so in a non-discriminatory manner, as between foreign investors and domestic investors."[162] Further, a criminal law exception has no basis in the treaty text. Such unwritten exceptions obscure the treaty language, contrary to the transparency principle, and, to the extent that they are created by a tribunal after a dispute has arisen, they constitute a retroactive, *de facto* revision of the treaty that undermines the security principle. A state that wishes to exempt enforcement of its criminal laws from the application of the national treatment provision should do so through treaty language explicitly creating such an exception, thereby giving notice of the limits of treaty protection to investors. Finally, criminal law embodies many of a state's most important public policies and certainly foreign investments are and should be subject to a state's criminal laws to the same extent as other investments. Rarely, however, should a state have a legitimate reason to enforce its criminal laws on the basis of nationality. Indeed, the more important the public policy behind the law, the greater the need for consistent application of the law. It is in the area of criminal law, where sanctions are often the most severe and where transgressions are met with moral condemnation as well as the imposition of penalties, that the need for transparency, security and nondiscrimination is particularly important.

Another claim that failed because of the claimant's inability to prove discrimination was *ADF Group v. United States*, a case arising under the NAFTA. In that case, a Canadian company challenged a U.S. government requirement that the steel used in government-funded highway construction projects be of U.S. origin. The tribunal observed that the law did not on its face discriminate against steel owned by Canadian investors or against Canadian steel fabricators. All steel used in the highway project was required to be of U.S. origin, regardless of ownership.[163] The tribunal noted that such a regulation could give rise to a claim for *de facto* discrimination if it were shown that U.S. companies were inherently advantaged by a domestic content requirement.[164] The claimant, however, had submitted no evidence that it would have benefited economically from being allowed to use steel fabricated in Canada and thus had not established a claim of *de facto* discrimination.

---

161 Award, para. 183.
162 Award, para. 169.
163 Award, para. 156.
164 Award, para. 157.

Although an investment or investor seeking national treatment normally seeks the treatment accorded by the host state to its own nationals in its territory, the tribunal in *Maffezini v. Spain*, a case arising under the Argentina-Spain BIT, commented that the national treatment obligation also can require the treatment that the host state obtains through BITs for its nationals abroad. For example, if Spain concluded BITs with third countries entitling Spanish investors to fair and equitable treatment of their investments abroad, then Spain would be required to provide fair and equitable treatment to investments in its territory that were covered by a national treatment guarantee. The tribunal in *ADF Group v. United States*, a case arising under the NAFTA, cited this language from *Maffezini*, but found it inapplicable because the national treatment obligation of the NAFTA does not apply to government procurement programs, such as the highway construction project at issue in that case.

The national treatment obligation sometimes explicitly prohibits discrimination only as among investments (or, in some treaties, investors) "in like circumstances" or "in like situations." The two phrases are used interchangeably here. Several tribunals have addressed the meaning of "like circumstances." In general, tribunals have treated investments as in like circumstances where they have no differences that are related to legitimate regulatory objectives. That is, if the host state has legitimate regulatory reasons for treating the investments differently, then they are not in like circumstances and treating them differently will not violate the national treatment obligation.

In *Pope and Talbot v. Canada*, a case arising under the NAFTA, the tribunal observed that the meaning of "in like circumstances" varies according to the factual and legal contexts. In that case, the context included the investment-liberalizing objectives of the NAFTA and the entire softwood lumber trade dispute between Canada and the United States that had given rise to the measures about which the claimant was complaining. The tribunal also noted that any comparison should be of investments in the same economic sector. The tribunal went on to observe, however, that the inquiry did not end with that question. Specifically, the tribunal held that differences in treatment will presumptively violate the national treatment provision unless they have a "reasonable nexus to rational government policies" that do not distinguish on their face or in their effects between foreign and domestic companies and do not otherwise "unduly undermine" the investment liberalization objectives of NAFTA.[165] The tribunal found that different treatment of softwood lumber producers in provinces not covered by the agreement or new entrants in other provinces covered by the agreement were justified by rational policies to avoid the threat of U.S. retaliation and to provide for new entrants into the market. Therefore, these producers were not in like circumstances with the claimants. Within British Columbia, where claimant's investment was located, the tribunal found that a history of different treatment of coastal and interior producers prior to Canada's efforts to resolve the trade dispute meant that these groups of producers were not in like circumstances.

The *Pope & Talbot* approach to defining like circumstances was followed in *Parkerings-Compagniet v. Lithuania*, a case involving the Norway-Lithuania BIT and

165 Award, para. 78.

one of the rare cases where the term "like circumstances" is discussed in the context of the MFN treatment provision. Although the BIT did not expressly limit the MFN treatment provision to investors in like circumstances, the tribunal held that "[t]he essential condition of the violation of a MFN clause is the existence of a different treatment accorded to another foreign investor in a similar situation. Therefore, a comparison is necessary with an investor in like circumstances."[166] The tribunal also held that "two investors will not be in like circumstances if a justification of the different treatment is established."[167] The tribunal found that the Norwegian claimant's parking project was not in like circumstances with another project performed by a Dutch foreign investor because the former was larger and in a culturally sensitive area. That is, the different impact of the two projects was related to the host state's legitimate archeological and environmental policies.

The tribunal also followed the *Pope & Talbot* approach in *GAMI Investments v. Mexico*, another case arising under the NAFTA. In that case, Mexico expropriated 22 sugar mills, including Mexican-owned mills and five 5mills owned by a company in which the claimant was a minority shareholder. The tribunal found that no violation of the national treatment provision occurred, seeming to rest the decision on multiple grounds. Although the tribunal acknowledged that GAMI's investment was treated differently than some Mexican mills, the tribunal found that GAMI had failed to demonstrate that its circumstances were sufficiently like those of the nonexpropriated mills for the disparate treatment to violate the national treatment provision of the NAFTA. Mexico's decision to expropriate certain sugar mills and not others was not based on a discriminatory motive, but was "plausibly connected" to a legitimate policy of ensuring that the sugar industry was owned by solvent enterprises.[168]

The same approach was followed in *Champion Trading v. Egypt*, a case arising under the United States-Egypt BIT. In that case, the parties agreed that the claimant, a cotton trading company, was in like situation with other publicly- or privately-owned cotton trading companies. All these companies, purchased, ginned, and sold cotton. The claimant alleged a violation of national treatment because some such companies had received payments from the Egyptian government while others had not. The tribunal found, however, that in fact the claimant was not in a like situation with those cotton trading companies that received the payment. The payments were made to two groups of companies. One set of payments was made to companies to extinguish debts incurred prior to 1994, before the claimant's investment existed. These debts had arisen because prior to 1994 the government controlled the price at which cotton was purchased from farmers as well as the price at which it was sold, in some cases forcing cotton trading companies to suffer a loss. Ordinarily, of course, the date of incorporation might seem a trivial difference between two investments, but in this case the fact that the claimant's investment came into existence after 1994 was relevant to advancing the state's legitimate, nondiscriminatory policy of reimbursing all companies for debts incurred prior to that date as a result of the government pricing system. Thus, that

166 Award, para. 369.
167 Award, para. 375.
168 Award, para. 114.

policy served to distinguish the claimant's investment from recipients of the first type of payment. After 1994, the government allowed cotton trading companies to choose whether to purchase and sell their cotton through a cotton exchange at government fixed prices or to purchase and sell on the open market. A second set of payments reimbursed companies that had chosen to purchase and sell their cotton through the cotton exchange. The claimant's investment had chosen not to purchase through the exchange. The tribunal found that the claimant's investment could not be compared with other cotton trading companies that did purchase through the exchange. The payments were intended to reimburse the companies for losses associated with their purchase through the exchange and thus, the tribunal might have said, were a measure reasonably related to a legitimate nondiscriminatory policy. Finding that none of the companies that were said to receive more favorable treatment in the form of reimbursements was in a like situation with the claimant's investment, the tribunal found that Egypt had not provided more favorable treatment to local investments in like situations.

In *S.D. Myers v. Canada*, yet another case arising under the NAFTA, the tribunal said that the phrase should be interpreted keeping in mind the overall legal context, which would include the policy objectives of the relevant agreement, in that case the desire to protect the environment while avoiding trade distortions, and the need to protect the public interest. The tribunal noted that the concept of "like circumstances" invites an examination of whether the investors are in the same sector. The tribunal also noted that S.D. Myers was providing the same service as the Canadian companies that were more favorably treated and was in competition with them. Therefore, it was in like circumstances with the Canadian companies. Thus, despite the tribunal's discussion of policy objectives, it appears that the dispositive consideration in *S.D. Myers* was that the companies receiving different treatment were in the same sector and in direct competition.

One difficulty involved in the inquiry whether two investments are in the same sector is that the term "sector" can be defined at different levels of generality. A broadly defined sector could include the covered investment and many potential comparators, while a narrowly defined sector might include only the covered investment. Another difficulty is that operations can be aggregated in different ways such that two companies may have overlapping, but not entirely identical, operations. No criteria exist for determining the extent of the overlap necessary for two companies to be treated as being in the same sector. Further, in the contemporary world, an enterprise is not unlikely to assign various tasks to different corporate entities, including both affiliates and contractors. A technical or formalist preoccupation with identifying and assigning businesses to particular sectors could fail to take account of the reality of how investments are structured.

These problems are illustrated by the award in *S.D. Myers*. It has been argued that the investment in that case was not in the same sector as the Canadian companies with which its circumstances were compared because the investment was in the business of obtaining contracts for waste remediation but did not itself provide such services. Rather, such services were provided by a corporate affiliate. The Canadian companies, by contrast, were in the business of providing waste remediation services. It could be argued in reply that the Canadian companies also would have needed to obtain contracts to perform their services and thus they were in the same sector as S.D. Myers (obtaining contracts), although they were in another sector (providing services) as well. Indeed, as the tribunal found, the Canadian companies had lobbied the Canadian governments to ban PCB exports precisely because the covered investment was in a position to take business away from them. As this discussion illustrates, it is possible to characterize a business operation as involving a number of discrete tasks, each of which is said to be in a different sector.

These issues are illustrated as well by the award in *UPS v. Canada*, still another case arising under the NAFTA. In that case, the claimant was an overnight courier service claiming that it had been granted less favorable customs treatment than Canada Post. The tribunal concluded that the two enterprises were not in like circumstances, noting differences between the operation of an overnight courier service and a postal service, including the need for expedited treatment of courier deliveries, the greater security associated with courier shipments, the existence of contractual relationships between couriers and their clients, and the more detailed documentation provided by couriers. The tribunal observed that the claimant was in like circumstances with Canadian courier companies, with which the claimant was treated identically. Dean Ronald Cass wrote a dissenting opinion in which he concluded that the claimant and Canada Post were in like circumstances with respect to certain products. Dean Cass thus would have compared the treatment given to those aspects of the enterprises that were similar, while the tribunal compared the enterprises as a whole. Canada Post was in like circumstances with the claimant with respect to its courier service, but in the view of the tribunal it was not in like circumstances with the claimant with respect to general postal services.

In *Methanex v. United State*, one more case arising under the NAFTA, the tribunal held that the correct comparators of the claimant, a Canadian methanol producer, were U.S. methanol producers, who were treated in identical fashion by California's ban on methyl tertiary-butyl ether (MTBE) in gasoline, which eliminated the market for methanol in California. Methanex argued that the correct comparator was U.S. producers of ethanol, who were favored by the ban on MTBE because ethanol was a substitute for MTBE. The tribunal disagreed with the claimant, noting that ethanol is used as a fuel, while methanol is not. Rather, methanol is merely an ingredient in MTBE, which is the alternative to ethanol. In the course of its discussion, the tribunal commented that the phrase "in like circumstances" is not the same as the phrase "like products" used in trade agreements, although decisions in trade disputes could be considered for possible guidance in interpreting the phrase "in like circumstances."

In contrast to the award in *Methanex* is the award in *Occidental v. Ecuador*, a case arising under the United States-Ecuador BIT. In that case, the tribunal compared the claimant, which exported petroleum, with domestic companies that exported other products that were not in the same economic sector. The tribunal explained that "the purpose of national treatment is to protect investors as compared to local producers, and this cannot be done by addressing exclusively the sector in which that particular activity is undertaken."[169]

---

169 Award, para. 173.

In *Feldman v. Mexico*, another case arising under the NAFTA, the claimant's investment purchased cigarettes for export. The tribunal held that firms that purchase cigarettes for resale or export were in like circumstances with claimant, but that firms that produce cigarettes are not in like circumstances, even if they also export them. The parties actually agreed that the claimant was in like circumstances with Mexican-owned resellers of cigarettes for export and presumably for this reason the tribunal did not discuss the basis of its holding in any detail.

The question arises as to the consequences of being unable to identify an investment or investor in like circumstances with the claimant. In *Loewen v. United States*, yet another case arising under the NAFTA, the claimant had been a defendant in a civil action in Mississippi state court that was characterized by numerous references to the claimant's Canadian nationality and that resulted in a jury verdict against the claimant for $500,000,000. In addressing whether this conduct violated the national treatment provision, the tribunal alluded to the "critical problem" that it did not have an example of the treatment accorded in like circumstances by a Mississippi court to U.S. investors or investments.[170] The claimants argued that the plaintiff in the state court action was in like circumstances with them because all were litigants in the state court action. The tribunal found, however, that the circumstances of a plaintiff and a defendant were "very different."[171] Unable to find an appropriate comparator, the tribunal declined to consider the claimed violation of national treatment.

The approach of the *Loewen* tribunal is questionable. The purpose of the like circumstances requirement is not to permit the host state to engage in discriminatory action whenever no sufficiently close comparator exists. Rather, the purpose is to prevent unjustified discriminations, the assumption being that treating unlike investments differently is justifiable. Certainly, as the tribunal indicates, the circumstances of the two litigants were different. Yet, they nevertheless can be "like" within the meaning of the BIT if none of the differences is relevant to legitimate nondiscriminatory policies of the host state. The like circumstances test supports the policy behind the nondiscrimination provisions by attempting to remove from consideration comparators whose different treatment was based on legitimate, nondiscriminatory policies, but it was not intended to provide a technical defense for adverse treatment resulting from a discriminatory motive. Thus, as discussed in Section 7.1, even where no plausible comparator exists, the tribunal should find a violation if the treatment of the covered investment was the result of a discriminatory motive, that is, was not in furtherance of a legitimate host-state regulatory interest.[172]

---

170 Award, para. 140.

171 *Id.*

172 The award in *Loewen* can be contrasted with those in *Pope & Talbot, GAMI Investments*, and *Champion Trading*, discussed above, where the tribunal found a reasonable basis for treating the covered investment or investor differently than the putative comparators and concluded, therefore, that these comparators were not in like circumstances with the covered investment or investor. In those cases, then, the tribunal did inquire into the justification for the discriminatory treatment and, having found a nondiscriminatory justification, held that no violation of the BIT had occurred. That is, the awards in those cases adopted the approach proposed in Section 7.1, in that they apparently would have found a violation had the claimant been able to demonstrate

Nevertheless, tribunals in at least two other cases, *BG Group v. Argentina*, applying the unreasonable or discriminatory measures provision of the United Kingdom-Argentina BIT, and *Parkerings-Compagniet v. Lithuania*, applying the fair and equitable treatment standard of the Norway-Lithuania BIT, also have refused to find discrimination where no appropriate comparator could be identified.[173] By contrast, in *Noble Ventures v. Romania*, a case arising under the United States-Romania BIT, the tribunal recognized that in such a case a violation could be demonstrated by proving the existence of a discriminatory motive.[174]

7.3 WAR AND CIVIL DISTURBANCE

Many BITs include a provision requiring MFN and national treatment with respect to any compensation paid for losses sustained as a result of war or civil disturbance.[175] Some BITs that require both MFN and national treatment specify that the treatment to be accorded is that which is more favorable.[176] Even where this language does not appear, however, requiring that both be accorded implicitly requires that the investor receive the benefit of the more favorable treatment. Some BITs require only MFN treatment with respect to any such compensation.[177]

The war and civil disturbance nondiscrimination provision might seem largely redundant of the general national and MFN treatment provisions of the BITs. The war and civil disturbance nondiscrimination provision may offer protection beyond that accorded by the general national and MFN treatment provisions, however, in the case of BITs that include exceptions to the general national and MFN treatment provisions, to the extent that those exceptions do not apply to the war and civil disturbance provision. Some BITs, though, define the protection to be accorded under the war and civil disturbance nondiscrimination provision by reference to the general national and MFN treatment provision and thus may incorporate into the war and civil disturbance nondiscrimination provision any exceptions in the general national and MFN treatment provisions.[178]

---

that the discriminatory treatment was not the result of any legitimate host state policy. In *Loewen*, by contrast, the tribunal never inquired into the host state's justification or motive for the treatment of the covered investment.

173 *See* Sections 7.4 and 7.5.

174 *See* Section 7.4.

175 *See, e.g.*, United Kingdom-Bosnia-Herzegovina BIT, Art. 5(1); Netherlands-Ethiopia BIT, Art. 7; Germany-Timor-Leste BIT, Art. 5(3)-(4); Switzerland-Algeria BIT, Art. 6(2); Austria-Armenia BIT, Art. 6(1); Finland-Armenia BIT, Art. 6(1); Sweden-Kazakhstan BIT, Art. 5(1); Denmark-Ethiopia, Art. 6; Chile-Indonesia BIT, Art. VII; Australia-India BIT, Art. 8; Argentina-Thailand BIT, Art. 6(3); Cambodia-Vietnam BIT, Art. V; Mexico-Iceland BIT, Art. 5; Canada-Uruguay BIT, Art. VII; India-Indonesia BIT, Art. 6.

176 *See, e.g.*, Denmark-Ethiopia BIT, Art. 6; Finland-Armenia BIT, Art. 6(1); Chile-Indonesia BIT, Art. VII; Cambodia-Vietnam BIT, Art. V.

177 *See, e.g.*, BLEU-Sudan BIT, Art. 7(4); Egypt-Zambia BIT, Art.4.

178 *See, e.g.*, Switzerland-Algeria BIT, Art. 6(2).

Another distinctive feature of the war and civil disturbance nondiscrimination provision is that it grants nondiscriminatory treatment to investors whose investments suffer losses. At the same time, however, the typical provision seems not to grant any rights to the investments. By contrast, in many BITs, the general national and MFN treatment provision applies to investments, rather than to investors. This further distinguishes the war and civil disturbance nondiscrimination provision from the general national and MFN treatment provisions in many BITs. Thus, the language suggests that only where damage to the investment causes losses to the investor is the right to nondiscriminatory treatment guaranteed by the war and civil disturbance nondiscrimination provision. The right is to nondiscriminatory treatment with respect to compensation paid to the investors for their losses.

The war and civil disturbance nondiscrimination provision generally applies regardless of the person or entity that is responsible for the losses. That is, it applies even if the losses are entirely attributable to the action of private parties acting without any involvement of the government.

The war and civil disturbance nondiscrimination provision sometimes is accompanied by a second provision that requires payment of compensation for certain losses attributable to war and civil disturbance. The origins of and arbitral practice with respect to both of these provisions are discussed in Section 6.6.

7.4 UNREASONABLE OR DISCRIMINATORY MEASURES

Many BITs include a prohibition on unreasonable or discriminatory measures. This provision constitutes a general prohibition on at least certain forms of discriminatory treatment. It was introduced in Section 5.3, which should be consulted for a more thorough discussion of this provision.

The analysis of discrimination is conceptually the same under the unreasonable or discriminatory measures provision as it is under the national and MFN treatment provisions, discussed in Section 7.2. Yet, numerous differences exist in the provisions.

First, the unreasonable or discriminatory measures provision does not explicitly identify the beneficiary of its protection. The language of the provision typically prohibits unreasonable or discriminatory measures that impair the operation, maintenance, management, use, enjoyment, disposal and, in some cases, the establishment of the investment. Because the investor engages in all of these functions, the investor would seem to be a beneficiary of the provision. Yet the investment itself engages in some of these functions as well. Thus, both the investor and the investment may be a beneficiary of the provision.

Second, the unreasonable or discriminatory measures provision does not explicitly identify the relevant comparator. Obviously, a comparator must be used. If the provision is read to prohibit only unreasonable discriminations, then the correct comparators would be investments or investors that are different from the covered investment or investor only in ways irrelevant to the host state's legitimate regulatory objectives, essentially the same test as that which should be applied to determine whether investments are in like circumstances within the meaning of the national and MFN treatment provisions.

Thus, if two investments differ in ways relevant to a legitimate regulatory objective, then one investment is not an appropriate comparator for the other. This simply is another way of saying that any discrimination between the two investments with respect to those differences is not unreasonable.

As in the case of the national and MFN treatment provisions, one problem that may arise in the application of this provision is the absence of an appropriate comparator. In such a case, however, unreasonable or discriminatory treatment should be found where the host state's treatment of the investment is the result of an illegitimate motive or policy. For example, if the host state acted adversely to the covered investment solely for reasons of racial animosity, such conduct should be regarded as a violation of the unreasonable or discriminatory measures provision, even if no appropriate comparator can be found.

Third, the unreasonable or discriminatory measures provision makes no reference to nationality and thus any kind of discrimination would violate the literal language of the provision. Occasionally language can be found that seems to limit the provision to discrimination based on nationality,[179] but most awards do not mention such a limitation. In very few cases, however, has the tribunal discussed the meaning of the term "discriminatory" within the meaning of this provision. Tribunals appear to assume that the meaning of the term is self-evident. One case where the tribunal suggested a definition was *Saluka Investments v. Czech Republic*, a case arising under the Netherlands-Czech Republic BIT, where the tribunal held that nondiscrimination "requires a rational justification of any differential treatment of a foreign investor."[180] The tribunal also noted that the term has the same meaning in the application of this provision as it does in the application of the fair and equitable treatment provision. Thus, the language should be interpreted to prohibit only unreasonable discriminations. Even so, the provision could apply to discrimination among investors of the same nationality, if the discrimination was unreasonable.

Indeed, the unreasonable or discriminatory measures provision may reflect a more complex understanding of equivalency than the national and MFN treatment provisions. The national and MFN treatment provisions typically require treatment no less favorable than that accorded to the comparators. The assumption is that the covered investment and the comparator are similar and, therefore, should receive similar treatment. The prohibition on unreasonable or discriminatory measures, however, also may prohibit treating dissimilar investments similarly.[181] That is, it may be violated where the host state fails to recognize legitimate differences between investments. Disregarding legitimate differences in some cases could be regarded as a form of arbitrariness and thus an unreasonable or discriminatory measure.

---

179 *See LG&E v. Argentina*, discussed below.

180 Award, para. 460.

181 The tribunal suggested that such treatment would violate a prohibition on discriminatory treatment in *Parkerings-Compagniet v. Lithuania*, a case arising under the Norway-Lithuania BIT, although the tribunal also suggested that this would be true even under a national or MFN treatment provision. Award, para. 368.

Finally, unlike the national and MFN treatment provisions, the unreasonable or discriminatory measures provision is often subject only to any general treaty exceptions. The national and MFN treatment provisions, by contrast, often are subject to special exceptions for treatment provided under an economic integration agreement or tax treaties and legislation.

Most of the discussion in the awards generally involves either the identification of the proper comparative or a discussion of whether the discrimination is unreasonable. As has been noted, these two issues are conceptually the same. That is, the same analysis should determine whether a differently treated comparator is the appropriate comparator and whether the different treatment was reasonable. In most cases, the tribunals have found that any difference in treatment was justified by reasonable regulatory objectives. Thus, no violation of the provision was found.

For example, in *Enron v. Argentina*, a case arising under the United States-Argentina BIT, Argentina responded to an economic crisis by modifying the tariff structure applicable to the claimant's investment. The tribunal found that there had been no "capricious, irrational or absurd differentiation in the treatment accorded to the Claimant as compared to other entities or sectors."[182] Similarly, in *Sempra Energy v. Argentina*, another case arising under that BIT, the tribunal echoed *Enron* in finding no "capricious, irrational or absurd differentiation" in the treatment of the claimant in relation to enterprises in other sectors of the economy.[183] In *CMS Gas Transmission Company v. Argentina*, a case arising under the same BIT and involving the same economic crisis, the tribunal noted that discrimination exists only if similarly situated investments are treated differently, but found no discrimination on the facts of the case. Thus, in none of these cases did the tribunal limit its inquiry to discrimination based on nationality. Rather, the tribunals focused on the reasonableness of any discrimination. Notably, tribunals in these cases were prepared to employ comparators in different economic sectors than the beneficiary.

In *National Grid v. Argentina*, a case arising under the United Kingdom-Argentina BIT, the tribunal noted explicitly that the provision applies to discrimination on grounds of nationality as well as on other grounds. The tribunal found no discrimination based on nationality because the emergency measures adopted by Argentina affected both local and foreign investors. With respect to other forms of discrimination, the tribunal considered whether the relevant comparators were investments in the same economic sector or whether investments in other sectors could serve as comparators. The tribunal noted that comparisons across sectors were possible, but that the different treatment of investments in different sectors was more likely to be justified by legitimate host state policies. For example, while Argentina's devaluation undoubtedly favored the export sector over investments in the electrical distribution sector, promoting exports is a principal reason to devalue the currency. That is, Argentina had a rational justification for a policy that favored the export sector. The tribunal found rational policy reasons for treating other sectors favorably as well. Hence, no violation of the provision had occurred.

---

182 Award, para. 282.

183 Award, para. 319.

The tribunal did find an unjustified discrimination in *Lauder v. Czech Republic*, a case arising under the United States-Czech Republic BIT. In that case, the tribunal found that the host state's requirement that the claimant participate in the operation of a television station as a co-venturer with a local company rather than as an equity investor in that local company was discriminatory because it was based on the claimant's foreign nationality. The Czech Republic was reacting to a public outcry that the tribunal concluded would not have occurred had the claimant been a domestic investor.[184] The tribunal also found, however, that no objection to the discriminatory treatment had been raised at the time.

In *Plama Consortium v. Bulgaria*, a case arising under the Energy Charter Treaty, the tribunal explained that discriminatory treatment "entails like persons being treated in a different manner in similar circumstances without reasonable or justifiable grounds."[185] In that case, some evidence suggested that some companies had received state assistance in complying with new environmental regulations, while the claimant's investment had not. The evidence was insufficient for the tribunal to make a finding, however.

Although most of the awards would limit violations of the provision to situations of unreasonable discrimination, a couple of tribunals seemed prepared to find a violation based merely on a discriminatory effect. For example, in *LG&E v. Argentina*, a case arising under the United States-Argentina BIT, the tribunal held that the obligation imposed by the unreasonable or discriminatory measures provision was not to discriminate against foreign investors and that "a measure is considered discriminatory if the intent of the measure is to discriminate or if the measure has a discriminatory effect."[186] Citing the *ELSI* case, the tribunal held that to establish discrimination, there must be an intentional discrimination in favor of a national against a foreign investor that is not taken under similar circumstances against another national. The tribunal found that Argentina had treated gas distribution companies more harshly than other utilities. Although the claimant had failed to prove that the discrimination was based on nationality, the tribunal nevertheless found a violation of the provision.[187] The award does require, however, that the beneficiary be compared to a comparator in similar circumstances. As has been noted, identifying a comparator in similar circumstances typically entails examining the justification for any difference in treatment and thus the discriminatory motive becomes relevant to that determination. The tribunal avoided the issue by assuming that the beneficiary was in similar circumstances with other utilities.[188]

In *Siemens v. Argentina*, a case arising under the Germany-Argentina BIT, the tribunal commented that "intent is not decisive or essential for a finding of discrimination, and that the impact of the measure on the investment would be the determining

184 Award, para. 231.
185 Award, para. 184.
186 Award, para. 146.
187 Award, paras. 147–148.
188 Award, para. 148.

factor to ascertain whether it had resulted in nondiscriminatory treatment."[189] The comment was *dictum*, however, because the tribunal found that in light of its holdings with respect to other provisions of the BIT, a determination whether the nondiscriminatory treatment obligation was breached was unnecessary.

In some cases, the tribunal simply observes that the action of the host state was not discriminatory.[190] Alternatively, the tribunal may find discrimination without an elaborate analysis. For example, in *CME v. Czech Republic*, a case arising under the Netherlands-Czech Republic BIT and involving the same facts as the *Lauder* claim, the tribunal noted that the Czech government's action "smacks of discrimination" against the foreign investor.[191]

In at least two cases, the tribunal has considered the situation where no comparator exists. In *Noble Ventures v. Romania*, a case arising under the United States-Romania BIT, the claimant alleged that the host state's institution of judicial reorganization proceedings with respect to its investment violated the prohibition on arbitrary or discriminatory measures. The tribunal noted the absence of any evidence in the record that comparable proceedings had been instituted with respect to other investors. The tribunal continued,

> But that in itself does not exclude the possibility that the proceedings constituted a discriminatory measure because it is possible for a single measure to be discriminatory if proof to that effect is given. As one cannot rely on objective criteria in such situations, the Claimant has to demonstrate that a certain measure was directed specifically against a certain investor by reason of his, her, or its nationality.[192]

No such demonstration was made, however, and thus the tribunal found no violation of the standard. The award, however, reflects a recognition that the claimant may prove discriminatory treatment where no comparator exists by demonstrating that measures were adopted with a discriminatory motive.

A different approach was taken, however, in *BG Group v. Argentina*, a case arising under the United Kingdom-Argentina BIT. In that case, the tribunal accepted "for the sake of analysis" that a measure in breach of the national or MFN treatment standards would be discriminatory within the meaning of the prohibition on unreasonable or discriminatory measures.[193] In determining whether discrimination had occurred, the tribunal adopted the analytical framework used in *International Thunderbird v. Mexico*, a case arising under the NAFTA, to determine whether the national treatment standard was violated. The tribunal found that, while the claimant's gas distribution company may have been treated less favorably than other utilities, such as companies distributing electricity, these other companies were not shown to be in like circumstances with the claimant's investment. Thus, the tribunal could not hold that Argentina had discriminated

---

189 Award, para. 321.

190 *See, e.g., Genin v. Estonia* (United States-Estonia BIT), Award, para. 370; *MTD Equity v. Chile* (Malaysia-Chile BIT), Award, para. 196; *ADF Group v. United States* (NAFTA), Award, para. 194.

191 Partial Award, para. 612.

192 Award, para. 180.

193 Award, para. 355.

against the claimant.[194] As noted in Section 7.2.5, a similar approach was taken in *Loewen v. United States*, a case arising under the NAFTA, and in *Parkerings-Compagniet v. Lithuania*, a case arising under the Norway-Lithuania BIT, although the language in *Noble Ventures* seems sounder as a matter of principle.

Occasionally, a tribunal may not distinguish between unreasonable and discriminatory measures. This situation is discussed in Section 5.3.3. Further, because the fair and equitable treatment standard has been held to prohibit both unreasonable conduct and discriminatory conduct, tribunals do not always analyze the application of the prohibition on unreasonable and discriminatory measures separately from the application of the fair and equitable treatment standard. This too is further discussed in Section 5.3.3.

7.5 FAIR AND EQUITABLE TREATMENT

The vast majority of BITs require that the host state provide covered investment with fair and equitable treatment. This provision was introduced in Section 5.2. As was discussed there, some arbitral awards have held that the fair and equitable treatment standard includes a requirement of nondiscriminatory treatment. Further, fair and equitable treatment has been, from the beginning, linked to the nondiscrimination principle. Many BITs place the two standards in the same sentence. The notes to the 1967 OECD Draft Convention on the Protection of Foreign Property suggested that fair and equitable treatment included the nondiscrimination obligation and in the early 1980s the OECD queried its members as to whether it required more than that.[195] As in the case of the unreasonable or discriminatory treatment provision,[196] however, the fair and equitable treatment standard appears to prohibit only unreasonable discriminations.

For example, in *Eureko v. Poland*, a case arising under the Netherlands-Poland BIT, the tribunal held that Poland violated the fair and equitable treatment standard by failing to adhere to its privatization commitments. That failure was attributable to what the tribunal referred to as "purely arbitrary reasons linked to the interplay of Polish politics and nationalistic reasons of a discriminatory character."[197]

Similarly, in *Saluka Investments v. Czech Republic*, a case arising under the Netherlands-Czech Republic BIT, four major banks in the Czech Republic were in the process of privatization. The Czech government provided financial assistance to three of the banks, but not the one in which claimant had invested. The tribunal found no reasonable basis for the discrimination.

In *Parkerings-Compagniet v. Lithuania*, a case arising under the Norway-Lithuania BIT, the tribunal held that discriminatory conduct violates the fair and equitable treatment standard, although the claimant or its investment must be in like circumstances

194 Award, para. 360.
195 *See* Section 5.2.2.
196 *See* Section 5.3.1.
197 Award, para. 233.

with the comparator.[198] In that case, however, no comparator existed. The tribunal held, therefore, that it could not determine the existence of a violation.[199] As noted in Section 7.1, the dismissal of a claim because the tribunal cannot identify a comparator is a questionable result, although tribunals also have refused to find discrimination where no comparator exists in *Loewen v. United States*, a case arising under the NAFTA,[200] and *BG Group v. Argentina*, a case arising under the United Kingdom-Argentina BIT.[201] In any event, the tribunal noted that other discrimination claims on the basis of nationality would require the same analysis as under the MFN treatment provision clause and thus would be analyzed under that doctrine.[202]

In *Loewen v. United States*, a case arising under the NAFTA, a Canadian investor was sued by a U.S. company in a Mississippi state court. The trial featured numerous references to the Canadian nationality of the investor and the jury ultimately rendered a $500,000,000 verdict against the investor. The tribunal observed that, under Article 1105[203] of the NAFTA, the United States had a duty to provide a fair trial, free of sectional or local prejudice.[204] That is, the tribunal recognized the principle of nondiscrimination. Further, the tribunal found that the trial was "improper and discreditable and cannot be squared with minimum standards of international law and fair and equitable treatment."[205] The claimant, however, had failed to appeal the adverse judgment. The tribunal held that the BIT protects foreign investment and investors against wrongful conduct by the judicial system as a whole.[206] The claimant had not allowed the U.S. judicial system the opportunity to remedy any deficiencies in the trial and therefore could not complain of a treaty violation.

In *Methanex v. United States*, a case arising under the NAFTA, the tribunal in *obiter dictum* observed that discriminatory treatment of investment generally would not violate NAFTA article 1105, which includes a requirement of fair and equitable treatment, although discrimination based on sectional or racial prejudice might constitute a violation. Thus, the *Methanex* tribunal questioned whether fair and equitable treatment requires nondiscriminatory treatment, although it did not dismiss the possibility entirely. To hold that the standard does not include the principle of nondiscrimination would represent a unique view of the standard. In any event, as has been noted, the remark was *dictum*. The tribunal found that California's ban on MTBE, which was the

198 Award, paras. 287–288. The tribunal relied on *Goetz v. Burundi* (BLEU-Burundi BIT), Award, para. 121.

199 Award, para. 290.

200 *See* Section 7.2.5.

201 *See* Section 7.4. *But see Noble Ventures v. Romania*, a case arising under the United States-Romania BIT, in which the tribunal reached a different result. The *Noble Ventures* award is discussed in Section 7.4.

202 Award, para. 291.

203 That article prohibits treatment inconsistent with customary international law, including fair and equitable treatment.

204 Award, para. 123.

205 Award, para. 137.

206 Award, para. 143.

basis of the dispute, applied equally to all investments and thus no discrimination had occurred.

7.6 THE INTERNATIONAL MINIMUM STANDARD

As noted in Section 5.4, some BITs require that investment be treated no less favorably than is required by customary international law. Treatment in accordance with customary law also may be required by several other BIT provisions.

Quite clearly, both the fair and equitable treatment provision and the prohibition on unreasonable or discriminatory measures include prohibitions on unreasonable discriminations. Moreover, some authority exists for concluding that both provisions are elements of customary law.[207] To the extent that either provision is part of customary law, customary law would include a general prohibition on discrimination.

A few cases have discussed briefly whether customary law includes a general prohibition on discriminatory treatment of foreign investment., apart from these treaty standards. The awards have not produced a consensus.

A couple of awards have suggested that no such prohibition exists. For example, in *Genin v. Estonia*, a case arising under the United States-Estonia BIT, in the course of its discussion of the prohibition on arbitrary and discriminatory measures in that BIT, the tribunal observed that

> [c]ustomary international law does not, however, require that a state treat all aliens (and alien property) equally, or that it treat aliens as favourably as nationals. Indeed, "even unjustifiable differentiation may not be actionable."[208]

In any event, the tribunal found no evidence of discrimination in the case before it.

Similarly, in *Methanex v. United States*, a case arising under the NAFTA, the tribunal observed that

> international law is clear. In the absence of a contrary rule of international law binding on the State parties, whether of conventional or customary origin, a State may differentiate in its treatment of nationals and aliens.[209]

The tribunal went on to observe that customary law has established some exceptions to this broad rule. The claimant had cited language from the NAFTA award in *Waste Management v. Mexico*, referring to a customary law prohibition on conduct that is discriminatory and exposes the investment or investor to sectional or racial prejudice,[210] which the tribunal interpreted as a reference to the award in *Loewen v. United States*,

---

207 As discussed in Section 5.2.1, considerable debate has occurred concerning whether fair and equitable treatment is an element of customary law. The OECD in its 1967 Draft Convention on the Protection of Foreign Property stated the view that both standards are required by customary law and the United States has taken that position as well. *See* Section 5.2.2.

208 Award, para. 368. The internal quotation was from Rudolf Dolzer and Margrete Stevens, *Bilateral Investment Treaties* 61–62 (1995).

209 Award, Part IV, Chapter C, para. 25.

210 *See* Section 5.4.

discussed below. The tribunal declined to address whether *Waste Management* was correct in asserting the existence of such a prohibition because, in any event, the claimant in *Methanex* had failed to demonstrate that it was the victim of discrimination.

A couple of other awards have suggested that such a prohibition does exist. For example, in *Loewen v. United States*, another case arising under the NAFTA, the tribunal held that a judicial decision that is "in breach of municipal law and is discriminatory against the foreign litigant amounts to manifest injustice according to international law."[211] Further, as noted in Section 7.5, the tribunal found that the trial was "improper and discreditable and cannot be squared with minimum standards of international law and fair and equitable treatment,"[212] although the claimants' failure to exhaust local remedies precluded their submitting a claim to investor-state arbitration.

Similarly, in *Parkerings-Compagniet v. Lithuania*, a case arising under the Norway-Lithuania BIT, the tribunal observed that the national and MFN treatment provisions "are treaty clauses that have the same substantive effect as the international treatment standard."[213] A violation would occur where the discrimination was unreasonable or lacking proportionality.[214] The tribunal found that the differences in treatment in that case were justified by legitimate host-state regulatory concerns. For example, the Norwegian claimant's parking facility was treated differently than a Dutch investor's parking facility because it was larger and located in a culturally sensitive area and thus the difference in treatment was justified by legitimate policies in favor of archeological and environmental preservation.[215]

The issue, however, rarely arises in BIT arbitrations. Virtually every BIT has a fair and equitable treatment standard and most have national and MFN treatment provisions. Many have prohibitions on unreasonable or discriminatory measures. Thus, a claimant in nearly every BIT claims has ample grounds under specific BIT provisions to allege an unlawful discrimination without the need to discuss customary law.

211 Award, para. 135.
212 Award, para. 137.
213 Award, para. 367.
214 Award, para. 368.
215 Award, para. 396.

Chapter 8

Transparency

8.1 INTRODUCTION

Transparency exists where the operation of a system is visible or discoverable to observers without undue burden. The principle of transparency generally requires the removal of barriers to information. Thus, while most BIT principles can be promoted merely by state inaction, such as where the state declines to discriminate or to interfere with the operation of an investment, promoting transparency may necessitate action to disseminate information.

Transparency promotes the rule of law in that a basic element of the concept of the rule of law is that laws be known.[1] Thus, transparency is necessary for the creation of a rules–based investment regime. Transparency inhibits corruption, a classic form of government failure that is the antithesis of the rule of law and that has been demonstrated to inhibit investment flows.[2] More generally, transparency improves governance, which promotes development.[3] Transparency may reduce the probability of disputes over the interpretation and application of the law.

Transparency also promotes a liberal investment regime. Because market theory assumes that parties are knowledgeable, transparency is necessary to a properly functioning market. Information asymmetries are a classic form of market failure.

Lack of information increases risk, which increases the cost of capital and reduces the quantity of investment.[4] Lack of transparency also encourages herding behavior.[5] Thus, the Asian financial crisis of 1997–98[6] has been attributed in part to insufficient

1 *See* Kenneth J. Vandevelde, "A Unified Theory of Fair and Equitable Treatment," (forthcoming).

2 Bellver and Kaufman, *supra* note 1, at 8.

3 *Id.* at 10.

4 R. Gason Gelos and Shang-Jin Wei, "Transparency and International Investor Behavior," February 10, 2002, available at http://www.ssrn.com; Ana Bellver and Daniel Kaufman, "Transparenting Transparency: Initial Empirics and Policy Applications," September 2005, at 7, available at http://www.ssrn.com.

5 Belver and Kaufman, *supra* note 1, at 8; Gelose and Wei, *supra* note 1 (defining herding behavior as investment decisions made because others are observed making them).

6 *See* Section 2.3.

transparency in the financial market.[7] Distortions of information can cause sudden influxes as well as sudden withdrawals of capital.

Lack of transparency may have distributional consequences. More specifically, transparency can contribute to preventing the appropriation of resources by those in power and to ensuring a broader distribution of the benefits of economic growth.[8]

Information asymmetries in many cases disfavor foreign investors, if for no other reason than the geographic and cultural distance between the home and host countries. Thus, the absence of transparency tends inherently to discriminate against foreign investment. That is, as a practical matter, in the context of foreign investment, the transparency principle reinforces the nondiscrimination principle.

Despite the importance of transparency, few BITs have provisions that explicitly require transparency. Indeed, the BITs do not appear to have included any explicit provisions on transparency until 1982, when the United States concluded its first BITs.[9]

One reason for the lack of transparency provisions is that providing transparency imposes costs on a system that states may be reluctant to assume. Transparency may require that information be collected. Much of the information to be made available may be generated at the regional or local level, which increases substantially the burden of collection. Because users of information are widely dispersed, transparency requires some mechanism for disseminating information. Either sites must be established where information is available or the information must be distributed, electronically or otherwise. These tasks can impose significant costs. For example, the WTO imposes publication and notification requirements[10] that some developing countries already find burdensome. In any given case, the cost of transparency could exceed the usefulness of the information. Judgments thus must be made about which information shall be made available and how it shall be made available.

Further, most BIT obligations prevent very specific kinds of conduct by host states that often have had substantial adverse, even devastating, consequences for foreign investment, such as seizures or destruction of property, the imposition of exchange controls, or the adoption of discriminatory policies directed at foreign investment. Lack of transparency, by contrast, tends to be reflected less in specific, discrete host–state actions and more in a pervasive and permanent condition that may raise the cost of business significantly, but that can be taken into account in making the initial investment decision. That is, a lack of transparency may seem to resemble other persistent deficiencies in the investment climate, such as lack of infrastructure, lack of developed human capital, or lack of sound macroeconomic policies, that affect all investors and

---

7 Bellver and Kaufman, *supra* note 1; Gelos and Wei, *supra* note 1.

8 Bellver and Kaufman, *supra* note 1.

9 *See* Section 8.2. On the transparency principle generally, *see* Akira Kotera, "Regulatory Transparency," in Peter Muchlinski, Frederico Ortino, and Christoph Schreuer, eds., *The Oxford Handbook of Internatonal Investment Law* (2008).

10 These include Article X of the General Agreement on Tariffs and Trade, Art. III of the General Agreement on Trade in Services, and Article 63 of the Agreement on Trade-Related Aspects of Intellectual Property Rights.

that require significant resources to rectify, rather than the kind of sudden changes in government policy, often directed at foreign investment specifically, that triggered investment disputes in the past.

Yet, as has been noted, transparency is a critical element of the rule of law and a liberal investment regime and thus is a principle that is entirely consistent with the purposes of the BIT. A BIT itself, of course, contributes to transparency by publicly committing host states to certain standards of treatment of covered investment. Indeed, as discussed in Section 10.2.1.8, one of the principle criticisms of BITs has been that the investor-state disputes provision created by the BITs lacked sufficient transparency. Thus, much of the discussion of the transparency principle as it relates to BITs has concerned whether the procedures created by BITs were sufficiently transparent.

BITs do, however, also promote the transparency of host-state treatment of covered investment. Most BITs contain a requirement of fair and equitable treatment, which, as will be seen, has been interpreted to include an obligation of transparency, although this obligation is only implicit. Some BITs include provisions that explicitly require some form of action by the host state to promote transparency. No tribunal thus far has found a violation of any of the specific transparency provisions, but, as will be seen, several tribunals have held that host states have violated the transparency principle embraced within the fair and equitable treatment standard.

A few BITs have extended the concept of transparency to include participation in decision making. In this understanding of transparency, an investor has the right not only to obtain information, but to submit information to the decision maker. Such provisions, although often designated as transparency provisions, in some respects promote the principle of due process. BITs that contain the most elaborate transparency provisions sometimes exclude those provisions from the scope of the investor-state disputes provision.[11] In any event, no tribunal has yet found a violation of this type of transparency provision.

8.2 PUBLICATION

The earliest transparency provisions appeared in trade-related agreements. For example, the GATT required parties to publish or make publicly available certain laws, regulations, judicial decisions, and administrative rulings related to trade.[12] The post-war U.S. FCNs had a similar provision that also was limited to trade related laws.[13]

When the United States concluded its first BITs in the early 1980s, these treaties included a provision based on the publication provision of the post-war U.S. FCNs, except that the provision was investment- rather than trade-related. Such a provision appears in the BITs of a few other countries as well.

---

11 *See, e.g.*, 2003 Canadian Model BIT, Art. 19, footnote 7; United States-Uruguay BIT, Art. 24.

12 General Agreement on Tariffs and Trade, Art. X(1). Under Art. X(2), such laws cannot be enforced until they are published or make publicly available.

13 *See, e.g.*, Netherlands-United States FCN, *supra* chapter 2, note 179, Art. XV.

A typical formulation requires each party to "promptly publish or otherwise make publicly available" certain laws.[14] Most commonly, these are laws that pertain to or affect investments.[15] In some BITs, these are laws respecting matters covered by the BIT[16] or that may affect the operation of the BIT.[17] Such provisions may apply not only to legislation, but to judicial decisions and administrative regulations and decisions.[18]

A variation of this provision requires publication of laws prior to their adoption. For example, a few recent U.S. BITs require each party, to the extent possible, to publish in advance laws respecting matters covered by the BIT that it proposes to adopt.[19]

The publication provision was at issue in *Azurix v. Argentina*, a case arising under the United States-Argentina BIT. The tribunal found in that case that the investor's claim in actuality was based on the application of the regulatory framework rather than Argentina's failure to make public its regulations. Although the tribunal observed that publication of the regulations in that case would have been a *desirable* improvement, Argentina's failure to publish the regulations was not sufficient to constitute a breach of the publication provision.

8.3 INFORMATION EXCHANGE

Several transparency provisions that appear in some BITs are directed not at making information available to investors or investments generally, but at promoting information exchange between the two BIT parties themselves. For example, one such provision requires each party, upon request, to provide information relating to covered investment to the other party.[20] A variation requires each party, upon request, to provide information relating to its measures affecting covered investment.[21] These kinds of provisions may have exceptions for information the disclosure of which would impede law enforcement, contravene laws protecting privacy[22] or impede legitimate commercial interests.[23] A few U.S. BITs from the 1980s have an even weaker provision under which, if one party requests information concerning covered investments, the other party shall

14 *See, e.g.*, Austria-Armenia BIT, Art. 4(1). *See also* Sweden-Kazakhstan BIT, Art. 2(6) ("promptly published or otherwise made publicly known"); Australia-India BIT, Art. 6 ("make public and readily accessible"); Finland-Armenia BIT, Art. 15(1) ("promptly public or make publicly available"); United States-Egypt BIT, Art. II(8) ("make public"); 2003 Canadian Model BIT, Art. 19(1) ("promptly published or otherwise made available").

15 *See, e.g.*, United States-Senegal BIT, Art. II(10); Sweden-Kazakhstan BIT, Art. 2(6); Australia-India BIT, Art. 6; Finland-Armenia BIT, Art. 15(1) (may affect investment).

16 *See, e.g.*, United States-Uruguay BIT, Art. 10(1); 2003 Canadian Model BIT, Art. 19(1).

17 *See, e.g.*, Austria-Armenia BIT, Art. 4(1).

18 *See, e.g.*, United States-Uruguay BIT, Art. 10(1).

19 *See, e.g.*, United States-Uruguay BIT, Art. 10(2).

20 *See, e.g.*, Austria-Armenia BIT, Art. 4(2).

21 *See, e.g.*, 2003 Canadian Model BIT, Art. 19(3).

22 *See, e.g.*, Austria-Armenia BIT, Art. 4(3); Finland-Armenia BIT, Art. 15(2).

23 *See, e.g.*, Finland-Armenia BIT, Art. 15(2).

endeavor to establish appropriate procedures for providing such information.[24] Even this limited obligation is subject to the laws of the party supplying the information and is to be performed with due regard for business confidentiality.

To facilitate information exchange, a few BITs require each party to designate a contact point for communication between the parties on any matter covered by the treaty.[25] Occasionally, BITs may require the designation of a contact point for investors seeking information about investment opportunities or host state laws and policies relating to investment.[26]

A few BITs impose on each party an affirmative obligation to notify the other party of its intent to adopt measures that might affect the interests of the other party under the treaty.[27] That is, the notification obligation exists regardless of whether the information has been requested.

These information exchange provisions have not been at issue in any dispute for which an award is publicly available.

8.4 PARTICIPATION IN DECISION MAKING

In a small number of BITs, the principle of transparency has been expanded to include obligations more traditionally associated with due process. Under this expanded conception of transparency, a host state has an obligation to permit certain actors, such as investors, investments, or even the other BIT party, to participate in decision making.

For example, under recent U.S. BITs, each party is obligated to ensure that, in its administrative proceedings applying measures to particular covered investments or investors, whenever possible such investments or investors that are directly affected by the proceeding are provided with reasonable notice when the proceeding is initiated and a reasonable opportunity to present facts and arguments before any final administrative action.[28] Further, each party shall establish or maintain an independent and impartial system for appellate review of administrative decisions and permit parties to the administrative proceeding an opportunity to support their positions and the right to a decision based on the record, which decision shall be binding on the administrative agency.[29] A few BITs provide that, to the extent possible, each party shall provide interested persons and the other party a reasonable opportunity to comment on proposed measures respecting any matter covered by the BIT.[30]

None of these provisions has yet been at issue in any dispute for which an award is publicly available.

---

24 *See, e.g.*, United States-Egypt BIT, Art. VI(3).

25 *See, e.g.*, United States-Uruguay BIT, Art. 11(1).

26 *See, e.g.*, United States-Czech Republic BIT, exchange of letters dated October 22, 1991.

27 *See, e.g.*, United States-Uruguay BIT, Art. 11(3).

28 *See, e.g.*, United States-Uruguay BIT, Art. 11(4).

29 *See, e.g.*, United States-Uruguay BIT, Art. 11(5).

30 *See, e.g.*, United States-Uruguay BIT, Art. 11(2); 2003 Canadian Model BIT, Art. 19(2).

8.5 FAIR AND EQUITABLE TREATMENT

The fair and equitable treatment provision was introduced in Section 5.2, where it is discussed in some detail. As is noted there, tribunals have held that the fair and equitable treatment standard embraces the principle of transparency.

The transparency principle, however, has been the most conceptually troubled aspect of the fair and equitable treatment cases and no rule that describes the extent of transparency required has emerged. In any event, a few awards have found violations of the fair and equitable treatment standard where the state did not disclose the rules to be applied, whether substantive or procedural, or where the state failed to disclose the reasons for measures that it had taken or declined to take. Thus, the transparency principle applies not only to host-state law, but to host-state policy. With respect to policy disclosures, the transparency principle does not seem to require disclosure of internal deliberations, but has been violated where a government refused to disclose its policy once the policy had been adopted. Finally, at least one award has found a violation of the standard where the host state failed to allow access to information needed by the claimant to prosecute an appeal. Presumably because the laws are more readily accessible than host-state policies, claimants have succeeded more often with claims based on nondisclosure of policies than nondisclosure of laws, though the awards are insufficiently numerous to draw any firm conclusions.

In *MTD Equity v. Chile*, a case arising under the Malaysia-Chile BIT, the Chilean government had induced a Malaysian investor to invest in the construction of a planned community, although such construction was in violation of local zoning laws. The tribunal held that Chile's inconsistent conduct violated the fair and equitable treatment standard.[31] Alternatively, the tribunal held that the lack of transparency also violated the standard. At the time that Chile induced the investors to invest, it had not disclosed that the project would violate local law. In effect, had Chile made this disclosure, the investor could have made an informed decision whether to invest in light of the risk that the required local approval would not be received. That is, Chile could have complied with the BIT in either of two ways, by having a consistent policy or by disclosing its inconsistent policy. Chile did neither and thus violated the fair and equitable treatment standard. Ordinarily, an investor might be expected to ascertain for itself the extent to which a proposal would be consistent with local law, but the *MTD Equity* case involved affirmative efforts by Chilean officials to persuade the investor to invest.

One might contrast the *MTD Equity* award with that in *Parkerings-Compagniet v. Lithuania*, a case arising under the Norway-Lithuania BIT. In that case, the tribunal rejected a claim that the BIT was violated by the host state's failure to disclose its intention to modify local law in ways that would adversely affect the claimant's investment. The tribunal explained that the claimant should have known that the legal situation was changing in Lithuania because of the transitional nature of the economy and that the claimant could have retained local counsel to advise it about the amendment process.[32] The tribunal compared the situation before it with the situation, such as in *MTD Equity*,

---

31 *See* Section 5.2.3.

32 Award, para. 342.

where the state "made assurances or representation [sic] that the investors took into account in making the investment."[33]

In *Champion Trading Company v. Egypt*, a case arising under the United States-Egypt BIT, Egypt had entered into a series of agreements to provide financial assistance to certain companies in Egypt's troubled cotton industry, but had not included the claimants in these settlements. The claimants originally asserted that these agreements violated the fair and equitable treatment standard, but abandoned that claim in favor of an argument that they violated the principle of transparency under international law. The claimants' authority for the existence of a principle of transparency was a WTO case[34] unrelated to the protection of foreign investment and the *Tecmed* award, discussed below, which applied the fair and equitable treatment standard. Thus, the claimants ultimately were relying on the requirement of fair and equitable treatment. The tribunal did not question the existence of a transparency principle, but found that the claimants "were in a position to know beforehand all rules and regulations that would govern their investments for the respective season to come."[35]

While *MTD, Parkerings-Compagniet*, and *Champion Trading* discussed possible failures to disclose law, *Tecmed v. Mexico*, a case arising under the Spain-Mexico BIT, involved a failure to disclose policy. In that case, Mexican officials decided, largely because of community opposition, not to renew a permit held by the claimant's investment to operate a landfill. Mexican officials and the investment had engaged in lengthy discussions concerning the possible relocation of the landfill. Yet, throughout all of these discussions, the officials never revealed that they already had decided not to renew the permit. The tribunal found that Mexico's lack of transparency about its true intentions and the real basis upon which renewal of the permit depended violated the fair and equitable treatment standard.

Similarly, in *Saluka Investments v. Czech Republic*, a case arising under the Netherlands-Czech Republic BIT, the Czech government refused to discuss with the claimant its reasons for declining to provide claimant's bank with the same assistance that it had provided other, similarly situated banks. The tribunal found this refusal to disclose the rationale for its conduct to violate fair and equitable treatment.

Again, in *PSEG v. Turkey*, a case arising under the United States-Turkey BIT, the tribunal held that Turkey's "negligence" in handling negotiations with the claimants violated the fair and equitable treatment obligation. The specific behavior that constituted the negligence seemed largely to be a lack of transparency during negotiations to revise the terms under which the claimants would build a power generating plant. Turkey had failed during negotiations to disclose points of disagreement or to respond to important communications. The tribunal referred to "a cumulative lack of transparency that, short of bad faith, comes at the very least close to negligence. . . ."[36] Although the tribunal used the term "negligence," that does not seem to have been critical to

---

33 Award, para. 331.

34 United States—Restrictions on Imports of Cotton and Man-made Fibre Underwear, (WT/DS24/AB/R), February 10, 1997.

35 Award, para. 164.

36 Award, para. 174.

the decision. Rather, the award seemed to rest on the lack of transparency with respect to Turkey's position in the negotiations.

One case involved in part a denial of access to documents. In *Siemens v. Argentina*, a case arising under the Germany-Argentina BIT, the claimant's investment was awarded a contract to produce national identity cards. When it delayed compensation owed to the investment, Argentina advanced unsupported arguments to justify the delay and, after terminating the contract, Argentina denied the investment access to the administrative file so that an appeal could be filed. The tribunal found both of these acts to violate the principle of transparency and thus the fair and equitable treatment standard.[37]

One case invoked the transparency principle in a setting in which its application is puzzling. In *Maffezini v. Spain*, a case arising under the Argentina-Spain BIT, an official whose conduct was attributable to Spain transferred money from the claimant's bank account without his prior knowledge or approval. The tribunal held that this conduct violated the transparency principle of the fair and equitable treatment standard. The award is puzzling because the true basis for objection would seem not to be a violation of the transparency principle, but of the security principle. The government, in effect, had seized claimant's property. The lack of transparency with which it was done would seem to be an aggravating factor, but the seizure presumably still would have been wrongful even if the government had disclosed it.

In one case, the tribunal found a violation of the transparency principle, but the award was set aside on the ground that international law, including the fair and equitable treatment standard, does not include a transparency principle. In *Metalclad v. Mexico*, a case arising under the NAFTA, the state of San Luis Potosi denied to the claimant's investment a construction permit needed to operate a hazardous waste disposal site. The claimant had invested initially based on assurances that the site had been approved, but then subsequently was told that a construction permit would be necessary. The permit ultimately was denied at a meeting of which the claimant received no notice. Thus, Mexico failed to provide transparency with respect to the rules to be applied or the process by which the rules were to be applied. The tribunal found this lack of transparency to violate the fair and equitable treatment standard. This portion of the award subsequently was set aside by the British Columbia Supreme Court, which held that transparency is not an element of customary international law. Because the NAFTA explicitly provides that the fair and equitable treatment standard is part of customary law, transparency could not be an element of that standard either, according to the court. As this section has demonstrated, however, the set-aside decision is not consistent with the body of arbitral awards.

---

37 Award, para. 308.

Chapter 9

Access

9.1 INTRODUCTION

Customary international law imposes no obligation on a state to admit people, goods, information, or capital into its territory. Until 1914, states rarely imposed restrictions on the admission of capital into their territory.[1] Developing countries in particular regarded foreign capital as a vital element of their economic development. Even after 1870, when some countries increasingly embraced trade protectionism, they continued to welcome foreign investment. In the aftermath of World War I, however, most countries adopted autarkic policies that included restrictions on the establishment of foreign investment and the movement of capital.[2] The developed countries began to remove some of these restrictions after World War II, but only in the 1990s did much of the rest of the world begin to pursue a vigorous policy of liberalization.[3] Even as the world pursued the integration of capital markets in the 1990s, however, most countries remained reluctant to bind themselves to an open capital account through BIT commitments.

Although access is one of the core principles found in BITs, the vast majority of BITs provide only a very limited right of access. As will be seen, the most common provision guaranteeing the right to establish investment is subject to the law of the host state. A small minority of BITs, however, do guarantee to the covered investors of one party national and MFN treatment with respect to the right to establish investment, although these BITs generally permit each party to make exceptions to the national and MFN treatment obligations. Similarly, a few BITs prohibit the host state from imposing performance requirements on foreign investment as a condition of admission. Some BITs contain provisions for entry and employment of foreign nationals in connection with the establishment or operation of an investment.

The access provisions of a BIT are critical because they may counterbalance the scope and other operational provisions of the BIT. A state seeking to retain regulatory

1 *See* Section 2.1.

2 *See* Section 2.1.2.

3 *See* Section 2.3.

discretion may agree to a broad scope of application for its BIT and to strong provisions on reasonableness, security, nondiscrimination, transparency, and due process, anticipating that it will exclude or admit only conditionally those investments to which it is not prepared to extend the full panoply of BIT rights. Yet a narrow access provision is not a perfect substitute for a narrow scope provision or narrow reasonableness, security, nondiscrimination, transparency, and due process provisions. A state that preserves its regulatory discretion through exclusion forfeits all of the benefits that would have been conferred by entry of a foreign investment. Preserving regulatory discretion through exclusion thus may be costly. Admission of the investment subject to conditions allows the host state to reap some of the benefits of the investment while potentially retaining such regulatory discretion as the conditions permit, but certain conditions may not be permissible under the BIT. For example, some BITs prohibit certain performance requirements even if accepted by an investor in exchange for an incentive or other benefit.

Despite the crudeness of investment exclusion as an instrument of foreign investment policy, it may be the approach that best furthers the development of the rule of law and an investment climate characterized by reasonableness, security, nondiscrimination, transparency, and due process. The alternative to excluding the investment may be to curtail investment security, for example, in order to preserve the discretion to regulate the admitted investment more strictly. Such an approach undermines the host state's commitment to security in principle and may encourage or set a precedent for further derogations. The better policy from a rule of law perspective may be for a host state to create an excellent investment climate for those investments admitted, while excluding those investments that it does not wish to treat fully in accordance with other BIT principles. Sound BIT policy militates in favor of well-defined exceptions rather than erosive interpretations of BIT principles. If a particular investment cannot be admitted and treated in accordance with BIT principles, for purposes of promoting the rule of law perhaps the investment is better excluded than introduced into a setting where it will encourage the host state to erode generally applicable BIT rights in order to address the special circumstances of that investment.

The principle of access in some respects is in philosophical tension with the principle of security. Access is dynamic while security is static. The principle of security means that the rules cannot be changed in the middle of the game, but the principle of access means that the players can be. Thus, the principle of security is stabilizing, while the principle of access is destabilizing.

Despite this philosophical tension, greater access is often associated with greater security in practice. As an empirical matter, economies that grant less access are also more likely to expropriate property and to repudiate contracts.[4] The tendency is to grant security followed by access because a liberal investment regime seeks precisely the balance of stability and dynamism that the combination of security and access brings. That is, host states do not adopt these principles as substitutes, but as complements. Access builds on security.

---

4 John Garen and Kathleen Trask, "Do More Open Economies Have Bigger Governments? Another Look," June 2001, available at http://www.ssrn.com.

The principle of access also may be difficult to separate from other BIT principles in practice because conditions imposed upon the admission of investment typically have long term effects on the operation of the investment once established. Such conditions may include requirements of local participation in ownership and performance requirements. These conditions on access may undermine the long-term security of the investment.

Some commentators distinguish between the "admission" and the "establishment" of investment. In this view, "admission" refers to the right of foreign investment to cross the border, while "establishment" refers to the right to be present indefinitely for the purpose of doing business. This distinction seems unhelpful. All investment by definition is present for some period of time for the purpose of earning a return and thus whether it is described as admitted or established seems of no significance. The BITs themselves do not recognize the distinction. BITs typically protect investment as long as it is present in the territory. This book uses the term "establishment" to refer to the act of becoming the owner or controller of an asset, regardless of the duration of that ownership or control. That is, every act of investing is treated as an act of establishment.

The term "establishment" applies whether the investment is acquired through a merger or acquisition or represents greenfield investment.[5] The distinction between acquired investment and greenfield investment is also one that generally has no significance under the BITs. Investment is protected as long as it is in the territory of one BIT party and owned or controlled by investors of the other BIT party, regardless of whether it existed before the investor acquired ownership or control of it.

Though it appears that every country maintains at least some restrictions on inward foreign investment, especially since the 1990s, states have been dismantling many of their restrictions on access to the local economy by foreign capital, a process that is referred to as liberalization of the capital account. In some cases, they have incorporated liberalization commitments into their BITs.

The principle of access requires not only that host states admit inward investment, but that home states permit outward investment flows. BITs, however, virtually never impose obligations on home states, including in particular obligations to permit outward investment. Home states have a variety of potential reasons for wishing to control outward investment flows. Most notably, some groups, particularly organized labor groups, fear that outward investment will result in the loss of employment in the home state. Some of the empirical evidence on this issue was summarized in Section 3.4.3. Home state business groups may be concerned that capital needed in the home economy for domestic investment is being sent abroad in search of a higher return or reduced risk. Indeed, capital flight has been a significant problem for some developing countries.[6] In addition, home states may fear that sensitive technology, such as technology with important military applications, could be exported to foreign territory where it

---

5 As discussed in Section 3.1, the term "greenfield investment" refers to newly created investment.

6 *See* Valerie Cerra, Meenaskshi Rishi, and Sweta C. Saxena, "Robbing the Riches: Capital Flight, Institutions, and Instability," IMF Working Paper, October 2005, available at http://www.ssrn.com. The authors note that many poor countries lose more resources through capital flight than through debt service. *Id.* at 3.

may come into the possession of hostile governments or even terrorists. In any event, while BIT access obligations on host states are quite limited, access obligations on home states are virtually non-existent.

9.2 THE ECONOMICS OF AN OPEN CAPITAL ACCOUNT

Economic theory holds that a country cannot simultaneously have an open capital account, fixed exchange rates, and control over its monetary policy, although it can have any two of the three. In the period before 1914, many countries were on the gold standard and gave up control over their internal monetary policy in order to maintain the free movement of capital at fixed exchange rates.[7] After World War II, the Bretton Woods system called for at least some restrictions on capital movements to give states greater control over monetary policy, again with fixed exchange rates.[8] Since 1971, many states have abandoned fixed exchange rates, allowing them to permit free movement of capital while also maintaining control over their monetary policy.[9] Especially since the early 1990s, many countries have moved aggressively to eliminate restrictions on access, requiring them either to abandon fixed exchange rates or surrender control over their monetary policy. Generally, the most highly developed countries have the most open economies and thus capital account liberalization has become identified with economic development.

The removal of barriers to access, of course, hardly ensures an increase in foreign investment. Foreign investors may be deterred by a lack of security and transparency in the investment climate, poor infrastructure, undeveloped human capital, high exchange risk, or government corruption, among other factors. Thus, the removal of controls is a necessary, but not a sufficient, condition for promoting inward investment. For this reason, the argument against liberalization is perhaps strongest in the case of the least-developed countries. These countries typically have poorly developed human capital and physical infrastructure and the weakest prospects for attracting significant investment. Further, their financial and legal institutions may be so weak that such investment could not be adequately supervised, were it to come.

In any event, the liberalization of the capital account remains one of the most controversial policies of the early twenty-first century.[10] Studies investigating whether liberalization of the capital account promotes growth have produced mixed results and thus far no consensus has emerged.[11] Many countries remove capital controls

---

7 *See* Section 2.1.1.

8 *See* Section 2.1.2.

9 *See* Section 2.2.

10 Kristin J. Forbes, "Capital Controls: Mud in the Wheels of Market Efficiency" 25 *Cato Journal* 153 (2005).

11 The literature is summarized in Hali J. Edison, Michael W. Klein, Luca Ricci, and Torsten Slok, "Capital Account Liberalization and Economic Performance: Survey and Synthesis," June 2002, available at http://www.ssrn.com. *See generally* M. Ayhan Kose, Eswar Prasad, Kenneth Rogoff, and Shang-Jin Wei, "Financial Globalization: A Reappraisal," IMF Working

while undertaking other measures, so that the effect of any one policy cannot be easily isolated.[12] The benefits of liberalization may vary across countries depending on other factors, such as the level of their institutional development.[13] For example, capital account liberalization is positively associated with growth in countries with strong support for the rule of law[14] and with a good macroeconomic environment.[15] One reason that capital account liberalization may fail is that investors may lack confidence in the host country's long term commitment to its policies. Thus, liberalization commitments in BITs can play a role not only in the promotion of the rule of law generally, but more particularly in bolstering the credibility of liberalization policies.

The controversy over the benefits of liberalization has led to efforts to identify more precisely the circumstances in which openness promotes growth and those in which it does not. Such efforts have focused, for example, on comparing countries at different income levels, as well as comparing those that have sequenced capital account opening differently[16] or looking only at those with developed financial markets.[17] For example, studies have found that financial openness contributes to financial development,[18] which is associated with economic growth,[19] but some studies suggest that this occurs only when a threshold level of development of legal institutions has been attained[20] and those with a more developed legal system benefit more.[21] Financial liberalization is also more strongly associated with growth where accompanied by the elimination of corruption.[22] In short, financial liberalization is beneficial only under the proper conditions.[23]

Liberalization has raised special concerns in the case of portfolio investment, because of concerns that portfolio investment is volatile, that is, it may be transferred out of the host country abruptly during a financial or currency crisis, thereby aggravating

---

Paper WP/06/189, August 2006, available at http://www.ssrn.com; Maurice Obstfeld and Alan M. Taylor, *Global Capital Markets: Integration, Crisis, and Growth* 271 (2004).

12 Forbes, *supra* note 10.

13 *Id.*

14 Barry Eichengreen, *Capital Flows and Crises* 83, 93 (2003).

15 *Id.* at 94.

16 Mihir A. Desai, C. Fritz Foley, and James R. Hines, Jr., "Capital Controls, Liberalizations, and Foreign Direct Investment," Harvard NOM Research Paper No. 04-24, February 2004, available at http://www.ssrn.com.

17 Aaron Tornell, Frank Westerman, and Lorenza Martinez, "Liberalization, Growth and Financial Crises: Lessons from Mexico and the Developing World," November 4, 2003, available at http://www.ssrn.com.

18 Kose et al., *supra* note 11.

19 Obstfeld and Taylor, *supra* note 11, at 272.

20 Menzie Chinn and Hiro Ito, "What Matters for Financial Development? Capital controls, Institutions and Interactions," available at http://www.ssrn.com; Obstfeld and Taylor, *supra* note 11, at 280–282.

21 Menzie D. Chinn and Hiro Ito, "Capital Account Liberalization, Institutions and Financial Development: Cross Country Evidence," May 5, 2002, available at http://www.ssrn.com.

22 Obstfeld and Taylor, *supra* note11, at 280–282. Some evidence exists that equity market opening in particular is associated with economic growth, perhaps because bank lending is heaviest in more corrupt countries. Obstfeld and Taylor, at 277.

23 Obstfeld and Taylor, *supra* note 11, at 300.

the crisis. Capital flows often are volatile because information is incomplete. The problem is especially severe in the case of foreign investors because of their physical and cultural separation from the host state.[24] When investors lack adequate information, they are more likely to take cues from the behavior of other investors. In such a setting, false rumors routinely become self-fulfilling prophecies. Fears of a crisis trigger the very crisis that was feared. Sudden inflows of investment also can be harmful to an economy. For example, inflows of large amounts of capital may cause the local currency to appreciate, reducing the competitiveness of exports.[25] Further, one study found that surges of inward portfolio (but not direct) investment are strong predictors of currency crises resulting from sudden stops of investment flows, an effect that is magnified by weak economic fundamentals.[26]

A synthesis of the literature found "little systematic evidence that capital account liberalization, by itself, increases vulnerability to financial crises," although the combination of capital account liberalization and other policy choices could promote volatility.[27] Another study found that liberalizing equity markets does not lead to increased volatility, although the results again were weaker for liberalizing emerging markets, indicating again the context specific nature of generalizations in development economics.[28] The argument that liberalization of investment flows causes currency crises has been met by the observation that countries with capital controls also experience crises. That is, the crises may be the result of poor macroeconomic policies rather than capital account liberalization.[29] Yet, the repeated financial crises of the 1990s[30] clearly demonstrated the fact of volatility within economies that had liberalized their capital account, whatever its cause. The concern is that, even if liberalization does not cause volatility, it permits it.

The evidence is that debt flows are more volatile than equity flows.[31] For example, most lending to emerging markets is in the form of short-term bank loans.[32] These are loans with a maturity of less than a year. Yet, these loans may be used to finance projects that are long-term. Thus, the borrowers are dependent upon a continuous supply of new lending. An event that prompts one bank to call in existing loans and to refuse to issue new loans is likely to trigger a similar response on the part of other banks. The result will be a sudden contraction in liquidity. More generally, bank loans

---

24 Eichengreen, *supra* note 14, at 49–50.

25 Sweta C. Saxena, "A Survey of Issues Related to Capital Account Liberalization," available at http://www.ssrn.com.

26 Ozan Sula, "Surges and Sudden Stops of Capital Flows to Emerging Markets," available at http://www.ssrn.com.

27 Kose et al., *supra* note 11.

28 Geert Bekaert, Campbell R. Harvey, Christian Lundblad, "Growth Volatility and Financial Liberalization," June 2, 2004, available at www.ssrn.com.

29 Peter Blair Henry, "Capital Account Liberalization: Theory, Evidence and Speculation," Stanford Graduate School of Business Research Paper No. 1951, November 2006, available at http://www.ssrn.com.

30 *See* Section 2.3.

31 Kose et al., *supra* note 11.

32 Henry, *supra* note 29.

are procyclical and thus tend to increase during expansions and rapidly decrease during contractions.[33] Accordingly, they will aggravate a financial crisis.

Equity flows operate differently. While the holder of a debt is entitled to payment from the borrowing enterprise regardless of the circumstances of the enterprise, a shareholder participates in the risk assumed by the enterprise.[34] If the enterprise operates at a loss, the shareholder's only recourse is to sell its stock. The availability of stock for sale will tend to lower the price and as prices fall, shareholders will lose the incentive to sell.

In short, debt and equity flows respond differently to bad news. Equity flows adjust through changes in price, while debt flows adjust through reductions in quantity.[35] Thus, where a host state has large quantities of investment in the form of debt, the effect of a shock will be to induce large outflows. Equity may not respond the same way, however. For example, during the Asian crisis of 1997, abrupt reversals of bank flows were accompanied by positive flows of equity investment.[36]

One policy response to the volatility of debt could be to limit offshore borrowing. Developing countries, however, tend to rely disproportionately on banks. Banks have a history with customers and thus have a comparative advantage in overcoming information gaps,[37] which are often severest in developing countries. Developing countries also may rely more on debt than equity financing because stock markets require substantial resources to regulate properly, such as to require disclosure, prevent fraud, and protect minority shareholders.[38]

In any event, countries may consider various capital controls to limit the volatility of portfolio investment. Capital controls, it may be thought, provide insulation against financial turbulence.[39] Economic analyses, however, have identified a number of potential problems with capital controls.

First, capital controls are only partially effective in controlling capital movements. In particular, they are least effective against multinational firms, which can circumvent them through the use of internal markets.[40] Capital controls have their greatest impact on smaller, domestic enterprises. That is, capital controls have distributional consequences.

Second, capital controls may actually render countries more vulnerable to an exchange rate crisis.[41] In particular, capital controls reduce market discipline.[42] They allow more lax macroeconomic policy and increase the incidence of attacks on the currency.[43] Indeed, the mere expectation of controls may actually increase the likelihood

---

33 Kose *et al., supra* note 11.

34 Henry, *supra* note 32.

35 *Id.*

36 *Id.*

37 Eichengreen, *supra* note 14, at 297.

38 *Id.*

39 Obstfeld and Taylor, *supra* note 11, at 285.

40 Desai et al., *supra* note 16.

41 Reuven Glick and Michael Hutchison, "Capital Controls and Exchange Rate Instability in Developing Countries," June 15, 2000, http://www.ssrn.com.

42 Kose *et al., supra* note 11.

43 Eichengren, *supra* note 14, at 139.

of a crisis.[44] One study concluded that financial openness, by contrast, reduces the likelihood of a currency crisis for industrialized and less-developed countries (although not for emerging markets).[45] It also concluded that capital controls imposed immediately after a crisis begins are not effective.

Third, capital controls are costly. In particular, they increase the cost of finance,[46] especially for smaller firms without access to international markets. They distort the behavior of firms seeking to evade them, while imposing costs on governments trying to halt evasion.[47] Because they increase the cost of borrowing and create inefficiencies,[48] capital controls reduce effective returns and thus lower the quantity of investment.[49] That is, they may discourage not only portfolio investment, but direct investment as well. Even if they are targeted only at portfolio investment, most studies have found that portfolio equity flows have a significant positive impact on growth.[50] Capital controls, in short, reduce growth.[51]

Fourth, capital controls encourage corruption. One study found that the capital controls imposed by Malaysia in September 1998 during the East Asian financial crisis primarily benefited firms with strong ties to the prime minister.[52]

As this indicates, the empirical evidence casts considerable doubt on the wisdom of capital controls, suggesting that states are better served by building strong institutions and pursuing sound macroeconomic policies. Unfortunately, pursuing the right policies is no guarantee against speculative attacks on a currency or against the success of speculative attacks.[53] Such attacks are not necessarily preceded by reckless expansionary policies.[54] They may be prompted merely by a belief that the government will not defend the currency because to do so would require unacceptable levels of unemployment.[55]

Countries continue to struggle with the choices among capital mobility, currency stability, and control over monetary policy. The principle of access poses the unavoidable problem that, if a country allows capital mobility, it must accept some trade-off between control over its monetary policy and currency stability. A confluence of circumstances described in Section 2.3 brought countries to the belief that an open capital account was desirable and the last two decades have witnessed a continuing process of dealing with the consequences of acting upon that belief, including both economic growth and periodic crises. One lesson, however, is that the benefits of an open capital

---

44 Obstfeld and Taylor, *supra* note 11, at 287.

45 Hiro Ito, "Is Financial Openness a Bad Thing? An Analysis on the Correlation Between Financial Liberalization and the Output Performance of Crisis-Hit Economies," August 2004, available at http://www.ssrn.com.

46 Kose *et al, supra* note 11; Desai et al., *supra* note 16.

47 Kose *et al, supra* note 11.

48 Forbes, *supra* note 10.

49 Kose *et al., supra* note 11; Desai *et al., supra* note 16.

50 The literature is surveyed in Kose *et al, supra* note 11.

51 Obstfeld and Taylor, *supra* note11, at 285.

52 Simon Johnson and Todd Mitton, "Cronyism and Capital Controls: Evidence from Malaysia," August 20, 2001, available at http://www.ssrn.com.

53 Eichengreen, *supra* note 14, at 152.

54 *Id.*, at 150.

55 *Id.*

account are more likely realized and the adverse consequences are more likely avoided where a country has sound institutions, including the rule of law. That is, the core principles embodied in BITs are critical to realizing the economic benefits of international investment flows.

9.3 ESTABLISHMENT

9.3.1 Structure and Policy

Most BITs include a very limited right of establishment.[56] By far the most common commitment is a commitment that the host state will admit investment in accordance with its laws.[57] Such a provision merely obligates the host state to adhere to its own laws with respect to establishment. That is, access is guaranteed only if the host state's domestic law guarantees access, but host state law may be changed at any time. Indeed, this fact is acknowledged explicitly by the Australia-Egypt BIT, which provides that "Each Party shall encourage and promote investment in its territory by investors of the other Party and shall, in accordance with its laws and investment policies, applicable from time to time, admit investments."[58]

The provision is not entirely without effect, however. It incorporates local law with respect to establishment into the BIT so that a failure by the host state to adhere to its own law violates the BIT, potentially allowing the investor to seek a remedy through the investor-state disputes provision or the home state to seek a remedy through the state-state disputes provision. Thus, while the host state may change its law at any time, it must adhere to its own law until such time as that law has been changed.

As illustrated by the language of the Australia-Egypt quoted above, this provision is virtually always coupled with an obligation to "promote" or "encourage" in its territory investment of investors of the other party.[59] This may be the vaguest provision of all of

56 On the right of admission and establishment, *see generally* Anna Joubin-Bret, "Admission and Establishment in the Context of Investment Protection," in August Reinisch, *Standards of Investment Protection* (2008); Ignacio Gomez-Palacio and Peter Muchlinski, "Admission and Establishment," in *The Oxford Handbook of International Investment Law* (Peter Muchlinski, Frederico Ortino, and Christoph Schreuer, eds. 2008). Apart from the BITs, the General Agreement on Trade in Services imposes liberalization obligations on WTO members with respect to trade in services. Because services sometimes are delivered through a commercial presence in a state, the right to permit trade in services in some cases amounts to a right to establishment investment for the purpose providing the service.

57 *See, e.g.*, BLEU-Sudan BIT, Art. 2(1); Australia-India BIT, Art. 3(1); France-Uganda BIT, Art. 2; Austria-Armenia BIT, Art. 2(1); Sweden-Kazakhstan BIT, Art. 2(1); United Kingdom-Bosnia-Herzegovina BIT, Art. 2(1); Netherlands-Ethiopia BIT, Art. 2; Indonesia-India BIT, Art. 3(1); Cambodia-Vietnam BIT, Art. II(1); Egypt-Zambia BIT, Art. 2(1); Germany-Timor-Leste BIT, Art. 2(1); Switzerland-Algeria BIT, Art. 3(1).

58 Australia-Egypt BIT, Art. 3.

59 *See, e.g.*, BLEU-Sudan BIT, Art. 2(1); Australia-India BIT, Art. 3(1); France-Uganda BIT, Art. 2; Austria-Armenia BIT, Art. 2(1); Sweden-Kazakhstan BIT, Art. 2(1); United Kingdom-Bosnia-Herzegovina BIT, Art. 2(1); Netherlands-Ethiopia BIT, Art. 2; Indonesia-India BIT,

those commonly appearing in the BITs. Each party appears to be committing itself generally to providing a favorable investment climate, but no specific action is required. In some cases, the language explicitly requires the party to create "favourable conditions" for investment.[60] At a minimum, such language provides guidance in interpreting other more specific provisions of the BIT. That is, other provisions should be interpreted in light of each party's commitment to providing a favorable investment climate. Yet, the provision should not be presumed to lack independent significance. Under some circumstances, a host state's mistreatment of an investor seeking to establish a lawful investment in the territory of that state might be deemed to violate the state's obligation to promote investment. Occasionally, a more specific obligation is included, such as facilitating the establishment of representative offices[61] or the granting of certain permissions.[62]

Far less common, but present in a significant number of BITs, is a commitment to provide national treatment with respect to the establishment of investment.[63] A national treatment obligation in this context requires the host state to grant to covered investors the right to establish investment in any circumstance where domestic investors are permitted to establish investment, a commitment that obviously has a strong liberalizing effect. In the case of this provision, the definition of "investor" establishes in part the substance of the obligation. Host states may restrict certain sectors of the economy to state enterprises. Thus, if the term "investor" includes only private entities, then the national treatment provision will not guarantee to foreign investors the right to establish investment in sectors of the economy open only to state enterprises.

BITs that guarantee national treatment with respect to the establishment of investment virtually always guarantee MFN treatment as well with respect to the establishment of investment.[64] A guarantee of MFN treatment essentially requires the host state to allow a covered investor to establish investment in any circumstance in which another foreign investor is permitted to establish investment. Such a provision offers only a weak form of liberalization because it applies only to sectors that already have been opened to foreign investment. It levels the playing field among foreign investors without expanding the size of the field on which the game may be played.

BITs that grant national (and MFN) treatment with respect to the right to establish investment virtually always reserve for each party the right to designate sectors of the economy within which exceptions to national (and MFN) treatment may be made.[65] Typically, the host state may maintain existing exceptions and adopt future exceptions.

Art. 3(1); Cambodia-Vietnam BIT, Art. II(1); Egypt-Zambia BIT, Art. 2(1); Germany-Timor-Leste BIT, Art. 2(1); Switzerland-Algeria BIT, Art. 3(1).

60 *See, e.g.*, Indonesia-India BIT, Art. 3(1); Cambodia-Vietnam BIT, Art. II(1); United Kingdom-Bosnia-Herzegovina BIT, Art. 2(1); Australia-India BIT, Art. 3(1); Egypt-Zambia BIT, Art. 2(1).

61 *See, e.g.*, Denmark-Ethiopia BIT, Art. 2(1).

62 *See, e.g.*, BLEU-Sudan BIT, Art. 2(2); Mexico-Iceland BIT, Art. 2(2) (host state will give "sympathetic consideration" to applications for necessary permits); Finland-Armenia BIT, Art. 11(1) ("grant expeditiously the necessary permits required . . . in connection with investments").

63 *See, e.g.*, Canada-Uruguay BIT, Art. III; United States-Argentina BIT, Art. II.

64 *See, e.g.*, Canada-Uruguay BIT, Art. III; United States-Argentina BIT, Art. II.

65 *See, e.g.*, Canada-Uruguay BIT, Annex I, Paragraphs (I)–(II).

Sometimes these provisions require the parties to notify each other of existing measures[66] or the treaty itself may identify the existing measures with some degree of particularity.[67]

Some BITs guarantee MFN treatment, but not national treatment, with respect to the right of establishment.[68] These BITs typically do not include sectoral exceptions to the right of establishment.

These national and MFN treatment provisions, like other national and MFN treatment provisions, raise a number of general problems. One such problem is to identify the appropriate comparators. This problem may arise where a host state contends that a covered investor should not be treated the same as a domestic investor because of differences in their circumstances that justify different treatment. Another such problem is to determine the effect of discrimination among comparators. This problem may arise where a host state treats some domestic investors differently than others. The question presented in that situation is whether the foreign investor who has been granted national treatment is entitled to the best treatment accorded to any domestic investor, the worst treatment accorded to any domestic investor, or some other treatment, such as the typical treatment accorded to a domestic investor. These general problems are discussed in Section 7.2.

Access commitments raise special difficulties with respect to enforcement. Where principles of reasonableness, security, nondiscrimination, transparency, or due process are violated, the normal remedy is to award compensation sufficient to eliminate the effects of the wrongful conduct. Where a guarantee of access is violated, the calculation of compensation is complicated by the speculative nature of the injury. The claimant must establish that had access been permitted, it would have established an investment and that the investment would have generated a return. Otherwise the claimant has suffered no injury. Precisely because the investment was not permitted, the investment likely will not have progressed beyond the planning stage. Many of the facts that mustbe proven to warrant an award of compensation may not yet have been finally determined.

9.3.2 Origins

Access was an important principle of the early FCNs, which had as their purpose the establishment of commercial relations between the parties. Early FCNs granted to nationals of each party the right to enter and remain in the territory of the other for the purpose of engaging in various business activities.[69] The establishment of some forms of investment, such as a warehouse, could have been an incident of such activities and thus these treaties guaranteed the right to establish at least those forms of investment.

66 *See, e.g.*, Canada-Uruguay BIT, Annex I, Paragraph (I)-(II).

67 *See, e.g.*, United States-Uruguay BIT, Annexes I and III.

68 *See, e.g.*, Japan-Bangladesh BIT, Art. 2.; BLEU-Indonesia BIT, Art. 1(3); Italy-Nicaragua BIT, Art. II(2).

69 *See* Section 2.1.1.

At that time, countries rarely, if ever, erected legal barriers to inward investment and so no country would have felt the need for a separate treaty right to establish investment as such. Rather, the purpose of the provision largely was to permit the establishment of trade. The right of nationals of one party to engage in various kinds of economic activities continued to be a common element of FCNs in the twentieth century, even as countries began to erect barriers to inward investment in the 1920s.[70] In the early twentieth century, the right to engage in commerce and manufacturing was extended to companies as well as to individuals.[71]

The principle of access represents one area in which the BITs are often weaker than some of the FCNs. When the first BITs appeared, they included a right of access, but it invariably was subject to local law. That is, investors of one party had a right to invest in the territory of the other party only if local law permitted such investment. Many of the earliest BITs did not include even this limited provision. The 1959 Abs-Shawcross Draft Convention on Investments Abroad did not incorporate any right of access. Further, a commentary on the convention prepared by its authors noted that the general absolute standards of treatment included in Article I of the convention, which were derived from U.S. post-war FCN practice, had been "slightly modified to make it clear that the treaty does not deal with questions of establishment."[72] The 1967 OECD Draft Convention on the Protection of Foreign Property expressly disclaimed a right of access. Article 1(b) provided that "[t]he provisions of this Convention shall not affect the right of any Party to allow or prohibit the acquisition of property or the investment of capital, within its territory by nationals of another Party." Note 9(a) to Article 1 explained that the convention was "designed to safeguard property *after* its acquisition or investments *after* they have been made." That same note confirmed that "no State is bound—unless it agrees otherwise—to admit aliens into, or permit the acquisition of property by aliens in, its territory."

The first BIT, the 1959 treaty between Germany and Pakistan, required each party only to endeavor to admit capital of investors of the other party and even this minimal obligation was subject to the host state's local law.[73] The same provision required "sympathetic consideration" of requests for permits. Italy's first BIT, concluded in 1964 with Guinea, committed the parties to facilitating investment, subject to local law.[74]

As early as 1968, the Danish BITs required each party to "consider favourably" applications for investment for the purpose of establishing lasting economic relations.[75] In 1980, Denmark added language requiring that each party encourage investment and admit investments in accordance with its laws.[76] That remains Denmark's practice,

---

70 *See* Section 2.1.2.

71 *See* Section 2.1.2.

72 Hermann Abs and Lord Shawcross, "Comment on the Draft Convention By Its Authors," 9 *Journal of Public Law* 115, 119–120 (1960).

73 Germany-Pakistan BIT, Art. 1(1).

74 Italy-Guinea BIT, Art. II.

75 *See, e.g.*, Denmark-Indonesia BIT, Art. I.

76 *See, e.g.*, Denmark-Romania BIT, Art. 1.

although recent Danish BITs include a specific reference to facilitating the establishment of representative offices.[77]

By 1970, the Belgium-Luxembourg Economic Union (BLEU) was including in its BITs an obligation to admit investment in accordance with its law,[78] a provision that remains in the BLEU BITs.[79] A novel provision calling upon the parties to authorize license contracts and commercial, administrative, or technical assistance agreements in connection with investments that had appeared by 1970[80] also remains in the BLEU BITs.[81]

In 1973, France concluded a BIT with Indonesia that required each party to authorize investment in accordance with its laws.[82] By 1977, the French BITs used the term "admit."[83] An obligation to admit investment in accordance with local law appeared in the Swiss BITs by 1974.[84]

The first U.K BIT, concluded in 1975 with Egypt, required each party to admit investment of nationals and companies of the other party, but subject to the laws of the host state.[85] The parties also undertook to encourage and create favorable conditions for investment. This provision remains unchanged.[86] The first Austrian BIT, concluded in 1976 with Romania, was similar[87] and the Austrian BITs continue to employ that approach.[88] Similar language began to appear in the Italian BITs in 1985.[89]

Although its BIT program dated from 1965, Sweden did not incorporate a right of establishment into its BITs until 1983, but the right was subject to host state law,[90] the same approach used in the most recent Swedish BITs.[91] Kuwait's BIT program dates from 1964, but Kuwait incorporated a right of establishment, subject to local law, in its BITs only in the 1980s.[92] In some cases, this provision covers activities associated with an investment as well.[93] Finland, which began its BIT program in 1980, did not address

---

77 *See, e.g.*, Denmark-Ethiopia BIT, Art. 2(1); Denmark-Croatia BIT, Art. 2(1); Denmark-Cuba BIT, Art. 2(1); Denmark-Kyrgyz Republic BIT, Art. 2(1).

78 *See, e.g.*, Belgium-Indonesia BIT, Art. 1(1).

79 *See, e.g.*, Belgium-Nicaragua BIT, Art. 2(1).

80 *See, e.g.*, Belgium-Indonesia BIT, Art. 2(2).

81 *See, e.g.*, Belgium-Nicaragua BIT, Art, 2(2).

82 France-Indonesia BIT, Art. 1.

83 *See, e.g.*, France-Malta BIT, Art. 2.

84 *See, e.g.*, Switzerland-Indonesia BIT, Art. 1; Switzerland-Sudan BIT, Art. 2.

85 United Kingdom-Egypt BIT, Art. 2(1).

86 *See, e.g.*, United Kingdom-Vietnam BIT, Art. 2(1); United Kingdom-Bosnia- Herzegovina BIT, Art. 2(1).

87 Austria-Romania BIT, Art. 2.

88 *See, e.g.*, Austria-Jordan BIT, Art. 2(1); Austria-Libya BIT, Art. 2(1); Austria-Bosnia-Herzegovina BIT, Art. 2(1); Austria-Armenia BIT, Art. 2(1).

89 *See, e.g.*, Italy-Tunisia BIT, Art. 2(1).

90 *See, e.g.*, Sweden-Yemen BIT, Art. 2(1); Sweden-Hungary BIT, Art. 3(2); Sweden-Poland BIT, Art. 2(4); Sweden-Bolivia BIT, Art. 2(4); Sweden-Czechoslovakia BIT, Art. 2(2).

91 *See, e.g.*, Sweden-Kazakhstan BIT, Art. 2(1); Sweden-Croatia BIT, Art. 2(1); Sweden-Bosnia-Herzegovina BIT, Art. 2(1).

92 *See, e.g.*, Kuwait-China BIT, Art. 2(1); Kuwait-Hungary BIT, Art. 2(1).

93 *See, e.g.*, Kuwait-Hungary BIT, Art. 2(1); Kuwait-Croatia BIT, Art. 2(1); Kuwait-Czech Republic BIT, Art. 2(1).

the right of establishment until 1993. The provision that it adopted at that time requires admission of investment in accordance with host state law,[94] which is the approach still followed in the Finnish BITs.[95]

An important innovation with respect to the right of establishment appeared in 1982 with the conclusion of the first U.S. BITs. These BITs guaranteed national and MFN treatment with respect to the right to establish investment, subject to the right of each party to specify sectors or matters in an annex with respect to which the party reserved the right to deny national treatment.[96] In 1991, the U.S. model negotiating text was modified to permit derogations to MFN, as well as national, treatment.[97]

The U.S. innovation eventually was adopted by Canada[98] and Japan.[99] Further, some of the later Italian BITs have guaranteed MFN treatment with respect to the right to establish investment.[100] Even most developed countries, however, have declined to follow the U.S. example.

9.3.3 Arbitral Practice

In a couple of cases, tribunals have held that provisions requiring that investment be admitted in accordance with host-state law had the effect of conditioning BIT protection on compliance with local law at the time the BIT is established. That is, they have interpreted a provision that purports to expand investor rights as actually imposing a limitation on them. These cases are discussed in Section 4.2.3.5.

In *Aguas del Tunari v. Bolivia*, a case arising under the Netherlands-Bolivia BIT, Bolivia argued that the language subordinating the right of establishment to local law meant that the investment was subject to Bolivian law and the exclusive jurisdiction of the Bolivian courts, with the result that the tribunal had no jurisdiction over the claim. The tribunal rejected this argument, noting that Bolivia's proposed interpretation would defeat the purpose of the BIT in providing for investor-state arbitration before ICSID.[101]

In *MTD Equity v. Chile*, a case arising under the Malaysia-Chile BIT, the claimant argued that the MFN provision of that BIT entitled it to the benefit of Article 3(2) of the Croatia-Chile BIT, which required Chile "to grant the necessary permits in accordance with its laws and regulations." In that case, the claimant was seeking to build a housing development that was inconsistent with local zoning laws. The tribunal

94 *See, e.g.*, Finland-Turkey BIT, Art. 2(1); Finland-Chile BIT, Art. 2(1); Finland-Vietnam BIT, Art. 2(1); Finland-Republic of Korea BIT, Art. 2(1); Finland-Argentina BIT, Art. 2(1).
95 *See, e.g.*, Finland-Algeria BIT, Art. 2(1); Finland-Belarus BIT, Art. 2(1).
96 *See, e.g.*, United States-Egypt BIT, Art. II(1)-(3).
97 *See* Kenneth J. Vandevelde, *U.S. International Investment Agreements* 246 (2009).
98 See, e.g., 2003 Canadian Model BIT, Arts. 3-4.
99 See, e.g., Japan-Vietnam BIT, Art. 2(1).
100 *See, e.g.*, Italy-Jordan BIT, Art. 2(2).
101 Decision on Jurisdiction, paras. 153–154.

rejected the claimant's argument, holding that the provision entitled the claimant to a permit only if the permit was consistent with local law.[102]

9.4 CURRENCY TRANSFERS

The vast majority of BITs include a provision guaranteeing the free transferability of payments related to an investment. In many cases, this provision applies to transfers into the state as well as out of the state. Such a provision thus may provide a right of access for capital under certain circumstances. The currency transfers provision is discussed in Section 6.7.

9.5 PERFORMANCE REQUIREMENTS

Countries permit access to their economies for foreign investment because they believe that foreign investment can contribute to their economic development and prosperity. Foreign investment, for example, can increase employment, bring new technology and expertise into the economy, and develop trade linkages, particularly for exports, which will generate foreign exchange and improve the balance of payments. As discussed in Section 3.2, however, countries sometimes are skeptical that foreign investment necessarily will contribute to their development in these and other ways. Accordingly, many countries impose certain requirements, often known as performance requirements, on foreign investment as a condition of granting access to their economy.[103] These requirements are intended to ensure that foreign investment operates in a way that contributes to economic development and prosperity.

A small number of BITs contain prohibitions on performance requirements. Typically, no definition of the term "performance requirements" appears in a BIT. Prohibited performance requirements usually are host-state restrictions on the use of inputs and outputs by investments. Examples include local hiring requirements, domestic content requirements, import restrictions, technology transfer requirements, and export requirements. BITs that prohibit performance requirements most often prohibit only those requirements that are included in an exhaustive list. Those performance requirements not on the list are permitted.

At least two justifications for the prohibition on performance requirements exist. One is that such requirements interfere with the investor's control of the investment and thus potentially the security of the investment. That is, to gain access, investors must sacrifice a degree of security, in the form of operational control. As has been noted, the critical distinction between direct and portfolio investment is that the former provides control over the enterprise to the investor.[104] Control thus is sometimes a

---

102 Award, para. 205.

103 *See* Section 9.5.

104 *See* Section 3.1.1.

critical element of the investment. Performance requirements represent a limited diminution of that control.

In many cases, however, performance requirements are accepted by the investor at the time the investment is established in exchange for some incentive, such as favorable tax treatment. In those cases, the investor, in effect, has bargained away control. It has lost control in the same sense that any business that enters into a contract whereby a right is exchanged for a privilege has lost the control provided by the right. Certainly, the investor will have calculated the cost of the performance requirements and concluded that the benefits received from the incentives exceed the costs imposed by the requirements. Yet, some BITs prohibit performance requirements even in situations where they are accepted by the investor. Thus, the loss of control is not the sole, or even necessarily the principal, justification for a performance requirements prohibition. Host states impose countless regulations on investments all of which by definition limit the control that the investor can exercise over the investment and these regulations are not on that ground alone prohibited by BITs.

A second justification for the prohibition on performance requirements is that they are trade distorting. Because performance requirements often regulate the source or use of inputs or the destination of outputs, they restrict international trade. Performance requirements thus have an impact not merely on the covered investment, but on international trade flows. Accordingly, the covered investor is not the only beneficiary of the prohibition on performance requirements. Exporters in the home country (or in any other country) whose ability to export inputs to the covered investment or to other investments in the host state is curtailed by performance requirements are also important beneficiaries of the prohibition. For this reason, some BITs prohibit even performance requirements to which the investor agrees.[105] Indeed, some BITs prohibit performance requirements imposed on any investment, not merely covered investment,[106] because such requirements may be trade distorting when imposed on the investment of any nationality.

Because of their trade distorting character, certain performance requirements also are prohibited by the WTO's Agreement on Trade Related Investment Measures (TRIMs), which entered into force in 1995. The TRIMs agreement applies to performance requirements that are inconsistent with the obligation of national treatment or the prohibition on quantitative restrictions in the General Agreement on Tariffs and Trade.

The FCNs generally did not include prohibitions on performance requirements. When the United States inaugurated its BIT program in 1982, the U.S. BITs included a brief prohibition on performance requirements that are imposed as a condition of the establishment, expansion or maintenance of an investment. Perhaps reflecting its innovative nature, the first U.S. provision was brief and vague. The performance requirements to which the prohibition applied were those that required the export of goods or the local purchase of goods or services or that imposed "similar requirements."[107]

105 *See, e.g.*, United States-Uruguay BIT, Art. 8.

106 *See, e.g.*, United States-Uruguay BIT, Art. 8.

107 *See, e.g.*, Senegal-United States BIT, Art. II(8); United States-Cameroon BIT, Art. II(6).

In the 1980s, such a provision was difficult to negotiate and most of the U.S. BITs in the 1980s ultimately included compromise language that requires host states only to endeavor to avoid such requirements.[108] A few other countries that have introduced performance requirements provisions into their BITs more recently have followed the early U.S. model in prohibiting a short, non-exhaustive list of requirements. For example, the Finland-Armenia BIT provides that neither party may impose mandatory measures on covered investments "concerning purchase of materials, means of production, operation, transport, marketing of its products or similar orders having unreasonable or discriminatory effects."[109]

The change in the global investment climate at the end of the 1980s, however, resulted in a much greater willingness on the part of developing countries to agree to performance requirements prohibitions. In 1994, the U.S. model BIT incorporated a more elaborate provision that set forth an exhaustive list of performance requirements, though such requirements were permitted if accepted by the investor in exchange for some benefit.

A decade later, the United States incorporated into its model BIT an even more elaborate provision that was similar in many respects to the 1994 language, but that was influenced by the OECD draft Multilateral Agreement on Investment. Thus, the 2004 U.S. model negotiating text, at Article 8, prohibits certain performance requirements whether imposed on an investment or accepted by the investment in exchange for a benefit. Such performance requirements include local content requirements, restrictions on imports, and restrictions on local sales. The United States considered these performance requirements so trade-distorting that they are not permitted even if the investor voluntarily agrees to them. In addition, the 2004 model prohibits export requirements and technology transfer requirements, when imposed by the government, but allows them if accepted as a condition of receiving a benefit. The 2004 U.S. model BIT also includes a number of exceptions in the text and allows the parties to reserve the right to maintain or adopt other exceptions by specifying them in an annex to the treaty. The 2003 Canadian model BIT, at Article 7, is similar in its two-tier structure of prohibited performance requirements as well as in its exceptions. Japan also has adopted a two-tiered approach.[110]

The recent U.S., Canadian, and Japanese model BITs, with their complex combination of carefully drafted prohibitions and exceptions, reflect the pragmatic nature of the performance requirements provision. The prohibitions are based on the kinds of requirements that actually have created problems for investors or traders in the past, but the practical reality that many states use, or wish to retain the discretion to use, performance requirements has resulted in the omission of performance requirements provisions from most BITs entirely. Where these provisions do appear, they often consist of language that is carefully drawn and subject to exceptions.

The performance requirements provisions have been the subject of very few international arbitrations. All three publicly available awards involving the performance

108 *See* Vandevelde, *supra* note 97, at 397.

109 Finland-Armenia BIT, Art. 3(4).

110 *See, e.g.*, Japan-Vietnam BIT, Art. 4.

requirements provision were issued in cases arising under the NAFTA. These awards suggest that tribunals are giving a literal reading to the performance requirements provision, applying it only to requirements that are explicitly included in the exhaustive list and declining to apply the prohibition to requirements that might be analogous or similar in their effect to those explicitly prohibited. Given that the list in NAFTA is exhaustive and given the specific nature of the language, a literal approach would seem appropriate.

In *Pope & Talbot v. Canada*, the claimant challenged a Canadian measure that required payment of a fee for softwood lumber exports that exceeded the exporter's assigned quota. The measure had been adopted by Canada pursuant to an agreement with the United States to limit softwood lumber exports. The tribunal found the measure not to fall within the terms of any of the prohibited performance requirements. More specifically, the measure did not require the claimant to export a given level or percentage of its product. In fact, the measure limited exports. Neither did it restrict the claimant's sales in Canadian territory.

In *S.D. Myers v. Canada*, the claimant, a U.S. company, sought to export toxic substances known as polychlorinated biphenyls (PCBs) from Canada to the United States, where it had a facility engaged in the business of disposing of PCBs. Canada imposed a ban on the export of PCBs in order to preserve the business of PCB disposal for Canadian companies. The claimant argued that this prohibition, in substance, amounted to a violation of the NAFTA's prohibition on performance requirements to utilize domestic content or purchase local goods or services. The tribunal held, however, that an export ban clearly was not either a domestic content requirement or a requirement to purchase local goods or services. One arbitrator, Professor Bryan Schwartz, dissented.

In *ADF Group v. United States*, the United States conceded that its law requiring that steel used in federally funded highway construction projects be of U.S. origin was a domestic content performance requirement and therefore a prohibited performance requirement under the NAFTA. Nevertheless, the tribunal found, as the United States argued, that the requirement did not violate the performance requirement provision of the NAFTA because the NAFTA contains an exception to the performance requirements prohibition for measures relating to government procurement.

Where a BIT does not contain a performance requirements provision, such requirements nevertheless may be precluded by other provisions of the BIT, notably the MFN and national treatment provisions, which prohibit measures that are imposed on a discriminatory basis.

9.6 ENTRY AND SOJOURN

Countries have the right under customary international law to exclude persons, just as they have the right to exclude capital. The establishment and operation of an investment, however, particularly a foreign direct investment, often require the entry into the host state's territory of investors or their agents and employees, perhaps for an extended period of time. Indeed, one of the benefits of foreign direct investment is that it may bring technology and expertise to an economy, the beneficial use of which generally requires the presence of individuals who have expertise or understand a technology. Thus, obtaining the benefits of providing access to capital may necessitate providing at least limited access to persons.

The earliest investment-related access provisions were those guaranteeing to nationals of one FCN party the right to enter the territory of the other FCN party and to carry on business there.[111] These provisions, which were already common by the early nineteenth century, clearly were intended to promote trade, but they would have incidentally protected some investment-related activities as well. At that time, restrictions on immigration were virtually unknown and thus foreigners generally would have been able at least to gain entry to the territory of a host state even in the absence of such a provision.

As early as the last decades of the nineteenth century, and particularly at the time of World War I and immediately thereafter, countries began to impose restrictions on immigration. Thus, many countries no longer could provide the same commitment to free entry in their FCNs.

U.S. immigration laws authorize a special visa for persons who enter the United States for the purpose of establishing or directing their investment or their employer's investment, provided that such visas are authorized by a U.S. treaty.[112] Thus, the U.S. post-war FCNs included an entry and sojourn provision that renders investors of the other party eligible for these "treaty investor visas."[113] The provision was expressly subordinate to domestic law, however, allowing either party to modify its immigration laws at any time to prevent entry of any person. When the United States concluded its first BITs in 1982, a successor provision appeared in them.[114]

Most BITs contain no provision specifically addressing the right of entry of persons. A few BITs provide only a very limited right of access for investors or persons associated with an investment. A typical provision states that, in accordance with national legislation relating to the entry and sojourn of aliens, individuals working for an investor of one party, as well as members of their household, shall be permitted to enter into, remain in, and leave the territory of the other party for the purpose of carrying out activities associated with an investment.[115] Some BITs limit the provision to persons in a managerial or technical position.[116] Although such provisions typically require that the individuals be nationals of the other BIT party, in some BITs the entry and sojourn provision applies to employees of an investment who may not be nationals of a BIT party.[117] A weak version of the provision simply requires each party to give

111 *See* Section 2.1.1.

112 *See* Vandevelde, *supra* note 97, at 361–362.

113 *See, e.g.*, Treaty of Friendship, Commerce, and Navigation, United States-Netherlands, Art. II(1), 8 U.S.T. 2043, T.I.A.S. No. 3942.

114 *See, e.g.*, United States-Panama BIT, Art. III(1).

115 *See, e.g.*, Sweden-Kazakhstan BIT, Art. 2(2); Australia-India BIT, Art. 5(1) (investors and employees for purposes of engaging in activities connected with investments); India-Indonesia BIT, Art. 11 (same).

116 *See, e.g.*, Canada-Uruguay BIT, Art. V(3); Finland-Armenia BIT, Art. 11(2).

117 *See, e.g.*, Australia-India BIT, Art. 5(1).

sympathetic consideration to applications for entry of persons in connection with an investment.[118]

The entry and sojourn provision has not been the subject of any publicly available arbitral awards issued pursuant to a BIT.

9.7 EMPLOYMENT

One of the potential benefits of foreign direct investment is the creation of employment in the host state. Host state governments, however, sometimes fear that many of these positions, particularly those involving managerial, professional, or technical skills, will be awarded to nationals of the investor's home state, thereby depriving host state nationals of the opportunity to obtain expertise and experience.

The FCNs of the early nineteenth century commonly contained provisions guaranteeing to nationals of one party engaged in business in the territory of the other party the right to hire agents and employees.[119] Such provisions, however, eventually disappeared from the FCNs and essentially were no longer used in the early twentieth century. The U.S. post-war FCNs, however, did contain a provision guaranteeing to nationals and companies of either party the right to engage, within the territory of the other party, "accountants and other technical experts, executive personnel, attorneys, agents, and other specialists of their choice."[120] Some of these FCN provisions were broader, permitting engagement of "other employees of their choice," not merely specialists.[121]

The U.S. BITs of the early 1980s contained a successor provision[122] and some other countries since have incorporated an employment provision into their BIT practice. The most common form of this provision guarantees to an investment the right to hire top managerial personnel of its choice, regardless of nationality.[123] The language thus prohibits the host state from prescribing the nationality of those who hold certain positions within the enterprise. It is typical that such a provision is subject to the immigration laws of the host state. That is, as a practical matter, the investor in choosing its employees may consider only those who have gained lawful entry into the territory of the host state. Thus, the host state retains some ability to control the nationality of employees by the application of its immigration laws.

Having introduced this provision into BIT practice, the United States also has been responsible for creating exceptions to it. First, the United States added an exception that allowed host states to require that a majority of the members of the board of directors be of a particular nationality, provided that the requirement does not materially impair

---

118 *See, e.g.*, Germany-Timor-Leste BIT, Protocol, Para. 3(c); Mexico-Iceland BIT, Art. 2(2).

119 *See* Section 2.1.1.

120 *See, e.g.*, Treaty of Friendship, Commerce, and Navigation, United States-Japan, Art. VIII(1), 4 U.S.T. 2063, T.I.A.S. No. 2863.

121 *See, e.g.*, Treaty of Friendship, Commerce, and Navigation, United States-Greece, Art. XII(4), 5 U.S.T. 1829, T.I.A.S. No. 3057, 224 U.N.T.S. 279.

122 *See, e.g.*, United States-Cameroon BIT, Art. II(5)(b).

123 *See, e.g.*, Canada-Uruguay BIT, Art. V(1) (senior management positions); Australia-India BIT, Art. 5(2)(key technical and managerial personnel—but subject to its laws).

the ability of the investor to exercise control over its investment.[124] Second, the U.S. BITs concluded in 2004 and thereafter allow the parties to specify exceptions to this provision in an annex to the treaty. A few BITs of other countries have adopted these exceptions as well.[125]

The employment provision has not been the subject of any publicly available arbitral awards issued pursuant to a BIT.

124 *See, e.g.*, United States-Uruguay BIT, Art. 9(2). *See also* Canada-Uruguay BIT, Art. V(2).

125 *See, e.g.*, Canada-Uruguay BIT, Annex I, Paragraph 2.

Chapter 10

Due Process

10.1 INTRODUCTION

An ancient maxim of Roman law holds that where there is no remedy, there is no right.[1] As this maxim suggests, the protections accorded by the BITs are effective only to the extent that they are enforceable through the BITs' dispute resolution provisions. Thus, due process, the BIT principle underlying dispute resolution, is the principle upon which rests the effectiveness of the other principles. Indeed, investor-state dispute resolution is the principal way in which the BITs represent an advance—in promoting the rule of law, in creating a liberal investment regime and in providing a favorable investment climate—relative to the post-war FCNs.

Foreign investors, at least where they own direct investment, generally intend to have a long-term presence in the host state and are benefited by a cordial working relationship with the host-state government. In this situation, the best method of dispute resolution is usually through negotiation. Failing that, foreign investors often resort to local courts to resolve disputes with the host state.

Local courts, however, are not always an effective method of dispute resolution. Particularly in a developing country, the courts may have insufficient resources, with the result that the process is slow, and the judges may lack expertise in complex financial transactions. The procedures may be unfamiliar to the investor, the judge may not be impartial in a dispute between a foreign investor and the host-state government, and the court usually will apply host-state law, which may not be favorable to the investor. Indeed, the investor's claim may have arisen from an adverse change in host-state law. Finally, the host-state government may have sovereign immunity to the claim or at least to any enforcement actions.

To assist foreign nationals in obtaining justice in local courts, FCN treaties long have included provisions granting nationals of one party the right of access to local

1 Edward Poste, *Gaius' Elements of Roman Law* 485 (1875). The principle is also well established in the common law system as well. For example, Lord Coke wrote in 1628 that "want of remedy and want of right is all one." Edward Coke, *Institutes of the Laws of England, vol. 1*, 95 b. (1794 ed.).

courts and guaranteeing them national treatment in those courts and the right to choose their advocates.[2] In the twentieth century, provisions were added guaranteeing to companies the right to appear in local courts.[3] Such provisions, however, hardly remedied the deficiencies of proceeding in local courts, particularly where large, complex investment claims were concerned. For these reasons, investors sometimes seek dispute resolution through international law.

One of the earliest forms of dispute resolution available to investors under international law was diplomatic protection, also known as espousal. The theory was that a wrong committed against a country's national was a wrong committed against the country itself.[4] Thus, where the host state wrongfully injured foreign investment, the investor's own state could assert a claim for the injury.[5] That is, the investor's government could espouse the claim of its investor, which essentially would mean that the government would present a claim through diplomatic channels.

Espousal, however, is a potentially ineffective remedy for the investor. First, the investor's state has no duty to espouse a claim.[6] Thus, the investor cannot be assured that the remedy will be available. In fact, governments generally are reluctant to espouse claims because a single investor's claim thereby becomes an irritant in that government's relations with the host-state government.

Second, states generally require that their investors have exhausted local remedies as a condition of espousal.[7] This policy conserves the resources of the home-state government by deflecting claims that could be resolved by the investor in local courts without the involvement of the home state. It also preserves the dignity of the host state by providing it with an opportunity to rectify a violation of law and to accord justice to the investor under its own law. Moreover, it minimizes the number of disputes that can become irritants in the bilateral relations between the home and host states. Although the exhaustion requirement may be excused where pursuing local remedies would be futile,[8] the investor may not be able to demonstrate in advance their futility. Thus, several years of wasteful litigation in local courts may elapse before the investor's state is willing even to consider espousing the claim.

Third, if the investor's state does espouse the claim, it may resolve the claim on any terms it deems appropriate, perhaps settling the claim for far less compensation than the investor believes should be paid.[9] In effect, the investor loses all control over the prosecution of the claim.

---

2 *See* Section 2.1.1.

3 *See* Section 2.1.1.

4 *See* Marion Whiteman, 8 *Digest of International Law* 1216–1219 (1967).

5 *Id.*

6 *Id.*

7 *See, e.g., Interhandel* (Switzerland v. United States), 1959 I.CJ. 6, 27; *Ambatielos Claim* (Greece v. United Kingdom) 23 International Law Reports 306, 344 (1956); Whiteman, *supra* note 4, at 769–807.

8 *See generally Restatement (Third) Foreign Relations Law* Section 713, comment f (1987); *Panevezys-Saldutiskis Ry.* (Est. v. Lith.) 1939 P.C.I.J. Ser. A/B No 76 at 18.

9 Whiteman, *supra* note 4, at 1216–1219.

Fourth, even if the investor's state espouses the claim and seeks a level of compensation that would satisfy the investor, the host state may refuse to negotiate a settlement or pay any compensation. Especially if the home state has a large number of claims against the host state, the formation of an arbitral tribunal might be proposed, but under customary international law a tribunal has jurisdiction over a state only with the consent of the latter.[10] Thus, diplomacy cannot resolve the dispute in the absence of an agreement by the host state.

Given the potential ineffectiveness of diplomacy, home states sometimes have resorted to extralegal remedies. Most commonly, they have threatened or utilized force to compel payment of compensation. As discussed in Section 2.1, military force often was used in the nineteenth and early twentieth centuries to protect foreign investment, but after the entry into force of the U.N. Charter at the end of World War II, the use of force except in self-defense became unlawful. Although states in fact have used force in situations where the security of their investment abroad was threatened, in the post-war world that is rarely, if ever, the public justification for military action.

With the use of force to protect foreign investment no longer lawful, some countries, notably the United States, have imposed economic sanctions on countries that expropriate foreign investment. The United States, for example, in 1959 enacted legislation requiring the suspension of foreign assistance to states that expropriate U.S. investment without payment of prompt, adequate, and effective compensation.[11] Subsequent legislation enacted in the 1960s and 1970s required opposing loans from international financial institutions and eliminating favorable trade treatment to such states.[12] Although these kinds of sanctions may be effective on occasion,[13] they did not prevent the massive number of expropriations that occurred in the late 1960s and early 1970s, after most of this legislation had been adopted. One reason for the ineffectiveness of such legislation is that the executive branch may be reluctant to impose sanctions because, like espousal of claims, sanctions become an irritant in bilateral relations. Further, where sanctions are imposed, host-state governments may resist appearing to have been coerced by another country. The United States did eliminate foreign assistance for a time to two countries that expropriated U.S. property: Sri Lanka in 1963 and Ethiopia in 1979. In both cases, however, bilateral relations already were poor and compensation for the expropriation was paid only after a general improvement in those relations.[14] In a more successful use of sanctions, the United States voted against a $175 million Inter-American Development Bank loan to Costa Rica to compel Costa Rica to submit to arbitration a dispute over the value of land expropriated for a national park. Subsequently, Costa Rica

---

10 Advisory Opinion of International Court of Justice on Reparation of Injuries, 1949 I.C.J. Rep. 177–78.

11 *See generally* Kenneth J. Vandevelde, "Reassessing the Hickenlooper Amendment," 29 *Virginia Journal of International Law* 115 (1988).

12 *Id.*

13 For example, Costa Rica agreed to submit an investment dispute with a U.S. investor to arbitration after the United States opposed developmental assistance loans to Costa Rica by the World Bank.

14 Vandevelde, *supra* note 11, at 159.

and the U.S. investor who owned the land reached an agreement to submit the claim to arbitration.[15]

Prior to the twentieth century, states sometimes agreed to the arbitration of disputes that had arisen, often because of a war or other circumstances involving violence.[16] Following the conclusion of the 1899 Hague Peace Conference and the formation of the Permanent Court of Arbitration, numerous countries concluded bilateral arbitration agreements in which they agreed to submit disputes to arbitration for peaceful resolution. Arbitration clauses also commonly were included in FCN treaties. After the creation of the Permanent Court of International Justice at the end of World War I, FCN treaties sometimes provided for the submission to the court of disputes involving the interpretation or application of the treaty.[17] Following World War II, the International Court of Justice was designated as the means of dispute resolution under some FCNs.[18]

International arbitration may be superior to the use of national courts in a number of respects. The parties can ensure that the dispute will be resolved by experts in the subject matter, rather than judges whose expertise may be in routine matters of domestic law. The arbitrators may have greater impartiality than a judge deciding a case between a foreign investor and the judge's own state. The tribunal is likely to apply international law, rather than the law of the host state. International arbitral procedure may be less complex than domestic procedure and, even if it is not, it at least will seem more neutral to the investor than the procedure of the host state. Indeed, in some cases, host states have been at a disadvantage before international tribunals because investors have retained experienced attorneys who have served as both claimants' counsel and arbitrators, while the host state may rely on attorneys already employed by the government, who may have no prior experience with investor-state arbitration and who may lack the resources of the investors and their counsel.[19] Finally, arbitral awards, unlike domestic court judgments, are enforceable through the United Nations Convention on the Recognition and Enforcement of Foreign Arbitral Awards, generally known as the New York Convention.[20]

This form of dispute resolution was superior to diplomacy because, once the treaty entered into force, an effective remedy was available. Yet, like espousal, the remedy might still require the exhaustion of local remedies. It also would depend upon the willingness of the home state to espouse the claim before the tribunal, although submission of a claim to an impartial tribunal might interfere with bilateral relations less than an attempt to negotiate a claim.

Because state-state arbitration still retained some of the disadvantages of espousal, in the mid-twentieth century the idea emerged of obtaining host-state consent in

---

15 *See Santa Elena v. Costa Rica*, Award, paras. 25–26.

16 *See* Section 2.1.1.

17 *See* Section 2.1.2.

18 *See* Section 2.2.

19 *See* Eric Gottwald, "Leveling the Playing Field: Is It Time for a Legal Assistance Center for Developing Nations in Investment Treaty Arbitration," 22 *American University International Law Review* 237, 261–264 (2007).

20 21 U.S.T. 2517, T.I.A.S. No. 6997, 330 U.N.T.S. 3.

advance to the jurisdiction of a tribunal to which the investor itself could submit a claim. For example, in 1948 the International Law Commission published the Draft Statute of the Arbitral Tribunal for Foreign Investment and the Draft Statute of the Foreign Investment Court,[21] both of which provide for investor-state arbitration of certain investment disputes. The 1959 Abs-Shawcross Draft Convention on Investments Abroad[22] contemplated investor-state arbitration of disputes involving alleged violations of the convention. The 1967 OECD Draft Convention on the Protection of Foreign Property, at Note 1 to Article 7, described the "vital need" to create a dispute resolution mechanism "in view of the nature of the provisions of the Convention, the generality of the terms employed therein, and the complexity of the facts that might have to be elaborated."

As will be seen, investor-state arbitration offers many of the benefits of state-state arbitration. Both provide for arbitration before impartial arbitrators, who can be selected for their expertise. Both provide for the application of international law, can be confidential, and have mechanisms for the enforcement of the awards. Investor-state arbitration offers the additional advantage, however, that it can remove the home state from the dispute resolution process entirely, thereby eliminating the disadvantages of espousal. The investor has an assured remedy, need not exhaust local remedies, and will not lose control over the prosecution of the claim.

No progress was made toward establishing an investor-state arbitral mechanism prior to the beginning of the first BIT program. At their inception, the BITs did include a provision for state-state dispute resolution, typically before an *ad hoc* arbitral tribunal. No reason existed why a disputes provision could not provide a virtually identical procedure for establishing an investor-state arbitral tribunal. Indeed, a few BITs use the same mechanism for investor-state and state-state dispute resolution.[23]

Investor-state arbitration, however, did not become a feature of the BITs until the conclusion in 1965 of the Convention on the Settlement of Investment Disputes Between States and Nationals of Other States. This convention established the International Centre for Settlement of Investment Disputes, also known as ICSID, an entity of the World Bank. ICSID has adopted rules for the arbitration of investor-state investment disputes and provides administrative support for investor-state arbitral tribunals. ICSID does not itself arbitrate the disputes, however. Rather, the arbitration is conducted by one or more arbitrators designated by the disputing parties.

Following entry into force of the ICSID Convention, countries began gradually to provide for investor-state arbitration in their BITs, beginning with a 1968 BIT between the Netherlands and Indonesia. The practice did not become widespread, however, until the 1970s and did not become virtually universal until the 1980s.

The emergence of investor-state arbitration represented not merely the creation of a more effective remedy for investors, but an important philosophical change in international investment law. Prior investment-related agreements, such as the FCNs or

21 Reprinted in United Nations Conference on Trade and Development, 3 International Investment Instruments: A Compendium 259 (1996).

22 9 *Journal of Public Law* 115 (1960).

23 *See, e.g.*, Finland-Egypt BIT, Art. 7; Germany-Bolivia BIT, Art. 11(2).

the early BITs, had required the investor's government to become involved in an investment dispute if the investor was to receive compensation for a treaty violation. As has been noted, the investor's government inevitably would treat the resolution of the dispute as only one factor in its overall political relationship with the host-state government. Claims, in other words, would be resolved only if it was politically expedient to do so. Providing a mechanism whereby claims could be submitted to binding arbitration without the involvement of the investor's own government depoliticized the dispute. That is, it shifted the resolution of the dispute from the realm of politics to the realm of law. This shift became a critical element of the BIT's function not only as a device for investment protection, but also as an instrument for the promotion of the rule of law.

One consequence of depoliticizing dispute resolution is that claims are much more likely to be arbitrated, because the home state no longer stands as a potential barrier to arbitration. The investor is more likely to receive compensation for an injury, but the host state is more likely to face frivolous claims that never would have been espoused. While the host state is more likely to find itself a respondent, its adversary in the proceedings will be a private claimant, not another sovereign state. The dispute therefore is less likely to disrupt the political relations between the two BIT parties. Indeed, the home state may find itself in support of the host state's position, fearing that a decision adverse to the host state will set a precedent that will prejudice the interests of the home state in a future dispute. This appears to not yet be a widespread phenomenon in investor-state arbitration under the BITs, but in several NAFTA arbitrations the two non-disputing NAFTA parties have submitted statements supporting the respondent with respect to specific issues.[24] The NAFTA explicitly authorizes such submissions, while few BITs do, but the existence of a mechanism for comments from the non-disputing parties in the NAFTA has provided a glimpse of the ways in which the two BIT parties may find their interests aligned against those of the investor.

Another consequence of depoliticizing dispute resolution is that it shifts the blame for the result from the political branches to the legal system. Where large awards are issued against host-state governments, the existence of BITs and their provisions for investor-state arbitration, rather than the host state's wrongful conduct, can be portrayed as the cause of the host state's misfortune. The benefits of a BIT are difficult to quantify, but arbitral awards adverse to the host state readily quantify at least some of their costs. In time, the investor-state arbitral process may place more weight on the BIT system than it can bear and some states may look for ways to shrink their BIT programs, if not to abolish them entirely, or at least to diminish or eliminate resort to investor-state arbitration. Such moves, of course, would be strongly resisted by the investor community. As discussed in Section 2.3, by 2007, some steps in this direction were already evident in Latin America.

---

24 Article 1128 of the NAFTA authorizes the NAFTA parties who are not parties to the dispute to submit comments on a question of interpretation of the agreement.

10.2 INVESTOR-STATE DISPUTE RESOLUTION

10.2.1 Structure and Policy

10.2.1.1 Consent to Arbitration The most important element of an investor-state disputes provision is the host state's consent to arbitration.[25] If an investor-state disputes provision includes nothing else, it should include this. The consent must contain two elements. First, it must identify the types of disputes that are within the consent, because the tribunal's jurisdiction is limited by the terms of the parties' consent. Second, it must specify the means by which a dispute is to be arbitrated.

The most common BIT provision sets forth the host state's consent to arbitration of any dispute "concerning an investment."[26] This consent is quite broad. It does not require that the dispute involve an alleged violation of a provision of the BIT. All that is required is that the dispute concern an investment. In practice, however, claims submitted to arbitration under investor-state disputes provisions in BITs usually allege violations of the BIT. Occasionally the consent applies to "any dispute,"[27] which clearly is even broader than the more common language.

Some BITs limit the consent to disputes arising out of an alleged violation of a BIT provision.[28] Occasionally, they further specify that the breach must have caused loss to the investor or the investment.[29] The U.S. BITs include disputes arising out of an alleged breach of an investment agreement or investment authorization in the parties' consent to arbitration.[30] In other words, the U.S. BITs permit the investor to use the investor-state disputes provision to enforce investment agreements and investment authorizations. A few BITs limit the jurisdiction of the tribunal to disputes concerning a violation of only certain provisions of the BIT, such as the expropriation provision.[31]

---

25 *See generally* Christoph Schreuer, "Consent to Arbitration," in *The Oxford Handbook of International Investment Law* (Peter Muchlinski, Frederico Ortino, and Christoph Schreuer, eds. 2008).

26 *See, e.g.*, Netherlands-Ethiopia BIT, Art. 9(1), (5); Sweden-Kazakhstan BIT, Art. 8(1); Cambodia-Vietnam BIT, Art. VIII(1); Denmark-Ethiopia BIT, Art. 9(1); Switzerland-Algeria BIT, Art. 8(1); BLEU-Sudan BIT, Art. 12(1)–(2) ("investment dispute"); Finland-Armenia BIT, Art. 9(1),(5) ("dispute arising directly from an investment"); Australia-India BIT, Art. 12(1) ("in relation to an investment"); France-Uganda BIT, Art. 7; Germany-Timor-Leste BIT, Art. 11(1); Indonesia-India BIT, Art. 9(1).

27 *See, e.g.*, Egypt-Zambia BIT, Art. 8(1).

28 *See, e.g.*, United Kingdom-Bosnia-Herzegovina BIT, Art. 8(1) (disputes "concerning an obligation" of the BIT); Austria-Armenia BIT, Art. 11; Canada-Uruguay BIT, Art. 9.

29 *See, e.g.*, Austria-Armenia BIT, Art. 11; Mexico-Iceland BIT, Art. 10(1).

30 *See, e.g.*, United States-Argentina BIT, Art. VII(1).

31 *See, e.g.*, Bulgaria-Cyprus BIT, Art. 4.1 (authorizing investor-state arbitration of dispute concerning the amount of expropriation compensation); Norway-Hungary BIT, Art. XII (authorizing investor-state arbitration of disputes under the expropriation, war and civil disturbance and transfers provisions); Italy-Bangladesh BIT, Art. 9 (expropriation compensation); Italy-Pakistan BIT, Art. 9 (expropriation compensation); Austria-Romania BIT, Art. 5 (expropriation compensation).

Some BITs provide that, in the event of an investment dispute, the parties "shall" consent to investor-state arbitration.[32] This implies that the BIT itself does not constitute the host state's consent. Refusal of the host state to consent, however, would itself violate the BIT and would give rise to a claim under the state-state disputes provision.

A very few BITs provide that consent is subject to agreement between the investor and the host state, without specifically requiring that consent be given.[33] In such a case, it would appear that neither party has consented nor is either party required to consent.

Under the ICSID convention, recourse to ICSID is available only where the home and host states are parties to the ICSID convention.[34] Thus, where the parties consent to ICSID arbitration in the BIT, but one of them does not adhere to the ICSID convention or later withdraws its adherence to the ICSID convention, the consent to arbitrate is effectively meaningless because an ICSID tribunal must decline jurisdiction. In such a case, however, the other party may submit a claim to state-state dispute resolution alleging that, in failing to adhere to the ICSID convention and thereby thwarting the intended operation of the BIT, the party has breached its obligation of good faith.

While the host state's consent to arbitration typically is given in the BIT, the common practice is that the investor consents by submitting a claim to arbitration. Some BITs provide that the investor may consent in writing to arbitration, after which either party may submit the dispute to arbitration.[35] In either case, no single instrument embodying the consents of both disputing parties ever exists, although some arbitral mechanisms condition the jurisdiction of the tribunal upon an agreement in writing to arbitrate. This practice has never resulted in a denial of jurisdiction by a tribunal in a case arising under a BIT, but some BITs,[36] from an abundance of caution, include language specifying that the host state's consent and the investor's submission of the claim to arbitration shall constitute a written agreement for purposes of various relevant agreements, including the ICSID convention, the Additional Facility Rules,[37] the UNCITRAL Rules[38] and the New York Convention[39]

10.2.1.2 Arbitral Mechanisms By far the most common means of arbitration to which host states consent is an arbitration administered by ICSID under the ICSID arbitration rules.[40] Most of the earliest investor-state disputes provisions included

---

32 *See, e.g.*, Netherlands-Philippines BIT, Art. 9(1); Japan-Egypt BIT, Art. 11; Japan-Sri Lanka BIT, Art.11.

33 *See, e.g.*, Sweden-Malaysia BIT, Art. 6.

34 ICSID convention, Art. 25(1).

35 *See, e.g.*, Switzerland-Pakistan BIT, Art. 9; United Kingdom-Egypt BIT, Art. 8(1).

36 *See, e.g.*, Sweden-Kazakhstan BIT, Art. 8(4).

37 The Additional Facility is an alternative arbitral mechanism under the auspices of ICSID and is discussed in Section 10.2.1.2.

38 Arbitration under the UNCITRAL Rules is discussed in Section 10.2.1.2.

39 The New York Convention is discussed in Section 10.2.1.7.

40 *See, e.g.*, United Kingdom-Bosnia-Herzegovina BIT, Art. 8(2); Netherlands-Ethiopia BIT, Art. 9(2); BLEU-Sudan BIT, Art. 12; Finland-Armenia BIT, Art. 9(2); Australia-India BIT,

the parties' consent to only this single method of arbitration. By the 1980s, some countries began to negotiate BITs that provided investors with other means of dispute resolution and this practice became common in the 1990s. The great majority of investor-state arbitrations to date, however, have been before ICSID. In fact, of the 317 claims submitted to investor-state arbitration under a BIT as of the end of 2008, 202 were submitted to arbitration before ICSID or the ICSID Additional Facility, discussed below.[41]

The most common alternative to ICSID arbitration is arbitration under the rules of the United Nations Commission on International Trade Law (UNCITRAL).[42] Arbitration under the UNCITRAL rules differs from ICSID arbitration in that UNCITRAL does not provide an institution to administer the arbitration. For this reason, UNCITRAL arbitration is described as ad hoc arbitration, meaning that a tribunal, support staff, and appropriate facilities must be assembled for each arbitration. Of the 317 disputes submitted to investor-state arbitration under a BIT by the end of 2008, 83 were submitted to arbitration under the UNCITRAL Rules.[43]

The second most common alternative to ICSID arbitration is arbitration before the ICSID Additional Facility.[44] The Additional Facility was created by ICSID in 1978 to arbitrate disputes that are outside the scope of ICSID's jurisdiction as defined by the ICSID convention. Because the Additional Facility is not a creation of the ICSID convention, it is not subject to any of the limitations of that convention. One such limitation is that ICSID has jurisdiction over a claim only if the home and host states both are parties to the ICSID convention. The Additional Facility, by contrast, has jurisdiction if either state, but not both, is a party to the ICSID Convention. In other words, the jurisdiction of ICSID and of the Additional Facility are mutually exclusive. Another limitation in the ICSID convention that does not apply to Additional Facility arbitrations is that the dispute must be one arising directly out of an investment.[45]

Art. 12(3); Sweden-Kazakhstan BIT, Art. 8(2); Egypt-Zambia BIT, Art. 8(2); Vietnam-Cambodia BIT, Art. VIII(3); Argentina-Thailand BIT, Art. 9(5); Denmark-Ethiopia BIT, Art. 9(2); France-Uganda BIT, Art. 7; Germany-Timor-Leste BIT, Art. 11(2); Indonesia-India BIT, Art. 9(3); Switzerland-Algeria BIT, Art. 8(2); Austria-Armenia BIT, Art. 12; Mexico-Iceland BIT, Art. 10.

41 United Nations Conference on Trade and Development, *Latest Developments in Investor-State Dispute Settlement* 2 (2009).

42 *See, e.g.*, United Kingdom-Bosnia-Herzegovina BIT, Art. 8(2); Netherlands-Ethiopia BIT, Art. 9(2); BLEU-Sudan BIT, Art. 12; Finland-Armenia BIT, Art. 9(2); Australia-India BIT, Art. 12(3)(as amended by the BIT); Sweden-Kazakhstan BIT, Art. 8(2); Egypt-Zambia BIT, Art. 8(2); Vietnam-Cambodia BIT, Art. VIII(3); Argentina-Thailand BIT, Art. 9(5); Denmark-Ethiopia BIT, Art. 9(2); Indonesia-India BIT, Art. 9(3) (as amended by the BIT); Switzerland-Algeria BIT, Art. 8(2); Austria-Armenia BIT, Art. 12; Mexico-Iceland BIT, Art. 10.

43 UNCTAD, *supra* note 40, at 2.

44 *See, e.g.*, United Kingdom-Bosnia-Herzegovina BIT, Art. 8(2); Netherlands-Ethiopia BIT, Art. 9(2); BLEU-Sudan BIT, Art. 12; Finland-Armenia BIT, Art. 9(2); Australia-India BIT, Art. 12(3); Sweden-Kazakhstan BIT, Art. 8(2); Argentina-Thailand BIT, Art. 9(5); Denmark-Ethiopia BIT, Art. 9(2); Austria-Armenia BIT, Art. 12; Mexico-Iceland BIT, Art. 10.

45 ICSID convention, Article 25(1).

Other arbitral mechanisms sometimes appear in the parties' consent to arbitration. The most common are arbitration before the Stockholm Chamber of Commerce[46] or the International Chamber of Commerce.[47] As of the end of 2008, 17 of the disputes submitted under a BIT to investor-state arbitration were submitted to the Stockholm Chamber of Commerce, while 5 were submitted to the International Chamber of Commerce. Other alternatives to ICSID, the Additional Facility, and the UNCITRAL rules are used only occasionally in investor-state arbitration.[48] A few BITs provide for the creation of an ad hoc tribunal without reference to any specific set of rules.[49]

Many BITs specify that, if multiple fora for international arbitration are available, the investor may choose among them.[50] Even where such language does not appear, as a practical matter the investor generally controls the choice. The reason is that BITs typically include the host state's consent to each of the available alternatives, but never the investor's consent because the investor is not a party to the BIT. The investor thus may control the choice by consenting to only one of the alternatives. A small number of BITs leave the choice of mechanisms to the mutual agreement of the parties. Some of these specify which mechanism shall be used in the event that the parties are unable to reach agreement,[51] but others do not.[52]

Arbitration under the various sets of rules is similar in many respects. In the case of ICSID arbitration, each disputant selects an arbitrator and the disputants mutually agree upon a third arbitrator, who serves as the chair of the tribunal. Under the UNCITRAL rules, each disputant selects an arbitrator and the two arbitrators chose a third arbitrator, who serves as chair. If a party does not designate an arbitrator or if agreement cannot be reached on the third arbitrator, the rules typically identify an official affiliated with another international organization, such as the World Bank or the United Nations, who serves as an appointing authority and, in that capacity, appoints the unappointed arbitrator.

Some BITs explicitly identify local remedies[53] or, less often, previously-agreed disputes procedures[54] as alternatives to international arbitration. Again, these BITs

---

46 *See, e.g.*, BLEU-Sudan BIT, Art. 12(3).

47 *See, e.g.*, United Kingdom-Bosnia-Herzegovina BIT, Art. 8(2); BLEU-Sudan BIT, Art. 12(3); Austria-Armenia BIT, Art.12.

48 *See, e.g.*, Egypt-Zambia BIT, Art. 8 (Regional Center for International Commercial Arbitration in Cairo).

49 *See, e.g.*, Mexico-Iceland BIT, Art. 12.

50 *See, e.g.*, Netherlands-Ethiopia BIT, Art. 9(2); United Kingdom-Bosnia-Herzegovina BIT, Art. 8(2); BLEU-Sudan BIT, Art. 12(3); Sweden-Kazakhstan BIT, Art. 8(2); Egypt-Zambia BIT, Art. 8(2); Switzerland-Algeria BIT, Art. 8(2); Austria-Armenia BIT, Art. 12.

51 *See, e.g.*, Argentina-Thailand BIT, Art. 9(6).

52 *See, e.g.*, Denmark-Ethiopia BIT, Art. 9(2).

53 *See, e.g.*, Finland-Armenia BIT, Art. 9(2); BLEU-Sudan BIT, Art. 12(2); Netherlands-Ethiopia BIT, Art. 9(2); Egypt-Zambia BIT, Art. 8(2); Vietnam-Cambodia BIT, Art. VIII(2); Thailand-Argentina BIT, Art. 9(2); Denmark-Ethiopia BIT, Art. 9(2); Indonesia-India BIT, Art. 9(2); Austria-Armenia BIT, Art. 12; Mexico-Iceland BIT, Art. 9.

54 *See, e.g.*, Finland-Armenia BIT, Art. 9(2); Austria-Armenia BIT, Art. 12; Mexico-Iceland BIT, Art. 9.

typically make clear that the choice between local remedies (or previously-agreed procedures) and international arbitration belongs to the investor.[55]

While BITs sometimes specify that the dispute may be submitted by either party once the investor consents, in actual practice investors rarely consent prior to their submission of the claim to arbitration. That is, investors typically consent by the act of submitting the claim to arbitration. Thus, the investor retains complete control over the issues of whether a dispute shall be submitted to arbitration, when the dispute shall be submitted, and which arbitral mechanism shall be utilized, if more than one is available.

Some BITs provide for conciliation as well as arbitration.[56] Conciliation is a nonbinding, third-party dispute settlement process. ICSID has a separate set of rules for conciliation and BITs usually refer to these rules when they provide for conciliation. Although the ICSID conciliation process has been invoked on at least five occasions, investors overwhelmingly have chosen binding arbitration instead. Investors very often prefer a negotiated solution not only because such a solution may be less costly to achieve and eliminates the risk of an adverse tribunal decision, but also because in many cases they wish to continue to operate in the host country and thus would prefer to reach an amicable resolution. Yet the likelihood is that, by the time the investor decides to seek third-party dispute resolution, it is already convinced that a negotiated settlement is not possible, at least in the absence of the threat of an adverse arbitral award, and therefore a nonbinding process such as conciliation may be perceived as unlikely to succeed.[57] Further, the efficient conduct of business necessitates that contingencies, where possible, be replaced with certainties. Investors seek security and transparency in an investment climate for precisely this reason. When an investor initiates an arbitration, the investor can be virtually certain that if the tribunal has jurisdiction, the claim will be decided. When an investor initiates a conciliation, the investor knows that the process may not yield a resolution. The investor may believe that it cannot afford the expense, time, and continued uncertainty associated with a process that may not yield a final resolution. Further, an arbitral award is enforceable in domestic courts through the New York Convention or the ICSID convention, while an agreement reached through conciliation is not. Moreover, a dispute with a foreign investor, especially a large dispute with a highly visible foreign investor, may be politically controversial. The investor typically is seen as challenging the legitimate regulatory power of the host-state government and perhaps its integrity and competence. If the investor prevails, the host state may be required to pay a large sum to the investor.

---

55 *See, e.g.*, Finland-Armenia BIT, Art. 9(2); BLEU-Sudan BIT, Art. 12(2); Netherlands-Ethiopia BIT, Art. 9(2); Egypt-Zambia BIT, Art. 8(2); Vietnam-Cambodia BIT, Art. VIII(2); Thailand-Argentina BIT, Art. 9(3); Denmark-Ethiopia BIT, Art. 9(2) Indonesia-India BIT, Art. 9(2); Austria-Armenia BIT, Art. 12; Mexico-Iceland BIT, Art. 9.

56 *See, e.g.*, Australia-India BIT, Art. 12(2); Indonesia-India BIT, Art. 9(3).

57 For example, in *Wintershall v. Argentina*, a case arising under the Germany-Argentina BIT, when the claim was submitted, ICSID informed that parties that the claim might be outside its jurisdiction and invited the parties to consider conciliation. The claimants replied that they did not believe that conciliation would be productive because they already had sought unsuccessfully to negotiate a resolution with the Argentine government. Award, paras. 12–13.

The host-state government thus has reason to resist the claim vigorously to protect its treasury, its reputation as a competent and honest administration, the reputation of the country's investment climate and even its national honor. A negotiated settlement or one reached through a nonbinding procedure may be politically very difficult for the host state government to accept. The government must concede wrongdoing, at least implicitly, by agreeing to pay compensation and it must reallocate perhaps much needed funds to pay the settlement. Rare is the country that has large sums budgeted to pay international claims should they arise. No constituency within the host state is benefited by payment of the settlement and thus those who authorize payment of it can expect little reward or gratitude. Particularly in smaller developing countries where resources are scarce, political opponents may claim that too much was paid and perhaps charge the responsible officials with collusion with a foreign government, capitulation to foreign pressure, or even an almost treasonous betrayal of the national interest. By contrast, if the host-state government vigorously contests the claim, forces the claim into arbitration and loses, it is faced with a legally binding obligation enforceable in domestic courts. The blame for the result can be placed on the tribunal that issued the award and the same desire to protect reputation and honor that required contesting the claim now requires paying the legal obligation. Forcing the claim to arbitration also opens the possibility of a complete vindication of the host state's conduct and, if the claim appears meritorious, efforts to create a consensus within the government to settle the claim can be buttressed by outside legal counsel's opinion about the government's exposure to liability. In short, investors may well believe that only a legally binding award, or at least the threat of a legally binding award, can provide a basis upon which the host state government can pay compensation.

The differences among the various arbitral processes can be significant. First, ad hoc arbitration places a heavy burden on the tribunal to arrange the logistics of the proceedings. An arbitral tribunal operating under the UNCITRAL rules typically must attend to a full range of organizational matters, such as creating a system to manage documents, locating a facility, and hiring clerical staff and, where necessary, interpreters for the hearing. Arbitration before ICSID eliminates this problem. In some cases, tribunals arbitrating pursuant to the UNCITRAL rules have utilized ICSID to administer the arbitration. ICSID charges a fee for the use of its facilities, but an ad hoc arbitral tribunal will also require the parties to pay its administrative costs.

Arbitration before ICSID requires that both home and host states adhere to the ICSID convention. Arbitration before the Additional Facility, as noted above, requires that either the home or host state, but not both, adhere to the ICSID convention Arbitration under the UNCITRAL rules does not require that the home and host states adhere to any convention and is not precluded by their adherence to any convention.

Some developing countries have reservations about ICSID arbitration because ICSID is affiliated with the World Bank and sometimes is perceived as having a bias in favor of investors. In the event that an arbitrator is not appointed in the manner contemplated by the applicable rules, the president of the World Bank, in his capacity as chairman of the Administrative Council, shall act as an appointing authority and make the necessary appointment. By contrast, under the UNCITRAL rules, if the BIT does not designate an appointing authority, the Secretary-General of the Permanent Court of

Arbitration shall designate one. Thus, the choice of arbitral mechanisms can influence directly the composition of the tribunal. In any event, the evidence is that investors do not fare better before ICSID tribunals than they do before other tribunals.[58]

ICSID arbitration differs from other forms of arbitration in that ICSID awards are reviewable under an annulment proceeding in which a separate tribunal is formed to determine whether one of the grounds of annulment is present. Other awards often may be challenged through set-aside proceedings under the arbitration law of the state where the arbitration takes place. This difference will be further discussed in Section 10.2.1.7. Another difference is that ICSID awards are enforceable under the ICSID convention, while awards issued by other tribunals generally are enforced under the New York Convention. This difference is also discussed further in Section 10.2.1.7.

10.2.1.3 Prerequisites to Arbitration Many BITs call upon the disputing parties, prior to submitting the dispute to arbitration, to seek to resolve the dispute through negotiations.[59] This language reflects the general preference of BIT parties for negotiated settlements, but typically is not treated as requiring any specific action by either party. No tribunal formed pursuant to a BIT has yet declined jurisdiction because the parties failed to seek a negotiated settlement. A negotiated settlement cannot be compelled and, if either party does not wish to negotiate, little is achieved by requiring them to engage in futile and purely formal negotiations.

Some BITs provide that the dispute may be submitted to arbitration if it cannot be[60] or has not been[61] resolved through negotiation. The former of these two formulations

---

58 UNCTAD maintains a comprehensive database of investor-state arbitral awards that provides extensive information about each award, including the nature of the tribunal and whether the award was in favor of the investor or the state. A review of the data in mid 2009 indicated that ICSID tribunals had ruled in favor of the investor in 24 out of 57 awards, or 42 percent of the time. ICSID Additional Facility tribunals had ruled in favor of the investor in 5 out of 11 awards, or 45 percent of the time. Thus, grouping all awards under ICSID auspices together, investors prevailed in 29 out of 68 awards, or 43 percent of the time. By contrast, investors prevailed in 11 out of 20 UNCITRAL awards, or 55 percent of the time. They prevailed in 5 out of 9 Stockholm Chamber of Commerce Awards, or 56 percent of the time. They prevailed before other tribunals in 2 out of 3 awards, or 67 percent of the time. Thus, ICSID is the only form of investor-state arbitration in which investors have prevailed less than half of the time. Aggregating the numbers, investors have prevailed in nonICSID arbitration in 56 percent of the awards, compared with 43 percent of the awards by ICSID and Additional Facility tribunals.

59 *See, e.g.*, Netherlands-Ethiopia BIT, Art. 9(1); BLEU-Sudan BIT, Art. 12(1); Finland-Armenia BIT, Art. 9(1); Australia-India BIT, Art. 12(1); Sweden-Kazakhstan BIT, Art. 8(1); Egypt-Zambia BIT, Art. 8(1); Vietnam-Cambodia BIT, Art. VIII(1); Denmark-Ethiopia BIT, Art. 9(1); France-Uganda BIT, Art. 7; Germany-Timor-Leste BIT, Art. 11(1); Indonesia-India BIT, Art. 9(1); Switzerland-Algeria BIT, Art. 8(1); Austria-Armenia BIT, Art. 12; Mexico-Iceland BIT, Art. 9.

60 *See, e.g.*, Egypt-Zambia BIT, Art. 8(2); Vietnam-Cambodia BIT, Art. VIII(2); Thailand-Argentina BIT, Art. 9(2); Germany-Timor-Leste BIT, Art. 11(2); Indonesia-India BIT, Art. 9(2).

61 *See, e.g.*, United Kingdom-Bosnia-Herzegovina BIT, Art. 8(1); BLEU-Sudan BIT, Art. 12(2); Australia-India BIT, Art. 12(3); France-Uganda BIT, Art. 7; Switzerland-Algeria BIT, Art. 8(2); Austria-Armenia BIT, Art. 12; Mexico-Iceland BIT, Art. 9.

has not been interpreted to require a party to prove that the dispute cannot be resolved through negotiation. The evidence that it cannot be resolved through negotiation is simply the fact that it has not been resolved through negotiation. Other BITs provide that the dispute may be submitted to arbitration if it has not been resolved through negotiation after a specified period of time. The most common such period of time is six months,[62] but other periods are occasionally utilized.[63] This waiting period provides the disputing parties with sufficient time to effect a negotiated settlement. A host state also may use this time to evaluate the claim against it and to prepare for arbitration, such as by collecting evidence, retaining counsel, and identifying potential arbitrators. Some states are especially reluctant to consent to investor-state arbitration and they seek a longer waiting period to provide the disputing parties with a more abundant opportunity to negotiate a settlement and avoid arbitration. Moreover, if it appears that negotiations will not be successful and that arbitration is likely, a longer waiting period provides the host state with more time to prepare its defense and to identify potential arbitrators. Delay may cause the loss of evidence needed by the claimant to meet its burden of proof. Further, if the period is long enough, an investor may prefer to compromise rather than waiting so long to begin an arbitral process that also will likely take a couple of years to complete. Thus, a longer waiting period generally benefits the host state. As discussed in Section 10.2.3.4, tribunals have divided over the issue of whether the claimant's submission of a claim to arbitration prior to expiration of the waiting period deprives the tribunal of jurisdiction. To allow the claimant to disregard the waiting period seems to deprive the clause requiring the period of any effect, a highly disfavored interpretation. Further, as has been noted, even if negotiations would be completely futile, a host state may have other reasons for requiring a lengthy waiting period. To disregard the language deprives the host state of the benefit of one of the terms for which it may have made concessions during negotiations. From a strictly technical perspective, adherence to a waiting period of a certain duration is sometimes phrased as a condition to the host state's consent to arbitration and thus the host state justifiably can insist that, until the waiting period has elapsed, its consent to jurisdiction is not effective. Yet to dismiss a claim because insufficient time elapsed before it was submitted is wasteful because by the time the tribunal has been formed and has reached the decision to dismiss the claim, the required waiting period almost certainly will have elapsed. At that point, the claimant may submit the same claim immediately to a new tribunal. In effect, the dismissal results in nothing more than a duplication of effort. One way to resolve this dilemma is to permit the claim to proceed despite the failure to observe the waiting period, but to take the claimant's failure to observe the period into account in deciding how the costs of the proceeding are to be paid. Thus, a claimant that fails to observe the waiting period must pay for

---

62 *See, e.g.*, Netherlands-Ethiopia BIT, Art. 9(1); Sweden-Kazakhstan BIT, Art. 8(2); Egypt-Zambia BIT, Art. 8(2); Vietnam-Cambodia BIT, Art. VIII(2); Argentina-Thailand BIT, Art. 9(3); Denmark-Ethiopia BIT, Art. 9; France-Uganda BIT, Art. 7; Germany-Timor-Leste BIT, Art. 11(2); Switzerland-Algeria BIT, Art. 8(2); Mexico-Iceland BIT, Art. 9.

63 *See, e.g.*, United Kingdom-Bosnia-Herzegovina BIT, Art. 8(1)(30 days); Finland-Armenia BIT, Art. 9(2) (30 days); Austria-Armenia BIT, Art. 12 (60 days).

the privilege. Where the host state can show irreparable harm from the failure of the investor to observe the waiting period, dismissal of the claim may be the only just result.

Some BITs provide that the waiting period begins with the delivery of a written notice of a dispute.[64] The notice typically must provide information about the basis of the claim and the relief sought and be delivered by a specified date, such as ninety days prior to the submission of the claim to arbitration.[65]

The great majority of BITs do not require the exhaustion of local remedies. Some BITs explicitly so state,[66] while others are silent. Silence is understood to mean that exhaustion is not required. A few BITs, however, do require exhaustion of,[67] or at least some recourse to, local remedies.[68] The most common approach, if recourse to local remedies is to be required, is to require that the dispute be submitted to local remedies for a specified period of time, after which the investor may submit the dispute to investor-state arbitration if it has not been resolved. Investors or investments in some cases prefer that a dispute be resolved in the local courts, if possible. As discussed in Section 10.1, one traditional reason for preferring this remedy over espousal was that resort to local remedies may be regarded as a less provocative way of resolving the dispute, which could be important to an investor that wishes to continue to operate in the host state. It suggests a continued confidence in the institutions of the state, despite the existence of a particular dispute. Investors or investments may have other reasons to utilize local remedies. For example, the investor or investment may have local counsel who is familiar with local courts and accustomed to resolving disputes in that way. Recourse to international arbitration would require operating in an unfamiliar environment. Many covered investments or investors may be unaware of the availability of international arbitration. With the large number of investor-state arbitrations pending or resolved, awareness of the availability of the remedy is spreading and a growing number of law firms justifiably can claim expertise in this area, thus giving investors access to experienced counsel, although the elite nature of the practice means that attorneys' fees are unlikely to be modest and arbitrators' fees and expenses must be paid as well. For relatively small claims, investor-state arbitration may not be a financially feasible alternative. Thus, investor-state arbitration has by no means displaced local courts as a method of investment dispute resolution. Indeed, the rule of law rationale for BITs militates in favor of promoting effective remedies in local courts, such that recourse to investor-state arbitration would be regarded as an exceptional, rather than a routine, remedy.

Some BITs nevertheless may actually discourage resort to local remedies. These BITs have an election of remedies clause, sometimes known as a "fork in the road"

---

64 *See, e.g.*, Indonesia-India BIT, Art. 9(2); Lebanon-Chile BIT, Art. IX(2); Cambodia-Vietnam BIT, Art. VIII(2); Denmark-Ethiopia BIT, Art. 9(2).

65 *See, e.g.*, Mexico-Iceland BIT, Art. 10.

66 *See, e.g.*, BLEU-Sudan BIT, Art. 12(2); Austria-Armenia BIT, Art. 13(2).

67 *See, e.g.*, Ghana-Romania BIT, Art. 4(3).

68 *See, e.g.*, Spain-Argentina BIT, Art. X(3); United Kingdom-Argentina BIT, Art. 8(2); Germany-Argentina BIT, Art. 10(3).

clause, whereby an investor's choice of one remedy precludes the invocation of another.[69] For example, under this clause, a claim may not be submitted to investor-state arbitration if it previously has been submitted to local remedies. The clause may have less effect than might initially seem to be the case because a dispute generally is defined by the identity of the parties and by the cause of action. Thus, if a claim under local law is submitted to local courts, a claim under the BIT likely may be submitted to investor-state arbitration because the different cause of action creates a different dispute, even though both claims arose out of the same events. If the parties in the two proceedings are different, the case for treating the disputes as different is strengthened. Nevertheless, the existence of this election of remedies clause and the possibility that recourse to local remedies could preclude investor-state arbitration in some situations at least must be taken into account in deciding whether to invoke local remedies.

Discouraging resort to local remedies would be inconsistent with the purpose of the BITs in promoting the rule of law. So as not to discourage resort to local remedies, some BITs have adopted a different election of remedies clause. Under this second type of election of remedies clause, submission of the dispute to local remedies does not preclude subsequent submission of the dispute to investor-state arbitration under the BIT, provided that at the time the investor submits a claim to investor-state arbitration the investor waives the right to initiate or continue any other proceeding with respect to the same measure, a proviso intended to limit multiple proceedings.[70] Obviously, the proviso does not preclude multiple proceedings entirely, because the investor may choose to initiate and then discontinue local proceedings before submitting the dispute to investor-state arbitration. This second type of election of remedies clause has become known as the "No U Turn" clause because, once the claim is submitted to investor-state arbitration, it may not be submitted to local courts. The "No U Turn" clause places less emphasis on avoiding multiple proceedings than the "Fork in the Road" election of remedies clause, but more emphasis on encouraging resort to local remedies. The "No U Turn" clause also reduces the possibility that an investor may inadvertently waive the right to investor-state arbitration by submitting a dispute to local courts before realizing that the BIT remedy is available. Even if a BIT does not contain an election of remedies clause, where the dispute is submitted to ICSID arbitration, Article 26 of the ICSID convention provides that submission of a dispute to ICSID arbitration excludes all other remedies.

A small number of BITs impose a limitation on the time within which the claim must be submitted. Typically, the limitations period begins when the investors first acquired

---

69 *See, e.g.*, Argentina-Thailand BIT, Art. 9(4); Indonesia-India BIT, Art. 9(2); Austria-Armenia BIT, Art. 13(1) (dispute may not be submitted to arbitration if a local court has rendered a decision); Mexico-Iceland BIT, Art. 10 (dispute may be submitted to arbitration provided that it has not been submitted to local remedies or previously-agreed procedures; submission to arbitration requires waiver of other disputes mechanisms with respect to the same measure, except for actions for extraordinary relief). *See generally* Christoph Schreuer, "Traveling the BIT Route: Of Waiting Periods, Umbrella Clauses and Forks in the Road," 5 *Journal of World Investment and Trade* 231 (2004).

70 *See, e.g.*, Finland-Armenia BIT, Art. 9 (provided that no judgment has been issued by the national court).

or should have acquired knowledge of the events giving rise to the dispute.[71] A typical limitations period is three years,[72] but other periods are sometimes specified.[73]

10.2.1.4 Investment-State Arbitration Clauses One clause commonly found in BITs is based on Article 25(2)(b) of the ICSID convention. Under Article 25 of that convention, a national or company may not submit a claim to arbitration against its own state. BITs commonly ascribe nationality to a company based on its place of incorporation or the location of its seat.[74] Covered investments that are companies, such as a local subsidiary of a foreign company, typically are incorporated under the law of the host state and have their seat in that state as well. The result is that, under the typical BIT, the covered investment is considered a national of the host state and therefore is unable to submit a claim against the host state to ICSID arbitration. To permit locally incorporated foreign investments to submit claims to ICSID arbitration, Article 25(2)(b) of the ICSID convention provides that a company that is a national of the host state may be treated for purposes of ICSID arbitration as a national of the home state if the company is owned or controlled by nationals of the home state and the home and host states have agreed to this ascription of nationality. Many BITs contain a clause that constitutes this agreement.[75] Effectively, it allows investments to submit claims to arbitration against the host state. Thus, although the common usage is to refer to investor-state arbitration, in fact many BITs also provide for investment-state arbitration.

Submission of a claim by the investment rather than the investor offers certain benefits. One benefit is that it prevents an investor from appropriating the assets of its investment, to the detriment of other investors in, or creditors of, the investment. This potentially can occur where an investor submits to arbitration a claim on behalf of an investment that it controls, but does not completely own. The tribunal will award to the investor the full value of the loss. Because international law requires a wrongdoer to pay compensation only once, the effect of the award will be to preclude payment of any other claim against the host state for the same loss. If the investor who has received the compensation chooses to retain all of it, the investor may thereby deprive other investors in, or creditors of, the investment of any part of the recovery. If instead the investment submits the claim to arbitration, the compensation will be paid to the investment. The asset may then be divided among the investment's investors and creditors in accordance with the domestic law of the host state.

A few BITs state explicitly that a claim may be submitted to arbitration by an investor on behalf of an investment that it owns or controls.[76] For example, U.S. and

---

71 *See, e.g.*, Austria-Armenia BIT, Art. 12; Mexico-Iceland BIT, Art. 10; United States-Uruguay BIT, Art. 26.

72 *See, e.g.*, Austria-Armenia BIT, Art. 12; Mexico-Iceland BIT, Art. 10; United States-Uruguay BIT, Art. 26.

73 *See, e.g.*, Austria-Macedonia BIT, Art. 12 (five years).

74 *See* Section 4.3.1.

75 *See, e.g.*, Netherlands-Ethiopia BIT, Art. 9(3); Denmark-Ethiopia BIT, Art. 9(3); Japan-Vietnam BIT, Art. 14(4).

76 *See, e.g.*, Mexico-Iceland BIT, Art. 10.

Canadian BITs based on their 2004 and 2003 model negotiating texts, respectively, authorize an investor to submit a claim on its own behalf or on behalf of an investment that it owns or controls.[77] To prevent the investor from appropriating the assets owed to others, these BITs provide that any compensation for losses suffered by the investment itself shall be paid to the investment, even where the claim is brought by an investor on behalf of an investment that it owns or controls.[78] Even where a BIT does not state explicitly that a controlling investor may submit to arbitration a claim on behalf of the investment, the universal practice is to permit the controlling investor to do so.[79]

10.2.1.5 Choice of Law Clauses The investor-state disputes provision sometimes includes a choice of law clause. International tribunals generally give effect to a clause in which the disputing parties specify the law to be applied. Where the claim arises under a contract, the contract may specify the law to be applied, which typically is the law of the host state. Investors generally prefer to have international law apply to any dispute because international law often provides greater protection for investment than national law and because the host state can alter national law to the detriment of the investor. In fact, investment disputes sometimes arise from the host state's modification of national law to the detriment of the investor. Host states for the same reasons generally prefer that national law be applied.

BITs generally do not designate local law as the governing law, although individual substantive provisions are sometimes subordinate to local law.[80] Thus, a choice of law clause in a BIT is likely to specify either that international law applies or that both international law and local law apply.[81] In some cases, a BIT provides that investment shall receive treatment no less favorable than that required by international law,[82] a provision that effectively requires application of international law in order to ensure that the investment receives the required treatment. International law addresses only a limited range of issues and, of course, investment located in the territory of a state generally is subject to the law of that state, in the absence of an agreement to the contrary.[83] Thus, even where international law is designated, national law may be applicable to the extent that it is consistent with international law. Accordingly, irrespective of the presence of a choice of law clause or the language of the clause, the situation that nearly always exists in an investor-state arbitration is that international law, including in particular the provisions of the BIT, applies where it exists, while national

77 *See, e.g.*, United States-Uruguay BIT, Art. 24(1); 2003 Canadian Model BIT, Arts. 22-23.

78 *See, e.g.*, Mexico-Iceland BIT, Art. 17(2).

79 *See* Section 10.2.3.1.2.

80 This is particularly true of provisions on the admission of investment. *See* Section 9.3.1.

81 *See, e.g.*, Egypt-Zambia BIT, Art. 8(3) (international and national law); Argentina-Thailand BIT, Art. 9(7); Austria-Armenia BIT, Art. 16 (except that local law and international law apply to disputes under the observance of obligations provision and the preservation of rights provision); Mexico-Iceland BIT, Art. 16 (international law).

82 *See* Section 5.4.

83 *On the choice of law, see generally* Ole Spiermann, "Applicable Law," in *The Oxford Handbook of International Investment Law* (Peter Muchlinski, Frederico Ortino, and Christoph Schreuer, eds. 2008).

law applies to the extent that it is not inconsistent with or displaced by international law. The significance of national law is greatly diminished by the fact that most investment disputes submitted to investor-state arbitration arise out of an alleged breach of a BIT, an issue that in its nature is governed by international law.

Where the dispute is submitted to ICSID, the arbitration is governed by Article 42 of the ICSID convention, which states that, in the absence of agreement between the disputing parties with respect to the choice of law, the tribunal shall apply the law of the host state and any applicable rules of international law. Thus, Article 42 is consistent with the practice of tribunals not subject to the ICSID convention.

10.2.1.6 Collateral Sources of Compensation Many BITs include a clause on collateral sources of compensation.[84] This clause provides that the host state may not raise as a defense that the investor has received partial or total compensation under an insurance or guarantee program. That is, the host state remains liable for compensation, even if the investor already has been compensated through such a program. This clause seems merely to make explicit that which would be the rule even in the absence of the clause. Without such a rule, the host state would be able to avoid liability for its wrongful conduct merely because the investor had been prudent enough to obtain insurance. Insurance, of course, is funded at least in part by the premiums paid by investors. Thus, the effect would be to shift the burden of compensation from the host state to a fund created by investor payments.

10.2.1.7 Awards A few BITs specify the forms of relief that a tribunal may award. Typically, these include a declaration that a party has failed to comply with the BIT, compensation that includes interest,[85] and restitution, provided in the last case that compensation may be paid in lieu of restitution where restitution is not practicable.[86] In a few BITs, punitive damages are explicitly disallowed.[87]

A large number of BITs provide that any award under the investor-state disputes provision shall be final[88] and binding.[89] This clause makes explicit that an award is

---

84 *See, e.g.*, BLEU-Sudan BIT, Art. 12(4); Finland-Armenia BIT, Art. 9(6); Sweden-Kazakhstan BIT, Art. 8(5); Denmark-Ethiopia BIT, Art. 9(5); Germany-Timor-Leste BIT, Art. 11(4); Switzerland-Algeria BIT, Art. 8(4); Austria-Armenia BIT, Art. 15; Mexico-Iceland BIT, Art. 15.

85 Tribunals rather consistently award interest and compound interest is increasingly common, but the rate of interest awarded varies. No uniform approach has emerged. For an argument that prejudgment interest should be awarded at a rate consistent with the investor's unsecured borrowing rate, *see* Jeffrey M. Colon and Michael S. Knoll, "Prejudgment Interest in International Arbitration," undated manuscript available at http://www.ssrn.com.

86 *See, e.g.*, Austria-Armenia BIT, Art.17; Mexico-Iceland BIT, Art. 17.

87 *See, e.g.*, Mexico-Iceland BIT, Art. 17(5).

88 *See, e.g.*, Netherlands-Ethiopia BIT, Art. 9(4); BLEU-Sudan BIT, Art. 12(5); Finland-Armenia BIT, Art. 9(7); Sweden-Kazakhstan BIT, Art. 8(6); Egypt-Zambia BIT, Art. 8(4); Argentina-Thailand BIT, Art. 9(8); Denmark-Ethiopia BIT, Art. 9(6); Germany-Timor-Leste BIT, Art. 11(3); Switzerland-Algeria BIT, Art. 8(6); Austria-Armenia BIT, Art. 17; Mexico-Iceland BIT, Art. 17(4).

89 *See, e.g.*, Netherlands-Ethiopia BIT, Art. 9(4); BLEU-Sudan BIT, Art. 12(5); Finland-Armenia BIT, Art. 9(7); Sweden-Kazakhstan BIT, Art. 8(6); Egypt-Zambia BIT, Art. 8(4); Argentina-Thailand BIT, Art. 9(8); Denmark-Ethiopia BIT, Art. 9(6); Germany-Timor-Leste BIT,

res judicata and not subject to appeal. It also obligates the host state to comply with the award. The failure of the host state to comply would give rise to a claim under the state-state disputes provision.

Although investor-state arbitral awards are not subject to appeal,[90] awards issued by ICSID tribunals are subject to an annulment proceeding. Annulment proceedings are authorized by the ICSID convention. Under this process, an award may be annulled on any of several grounds, which are that the tribunal was not properly constituted, the tribunal manifestly exceeded its powers, a tribunal member was corrupt, the tribunal departed seriously from a fundamental rule of procedure, or the award did not state the reasons on which it was based.[91]

Awards that are not governed by the ICSID convention may be subject to review under the arbitration law of the state where the arbitration takes place. In order to control which arbitration law shall apply, a tribunal may designate a particular state as the place of arbitration, even if the hearings are held elsewhere. The grounds for set aside vary, but are often similar to the grounds for annulment. Such grounds include that the tribunal has exceeded its authority, such as where it has arbitrated an issue outside the scope of the parties' consent, that the tribunal engaged in a manifest disregard of the law, that the tribunal has violated the rules of procedure, or that the award violates public policy.[92] Thus, these proceedings are not the equivalent of an appeal.

One important difference between set aside and ICSID annulment is that an ICSID annulment proceeding is decided by an international arbitral tribunal similar to that which decided the original claim, while a set-aside proceeding generally is decided by a judge of the state where the arbitration was situated. Another is that the grounds for set aside are prescribed by the arbitration law of the state where the set-aside proceeding occurs, while the grounds for annulment are prescribed by the ICSID convention. Because the annulment proceeding does not rely upon local courts and is not governed by local law, ICSID arbitration is sometimes said to be "de-nationalized." That is, ICSID tribunals function without regard to the specific terms of the arbitration law of the state where the arbitration occurs. As this discussion indicates, where an arbitration is not an ICSID arbitration, the choice of the location of the arbitration is important because that choice determines which courts will conduct any set-aside proceedings and the grounds upon which an award may be set aside.

Some BITs include clauses to facilitate the enforcement of awards.[93] ICSID awards are enforceable under the ICSID convention in the territory of any state that is a party

---

Art. 11(3); Switzerland-Algeria BIT, Art. 8(6); Austria-Armenia BIT, Art. 17; Mexico-Iceland BIT, Art. 17.

90 *See generally* Vladimir Balas, "Review of Awards," in *The Oxford Handbook of International Investment Law* (Peter Muchlinski, Frederico Ortino, and Christoph Schreuer, eds. 2008).

91 ICSID convention, Art. 52.

92 *See generally* Christopher F. Dugan, Don Wallace, Jr., Noah D. Rubins, and Borzu Sabahi, *Investor-State Arbitration* 637-647 (2008).

93 On enforcement generally, *see* Alan S. Alexandroff and Ian A. Laird, "Compliance and Enforcement," in *The Oxford Handbook of International Investment Law* (Peter Muchlinski, Frederico Ortino, and Christoph Schreuer, eds. 2008).

to that convention. The ICSID convention, however, does not require enforcement of any other awards. Awards issued as a result of arbitration before the Additional Facility, under the UNCITRAL Rules, or through some other mechanism may be enforced through the United Nations Convention on the Recognition and Enforcement of Foreign Arbitral Awards,[94] also known as the New York Convention. The New York Convention allows parties to declare at the time of their accession that they will apply the Convention only to awards issued in the territory of another party to the Convention.[95] Thus, the Additional Facility Rules require that arbitrations before the Additional Facility take place in the territory of a state that is a party to the New York Convention.[96] Some BITs impose this requirement as well.[97] Because the New York Convention allows parties to apply the Convention only to disputes arising out of commercial relationships,[98] some BITs provide that the disputes shall be considered to arise out of a commercial relationship or transaction.[99] Further, some BITs require that each party shall provide for enforcement of the award in its territory.[100] A few BITs require a certain period of time to pass before an investor may seek to enforce an award,[101] thereby providing an opportunity for the host state to commence an annulment or set-aside proceeding before the investor initiates enforcement action.

Some BITs provide that once a dispute has been submitted to investor-state arbitration, the same dispute may not be pursued through diplomatic channels or the state-state disputes provision unless the arbitral tribunal decides that it has no jurisdiction or the host state has failed to comply with the award. [102] A few BITs instead include a clause providing that, in the event that the host state fails to comply with an award of an investor-state arbitral tribunal, a state-state arbitral tribunal may be formed.[103]

10.2.1.8 Innovations in Investor-State Arbitration Beginning in the late 1990s, several of the features of investor-state arbitration that had been regarded as benefits of the process came under criticism. One occasion for the criticism was that several

---

94 21 U.S.T. 2517, T.I.A.S. No. 6997, 330 U.N.T.S. 3.

95 New York Convention, Art. I(3).

96 Additional Facility Arbitration Rules, Rule 19.

97 *See, e.g.*, Finland-Armenia BIT, Art. 9(3) (at the request of either party to the dispute); Sweden-Kazakhstan BIT, Art. 8(3) (in the case of UNCITRAL arbitrations); Denmark-Ethiopia BIT, Art. 9(4) (at the request of either party to the dispute); Mexico-Iceland BIT, Art. 14.

98 New York Convention, Art. I(3).

99 *See, e.g.*, Finland-Armenia BIT, Art. 9(3); Vietnam-Cambodia BIT, Art. VIII(4); Austria-Armenia BIT, Art. 14.; Mexico-Iceland BIT, Art. 14.

100 *See, e.g.*, Netherlands-Ethiopia BIT, Art. 9(4); BLEU-Sudan BIT, Art. 12(5); Finland-Armenia BIT, Art. 9(7); Sweden-Kazakhstan BIT, Art. 8(6); Egypt-Zambia BIT, Art. 8(4); Argentina-Thailand BIT, Art. 9(8); Denmark-Ethiopia BIT, Art. 9(6); Germany-Timor-Leste BIT, Art. 11(3); Switzerland-Algeria BIT, Art. 8(6); Austria-Armenia BIT, Art. 17; Mexico-Iceland BIT, Art. 17(6).

101 *See, e.g.*, Mexico-Iceland BIT, Art. 17(8).

102 *See, e.g.*, Australia-India BIT, Art. 12(4); Vietnam-Cambodia BIT, Art. VIII(4); Switzerland-Algeria BIT, Art. 8(5) (no reference to lack of jurisdiction).

103 *See, e.g.*, Mexico-Iceland BIT, Art. 17(9).

investor-state arbitrations, particularly under the NAFTA, arose out of claims that host state environmental measures violated the NAFTA. Some environmental nongovernmental organizations (NGOs) feared that the investors would prevail in these claims and that, if host states were required to compensate investors for losses suffered as a result of environmental measures, states would be reluctant or unable to enact or enforce such measures. The change in the perception of the investor-state arbitral process is perhaps easily explained. When the first BITs were being negotiated, a typical investment dispute contemplated by BIT drafters arose out of a direct expropriation of covered investment, whether in the form of a concession agreement or tangible assets, by the host state. Although many in the communist and the developing world questioned the extent to which compensation should be paid, in the developed world a broad consensus existed that a state that seizes private property should compensate the owner. The critical issue was the amount of compensation, which was regarded at least in the developed world largely as a technical matter of ascertaining the fair market value of the property. Another typical investment dispute was one arising out of a failure to use reasonable care to protect the investment. Such claims were most likely to arise during periods of civil disturbance, which in developed countries are extraordinary situations. Again, within the developed world, the issue of whether to provide compensation for official nonfeasance or misfeasance during a civil disturbance was not the kind of issue in which major issues of public policy were at stake.

A number of claims submitted to investor-state arbitration in the late 1990s, however, did not fall within these categories. They involved allegations not of direct expropriations or government nonfeasance during periods of violence, but of regulatory measures that diminished the value of investment. These were not always the kinds of claims that were regarded by consensus as meritorious in the developed world. Further, while uncompensated direct expropriations or civil disturbances resulting in the destruction of foreign investment are relatively rare events in the developed world, governmental regulation is a daily and pervasive event. Thus, these disputes demonstrated that investment disputes would arise in which the conduct of a developed country with a highly favorable investment climate would be at issue. Thus, when criticisms of the investor-state disputes process arose in the 1990s, they often came from governments and NGOs in Canada and the United States. Features of investor-state arbitration previously regarded by proponents as advantages suddenly were regarded by critics as serious flaws.

First, one benefit of investor-state arbitration is that decisions are made by impartial arbitrators, rather than by judges of the national courts, who might well be biased in favor of their own governments and against foreign investors. Critics, however, saw the absence of a link between the arbitrators and a national court system not as an indication of impartiality, but rather as an indication of a lack of accountability. Investors had feared judges who were under the sway of their own governments. Critics feared arbitrators who were answerable to no one.

A second benefit of investor-state arbitration is that the parties can select arbitrators who are experts in the field of international investment law, rather than submitting their disputes to domestic court judges whose experiences might be in routine matters of national law. Critics, however, feared that with expertise would come conflicts of interest or bias. The number of potential arbitrators possessing expertise in international investment law and arbitration was not large in the 1990s. Thus, the tendency was for arbitral tribunals to be selected from a relatively small group of individuals, some of whom also served as advocates in other cases, perhaps involving similar legal issues.

A third benefit of investor-state arbitration is that it can be kept confidential. To the extent that it is, investors need not fear that proprietary business information will be made available to their competitors, while host states need not fear that potentially embarrassing conduct by some officials will be made public in a way that undermines the BIT's purpose as a signaling device or casts the officials in a poor light before their domestic constituencies. Critics, however, reviled a system in which decisions with important public policy implications were made in complete secrecy, a problem aggravated by the lack of accountability.

A fourth benefit of investor-state arbitration is that awards are final. An award is not subject to an appeal, although it can be set aside by local courts in certain limited circumstances that are sufficiently restrictive that awards issued by investor-state arbitral tribunals only very occasionally are set aside. Where the dispute is of the type contemplated when BITs first were conceived, both parties are likely to prefer a system that resolves a dispute efficiently either by awarding compensation to the claimant or by denying the claim. Where the dispute involves a challenge to the host state's regulatory discretion, however, resolution of the dispute adversely to the host state may have long term consequences for its ability to regulate in the future. Critics portrayed a system in which secret tribunals of biased arbitrators, accountable to no one, could issue non-reviewable decisions injurious to the public interest.

A fifth benefit of investor-state arbitration is that it permits resolution of investment disputes without the involvement of the investor's government. As tribunals in early NAFTA cases struggled with novel questions in international law, such as the extent of regulatory expropriations or the meaning of the fair and equitable treatment standard, a few developed country governments, particularly those of the United States and Canada, sought to create a role for the investor's government as well as the respondent in overseeing the dispute resolution process. They recognized that even one or two highly publicized adverse awards easily could shift public sentiment against investor-state arbitration and force the curtailment of a mechanism that generally served their interests well.

As will be seen in Sections 10.2.1.8.1 through 10.2.1.8.7, these criticisms have resulted in a few innovations. Some steps have been taken to increase the transparency of investor-state arbitration and to permit various kinds of participation in the arbitration by nondisputants, including the investor's home country and members of the public. Other innovations have resulted from efforts to improve efficiency.

10.2.1.8.1 PARTY PARTICIPATION IN THE ARBITRATION

Potentially the most important innovation in the investor-state disputes provisions is a series of new clauses in a very few BITs that essentially allow the BIT parties to remove certain issues from the power of the tribunal to decide. These kinds of clauses reflect a greater awareness of the BIT parties' potential dual capacities as both home and host states. They also reflect a greater awareness that an investor-state arbitral tribunal is not simply a device for obtaining compensation for an investor in a case where the legal rules are relatively well-settled, but also a mechanism by which uncertain treaty language is interpreted and the scope of host-state regulatory discretion is thereby defined.

Such clauses represent a partial shift away from one purpose of the investor-state disputes provision, which was to remove the home state from the process of resolving investment disputes. Allowing the BIT parties to become involved in resolving a dispute raises the possibility that investment disputes will be governed by political considerations rather than the rule of law, thus undermining the BIT's purpose of depoliticizing investment disputes.

The progenitor of these clauses is Article 1131(2) of the NAFTA, under which the NAFTA Free Trade Commission may issue interpretations of the NAFTA that are binding on any tribunal formed under the investor-state disputes provision. Thus, while concerns about certain arbitral awards issued in the mid-1990s may have contributed to the desire for these clauses, such a clause already was in the NAFTA before these awards were issued. Subsequently, the three NAFTA parties incorporated into their BITs similar clauses, authorizing the BIT parties, by mutual agreement, to decide any issue involving the interpretation of the BIT. In the U.S. BITs, their joint decision is binding on the investor-state arbitral tribunal as well as on any state-state arbitral tribunal.[104] In the Mexican and Canadian BITs, they are binding on any investor-state tribunal.[105]

Similar mechanisms may be created for the purpose of resolving a narrower set of issues. For example, the current U.S. and Canadian model BITs require that a host state that invokes a financial services exception refer to the financial authorities of both parties the issue of whether the exception applies. The financial authorities are authorized to issue a binding, joint determination of that issue.[106]

In addition, the 2004 U.S. and 2003 Canadian model BITs include a provision under which certain claims relating to taxation measures may be resolved by agreement of the taxation authorities of the two parties. Under the U.S. model, claims to which this provision applies are claims that a taxation measure constitutes an expropriation.[107] Under the Canadian model, claims to which this provision applies are claims that a taxation measure constitutes an expropriation and claims that a taxation measure contravenes an agreement between the investors and the host state.[108]

These kinds of provisions not only permit resolution of certain issues by agreement of the parties, but specify the agency within each government that shall make the determination for that party. Such provisions thus reflect both the desire of the BIT parties to retain greater control over the investor-state dispute resolution mechanism and the increased role of regulatory agencies in formulating foreign investment policy, a result of the heightened awareness in some developed countries about the potential impact of BITs on regulatory discretion.

---

104 *See, e.g.*, United States-Uruguay BIT, Arts. 30(3) and 37(4).

105 *See, e.g.*, Mexico-Iceland BIT, Art. 16(2); 2003 Canadian Model BIT, Art. 40(2).

106 2004 U.S. Model BIT, Art. 20(3); 2003 Canadian Model BIT, Art. 17.

107 2004 U.S. Model BIT, Art. 21(2).

108 2003 Canadian Model BIT, Art. 16(3)-(4).

Still another example of this kind of provision applies when a host-state party raises as a defense that a measure falls within certain exceptions to one or more BIT obligations.[109] By mutual agreement, the parties may make a binding determination that the exception applies.

An alternative to provisions allowing the BIT parties to decide an issue is to permit the non-disputing party to make submissions to the tribunal. This approach also was pioneered by the NAFTA, Article 1128 of which allows any party to the agreement to make a submission to the tribunal on a question of the interpretation of the agreement. The Article 1128 procedure has been used numerous times by all of the NAFTA parties. Some BITs now include such a clause.[110]

10.2.1.8.2 TRANSPARENCY

Concerns expressed about the lack of accountability of arbitrators and their potential conflicts of interest and bias have had little impact. Demands for greater transparency, however, have generated some reforms in the investor-state arbitral process.[111]

In *Loewen v. United States*, one of the early cases arising under the NAFTA, the United States received a request under the Freedom of Information Act for documents related to the dispute. The tribunal ruled that U.S. compliance with the request would not violate the NAFTA or the ICSID Additional Facility rules. Accordingly, the United States released the documents.

Clauses promoting transparency now appear in the investor-state disputes provisions of some BITs. Recent U.S. BITs include language requiring that certain specified documents relating to investor-state arbitrations be made publicly available, including the notice of intent to submit a claim to arbitration, the notice of arbitration, the written submissions of the parties, the minutes or transcripts of hearings where available, and the orders, decisions, and awards of the tribunal.[112] An exception is made for certain sensitive information. Although the NAFTA does not require disclosure of information about pending or resolved investor-state disputes, the NAFTA parties have adopted the practice of making public all documents submitted to or issued by tribunals formed under the investor-state dispute provision of the NAFTA, except for confidential business information.[113]

Under Article 48(5) of the ICSID convention, ICSID may publish the full text of an award only with the consent of both parties, although the ICSID arbitration rules permit ICSID to publish excerpts from the award without consent. Consent is obtained about

---

109 *See, e.g.*, United States-Uruguay BIT, Art. 31.

110 *See, e.g.*, United States-Uruguay BIT, Art. 28(2); 2003 Canadian Model BIT, Art. 35(1).

111 *See generally* Joachim Delaney and Daniel Barstow Magraw, "Procedural Transparency," in *The Oxford Handbook of International Investment Law* (Peter Muchlinski, Frederico Ortino, and Christoph Schreuer, eds. 2008).

112 *See, e.g.*, United States-Uruguay BIT, Art. 29.

113 The NAFTA Free Trade Commission on July 31, 2001, issued an interpretation of the NAFTA clarifying that the NAFTA imposed no general duty of confidentiality. *See* Meg N. Kinnear, Andrea K. Bjorklund, & John F. G. Hannaford, *Investment Disputes Under NAFTA: An Annotated Guide to Chapter 11* Appendices (2008).

half the time.[114] Nothing, however, precludes a party to an ICSID dispute from voluntarily publishing the contents of an award. In 2006, ICSID amended its rules to require prompt publication of excerpts from the legal reasoning in the award, pending the parties' consent to publication of the full award.[115] Other arbitral institutions, such as the International Chamber of Commerce, also publish at least some information about arbitrations conducted through those institutions.

Some investor-state arbitrations, however, remain shrouded in secrecy. For example, Article 32(5) of the UNCITRAL Rules provides that an award may be made public only with the consent of the parties. Further, unlike in the case of ICSID, the UNCITRAL Secretariat does not maintain a registry of cases conducted under the UNCITRAL rules and, in fact, there is no requirement that the Secretariat be notified when arbitration under the UNCITRAL rules is initiated. Thus, no one knows precisely how many investor-state arbitrations have been conducted.

A number of NGOs also have proposed that any oral proceedings be open to the public. In August 2000, the International Institute for Sustainable Development (IISD), a Canadian nongovernmental organization, submitted a petition to the tribunal in *Methanex v. United States*, a case arising under the NAFTA, requesting that hearings be open to the public and that IISD be permitted to make written and oral submissions. Earthjustice, a U.S. NGO, submitted a similar petition the following month. The Canadian Union of Postal Workers and the Council of Canadians, both nongovernmental organizations, sought permission to intervene in *UPS v. Canada*, another case arising under the NAFTA. Both cases were being arbitrated under the UNCITRAL rules. With the support of both Canada and the United States, who acknowledged that closed proceedings endangered public acceptance of the process, the tribunals in both cases permitted the written submissions and held open hearings at the World Bank headquarters on July 29–31, 2002, in the *UPS* case and on June 7–17, 2004, in the *Methanex* case.

The issue of open hearings arose with respect to ICSID proceedings in *Suez and Interaguas v. Argentina*, a case arising under France-Argentina and Spain-Argentina BITs, and *Suez and Vivendi v. Argentina*, a case arising under the France-Argentina, Spain-Argentina and United Kingdom-Argentina BITs. ICSID practice traditionally was that proceedings could be opened to other persons with the consent of the parties.[116] The tribunals, whose members were the same in both cases, held that ICSID Arbitration Rule 32(2) permitted open hearings only with the consent of the parties, which was lacking in that case. In 2006, ICSID amended its rules to provide that, unless either party objects, the tribunal may permit persons other than the parties, their agents, witnesses, experts, and tribunal personnel to attend or to observe the hearings, provided that proprietary information is protected and suitable logistical arrangements

---

114 Katia Yannaca-Small, "Transparency and Third Party Participation in Investor-state Dispute Settlement Procedures," in Organization for Economic Cooperation and Development, *International Investment Law: A Changing Landscape* 13 (2005).

115 ICSID Arbitration Rules, Rule 48(4).

116 Consent of the parties was necessary under ICSID Arbitration Rule 32(2) and Additional Facility Arbitration Rule 39(2).

can be made.[117] The NAFTA parties already have adopted the practice of holding public hearings and such hearings are required by the most recent U.S. and Canadian BITs.[118] Typically, public hearings do not involve the attendance of the public at the hearing, but rather permitting the public to observe the hearing on a monitor in a separate room.

10.2.1.8.3 PUBLIC PARTICIPATION

Because of their concern that investor-state arbitral tribunals might not give sufficient weight to the public interest, several NGOs in the 1990s sought approval of tribunals in a few cases to submit *amicus curiae*[119] briefs. In *Methanex v. United States* and in *UPS v. Canada*, both of which were cases arising under the NAFTA, the tribunal held that, at least under the UNCITRAL Rules, it had authority to accept *amicus curiae* submissions. In *Suez and Interaguas v. Argentina*, a case arising under France-Argentina and Spain-Argentina BITs, and *Suez and Vivendi v. Argentina*, a case arising under the France-Argentina, Spain-Argentina and United Kingdom-Argentina BITs, the tribunals, which were composed of the same three arbitrators, held that they had authority under Article 44 of the ICSID convention, to accept submissions from *amicus curiae*. By contrast, in *Aguas del Tunari v. Bolivia*, a case arising under the Netherlands-Bolivia BIT, an ICSID tribunal responded to a request by an NGO to intervene or, in the alternative, to submit an *amicus curiae* brief by stating that the request was beyond the power of the tribunal to grant absent the consent of the disputing parties.

The current U.S. and Canadian model BITs now include clauses authorizing tribunals to accept such submissions from individuals or entities not involved in the dispute.[120] Further, in 2006, ICSID modified its rules to permit a tribunal, after consulting the parties, to permit submissions from non-disputants. In deciding whether to permit these submissions, a tribunal shall consider factors such as whether the submission would assist the tribunal in the determination of a factual or legal issue by bringing a perspective or special knowledge or insight that is different from that of the disputing parties, whether the submission would address a matter within the scope of the dispute, and whether the non-disputant has a significant interest in the proceedings.[121] The ICSID language directs the tribunal to ensure that any such submissions will not disrupt the process or unduly burden or unfairly prejudice either party. The 2003 Canadian model BIT imposes very similar conditions. The ICSID amendment already has been employed by NGOs.[122]

One concern raised by allowing *amicus curiae* submissions is the potential burden it could place on the disputants. The disputing parties may believe that prudence

117 ICISD Arbitration Rules, Rule 32(2).

118 2004 U.S. Model BIT, Art. 29(2); 2003 Canadian Model BIT, Art. 38(1).

119 The Latin term *amicus curiae* means "friend of the court" and is derived from the domestic legal practice of some states in which nonparties to a dispute are permitted to make written submissions to the court concerning a case before it.

120 2004 U.S. Model BIT, Art. 28(3); 2003 Canadian Model BIT, Art. 39.

121 ICSID Arbitration Rules, Rule 37(2).

122 *See, e.g., Biwater v. Tanzania* (United Kingdom-Tanzania BIT), Procedural Order No. 5, February 2, 2007 (allowing participation by *amici*).

requires them to respond to these submissions, at least where the submissions support the opposing party. This, along with the additional time required by the arbitrators to consider the *amicus* submissions and any responses from the parties, could increase the cost of the attorneys' and arbitrators' fees. Concerns also have been expressed that *amici* not be accorded greater rights of participation than the non-disputing BIT party and that they be screened to ensure that they are independent and not merely acting covertly at the behest of one of the disputing parties.[123]

10.2.1.8.4 EXPEDITED CONSIDERATION OF CLAIMS

Some of the early NAFTA claims, such as that in *Methanex v. United States*, were regarded by some officials as clearly frivolous and yet no mechanism existed for disposing of these claims other than a full hearing on the merits. As a result, the most recent U.S. BITs now specifically authorize a tribunal to hear an objection that a claim, as a matter of law, is not one for which an award in favor of a claimant may be made.[124] To say that an award cannot be made in favor of claimant means that, even if all the factual allegations made by the claimant are true, the claimant would have no legal right to a remedy. The language in the U.S. BITs is based on Rule 12(b)(6) of the Federal Rules of Civil Procedure. This mechanism permits the early dismissal of certain non-meritorious claims before the parties have expended time and other resources developing the evidence that would be unnecessary to resolve the claim in any event. In 2006, ICSID amended its rules to allow a preliminary procedure for considering an objection that a claim is "manifestly without legal merit."[125] On May 12, 2008, a tribunal issued the first ruling on an objection under this rule, rejecting the host state's challenge to two of the claims, but granting it with respect to a third claim.[126]

These kinds of provisions could have multiple effects. Certainly, they will result in the early dismissal of some nonmeritorious claims. By exposing very weak claims to early dismissal, they may discourage the submission of such claims to arbitration merely to gain leverage in settlement negotiations. At the same time, by making an additional procedure available, they may add to the expense of arbitrating at least some claims that are strong enough to withstand expedited consideration, whether or not ultimately successful. Although they sometimes regard specific arguments advanced in a claim as frivolous, tribunals rarely characterize an entire claim as frivolous.[127]

10.2.1.8.5 CONSOLIDATION OF CLAIMS

When Canada, Mexico, and the United States negotiated the NAFTA in the early 1990s, they inserted an innovative provision to permit the consolidation of related cases. Specifically, Article 1126 provides that where a tribunal determines that claims

---

123 Yannaca-Small, *supra* note 112, at 26.

124 2004 U.S. Model BIT, Art. 28(4).

125 ICSID Arbitration Rules, Rule 41(5).

126 *See Trans-Global Petroleum v. Jordan* (United States-Jordan BIT), Decision on Rule 41(5) Objection, para. 124.

127 But note the claim in *Methanex v. United States*, a claim arising under the NAFTA, in which the claimant, because of the weakness of its claim, was ordered to pay the attorneys' fees of the United States government.

submitted have a question of law or fact in common, in the interest of fair and efficient adjudication the tribunal may assume jurisdiction over the claims and determine all or part of them.

Subsequently, the three NAFTA parties have inserted similar provisions in their BITs. For example, the Mexico-Iceland BIT provides that proceedings shall be consolidated when two or more investors in relation to the same investment submit a claim to arbitration or when two or more claims arising from common legal and factual issues are submitted to arbitration.[128] The claims shall not be consolidated if the tribunal determines that the interests of any disputing party would be seriously harmed. Claims may be consolidated under the 2003 Canadian model where they have a question of law or fact in common and the tribunal determines that consolidation would be in the interests of the fair and efficient resolution of the claims.[129] Under the 2004 U.S. model, claims may be consolidated if they have a question of law or fact in common and arise out of the same events or circumstances and the tribunal determines that consolidation would be in the interest of the fair and efficient resolution of claims.[130] Under all of these provisions, the tribunal shall follow the UNCITRAL Arbitration Rules.

The benefits of consolidation are obvious. First, a single tribunal deciding multiple cases can ensure that the results in those cases are consistent. Second, the cost and time involved in arbitrating the disputes may be reduced because the host state may be able to submit a common response to all claimants on certain issues and only one set of proceedings is needed to resolve the claims. The savings for claimants may be less certain, because each claimant presumably will wish to submit its own separate argument, although claimants' counsel may be able to coordinate their work and achieve some savings.[131] In any event, all parties may be able to reduce expenses by sharing the costs of a single tribunal, which must decide certain common issues only once, rather than bearing the costs of multiple tribunals, each of which must duplicate much of the work of the others.

Consolidation, however, raises concerns. First, because a single tribunal is deciding multiple cases, the adverse consequences of a poor decision are greatly increased. In a sense, submitting cases to different tribunals diversifies the risk inherent in arbitration. Second, although cases may be consolidated because they are related, they are unlikely to be identical. Thus, the consolidated claim is likely to be more complex and more costly and time-consuming to arbitrate than would any single case. Third, the host state may not wish to face the united force of several claimants in one proceeding or may wish to resolve one claim before the others. Fourth, any one investor may believe that it can arbitrate its claim more quickly and at less cost separately than it can as part of

128 Mexico-Iceland BIT, Art. 13.

129 2003 Canadian Model BIT, Art. 32.

130 2004 U.S. Model BIT, Art. 33.

131 In the early years of the Iran-U.S. Claims Tribunal, for example, a number of law firms representing private claimants met regularly and freely shared research and arguments with each other, to ensure that every claim would be as well argued as possible and to reduce the risk of adverse decisions based on poorly presented claims.

a much larger consolidated proceeding. In short, consolidation may not be in every party's interest. Thus, in any given dispute, one or more parties could be expected to oppose consolidation. Nevertheless, consolidation procedures typically allow consolidation of claims even over the opposition of one or more of the disputants.

That consolidation may more often be in the interest of the host state than in the interests of all of the claimants is indicated by the fact the earliest uses of the NAFTA consolidation procedure have been at the request of the respondents. In 2004, Archer Daniels Midland and Co. and A. E. Staley Manufacturing Co. (which was succeeded by Tate & Lyle Ingredients Americas, Inc.) submitted to arbitration a claim under the NAFTA against Mexico arising out of a tax on high fructose corn syrup. Corn Products International submitted a separate claim under NAFTA with respect to the same tax. Mexico sought to consolidate the claims, but the request was denied by the tribunal on the grounds that the claims involved numerous issues that were not common to all parties and that the fact that the parties were competitors would require cumbersome procedures to protect the confidentiality of business information.[132] By contrast, a tribunal granted a request by the United States that three claims under the NAFTA arising out of measures that it took with respect to its softwood lumber trade dispute with Canada be consolidated.[133] One of the claimants, Tembec International, which had opposed consolidation, subsequently withdrew its claim, although it was required to pay costs associated with the arbitration.

The potential advantages of consolidation for all parties, however, are evidenced by the fact that some disputants have sought to consolidate cases even where no treaty provides for consolidation. This can be done where the claimants and the host state agree to appoint the same tribunal to hear each of the claims. Where they are unable to agree on the third arbitrator, they also may request the appointing authority to designate the same arbitrator in each of the claims. For example, the same tribunal was appointed to arbitrate the claims in *Sempra Energy v. Argentina*, a case arising under the United States-Argentina BIT, and *Camuzzi International v. Argentina*, a case arising under the Belgium-Luxembourg Economic Union-Argentina BIT. The same tribunal also was appointed to decide the claims in *Suez and Interaguas v. Argentina*, a case arising under France-Argentina and Spain-Argentina BITs, and *Suez and Vivendi v. Argentina*, a case arising under the France-Argentina, Spain-Argentina and United Kingdom-Argentina BITs. This latter case is noteworthy because one of the BITs, the United Kingdom-Argentina BIT, provided for arbitration under the UNCITRAL rules, unless the parties agreed to ICSID arbitration, while the other two BITs authorized ICSID arbitration. Argentina refused to agree to ICSID arbitration of the claim under the U.K. BIT, but did agree to allow the arbitration to be administered by ICSID. By contrast, the Czech Republic refused to allow the same tribunal to be appointed to hear both the claims against it in *Lauder v. Czech Republic*, a case arising under the

132 *See Corn Products International v. Mexico* and *Archer Daniels Midland Company and Tate & Lyle Ingredients America, Inc. v. Mexico*, Order of the Consolidation Tribunal, May 20, 2005.

133 *See Canfor Corporation v. United States of America, Terminal Forest Products Ltd. v. United States*, and *Tembec International v. United States*, Order of the Consolidation Tribunal, September 7, 2007.

United States-Czech Republic BIT, and in *CME v. Czech Republic*, a case arising under the Netherlands-Czech Republic BIT, with the result that two different tribunals reached different conclusions regarding virtually identical claims.

10.2.1.8.6 APPELLATE MECHANISMS

Some critics of investor-state arbitration have advocated the establishment of an appellate mechanism[134] to bring consistency to arbitral awards while also providing a remedy for erroneous decisions. The issue of consistency became particularly salient as a result of a couple of instances in which different tribunals reached different conclusions regarding similar facts. One such instance is the awards in *CME v. Czech Republic* and *Lauder v. Czech Republic*, where identical claims were submitted by different claimants to two different tribunals. The *CME* tribunal issued an award in favor of the claimant, while the *Lauder* tribunal issued its award in favor of the respondent. Another such instance is the decisions on jurisdiction in *SGS v. Pakistan* and SGS *v. Philippines*, in which two tribunals gave different interpretations to two Swiss BITs as they applied to similar factual circumstances. In addition, a few issues of law have arisen in which tribunals are divided, such as whether the full protection and security provision applies to nonphysical harm,[135] whether the observance of obligations provision shall be given its ordinary meaning,[136] or whether the MFN treatment provision applies to procedural provisions.[137]

Recent U.S. BITs include clauses calling for future consideration of the establishment of an appellate mechanism.[138] No such mechanisms, however, have yet been established. At the multilateral level, the ICSID Secretariat in October 2004 proposed the possible creation of an appellate body that would review ICSID awards. The proposal met with mixed reactions, however, and was not adopted. Many ICSID parties believed that an appellate mechanism would best be implemented at the multilateral level, but were not yet convinced that such a mechanism should be established. A consensus has not emerged that the problems of inconsistency and error in awards are sufficient to warrant the additional expense and delay that an appellate mechanism would created.

10.2.2 Origins

Investor-state arbitration provisions had not appeared in the FCNs. The first BIT to include an investor-state disputes provision was the 1968 BIT between the Netherlands

---

134 *See* Asif H. Qureshi, "An Appellate System in International Investment Arbitration?" in *The Oxford Handbook of International Investment Law* (Peter Muchlinski, Frederico Ortino, and Christoph Schreuer, eds. 2008); David A. Gantz, "An Appellate Mechanism for Review of Arbitral Decisions in Investor-State Disputes: Prospects and Challenges," 39 *Vanderbilt Journal of Transnational Law* 39 (2006).

135 *See* Section 6.3.3.

136 *See* Section 6.4.3.

137 *See* Section 7.2.3.

138 *See, e.g.*, United States-Uruguay BIT, Annex E.

and Indonesia. Article 11 of that BIT contained a very brief provision stating that "[t]the Contracting Party in the territory of which a national of the other Contracting Party makes or intends to make an investment, shall assent to any demand on the part of such national and any such national shall comply with the request of the former Contracting Party, to submit, for conciliation or arbitration, to the Centre established by the Convention of Washington of March 18, 1965, any dispute that may arise in connection with the investment." The language referring to the national's compliance with a host state demand for arbitration quickly disappeared from the provision.[139] By the early 1970s, some Dutch BITs included a requirement that the investor exhaust local remedies.[140]

Italy incorporated investor-state arbitration into its BITs in 1969, when it concluded a BIT with Chad. That treaty provided that any dispute concerning investment may be submitted to the jurisdiction of ICSID.[141] Interestingly, the Italy-Chad BIT eliminated the state-state disputes provision and stated that disputes between the two parties were to be resolved diplomatically. Some Italian BITs narrow the scope of the investor-state disputes provision to apply only to disputes relating to compensation for expropriation.[142] The investor-state disputes provisions of the Italian BITs generally are not elaborate. As these provisions have evolved, typical features include a six-month waiting period, a choice of dispute resolution mechanisms, including ICSID, ad hoc arbitration using the UNCITRAL Rules, and submission to local remedies, and a commitment not to submit to diplomatic remedies a dispute previously submitted to investor-state dispute resolution unless the host state has failed to comply with the award or judgment.[143]

The Belgium-Luxembourg Economic Union (BLEU) BITs began to address investor-state arbitration at the beginning of the 1970s. For example, Article 10 of the 1970 BLEU-Indonesia BIT provided that each party consented to conciliation and arbitration of any dispute "relating to a measure contrary to" the BIT at the initiative of a national or legal person of the other party "who considers himself to have been affected by such a measure." Article 10 further provided that the consent implied the renunciation of the exhaustion of local remedies requirement. At the end of the decade, the BLEU BITs broadened the consent to extend to "any investment dispute," not merely disputes alleging a breach of the BIT.[144] The new provision generally prescribed a three-month waiting period, soon lengthened to six months,[145] and included a collateral source rule. In the 1980s, BLEU BITs began to offer investors a choice of arbitral mechanisms, including ICSID arbitration and arbitration before the Stockholm Chamber

139 *See, e.g.*, Netherlands-Uganda BIT, Art. XII.

140 *See, e.g.*, Netherlands-Malaysia BIT, 1971, Art. XII.; Netherlands-Republic of Korea BIT, Art. VI.

141 *See, e.g.*, Italy-Chad BIT, Art. VII.

142 *See, e.g.*, Italy-Bangladesh BIT, Art. 9; Italy-Pakistan BIT, Art. 9.

143 *See, e.g.*, Italy-Bangladesh BIT, Art. 9; Italy-Nicaragua BIT, Art. X; Italy-Jordan BIT, Art. 9; Italy-Pakistan BIT, Art. 9.; Italy-Lebanon BIT, Art. 7; Italy-Croatia BIT, Art. 9; Italy-Vietnam BIT, Art. 9.

144 *See, e.g.*, BLEU-Cameroon BIT, Art. 10(1); BLEU-Bangladesh BIT, Art. 6(1) (excluding tax disputes).

145 *See, e.g.*, BLEU-Sri Lanka BIT, Art. 10(2).

of Commerce and the International Chamber of Commerce, and to include specifications that awards shall be final and binding and that each party shall execute the awards in accordance with its legislation.[146] These changes remain typical of the BLEU BITs today, although UNCITRAL arbitration is now provided as an alternative.[147]

The 1973 BIT between France and Indonesia provided for recourse to ICSID after a five-month waiting period,[148] but later BITs often specified no waiting period.[149] When they did specify a period, six months was typical.[150] Beginning in 1977 France sometimes would agree to arbitration before the International Chamber of Commerce in Paris in the event that ICSID was not available.[151] The French BITs, however, generally have featured short investor-state disputes provisions that in most cases provide for ICSID arbitration after a six-month waiting period.

The U.K. BITs included an investor-state disputes provision from the beginning. Article 8(1) of the 1975 United Kingdom-Egypt BIT contained the parties' consent to ICSID conciliation or arbitration of any legal dispute concerning an investment. The provision required that three months must elapse before the dispute may be submitted to arbitration and authorized submission of a claim by the locally incorporated investment under Article 25(2)(b) of the ICSID convention. In the event of a dispute concerning whether the claim was to be submitted to arbitration or conciliation, the preference of the investor or investment would prevail. No claim submitted to investor-state arbitration could be pursued through diplomatic channels unless the host state did not comply with the award. Within a year, the United Kingdom had added a collateral source rule to its BITs.[152] In the early 1980s, the United Kingdom modified its provision in two critical respects. First, the new provision gave investors the choice of arbitration before ICSID, the International Chamber of Commerce, a sole arbitrator or a tribunal formed under the UNCITRAL Arbitration Rules.[153] The reference to conciliation was omitted. Second, the jurisdiction of the tribunal or arbitrator was narrowed to include only disputes concerning the host state's obligations under the BIT. In this new provision, the reference to Article 25(2)(b) of the ICSID convention was deleted, as was the prohibition on pursuing claims through diplomatic channels and the collateral source rule. The three-month waiting period remained. The investor-state disputes provision of the U.K. BITs has remained essentially unchanged since that time.[154]

Austria included an investor-state disputes provision in its first BIT, concluded with Romania in 1976, although the provision applied only to disputes concerning

---

146 *See, e.g.*, BLEU-Hungary BIT, Art. 9; BLEU-Bolivia BIT, Art. 11.

147 *See, e.g.*, BLEU-Sudan BIT, Art. 12; BLEU-D.R. Congo BIT, Art. 11.

148 *See, e.g.*, France-Indonesia BIT, Art. 3.

149 *See, e.g.*, France-Mauritius, Art.9; France-Egypt BIT, Art. 7; France-Paraguay BIT, Art. 8.

150 *See, e.g.*, France-Pakistan BIT, Art. 8; France-Equatorial Guinea BIT, Art. 8; France-Pakistan BIT, Art. 8.

151 *See, e.g.*, France-Syria BIT, Art. 8; France-El Salvador BIT, Art. 8.

152 *See, e.g.*, U.K.-Republic of Korea BIT, Art. 8(1).

153 *See, e.g.*, U.K.-Belize BIT, Art. 8.

154 *See, e.g.*, U.K.-Bosnia-Herzegovina BIT, Art. 8.

expropriation compensation.[155] It authorized ICSID arbitration. When Austria resumed BIT negotiations in the mid 1980s, it began to conclude BITs with an investor-state disputes provision applicable to any dispute arising directly out of an investment. The provision authorized ICSID arbitration, explicitly renounced the exhaustion of remedies requirement, and adopted a collateral source rule.[156] In many of its more recent BITs, Austria has created a separate chapter on dispute settlement with a half dozen or more articles on investor-state dispute resolution.[157] Under this new approach, the jurisdiction of the tribunal is narrowed to apply to disputes concerning an alleged breach of the BIT that causes loss to the investment or investor. The investor may submit the dispute to ICSID, the Additional Facility if one BIT party is not a party to the ICSID Convention, ad hoc arbitration under the UNCITRAL Rules, or arbitration before the International Chamber of Commerce, although some of these BITs require the expiration of a waiting period, typically sixty days. The new language continues to renounce the exhaustion of remedies requirement, but also provides that international arbitration is not available if the dispute has been submitted to a local court and the court has rendered its decision. The collateral source rule also remains. The new provision includes a choice of law clause, a clause requiring that the arbitration take place in the territory of a state that is a party to the New York Convention, and a clause essentially limiting the relief available to an award of monetary payment. Some of these BITs require that a claim be submitted within a certain number of years, such as three or five, from when the claimant acquired or should have acquired knowledge of the events giving rise to the claim.

The first Swedish BITs were concluded between 1965 and 1967, after which the Swedish BIT program went into a hiatus. When the program resumed in 1978, the Swedish BITs included a provision for investor-state arbitration before ICSID, but only upon the agreement of both parties.[158] In 1981, the Swedish BITs incorporated the host state's consent to ICSID arbitration or conciliation. The new language authorized the locally incorporated investment to submit a claim under Article 25(2)(b) of the ICSID convention and contained a collateral source rule and a prohibition on diplomatic protection with respect to any claim that had been submitted to investor-state arbitration unless the claim was outside the tribunal's jurisdiction or the host state failed to abide by the award,[159] although other versions of the clause were sometimes used.[160] In the late 1990s, the Swedish BITs began to permit arbitration before the ICSID Additional Facility or ad hoc arbitration under the UNCITRAL rules in the event that ICSID arbitration was not available.[161] In Sweden's more recent BITs, the investor

155 *See, e.g.*, Austria-Romania BIT, Art. 5.

156 *See, e.g.*, Austria-Malaysia BIT, Art. 9; Austria-Republic of Korea BIT, Art. 8.

157 *See, e.g.*, Austria-Lebanon BIT, Chapter 2; Austria-Libya BIT, Chapter 2; Austria-Jordan BIT, Chapter 2; Austria-Bosnia-Herzegovina BIT, Chapter 2; Austria-Armenia BIT, Chapter 2.

158 *See, e.g.*, Sweden-Yugoslavia BIT, Art. 6; Sweden-Egypt BIT, Art. 6.

159 *See, e.g.*, Sweden-Pakistan BIT, Art. 7; Sweden-Sri Lanka BIT, Art. 9; Sweden-Yemen BIT, Art. 7.

160 *See, e.g.*, Sweden-Tunisia BIT, Art. 5; Sweden-Czechoslovakia BIT, Art. 8.

161 *See, e.g.*, Sweden-South Africa BIT, Art. 7; Sweden-Turkey BIT, Art. 8.

may choose UNCITRAL arbitration even if ICSID arbitration is available.[162] These BITs also contain a few additional clauses, including a requirement that the arbitration be held in a state that is a party to the New York Convention.

Switzerland began to include a provision for investor-state arbitration in 1981[163] The Swiss BITs initially varied considerably in the content of their investor state disputes provision,[164] although certain clauses now have become common (albeit not universally present) in the Swiss BITs, such as a requirement of a six-month waiting period, a choice of arbitral mechanisms among alternatives such as ICSID arbitration or ad hoc arbitration under the UNCITRAL Rules, a collateral source rule, a commitment not to seek diplomatic protection with respect to a claim submitted to investor-state arbitration unless the host state does not comply with the arbitral award, and a provision stating that the arbitral award is final and binding and shall be enforced under domestic law.[165] The jurisdiction of the tribunal typically extends to any dispute concerning an investment.

The U.S. BITs included an investor-state disputes provision from the beginning. The U.S. BITs contained relatively elaborate provisions that conferred on the tribunal jurisdiction over disputes involving an alleged violation of the BIT, but also involving the interpretation or application of an investment agreement or investment authorization. The U.S. BITs authorized arbitration before ICSID or the Additional Facility. They also included an election of remedies clause that precluded investor-state arbitration of disputes submitted to local remedies or previously agreed dispute procedures. Like many other BITs, they included a waiting period, a collateral source rule, and a clause authorizing claims by the locally incorporated investment. In the 1990s, the U.S. BITs authorized ad hoc arbitration under the UNCITRAL rules as well. In 2004, the investor-state disputes provision of the U.S. model BIT was extensively revised. The new model includes provisions allowing the BIT parties to resolve a number of different kinds of issues by mutual agreement, to increase the transparency of investor-state arbitral proceedings, and to improve efficiency by permitting expedited dismissal of frivolous claims and consolidation of related claims.[166]

Kuwait, which had started its BIT program in 1964, incorporated an investor-state disputes provision authorizing ICSID arbitration into its 1983 BIT with Pakistan.[167] The provision applied to any dispute between the investor and the host state. Soon, however, the tribunal's jurisdiction was narrowed to include only disputes concerning an investment[168] and by the 1990s the Kuwaiti BITs offered investors a choice of mechanisms, including not only ICSID, but the Additional Facility, ad hoc arbitration

---

162 *See, e.g.*, Sweden-Bosnia-Herzegovina BIT, Art. 8; Sweden-Kazakhstan BIT, Art. 8; Sweden-Ecuador BIT, Art. 8.

163 *See, e.g.*, Switzerland-Sri Lanka BIT, Art. 9.

164 *Compare, e.g.*, Switzerland-Sri Lanka BIT, Art. 9; Switzerland-Panama BIT, Art. 9; Switzerland-China BIT, Art. 12; Switzerland-Jamaica BIT, Art. 9.

165 *See, e.g.*, Switzerland-Djibouti BIT, Art. 8; Switzerland-Guatemala BIT, Art, 8; Switzerland-Libya BIT, Art. 8; Switzerland-Algeria BIT, Art. 8.

166 *See* Section 10.2.1.8.

167 *See, e.g.* Kuwait-Pakistan BIT, Art. 8(1).

168 *See, e.g.*, Kuwait-Hungary BIT, Art. 11(1).

under the UNCITRAL Rules, or arbitration in any other forum to which the parties agree.[169] These provisions sometimes also authorize claims by locally incorporated investors, include a collateral source rule, and provide for interim injunctive relief in local courts [170]

Denmark incorporated an investor-state disputes provision in its BITs for the first time in 1985, when it concluded a BIT with China.[171] The provision applied to any dispute in connection with an investment. It provided for arbitration, after a six-month waiting period, by an ad hoc tribunal, which was to determine its own procedures "with reference to" the ICSID Convention. The appointing authority was the Chairman of the International Arbitration Institute of the Stockholm Chamber of Commerce. Each party was to bear the costs of its own representation and of the arbitrator it appointed, while the other costs were to be borne equally by the parties. The decision of the tribunal would be final, binding, and enforceable in accordance with domestic law. The tribunal was to state the basis of its decision. This provision, however, was not to become part of routine Danish practice. When Denmark concluded its next BITs, in 1988, the new provision provided that disputes in connection with investment may be submitted to ICSID following a three-month waiting period.[172] By 1990, the Danish BITs offered parties a choice of mechanisms, typically between ICSID and ad hoc arbitration under the UNCITRAL rules.[173] In some of its most recent BITs, Denmark has lengthened the waiting period to six months, added the Additional Facility as an alternative, authorized the locally incorporated investment to submit a claim to arbitration, required that an arbitration other than before ICSID at the request of either disputing party be held in a state that is a party to the New York Convention, incorporated a collateral source rule, and provided that any award is final and binding and shall be carried out without delay.[174]. In others, the investor-state disputes provision remains very brief, providing for a three-month waiting period and a choice of two mechanisms.[175] Even these approaches, however, are not exhaustive of the possibilities. The Denmark-Kuwait BIT, for example, provides for a six-month waiting period and arbitration only before ICSID, although an ad hoc tribunal is authorized if ICSID is not available.[176]

The German BITs began to acknowledge the possibility of investor-state arbitration in the late 1970s. They included a provision that excluded from the jurisdiction of an arbitral tribunal formed under the state-state disputes provision any claim submitted to

---

169 *See, e.g.*, Kuwait-Ethiopia BIT, Art. 9; Kuwait-Croatia BIT, Art. 9; Kuwait-Czech Republic BIT, Art. 9 (ICSID and UNCITRAL only); Kuwait-Bulgaria BIT, Art. 10 (ICSID and UNCITRAL only).

170 *See, e.g.*, Kuwait-Croatia BIT, Art. 9; Kuwait-Ethiopia BIT, Art. 10.

171 *See, e.g.*, Denmark-China BIT, April 29, 1985, Art. 8.

172 *See, e.g.*, Denmark-Republic of Korea BIT, Art. 8.

173 *See, e.g.*, Denmark-Poland BIT, Art. 9; Denmark-Peru BIT, Art. 9; Denmark-Mongolia BIT, Art. 9; Denmark-Venezuela BIT, Art. 9 (also providing for arbitration before the ICSID Additional Facility).

174 *See, e.g.*, Denmark-Ethiopia BIT, Art. 9; Denmark-Croatia BIT, Art. 9.

175 *See, e.g.*, Denmark-Kyrgyz Republic BIT, Art. 9; Denmark-Cuba BIT, Art. 10.

176 *See, e.g.*, Denmark-Kuwait BIT, Art. 10.

ICSID arbitration, unless an award had been issued and the host state had failed to comply with the award. This was consistent with Article 27(1) of the ICSID convention. The German BITs began to include consent to investor-state arbitration in the mid-1980s. For example, Germany's 1987 BIT with Bolivia provided at Article 11 that any disputes between in investor and a host state "in connection with investments" shall, upon the request of either party, be submitted to arbitration. The provision stated that the dispute should as far as possible be settled amicably and permitted resort to arbitration only after six months had elapsed since the claim was first raised by a party. The Germany-Bolivia BIT required that the dispute be submitted to ICSID if both BIT parties were parties to the ICSID convention, but otherwise authorized ad hoc arbitration using essentially the same procedure as was authorized for state-state dispute resolution.[177] German BITs would continue to make provision for ad hoc arbitration in lieu of ICSID arbitration in some cases.[178] Minor evolutions in this provision occurred over the next twenty years. By 1989, the Germany BITs included a collateral source rule[179] and a clause stating that the award shall be binding, final, unreviewable except to the extent permitted in the ICSID convention, and enforced under national law. By the mid-1990s, the German BITs included a choice of law provision, designating the BIT, treaties, international law, and the law of the host state as applicable law.[180] A decade later, the provision as it had emerged in the 1990s still was in use in the German BITs.[181] Germany, however, occasionally would agree to substantive departures from its standard provision. For example, in its 2004 BIT with Ethiopia, it agreed that a dispute submitted to local courts could be submitted to investor-state arbitration only if the local court had not rendered a decision finally disposing of the case and only if 18 months had elapsed.[182]

When Finland commenced its BIT program in 1980, the Finnish BITs included an investor-state disputes provision. This early provision called for ad hoc arbitration of any dispute in connection with an investment, with ICSID as the appointing authority, which was the same mechanism used for state-state dispute resolution.[183] By 1985, however, Finland replaced ad hoc arbitration with ICSID arbitration or conciliation, authorized claims by locally incorporated investments under Article 25(2)(b) of the ICSID convention, required a three-month waiting period, included a collateral source rule, and prohibited diplomatic protection with respect to a claim submitted to investor-state arbitration unless the tribunal held that it had no jurisdiction or the host state failed to comply with the award.[184] The new provision applied to any dispute between an investor and host state, without an explicit requirement that the dispute be in connection with an investment. Finnish BIT practice in the 1990s varied. In some cases,

---

177 Germany-Bolivia BIT, Art. 11(2).

178 *See, e.g.*, Germany-Qatar BIT, Art. 11(3). Germany-Hong Kong BIT, Art. 11(2); Germany-Ethiopia BIT, Art. 11.

179 *See, e.g.*, Germany-Poland BIT, Art. 11(5); Germany-Serbia BIT, Art. 9(4).

180 *See, e.g.*, Germany-Zimbabwe BIT, Art. 11(2).

181 *See, e.g.*, Germany-Timore-Leste BIT, Art. 11.

182 Germany-Ethiopia BIT, Arts. 11(2), 11(7).

183 *See* Finland-Egypt BIT, Art. 7.

184 *See, e.g.*, Finland-Malaysia BIT, Art. 7; Finland-Sri Lanka BIT, Art. 9.

the investor-state disputes provision applied to any dispute,[185] while in other cases it applied to disputes concerning an investment.[186] In some cases the BIT provided a choice of arbitral mechanisms,[187] typically between ICSID and ad hoc arbitration under the UNCITRAL Rules, while in other cases only ICSID arbitration was authorized.[188] Some Finnish BITs provided that, where a dispute was submitted to local remedies, it could not be submitted to investor-state arbitration.[189] In Finland's more recent BITs, the jurisdiction of the tribunal has been limited to disputes arising directly from an investment.[190] The waiting period, which was often six months in the 1990s, is again three months. The right of the locally incorporated investment to submit a claim to arbitration under Article 25(2)(b) of the ICSID convention largely disappeared from the Finnish BITs in the 1990s and typically has not reappeared in the more recent BITs. In some recent BITs, resort to local remedies does not foreclose submission of the same dispute to investor-state arbitration provided that the disputes is withdrawn from local courts before judgment is entered and further recourse to them is waived by the investor.[191] In other recent Finnish BITs, resort to local remedies does foreclose submission of the same dispute to investor-state arbitration.[192] Some of the recent Finnish BITs also broaden the investor's choices to include the Additional Facility when ICSID is not available.[193]

As indicated by this survey of the BIT practice of the earliest states to inaugurate BIT programs, investor-state arbitration provisions first appeared in BITs in the late 1960s. They appeared first in the Dutch BITs and were soon employed in the Italian and BLEU BITs. They appeared in the French and English BITs in the first half of the 1970s, but such provisions did not become routine in BITs until the 1980s. The earliest provisions provided for ICSID arbitration, but by the 1990s it was common to provide investors with a choice of arbitral mechanisms. The principle that investor-state arbitration does not require exhaustion of local remedies appeared explicitly within a couple of years. Most of the clauses that commonly appear in BITs—such as the waiting period, the collateral source rule, the authorization of claims by locally incorporated subsidiaries, and the prohibition on diplomatic protection for claims submitted to investor-state arbitration—all had appeared in the BITs by the 1970s. The two main jurisdictional clauses—that providing for arbitration of disputes involving a BIT

185 *See, e.g.*, Finland-Chile BIT, Art. 8; Finland-Republic of Korea BIT, Art. 9; Finland-Brazil BIT, Art.8.

186 *See, e.g.*, Finland-Czechoslovakia BIT, Art. 8.

187 *See, e.g.*, Finland-Czechoslovakia BIT, Art. 8; Finland-Estonia BIT, Art. 8; Finland-Latvia BIT, Art. 8; Finland-Uzbekistan BIT, Art. 8; Finland-Argentina BIT, Art. 9.

188 *See, e.g.*, Finland-Romania BIT, Art. 8; Finland-Turkey BIT, Art. 8; Finland-Chile BIT, Art. 8; Finland-Republic of Korea BIT, Art. 9; Finland-Thailand BIT, Art. 8.

189 *See, e.g.*, Finland-Turkey BIT, Art. 8; Finland-Chile BIT, Art. 8; Finland-Argentina BIT, Art. 9.

190 *See, e.g.*, Finland-Belarus BIT, Art. 9; Finland-Croatia BIT, Art. 10; Finland-Armenia BIT, Art. 9; Finland-Algeria BIT, Art. 8; Finland-Azerbaijan BIT, Art. 11.

191 *See, e.g.*, Finland-Belarus BIT, Art. 9; Finland-Croatia BIT, Art. 10; Finland-Armenia BIT, Art. 9.

192 *See, e.g.*, Finland-Algeria BIT, Art. 8; Finland-Azerbaijan BIT, Art. 11.

193 *See, e.g.*, Finland-Azerbaijan BIT, Art. 11; Finland-Algeria BIT, Art. 8.

violation and that providing for arbitration of disputes concerning an investment—also were both in use during the 1970s. The election of remedies clause appears in the early 1980s, with the inauguration of the U.S. BIT program. As indicated in Section 10.2.1.8, a number of innovations in BIT practice appeared after 2000, but these have been limited to a small number of countries.

10.2.3 Arbitral Practice

10.2.3.1 The Tribunal's Jurisdiction The host state in an investment arbitration very often challenges the jurisdiction of the tribunal. In most cases, these challenges are unsuccessful.[194] Usually, the tribunal holds that it has jurisdiction over at least some of the claims.

Clearly, the tribunal's jurisdiction under the BIT is limited to disputes within the scope of the investor-state disputes provision of the BIT.[195] As noted in Section 10.2.1.1, in most BITs, the investor-state disputes provision applies to any dispute concerning an investment. Thus, in these BITs, disputes that do not involve an alleged breach of a BIT may be submitted to arbitration under the investor-state disputes provision, if they concern an investment.[196]

The general rule is that, in determining whether it has jurisdiction, a tribunal shall take the allegations of the pleadings as true.[197] In effect, the tribunal asks whether, assuming that the alleged facts are true, the investor has a legitimate claim against the host state. Tribunals have not been entirely clear concerning the extent to which they will interpret a BIT's substantive provisions at the jurisdictional phase. On the one hand, to determine that the facts alleged could constitute a violation of the BIT unquestionably requires the tribunal to interpret the BIT. On the other hand, tribunals in a number of cases have declined to resolve questions concerning the interpretation of a

---

194 One study of awards made public as of June 1, 2006, found that tribunals denied jurisdiction over a claim in its entirety about 10 percent of the time. *See* Susan D. Franck, "Empirically Evaluating Claims About Investment Treaty Arbitration," 86 *North Carolina Law Review* 1, 52 (2007). The exact figure was 11.5 percent. In 31 percent of the cases, the tribunal dismissed some part of the claim on jurisdictional grounds, but proceeded to decide the rest of the claim on the merits.

195 *Generation Ukraine v. Ukraine* (United States-Ukraine BIT), Award, para. 8.10.

196 *Jan de Nul v. Egypt* (1977 BLEU-Egypt BIT and 2002 BLEU-Egypt BIT), Award, para. 137; *BG Group v. Argentina* (United Kingdom-Argentina BIT), Award, para. 181; *Salini v. Morocco* (Italy-Morocco BIT), Decision on Jurisdiction, paras. 59–62; *SGS v. Philippines* (Switzerland-Philippines BIT), Decision on Jurisdiction, paras. 130–135. The awards not unanimous, however. *See SGS v. Pakistan* (Switzerland-Pakistan BIT), Decision on Jurisdiction, paras 160–161.

197 *See, e.g., Wena Hotels v. Egypt* (United Kingdom-Egypt BIT); Proceedings on Jurisdiction, Section VI; *Desert Line v. Yemen* (Oman-Yemen BIT), Award, para. 129; *Kardassopoulos v. Georgia* (Greece-Georgia BIT), Decision on Jurisdiction, paras. 103–104; *Micula v. Romania* (Sweden-Romania BIT), Decision on Jurisdiction, para. 66; *Chevron v. Ecuador* (United States-Ecuador BIT), Interim Award, paras. 103–105. *See generally* Audley Sheppard, "The Jurisdictional Threshold of a Prima-Facie Case," in *The Oxford Handbook of International Investment Law* (Peter Muchlinski, Frederico Ortino, and Christoph Schreuer, eds. 2008).

BIT provision on the ground that such questions are left to the merits phase. Perhaps the most accurate characterization of arbitral practice is that the tribunal at the jurisdictional phase will engage in an inquiry into the meaning of the BIT sufficient to determine whether the claim is frivolous or abusive, but will defer any more searching inquiry to the merits phase.[198] Where some doubt exists as to whether the allegations could state a claim under the BIT, the tribunal may defer the jurisdictional issue to the merits phase, issuing a final award that resolves the issues of both jurisdiction and the merits.[199]

Tribunals, however, do not invariably assume the facts to be true, at the jurisdictional stage. A few tribunals have rejected this approach in cases where the parties disagreed greatly concerning the relevant facts, although these tribunals typically acknowledged that in so doing they were deviating from the general practice.[200] If the host state demonstrates at the jurisdictional phase that the facts on which jurisdiction is based are not true, then the tribunal will decline jurisdiction.[201]

The next five sections discuss common jurisdictional objections.

10.2.3.1.1 EXISTENCE OF AN INVESTMENT

Host states in many cases have argued that the tribunal lacked jurisdiction because the claim submitted by the claimant did not concern an investment. Tribunals typically discuss this as an issue of jurisdiction *ratione materiae*.

The existence of an investment is a necessary condition of the tribunal's jurisdiction potentially for two reasons. First, the investor-state disputes provision of a BIT generally confers on a tribunal jurisdiction only over disputes concerning an investment or over disputes involving an alleged violation of the BIT's obligations to investments or to investors that have made or are making an investment. Without an investment, no claim within the tribunal's jurisdiction as described in the BIT can arise. Second, the ICSID convention provides that an ICSID tribunal has jurisdiction only over a dispute arising directly from an investment.[202] Thus, in cases before ICSID, the dispute must arise from an investment within the meaning of both the BIT and the ICSID convention. The meaning of the term "investment" under both has been extensively discussed in Sections 4.2.1., 4.2.3.1 and 4.2.3.2.

10.2.3.1.2 EXISTENCE OF AN INVESTOR OR INVESTMENT WITH STANDING

Host states often challenge the jurisdiction of the tribunal on the ground that the claimant is not an investor or investment authorized by the BIT to submit a claim. Such challenges sometimes are described as challenges to the jurisdiction of the tribunal *ratione personae* and sometimes are described as challenges to the standing of the claimant.

---

198 *See, e.g., El Paso Energy v. Argentina* (United States-Argentina BIT); *Pan American Energy v. Argentina* (United States-Argentina BIT).

199 *See, e.g., Société Générale I v. Dominican Republic*, (France-Dominican Republic BIT), Award on Jurisdiction, para. 59.

200 *See, e.g., Joy Mining v. Egypt* (United Kingdom-Egypt BIT), Award on Jurisdiction, para. 30.

201 *See, e.g., Total v. Argentina* (France-Argentina BIT); *Continental Casualty v. Argentina* (United States-Argentina BIT); *Chevron v. Ecuador* (United States-Ecuador BIT), Interim Award, para. 110.

202 ICSID convention, Art. 25(1).

All BITs authorize an investor to submit a claim for injuries that they have suffered as a result of the host state's unlawful conduct. The definition of the term "investor" was discussed in Section 4.3.1 and 4.3.3. Some BITs also authorize the investment to submit a claim for injuries they have suffered as a result of the host state's unlawful conduct.[203] The definition of the term "investment" was discussed in Sections 4.2.1., 4.2.3.1 and 4.2.3.2.

Moreover, the earliest BIT cases held that an investor that owns or controls an investment may bring a claim on behalf of the investment for injury to the investment, regardless of whether the investor itself was injured. In *American Manufacturing & Trading v. Zaire*, a claim arising under the United States-D.R. Congo BIT, a company organized under U.S. law and therefore a U.S. investor owned 94 percent of a company located in the D.R. Congo (then Zaire) that was damaged by government troops. The tribunal held that the U.S. investor had standing to bring a claim for the injury to the Congolese company. This holding, which rejects the approach taken in *Barcelona Traction*,[204] is now the uniform rule.[205]

The rule is the same where the claim is based on a breach of an agreement between the investment and the host state. For example, in *Azuriz v. Argentina*, a case arising under the United States-Argentina BIT, the U.S. claimant owned 90 percent of an Argentine company and was permitted to bring a claim for breach of a concession agreement between the company and Argentina. Similarly, in *Telenor v. Hungary*, a case arising under the Norway-Hungary BIT, the claimant was allowed to submit a claim for violations of a concession agreement with its wholly owned subsidiary. In *Continental Casualty v. Argentina*, a case arising under the United States-Argentina BIT, the tribunal observed that where a claim is brought for violation of the observance of obligations provision, it is immaterial whether the claim is brought by the investor or by its local subsidiary.[206] Again, in *Parkerings-Compagniet v. Lithuania*, a case arising under the Norway-Lithuania BIT, the claimant alleged that the failure of the city of Vilnius to honor its agreement with the claimant's wholly owned subsidiary violated the BIT. The tribunal explained, "That the Claimant was not a party to the Agreement is irrelevant as the Arbitral Tribunal is not ruling on breaches of the Agreement but on violations of the BIT."[207]

A shareholder that does not control the investment may be treated as a controlling shareholder if it has gained control through a shareholders' agreement with other shareholders. In *Sempra Energy v. Argentina*, a case arising under the United States-Argentina BIT, the claimant, which was a minority shareholder in the investment, had entered into a shareholders' agreement with the majority shareholder, a company of

---

203 *See* Section 10.2.1.4.

204 (Belgium v. Spain), 1970 I.C.J. Rep. 3.

205 *See, e.g., Santa Elena v. Costa Rica* (no BIT at issue); *Maffezini v. Spain* (Argentina-Spain BIT); *Pope & Talbot v. Canada* (NAFTA); *Siemens v. Argentina* (Germany-Argentina BIT); *AES v. Argentina* (United States-Argentina BIT); *Pan American Energy v. Argentina* (United States-Argentina BIT); *Continental Casualty v. Argentina* (United States-Argentina BIT); *GAMI Investments v. Mexico* (NAFTA), Award, para. 30.

206 Award, para. 98.

207 Award, para. 259.

different nationality than the claimant. The tribunal observed in *dictum* that there would be no objection to jurisdiction if the two shareholders were of the same nationality and therefore covered by the same BIT. Where, as in that case, they were of different nationalities, the tribunal believed that the minority shareholder could submit a claim as a controlling shareholder on the basis of the shareholders' agreement only if the two investors were "operating jointly."[208] The tribunal found that such joint operation existed in that case.

At the same time, a non-controlling shareholder may not obtain standing merely by agreement of the parties. In *Impregilo v. Pakistan*, a case arising under the Italy-Pakistan BIT, the claimant was a member of a joint venture, but the venture was not a juridical person and therefore, under Article 25(1) of the ICSID convention, was not eligible to be a claimant before an ICSID tribunal. The joint venture agreement, however, designated the claimant as the "leader," a designation that allowed it to act on behalf of the joint venture for certain purposes. The tribunal held, however, that the claimant could not assert a claim on behalf of the joint venture because the co-venturers could not expand the scope of the host state's consent through their joint venture agreement.[209] The claimant could assert a claim for its *pro rata* share of the losses.[210]

Where the claimant is an investor that does not control the investment, tribunals have held that the claimant may submit a claim based on host-state measures, although only for the losses suffered by the claimant. For example, in *Lanco v. Argentina*, a case arising under the United States-Argentina BIT, the claimant owned 18.3 percent of the stock in the investment. The tribunal held that the claimant had standing to bring a claim based on wrongful acts affecting the company. The claimant also had standing, however, because it was a party to the concession agreement on which the claim was based. Thus, the claim did not rest on the investor's minority ownership alone.

In *CMS v. Argentina*, another case arising under the United States-Argentina BIT, the investor owned 29.42 percent of an Argentine company that had suffered losses as a result of Argentina's breach of a concession agreement to provide gas transmission services. The tribunal held that investor could submit a claim for losses suffered as a result of the breach. Further, the tribunal found that "[w]hether the protected investor is in addition a party to a concession agreement or a license agreement with the host State is immaterial for the purpose of finding jurisdiction . . . since there is a direct right of action of shareholders."[211]

Similarly, in *LG&E v. Argentina*, a third case arising under the United States-Argentina BIT, the claimant owned a 45.9 percent interest in one Argentine company, a 14.4 percent interest in a second Argentine company, and a 19.6 percent interest in a third Argentine company. The tribunal held that it had jurisdiction over a claim submitted by LG&E for violations of concession agreements with those three companies.[212]

---

208 Decision on Jurisdiction, para. 54.

209 Decision on Jurisdiction, para. 136.

210 Decision on Jurisdiction, para. 173.

211 Decision on Jurisdiction, para. 65.

212 *Accord El Paso Energy v. Argentina* (United States-Argentina BIT), Decision on Jurisdiction, para. 138.

In *Suez and Vivendi v. Argentina*, a case arising under the France-Argentina BIT, the Spain-Argentina BIT, and the United-Kingdom-Argentina BIT, the tribunal held that foreign investors owning 39.93, 25.01, 7.55 and 4.25 percent, respectively, of an Argentine company had standing to submit claims for violations of a concession agreement between the company and Buenos Aires to provide water and waste water services. In *Suez and InterAguas v. Argentina*, a case arising under the France-Argentina BIT and the Spain-Argentina BIT, a tribunal with the same composition, held that investors owning 51.69, 14.92 and 10.89 percent of the shares of an Argentine company had standing to submit claims for violations of a concession agreement between the company and the province of Santa Fe to provide water and waste water services.

In *Total v. Argentina*, a case arising under the France-Argentina BIT, the tribunal held that an investor that owned indirectly a 19.21 percent share in an Argentine company that had a concession agreement to exploit oil and gas had standing to submit a claim for violation of the agreement.

In *GAMI v. Mexico*, a case arising under the NAFTA, the investor owned 14.18 percent of a local company whose principal assets, five sugar mills, were expropriated. The tribunal held that "the fact that GAMI is only a minority shareholder does not affect its right to seek the international arbitral remedy."[213] Further, the tribunal explained that

> The fact that a host state does not explicitly interfere with share ownership is not decisive. The issue is rather whether a breach of NAFTA leads with sufficient directness to loss or damage in respect of a given investment.[214]

GAMI's right to submit a claim was unaffected by the fact that the controlling shareholder had sought redress in Mexican courts.

In *BG Group v. Argentina*, a case arising under the United Kingdom-Argentina BIT, the claimant owned 45.11% of an Argentine company, MetroGas. The tribunal held that the claimant was not entitled to raise any claims for violation of a license issued to MetroGas because the claimant had not alleged any separate loss attributable to any such violations.[215] The tribunal noted that any loss would be reflected in the value of the claimant's shares in MetroGas and the claimant did have standing to submit a claim for violations of the BIT relating to its shareholding interest.

In *Enron v. Argentina*, a case arising under the United States-Argentina BIT, the claimants owned approximately 35 percent of the investment through intermediary corporations. The tribunal held that minority investors may submit claims to international arbitration. As the tribunal explained, "claims made by investors that are not in the majority or in control of the affected corporation when claiming for violations of their rights under such treaty are admissible."[216] Further, they may do so even if they own the stock through intermediary companies. That is, they need not be shareholders

---

213 Award, para. 37.

214 Award, para. 33.

215 Award, paras. 213–215.

216 Decision on Jurisdiction, para. 49.

in the company that was injured by the host state's conduct in violation of the BIT, as long as they have at least an indirect ownership interest in the company. The tribunal did note that shareholders with only a remote connection to the affected company should not be permitted to submit a claim for losses attributable to wrongful action to the company. In that case, however, the tribunal found that the claimants' participation in the company had been specifically sought and thus their claims were not too remote. The tribunal's *dictum* regarding remoteness seems inconsistent with the language of the BITs. The United States-Argentina BIT at issue in that case, for example, explicitly allows claims for breaches of the treaty that cause injury to investment owned or controlled directly or indirectly by the investor. The treaty text does not impose a proximity requirement and nothing in BITs suggests that such a requirement is generally contemplated by the parties. Certainly, nothing in the BITs indicates that only investors whose participation was invited or foreseen should be protected. To impose limitations on the ordinary language of the text undermines the very transparency and security that BITs are intended to create. In cases where the investor owns the investment through numerous intermediate companies, no reason exists in principle for extinguishing a claim merely because the number of intermediates exceeds some arbitrary figure. In cases where the remote investor owns the investment through numerous substantial companies (as opposed to shell companies), the likelihood is that adverse action taken against the investment will have only negligible impact on the remote investor, which could be difficult or impossible to prove in any event. International law does not permit recovery for damages that are too speculative to be susceptible of proof. This well-established rule seems the preferred way in which to address the tribunal's concern.

Nor is the standing of the investor affected by the nationality of the intermediary companies. In *Waste Management v. Mexico*, a case arising under the NAFTA, the claimant, a U.S. company, owned a Caymanian company, which owned a second Caymanian company, which owned the investment. When the U.S. claimant submitted a claim against Mexico, the tribunal held that it had jurisdiction. The tribunal explained that the claimant had the requisite nationality and owned or controlled the investment, albeit through intermediaries. Nothing in the text of the NAFTA required the intermediaries to have the nationality of a NAFTA party. As the tribunal held, "The nationality of any intermediate holding companies is irrelevant to the present claim."[217]

In *Siag and Vecchi v. Egypt*, a case arising under the Italy-Egypt BIT, the claimants were Italian nationals who had made investments in Egypt. The tribunal held that its jurisdiction was not affected by the fact that the claimants "managed their investment through the medium of companies incorporated under Egyptian law. . . ."[218]

In many cases, more than one party may submit a claim. As the tribunal explained in *Continental Casualty v. Argentina*, a case arising under the United States-Argentina BIT, the investor may submit a claim even if the investment also has standing to claim.[219] In *Sempra Energy v. Argentina*, another case arising under the United States-Argentina BIT, the tribunal similarly noted that the fact that the investment may submit

---

217 Award, para. 85.

218 Decision on Jurisdiction, para. 207.

219 Decision on Jurisdiction, para. 85.

a claim does not preclude the investor also from submitting a claim.[220] Thus, for example, in *Empresas Lucchetti v. Peru*, a case arising under the Chile-Peru BIT, both the investor and the investment submitted claims. Similarly, in *Pan American Energy v. Argentina*, a case arising under the United States-Argentina BIT, a claim was submitted by both the investors and the local companies in which they invested.

An investor is an investor within the meaning of the BIT only if it has the nationality of a BIT party. Tribunals have addressed the issue of the dates on which the claimant must have the nationality of the non-disputing BIT party. In *Loewen v. United States*, a case arising under the NAFTA, a Canadian claimant arbitrating a claim against the United States prior to the resolution of the claim had reorganized itself under the U.S. bankruptcy laws as a U.S. corporation. Recognizing that as a U.S. corporation it would not be able to arbitrate a claim against the United States, the claimant prior to its cessation of existence as a Canadian company assigned the claim to a newly created Canadian company, which had as its sole asset the claim and as its sole business activity the pursuit of the claim. The beneficiary of the claim thus remained the U.S. company that owned and controlled the newly created Canadian corporation. The tribunal noted that customary international law requires that the nationality requirement be met continuously from the date on which the claim arose until the date on which the claim is decided. The tribunal further observed that the customary rule could be relaxed by agreement and that the NAFTA was silent on this issue. In the absence of explicit language to such effect, the tribunal declined to interpret the NAFTA as modifying the customary rule. Because it did not have jurisdiction over a claim by a U.S. national against the United States, the tribunal held that, as a result of the reorganization of the Canadian claimant as a U.S. corporation, it lacked jurisdiction over the claim.

Most cases, however, have rejected the continuous nationality rule espoused in *Loewen*. In *National Grid v. Argentina*, an UNCITRAL arbitration arising under the United Kingdom-Argentina BIT, the investor had sold its shares in the investment after submitting the claim to arbitration. The tribunal doubted that the continuous nationality rule cited by *Loewen* existed. Rather, the tribunal found that precedent supported the principle that "the critical date to meet the jurisdiction requirements is the date when the proceedings are instituted"[221] rather than the date on which the claim is decided.[222]

Similarly, in *El Paso Energy v. Argentina*, an ICSID arbitration arising under the United States-Argentina BIT, the investor brought a claim for damage to Argentine companies in which it was a shareholder. Seventeen days later it sold its investment in two companies and then, less than four months later, it sold its investment in a third company. The tribunal held that its jurisdiction was not affected by the subsequent sale of the investment, finding that nothing required that the investor continuously own the

---

220 Decision on Jurisdiction, para. 42.

221 Decision on Jurisdiction, para. 118.

222 *See also Siemens v. Argentina* (Germany-Argentina BIT), Decision on Jurisdiction, para. 161 (under the ICSID Convention, the necessary nationality must exist at the time of the notice of arbitration, at the time the dispute is submitted to arbitration and at the time the claim is registered).

investment after the proceedings were instituted. Further, the sale of the investment was in mitigation of the investor's damages, a circumstance that illustrated the desirability of allowing an investor to divest itself of an investment following institution of a claim without defeating a tribunal's jurisdiction.

Again, in *CSOB v. Slovak Republic*, an ICSID arbitration arising under the Slovak Republic-Czech Republic BIT, the tribunal held that standing is to be determined as of the date on which the proceedings are instituted. In that case, the claimant assigned its claim after the arbitral proceedings had been initiated. Thus, the assignment would have no effect on the tribunal's jurisdiction. The tribunal went on to note that, even if it were to consider the effects of the assignment, the assignment by its terms was not to take effect until after the proceedings terminated. Further, the claimant would receive a portion of the award and thus continued to have a genuine interest in the result. Accordingly, even were the tribunal to consider the effects of the assignment, under these circumstances, the assignment would not defeat the tribunal's jurisdiction.

In *Encana v. Ecuador*, an UNCITRAL arbitration arising under the Canada-Ecuador BIT, the tribunal held that the investor's sale of the investment during the pendency of the arbitration did not affect the tribunal's jurisdiction. The tribunal noted that the investor's claim was not on behalf of the investment, but on its own behalf.[223] The tribunal did not need to address the question of whether a requirement of continuous ownership would apply to a claim on behalf of the investment.[224]

The result is the same where the investor ceases to exist during the pendency of the arbitration. For example, in *Link-Trading v. Moldova*, an UNCITRAL arbitration arising under the United States-Moldova BIT, the claimant was a Moldovan company controlled by a U.S. investor. About three months after the claim was submitted to arbitration, the parent went out of business. The tribunal, in an extremely brief discussion, rejected Moldova's argument that the termination of the U.S. investor divested it of jurisdiction. The tribunal explained that "the critical date for purposes of determining Claimant's standing to sue, as a company controlled by a U.S. investors, is the date on which the expropriation is alleged to have taken place. . . ."[225] Thus, the fact that the claimant's parent had ceased to exist was irrelevant.

A few awards have required that the claimant have the requisite nationality not only at the time the proceedings were instituted, but also at the time that consent to arbitration was given. For example, in *Siag & Vecchi v. Egypt*, an ICSID arbitration arising under the Italy-Egypt BIT, the claimants had been Egyptian nationals when the BIT entered into force and when the investment began. The tribunal held that the ICSID convention does not require that the claim be owned by a national of the host state continuously from the time the claim arose until some specified future date, such as the date the claim is submitted to arbitration or the date of an award. Rather, it requires that the claimant have the nationality of the home state on the date of consent to arbitration

223 Award, para. 126.

224 Award, para. 128.

225 Award, para. 55.

and the date that the claim is registered.[226] The tribunal designated as the date of consent the date on which the investor consented.[227] In a partial dissenting opinion, Professor Francisco Orrego Vicuna contended that the date of consent should be the date on which the host state consents to jurisdiction, i.e., the date on which the BIT enters into force.

In *BARI v. D.R. Congo*, a case arising under a mining concession agreement rather than a BIT, the tribunal noted that, for purposes of arbitration under the ICSID convention, the investor must have the nationality of an ICSID member on the date on which the claimant and the host state consented to arbitration. Where the consents are given on different days, then the relevant date is that on which the last of the parties gave consent,[228] essentially the same position taken by the tribunal in *Siag & Vecchi.* Because the last party to give consent to BIT arbitration is virtually always the investor and because the investor generally consents at the time it submits a claim to arbitration, the holding of these two tribunals in effect means that the date of consent and the date when proceedings are instituted is the same. As a practical matter, these two awards reach the same result as the majority of awards discussed above: the claimant must have the requisite nationality on the date that proceedings are instituted.

In a couple of cases, the tribunal rejected attempts to create standing by changes in the nationality of ownership of a claim after the claim arose. In *Mihaly v. Sri Lanka*, a case arising under the United States-Sri Lanka BIT, a Canadian company assigned its claim against Sri Lanka to a U.S. company, which then sought to submit the claim to arbitration under the BIT. The tribunal held that it had no jurisdiction over the claim. The Canadian company, not having U.S. nationality, was not protected by, and thus had no claim under, the U.S. BIT. It could not assign to a U.S. company a claim that it did not have. In *Société Générale v. Dominican Republic*, a case arising under the France-Dominican Republic BIT, the tribunal agreed. It held that, where a claim arises while the investment is owned by an investor unprotected by any BIT, transfer of the investment to a covered investor will not confer jurisdiction upon the tribunal.[229]

The claim in *Waste Management v. Mexico*, a case arising under the NAFTA, raised the question whether the investor must disclose its nationality, thereby putting the host state on notice of the investor's right to treaty protection. The tribunal held that the host state's ignorance of the investor's nationality was irrelevant. The absence of a duty of disclosure was discussed in a different context in *Saluka Investments v. Czech Republic*, a case arising under the Netherlands-Czech Republic BIT. In that case, the tribunal held that an investor was under no duty to disclose to the host state its ultimate investment objectives.[230]

---

226 *Accord Soufraki v. United Arab Emirates* (Italy-United Arab Emirates BIT; Claimant was not an Italian national at the date of parties' consent to arbitration or the date the request was registered with ICSID).

227 *Accord Soufraki v. United Arab Emirates* (Italy-United Arab Emirates BIT).

228 Award Excerpts, para. 1.

229 Award, para. 111.

230 Partial Award, para. 232.

Where a case is submitted to ICSID, the claimant must also satisfy any ICSID nationality requirements. Article 25(2)(a) of the ICSID convention excludes from ICSID jurisdiction claims by individuals against the state of their own nationality, even if they also possess the nationality of another state. In *Champion Trading v. Egypt*, a case arising under the United States-Egypt BIT, the tribunal held that it would apply this rule unless to do so would lead to a result that is manifestly absurd or unreasonable. In that case, Egyptian nationals had relied upon their Egyptian nationality in making an investment in Egypt and would not be permitted to bring a claim against Egypt, notwithstanding that they also were U.S. nationals. This result did not allow Egypt to escape responsibility, however. The tribunal held that a claim by a U.S. corporate investor was within its jurisdiction, notwithstanding that the same dual nationals were shareholders of the corporation. Had the shareholders been nationals of a third country, the denial of benefits clause of the BIT potentially would have been applicable. The denial of benefits clause of the United States-Egypt BIT, however, does not apply where the investor is owned or controlled by nationals of either BIT party.

The question also has arisen concerning the effect of the end of the investment. In *Mondev v. United States*, a case arising under the NAFTA, the United States argued that because the enterprise that constituted the investment had failed prior to the entry into force of the NAFTA, there was no investment in existence when the NAFTA entered into force and therefore the claimant, who had owned the enterprise, could not be considered an investor within the meaning of the NAFTA. The tribunal, however, rejected this argument. It held that once an investment exists, it is protected by the NAFTA even after the enterprise has failed. As long as the investor still had subsisting interests in the investment, the investor could bring a claim.

The tribunal followed the *Mondev* award in *Chevron v. Ecuador*, a case arising under the United States-Ecuador BIT, in which the investor had largely liquidated its investments in the form of oil concession agreements by transferring ownership to PetroEcuador, the national oil company of Ecuador. The claimants nevertheless retained some legal claims for money arising out of their oil extraction and production activities. Thus, the tribunal held, the claimants continued to own an investment and had standing to assert violations of the BIT with respect to those claims.

Similarly, in *Jan de Nul v. Egypt*, a case arising under the 2002 BLEU-Egypt BIT, the tribunal held that it had jurisdiction over a claim not withstanding that the investment had ceased to exist prior to the BIT's entry into force. In that case, the claimants had submitted breach of contract actions to local courts prior to the BIT's entry into force. After the treaty entered into force, the local court issued a judgment adverse to the claimants, on which they based their claim before the tribunal for violations of the BIT. The tribunal noted that to deny jurisdiction would defeat "the entire logic of investment protection treaties."[231]

Where the investor has standing to bring a claim, the nationality of the investment generally is irrelevant. In *Waste Management v. Mexico*, a case arising under the NAFTA, a U.S. company brought a claim for injury to its investment in Mexico.

231 Decision on Jurisdiction, para. 135 (quoting the claimants' reply).

Mexico objected that the investment did not have U.S. nationality and therefore the tribunal was without jurisdiction. The tribunal rejected that argument, holding that nothing in the NAFTA required that the investment have same nationality as the investor. The tribunal explained that

> When a treaty spells out in detail and with precision the requirements for maintaining a claim, there is no room for implying into the treaty additional requirements, whether based on alleged requirements of general international law in the field of diplomatic protection or otherwise.[232]

As noted in Section 10.2.1.4, many BITs include a clause pursuant to Article 25(2)(b) of the ICSID convention under which the locally incorporated investment may submit a claim to arbitration against the host state, as long as the investment is owned or controlled by the other BIT party. One issue that arises involving this clause concerns the meaning of "own" and "control" for purposes of Article 25(2)(b). Some tribunals have held that these words do not refer to ultimate or actual control. Thus, an intermediate company in the chain of ownership has been held to own or control the investment, notwithstanding that ultimate control was exercised by an investor that owned or controlled the intermediate company.

For example, in *Aguas del Tunari v. Bolivia*, a case arising under the Netherlands-Bolivia BIT, the claimant was a Bolivian company that had entered into a concession agreement to provide water and sewerage services to the Bolivian city of Cochabamba. The Bolivian company was owned by four Bolivian companies, a Uruguayan company, and a Luxembourgian company. The Luxembourgian company was owned by a Dutch company, which was owned by a second Dutch company, which was jointly owned by a third Dutch company and an Italian company. The third Dutch company was owned by a U.S. company. Public criticism of the concession agreement led Bolivia to rescind the agreement, whereupon the concessionaire submitted a claim to arbitration under the Netherlands-Bolivia BIT. The Bolivian claimant contended that the tribunal had jurisdiction under the Netherlands-Bolivia BIT because the claimant was owned or controlled by the Dutch company (that owned the Luxembourgian company), within the meaning of Article 25(2)(b) of the ICSID convention, and therefore should be treated as a Dutch national for purposes of arbitration. Bolivia responded that ultimate control lay not in any Dutch company, but the U.S. company that owned the Dutch companies, and thus the Dutch company did not own or control the concessionaire. The tribunal, however, rejected Bolivia's argument, finding that the reference to own or control in Article 25(2)(b) referred to the legal capacity to control the investment, not to the ultimate control in fact. The first and second Dutch companies had legal authority over the investment and therefore controlled it. The tribunal noted that the second Dutch company was not a mere shell and that it had other projects and employees of its own. Thus, the Bolivian company could claim the nationality of the Dutch companies for purposes of the arbitration and could submit a claim against Bolivia under the Netherlands-Bolivia BIT.

---

232 Award, para. 85.

The decision on jurisdiction in *Aucoven v. Venezuela*, a case arising under a concession agreement and not involving any BIT, similarly held that ownership and control should be defined according to the potential to control rather than actual control. In that case, the claimant was a Venezuelan company that initially was majority owned by Mexican companies. As a result of the peso crisis in Mexico, Mexican companies encountered difficulties conducting certain international operations. Accordingly, with the approval of Venezuela, 75 percent of the shares in Aucoven were transferred to a U.S. corporation that was wholly owned by one of Aucoven's Mexican owners. Thus, Mexican nationals continued to own or control Aucoven, but through a U.S. intermediary. Thereafter, Aucoven's shareholders adopted a resolution that Aucoven was controlled by the U.S. company for purposes of the ICSID convention. When disputes arose concerning the concession agreement, the Mexican government attempted to intervene on behalf of Aucoven. After such attempts proved unsuccessful, Aucoven submitted a claim to arbitration against Venezuela invoking Venezuela's consent to ICSID jurisdiction under Clause 64 of the agreement. The tribunal found that Clause 64 included Venezuela's consent to ICSID jurisdiction provided that Aucoven's stock was majority owned by a national of an ICSID party. Because the majority of Aucoven's stock was owned by a U.S. company and the United States was a party to the ICSID convention, the condition to Venezuela's consent appeared to have been satisfied, which meant that the tribunal had jurisdiction. Venezuela contended that Article 25(2)(b) of the ICSID convention required that the claimant, if incorporated under the laws of the host state, be owned or controlled by foreign nationals of a party to the ICSID convention and that Aucoven was not in reality owned or controlled by a U.S. national. Rather, "effective control" rested with the Mexican company that owned the U.S. company. Mexico was not an ICSID party. The tribunal held that the parties were free to define what was meant by "control" as long as the definition was reasonable and not inconsistent with the purposes of the ICSID convention. The tribunal found majority ownership to be a reasonable criterion for determining control because shareholding confers the possibility of exercising control. The tribunal rejected Venezuela's argument that Article 25(2)(b) of the ICSID convention requires that ownership or control be limited to ultimate control, saying that the parties were within their discretion in choosing a reasonable definition of ownership or control and that the tribunal would not disturb the parties' agreement. The tribunal went on to observe that the U.S. company was not a mere corporation of convenience, noting that it had about twenty subsidiaries in different countries and was subject to the regulatory authority of the United States, a country not considered to be a tax or regulatory haven.

At least one tribunal has disagreed, however. In *TSA v. Argentina*, a case arising under the Netherlands-Argentina BIT, the tribunal held that Article 25(2)(b) adopts the concept of a control as an exception to a formal test of nationality and that, consistent with this departure from formalism, the concept of control should be interpreted to refer to ultimate control.[233] In that case, the claimant was an Argentine company wholly owned by a Dutch company. The tribunal found that on the date of consent to arbitration

233 Decision on Jurisdiction, paras. 134–154.

the Dutch company was subject to the ultimate control of an Argentine national and thus the claimant was also ultimately controlled by an Argentine national. Accordingly, the claimant could not be treated as a Dutch company.[234]

In *PSEG v. Turkey*, a case arising under the United States-Turkey BIT, Turkey argued that the local company could not submit a claim because it had not existed at the time many of the events giving rise to the dispute occurred and therefore the BIT language requiring it to have been owned or controlled immediately prior to the events giving rise to the dispute could not apply to it. The tribunal rejected this argument, noting that the local company was a legal successor to a branch of the foreign investor that had existed at the time those disputes occurred. As an alternative ground for its decision that the local company had standing, the tribunal found that some of the events giving rise to the dispute arose after the local company was incorporated.

Questions of proof sometimes arise. For example, in *AES v. Argentina*, a case arising under the United States-Argentina BIT, Argentina argued that sworn statements were insufficient to demonstrate ownership or control, but the tribunal rejected that argument.

10.2.3.1.3 CONSENT TO ARBITRATION

As noted in Section 10.2.1.1, an investor-state arbitral tribunal has jurisdiction over a claim only if the disputing parties have consented. Tribunals have demanded little in the formalities of the parties' expression of consent, as long as the consent is evidenced in writing. In *American Manufacturing & Trading v. Zaire*, a case arising under the United States-D.R. Congo BIT, the tribunal held that the host state's consent to arbitration combined with the investor's implied consent to arbitrate in its notice of arbitration constituted the required agreement to arbitrate, including in particular the agreement in writing required by Article 25(6) of the ICSID convention. This is the rule universally followed. That is, the agreement to arbitrate may consist of the host state's consent expressed in a BIT and the investor's implied consent through its submission to arbitration. The agreement to arbitration need not be embodied in a single instrument.

In *Wena Hotels v. Egypt*, the United Kingdom-Egypt BIT provided that, if the investor consents in writing to submission of a dispute to investor-state arbitration, then either party may submit the dispute to arbitration. Egypt objected that the investor had not followed this procedure, but then withdrew its objection, acknowledging that the procedural defect was "easily rectified" and that sustaining the objection would have served only to delay the proceedings.[235] In *SGS v. Pakistan*, the Switzerland-Pakistan BIT included a provision similar to that in the United Kingdom-Egypt BIT. The claimant complied with the requirement of a separate consent, although it failed to observe the waiting period, a defect that the tribunal held not to defeat its jurisdiction.[236]

---

234 Decision on Jurisdiction, para. 162.

235 Decision on Jurisdiction, Section VII.

236 Decision on Jurisdiction, paras. 183–184.

In *CSOB v. Slovak Republic*, a case arising under the Czech Republic-Slovak Republic BIT, the tribunal held that a contract providing that it was to be governed by a BIT with an investor-state disputes provision would be construed as consent to arbitration by the host state regardless of whether the BIT ever entered into force.

Further, a host state's consent to ICSID arbitration is valid, even when given before the state has acceded to the ICSID convention, although it is conditioned on eventual accession.[237] Article 25(4) of the ICSID convention allows parties to notify ICSID of classes of disputes that they would or would not consider submitting to ICSID jurisdiction, but that notice does not qualify the terms of the consent given in a BIT.[238]

Once the consent is given, it may not be withdrawn unilaterally[239] nor may a party impose additional conditions on its consent.[240] Consent given by a subsidiary has been treated as if given by the parent.[241]

Not every tribunal has applied the language of consent to arbitration consistently with its ordinary meaning. In *SGS v. Pakistan*, the Switzerland-Pakistan BIT contained the parties' consent to "disputes with respect to investments." Thus, the language was not limited to disputes alleging violations of the BIT. The tribunal held, however, that this language described the factual, not the legal basis, of claims within the tribunal's jurisdiction. Accordingly, a claim not involving an allegation of a BIT violation and resting exclusively on contract that contained a choice of forum clause designating a different forum would not be treated as within the consent of the parties. The tribunal did assume jurisdiction over claims alleging BIT violations. The tribunal's narrow reading of the consent language has not been followed by other tribunals. Rather, other tribunals have held that language such as that in the Switzerland-Pakistan BIT permits claims not involving allegations of BIT violations to be submitted to investor-state arbitration,[242] although contract claims in many cases may be outside the tribunal's jurisdiction because of a choice of forum clause in the contract.[243]

10.2.3.1.4 EXISTENCE OF AN INVESTMENT DISPUTE

Under the ICSID convention, an ICSID tribunal has jurisdiction over any "legal dispute" arising directly out of an investment.[244] Tribunals thus have addressed on numerous occasions the question of whether a claim was a legal dispute.

In *Lanco v. Argentina*, a case arising under the United States-Argentina BIT, the tribunal relied on language from the Report of the Executive Directors of the World Bank

237 *Generation Ukraine v. Ukraine* (United States-Ukraine BIT).

238 *PSEG v. Turkey* (United States-Turkey BIT).

239 *Lanco v. Argentina* (United States-Argentina BIT), Preliminary Decision on Jurisdiction, para. 41; *Plama v. Bulgaria* (Energy Charter Treaty), Decision on Jurisdiction, para. 140; *Generation Ukraine v Ukraine* (United States-Ukraine BIT), Award, para. 12.6.

240 *Generation Ukraine v. Ukraine* (United States-Ukraine BIT).

241 *See B.A.R.I. v. D.R. Congo* (No BIT applicable), Award, paras.10–12.

242 *See, e.g., Jan de Nul v. Egypt* (1977 BLEU-Egypt BIT and 2002 BLEU-Egypt BIT), Award, para. 137; *BG Group v. Argentina* (United Kingdom-Argentina BIT), Award, para. 181.

243 *See* Section 10.2.3.2.4.

244 ICSID convention, Art. 25(1).

on the ICSID convention that since has been relied on by numerous other tribunals.[245] The language states that "[t]he expression 'legal dispute' has been used to make clear that while conflicts of rights are within the jurisdiction of the Center, mere conflicts of interest are not. The dispute must concern the existence or scope of a legal right or obligation, or the nature or extent of the reparation to be made for breach of a legal obligation."[246] The tribunal found that a legal dispute existed because the claimant had alleged violations of various BIT obligations.

Another commonly cited definition of a dispute is that applied in *AES v. Argentina*, another case arising under the United States-Argentina BIT. The definition, which is taken from the judgment of the Permanent Court of International Justice in the *Mavrommatis* case[247] and which was later adopted by the International Court of Justice judgment in the *Case concerning East Timor*,[248] defines a "dispute" as "a disagreement on a point of law or fact, a conflict of legal views or interests between parties." The claimant was alleging violations of several BIT provisions and thus the tribunal found a dispute to exist. In *El Paso Energy v. Argentina*, yet another case arising under the United States-Argentina BIT, applying the same definition the tribunal rejected Argentina's argument that the dispute was not a legal dispute because it involved contract rights. The claimant had formulated its claims as alleged violations of the BIT and this was sufficient to create a dispute for jurisdictional purposes. A tribunal composed of two of the three arbitrators that sat in the *El Paso* case applied the same definition and reached the same conclusion in *Pan American Energy v. Argentina*, yet another case arising under the United States-Argentina BIT.[249]

Still another approach is that taken in *Total v. Argentina*, a case arising under the France-Argentina BIT. In that case, the tribunal did not adopt either definition but found that the case involved a legal dispute because it involved an allegation of a violation of the BIT.[250]

Argentina has argued in a number of cases that an ICSID tribunal was without jurisdiction because the dispute concerned general measures adopted by Argentina, not measures directed specifically at the investment. Thus, Argentina alleged, the disputes was not one arising "directly" out of an investment. In *CMS Gas Transmission v. Argentina*, a case arising under the United States-Argentina BIT, the tribunal rejected this argument, finding that it had jurisdiction over measures that directly affect the

245 *Lanco v. Argentina* (United States-Argentina BIT), Preliminary Decision, para. 47. *See also Azuriz v. Argentina* (United States-Argentina BIT), Decision on Jurisdiction, para. 58; *National Grid v. Argentina* (United Kingdom-Argentina BIT), Decision on Jurisdiction, para. 160; *Jan de Nul v. Egypt* (1977 and 2002 Belgium-Luxembourg Economic Union-Egypt BITs), Decision on Jurisdiction, para. 74.

246 Report of the Executive Directors on the Convention on the Settlement of Investment Disputes between States and Nationals of Other States, para. 26.

247 (Greece v. Great Britain), Judgment of August 30, 1924, PCIJ Ser. A, No. 2.

248 1995 ICJ Rep. 89, section 99.

249 *See also Impregilo v. Pakistan* (Italy-Pakistan BIT), Decision on Jurisdiction, para. 302; *Empresa Lucchetti v. Peru* (Chile-Peru BIT), Award, para. 382.

250 Decision on Jurisdiction, para. 68.

investment and that violate legally binding commitments. Other tribunals have been in accord.[251]

10.2.3.1.5 HYPOTHETICALITY AND TIMING OF THE DISPUTE

Tribunals have held that a dispute must not be merely hypothetical, but must have some practical consequence.[252] In *AES v. Argentina*, for example, after citing this requirement, the tribunal found that Argentina's alleged violations of the United States-Argentina BIT were claimed to have adversely affected the claimant's $1 billion investment, thereby causing the claimant to incur certain losses. The tribunal found these allegations sufficient to meet the requirement that the dispute have practical consequences.

The question of whether the dispute was merely hypothetical also arose in *Enron v. Argentina*, still another case arising under the United States-Argentina BIT. In that case, the claimant was contesting Argentina's assessment of a tax, the collection of which had been enjoined by the Argentine Supreme Court. Argentina argued that the dispute was only hypothetical because the tax had not been collected and might never be. The tribunal observed that, once the tax has been assessed and the payment ordered, a liability exists irrespective of whether the taxes are actually collected. Thus, the tribunal found a sufficient dispute to establish its jurisdiction.

Argentina argued that the dispute was hypothetical in *Siemens v. Argentina*, a case arising under the Germany-Argentina BIT, on the ground that the claim was submitted while administrative appeals were pending in Argentine courts. Citing the definition of dispute adopted by the International Court of Justice in the *East Timor* case, discussed in Section 10.2.3.1.4, the tribunal found that the dispute was not hypothetical. The appeals had been rejected and, in any event, the claim before the tribunal addressed matters beyond the measures on which the appeal was based.

In *Pan American Energy v. Argentina*, a case arising under the United States-Argentina BIT, Argentina again argued that the dispute was hypothetical because no actual harm had yet occurred. The tribunal observed that investment disputes often arise from situations where continuing adverse effects on the claimant exist and that not all of the harm to the claimant will have occurred yet. In any event, the tribunal held that the claimant had made a prima facie case that some injury already had occurred and that the full extent of the injury would be a matter for the merits phase. The claimant was not limited to claiming compensation only for that damage that had occurred as of when the jurisdictional issue was under consideration.

In *Micula v. Romania*, a case arising under the Sweden-Romania BIT, Romania eliminated certain incentives previously available to the claimants, such as exemptions from customs duties. Romania objected that the tribunal lacked jurisdiction because no harm had been suffered. The tribunal rejected this argument, noting that the claimants

---

251 *See LG&E v. Argentina* (United States-Argentina BIT); *Total v. Argentina* (France-Argentina BIT); *Suez & Interaguas v. Argentina* (France-Argentina BIT, Spain-Argentina BIT); *Suez & Vivendi v. Argentina* (France-Argentina BIT, Spain-Argentina BIT, United Kingdom-Argentina BIT).

252 *See* Christoph Schreuer, *The ICSID Convention: A Commentary* 102 (2001).

had alleged that they had suffered losses and that, based on the facts alleged, Romania's measures were capable of having already caused loss to the claimants.[253]

In other cases, the respondent has argued that, while a dispute exists, the dispute arose before the BIT entered into force and, therefore, is outside the tribunal's jurisdiction. This problem is discussed in Section 4.4.

In still other cases, the respondent has argued that the dispute was submitted too late. A few BITs require that the dispute be submitted to arbitration within a certain number of years of when it arose. In *Feldman v. Mexico*, a case arising under the NAFTA, the tribunal held that the requirement that the claimant "make a claim" within three years is satisfied where the claimant submits its notice of arbitration within three years of when the claimant knew or should have known that the dispute existed. The tribunal in *Feldman* also rejected the claimant's argument that the limitations period was suspended as a result of an agreement reached with Mexico, although the tribunal did acknowledge that the limitations period could be suspended under some circumstances.[254]

The United States raised the three-year limitations period as a defense in *Grand River Enterprises v. United States*, another case arising under the NAFTA. In that case, the tribunal barred all claims with respect to measures of which the claimants were aware or should have been aware prior to the beginning of the period. In finding that these claims were barred, the tribunal explicitly relied upon the constructive notice language of the NAFTA.[255] The tribunal allowed claims regarding statutory amendments that occurred within the three-year period, even though those claims required consideration of events that occurred prior to the commencement of the three year period. In so holding, the tribunal relied upon the decision of the Permanent Court of Justice in *The Electricity Company of Sofia and Bulgaria*,[256] where it said that, while "a dispute may presuppose the existence of some prior situation or fact . . . it does not follow that the dispute arises in regard to the situation or fact."[257] Thus, the tribunal could consider events that occurred outside the three-year limitations period in assessing the legality of the measure adopted within the limitations period.

The United States also raised the defense of the three-year limitations period in *Mondev v. United States*, yet another case arising under the NAFTA. In that case, the claimant had brought an unsuccessful action in Massachusetts state court against the Boston Redevelopment Authority for alleged wrongful acts that had occurred prior to the entry into force of the NAFTA and outside the three-year limitations period. The tribunal held that NAFTA obligations did not apply to conduct prior to the agreement's entry into force and thus it had jurisdiction only over a claim for denial of justice in the Massachusetts courts, which had adjudicated claimant's action after the NAFTA's entry into force. Because any alleged denial of justice occurred within the limitations period, the tribunal found no time bar with respect to the denial of justice claim.

253 Decision on Jurisdiction, paras. 137–138.

254 Award, para. 65.

255 Decision on Jurisdiction, para. 83.

256 PCIJ Series A/B No. 77, at p. 82.

257 Decision on Jurisdiction, para. 86.

The tribunal addressed the application of the limitations period to a continuing course of conduct in *UPS v. Canada*, still another case arising under the NAFTA. The tribunal held that the continuing conduct restarts the limitations period, allowing a claimant to submit a claim even if more than three years has elapsed since the conduct began. The amount of compensation to be awarded, however, would be limited to that which was suffered during the three-year period and not that suffered since the conduct began.[258]

10.2.3.2 Submission of the Dispute to Local Remedies

10.2.3.2.1 THE EXHAUSTION OF LOCAL REMEDIES REQUIREMENT

One of the issues that arises with the greatest frequency in international investment arbitration is whether a claim must be resolved through local remedies rather than investor-state arbitration. As was held in *Generation Ukraine v. Ukraine*, a case arising under the United States-Ukraine BIT, the exhaustion of local remedies is not required as a condition of submitting a claim to ICSID arbitration, unless the instrument containing the parties' consent to arbitration so requires.[259] Indeed, in the case of ICSID arbitration, Article 26 of the ICSID convention explicitly excludes a requirement of exhaustion of remedies, unless demanded by the host country's consent to jurisdiction. Further, the tribunal held that once an investor has accepted the host state's offer to arbitrate set forth in the BIT, no further conditions on arbitration may be imposed unilaterally by either party. In that case, the BIT did not expressly require exhaustion of local remedies and therefore exhaustion was not required. At the same time, as the tribunal explained in *Siemens v. Argentina*, a case arising under the Germany-Argentina BIT, BITs do not restrict the right of an investor to submit a dispute to local courts, but merely provide an additional remedy otherwise unavailable.[260]

Some BITs require that a claim be submitted to local remedies before it may be submitted to arbitration, but do not require that those remedies be exhausted. Typically, the claimant must pursue local remedies for a period of time before the claim may be submitted to international arbitration, but then may submit the claim to international arbitration upon the expiration of the prescribed time.[261] Such a clause was at issue in *Siemens v. Argentina*. The tribunal held that the provision did not require exhaustion

---

258 Award, paras. 23–30.

259 Citing *Lanco v. Argentina* (United States-Argentina BIT). *Accord Metalclad v. Mexico* (NAFTA); *CME v. Czech Republic*, (Netherlands-Czech Republic BIT) Partial Award, para. 416; *AES v. Argentina* (United States-Argentina BIT), Decision on Jurisdiction, para. 69; *LG&E v. Argentina* (United States-Argentina BIT), Decision on Jurisdiction, para. 77; *Eastern Sugar v. Czech Republic* (Netherlands-Czech Republic BIT), Partial Award, 2007, para. 141; *RosInvestCo v. Russia* (United Kingdom-Russia BIT), Decision on Jurisdiction, para. 153; *Sedelmeyer v. Russia* (Germany-Russia BIT), Award, para. 3.7; *Saipem v. Bangladesh* (Italy-Bangladesh BIT), Decision on Jurisdiction, para. 151 (exhaustion still required for denial of justice claim).

260 Decision on Jurisdiction, para. 107. As discussed in Section 10.2.1.3, however, under some BITs submission of a dispute to investor-state arbitration may result in a loss of the right to pursue local remedies.

261 *See* Section 10.2.1.3.

of local remedies or even a prior decision by the local courts, but merely the passage of time and the continued existence of the dispute at the end of that time.[262]

An investor may seek to evade a requirement that local remedies be utilized. In *Maffezini v. Spain*, the Argentina-Spain BIT provided that, if an investment dispute could not be amicably settled, it "shall" be submitted to the courts of the host state.[263] The BIT further provided that the dispute could be submitted to international arbitration only if no decision had been rendered 18 months after the dispute had been submitted to local courts or a decision had been rendered but the dispute continued.[264] The claimant, however, had not submitted the dispute to local courts. The tribunal held that the claimant's failure to comply with the obligation to utilize local remedies ordinarily would defeat jurisdiction. The tribunal nevertheless could exercise jurisdiction in that case because the Argentina-Spain BIT included an MFN treatment provision that allowed the claimant to enjoy the benefit of a disputes provision in the Chile-Spain BIT under which claimants were authorized to proceed to arbitration without first submitting the dispute to local courts. As discussed in Section 7.2.3, the issue of whether a requirement to submit a dispute to local remedies can be avoided in this way has been addressed by several other tribunals, which generally have held that it may be. As discussed in Section 10.2.3.2.2, a tribunal has held that language providing that a dispute "shall" be submitted to previously-agreed procedures does not require the investor to utilize the procedures, but entitles the investor to utilize such procedures if it so wishes.

In *Wintershall v. Argentina*, a case arising under the Germany-Argentina BIT, the tribunal held that the word "shall" in a clause requiring submission of the dispute to local remedies was obligatory.[265] The claimant had declined to submit the dispute to local remedies on the ground that the Argentine courts would not have been able to resolve it in 18 months and that, in any event, the Argentine judiciary was not independent. The tribunal held that, because the claimant had not satisfied the requirement that it submit its dispute to local remedies for 18 months, the claim was outside the tribunal's jurisdiction.

In *BG Group v. Argentina*, a case arising under the United Kingdom-Argentina BIT, the BIT similarly required that a claim be submitted to local remedies for 18 months prior to submission to investor-state arbitration. The tribunal held, however, that this requirement would be excused where the host state prevented or hindered access to the local courts.[266] Further, the fact that a negotiation process was available to resolve the claims would not affect the jurisdiction of the tribunal.[267]

In *TSA v. Argentina*, a case arising under the Netherlands-Argentina BIT, the BIT again required submission of the dispute to local remedies for 18 months or until a

---

262 *See also Camuzzi v. Argentina* (Belgium-Luxembourg Economic Union-Argentina BIT), Decision on Jurisdiction.

263 Argentina-Spain BIT, Art. X(2).

264 Argentina-Spain BIT, Art. X(3).

265 Award, para. 119.

266 Award, para. 147.

267 Award, para. 239.

final decision was reached, whichever came first. The tribunal held that the investor was required to utilize local remedies to the extent that they provided a fair chance of satisfaction. The tribunal held that the term "final decision" should be interpreted independently of local law, but that nevertheless no final decision had been reached nor had 18 months elapsed. Only 3 of the 18 months remained, however, at the time the investor submitted the claim to arbitration and the tribunal found it unlikely local remedies could provide satisfaction in the time remaining. To dismiss the claim for failure to exhaust the entire 18 months under those circumstances would be formalistic and would serve little purpose, inasmuch as the claimant could merely reinstitute the claim after the three months passed.[268]

Although BITs typically do not require exhaustion of local remedies, exhaustion may be implicitly required in one situation: where the claim is for denial of justice. In *Loewen v. United States*, a case arising under the NAFTA, the Canadian claimant was sued by a U.S. company in a U.S. court, where the jury rendered a $500,000,000 verdict against the claimant following a trial characterized by numerous references to the claimant's foreign nationality. The claimant chose not to appeal the trial court's judgment and settled the dispute with the U.S. company. The claimant then submitted a claim for denial of justice to investor-state arbitration. The tribunal held that where the claimant has not exhausted all remedies provided by the judicial system, no claim for denial of justice can arise. As discussed in Section 10.4, other tribunals have concurred that a denial of justice claim may not be submitted to investor-state arbitration unless local remedies have been exhausted. In *Chevron v. Ecuador*, a case arising under the United States-Ecuador BIT, the tribunal agreed that exhaustion was required for a denial of justice claim and noted that whether exhaustion had occurred was an issue not of jurisdiction, but of the merits of the claim. [269]

10.2.3.2.2 PREVIOUSLY AGREED PROCEDURES

Some BITs require submission of a claim to "previously-agreed" procedures. The tribunal held in *Lanco v. Argentina*, a case arising under the United States-Argentina BIT, that the phrase refers to procedures to which the parties agreed prior to the time the dispute arose, as opposed to prior to the entry into force of the BIT. In *PSEG v. Turkey*, the United States-Turkey BIT provided, at Article VI(2), that in the event that a dispute could not be resolved amicably, it "shall" be submitted to previously-agreed dispute settlement procedures. Article VI(3) went on to state that, in the event that the dispute was not submitted to previously-agreed dispute procedures, the investor could submit the dispute to arbitration. The tribunal held that these provisions did not require submission of the dispute to previously-agreed procedures. Rather, the word "shall" meant only that the host state was bound to such procedures in the event that they were invoked by the investor. The investor had the discretion, however, to forego such procedures and to submit the claim to investor-state arbitration under the BIT. Otherwise, the language would nullify one of the principal features of the BIT, the right to investor-state arbitration. This interpretation is consistent with the underlying intent

268 Award, para. 112.
269 Interim Award, para. 235.

of that BIT.[270] By contrast, as discussed in Section 10.2.3.2.1, tribunals generally have held that BIT language requiring that a dispute shall be submitted to local remedies does require that local remedies be utilized.

10.2.3.2.3 VOLUNTARY SUBMISSION TO LOCAL REMEDIES

Host states sometimes have argued that prior submission of a dispute to local remedies deprived the investor-state arbitral tribunal of jurisdiction. In *Azinian v. Mexico*, a case arising under the NAFTA, the tribunal held that submission of a dispute to local remedies does not oust the tribunal of jurisdiction, in the absence of an election of remedies clause, such as those discussed below.

In *SGS v. Pakistan*, a case arising under the Switzerland-Pakistan BIT, the tribunal similarly noted that, in the absence of an election of remedies clause, the investor may submit a claim to the local courts and then, if dissatisfied, seek arbitration under the BIT. Because Article 26 of the ICSID convention provides that arbitration before ICSID is an exclusive remedy, once a claim is submitted to ICSID arbitration, the investor may not pursue the same claim before another forum.

Some BITs contain an election of remedies clause under which a dispute submitted to local courts may not thereafter be submitted to investor-state arbitration.[271] In *MCI Power v. Ecuador*, a case arising under the United States-Ecuador BIT, the tribunal observed that the choice under such a clause is irrevocable, even if the remedy chosen did not result in a final decision on the merits.[272] In several cases, the host state has sought to utilize the election of remedies clause to defeat the tribunal's jurisdiction by arguing that the dispute before the tribunal already had been submitted to local courts. These objections to jurisdiction generally have been unsuccessful because the tribunals have held that the dispute submitted to local courts was different from the dispute submitted to the tribunal, typically because the parties and causes of action were different.

For example, in *Genin v. Estonia*, a case arising under the United States-Estonia BIT, the claimant was a shareholder in an Estonian bank, which had lost its banking license. The bank had brought a local action on behalf of all shareholders, depositors, borrowers, and employees in the only available forum to have its license restored. The claimant, by contrast, brought a claim for losses he suffered as a result of BIT violations. Thus, the dispute in local courts was brought by a different claimant than the dispute before the tribunal and arose out of alleged violations of local law, while the dispute before the tribunal arose out of alleged BIT violations. The claimant also had filed a claim in U.S. courts, but the tribunal held that the U.S. litigation involved different issues than the claim before the tribunal. In short, the existence of these local proceedings did not divest the tribunal of jurisdiction under the election of remedies clause.

Similarly, in *Lauder v. Czech Republic*, a case arising under the United States-Czech Republic BIT, the respondent argued that the claimant should not be permitted to pursue remedies both in local courts and before an international tribunal. The tribunal

270 *See* Kenneth J. Vandevelde, *U.S. International Investment Agreements* 580 (2009).

271 *See* Section 10.2.1.3. *See generally* Schreuer, *supra* note 67.

272 Award, paras. 181–182.

held that the election of remedies clause did not divest it of jurisdiction because the claim submitted to local courts involved different parties and different causes of action and, therefore, the disputes were different. Double recovery would be prevented if the second deciding court or tribunal took into account any prior judgment or award in assessing compensation.

Similarly, in *Pan American Energy v. Argentina*, a case arising under the United States-Argentina BIT, the investor through its local company had submitted a claim to the Argentine courts seeking a declaration that a claim filed against the investor in U.S. courts was exclusively within the jurisdiction of the Argentine courts. The tribunal found that the submission of this dispute to the Argentine courts did not preclude the investor from submitting a dispute to international arbitration. The parties were different in that Argentina had not been a party to the local action. The causes of action also were different in that the local action was not based on an alleged violation of the BIT. Other tribunals reached the same result in, for example, *Champion Trading v. Argentina*, a case arising under the United States-Egypt BIT, *Azurix v. Argentina*, a case arising under the United States-Argentina BIT, and *LG&E v. Argentina*, another case arising under the United States-Argentina BIT[273].

In *CMS Gas Transmission v. Argentina*, yet another case arising under the United States-Argentina BIT, the local proceedings were initiated by the host state and the claimant's investment had intervened to protect its interests. That is, the investment's appearance in local courts was "defensive and reactive."[274] The tribunal held that its jurisdiction was not defeated by the local court proceedings. Not only were the parties and causes of action different, but the dispute before the local courts had not been submitted by the investor or the investment, but by Argentina.

Local proceedings were treated as defensive as well in *Enron v. Argentina*, still another case arising under the United States-Argentina BIT. In that case, the tribunal noted that the submissions made before the local courts were different from those before the tribunal, that they were submitted by the investment rather than by the investor, and that the investment's actions had mainly been in the defensive so as to oppose certain tax measures imposed upon it. The tribunal held that it had jurisdiction over the investor's claim,

In *Occidental v. Ecuador*, a case arising under the United States-Ecuador BIT, the tribunal held that the dispute submitted to local courts would be considered the same dispute as that submitted to investor-state arbitration only if it involved the same parties, object and cause of action. In that case, the dispute submitted to local courts arose out of an alleged breach of the tax laws of Ecuador, while the dispute submitted to the tribunal alleged violations of the BIT. The tribunal noted one further reason for allowing the dispute to be submitted to arbitration. Specifically, it noted that the "fork in the road" election of remedies clause[275] in the United States-Ecuador BIT presumes a choice and that the claimant in that case realistically had no choice, because local law required that the claim under local tax law be submitted to local courts within 20 days

273 Decision on Jurisdiction, paras. 75–76.

274 Decision on Jurisdiction, para. 78.

275 *See* Section 10.2.1.3.

or be lost, which as a practical matter compelled the claimant to pursue local remedies first in order to preserve its rights. Thus, the provision should not be permitted to divest the tribunal of jurisdiction.

In *MCI Power v. Ecuador*, another case arising under the United States-Ecuador BIT, the tribunal observed that the proceedings in local courts were commenced before the BIT entered into force and therefore the investor could not have made an election of remedies under the BIT. Thus, the election of remedies clause was not triggered by those proceedings.[276] The local proceedings did not divest the tribunal of jurisdiction over disputes that arose after the BIT entered into force.

In *Chevron v. Ecuador*, a case arising under the United States-Ecuador BIT, one of the claimants had filed several breach of contract actions against the Ecuadoran government in Ecuadoran courts. After well over a decade had passed without a decision in the cases, the claimants submitted a denial of justice claim to investor-state arbitration The tribunal held that the election of remedies provision of the BIT did not divest the tribunal of jurisdiction over a claim for denial of justice.[277]

Several cases involved the "No U Turn" election of remedies provision, which provides that, at the time the claimant submits the dispute to arbitration, the claimant must execute a waiver of the right to submit the dispute to local remedies.[278] In *Waste Management v. Mexico*, a case arising under the NAFTA, the tribunal dismissed the claim for lack of jurisdiction because the waiver was not sufficiently clear and categorical. Specifically, the waiver reserved to the claimants the right to submit to local remedies claims arising out of local law. The tribunal held that the purpose of the waiver was to prevent the claimant from submitting to local remedies claims arising out of the same measures, even if those claims were for violation of local law rather than the BIT. The tribunal found that the claimant's waiver failed to abandon local remedies to the extent required and thus the tribunal had no jurisdiction. The claim subsequently was resubmitted to arbitration accompanied by a different waiver.

Similarly, in *Methanex v. United States*, another case arising under the NAFTA, the tribunal held that a waiver submitted in May 2001 stated in the present tense could not be construed to apply to claims arising from a regulation not adopted until May 2003. Thus, no valid waiver of local remedies with respect to such claims had been made.

In *Vannessa Ventures v. Venezuela*, a case arising under the Canada-Venezuela BIT, an issue arose as to whether the claimant's waiver was sufficient to preclude further proceedings in local courts, as required by the "No U Turn" election of remedies clause. The tribunal held that the effect of the waiver was governed by Venezuelan law and that the interpretation of the Venezuelan Supreme Court would be determinative.[279]

In *Railroad Development v. Guatemala*, a case arising under the Central American Free Trade Agreement, the tribunal found the waiver defective as to a portion of the claim. Guatemala declined to permit the claimant to remedy its defective waiver and

---

276 The tribunal also held that it had no jurisdiction over disputes that arose prior to the BIT's entry into force.

277 Interim Award, para. 207.

278 *See* Section 10.2.1.3.

279 Decision on Jurisdiction, para. 88.

the tribunal held that it had no power to authorize remediation of a defective waiver.[280] The tribunal held that it had jurisdiction over the portion of the claim for which a valid waiver had been submitted.[281]

By contrast, in *International Thunderbird v. Mexico*, the tribunal held that failure to submit a waiver would not defeat the tribunal's jurisdiction, provided that the defect was remedied later. The tribunal noted that the goal of the waiver is to prevent inconsistent results and double recovery and that both of those goals had been satisfied by the claimant's subsequent submission of a waiver.

In *Encana v. Ecuador*, a case arising under the Canada-Ecuador BIT, the claimant did not execute a separate waiver, but included the waiver in the notice of arbitration. Ecuador requested that the tribunal order the claimant to execute a separate instrument formally attested by the claimant, which the tribunal found to be a reasonable request.[282] The tribunal also found that the language of the BIT expressly required, in the case of a claim on behalf of a locally incorporated subsidiary, that a waiver of local remedies be submitted by or on behalf of the subsidiary, but that nothing in the BIT required submission of a waiver by third country subsidiaries.[283] While the tribunal acknowledged that such a result might be thought anomalous, the tribunal found that the language of the BIT was clear and must be respected.

10.2.3.2.4 CHOICE OF FORUM CLAUSES DESIGNATING LOCAL REMEDIES

In numerous cases, the host state has argued that the claim is within the exclusive jurisdiction of the local courts because of a choice of forum clause in the contract on which the claim was based. Tribunals repeatedly have held, however, that they have jurisdiction over a claim involving a contract with a choice of forum clause conferring exclusive jurisdiction on a local forum if the claim is based on a violation of the BIT.

In *Lanco v. Argentina*, a case arising under the United States-Argentina BIT, the dispute arose out of a concession agreement under which the parties "agree[d] to the jurisdiction" of Argentine courts for all purposes derived from the agreement. The tribunal observed that the language of the concession agreement merely recognized the jurisdiction of the courts that would have existed even in the absence of the provision. Further, Article 26 of the ICSID convention provides that consent to ICSID jurisdiction is to the exclusion of any other remedy, unless otherwise stipulated. The consent to ICSID jurisdiction contained no such stipulation and, even to the extent that the language of the concession agreement were treated as such a stipulation, it did not divest the tribunal of jurisdiction, but merely diluted the presumption of the exclusivity of ICSID arbitration.[284]

In *Vivendi Universal v. Argentina*, a case arising under the France-Argentina BIT, the concession agreement provided that "For purposes of interpretation and application of this Contract the parties submit themselves to the exclusive jurisdiction of the

280 Decision on Jurisdiction, para. 61.
281 Decision on Jurisdiction, para. 75.
282 Decision on Jurisdiction, para. 19.
283 Decision on Jurisdiction, para. 20.
284 *Accord Siemens v. Argentina* (Germany-Argentina BIT), Decision on Jurisdiction, para. 181.

contentious Administrative Tribunals of Tucuman." The tribunal held that all of the claims arose from disputes concerning the alleged nonperformance of the contract and that, in accordance with the choice of forum clause in the contract, such disputes could be submitted only to local courts. The claimants could resort to ICSID arbitration only with respect to a claim for denial of justice by the local courts. An annulment committee, however, citing *Lanco*, held that the choice of forum clause did not affect the jurisdiction of the tribunal with respect to a claim based on the provisions of the BIT. It noted that the language of the choice of forum clause did not explicitly exclude the jurisdiction of an international tribunal. The committee went on to say that "[i]n a case where the essential basis of a claim brought before an international tribunal is a breach of contract, the tribunal will give effect to any valid choice of forum clause in the contract."[285] At the same time, "where 'the fundamental basis of the claim' is a treaty laying down an independent standard by which the conduct of the parties is to be judged, existence of an exclusive jurisdiction clause in a contract between the claimant and the respondent state or one of its subdivisions cannot operate as a bar to the application of the treaty standard."[286]

This has become the settled rule.[287] An investor may submit to investor-state arbitration disputes involving a contract with a choice of forum clause conferring exclusive jurisdiction on local fora if the claim is based on a violation of the BIT, even if the BIT was violated through a breach of contract. If the cause of action is breach of contract, the choice of forum clause in the contract will apply with respect to that cause of action and confer jurisdiction on the designated forum. At the jurisdictional phase, the tribunal will accept the claimant's characterization of its claim.[288]

As the discussion indicates, the earliest cases on this point involved contracts to which Argentina was a party. In response to the award in *Lanco* and the first award in *Vivendi*, Argentina added language to its choice of forum clauses expressly excluding all other fora. For example, in *Azurix v. Argentina*, a case arising under the United States-Argentina BIT, Clause 16.7 of the concession agreement provided that "[i]n the event of any dispute regarding the construction or execution of the Agreement" the

---

285 Decision on Annulment, para. 98.

286 *Id.* at para. 101.

287 *See, e.g., CMS v. Argentina* (United States-Argentina BIT); *Azurix v. Argentina* (United States-Argentina BIT); *Siemens v. Argentina* (Germany-Argentina BIT); *PSEG v. Turkey* (United States-Turkey BIT); *Camuzzi v. Argentina* (Belgo-Luxembourg Union-Argentina BIT); *Aguas del Tunari v. Bolivia* (Netherlands-Bolivia BIT); *Enron v. Argentina* (United States-Argentina BIT); *Occidental v. Ecuador* (United States-Ecuador BIT); *Eureko v. Poland* (Netherlands-Poland BIT); *Bayindir v. Pakistan* (Turkey-Pakistan BIT); *Sempra Energy v. Argentina* (United States-Argentina BIT); *AES v. Argentina* (United States-Argentina BIT); *LG&E v. Argentina* (United States-Argentina BIT); *Suez & Interaguas v. Argentina* (France-Argentina BIT, Spain-Argentina BIT); *Suez & Vivendi v. Argentina* (France-Argentina BIT, Spain-Argentina BIT, United Kingdom-Argentina BIT); *Total v. Argentina* (France-Argentina BIT); *National Grid v. Argentina* (United Kingdom-Argentina BIT); *Jan de Nul v. Egypt* (Belgo-Luxembourg Union-Egypt BIT); *Impregilo v. Pakistan* (Italy-Pakistan BIT), Decision on Jurisdiction, para. 287; *TSA v. Argentina* (Netherlands-Argentina BIT), Award, paras. 58–63.

288 *SGS v. Pakistan* (Switzerland-Pakistan BIT), Decision on Jurisdiction, para. 145; *Occidental v. Ecuador* (United States-Ecuador BIT), Award, para. 47.

parties "submit to the court for contentious-administrative matters of the city of La Plata, expressly waiving any other forum or jurisdiction that may correspond due to any reason." The tribunal held, however, that the additional language made no substantive difference. The designation of an exclusive forum by its nature implies the exclusion of all other fora and thus the waiver language was redundant. The tribunal also noted that the parties had disagreed concerning whether a private party even has capacity to waive treaty rights, but found that it did not need to resolve that issue given its interpretation of the choice of forum clause.[289]

In *Aguas del Tunari v. Bolivia*, a case arising under the Netherlands-Bolivia BIT, the tribunal did address in *dictum* the question avoided in *Azurix* and concluded that an investor could waive its rights to submit a claim to international arbitration, although the question did not need to be decided in that case because the choice of forum clause to which the parties agreed did not appear to constitute such a waiver. The clause provided that the concessionaire "recognizes the jurisdiction and competence" of the local courts. The tribunal held that a choice of forum clause should be treated as a waiver of the right to international arbitration only if it indicates that the parties "clearly" and "specifically" so intended.[290]

The tribunal adopted a unique approach in *SGS v. Philippines*, a case arising under the Switzerland-Philippines BIT. In that case, the tribunal held that the exclusive choice of forum clause in the contract did not divest it of jurisdiction for claims arising under the BIT. At the same time, however, the tribunal did not believe that the general language of the BIT's investor-state disputes provision was intended to override the more specific language in the choice of forum clause. Rather, the tribunal believed that the BIT was intended to reinforce contracts between the investor and the host state. Nor did the tribunal believe that the BIT should be treated as a subsequent agreement overriding the contract because the BIT and the contract were not instruments of the same character. Accordingly, the tribunal stayed its proceedings pending a determination of the amount payable under the contract, either by a judgment of the local courts or by agreement between the two disputing parties. Arbitrator Antonio Crivellaro dissented, taking the position that the tribunal should have determined the issue of whether the Philippines had violated the BIT provision requiring it to observe obligations with respect to an investment.

By contrast, in *SGS v. Pakistan*, a case arising under the Switzerland-Pakistan BIT and involving a similar choice of forum clause, the tribunal adopted the typical approach, under which it would exercise jurisdiction over claims that Pakistan's conduct with respect to the contract violated the BIT. The tribunal held that it had no jurisdiction over claims based on alleged breaches of the contract that did not also constitute alleged breaches of the BIT.

The general rule that investor-state arbitral tribunals have jurisdiction over claims for violation of the BIT, even in the face of an exclusive choice of forum clause in the

---

289 *See generally* Anne K. Hoffman, "The Investor's Right to Waive Access to Protection Under a Bilateral Investment Treaty," 22 *ICSID Review—Foreign Investment Law Journal* 69 (2007).

290 Decision on Jurisdiction, para. 119.

contract giving rise to the claim, has been followed where the BIT itself says that choice of forum clause shall apply. In *Salini v. Jordan*, Article 9(2) of the Italy-Jordan BIT provided that "the procedures foreseen in [an] investment agreement shall apply." The tribunal held that the dispute procedures prescribed by the contract applied only to claims based on breaches of the contract. Accordingly, the tribunal had jurisdiction over claims based on violations of BIT provisions, including provisions guaranteeing performance of contracts.

In the great the majority of cases, the tribunal has found the claim to be one for a violation of the BIT and thus the tribunal's jurisdiction was not precluded by the choice of forum clause. A notable exception, however, is *Joy Mining Machinery v. Egypt*, a case arising under the United Kingdom-Egypt BIT. The claimant had supplied letters of guarantee for the performance of mining equipment that it was selling to an Egyptian government agency. When a dispute arose concerning the performance of the equipment and the agency refused to release the guarantees, the claimant submitted the dispute to arbitration. The tribunal found that the dispute was an ordinary commercial dispute that did not involve even a prima facie claim of a treaty violation. Without an investment dispute, no ICSID tribunal could exercise jurisdiction. Thus, only the forum designated by the contract was available. The tribunal, in effect, followed the general rule, but found no claims based on the treaty.

10.2.3.3 Multiple Proceedings Where the claimant has alleged breaches of a contract that also violate the BIT, the possibility exists that a claimant will pursue its contracts claims in local courts and its BIT claims before an international tribunal simultaneously.[291] Several tribunals have held that the doctrine of *lis pendens* precludes arbitration of the BIT claims concurrently with the contract claims only if the parties and the causes of action are identical.[292] In *Sedelmeyer v. Russia*, a case arising under the Germany-Russia BIT, the claimant had submitted to local courts a claim for review of an expropriation, which had not been resolved. The tribunal noted that the right to expropriation review in the local courts was guaranteed by Article 4(3) of the BIT and that the pendency of such proceedings should not, under the *lis pendens* doctrine, preclude submission of a claim to investor-state arbitration.[293]

The possibility also exists that the same claim might be submitted to different international arbitral tribunals by different claimants. This occurred in *CME v. Czech Republic* and *Lauder v. Czech Republic*, where the investor, Ronald Lauder, submitted a claim to a tribunal under the United States-Czech Republic BIT, while CME Czech

291 *See generally* Katia Yannaca-Small, "Parallel Proceedings," in *The Oxford Handbook of International Investment Law* (Peter Muchlinski, Frederico Ortino, and Christoph Schreuer, eds. 2008); Giles Cuniberti, "Parallel Litigation and Foreign Investment Dispute Settlement," 21 *ICSID Review—Foreign Investment Law Journal* 381 (2006).

292 *See, e.g., SGS v. Pakistan* (Switzerland-Pakistan BIT; different causes of action); *Lauder v. Czech Republic* (different parties and different causes of action); *Azurix v. Argentina* (United States-Argentina BIT; different parties and causes of action); *Bayindir v. Pakistan* (Turkey-Pakistan BIT; tribunal will not stay claim absent compelling reason); *LLC AMTO v. Ukraine* (Energy Charter Treaty), Award, para. 71.

293 Award, para. 2.4.2

Republic B.V., a company owned by that investor, submitted a claim under the Netherlands-Czech Republic BIT. The claimants proposed that both claims be heard by the same tribunal, but the Czech Republic declined to consent to a consolidated proceeding. Both tribunals held that they had jurisdiction over the claims and neither tribunal stayed its proceedings pending resolution of the claim before the other tribunal. The *Lauder* tribunal observed that dual recovery would not be permitted and that the second tribunal to issue an award, if it was in favor of the claimant, would take account of any compensation already awarded by the first tribunal.

10.2.3.4 Other Procedural Conditions for Submission of a Claim

10.2.3.4.1 PRIOR CONSULTATIONS OR NEGOTIATIONS

Many BITs provide that, prior to submitting a claim to investor-state arbitration, the disputing parties shall or should seek to resolve the dispute amicably through consultations or negotiations. Some tribunals have addressed the question of whether the parties have sought to resolve the dispute amicably. No tribunal appears to have declined jurisdiction under a BIT because of a failure to consult or negotiate. First, a tribunal is likely to find virtually any effort to negotiate to constitute consultations or negotiations.[294] Typically, some effort at amicable resolution has been made and tribunals generally find such efforts sufficient. In *Salini v. Morocco*, a case arising under the Italy-Morocco BIT, the tribunal observed that the attempt to consult should include the existence of the grounds for the complaint and the desire to negotiate a resolution, but need not be complete or detailed.[295] Documents submitted to the Moroccan government were sufficient to put Morocco on notice of the dispute and that met the treaty's specification that any dispute "should, if possible, be resolved amicably." In *Ethyl Corp. v. Canada*, a case arising under the NAFTA, the tribunal found that the claimant had sought to resolve the dispute amicably, even though moments prior to the claimant's meeting with Canadian officials it received a fax stating that "apparently it needs to be clarified that, in our view, today's meeting is not a consultation" and that none of the officials present at the meeting purported to have authority to consult or negotiate.[296] In *Sedelmeyer v. Russia*, a case arising under the Germany-Russia BIT, the claimant had made numerous attempts to resolve his dispute with the Russian government, but the government had refused to meet with him. The tribunal rejected the respondent's

---

294 *See, e.g., Azurix v. Argentina* (United States-Argentina BIT; letter to Argentine president, repeated pleas for assistance sufficient); *Tokios Tokeles v. Ukraine* (Lithuania-Ukraine BIT; letter to Ukrainian president, exchanges of letters with Ukrainian central government officials sufficient, even if such officials not authorized to negotiate); *Bogdanov v. Moldova* (Russia-Moldova BIT; letter by claimant and two from respondent sufficient); *Petrobart v. Kyrgyz Republic* (Energy Charter Treaty; three letters to Prime Minister sufficient, even though claimant was aware that the responsibility for the case had been delegated to three other individuals); *El Paso Energy v. Argentina* (United States-Argentina BIT; letter to government offering to negotiate sufficient); *Pan American Energy v. Argentina* (United States-Argentina BIT; letter to President and other officials sufficient).

295 *Accord Bayindir v. Pakistan* (Turkey-Pakistan BIT), Decision on Jurisdiction, para. 98.

296 Award on Jurisdiction, para. 78.

argument that the necessary efforts at amicable settlement had not been made, observing that, having refused to communicate with the claimant, "[t]he Respondent cannot now complain that measures have not been taken with a view to finding an amicable solution of the dispute."[297]

In any event, the prevailing view is that a failure to consult does not deprive the tribunal of jurisdiction. In *SGS v. Pakistan*, a case a rising under the Switzerland-Pakistan BIT, the tribunal found that consultations provisions are usually "directory and procedural" rather than "jurisdictional and mandatory." Accordingly, the tribunal said, compliance with such provisions is not a condition precedent to tribunal jurisdiction. To dismiss a claim and require the parties to consult, after which they could resubmit the claim to arbitration, would be inefficient.[298] Similarly, in *Bayindir v. Pakistan*, a case arising under the Turkey-Pakistan BIT, the tribunal held that a failure to comply with a notice requirement, intended to give the parties an opportunity to settle the dispute, did not deprive the tribunal of jurisdiction.[299] The tribunal observed that to require formal notice would result only in restarting the entire arbitral process, which was to no one's benefit, and that, in any event, Pakistan had never sought to engage in negotiations even after it became aware of the claim. In *LG&E v. Argentina*, a case arising under the United States-Argentina BIT, no negotiations had occurred, but the tribunal held that inasmuch as the six-month waiting period had elapsed, no bar to jurisdiction existed. By contrast, in *Generation Ukraine v. Ukraine*, a case arising under the United States-Ukraine BIT, the tribunal observed that it would be reluctant to treat the obligation to consult as merely procedural, although it did not need to reach the issue because the claimant's efforts to resolve the dispute were sufficient. Thus, the observation was *dictum*.

Where the treaty language is merely precatory on its face, clearly the obligation to consult should not be regarded as jurisdictional. Where the language is mandatory, treating the requirement as discretionary for the claimant is inconsistent with the treaty language as well as the general intent of such provisions, which is to notify the host country of the existence of a claim and to provide the host country an opportunity to resolve the claim without resort to arbitration. Yet, to require that consultations actually occur would allow the host state to defeat tribunal jurisdiction merely by refusing to negotiate, which is also inconsistent with the general intent of BITs. Accordingly, where the provision is mandatory, the claimant should be required to notify the host state of the existence of a dispute, but providing such notification should discharge the claimant's obligation to consult. The question remains as to the consequences of failing to meet that obligation. The tribunal in *SGS v. Pakistan* was correct about the inefficiency of dismissing a claim only to allow resubmission once a letter has been sent notifying the host state of the dispute, particularly given that the notice of arbitration already will have provided notice of a dispute. At that point, the letter would serve no useful purpose. Thus, the tribunal should accept jurisdiction and proceed with the

---

297 Award, Part IV, para. 3.7.

298 *See also Ethyl Corp. v. Canada* (NAFTA); *Lauder v. Czech Republic* (United States-Czech Republic BIT); *Bayindir v. Pakistan* (Turkey-Pakistan BIT).

299 Decision on Jurisdiction, para. 100.

arbitration whether or not the claimant has sought to negotiate first. Nevertheless, where no attempt to negotiate was made, the claimant's failure to satisfy conditions imposed by the treaty may have prejudiced the host state, such as by exposing it to the needless embarrassment of a claim that it was prepared to resolve or by requiring it to prepare for a major arbitration with little warning, in contrast to the claimant, who may have spent months preparing for the arbitration before submitting the claim. Where prejudice has occurred, the tribunal should seek to ameliorate it or to award compensation to the host state by way of costs or an offset against any compensation awarded to the claimant. In most cases, it will be difficult to find prejudice arising from a mere failure to give notice because the effect of providing notice immediately prior to submission of a claim would be no different than providing no notice at all and thus failure to provide the notice would not have prejudiced the host state. The reality is that a negotiated settlement cannot be compelled and that a requirement to negotiate cannot reasonably be expected to require more than giving notice of a claim.

10.2.3.4.2 THE WAITING PERIOD

Many BITs require that a waiting period elapse before a claim may be submitted to investor-state arbitration. The prevailing view here again is that the failure to observe this requirement does not deprive the tribunal of jurisdiction.[300] If the waiting period is commenced by notice to the host state, the consequences of the claimant's failure to observe this requirement may be more substantial than the consequences of a failure to notify the host state of a dispute where no waiting period exists.

In *Ethyl Corporation v. Canada*, a case arising under the NAFTA, the tribunal found that the claimant had deliberately submitted a claim prior to the expiration of the waiting period for tactical reasons. The tribunal declined to dismiss the claim because, by the time of its decision, the waiting period had elapsed and the claimant could have resubmitted the claim immediately. Thus, the only effect of dismissal would have been to waste time and other resources. The tribunal found no prejudice to Canada, which had no intention of removing the measure of which the claimant complained. The tribunal, however, did require the claimant to pay the costs of the proceedings on the issue of whether the waiting period was a jurisdictional requirement.

In *Lauder v. Czech Republic*, a case arising under the United States-Czech Republic BIT, the tribunal agreed that the six-month waiting period was not a jurisdictional requirement. The tribunal allowed the claimant to submit a claim notwithstanding that only 17 days had elapsed from the date that the claimant first had notified the host state of the existence of a dispute, the event that triggered the beginning of the waiting period, and the date the claim was submitted to arbitration. The tribunal found no evidence that the host state intended to negotiate with the claimant and, therefore, to require further delay would "amount to an unnecessary, overly formalistic approach which would not serve to protect any legitimate interests of the Parties."[301]

---

300 *See generally* Schreuer, *supra* note 67.

301 Final Award, para. 190. *Accord Bayindir v. Pakistan* (Turkey-Pakistan BIT), Decision on Jurisdiction, para. 102.

In *Link-Trading v. Moldova*, a case arising under the United States-Moldova BIT, the tribunal held that where it was evident that the respondent had rejected the claimant's position, compliance with the six-month waiting period would only aggravate damages. Thus, the tribunal had jurisdiction notwithstanding that the claim was submitted prior to the expiration of the waiting period.

In *SGS v. Pakistan*, the Switzerland-Pakistan BIT permitted submission of a claim to investor-state arbitration only if consultations between the disputants do not result in a solution within twelve months. The claimant, however, had submitted the claim to arbitration only two days after informing the respondent that it had a claim under the BIT. The tribunal held that compliance with the twelve month waiting period was not a condition precedent to the tribunal's jurisdiction and that neither party had shown any inclination to consult or negotiate.[302] To halt the arbitration and require consultations would be inconsistent with the need for an "orderly and cost-effective procedure."[303]

In *Biwater v. Tanzania*, a case arising under the United Kingdom-Tanzania BIT, the dispute had arisen in May and June 2005, but the claimant had submitted the dispute to arbitration in August notwithstanding the existence of a six-month waiting period. The tribunal held that compliance with the waiting period was not a condition precedent to tribunal jurisdiction. It found that the purpose of the period was to facilitate amicable settlement, not to impede arbitration where settlement was not possible. In that case, the parties had engaged in a long process of negotiation that had failed. Further, the Tanzanian government already had deported the claimant's personnel and taken control of the operation of the investment. These events amply demonstrated the futility of further negotiation. Finally, the tribunal held that, even if the requirement of a waiting period were a condition of jurisdiction, the requirement was waived by virtue of Tanzania's own conduct, including the deportation and takeover, that precluded any further negotiations.

In *Sedelmeyer v. Russia*, a case arising under the Germany-Russia BIT, the tribunal could not determine whether the six-month waiting period had been satisfied because of uncertainty about the triggering event. It concluded, however, that it need not resolve the issue definitively because to decline jurisdiction solely on the ground of noncompliance with the waiting period would be "too far-reaching."[304]

In *Wena Hotels v. Egypt*, a case arising under the United Kingdom-Egypt BIT, Egypt initially objected that the claimant had failed to observe the three-month waiting period, but withdrew its objection during oral argument, noting that the only effect of sustaining the objection would be to delay the proceedings.

By contrast, in *Enron v. Argentina*, a case arising under the United States-Argentina BIT, the tribunal held that the waiting period is a jurisdictional requirement. In that case, however, following the submission of the initial claim the host state had engaged in additional, similar allegedly wrongful acts. The tribunal held that to require a new claim for each such act would be wasteful and therefore an additional waiting period

302 Decision on Jurisdiction, para. 184.

303 *Id.*

304 Award, para. 2.6.2.

with respect to the subsequent acts need not be observed, at least for subsequent claims of the same nature and scope as the original claim.

At least two other cases involving the United States-Argentina BIT—*El Paso v. Argentina* and *Pan American Energy v. Argentina*—raised the question of whether the requirement was jurisdictional or not. In both cases, however, the tribunal determined that it need not resolve the question.

A host state may be able to demonstrate significant prejudice from a failure to observe the waiting period, at least where the waiting period is commenced by notice of a claim. The waiting period provides the host state with an opportunity to evaluate the claim, to decide whether to offer compensation or some other remedy to the claimant, and to prepare for an arbitration should one occur, such as by selecting outside counsel, collecting evidence, and identifying arbitrators. Such tasks may require extended interagency discussions, particularly where the host state has never been the respondent in an arbitration. Failure to require the claimant to observe the waiting period may necessitate that the host state commence an arbitration with little, if any, time to prepare. By contrast, the claimant, perhaps long aware of its own intention of submitting a claim to arbitration, may have had abundant opportunity to prepare before commencing the arbitration and thereby may begin with a substantial tactical advantage. Compliance with the waiting period admittedly could serve to aggravate damages, but that should be a matter of concern principally to the respondent, who must pay the aggravated damages if it violated the BIT. Where the respondent wishes to waive the waiting period in order to mitigate damages, of course, it may choose to do so. Failure to observe the waiting period, however, does not result in prejudice in every case. Where a BIT does not require notice of a claim to commence the waiting period, the host state may not know that it is in a waiting period and the waiting period may serve little purpose.

Determining whether the requirement of a waiting period has been met generally requires determining when it began. In *Lauder v. Czech Republic*, the United States-Czech Republic BIT allowed a claim to be submitted "[a]t any time after six months from the date on which the dispute arose. . . ."[305] The tribunal held that the waiting period begins on the date on which the state is notified that a breach has occurred, not on the date on which the breach occurs.[306] This interpretation is consistent with the purpose of such a provision in allowing meaningful negotiations or at least an opportunity for the host state to review the claim against it and to prepare for arbitration, something that cannot occur until the host state learns that a dispute exists. It is also consistent with the purpose of the BITs generally to promote predictability because determining the precise date on which a state received notice of a dispute may be much easier than to determine the precise date on which a treaty breach occurred, particularly when the breach is the result of a continuing course of conduct, as in the case of a creeping expropriation. Indeed, under this interpretation, a claimant can trigger the commencement of the period on a date certain by sending notice of a dispute to the host state.

---

305 United States-Czech Republic BIT, Art. VI(3)(a).

306 *Accord El Paso Energy v. Argentina* (United States-Argentina BIT), Decision on Jurisdiction, para. 36.

The notice of a dispute may come from the respondent. In *Link-Trading v. Moldova*, a case arising from the United States-Moldova BIT, the tribunal held that the dispute arose at the latest on the date on which Moldova notified the claimant that it had decided to eliminate a customs exemption for claimant's customers, which was the decision that the claimant alleged to violate the BIT. The decision itself had taken effect eight days earlier and so the tribunal appeared to believe that the dispute arose when both parties became aware of the allegedly wrongful conduct, rather than when the conduct occurred. Thus, the award seems consistent with that in *Lauder*, where the waiting period was triggered by notice rather than by the breach.

In *Ethyl Corporation v. Canada*, the NAFTA required that six months must have elapsed since the "events giving rise to a claim." The parties disputed whether such events included all elements required to submit a claim or only some. As it happened, the tribunal decided that it did not need to reach the issue. In *LLC AMTO v. Ukraine*, a case arising under the Energy Charter Treaty, the tribunal held that the waiting period commenced once the claimant had submitted claim letters to the government. In *Sedelmeyer v. Russia*, a case arising under the Germany-Russia BIT, the tribunal expressed some doubt about the triggering event, but for reasons discussed above decided that it need not resolve the issue.

Where multiple claims are alleged, the question arises whether a separate waiting period must elapse for each claim. As already noted, the tribunal held in *Enron v. Argentina*, a case arising under the United States-Argentina BIT, the tribunal held that subsequent waiting periods need not be observed at least for subsequent claims of the same nature and scope as the original claim. Similarly, in *Metalclad v. Mexico*, a case arising under the NAFTA, the tribunal held that the waiting period was not intended to amend the applicable procedural rules relating to the amendment of claims so as to require that a new waiting period be observed with respect to each amendment.

Once the waiting period has elapsed, the tribunal may assume jurisdiction over a dispute even if negotiations have not been completed. In *AES v. Argentina*, a case arising under the United States-Argentina BIT, Argentina asserted that the claim was not yet ripe because settlement negotiations were continuing. The tribunal rejected this argument, holding that the six-month waiting period had elapsed prior to submission of the claim and that the BIT did not require "prior exhaustion of local negotiations."[307]

10.2.3.4.3 SUFFICIENCY OF NOTICE

Where a notice is required, the host state may challenge the sufficiency of the notice. In *Berschader v. Russia*, a case arising under the Belgium Luxembourg Economic Union-Russia BIT, the tribunal held that the purpose of notification requirements is to provide the parties an opportunity to negotiate a resolution of the dispute before submitting it to arbitration. Thus, the notice must be sufficient to inform the respondent of the existence of a dispute and to commence negotiations if it so desires.[308] The claimant had delivered three letters to various officials and, in fact, some negotiations

307 Decision on Jurisdiction, para. 65.
308 Award, para. 100.

had ensued. The tribunal rejected the respondent's argument that the notices were insufficient because they were not submitted through diplomatic channels.

The tribunal agreed in *LLC AMTO v. Ukraine*, a case arising under the Energy Charter Treaty. In that case, the respondent argued that the notice of a dispute defines the claim that may be submitted to arbitration. The tribunal held that the purpose of the notice is to provide an opportunity for settlement negotiations and that the notice must be sufficient for that purpose. The claimant, however, was not required to specify the legal grounds for its claim. To require that formal claims be stated might actually discourage good faith negotiations. Thus, a notice could be sufficient even if it did not identify any claims under the Energy Charter Treaty.

Similarly, in *Generation Ukraine v. Ukraine*, a case arising under the United States-Ukraine BIT, the tribunal explained that

> The requirement to consult and negotiate, however, does not serve to compel the investors to plead its legal case on multiple occasions. To insist upon a precise congruity in the investor's articulation of its grievances in these different fora would only have a chilling effect on consultation and negotiation between the investor and host State.[309]

A similar rationale applies in the case of BITs that require the investor to send the host state a notice of intent to submit a claim to arbitration prior to submission of the claim. In *ADF Group v. United States*, a case arising under the NAFTA, the notice of intent did not include a reference to Article 1103, the general MFN provision, of the NAFTA although it did refer to Article 1102, the general national treatment provision. The tribunal held, however, that it had jurisdiction over the MFN claim.[310] The investor had not omitted a reference to Article 1103 to surprise the host state and had not appreciated the relevance of that article until after the claim was submitted. Further, the host state was not prejudiced by the late claim. The tribunal also noted that Article 1104 of the NAFTA guarantees to covered investors the better of the treatment under Article 1102 and Article 1103. Thus, the reference to Article 1102 in the notice of intent implicated Article 1104, which in turn put Article 1103 at issue.[311]

10.2.3.5 Conduct of the Arbitration The conduct of a BIT arbitration is virtually always governed by an existing set of rules, most often the ICSID rules, the Additional Facility rules, or the UNCITRAL rules. Procedural issues concerning the conduct of the arbitration thus typically involve an interpretation of the applicable rules, rather than of the BIT.[312]

---

309 Award, para. 14.5.

310 Award, para. 139.

311 Award, para. 137. As discussed in Section 7.2.1, any BIT that requires both national and MFN treatment implicitly requires the better of each. That is, Article 1104 only makes explicit that which would have been implicit in its absence. Thus, the presence of Article 1104 arguably should not have affected the result. The issue should have been decided on other grounds.

312 An extensive body of law applying the ICSID and UNCITRAL arbitration rules already exists. On the ICSID convention, *see* Christoph H. Schreuer, *The ICSID Convention: A Commentary* (2001) and Lucy Reed, Jan Paulsson, and Nigel Blackaby, *Guide to ICSID Arbitration* (2004).

Tribunals universally hold that the BIT is to be interpreted in accordance with Articles 31 and 32 of the Vienna Convention on the Law of Treaties, which are declaratory of customary international law.[313] Tribunals also are in agreement that awards in prior cases are not binding, but that they should be taken into account by tribunals in subsequent cases.[314] The tribunal commented in *Duke Energy v. Ecuador*, a case arising under the United States-Ecuador BIT, that it had a duty to contribute to the harmonious development of investment law and thereby to promote certainty in the rule of law.[315]

BITs sometimes specify that certain arbitral rules apply except as modified by the BIT. Tribunals generally do not readily infer an intent to modify specified rules. For example, tribunals have rejected an argument that several NAFTA articles modified Article 48 of the ICSID Additional Facility Arbitration Rules relating to ancillary claims, where nothing in those NAFTA articles addressed ancillary claims.[316]

10.3 STATE-STATE DISPUTE RESOLUTION

10.3.1 Structure and Policy

Virtually all BITs contain a provision for binding arbitration of disputes between the parties, with only minor variations among them. Such provisions continue to appear in the most recent BITs, notwithstanding that disputes not settled through negotiation or submitted to local remedies invariably are submitted to investor-state arbitration rather than to state-state arbitration.

These provisions generally apply to any dispute concerning the interpretation or application of the BIT.[317] As discussed in Section 10.2.1.1, the investor-state disputes provision in many BITs applies to any dispute concerning an investment. Thus, in many BITs, the state-state disputes provision potentially has a narrower scope of application than the investor-state disputes provision.

On UNCITRAL arbitration, *see* David D. Caron, Lee M. Caplan, and Matti Pellonpaa, *The UNCITRAL Arbitration Rules: A Commentary* (2006).

313 *See, e.g., Wintershall v. Argentina* (Germany-Argentina BIT), Award, para. 77.

314 *See, e.g., RosInvestco v. Russia* (United Kingdom-Russia BIT), Decision on Jurisdiction, para. 49. *See generally* Christoph Schreuer and Matthew Weiniger, "A Doctrine of Precedent?" in *The Oxford Handbook of International Investment Law* (Peter Muchlinski, Frederico Ortino, and Christoph Schreuer, eds. 2008).

315 Award, para. 117.

316 *See Feldman v. Mexico* (NAFTA); *Metalclad v. Mexico* (NAFTA). *See also Ethyl Corp. v. Canada* (NAFTA did not modify UNCITRAL rule relating to amendment of claims); *Pope and Talbot v. Canada* (NAFTA), Award, paras. 22–29.

317 *See, e.g.*, Thailand-Argentina BIT, Art. 10(1); Australia-India BIT, Art. 13(1); Netherlands-Ethiopia BIT, Art. 12(10; United Kingdom-Bosnia-Herzegovina BIT, Art. 9(1); BLEU-Sudan BIT, Art. 13(1); Cambodia-Vietnam BIT, Art. IX(1); Germany-Timor-Leste BIT, Art. 10(1); Egypt-Zambia BIT, Art. 9(1); Mexico-Iceland BIT, Art. 18; Denmark-Ethiopia BIT, Art. 10; France-Uganda BIT, Art. 10(1); Chile-Lebanon BIT, Art. X(1); India-Indonesia BIT, Art. 10(1).

As in the case of investor-state disputes provisions, state-state disputes provisions commonly begin with a statement that any disputes within the scope of the provision should be settled through negotiation, if possible.[318] Again, as in the case of the investor-state disputes provision, the state-state disputes provision sometimes specifies some period of time that must elapse before the dispute may be submitted to binding arbitration, most commonly six months,[319] but other times are sometimes specified.[320] Occasionally, a reasonable time is specified.[321]

Some BITs include an entirely separate provision requiring each party, at the request of the other, to consult on matters concerning the treaty.[322] Such a provision may be used to resolve disputes and its presence is a way of indicating the importance that the parties place on the amicable resolution of disputes. Consultations provisions, however, generally are not limited to the resolution of disputes. They also may be used as a means of monitoring the implementation of the treaty. In any event, such provisions have not become widespread in the BITs. Nothing precludes the parties from consulting without such a provision and meaningful consultations cannot be compelled if a party does not wish to engage in them. In short, the provision is of little practical value, accomplishing nothing that cannot be accomplished without such a provision. Such provisions principally serve the symbolic value of affirming the parties' desire to resolve differences amicably.

If the dispute has not been[323] or cannot be[324] settled through negotiations, state-state disputes provisions generally provide for arbitration of disputes before an ad hoc tribunal of three arbitrators. Typically, the prescribed procedure for formation of the tribunal is that each party appoints one arbitrator, after which the two party-appointed

---

318 *See, e.g.*, Thailand-Argentina BIT, Art. 10(1); Australia-India BIT, Art. 13(1); United Kingdom-Bosnia-Herzegovina BIT, Art 9(1); BLEU-Sudan BIT, Art. 13(1); Cambodia-Vietnam BIT, Art. IX(1); Germany-Timor-Leste BIT, Art. 10(1); Egypt-Zambia BIT, Art. 9(1); Mexico-Iceland BIT, Art.18; Denmark-Ethiopia BIT, Art. 10(1); France-Uganda BIT, Art. 10(1); Chile-Lebanon BIT, Art. X(1); India-Indonesia BIT, Art. 10(1).

319 *See, e.g.*, Thailand-Argentina BIT, Art. 10(2); Australia-India BIT, Art. 13(2); United Kingdom-Bosnia-Herzegovina BIT, Art 9(2); Egypt-Zambia BIT, Art. 9(2); Denmark-Ethiopia BIT, Art. 10(2); France-Uganda BIT, Art. 10(2); Chile-Lebanon BIT, Art. X(2); India-Indonesia BIT, Art. 10(2).

320 *See, e.g.*, Mexico-Iceland BIT, Art.19(1) (four months); Austria-Romania BIT, Art. 15(2) (one year).

321 *See, e.g.*, Netherlands-Ethiopia BIT, Art. 12(1).

322 *See, e.g.*, Netherlands-Ethiopia Art. 11; Denmark-Ethiopia, Art. 11; Cambodia Vietnam, Art. XIII; Chile-Indonesia BIT, Art. XII; Finland-Armenia BIT, Art. 17; Australia-India Art. 11; Egypt-Zambia BIT, Art. 2(3) (to promote investment); India-Indonesia BIT, Art. 14(1).

323 *See, e.g.*, BLEU-Sudan BIT, Art. 13(2); France-Uganda BIT, Art.10(2).

324 *See, e.g.*, Thailand-Argentina BIT, Art. 10(2); Australia-India BIT, Art. 13(2); Netherlands-Ethiopia BIT, Art. 12(1); United Kingdom-Bosnia-Herzegovina BIT, Art 9(2); Cambodia-Vietnam BIT, Art. IX(3); Germany-Timor-Leste BIT, Art. 10(2); Egypt-Zambia BIT, Art. 9(2); Denmark-Ethiopia BIT, Art. 10(2); Chile-Lebanon BIT, Art. X(2); India-Indonesia BIT, Art. 10(2).

arbitrators choose a third arbitrator, who serves as the chair of the tribunal.[325] Some BITs condition the appointment of the chair on the approval of the two disputing parties.[326] BITs generally require that the chair be a national of a third state.[327]

The process of tribunal formation usually is governed by a prescribed schedule. Typically, the two parties are permitted two months within which to appoint an arbitrator and the two party-appointed arbitrators are permitted an additional two months to select the chair.[328] Some variations in this schedule do appear, however.[329]

The tribunal formation process may fail in either of two situations. The first situation occurs where a party does not appoint an arbitrator. The second situation occurs where the two party-appointed arbitrators cannot agree upon a chair. The BITs adopt the same solution for both situations: the designation of an appointing authority who is authorized to make the necessary appointments if the normal process fails.

By far, the most frequently designated appointing authority is the President of the International Court of Justice.[330] The typical provision specifies that, if the ICJ President is a national of a disputing party or is unable to make the appointment, then the Vice-President of the court shall serve as the appointing authority.[331] If the Vice-President

---

325 *See, e.g.*, Thailand-Argentina BIT, Art. 10(3); Australia-India BIT, Art. 13(3); Netherlands-Ethiopia BIT, Art. 12(1); United Kingdom-Bosnia-Herzegovina BIT, Art. 9(3); Cambodia-Vietnam BIT, Art. IX(3); Egypt-Zambia BIT, Art. 9(3); Mexico-Iceland BIT, Art.20(1); France-Uganda BIT, Art.10(3); Chile-Lebanon BIT, Art. X(3); India-Indonesia BIT, Art. 10(3).

326 *See, e.g.*, Thailand-Argentina BIT, Art. 10(3); Australia-India BIT, Art. 13(3); Chile-Lebanon BIT, Art. X(3); India-Indonesia BIT, Art. 10(3).

327 *See, e.g.*, Thailand-Argentina BIT, Art. 10(3); Australia-India BIT, Art. 13(3); Netherlands-Ethiopia BIT, Art. 12(1); United Kingdom-Bosnia-Herzegovina BIT, Art 9(3); Cambodia-Vietnam BIT, Art. IX(3); Germany-Timor-Leste BIT, Art. 10(3); Egypt-Zambia BIT, Art. 9(3); Mexico-Iceland BIT, Art.20(1); France-Uganda BIT, Art.10(3); Chile-Lebanon BIT, Art. X(3); India-Indonesia BIT, Art. 10(3).

328 *See, e.g.*, Netherlands-Ethiopia BIT, Art. 12(2)–(3); United Kingdom-Bosnia-Herzegovina BIT, Art 9; Mexico-Iceland BIT, Art. 20; Denmark-Ethiopia BIT, Art. 10(3).

329 *See, e.g.*, Thailand-Argentina BIT, Art. 10(3) (two party-appointed arbitrators to be selected within three months and the chair within four months of when arbitration is proposed); Australia-India BIT, Art. 13(3) (only one additional month to select the chair); Germany-Timor-Leste BIT, Art. 10(2) (only one additional month to appoint the chair); Egypt-Zambia BIT, Art. 9(3) (party-appointed arbitrators to be appointed within three months and chairman within five months of when one party notifies other of intent to arbitrate); France-Uganda BIT, Art. 10(3) (all arbitrators appointed within two months); Chile-Lebanon BIT, Art. X(3) (chairman appointed within 45 days).

330 *See, e.g.*, Thailand-Argentina BIT, Art. 10(4); Australia-India BIT, Art. 13(4); Netherlands-Ethiopia BIT, Art. 12(2); United Kingdom-Bosnia-Herzegovina BIT, Art 9(4); Cambodia-Vietnam BIT, Art. IX(4); Germany-Timor-Leste BIT, Art. 10(4); Egypt-Zambia BIT, Art. 9(4); Mexico-Iceland BIT, Art. 20(2); Denmark-Ethiopia BIT, Art.10(4); Chile-Lebanon BIT, Art. X(4); India-Indonesia BIT, Art. 10(4).

331 *See, e.g.*, Thailand-Argentina BIT, Art. 10(4); Australia-India BIT, Art. 13(4); Netherlands-Ethiopia BIT, Art. 12(4); United Kingdom-Bosnia-Herzegovina BIT, Art 9(4); Cambodia-Vietnam BIT, Art. IX(4); Germany-Timor-Leste BIT, Art. 10(4); Egypt-Zambia BIT, Art. 9(4); Mexico-Iceland BIT, Art. 20(2); Denmark-Ethiopia BIT, Art. 10(4); Chile-Lebanon BIT, Art. X(4).

of the court is a national of a party or unable to act, the most senior member of the court who is not disqualified by either circumstance shall make the appointment.[332] This process is taken from Article 3(2) of the International Law Commission's Model Rules of Arbitral Procedure, which were adopted by the commission in 1958, the year before the Germany-Pakistan BIT was signed. Some BITs designate other officials as the appointing authority, such as the Secretary-General of the United Nations.[333]

Occasionally BITs address the resignation or incapacitation of an arbitrator. The typical approach is to provide that the successor shall be appointed in the same manner as the original arbitrator.[334]

BITs often provide that the tribunal shall determine its own procedure.[335] Under customary international law, international tribunals have inherent authority to determine their own procedures and thus this clause is not necessary. Some BITs specify that a particular set of rules be used, generally either the International Law Commission's Model Rules of Arbitral Procedure or the UNCITRAL rules.

One common clause specifies that decisions of the tribunal shall be by a majority vote.[336] This is also the practice under customary law, but the clause is useful because it eliminates any doubt about the issue. Once this fundamental procedural issue is resolved, the tribunal by majority vote can resolve all other procedural issues.

Many BITs do not include a choice of law clause. Those that do commonly require that international law be applied.[337] A few BITs authorize the tribunal to decide a dispute *ex aequo et bono*.[338] The choice of law clause in the state-state disputes provision of a BIT may differ from that in the investor-state disputes provision of that BIT, with the result that a different body of law in theory could be applied depending upon whether a dispute is submitted to investor-state or state-state arbitration. As was noted in Section 10.2.1.5, however, investor-state arbitral tribunals virtually always apply international law to the extent that it exists, regardless of the presence or wording of the choice of law clause in the investor-state disputes provision, and thus textual differences

---

332 *See, e.g.*, Thailand-Argentina BIT, Art. 10(4); Australia-India BIT, Art. 13(4); Netherlands-Ethiopia BIT, Art. 12(4); United Kingdom-Bosnia-Herzegovina BIT, Art 9(4); Cambodia-Vietnam BIT, Art. IX(4);); Germany-Timor-Leste BIT, Art. 10(4); Egypt-Zambia BIT, Art. 9(4); Mexico-Iceland BIT, Art. 20(2); Denmark-Ethiopia BIT, Art. 10(4); Chile-Lebanon BIT, Art. X(4).

333 *See, e.g.*, France-Uganda BIT, Art. 10(4).

334 *See, e.g.*, Australia-India BIT, Art. 13(5).

335 *See, e.g.*, Thailand-Argentina BIT, Art. 10(5); Australia-India BIT, Art. 13(8); Netherlands-Ethiopia BIT, Art. 12(6); United Kingdom-Bosnia-Herzegovina BIT, Art 9(5); Cambodia-Vietnam BIT, Art. IX(5); Egypt-Zambia BIT, Art. 9(6); Denmark-Ethiopia BIT, Art. 10(4); France-Uganda BIT, Art. 10(5); Chile-Lebanon BIT, Art. X(5); India-Indonesia BIT, Art. 10(5).

336 *See, e.g.*, Thailand-Argentina BIT, Art. 10(5); Australia-India BIT, Art. 13(6); Netherlands-Ethiopia BIT, Art. 12(7); United Kingdom-Bosnia-Herzegovina BIT, Art ((5); Cambodia-Vietnam BIT, Art. IX(5);); Germany-Timor-Leste BIT, Art. 10(5); Egypt-Zambia BIT, Art. 9(6); Denmark-Ethiopia BIT, Art. 10(6); France-Uganda BIT, Art.10(5); Chile-Lebanon BIT, Art. X(5); India-Indonesia BIT, Art. 10(5).

337 *See, e.g.*, Netherlands-Ethiopia BIT, Art. 12(5); Egypt-Zambia BIT, Art. 9(5); Mexico-Iceland BIT, Art. 21; Denmark-Ethiopia BIT, Art. 10(6); Chile-Lebanon BIT, Art. X(5).

338 *See, e.g.*, Netherlands-Ethiopia BIT, Art. 12(5) (if the parties so agree).

between the choice of law clauses of the two provisions are likely to be of no practical significance.

State-state disputes provisions often provide that any award shall be final[339] and binding.[340] Similar language also frequently appears in the investor-state disputes provision.[341]

The final issue addressed in most state-state disputes provisions is the payment of the costs of arbitration. The most common approach is to provide that each party shall bear the costs of its own representation and of the arbitrator that it appoints, but that the remaining costs shall be shared by the two parties.[342] An alternative is to provide that each party shall bear the costs of its own representation, but that all costs of the tribunal shall be paid equally by the parties.[343] The latter approach seems preferable on policy grounds. Arbitrators are expected to be impartial and a tribunal should function as a collaborative body, rather than as two partisans and a neutral chair. Under the latter approach to payment of costs, the tribunal as an institution obtains payment of its fees and expenses and the funds are disbursed by the chair. The former approach would place the two party-appointed arbitrators in the position of negotiating separately with the party that appointed them for payment, which would tend to undermine the appearance of impartiality if not the actual fact. The investor-state disputes provision, by contrast, generally does not specify that each party shall pay the expenses of the arbitrator that it appoints, nor does such a specification appear in the International Law Commission's model rules, the UNCITRAL rules, or the ICSID convention.

Many BITs permit the tribunal, in its discretion, to impose a greater share of the costs on one party than the other.[344] Typically, these BITs do not articulate the criteria to be used in any such allocation, but leave the matter entirely to the tribunal's discretion. The expectation is that a tribunal may exercise this power in cases where one party has unduly increased the costs of arbitration, such as by raising frivolous arguments or engaging in obstructive behavior.

Occasionally, other issues are addressed in the state-state disputes provisions. For example, a few BITs provide that the arbitrators shall be independent and impartial

---

339 *See, e.g.*, Netherlands-Ethiopia BIT, Art. 12(7); Egypt-Zambia BIT, Art. 9(6); Denmark-Ethiopia BIT, Art. 10(6); France-Uganda BIT, Art. 10(5); Chile-Lebanon BIT, Art. X(7).

340 *See, e.g.*, Thailand-Argentina BIT, Art. 10(5); Australia-India BIT, Art. 13(6); Netherlands-Ethiopia BIT, Art. 12(7); United Kingdom-Bosnia-Herzegovina BIT, Art 9(5); Cambodia-Vietnam BIT, Art. IX(5);Germany-Timor-Leste BIT, Art. 10(5); Egypt-Zambia BIT, Art. 9(6); Denmark-Ethiopia BIT, Art. 10(6); France-Uganda BIT, Art. 10(5); Chile-Lebanon BIT, Art. X(7); India-Indonesia BIT, Art. 10(5).

341 *See* Section 10.2.1.7.

342 *See, e.g.*, Thailand-Argentina BIT, Art. 10(5); Australia-India BIT, Art. 13(7); United Kingdom-Bosnia-Herzegovina BIT, Art 9(5); Cambodia-Vietnam BIT, Art. IX(6);Germany-Timor-Leste BIT, Art. 10(5); Egypt-Zambia BIT, Art. 9(6); Denmark-Ethiopia BIT, Art.10(7); Chile-Lebanon BIT, Art. X(6); India-Indonesia BIT, Art. 10(5).

343 *See, e.g.*, Mexico-Iceland BIT, Art. 22.

344 *See, e.g.*, Thailand-Argentina BIT, Art. 10(5); Australia-India BIT, Art. 13(7); United Kingdom-Bosnia-Herzegovina BIT, Art 9(5); Cambodia-Vietnam BIT, Art. IX(6); Germany-Timor-Leste BIT, Art. 10(5); Denmark-Ethiopia BIT, Art.10(7); India-Indonesia BIT, Art. 10(5).

and have experience in international law and investment matters.[345] As noted in Section 10.2.1.7, investor-state disputes provisions sometimes provide that a dispute submitted to investor-state arbitration may not be submitted to state-state arbitration unless the tribunal declined jurisdiction or the host state failed to comply with the award. A few BITs include a similar clause in the state-state disputes provision.[346]

10.3.2 Origins

Provisions for state-state arbitration of disputes appeared in the FCNs at least as early as the 1794 agreement between Great Britain and the United States.[347] Such provisions were not common in the nineteenth century FCNs, however. Following the Hague Peace Conference of 1899, countries began to insert dispute resolution clauses into their FCNs and to conclude separate arbitration agreements calling for arbitration of their disputes generally.[348]

The state-state disputes provision appeared in the first BIT and has changed relatively little in the fifty years since. The 1959 Germany-Pakistan BIT provided that, in the event of a dispute concerning the interpretation or application of the treaty, the parties "shall" enter into consultations for the purpose of finding a solution.[349] If no such solution is reached, the dispute shall be submitted to arbitration or, if both parties agree, to the International Court of Justice. Arbitration shall be before an ad hoc tribunal consisting of three arbitrators, one appointed by each party within two months of the request for arbitration and a chairman appointed by the two party-appointed arbitrators within a month of their appointment. If an arbitrator is not appointed in the time prescribed, the President of the International Court of Justice shall act as appointing authority. If the President is unable to act or is a national of either party, the Vice-President shall make the appointment. If the Vice-President is unable to act or is a national of either party, the senior-most member of the court who is not a national of either party shall make the appointment. The tribunal shall decide by a majority vote and shall determine its own rules of procedure. Its decisions shall be binding on the parties.

The approach adopted in the Germany-Pakistan BIT was followed closely by other BITs with some variations, typically in the form of additional clauses. In one respect, most other early BITs were less detailed than the Germany-Pakistan BIT. In particular, they did not refer to ICJ adjudication as an alternative. The earliest U.S. BITs authorized resort to the court, but only if both parties agreed, and even this reference was abandoned by the United States in its 1984 model.

The first Swiss BIT, concluded with Tunisia in 1961, specified at Article 4 that the parties were entitled to submit a dispute to arbitration if the dispute had not been

345 *See, e.g.*, Mexico-Iceland BIT, Art. 20(3).
346 *See, e.g.*, Mexico-Iceland BIT, Art. 19(2).
347 *See* Section 2.1.1.
348 *See* Section 2.1.1.
349 Germany-Pakistan BIT, Art. 11(1).

resolved after a period of six moths. The Germany-Pakistan BIT had not specified any particular period of time during which negotiations should or must occur. The Swiss approach over the next decade was adopted by the Netherlands, Sweden, Denmark and France, but other countries followed the German approach. In its first BIT, Austria specified a one-year waiting period, but this did not become a common practice. Today, those BITs that specify a waiting period most often specify six months.

The Switzerland-Tunisia BIT allowed the two party-appointed arbitrators a period of two months, rather than one, to designate the chair of the tribunal. Over the next few years, this approach was adopted by the Netherlands, the Belgium-Luxembourg Economic Union (BLEU), Sweden, Denmark, France, United Kingdom, and Norway. It thus has become the typical, but certainly not universal, approach.

The Switzerland-Tunisia BIT also authorized the two BIT parties to designate rules of procedure. Failing such a designation, the tribunal was authorized to adopt its own rules. When the Netherlands launched its BIT program in 1963, also with Tunisia, it included the same language. Sweden also adopted this approach in its first BIT, with Ivory Coast, as did France in its 1965 BIT with Ivory Coast. This approach, however, has not become the general practice and most BITs provide that the tribunal shall determine its own procedure.

The first Dutch BIT, the 1963 Netherlands-Tunisia BIT, also brought some innovations to the state-state disputes provision of the BITs. Article 4 of that BIT provides that the tribunal shall decide on the basis of law, although if the parties agree the tribunal may decide *ex aequo et bono*. This provision was quickly adopted by the BLEU in its BIT with Tunisia, but has not become typical in the BITs. The first Kuwaiti BIT, concluded with Iraq in 1964, specified that the dispute shall be decided in accordance with international law, a not uncommon provision that soon appeared in the Austrian and U.S. BITs as well.

The Netherlands-Tunisia BIT included a provision under which the tribunal at any time may propose to the parties a settlement of the dispute. This provision also was adopted by the BLEU in its BIT with Tunisia, but has not become typical in the BITs.

The 1964 BLEU-Tunisia BIT specifies that the chair of the tribunal may not be a national of either party and this provision was adopted in due course by Sweden, Denmark, France, the United Kingdom, the United States, Finland, and Norway. It is now common among BITs. Italy's first BIT, with Guinea, provided at Article VII that the third state must be one uninvolved in the dispute, a variation that is not common. The Kuwait-Iraq BIT required that the third country must have diplomatic relations with both BIT parties and this language still occasionally appears in BITs.

The 1964 Kuwait-Iraq BIT introduced an innovation with respect to the identity of the appointing authority. Article 7 provides that the third arbitrator in all cases shall be appointed by the Secretary General of the Arab League. It does not designate an appointing authority to act in the event that a party fails to appoint an arbitrator. Since that time, other BITs occasionally have been concluded designating an appointing authority other than the President of the International Court of Justice, such as the Secretary-General of the United Nations.

Sweden, in its first BIT, concluded with Ivory Coast in 1965, included a new clause at Article VII specifying that each party shall pay the expenses of the arbitrator that it appoints, while the other expenses of the tribunal shall be borne equally by the parties. A decade later, the United Kingdom followed the Swedish precedent and this now has become the common practice.

The United Kingdom, in its first BIT, concluded with Egypt in 1975, introduced an innovation that the chairman must be approved by the two BIT parties,[350] an innovation adopted quickly by Austria[351] and then by Norway when it resumed BIT negotiations in the 1980s.[352] The United Kingdom-Egypt BIT also specified that each party must bear the expenses of its own representation, an innovation that was adopted by Norway[353] and the United States,[354] when they concluded their first BITs in the 1980s. It provided finally that the tribunal may direct that one party pay a higher proportion of the costs of the arbitration, another innovation adopted by Norway[355] and the United States[356] in their BITs in the 1980s.

By the time the United Kingdom BIT program began in 1975, most of the features of the state-state disputes provision that would become common in BITs were part of BIT practice. Finland and the United States in the next few years introduced some innovations, but these have not become typical of BIT practice.

The first Finnish BIT, with Egypt, at Article 7, explicitly authorized the parties to agree on a different appointing authority, a clause also adopted by the United States in its first BIT, with Egypt in 1982. The Finland-Egypt BIT designated ICSID as the appointing authority and English as the language of the tribunal. It explicitly authorized the tribunal to designate the place of arbitration. The Finland BIT, in contrast to the prevailing practice, provided that the costs shall be shared equally by the two disputing parties.

The United States, in its 1982 BIT with Egypt, introduced several innovations at Article VIII. First, the U.S. BIT provides for the situation in which an arbitrator is unable to act, specifying that the appointing authority shall designate a successor. Second, the United States-Egypt BIT provides that the Model Rules of the International Law Commission shall be used, although the tribunal has the authority to resolve procedural issues not addressed by those rules. Third, to ensure a prompt resolution of the dispute, the United State-Egypt BIT imposes deadlines on the parties for submission of their memorials and on the tribunal for the issuance of its award. None of these innovations has been widely adopted.

The state-state disputes provision was one area in which the BITs were not greatly influenced by the 1959 Abs-Shawcross convention. Most importantly, under Article VII of that convention, arbitration required the further consent of the parties. In the absence of such consent, the dispute could be submitted to the International Court of Justice.

---

350 United Kingdom-Egypt BIT, Art. 9.

351 *See* Austria-Malaysia BIT, Art. 10(2).

352 *See* Norway-Malaysia BIT, Art. 10(3).

353 *See* Norway-Malaysia BIT, Art. 10(5).

354 *See* United States-Egypt BIT, Art. VIII(3)(g).

355 *See* Norway-Malaysia BIT, Art. 10(5).

356 *See* United States-Egypt BIT, Art. VIII(3)(g).

Under the annex to the convention, the third arbitrator, referred to as the "Umpire," was to be appointed by the parties rather than by the party-appointed arbitrators. The appointing authority, who was authorized to act if the parties could not agree, was to be the President of the International Court of Justice or, failing an appointment by him, the Secretary-General of the United Nations. If a party failed to appoint an arbitrator, the Umpire was to make the appointment. The Abs-Shawcross convention, unlike the early BITs, provided for appointment of replacement arbitrators and addressed various other procedural matters not addressed in the early BITs.

The 1967 OECD Draft Convention on the Protection of Foreign Property actually was more influenced by the Abs-Shawcross convention than by the BITs concluded up to that point by the OECD members. The OECD draft convention, like the Abs-Shawcross convention, called for the appointment of the third arbitrator by the parties rather than by the party-appointed arbitrators. The appointing authority, who was to be the President of the International Court of Justice or, if he was unable to act, the Vice-President, was authorized to appoint the third arbitrator if the parties could not agree. If a party did not appoint an arbitrator, the chair was authorized to appoint that arbitrator. Again like the Abs-Shawcross convention, the OECD draft convention also provided for the appointment of replacement arbitrators. The OECD draft convention had clauses to allow the intervention of another party and for the consolidation of pending claims, innovations that generally do not appear in the state-state disputes provisions, although a few BITs have consolidation provisions in their investor-state disputes provisions.[357]

As this suggests, then, the state-state disputes provisions of most BITs were largely based on the provision adopted by Germany in 1959, with a few innovations from the early Swiss, Dutch, BLEU, and Swedish BITs, all concluded in the 1960s. Most of the more recent innovations in the state-state disputes provision have not become common practice,

10.3.3 Arbitral Practice

To date, only one dispute is known to have been submitted to arbitration by one BIT party against another. After the claim in *Empressa Luchetti v. Peru* was submitted to investor state arbitration, Peru submitted to arbitration a dispute with Chile, the home state of the claimant, under the Chile-Peru BIT, seeking to resolve differences with respect to the interpretation of the BIT. Peru requested that the investor-state arbitral tribunal suspend its proceedings pending the resolution of the dispute between the two BIT parties, but the tribunal declined. Subsequently, however, the tribunal dismissed the investor's claim for lack of jurisdiction on the ground that the dispute arose before the BIT entered into force.

---

357 *See* Section 10.2.8.1.5.

10.4 DENIAL OF JUSTICE

10.4.1 Treaty Texts

Under customary international law, a state incurs responsibility for a denial of justice.[358] Denial of justice also was a concern of the early FCNs. In the early nineteenth century, FCNs often included provisions granting nationals of one party national treatment with respect to the right to appear in the courts of the other party.[359] The right of nationals of the other party to hire the representatives of their choice was commonly included as well. By the early twentieth century, FCNs frequently granted to companies of one party the right to appear in the courts of the other party.[360]

The BITs, by contrast, generally do not include a provision explicitly addressing treatment in the courts, although the kinds of rights guaranteed by the early FCNs are guaranteed by the general national treatment provision. Denial of justice was not explicitly prohibited by the 1959 Abs-Shawcross convention or the 1967 OECD draft convention.

The United States did adopt in its early BITs a provision on access to courts that went beyond national treatment. Typical of the provision used in the early 1980s is Article II(9) of the 1983 U.S.-Senegal BIT, which provides that "each Party shall provide effective means of asserting claims and enforcing rights with respect to investment agreements, investment authorizations and properties." An additional sentence required national and MFN treatment with respect to the right of access to local courts and the right to employ persons for the purpose of asserting such claims, although this sentence was deleted from the U.S. model negotiating text in 1984. Similar language had appeared in the post-war U.S. FCNs.[361] The judicial access provision was deleted from the U.S. model negotiating text in 2004, although that same year the model was revised to provide, at Article 5, that the fair and equitable treatment standard includes the obligation not to deny justice.

Other BITs occasionally include such a provision. For example, Article 2(3) of the Finland-Algeria BIT provides that each party "shall provide effective means of

---

358 *See generally* Jan Paulsson, *Denial of Justice in International Law* (2005); Alwyn V. Freeman, *The International Responsibility of States for Denial of Justice* (1938); Andrea Bjorklund, "Reconciling State Sovereignty and Investor Protection in Denial of Justice Claims," 45 *Virginia Journal of International Law* 809 (2005); Sir Gerald Fitzmaurice, "The Meaning of the Term 'Denial of Justice,'" 13 *British Yearbook of International Law* 93 (1932); Clyde Eagleton, "Denial of Justice in International Law," 22 *American Journal of International Law* 538 (1928).

359 *See* Section 2.1.1.

360 *See* Sections 2.1.1 and 2.1.2.

361 *See, e.g.*, Treaty of Friendship and Commerce, United States-Pakistan, Nov. 12, 1959, Art. V(1), 12 U.S.T. 110, T.I.A.S. No. 4683, 404 U.N.T.S. 259; Treaty of Friendship. Commerce, and Navigation, United States-Japan, April 2, 1953, Art. IV(1), 4 U.S.T. 2063, T.I.A.S. No. 2863, 206 U.N.T.S. 143.

asserting claims and enforcing rights with respect to investments covered by this Agreement."[362]

As noted in Section 10.4.2, the fair and equitable treatment standard has been held to include an obligation not to deny justice. Further, such an obligation would be imposed by any BIT that requires treatment consistent with customary international law.

10.4.2 Arbitral Practice

The judicial access provision of the U.S. BITs has been the subject of at least one award. In *Duke Energy v. Ecuador*, a case arising under the United States-Ecuador BIT, the claimants had not challenged in local courts an adverse local arbitral award in a dispute between the claimants and the Minister of Energy and Mines, arguing that the tribunal had declined jurisdiction and that local courts provided no remedy for that decision. The claimants argued that Ecuador's refusal to honor its promise to arbitrate constituted a denial of justice. The tribunal first noted that the judicial access provision implements part of the general prohibition on denial of justice, but that the claim before it related to the performance of the Ecuadoran courts rather than their availability. The tribunal next found that a disputant's raising of a defense did not constitute a denial of justice, unless the courts improperly upheld it.[363] Thus, the question was whether the local courts had upheld the jurisdictional defense improperly. As already noted, however, the award had not been challenged in local courts. The tribunal agreed with the claimants that they were not required to pursue improbable remedies. Yet, the record did not clearly establish that no remedy in local courts was available. Hence, no violation of the judicial access provision occurred.

A similar provision in the Energy Charter Treaty was at issue in *LLC AMTO v. Ukraine*. The tribunal found that the fundamental criterion for "effective means" is the rule of law. To satisfy the requirement, a state must have publicly available legislation to enforce property and contract rights as well as rules of procedure in the courts. Further, this legislation must meet international minimum standards. The tribunal found that Ukraine clearly satisfied its obligation to have the requisite legislation and rules. The issue to be resolved was whether the legislation met international standards, which required that the legislation be "systematic, comparative, progressive and practical."[364] The claimant failed to establish that Ukrainian bankruptcy law did not meet these criteria.

The fair and equitable treatment standard also has been held to require due process and thus to prohibit a denial of justice.[365] The fair and equitable treatment standard was introduced in Section 5.2, which contains a detailed discussion of that standard.

---

362 *See also* Sweden-Kazakhstan BIT, Art. 2(5).

363 The tribunal relied on *Waste Management v. Mexico* (NAFTA), discussed below.

364 Award, para. 88.

365 *See, e.g., Waste Management v. Mexico* (NAFTA), Award, para. 98; *Jan de Nul v. Egypt* (BLEU-Egypt BIT), Award, para. 187; *LLC AMTO v. Ukraine* (Energy Charter Treaty), Award, para. 75.

Because, under the NAFTA, fair and equitable treatment is regarded as an element of the international minimum standard under customary law, several awards have discussed the denial of justice doctrine without distinguishing carefully between the fair and equitable treatment standard and the international minimum standard.

One of the most cited awards with respect to the denial of justice is *Azinian v. Mexico*, a case arising under the NAFTA. In that case, the city of Naucalpan de Juarzez had terminated a contract with the claimant's company because of alleged failures to perform as well as misrepresentations concerning the company's capacity to perform. When the termination was challenged in the Mexican courts, it was upheld. The claimant did not actually allege a denial of justice by the Mexican courts. To avoid any suggestion, however, that the claimant's failure to prevail was based merely on an error of pleading, the tribunal elected to consider whether the claimant could have established a denial of justice by the Mexican courts. The tribunal explained that

> [a] denial of justice could be pleaded if the relevant courts refuse to entertain a suit, if they subject it to undue delay, or if they administer justice in a seriously inadequate way. . . . There is a fourth type of denial of justice, namely, the clear and malicious application of the law.[366]

In applying this standard, the tribunal was not to act as a court of appeal:

> [t]he possibility of holding a State internationally liable for judicial decisions does not, however, entitle a claimant to seek international review of the national court decisions as though the international jurisdiction seised has plenary appellate jurisdiction. This is not true generally, and it is not true for NAFTA.[367]

The tribunal then inquired whether the decision of the Mexican courts constituted a "clear and malicious misapplication of the law."[368] The tribunal found that the misrepresentations concerning the company's capacity to perform were adequate grounds for termination of the contract under Mexican law and thus there was no misapplication of the law. Accordingly, the tribunal found no denial of justice.

In *Mondev v. United States*, another case arising under the NAFTA, the Boston Redevelopment Authority had terminated a contract with the claimant's company to perform urban redevelopment work. When the company sued the authority in Massachusetts state courts, the courts ruled against the claimant, which appealed the decision to the Massachusetts Supreme Judicial Court and lost before that court as well. In considering whether the decision of the Massachusetts courts constituted a denial of justice, the tribunal cited the language quoted above from the *Azinian* case describing the four types of denial of justice. The tribunal then noted that the International Court of Justice in its judgment in the *ELSI*[369] case had defined arbitrariness as "a wilful disregard of due process of law . . . which shocks, or at least surprises,

366 Award, paras. 102–103.

367 Award, para. 99

368 Award, para. 103.

369 (United States v. Italy), 1989 I.C.J. 15, 76.

a sense of judicial propriety" and found that to be a useful standard for evaluating denial of justice claims. The tribunal next observed that

> [t]he test is not whether a particular result is surprising, but whether the shock or surprise occasioned to an impartial tribunal leads, on reflection, to justified concerns as to the judicial propriety of the outcome, bearing in mind on the one hand that international tribunals are not courts of appeal, and on the other hand that Chapter 11 of NAFTA (like other treaties for the protection of investments) is intended to provide a real measure of protection. In the end the question is whether, at an international level and having regard to generally accepted standards of the administration of justice, a tribunal can conclude in the light of all the available facts that the impugned decision was clearly improper and discreditable, with the result that the investment has been subjected to unfair and inequitable treatment.[370]

The tribunal acknowledged that the standard was "somewhat open-ended," but thought that perhaps no more precise formula could be offered to cover the full range of possibilities.[371] The claimant alleged four grounds on which the decision of the Massachusetts courts constituted a denial of justice. Three of them related to allegations that the court had applied new law or had misapplied procedural law. The tribunal found the supposed new law to be within the limits of common law adjudication and the procedural issues to be within the discretion of the local courts. The fourth ground was that the Massachusetts courts had held that the public authorities possessed immunity from claims of tortious interference with contractual relations. This, within broad limits, was a matter for each state to decide and the tribunal was unpersuaded that the decision in this case constituted a denial of justice.

In *Loewen v. United States*, yet another case arising under the NAFTA, the claimants alleged that a state court jury trial in Mississippi in which one of them was the defendant had been tainted by appeals to local favoritism against a foreign party. The tribunal began by quoting the definition of arbitrariness from the *ELSI* case that was also quoted in *Mondev*.[372] It explained that

> [n]either State practice, the decisions of international tribunals nor the opinions of commentators support the view that bad faith or malicious intention is an essential element of unfair and inequitable treatment or denial of justice amounting to a breach of international justice. Manifest injustice in the sense of a lack of due process leading to an outcome which offends a sense of judicial propriety is enough. . . .[373]

The tribunal then adopted the standard from *Mondev*. It observed, however, that international law attaches special importance to discriminatory violations of municipal law and held that a decision that is both in breach of municipal law and discriminatory against a foreign litigant constitutes a manifest injustice. Taking account of the

370 Award, para. 127.

371 *Id.*

372 Award, para. 131, quoting *Case concerning Elettronica Sicula SpA (ELSI)* (United States v. Italy), 1989 I.C.J. 15, 76.

373 *Id.* at para. 132.

numerous references to the foreign nationality of the claimants followed by a jury verdict against the claimants for $500,000,000, the tribunal held that the trial was inconsistent with the minimum standards of international law. As the tribunal further explained, "it is the responsibility of the courts of a State to ensure that litigation is free from discrimination against a foreign litigant and that the foreign litigant should not become the victim of sectional or local prejudice."[374] Although the tribunal had said that it regarded only discrimination in violation of municipal law to be a denial of justice, the tribunal observed that trials characterized by appeals to local or sectional prejudice have been consistently condemned in the United States and other jurisdictions and constitute grounds for a mistrial. For reasons explained below, however, the claim ultimately was denied on the merits.

In *Waste Management v. Mexico*, another case arising under the NAFTA, the claimant's company had sought to arbitrate its contract dispute with the city of Acapulco. The city refused to advance its share of the costs of arbitration and the claimant's company, unwilling to bear the entire cost on its own, discontinued the arbitral proceedings. The tribunal found no wrongful conduct in Mexico's refusal to advance the costs. The claimant's company also had filed two separate legal actions in Mexican courts against the bank that had opened a line of credit to secure the contract payments, but it was unsuccessful in both actions. The tribunal found that the decisions of the Mexican courts were not arbitrary, unjust or idiosyncratic. Rather, the decisions had been reasoned and prompt. Accordingly, there was no denial of justice.

The claimant also alleged that the city's litigation strategy amounted to a denial of justice. The tribunal observed that it is not unusual for litigants to be difficult and obstructive, but that a litigant cannot commit a denial of justice unless its improper conduct is endorsed by the court or the law gives it some extraordinary privilege that results in a lack of due process. The tribunal found no such circumstances in that case. Contrasting its case with the *Loewen* case, the tribunal noted that there was no evidence of discrimination, bias on grounds of sectional or local prejudice, or clear failure of due process.

In *Jan de Nul v. Egypt*, a case arising under the Belgium-Luxembourg Economic Union-Egypt BIT, the tribunal adopted the language quoted above from *Loewen* and *Mondev*. It held that the local court's decision to join two claims related to the same contract, where not done for dilatory purposes, did not constitute a denial of justice. The fact that the court's 15-page (in English translation) written opinion was "fairly short" given that the proceedings had taken ten years to complete did not amount to a denial of justice either.[375] The appointment of a second panel of experts after a first panel had made findings unfavorable to the state similarly did not constitute a denial of justice. The decision to appoint a second panel was not arbitrary in light of deficiencies in the first panel's report and the claimant was given an opportunity to argue its position with respect to the appointment. The fact that the court allowed ten years to pass before issuing a judgment was not a denial of justice in light of the complex and technical nature of the dispute. The claimant's allegation that the second panel of

374 *Id.* at para. 123.

375 Award, para. 199.

experts acted in excess of its authority could not constitute a denial of justice because a tribunal will not review "the scope of the jurisdiction of national authorities or the application of the law" in the absence of discrimination or severe impropriety, neither of which was present in that case.[376] The ruling of the court did not evidence discrimination or a malicious misapplication of the law and the tribunal would not act as a court of appeal.

In *LLC AMTO v. Ukraine*, a case arising under the Energy Charter Treaty, the claimant alleged a denial of justice in six bankruptcy proceedings against its investment's debtor, none of which resulted in collection of the debt. The tribunal adopted as the standard for denial of justice the language from *Mondev* quoted above. The claimant was precluded from participating in three bankruptcy proceedings because it never received notice, but providing notice was the obligation of the applicant, not the court, and thus no denial of justice occurred. In any event, the claimant's remedy was to initiate its own proceeding, which it did. In that proceeding, the parties were properly heard and the decision was rendered without undue delay. Although the claimant alleged that the court's ruling incorrectly applied the law, the tribunal held that it was not a court of appeal. After this fourth proceeding did not result in payment of the debt, the investment initiated a fifth proceeding. The court ruled against the investment, but this ruling was overturned on appeal and the fifth proceeding was consolidated with a sixth proceeding, initiated by another creditor. Thus, any errors with respect to the fifth proceeding were rectified by the Ukrainian court system. The sixth proceeding also ended without payment of the debt to the investment, but the tribunal found no improper conduct or excessive delay. The tribunal also found no evidence that the courts were improperly influenced by a legislative resolution, which claimants alleged was intended as a signal to the court to rule adversely to the claimant's investment. The resolution affected a number of other enterprises as well as the claimant's investment and was not relied upon by the courts. Its issuance during the bankruptcy proceedings was a coincidence in time. Other legislation that affected the bankruptcy proceedings was *bona fide* regulatory legislation the enactment of which did not coincide with any significant date in the bankruptcy proceedings and that may actually have been beneficial to the investment's attempts to obtain payment.

A denial of justice exists only where the claimant has exhausted its local remedies,[377] including the pursuit of available appeals. That is, a denial of justice exists only where the judicial system as a whole has engaged in improper conduct. The decision of a single court, unless endorsed by the appellate courts, does not constitute a denial of justice. For example, in *Loewen v. United States*, a case arising under the NAFTA, one of the claimants had been successfully sued in a U.S. court by a U.S. company, whose attorney made repeated improper references to the claimant's foreign nationality, comments that the tribunal found to have affected the result. Although the tribunal found that the conduct of the court was inconsistent with the minimum standard of treatment

376 Award, para. 206.

377 *Saipem v. Bangladesh* (Italy-Bangladesh BIT), Award, para. 151; *Chevron v. Ecuador* (United States-Ecuador BIT), Interim Award, para. 235.

under international law, the claimant's failure to appeal the trial court's verdict meant that no denial of justice could be established.

In *Bayinder v. Pakistan*, a case arising under the Turkey-Pakistan BIT, the tribunal agreed that a claim for denial of justice "must take into account the system of justice as a whole, not only an individual decision in the course of proceedings."[378] The claimant argued that it did not receive due process before the Pakistani courts, citing a letter written by one government official to another predicting that Pakistan would prevail in a local court action brought by the claimant against a Pakistani government agency challenging the constitutionality of a contract termination. The tribunal rejected this argument. The claimant also alleged that the lack of independence of the Pakistani judiciary was notorious, but the tribunal found no evidence supporting that allegation.

In *Jan de Nul v. Egypt*, a case arising under the Belgium-Luxembourg Economic Union-Egypt BIT, the tribunal noted that the exhaustion of remedies requirement in denial of justice cases will not bar a claim in the case of excessive delays before the local courts.[379] It also noted that an exception might be made where no effective remedy existed or no remedy had a reasonable prospect of success.[380] In that case, an appeal was pending and no claim had been made that the appellate proceedings were dysfunctional. Thus, no denial of justice could be found.

In *Chevron v. Ecuador*, a case arising under the United States-Ecuador BIT, the claimants' denial of justice claim rested on their allegation of undue delay in the Ecuadoran courts. Several cases submitted to those courts had been pending for 9 to 15 years. The tribunal held that exhaustion of local remedies is required for a denial of justice claim and that whether exhaustion had occurred was an issue to be addressed on the merits, rather than as a matter of jurisdiction.[381] The tribunal found that the claimants had pursued their cases to the point that the cases were ready for a decision, except in one case that could not progress for reasons beyond the claimants' control.[382] Accordingly, the tribunal concluded that the claimants had made a prima facie showing of exhaustion and that a final determination would be made at the merits phase of the arbitration.

A denial of justice claim also can be raised with respect to an administrative proceeding. For example, in *International Thunderbird v. Mexico*, a case arising under the NAFTA, the claimant alleged that Mexico had violated Article 1105(1), requiring treatment in accordance with international law, when it determined that the claimant's gaming operation violated Mexican law, after having initially given an opinion that the operation would be lawful. The tribunal held that the international law minimum standard has evolved since *Neer v. Mexico*[383] was decided, but found that "the threshold for

378 Award, para. 252.

379 Award, para. 256.

380 Award, para. 258 (citing Jan Paulsson, *Denial of Justice in International Law* 125, 130 (2005).

381 Interim Award, para. 235.

382 Decision on Jurisdiction, para. 237.

383 *U.S.A. (L.F. Neer) v. United Mexican States*, (United States-Mexico), October 15, 1926, 3 *International Law Reports* 213.

finding a violation of the minimum standard of treatment still remains high."[384] The tribunal held that for purposes of the case before it, acts that would violate the standard are those that "amount to a gross denial of justice or manifest arbitrariness falling below acceptable international standards." Regarding Mexico's disregard of its earlier opinion, the tribunal noted that the opinion was based on misrepresentations made by the claimant's investment and thus could not have been reasonably relied upon by the claimant. Regarding the administrative proceeding at which the claimant's operation was found to be illegal, the tribunal found no arbitrariness or lack of due process. The claimant was given an opportunity to be heard and the decision rendered cited both the facts and the law upon which it was based. The claimant also had an opportunity for judicial review of the administrative decision, although the appeal was withdrawn. The tribunal noted that "[t]he administrative due process requirement is lower than that of a judicial process."[385] Although the administrative proceeding may have been affected by some irregularities, they were not "grave enough to shock a sense of judicial propriety" and thereby breach the minimum standard.[386] Accordingly, no denial of justice occurred.

In *Genin v. Estonia*, a case arising under the United States-Estonia BIT, the Estonian Banking Supervision Department had revoked the banking license of claimant's investment, an Estonian bank. The bank was given no notice that its license was in danger of revocation and no opportunity to be heard with respect to the proposed revocation. Further, the revocation was effective immediately, leaving the bank with no opportunity to obtain judicial review of the revocation prior to its public announcement. The tribunal nevertheless found that these procedures, although they invited criticism, conformed to Estonian law and did not constitute a denial of due process.[387]

By contrast, in *Middle East Cement v. Egypt*, a case arising under the Greece-Egypt BIT, the host state seized and auctioned the claimant's vessel without prior notice to the claimant. The tribunal found that this taking of the claimant's property was not in accordance with due process of law and thus violated the fair and equitable treatment provision.[388]

384 The tribunal cited *Genin v. Estonia*, discussed below, and *Waste Management v. Mexico*, discussed above.

385 Award, para. 200.

386 *Id.* at para. 200.

387 Award, para. 365.

388 Award, para. 143.

Table of Cases

Table of Treaties and Other International Instruments

Index